Springer Proceedings in Business and Economics

Springer Proceedings in Business and Economics brings the most current research presented at conferences and workshops to a global readership. The series features volumes (in electronic and print formats) of selected contributions from conferences in all areas of economics, business, management, and finance. In addition to an overall evaluation by the publisher of the topical interest, scientific quality, and timeliness of each volume, each contribution is refereed to standards comparable to those of leading journals, resulting in authoritative contributions to the respective fields. Springer's production and distribution infrastructure ensures rapid publication and wide circulation of the latest developments in the most compelling and promising areas of research today.

The editorial development of volumes may be managed using Springer Nature's innovative EquinOCS, a proven online conference proceedings submission, management and review system. This system is designed to ensure an efficient timeline for your publication, making Springer Proceedings in Business and Economics the premier series to publish your workshop or conference volume.

This book series is indexed in SCOPUS.

Nicholas Tsounis • Aspasia Vlachvei
Editors

Advances in Quantitative Economic Research

2021 International Conference on Applied Economics (ICOAE), Heraklion Crete, Greece

Springer

Editors
Nicholas Tsounis
Department of Economics
University of Western Macedonia
Kastoria, Greece

Aspasia Vlachvei
Department of Economics
University of Western Macedonia
Kastoria, Greece

ISSN 2198-7246 ISSN 2198-7254 (electronic)
Springer Proceedings in Business and Economics
ISBN 978-3-030-98178-5 ISBN 978-3-030-98179-2 (ebook)
https://doi.org/10.1007/978-3-030-98179-2

This Springer imprint is published by the registered company Springer Nature Switzerland AG
The registered company address is: Gewerbestrasse 11, 6330 Cham, Switzerland

Preface

This year's conference is co-organised by the Department of Accounting and Finance at the Hellenic Mediterranean University (HMU) and the Department of Economics at the University of Western Macedonia, Heraklion, Crete, Greece, hosted by the HMU after the kind invitations by Prof. George Agiomirgianakis and Christos Floros who are also co-chairs of the conference.

The aim of the conference is to bring together economists from different fields of applied economic research in order to share methods and ideas.

The topics covered include:

- Applied macroeconomics
- Applied international economics
- Applied microeconomics including industrial organisations
- Applied work on international trade theory including European integration
- Applied financial economics
- Applied agricultural economics
- Applied labour and demographic economics
- Applied health economics
- Applied education economics

In total, 55 works were submitted from 13 countries while 39 papers were accepted for publication in the conference proceedings. All papers accepted for publication in the conference proceedings were peer reviewed by at least two anonymous referees.

The Acceptance Rate for ICOAE 2021 Was 71%

The full text articles will be published online by Springer in the series Springer Proceedings in Business and Economics.

The organisers of ICOAE 2021 would like to thank

- The scientific committee of the conference for their help and their important support for carrying out the tremendous workload organising and synchronising the peer-reviewing process of the submitted papers in a very specific short period of time
- The anonymous reviewers for accepting to referee the submitted conference papers and providing their reviews on time for the finalisation of the conference programme
- The keynote speaker, Prof Constantin Zopounidis from the Technical University of Crete, for accepting to present his work on environmental social governance
- The organising committee for its help for the success of the conference
- Dr Eirini Arvanitaki, Mr Gerassimos Bertsatos, Mr Lazaros Markopoulos and Mr. Stelios Angelis for secretarial and technical support

Kastoria, Greece Nicholas Tsounis
Kastoria, Greece Aspasia Vlachvei

Contents

1 **Cooperators Are Faster but Not More Accurate in Social Exchange Decisions Compared to Defectors** 1
Adam Karbowski, Jerzy Osiński, and Bartłomiej Wiśnicki

2 **Interest Rate Changes and Investors' Activity: Evidence from Poland During the Pandemic Period** 15
Joanna Olbrys

3 **Volatility Modelling of Volatility Indices: The Case of Emerging Markets** 31
Nadia de Villiers and Pierre J. Venter

4 **Quantitative Analysis of Corruption Political Factors** 47
Beáta Mikušová Meričková, Michal Lendvorský, and Nikoleta Jakuš Muthová

5 **Impact of COVID-19 Pandemic on Financial Health of SMEs** 63
Lenka Papíková, Mário Papík, and Jana Kajanová

6 **Preference Reversal and Impulsivity in Discounting of Monetary Losses** 77
Bartlomiej Wisnicki and Adam Karbowski

7 **Loss Sharing and Social Distance: An Experimental Study** 85
Bartłomiej Wiśnicki and Adam Karbowski

8 **Impatience and Altruism Over Hypothetical Monetary Losses** 99
Adam Karbowski, Bartłomiej Wiśnicki, and Jerzy Osiński

9 **Comparative Study of Static and Dynamic ARIMA Models in Forecasting of Seasonally Headline Inflation** 113
Melina Dritsaki and Chaido Dritsaki

10 The Destabilizing Effects of Political Budget Cycles: The Case of Greece 129
George Petrakos, Konstantinos Rontos, Chara Vavoura, and Ioannis Vavouras

11 *Beautification for Tourism!* Economics and Marketing of the Italian Cultural Foundation During and After Pandemic Times 143
Angela Besana and Annamaria Esposito

12 For Heritage Memory and Survival, Though Pandemic Times! Philanthropy of Leading Trust and Foundation in Italy and UK 153
Angela Besana and Maria Cristina Vannini

13 Sectoral and Occupational Employment Analysis in Greece: Evidence From Labor Market 165
Kostas Karamanis and Georgios Kolias

14 Cognitive/Emotional Errors and Financial Education 189
Anastasios D. Konstantinidis, Spinthiropoulos Konstantinos, Garefalakis Alexandros, and Hara Haritaki

15 Application of the Experiential Value Scale in Online Booking Conditions: Are There Consumer Demographic Characteristic Differences? 203
Aikaterini Stavrianea, Irene (Eirini) Kamenidou, Spyridon Mamalis, and Ifigeneia Mylona

16 Firm Conduct in a Duopolistic Industry with Product Innovation 217
Jacek Prokop

17 Gender Equality Issues in Labor Markets: Lessons for COVID-19 Era 229
Nihal Bayraktar

18 Interrelation Between Reinsurance and Financial Performance in Slovak Insurance Companies 255
Janka Grofčíková, Katarína Izáková, and Dagmar Škvareninová

19 Trends in the Use of Social Media in Cultural Centres in Developing Audiences 273
Tatiana Corejova, Andrea Pilatikova, Maria Rostasova, and Alexandra Valicova

20 Investigation of the Redesigning Process of the Development Identity of a Local Government Regional Unit (City): A Case Study of Kozani Regional Unit in Greece 285
Stavros Kalogiannidis, Stamatis Kontsas, George Konteos, and Fotios Chatzitheodoridis

21 Role of Management in Optimising the Quality of Education in Educational Organisations 299
Stavros Kalogiannidis, Stavroula Savvidou, Olympia Papaevangelou, and Fotini Pakaki

22 Simple and Transparent: A Positive Correlation for Virtuous Public Administrations 315
Anna Maria Bagnasco and Tiziana Alti

23 Circular Economy and the Clothing Industry 327
E. Pitoska, A. Kataraxia, and I. Araviadi

24 Working Capital Management in Relation to the Size and Profitability of Companies in the Czech Republic 339
Markéta Šeligová

25 Bankruptcy and Business Consolidation in Greece: An Exploratory Approach 361
I. Araviadi and A. Kataraxia

26 The European Case: Are There Externalities from the National Toward the Regional R&D Systems That Enhance Their Efficiency? 371
Cristián Gutiérrez Rojas and Thomas Baumert

27 Tracking Price Trends Using User–Product Interaction Data From a Price Comparison Service 393
Mattias Rydenfelt

28 Differences in Generational Cohort Satisfaction from a Public Hospital Medical Personnel: Insights from Generation Cohorts X, Y, and Z 409
Irene Kamenidou, Spyridon Mamalis, Aikaterini Stavrianea, and Ifigeneia Mylona

29 An Engineering Financial Analysis of a Research Sea Platform 425
Fotis Mavromatakis, Ioannis Katsigiannis, Hara Haritaki, Kyriakos Siderakis, and Giorgos Stavrakakis

30 Identification of Environmental and Economic Indicators: A Case Study of EU Countries with the Use of the DEA Method 439
Dimitrios Niklis, Pavlos Stamatiou, and Chaido Dritsaki

31 Application of Methods of Comprehensive Evaluation of a Company in the Conditions of the Visegrad Group's Countries . 451
Tomáš Pražák

32 Determinants of Customer Loyalty Toward Internet Service Providers in Albania 465
Alma Braimllari (Spaho) and Sauda Nerjaku

33 Strategic Agility and Economic Environment's Friendliness-Hostility in Explaining Performance of Polish SMEs in the Phase of COVID-19 Pandemic 477
Tomasz Sikora and Ewa Baranowska-Prokop

34 Brand Evangelism as an Emerging Marketing Approach Among Fashion Businesses 497
Eleni Mavragani, Fragiskos Archontakis, Maria Koiou, and Stavroula Laspita

35 Income Inequality and Shadow Economy in the EU. A Panel Cointegration and Causality Analysis 513
Simona-Gabriela Masca, Madalina Drutu, and Andrada-Maria Pojoca

36 Social Media Usage and Business Competitiveness in Agri-Food SMEs 531
Ourania Notta, Venetia Raikou, and Aspasia Vlachvei

37 Cultural Production as a Means of Acculturation of Global Consumer Culture for Luxury Brands: A Content Analysis 539
Koronaki Eirini, Aspasia Vlachvei, and Anastasios Panopoulos

38 Clustering the Social Media Users Based on Users' Motivations and Social Media Content 553
E. Iliopoulou and A. Vlachvei

Index 569

Chapter 1
Cooperators Are Faster but Not More Accurate in Social Exchange Decisions Compared to Defectors

Adam Karbowski, Jerzy Osiński, and Bartłomiej Wiśnicki

Abstract In this study, we focus on decision-making in social exchange. In particular, we test the effectiveness (measured by speed and accuracy of decisions) of the decision-making in social exchange. Experimental results show that persons who cooperate in a prisoner's dilemma game (cooperators) are faster but not more accurate at solving the social contract version of the Wason selection task compared to persons selecting in a prisoner's dilemma game a defection strategy (defectors). Differences between cooperators and defectors in speed or accuracy of decision-making have not been observed in the abstract version of the Wason selection task. The obtained results provide empirical support to the claim that the social exchange heuristic works as an optimizing tool of the human mind.

Keywords Social cooperation · Social exchange · Decision-making · Behavioral economics

1.1 Introduction

Social exchange (cf., e.g., cf., e.g., Kirchler et al., 1996; Kanazawa & Savage, 2009; Yamagishi & Mifune, 2009; Karbowski, 2012; Cook et al., 2013; Ohtsubo et al., 2014; Schilke et al., 2015; Bulbulia, 2017; Kim et al., 2019) is a phenomenon universal for the humankind. This behaviour is common in all cultures, including

Part of this paper was supported by funds from the National Science Centre, Poland, through grant number 2018/31/D/HS4/00203.

A. Karbowski (✉) · B. Wiśnicki
SGH Warsaw School of Economics, Warsaw, Poland
e-mail: akarbo1@sgh.waw.pl

J. Osiński
Faculty of Psychology, University of Warsaw, Warsaw, Poland

N. Tsounis, A. Vlachvei (eds.), *Advances in Quantitative Economic Research*, Springer Proceedings in Business and Economics,
https://doi.org/10.1007/978-3-030-98179-2_1

those that developed many years ago. Anthropological evidence to support the latter claim may be found, e.g., in Isaac (1978), Tooby and DeVore (1987), Cashdan (1989), McGrew and Feistner (1992), Sussman and Cloninger (2011) or Johnson (2016).

Cognitive psychology often assumes that the human mind consists of general rules of reasoning, independent from the object or the content of cognition (content-free rules; see, e.g., Fodor, 1983; Overton & Ricco, 2011). Evolutionary science challenges this assumption. According to evolutionary scientists, natural selection has led to the formation of many specific (content dependent) rules of reasoning, responsible for such areas of life as exchange, cooperation, danger or parenthood and care (Cosmides & Tooby, 1992; Overton & Ricco, 2011). Possessing these specific systems of reasoning has adaptive significance. Where, for example, two problems have different optimal solutions, a general principle for problem-solving would be worse off than two specific rules (Cosmides & Tooby, 1992).

Social exchange is the situation where the individuals are obliged to meet a particular requirement, usually at their costs, in exchange for which they acquire the right to gain a measurable benefit from another individual or a group (Cosmides & Tooby, 1992; Kim et al., 2019). The cost borne by the individual is always at least compensated by the received benefit. Social exchange is governed by the laws of interdependence, which makes it a form of a social contract. A failure to comply with the conditions of a social contract will be called "cheating".

According to Cosmides and Tooby (1992), social contracts have the logical structure of implication. This implication may be put down as follows: "If you have accepted a benefit from other persons, bear the cost for their account". While Cosmides and Tooby (1992) focused on the cheater detection device and its activation in the social context, Kiyonari et al. (2000) highlighted another fundamental precondition for the social exchange, i.e. willingness to cooperate. The ability to distinguish between defectors and cooperating persons is particularly useful to those who are going to cooperate (Kiyonari et al., 2000; Hiraishi & Hasegawa, 2001; Pothos et al., 2011; Barclay, 2013; Declerck et al., 2013; Reed et al., 2018). The effective social exchange module should then embrace both:

- a personal willingness (readiness) to cooperate and
- the cognitive ability to distinguish between defectors and cooperating persons (cheater detection device).

These two conditions may be described with the language of the theory proposed by Pruitt and Kimmel (1977). In the light of this theory, achieving cooperation in the social interaction requires: (1) a subjective transformation of the goal perception, from individual to common, and (2) a verification of the expectations that the common goal perception is shared by all the decision-makers involved. The social contract theory of Cosmides and Tooby concentrates on component (2), whereas the arguments of Kiyonari and others (2000) focus on component (1).

Let us now take a closer look at component (1). According to Kiyonari et al. (2000), in a social context, the subjective transformation involves a mental reshaping of the prisoner's dilemma game into the trust dilemma (assurance game). What is particularly surprising, this also applies to one-off prisoner's dilemma game. There is abundant empirical evidence that shows that people perceive one-shot prisoner's dilemma as the trust dilemma (cf., e.g., Watabe et al., 1996; Kollock, 1997; Hayashi et al., 1999; Kiyonari et al., 2000; Yamagishi et al., 2007).

The personal willingness to cooperate works with the specialized cheater detection module. The ultimate purpose of this module is to limit cooperation to the cooperating individuals. So, on the one hand, the personal willingness to cooperate allows and initiates cooperative behaviour, and on the other hand, the cheater detection device supervises social interaction.

Kiyonari et al. (2000) explain social cooperation in terms of a social exchange heuristic. The Japanese researchers experimentally demonstrated the operation of this heuristic. Participants of the experiment committed a logical error in the direction of favouring cooperation as the situation involved more serious consequences. This suggests the operation of a domain-specific heuristic that encourages the pursuit of cooperation in social exchange (Kiyonari et al., 2000).

We further hypothesize: if such a heuristic works, it should streamline the decision-making process in social exchange. As a result, cooperators should be faster and at least not worse at solving social exchange tasks compared to defectors. Our objective is to test the latter claim experimentally.

Our research problem is then the effectiveness of cooperators' decision-making in social exchange in comparison to defectors' decision-making in such circumstances. We measure the effectiveness of decision-making by the accuracy and speed of decisions.

We hypothesize that cooperation-seeking persons solve the social contract version of the Wason selection task (cf., Cosmides & Tooby, 1992; Evans, 2016) faster and more accurately than defectors. As we noticed earlier, the effective social exchange mechanism (heuristic) entails subject's cooperative behaviour and the expectation that the other decision-makers share common goal perspective. As a result, in a prisoner's dilemma game, the cooperators should expect a higher degree of cooperation on the part of the other players compared to the defectors.

It should also be noted that social exchange heuristic works only in the relevant social context (cf., Yamagishi et al., 2007; Glowacki & Molleman, 2017). In solving the abstract version of the Wason selection task (Green & Larking, 1995), the heuristic remains dormant (Cosmides & Tooby, 1992). Therefore, there are no theoretical grounds to expect the directional differences in respect of accuracy and speed of decisions when the subjects solve the abstract version of the Wason selection task.

Finally, we formulate the following hypotheses.

Hypothesis 1 The persons who select cooperation strategy in a prisoner's dilemma game declare a higher percentage of cooperative decisions on the part of their partners compared to the persons selecting the defection strategy.

Hypothesis 2 In the social contract version of the Wason selection task, the solving time for the persons who cooperate in a prisoner's dilemma game is shorter than for the persons who decide to select the defection strategy.

Hypothesis 3 The rate of correct answers provided in the social contract version of the Wason selection task is higher among the persons who cooperate in a prisoner's dilemma game than among the persons who select the defection strategy.

Hypothesis 4 In the abstract version of the Wason selection task, the solving time for the persons who cooperate in a prisoner's dilemma game is equal to the solving time for the persons who decide to select the defection strategy.

Hypothesis 5 The rate of correct answers provided in the abstract version of the Wason selection task by the persons who cooperate in a prisoner's dilemma game is equal to the rate of correct answers provided by the persons who decide to select the defection strategy.

1.2 Material and Methods

1.2.1 Participants

The research was carried out with the participation of 126 university students (63 women and 63 men). Participants were between 19 and 26 years old (mean 21.7, standard deviation 2.11). They received a fixed remuneration (in national currency, ca. 13 USD).

1.2.2 Material

For the needs of the experiment, an appropriate computer programme (application) was prepared in JavaScript. The programme displayed a series of screens with instructions and fields to fill in by the subjects. The programme allowed us to collect information about the age and sex of the participants. Further, the application allowed to present a description of the prisoner's dilemma task for the subjects (in a task description, we referred to the research done by the Japanese scientists and used the payoff matrix proposed by Kiyonari et al. (2000), p. 421, though we changed the currency since yens in the country where the experiment was run are used less frequently compared with dollars). The participants were informed that they are going to play in pair with another student in the following game with hypothetical payoffs.

		The choice of the other player	
		K	P
Your choice	L	You get 10 USD; The other player gets 10 USD	You get 0 USD; The other player gets 15 USD
	S	You get 15 USD; The other player gets 0 USD	You get 5 USD; The other player gets 5 USD

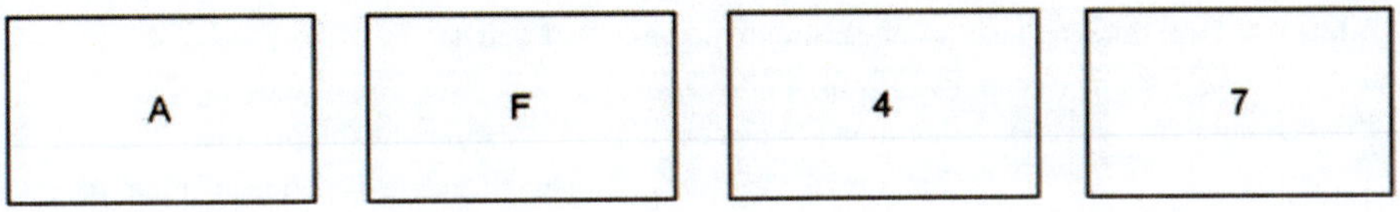

Fig. 1.1 Cards presented in the abstract version of the Wason selection task

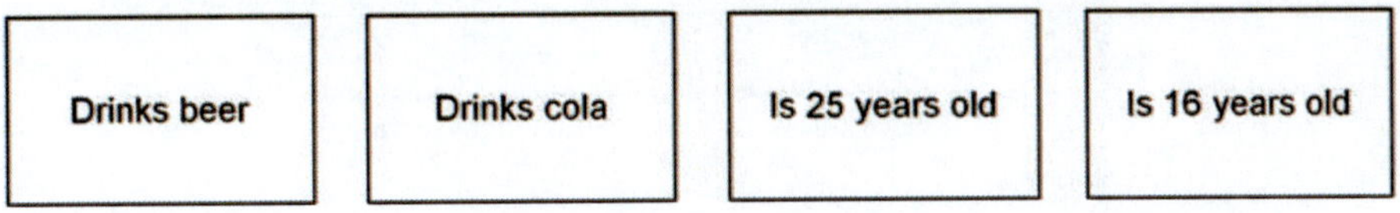

Fig. 1.2 Cards presented in the social contract version of the Wason selection task

> "Thus, if you select 'L' and the other player selects 'K', both of you will receive 10 USD. If you select 'L' and the other player selects 'P', you will not get the money, and the other player will receive 15 USD. If you select 'S' and the other player selects 'K', you will receive 15 USD, and the other player will not get the money. If you select 'S' and the other player selects 'P', both of you will receive 5 USD".

The participants were informed that the game is carried out once. Further, a computer application allowed the subjects to select "L" or "S". Then, the following question was addressed to the participants:

> "What do you think, how many people in the position of the second player would choose 'K'? Enter the estimated number in the box below: _ in 100 subjects".

The next screens presented the Wason selection task (in the abstract or the social contract version; the order depended on the experimental condition) preceded by appropriate instructions. These tasks offered the sets of cards like those shown in Figs. 1.1 and 1.2, respectively.

In the abstract task, the subject was asked to verify whether the logic rule—"if there is a vowel on one side of the card, there is an even number on the other side"—is violated for any of the four presented cards. For the task in the social contract version, the participant was asked to verify whether the rule—"if the person drinks beer, this person is more than twenty years old"—is violated for any of the four presented cards.

Finally, the programme allowed the subjects to select cards from those presented in the selection task.

1.2.3 Procedure

Before the beginning of the experiment, the experimenters indicated that they could assist if any part of the task were difficult to understand for the subjects. The subjects

Table 1.1 Experimental results concerning hypotheses 1, 2 and 4

Concerning hypothesis no.	Cooperators in a prisoner's dilemma (76 persons)	Defectors in a prisoner's dilemma (50 persons)
1	Declare 56.8 (mean value) per cent of cooperative decisions on the part of other players	Declare 44.7 (mean value) per cent of cooperative decisions on the part of other players
2	34.6 seconds (solving time; mean value)	48.7 seconds (solving time; mean value)
4	26.7 seconds (solving time; mean value)	33.1 seconds (solving time; mean value)

Source: Own calculations

were randomly assigned to one of the two experimental conditions. These conditions differed as regards the order in which the Wason selection task appeared on the screen, in its abstract or social contract version. The first task to solve for all subjects was a prisoner's dilemma game (exactly in the form given in the previous section). Then, they solved the selection task in the social contract version followed by the selection task in the abstract version (65 persons) or proceeded with the selection task in the abstract version followed by the selection task in the social contract version (61 persons). All the screens were displayed without a time limit, so the subjects decided by themselves when to proceed to the next screen. The time spent on solving the tasks by the subjects was automatically recorded (Table 1.1).

1.3 Results

Below are the results concerning hypotheses 1, 2 and 4. Next, the appropriate parametric tests are executed. In order to verify hypotheses 1, 2 and 4, we use Welch's t-test (which is a generalization of the standard t-test for unequal variances). The null hypothesis of the test is as follows:

$$H_0 : m_1 = m_2$$

where m_1 *and* m_2 are the means of cooperation declaration (for hypothesis 1) or solution time (hypotheses 2 and 4) for the participants who chose cooperation or defection in the prisoner's dilemma game, respectively. The alternative hypothesis is that the means are not equal (for hypothesis 4), or that $m_1 < m_2$ (for hypothesis 2) or that $m_1 > m_2$ (for hypothesis 1). The test uses t-statistic with calculated degrees of freedom. Table 1.2 provides the results with degrees of freedom and p-values for tested hypotheses. The decision to reject the null hypothesis (and thus declare rejection or no rejection of the research hypothesis) is made for the significance level of 0.05. Before the statistical procedure, the outliers (for which the answers lay above three times standard deviation value outside of mean of the respective groups of cooperators or defectors) were dismissed. By that, we lowered the sample

Table 1.2 Statistical testing of hypotheses 1, 2 and 4

Hypothesis no.	*t*-statistic value	Degrees of freedom	*p*-value	Decision concerning hypothesis
1	2.450	90.259	0.008	Not rejected
2	−2.003	71.752	0.024	Not rejected
4	−1.551	90.357	0.124	Not rejected

Source: Own calculations. Significance level: 0.05

size for hypothesis 2 by 2 (1 for each group) and hypothesis 4 by 3 (2 in the group that cooperated). Based on the statistical tests, research hypotheses 1, 2 and 4 cannot be rejected.

Next, let us present the experimental results concerning hypotheses 3 and 5 and the appropriate statistical testing. For that purpose, the following method was used. Hypotheses 3 and 5 concern the proportion of the sample that answered correctly in the Wason task. Thus, to verify the hypotheses, we use the two-proportion z-test (with Yates continuity correction) with the null hypothesis of the following form:

$$H_0 : p_1 = p_2$$

where $p_1$and p_2 are the fractions of persons who solved the Wason task correctly, given their cooperation or defection in the prisoner's dilemma game, respectively. The alternative hypothesis is $p_1 > p_2$ for hypothesis 3 and $p_1 \neq p_2$ for hypothesis 5. The test gives us a χ^2-statistic with 1 degree of freedom. We reject the null hypothesis with the significance level equal to 0.05. Based on the statistical tests, research hypothesis 5 cannot be rejected, but we reject research hypothesis 3 (Table 1.3).

The same procedure as in Table 1.4 can be used to statistically verify the significance of the difference in the accurate decisions in selecting a single card. For each card, the general population has a zero-one distribution; i.e., a correct decision may be taken, which involves inverting the card that needs to be inverted or leaving the card that need not be inverted. An incorrect decision involves inverting the card that does not allow checking the implication or leaving the card that should be inverted to check the implication. Next, we can make a comparison (between the group whose members decided to cooperate in a prisoner's dilemma game and the group whose members chose the defection strategy) of the fractions (or probabilities) of correct decisions concerning each card (Table 1.5).

Observe that in the social contract task, for three cards fraction differences are not significant, but for the card "drinks cola" significantly higher probability of making the correct decision occurred for the persons who chose to cooperate in a prisoner's dilemma game. In the abstract task, there are no significant differences in the fractions for all cards. Interestingly enough, the single card approach shows some evidence, which could be interpreted in line with the research hypothesis

Table 1.3 Experimental results concerning hypotheses 3 and 5

Type of Wason selection task	Percentage of correct answers by cooperators	Percentage of correct answers by defectors
Social contract	47.4%	40%
Abstract	35.5%	48%

Source: Own calculations

Table 1.4 Statistical testing of hypotheses 3 and 5

Hypothesis	χ^2-statistic value	Degrees of freedom	p-value	Decision concerning hypothesis
3	0.398	1	0.264	Rejected
5	1.464	1	0.226	Not rejected

Source: Own calculations. Significance level: 0.05

3, though the statistical testing (Table 1.4)—consistent with the formulation of hypothesis 3—leads to the rejection of this hypothesis.

1.4 Discussion

Hypothesis 1 was designed to check whether the subjects cooperating in a prisoner's dilemma game were to a greater extent than defectors expecting that the partners share a common goal perspective, as it is required by the effective social exchange mechanism (see Introduction). Note that the experimental results indicate that the subjects who decided to cooperate in a prisoner's dilemma game expected a higher degree of cooperation on the part of the partners compared to the persons who chose the defection strategy. Such a decision and revealed expectations of the cooperators are not consistent with the rational choice in a prisoner's dilemma game, but with the rational choice in a trust dilemma game, as Kiyonari et al. (2000) point out. As we remember, according to Kiyonari et al. (2000), in a social context, the subjective transformation of the goal perception involves a mental reshaping of the prisoner's dilemma into the trust dilemma (assurance game).

The purpose of the remaining hypotheses was to verify whether cooperators are better decision-makers in social exchange compared to defectors. To put it differently, the purpose of hypotheses 2–5 was to find out whether and what adaptive qualities are offered by the social exchange mechanism.

Biologists established criteria that allow determining which mechanisms are adaptive (Dawkins, 1982; Thornhill, 1991; Williams, 1966, 1985; Hauser et al., 2015). According to Williams (1985), adaptations are specially designed biological devices, which allow solving specific classes of problems (the special design problem-solving machinery). The criteria of evaluation are as follows: efficiency, precision, specialization and reliability (Williams, 1985).

Table 1.5 Statistical testing related to hypotheses 3—a single card approach

Type of Wason task	Card	Percentage of correct answers by cooperators	Percentage of correct answers by defectors	χ^2-statistic value	*p*-value
Social contract	"Drinks beer"	81.6%	86%	0.166	0.658
	"Drinks cola"	94.7%	84%	2.885	0.045
	"Is 25 years old"	77.6%	68%	0.992	0.160
	"Is 16 years old"	59.2%	56%	0.030	0.431
Abstract	"A"	84.2%	88%	0.111	0.738
	"F"	85.5%	92%	0.667	0.414
	"4"	61.8%	72%	0.969	0.325
	"7"	50%	56%	0.228	0.633

Source: Own calculations. Significance level: 0.05

Efficiency should be understood as the high speed and low cost associated with the functioning of the given mechanism. Precision should be seen as the high accuracy of the achieved solution. Specialization is the degree of the adjustment of the given mechanism to the requirements of the given class of social or biological problems. Reliability is the resistance of the given mechanism to errors.

The purpose of hypotheses 2–5 was to test the adaptive qualities of social exchange mechanism. We focused on the two dimensions stipulated by Williams, i.e. the efficiency of the mechanism (and specifically its speed) and its reliability. These qualities could be tested directly with the use of a properly designed experimental procedure.

The obtained results show that persons cooperating in a prisoner's dilemma game were faster and equally accurate at solving the social contract version of the Wason selection task compared to persons choosing in a prisoner's dilemma game the defection strategy. Intergroup differences in speed or accuracy of decision-making have not been observed in the abstract version of the Wason selection task.

These results provide empirical support to the claim that the social exchange mechanism works as an optimizing tool of the human mind. Such a device allows solving problems and takes decisions related to social cooperation more effectively (higher speed, not worse accuracy). Hence, such a mechanism has a measurable adaptive significance. The above results suggest that cooperators can respond faster than defectors to public policies based on social contract (e.g. redistributive policy, welfare policy, policy for sustainable development, cf., Benabou, 2000; Rhodes & Meny, 2016; Haagh, 2019).

The results presented in this paper are worth to be discussed in the light of another, more recent, experiment run by Karbowski and Wiśnicki (2021). The latter experiment shows that the social distance between players in games (i.e. social closeness to another player—from socially closest person to stranger) exerts a significant impact on prosocial/defection decisions made in the dictator and ultimatum games. Interestingly enough, for relatively close persons (up to no. 20 in the social distance scale), the participants were eager to accept a higher monetary loss from those persons than they transferred to them (Karbowski & Wiśnicki, 2021). For persons occupying further positions on the social distance scale (further than no. 20), participants were eager to transfer a higher monetary loss to them than they would accept from them. These findings show that prosocial/defection behaviour depends on social distance between players. Higher social distance between players makes subjects less cooperative.

Knowing that, we can reinterpret the results presented in the main body of the paper. The proportion of L/S decisions should depend on the perception of social distance to another student. If a decision-maker perceives other students as relatively close, the risk of obtaining LP outcome should be more tolerable compared with a decision-maker who feels socially detached from other students. The following is a speculation, but it is not excluded that decision-makers who perceive others as relatively close in general feel psychologically safe and are more eager to cooperate with others and perform it without deeper reflection (simply put, faster and with lower cognitive capacity use). The latter hypothesis needs a separate study.

1.5 Conclusion

In this study, we confirm the adaptive qualities of the social exchange heuristic. Persons who follow this cognitive and behavioural mechanism (and cooperate in the prisoner's dilemma game) turn out to be better decision-makers in the social version of the Wason selection task compared to defectors. The present study complements a work by Kiyonari et al. (2000) who presented the social exchange heuristic but did not test its adaptive qualities. A recent work by Karbowski and Wiśnicki (2021) sheds a new light on the incentives to launch a social exchange heuristic in decision-making. We hypothesize that the perception of a relatively small social distance to the other subject promotes social exchange heuristic and allows to optimize the process of decision-making in the social context. In turn, the relatively large social distance to another subject hampers the activation of social exchange heuristic, and as a result, defection rather than cooperation is expected. This hypothesis is important to environmental challenges (He et al., 2017) and sustainable development. Facing environmental challenges needs social cooperation, and now, we can add that such cooperation is—due to cognitive mechanisms—much easier to achieve in socially closer groups (where members perceive themselves as socially close or social distance to others is relatively small). It seems that solving global challenges starts locally.

References

Barclay, P. (2013). Strategies for cooperation in biological markets, especially for humans. *Evolution and Human Behavior, 34*, 164–175.

Benabou, R. (2000). Unequal societies: Income distribution and the social contract. *American Economic Review, 90*, 96–129.

Bulbulia, J. (2017). Anthropology: Tradition's hidden economy. *Nature Human Behaviour, 1*, 0070.

Cashdan, E. (1989). Hunters and gatherers: Economic behavior in bands. In S. Plattner (Ed.), *Economic anthropology* (pp. 21–48). Stanford University Press.

Cook, K. S., Cheshire, C., Rice, E. R., & Nakagawa, S. (2013). Social exchange theory. In J. DeLameter & A. Ward (Eds.), *Handbook of social psychology*. Springer.

Cosmides, L., & Tooby, J. (1992). Cognitive adaptations for social exchange. In J. H. Barkow, L. Cosmides, & J. Tooby (Eds.), *The adapted mind: Evolutionary psychology and the generation of culture*. Oxford University Press.

Dawkins, R. (1982). *The extended phenotype*. Freeman.

Declerck, C. H., Boone, C., & Emonds, G. (2013). When do people cooperate? The neuroeconomics of prosocial decision making. *Brain and Cognition, 81*, 95–117.

Evans, J. (2016). Wason selection task (chapter 8). In R. Pohl (Ed.), *Cognitive illusions*. Routledge.

Fodor, J. A. (1983). *The modularity of mind*. MIT Press.

Glowacki, L., & Molleman, L. (2017). Subsistence styles shape human social learning strategies. *Nature Human Behaviour, 1*, 0098.

Green, D., & Larking, R. (1995). The locus of facilitation in the abstract selection task. *Thinking & Reasoning, 1*, 183–199.

Haagh, L. (2019). The developmental social contract and basic income in Denmark. *Social Policy and Society, 18*, 301–317.

Hauser, T., Iannaccone, R., Walitza, S., Brandeis, D., & Brem, S. (2015). Cognitive flexibility in adolescence: Neural and behavioral mechanisms of reward prediction error processing in adaptive decision making during development. *NeuroImage, 104*, 347–354.

Hayashi, N., Ostrom, E., Walker, J., & Yamagishi, T. (1999). Reciprocity, trust, and the sense of control: A cross-societal study. *Rationality and Society, 11*, 27–46.

He, G., Yang, X., & Jiang, D. (2017). The effect of altruism on social discounting of environmental gain and loss. *Acta Psychologica Sinica, 49*, 1334–1343.

Hiraishi, K., & Hasegawa, T. (2001). Sharing-rule and detection of free-riders in cooperative groups: Evolutionarily important deontic reasoning in the Wason selection task. *Thinking & Reasoning, 7*, 255–294.

Isaac, G. (1978). The food-sharing behavior of protohuman hominids. *Scientific American, 238*, 90–108.

Johnson, D. (2016). Hand of the gods in human civilization. *Nature, 530*, 285–287.

Kanazawa, S., & Savage, J. (2009). An evolutionary psychological perspective on social capital. *Journal of Economic Psychology, 30*, 873–883.

Karbowski, A. (2012). The adaptive meaning of social exchange heuristic. *Mimeo.*

Karbowski, A., & Wísnicki, B. (2021). Behavioral economics of monetary loss sharing. Submitted to *Gospodarka Narodowa. The Polish Journal of Economics.*

Kim, T., Zhang, T., & Norton, M. (2019). Pettiness in social exchange. *Journal of Experimental Psychology: General, 148*, 361.

Kirchler, E., Fehr, E., & Evans, R. (1996). Social exchange in the labor market: Reciprocity and trust versus egoistic money maximization. *Journal of Economic Psychology, 17*, 313–341.

Kiyonari, T., Tanida, S., & Yamagishi, T. (2000). Social exchange and reciprocity: Confusion or a heuristic? *Evolution and Human Behavior, 21*, 411–427.

Kollock, P. (1997). Transforming social dilemmas: Group identity and cooperation. In P. Danielson (Ed.), *Modeling rational and moral agents*. Oxford University Press.

McGrew, W., & Feistner, A. (1992). Two nonhuman primate models for the evolution of human food sharing: Chimpanzees and Callitrichids. In J. H. Barkow, L. Cosmides, & J. Tooby (Eds.), *The adapted mind: Evolutionary psychology and the generation of culture*. Oxford University Press.

Ohtsubo, Y., Matsumura, A., Noda, C., Sawa, E., Yagi, A., & Yamaguchi, M. (2014). It's the attention that counts: Interpersonal attention fosters intimacy and social exchange. *Evolution and Human Behavior, 35*, 237–244.

Overton, W., & Ricco, R. (2011). Dual-systems and the development of reasoning: Competence-procedural systems. *Wiley Interdisciplinary Reviews: Cognitive Science, 2*, 231–237.

Pothos, E., Perry, G., Corr, P., Matthew, M., & Busemeyer, J. (2011). Understanding cooperation in the Prisoner's Dilemma game. *Personality and Individual Differences, 51*, 210–215.

Pruitt, D. G., & Kimmel, M. J. (1977). Twenty years of experimental gaming: Critique, synthesis, and suggestions for the future. *Annual Review of Psychology, 28*, 363–392.

Reed, L., Best, C., & Hooley, J. (2018). Cooperation with characters: How a partner's personality disorder decreases cooperation in two economic games. *Personality and Individual Differences, 126*, 33–37.

Rhodes, M., & Meny, Y. (2016). *The future of European welfare: A new social contract?* Palgrave.

Schilke, O., Reimann, M., & Cook, K. (2015). Power decreases trust in social exchange. *Proceedings of the National Academy of Sciences, 112*, 12950–12955.

Sussman, R., & Cloninger, C. R. (2011). *Origins of altruism and cooperation*. Springer.

Thornhill, R. (1991). The study of adaptation. In M. Bekoff & D. Jamieson (Eds.), *Interpretation and explanation in the study of behavior*. West View Press.

Tooby, J., & DeVore, I. (1987). The reconstruction of hominid behavioral evolution through strategic modeling. In W. Kinzey (Ed.), *Primate models of hominid behavior*. SUNY Press.

Watabe, M., Terai, S., Hayashi, N., & Yamagishi, T. (1996). Cooperation in the one-shot prisoner's dilemma based on expectations of reciprocity. *Japanese Journal of Experimental Social Psychology, 36*, 183–196.

Williams, G. (1966). *Adaptation and natural selection: A critique of some current evolutionary thought*. Princeton University Press.

Williams, G. (1985). A defense of reductionism in evolutionary biology. *Oxford Surveys in Evolutionary Biology, 2*, 1–27.

Yamagishi, T., & Mifune, N. (2009). Social exchange and solidarity: In-group love or out-group hate? *Evolution and Human Behavior, 30*, 229–237.

Yamagishi, T., Terai, S., Kiyonari, T., Mifune, N., & Kanazawa, S. (2007). The social exchange heuristic. Managing errors in social exchange. *Rationality and Society, 19(3)*, 259–291.

Chapter 2
Interest Rate Changes and Investors' Activity: Evidence from Poland During the Pandemic Period

Joanna Olbrys

Abstract During the COVID-19 pandemic period in Poland, interest rates have been substantially reduced by National Bank of Poland (NBP). Within three months, the WIBOR 1Y rate fell from 1.84% (27 February 2020) to 0.3% (4 June 2020). The consequences of the Central Bank decision have been crucial for investors, as a one-time increase (decrease) in rates decreases (increases) the market value of assets. Changes in the term structure of interest rates unknown a priori to investors arise particularly often in economic downturns. According to the literature, investors have a greater appetite for risk-taking when interest rates are low, and it is not confined to institutions. Generally speaking, low-interest rates lead to significantly higher allocations to risky assets among diverse groups of investors. In this context, the goal of this study is to investigate whether shifts in interest rates affected investors' activity on the Warsaw Stock Exchange (WSE) within the pandemic period in 2020. Daily trading volume is utilized as a measure of investors' activity. The event window method is used to assess whether the mean results of daily trading volume during the pre-event, event and post-event time windows significantly differ between each other in the case of all event windows. A particular event window includes consecutive considerable declines in interest rates. Moreover, robustness tests are conducted. The empirical findings confirm that interest rate cuts during the pandemic period increased investors' activity on the Polish stock market.

Keywords COVID-19 pandemic period · Declining interest rates · Event window · Trading volume · Warsaw Stock Exchange

J. Olbrys (✉)
Bialystok University of Technology, Bialystok, Poland
e-mail: j.olbrys@pb.edu.pl

N. Tsounis, A. Vlachvei (eds.), *Advances in Quantitative Economic Research*, Springer Proceedings in Business and Economics,
https://doi.org/10.1007/978-3-030-98179-2_2

2.1 Introduction

During the coronavirus pandemic, central banks have been entrenched as the first and main line of defence against economic and financial crises (Stiglitz et al., 2020). Cochrane (2020) indicates that there are some arguments for a sharp interest rate cut when serious economic disruption hits, but first of all governments need detailed, pandemic-induced financial crisis plans. The pandemic period constitutes a powerful reminder that the basic political and economic unit is the nation-state, and the borders suddenly do matter (Stiglitz et al., 2020). In March and April 2020, 21 central banks in advanced and emerging economies made quantitative easing announcements on government or government-backed securities. Some of these interventions were coupled with the substantial interest rates cuts, for instance, in Poland (Rebucci et al., 2020).

Changes in interest rates are crucial for investment decisions because a one-time increase (decrease) in rates decreases (increases) the market value of assets. Bae (1990) distinguishes current (anticipated) from unanticipated changes in interest rates. Ehrmann and Fratzscher (2004) document that equity returns react more strongly to monetary policy shocks when changes in interest rates are unexpected. Nissim and Penman (2003) point out that unanticipated shifts in interest rates should revise expectations of current and near-future revenues, expenses and earnings according to the direction of the interest rate change.

Unexpected changes in the term structure of interest rates unknown a priori to investors arise particularly often in economic downturns (Cieslak, 2018). According to the literature, investors have a greater appetite for risk-taking when interest rates are low, and it is not confined to institutions. In the recent paper, Lian et al. (2019) demonstrate that low-interest rates lead to significantly higher allocations to risky assets among diverse populations of institutional and individual investors. As a consequence, even rather conservative investors that usually exhibit a medium level of risk aversion seek more risky alternative investment opportunities. Several studies provide empirical evidence that banks, pension funds and mutual funds invest more in riskier assets when spot rates are low (e.g. Maddaloni & Peydró, 2011; Hanson & Stein, 2015; Andonov et al., 2017; Di Maggio & Kacperczyk, 2017; Daniel et al., 2018). In this context, a substantial rise of investors' activity on a stock market is not surprising when interest rates are low. Therefore, the proposed research question is as follows:

- *Did declining interest rates during the pandemic period affect investors' activity on the Polish stock market?*

To answer the research question, daily trading volume is used to investigate investors' activity on the Warsaw Stock Exchange (WSE). Trading volume is treated as a proxy of stock liquidity, and it is defined as a number of shares traded over a particular period of time (Olbryś & Oleszczak, 2020). The event window method is used to assess whether the mean results of daily trading volume during the pre-event, event and post-event time windows significantly differ between each other in the case of all event windows. An event means a particular considerable decline in spot rates. However, a particular event window includes consecutive declines in interest rates. As a robustness check, we compare the empirical findings within the whole sample period and the event windows.

It is well documented in the literature that volume displays significant differences across trading hours of the day and across days of the week. Quite extensive studies of this topic have been conducted on the WSE (e.g. Będowska-Sójka, 2014; Nowak & Olbryś, 2015; Miłobędzki & Nowak, 2018; Olbryś & Oleszczak, 2020). However, to the best of the author's knowledge, the empirical findings concerning investors' activity measured by daily trading volume on the WSE during the COVID-19 pandemic period are novel and have not been reported in the literature thus far.

The remainder of this study is organized as follows: Section 2.2 presents the problem of unexpected changes in interest rates during the COVID-19 pandemic period in Poland. Section 2.3 describes the methodological background of the event window approach. Section 2.4 contains data description and discusses the empirical results of investors' activity on the WSE. The last section recalls the main findings, concludes and indicates further directions of the research.

2.2 Changes in Interest Rates During the Pandemic Period in Poland

During the pandemic period in Poland, interest rates have been substantially reduced by National Bank of Poland (NBP) to support economy and to enable the entrepreneurs to take out low-interest loans. As a consequence, within three months, the WIBOR 1Y (Warsaw Interbank Offered Rate 1Y) fell from 1.84% (27 February 2020) to 0.30% (4 June 2020). Table 2.1 reports details concerning daily percentage changes in WIBOR 1Y. The shifts that arose on 16 March 2020, 17 March 2020, 18 March 2020, 9 April 2020 and 29 May 2020 were the most critical.

Figures 2.1 and 2.2 illustrate the term structure of the WIBOR 1Y rates. For instance, Fig. 2.1 shows the almost flat interest rate structure in Poland during the one year period from 12 June 2019 to 12 June 2020. Figure 2.2 displays results reported in Table 2.1. Percentage changes in WIBOR 1Y within the period from 20 February 2020 to 5 June 2020 are presented.

It is important to note that after the quite long time period of almost flat interest rate structure in Poland, the topic regarding financial market risk caused by changes in interest rates has become significant again in 2020.

Table 2.1 Daily percentage changes in WIBOR 1Y during the period from 20 February 2020 to 12 June 2020

Date	WIBOR 1Y	Daily change in WIBOR 1Y (%)
2020-02-20	1.84%	0
....		
2020-02-27	1.84%	0
2020-02-28	1.83%	−0.54%
....		
2020-03-13	1.78%	0
2020-03-16	1.66%	**−6.74%**
2020-03-17	1.53%	**−7.83%**
2020-03-18	1.26%	**−17.65%**
2020-03-19	1.25%	−0.79%
2020-03-20	1.24%	−0.8%
2020-03-23	1.23%	−0.81%
2020-03-24	1.23%	0
....		
2020-04-07	1.23%	0
2020-04-08	1.23%	0
2020-04-09	0.76%	**−38.21%**
2020-04-10	0.76%	0
2020-04-14	0.76%	0
....		
2020-04-28	0.75%	−1.32%
2020-04-29	0.75%	0
....		
2020-05-14	0.74%	−1.33%
....		
2020-05-28	0.74%	0
2020-05-29	0.33%	**−55.41%**
2020-06-01	0.32%	**−3.03%**
2020-06-02	0.31%	**−3.13%**
2020-06-03	0.31%	0
2020-06-04	0.3%	**−3.23%**
2020-06-05	0.3%	0
....		
2020-06-12	0.3%	0

Notes: The most critical changes in interest rates are marked in bold
Source: Olbryś (2020)

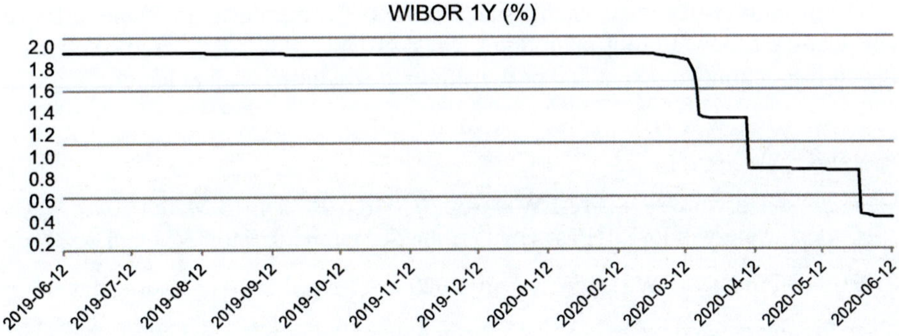

Fig. 2.1 WIBOR 1Y during the one year period from 12 June 2019 to 12 June 2020. (Source: Olbryś, 2020)

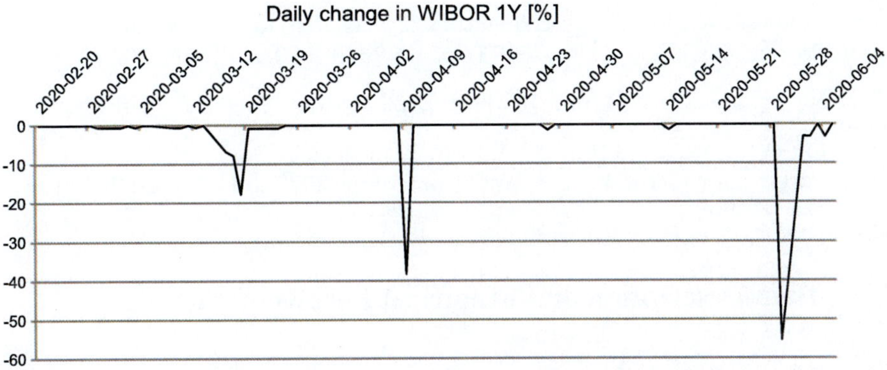

Fig. 2.2 Daily changes in WIBOR 1Y within the period 20 February 2020–5 June 2020. (Source: Olbryś, 2020)

2.3 The Event Window Approach

The event window framework is typical for event studies in economics and finance (MacKinlay, 1997). The event window approach requires constructing reasonable windows around the event dates (Di Maggio & Kacperczyk, 2017).

The aim of our event window study is to deeply investigate and compare daily trading volume behaviour around events related to the most critical changes in interest rates reported in Table 2.1. Defining $[T_1, T_2]$ as the event window that contains k-trading days, we base on MacKinlay (1997) and propose the following procedure for constructing the non-overlapping pre-event, event and post-event windows of equal length for daily data:

- Pre-event window $[T_1 - k, T_1 - 1]$ (k-trading days),
- Event window $[T_1, T_2]$ (k-trading days),
- Post-event window $[T_2 + 1, T_2 + k]$ (k-trading days).

Given daily percentage changes in WIBOR 1Y presented in Table 2.1, we consider the following four main event windows EW1, EW2, EW3 and EW4, with the corresponding pre-event and post-event time windows of equal length:

1. Event window 1 (EW1) from 16 March 2020 to 23 March 2020 (6 trading days)
   - Pre-event window 1 (Pre-EW1) from 6 March 2020 to 13 March 2020,
   - Post-event window 1 (Post-EW1) from 24 March 2020 to 31 March 2020.
2. Event window 2 (EW2) from 8 April 2020 to 14 April 2020 (3 trading days)
   - Pre-event window 2 (Pre-EW2) from 3 April 2020 to 7 April 2020,
   - Post-event window 2 (Post-EW2) from 15 April 2020 to 17 April 2020.
3. Event window 3 (EW3) from 29 May 2020 to 4 June 2020 (5 trading days)
   - Pre-event window 3 (Pre-EW3) from 22 May 2020 to 28 May 2020,
   - Post-event window 3 (Post-EW3) from 5 June 2020 to 12 June 2020.
4. Event window 4 (EW4) from 16 March 2020 to 4 June 2020 (55 trading days)
   - Pre-event window 4 (Pre-EW4) from 2 January 2020 to 13 March 2020,
   - Post-event window 4 (Post-EW4) from 5 June 2020 to 17 August 2020.

2.4 Data Description and Empirical Results on the WSE

This section describes the data set and presents empirical findings concerning comprehensive investigation of investors' activity on the WSE during the whole sample period from 2 January 2020 to 30 December 2020 (252 trading days), including the period of considerable declines in interest rates on Polish financial market, i.e. from 16 March 2020 to 4 June 2020.

2.4.1 Data Description

The data set consists of daily data and contains the opening, high, low and closing prices and volume for each security. The free historical market data come from the Stooq.pl (available at https://stooq.com/db/h/). The 18 major and most actively traded WSE companies and the WIG20 index as a benchmark are investigated. The equities were incessantly included in the WIG20 index within the whole sample period from 2 January 2020 to 30 December 2020. This information is based on the historical index portfolios (available at https://gpwbenchmark.pl/en-historyczne-portfele). Table 2.2 reports the basic information about all selected companies.

The whole sample period can be divided into the following two sub-periods: (1) before the COVID-19 pandemic lockdown from 2 January 2020 to 12 March 2020

Table 2.2 Basic information about the 18 major and most liquid WSE-listed companies included in the WIG20 index within the whole sample period

	Company	MV PLN m. (30 December 2020)	Average trading volume per session in 2020	Average no. of trades per session in 2020
1	KGH	24963.03	720721	5344
2	PKO	24630.07	3307051	7160
3	CDR	18500.50	536374	11307
4	PZU	18390.35	2362287	6045
5	PKN	16683.91	1512842	8262
6	DNP	13856.47	204769	3003
7	PEO	10776.76	1108242	5576
8	LPP	9154.93	3050	1131
9	PGN	9003.58	5830908	3314
10	CPS	8336.11	568826	1863
11	SPL	6185.30	92697	2028
12	PGE	5179.04	3668448	3549
13	OPL	4266.08	1899878	1781
14	LTS	3587.21	629846	3799
15	CCC	3307.38	586652	4848
16	TPE	2840.65	6807622	2523
17	ALR	1508.55	685050	2416
18	JSW	1365.90	1214032	4193

Notes: The 18 WSE-traded companies are labelled by ticker symbols and presented in decreasing order of the market value (MV in PLN million) on 30 December 2020
Source: The WSE website

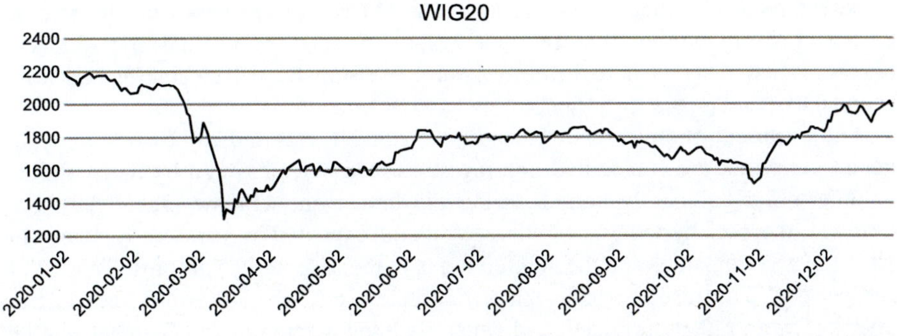

Fig. 2.3 Daily values of the WIG20 index within the whole sample period from 2 January 2020 to 30 December 2020

and (2) during and after the lockdown from 13 March 2020 to 30 December 2020. Daily values of the WIG20 index are presented in Fig. 2.3. It is pertinent to note that after the quite short period when the WIG20 index moved down substantially (with the lowest value equal to 1305.73 on 12 March 2020—the first day of the lockdown), the market index moved up within the subsequent sub-period.

2.4.2 Empirical Results on the WSE Based on the Event Window Approach

The main idea of the event window approach is to investigate a particular stock market characteristic's behaviour around events. Therefore, the goal of this study is to assess whether the mean results of daily trading volume during the pre-event, event and post-event time windows significantly differ compared to each other in the case of all event windows. To address this issue, the t-statistic for sample means is utilized:

$$t = \frac{\overline{x_1} - \overline{x_2}}{\sqrt{\frac{s_1^2(n_1-1)+s_2^2(n_2-1)}{n_1+n_2-2} \cdot \left(\frac{1}{n_1} + \frac{1}{n_2}\right)}}, \tag{2.1}$$

where $\overline{x_1}$ and $\overline{x_2}$ are sample means, s_1^2 *and* s_2^2 are sample variances, and n_1 and n_2 denote sample size, respectively. The following two-tailed hypothesis is tested:

$$\begin{aligned} H_0 &: \mu_1 = \mu_2 \\ H_1 &: \mu_1 \neq \mu_2 \end{aligned}, \tag{2.2}$$

where μ_1 and μ_2 are the expected values of daily trading volume during the compared periods, and the null hypothesis states that two expected values are equal. Tables 2.3, 2.4, 2.5, and 2.6 contain the summarized findings of the significance test for differences between two means for four event windows EW1, EW2, EW3 and EW4 in the chronological order based on Table 2.1. Standard deviations are given in parentheses. Calculations of the t-statistic (1) values are based on the sample empirical results presented in Tables 2.3, 2.4, 2.5, and 2.6. The null hypothesis is rejected when $|t| > t^*$, where the critical value of t-statistic at 10% significance level is equal to $t^* = t_{0,10;n_1+n_2-2}$.

The empirical findings reported in Tables 2.3, 2.4, 2.5, and 2.6 are not homogeneous. As would be anticipated, the investors' activity measured by daily trading volume was significantly higher during the first event window (Table 2.3). For instance, the null hypothesis of the equality of expected values was rejected for 14 out of 18 companies and the WIG20 index in the case of the pair post-EW1/EW1 sub-periods. The results suggest that the interest rate changes were unexpected, investors were rather surprised, and generally, they reacted violently to substantial interest rates cut. Tests for differences between two means for the second (EW2) and third (EW3) event windows are presented in Tables 2.4 and 2.5, and they show that these differences are not significant in the most cases. It is not surprising as the second pre-event, event and post-event time periods included the Easter holiday in Poland. The third event was the last one, and, less formally speaking, it seems that investors have accepted interest rate cuts.

Table 2.6 presents summarized results of the significance test for differences between two means for the fourth event window (EW4), which includes the whole

Table 2.3 Summarized results of the average daily trading volume, standard deviation and the significance test for differences between two means for the first event window (EW1)

	Company	Average daily trading volume (standard deviation)			Hypothesis		
		Pre-event window	Event window 1 (EW1)	Post-event window	Pre-EW1 /EW1	Post-EW1 /EW1	Pre-EW1 /Post-EW1
1	KGH	1318284.2(360765.4)	1695954.3(443975.4)	919140.7(259624.4)	H0	H1	H1
2	PKO	3964663.7(1421857.3)	6130055.2(1587269)	3293462.2(747492.5)	H1	H1	H0
3	CDR	815230.7(397957.5)	740655.5(225567)	338275(62824.7)	H0	H1	H1
4	PZU	3193154.8(1001207)	4188794.3(1139469)	2813320.5(602022.6)	H0	H1	H0
5	PKN	2433651.2(488011)	2487493.3(813423.5)	1759302.3(552576.4)	H0	H1	H1
6	DNP	370769.2(201750.8)	432834.7(136872.9)	230098.5(72609.3)	H0	H1	H0
7	PEO	1101058.5(457518.8)	1676369(466359.6)	861188(212601.9)	H1	H1	H0
8	LPP	5864.5(1466.63)	8264.33(3154.94)	3420.5(957.87)	H0	H1	H1
9	PGN	10110307.7(2310598.8)	15241999(5200387)	11599021(8767743)	H1	H0	H0
10	CPS	1205310.2(535202.6)	1433322.3(518098)	781429.3(444670.5)	H0	H1	H0
11	SPL	107873.2(44045.7)	158479.3(70144.2)	118907.5(44553.2)	H0	H0	H0
12	PGE	5175149.2(2442760)	9751551.3(4056472)	4553622.2(884153.8)	H1	H1	H0
13	OPL	3941452.2(1216222)	3568289.8(1328982)	2127740.7(931748)	H0	H1	H1
14	LTS	640689.2(210909.9)	701515.8(256866.4)	655976(129863.8)	H0	H0	H0
15	CCC	499833.5(479629.4)	2237457.2(708452.9)	774915.2(375715.3)	H1	H1	H0
16	TPE	10151277.3(4851047)	17183343.8(10027134)	7534241.8(1401942)	H0	H1	H0
17	ALR	997482(167159)	994104.3(321315.1)	870222.8(286411)	H0	H0	H0
18	JSW	1689321.7(555531.9)	2352053.7(886755.6)	1007259.7(212430.9)	H0	H1	H1
index	WIG20	48422554(14773523)	71585113(23636260)	40498573(11320598)	H1	H1	H0
No. of H1					6	15	6

Notes: The companies are presented in Table 2.2
H0—the null hypothesis; H1—the alternative hypothesis
EW1: 16.03.2020–23.03.2020 (6 trading days)
Pre-EW1: 6.03.2020–13.03.2020
Post_EW1: 24.03.2020–31.03.2020

Table 2.4 Summarized results of the average daily trading volume, standard deviation and the significance test for differences between two means for the second event window (EW2)

	Company	Average daily trading volume (standard deviation)			Hypothesis		
		Pre-event window	Event window 2 (EW2)	Post-event window	Pre-EW2 /EW2	Post-EW2 /EW2	Pre-EW2 /Post-EW2
1	KGH	1493043.3(473913.8)	1394585.7(947601)	1383785(541888.1)	H0	H0	H1
2	PKO	4774935.3(2023629.6)	5186777.3(2134481.5)	4864929.3(207458.9)	H0	H0	H0
3	CDR	459955.7(92803.7)	468782(198071.8)	407094.3(169533.8)	H0	H0	H0
4	PZU	2370520(481481)	3432189.3(499258.8)	3351073(1505531.9)	H1	H0	H0
5	PKN	4258645.3(2925377.1)	2265526.3(257619.8)	2458885.7(745688.4)	H0	H0	H0
6	DNP	235044(37984.7)	182802.3(25740.9)	298705.7(207709)	H0	H0	H0
7	PEO	1208728(619507.9)	3126350(538221.6)	1262299.3(239873.9)	H1	H1	H0
8	LPP	4140(1365)	3993(330)	3278.7(504.7)	H0	H0	H0
9	PGN	13394533(2823218.9)	10450321.7(1183764.2)	5757780(1437499.3)	H0	H1	H1
10	CPS	811099.7(136521.8)	961895.3(644252.2)	853643.3(374307.4)	H0	H0	H0
11	SPL	168214.3(16918.1)	165463.3(18383.8)	165119.3(34153.9)	H0	H0	H0
12	PGE	6384640(1050919.8)	6092275.3(708919.9)	6442521.7(2034605.8)	H0	H0	H0
13	OPL	1757677.7(517657.7)	2447353.3(1283630.6)	1502673.3(526141.5)	H0	H0	H0
14	LTS	901005.7(134268.5)	686117.3(215107.1)	605846.7(200549.2)	H0	H0	H0
15	CCC	1369114.3(642747)	1095918.7(543437.4)	2148231.7(1445428.9)	H0	H0	H0
16	TPE	10492365(2829502.7)	8789022.3(1323263.6)	10039507(3302804.1)	H0	H0	H0
17	ALR	1670917.3(894547.3)	2451843.7(1442481.4)	1742154.7(572784.1)	H0	H0	H0
18	JSW	1403336.7(473913.8)	1394585.7(947601)	1383785(541888.1)	H0	H0	H0
index	WIG20	53338987(10052333)	50918988(4764116.4)	45248136.7(4717268.6)	H0	H0	H0
No. of H1					2	2	2

Notes: The companies are presented in Table 2.2
H0—the null hypothesis; H1—the alternative hypothesis
EW2: 8.04.2020–14.04.2020 (3 trading days)
Pre-EW2: 3.04.2020–7.04.2020
Post_EW2: 15.04.2020–17.04.2020

Table 2.5 Summarized results of the average daily trading volume, standard deviation and the significance test for differences between two means for the third event window (EW3)

	Company	Average daily trading volume (standard deviation)			Hypothesis		
		Pre-event window	Event window 3 (EW3)	Post-event window	Pre-EW3 /EW3	Post-EW3 /EW3	Pre-EW3 /Post-EW3
1	KGH	730377.8(427613)	751879.8(277039.2)	734354,2(171877.2)	H0	H0	H0
2	PKO	5387389.6(5309144.3)	6877376.4(3051587.8)	7113249(1307693.9)	H0	H0	H0
3	CDR	371140.2(226222.8)	420750.6(257836.7)	369764(68947.7)	H0	H0	H0
4	PZU	2382568.2(1373812.8)	2914328.4(1255817.7)	2678489.4(551131.8)	H0	H0	H0
5	PKN	1046944.4(643790.7)	1501975(670620.3)	1824906.2(405960)	H0	H0	H1
6	DNP	218084.2(50179.5)	315405(151013.9)	224757.2(118796.9)	H0	H0	H0
7	PEO	3135569.8(2442806.3)	2725592.8(1780667.7)	2484646.8(736394.1)	H0	H0	H0
8	LPP	2742(1230.1)	3917.2(2362.7)	3961.6(881.3)	H0	H0	H0
9	PGN	11583277(10926558)	8001728.8(4350809.6)	5726270.6(1338455.6)	H0	H0	H0
10	CPS	579311.2(359770.7)	1397230.8(1445820.1)	688206.2(159127.1)	H0	H0	H0
11	SPL	198973.2(163208.7)	185360.2(102846.9)	151921.4(35854.9)	H0	H0	H0
12	PGE	3641426.8(2053599.1)	7709299(1525358.3)	11378102.6(5189339.3)	H1	H0	H1
13	OPL	1927561.6(1317917.7)	3633220.2(2367038.9)	1746645.4(539593)	H0	H0	H0
14	LTS	409506(282356.8)	650659(274748,8)	467008.8(212790.9)	H0	H0	H0
15	CCC	820800.6(510151.6)	2198973.6(1033415.6)	1372478(1150619.3)	H1	H0	H0
16	TPE	5195695.8(3807165.4)	11504588(5595983)	29527138.4(21852611)	H1	H0	H1
17	ALR	1659558(1211671)	1318216.8(378593.4)	2103426(1162920.4)	H0	H0	H0
18	JSW	1676613.4(1003044.4)	1809568(475022.8)	2739279.6(1447781.7)	H0	H0	H0
index	WIG20	41897899(23776764)	54492201.6(15308595)	72024145.4(21799664)	H0	H0	H1
No. of H1					3	0	4

Notes: The companies are presented in Table 2.2
H0—the null hypothesis; H1—the alternative hypothesis
EW3: 29.05.2020–4.06.2020 (5 trading days)
Pre-EW3: 22.05.2020–28.05.2020
Post_EW3: 5.06.2020–12.06.2020

Table 2.6 Summarized results of the average daily trading volume, standard deviation and the significance test for differences between two means for the fourth event window (EW4)

		Average daily trading volume (standard deviation)			Hypothesis		
	Company	Pre-event window	Event window 4 (EW4)	Post-event window	Pre-EW4 /EW4	Post-EW4 /EW4	Pre-EW4 /Post-EW4
1	KGH	694006(404036.5)	875199.9(488611.3)	803604(344971.1)	H1	H0	H0
2	PKO	2743302(1256227.6)	4380278(2438456)	3019648.7(1938472.6)	H1	H1	H0
3	CDR	477268.4(429410.6)	385561.3(194782.7)	346916.6(162862.7)	H0	H0	H1
4	PZU	2060714.7(900521)	2678266.3(1135372.1)	1970064.1(930484.8)	H1	H1	H0
5	PKN	1468119(675954.8)	1876248.4(1114062.7)	1296410.4(928581.2)	H1	H1	H0
6	DNP	203498.7(127978.9)	262811.8(127527.6)	163693.6(86431.7)	H1	H1	H1
7	PEO	689348.4(418390.5)	1852070(1229508.5)	977385.2(658549.5)	H1	H1	H1
8	LPP	2544(1856.1)	3936(2401.8)	3474.8(1759.1)	H1	H0	H1
9	PGN	5970444.4(2972211.1)	8315920.6(6180950.3)	5832263.3(3488933.4)	H1	H1	H0
10	CPS	551908.5(416506.8)	805418(603577.2)	515594(318984.6)	H1	H1	H0
11	SPL	69222(39625.3)	143232.8(72708.2)	88168.7(57696.7)	H1	H1	H1
12	PGE	2518705.5(1647675.5)	5119910.3(2751211.1)	4743267.9(4259850.9)	H1	H0	H1
13	OPL	2259336.5(1300709.4)	2128203.9(1316684.9)	1713027.4(1431518.4)	H0	H0	H1
14	LTS	367016.8(199881.5)	489345.6(261308.6)	437012.4(284456.7)	H1	H0	H0
15	CCC	274505.6(231542.6)	1390467.9(988971.2)	434356(493779.4)	H1	H1	H1
16	TPE	4609467.7(3487431.3)	7894857.6(5532355.2)	12283139.3(12587410)	H1	H1	H1
17	ALR	503948.9(347782.2)	1148188.9(730445.4)	679828(630810.8)	H1	H1	H1
18	JSW	1277019.8(680971.7)	1237215.3(739113.5)	783697.2(828113)	H1	H1	H1
index	WIG20	27185445(12738152)	41568467.4(18810324)	36503170.2(22073742)	H1	H0	H1
No. of H1					16	12	12

Notes: The companies are presented in Table 2.2
H0—the null hypothesis; H1—the alternative hypothesis
EW4: 16.03.2020–4.06.2020 (55 trading days)
Pre-EW4: 2.01.2020–13.03.2020
Post_EW4: 5.06.2020–17.08.2020

period of considerable declines in interest rates on Polish financial market, i.e. from 16 March 2020 to 4 June 2020. The empirical findings are interesting and worth special notice as they confirm that daily trading volume was significantly higher during this period for 14 out of 18 companies, namely KGH, PKO, PZU, PKN, DNP, PEO, LPP, PGN, CPS, SPL, PGE, LTS, CCC and ALR. This evidence is consistent with the hypothesis that declining interest rates during the pandemic period affected investors' activity on the Polish stock market.

2.4.3 Robustness Analyses

The additional goal of the study is to conduct robustness tests and assess whether the mean results of daily trading volume during the whole sample period and the event windows (EW1, EW2, EW3 and EW4) significantly differ compared to each other. To address this issue, the t-statistic (1) is utilized, and the two-tailed hypothesis (2) is tested. Summarized findings are reported in Table 2.7, and they require some comments. The null hypothesis H0 is outweighed by the hypothesis H1 in 10 out of 19 cases for the pair WS/EW1 and in 15 out of 19 cases for the pair WS/EW4, including the WIG20 index. It indicates that the mean results of daily trading volume during these periods significantly differ compared to each other. The evidence is that the influence of the first interest rate changes was the most crucial. The further changes were less important. Moreover, taking into consideration the whole sample period (WS) and the period including all interest rate cuts (EW4), the results confirm that trading volume was significantly higher during the EW4 time window. All these observations are in accordance with expectations.

2.5 Concluding Discussion

This paper is geared towards practical implications of changes in the term structure of interest rates unknown a priori to investors. Lian et al. (2019) investigate a phenomenon referred to as 'reaching for yield', which means that individuals invest more in risky assets when risk-free rate is low. The authors propose to explain this phenomenon by mechanisms related to investor's preferences and psychology rather than by conventional portfolio choice theory. They document that preferences and psychology may affect financially well-educated individuals as well as professional investors. The authors conclude that increased risk-taking may help stimulate the economy, but may also pose challenges for financial stability.

The low-interest-rate monetary policy is crucial for investors' decisions. Daniel et al. (2018) study the impact of monetary policy on investors' portfolio choices and asset prices. Their findings suggest that low-interest-rate policy may affect the risk premium of income-generating assets, lead to under-diversification of portfolios and cause redistributive effects across companies that differ in dividend policy.

Table 2.7 Summarized results of the significance test for differences between two means of the average daily trading volume for the group of companies

		The whole sample average daily trading volume (standard deviation)	Hypothesis			
	Company	WS/EW1	WS/EW2	WS/EW3	WS/EW4	
1	KGH	720721.2(371443.3)	H0	H0	H0	H1
2	PKO	3307050.8(1972772.1)	H1	H1	H1	H1
3	CDR	536374.2(623905.1)	H0	H0	H0	H1
4	PZU	2362286.9(1247000)	H0	H0	H0	H1
5	PKN	1526883.4(964467.7)	H0	H0	H0	H1
6	DNP	204768.8(129917.7)	H1	H0	H0	H1
7	PEO	1108241.8(856628.9)	H1	H1	H1	H1
8	LPP	3049.7(1905.3)	H0	H0	H0	H1
9	PGN	5896585.9(4092393.2)	H0	H1	H0	H1
10	CPS	586182.2(428849.3)	H1	H0	H0	H1
11	SPL	9269.7(60342.9)	H1	H1	H1	H1
12	PGE	3668448.3(2814256.5)	H1	H0	H1	H1
13	OPL	1899877.5(1248510.6)	H1	H0	H0	H0
14	LTS	637717.2(858793.7)	H0	H0	H0	H0
15	CCC	586651.8(699532.8)	H1	H0	H1	H1
16	TPE	6807621.8(7297218.2)	H0	H0	H1	H0
17	ALR	685049.5(568666.7)	H1	H1	H1	H1
18	JSW	1214032(922164.1)	H0	H0	H1	H0
index	WIG20	33313843.6(17035511.5)	H1	H0	H1	H1
No. of H1			10	5	9	15

Notes: The companies are presented in Table 2.2
H0—the null hypothesis; H1—the alternative hypothesis
WS: 2.01.2020–30.12.2020 (252 trading days)
EW1: 16.03.2020–23.03.2020 (6 trading days)
EW2: 8.04.2020–10.04.2020 (3 trading days)
EW3: 29.05.2020–4.06.2020 (5 trading days)
EW4: 16.03.2020–4.06.2020 (55 trading days)

Di Maggio and Kacperczyk (2017) stress that monetary authorities worldwide introduce a policy of keeping short-term interest rates at record low level.

Taking the above into consideration, the goal of this research was to assess whether considerable declines in interest rates increased the Polish stock market activity during the pandemic period. The empirical findings based on the event window approach confirm that daily trading volume within the period of the rate cuts was significantly higher for the most analysed companies. It means that low-interest rates led to significantly higher allocations to risky assets on the Warsaw Stock Exchange. This evidence is consistent with the literature. For instance, Brzeszczyński and Kutan (2015) suggest that the Polish Central Bank actions increase investors' activity. Gurgul and Majdosz (2005) examine whether base rate announcements released by the National Bank of Poland have a significant impact on stock returns and trading volume, but their findings are not such homogenous.

Di Maggio and Kacperczyk (2017) assess the influence of low-interest-rate policy on the U.S. money fund industry, and their empirical findings come from an event study analysis of monetary authority announcements. Therefore, one of the possible directions for further research could be to conduct a full event study to identify the impact of low-interest-rate policy during the pandemic period on asset returns on the WSE. To the best of the author's knowledge, no such investigation has been conducted on the Polish equity market thus far.

Acknowledgements The study was supported by the grant WZ/WI/1/2019 from Bialystok University of Technology and funded by the Ministry of Education and Science.

References

Andonov, A., Bauer, R. M. M. J., & Cremers, K. J. M. (2017). Pension fund asset allocation and liability discount rates. *The Review of Financial Studies, 30*(8), 2555–2595.

Bae, S. C. (1990). Interest rate changes and common stock returns of financial institutions: revisited. *The Journal of Financial Research, 13*(1), 71–79.

Będowska-Sójka, B. (2014). Intraday stealth trading. Evidence from the Warsaw Stock Exchange. *Poznan University of Economics Review, 14*(1), 5–19.

Brzeszczyński, J., & Kutan, A. M. (2015). Public information arrival and investor reaction during a period of institutional change: An episode of early years of a newly independent central bank. *Journal of Comparative Economics, 43*, 727–753.

Cieslak, A. (2018). Short-rate expectations and unexpected returns in treasury bonds. *The Review of Financial Studies, 31*(9), 3265–3306.

Cochrane, J. H. (2020). Coronavirus monetary policy. In R. Baldwin & B. Weder di Mauro (Eds.), *Economics in the Time of COVID-19* (pp. 112–114). CEPR Press.

Daniel, K., Garlappi, L., & Xiao, K. (2018). *Monetary policy and reaching for income* (NBER Working Paper No. 25344). National Bureau of Economic Research.

Di Maggio, M., & Kacperczyk, M. (2017). The unintended consequences of the zero lower bound policy. *Journal of Financial Economics, 123*(1), 59–80.

Ehrmann, M., & Fratzscher, M. (2004). Taking stock: Monetary policy transmission to equity markets. *Journal of Money, Credit and Banking, 36*(4), 719–737.

Gurgul, H., & Majdosz, P. (2005). Do NBP base rates announcements convey valuable information? *Systems Science, 31*(1), 105–116.

Hanson, S. G., & Stein, C. (2015). Monetary policy and long-term rates. *Journal of Financial Economics, 115*(3), 429–448.

Lian, C., Ma, Y., & Wang, C. (2019). Low interest rates and risk-taking: Evidence from individual investment decisions. *The Review of Financial Studies, 32*(6), 2107–2148.

MacKinlay, A. C. (1997). Event studies in economics and finance. *Journal of Economic Literature, 35*(1), 13–39.

Maddaloni, A., & Peydró, J.-L. (2011). Bank risk-taking, securitization, supervision, and low interest rates: Evidence from the Euro-area and the U.S. lending standards. *The Review of Financial Studies, 24*(6), 2121–2165.

Miłobędzki, P., & Nowak, S. (2018). Intraday trading patterns on the Warsaw Stock Exchange. In K. Jajuga, H. Locarek-Junge, & L. T. Orlowski (Eds.), *Contemporary trends and challenges in Finance* (Springer Proceedings in Business and Economics) (pp. 55–66). Springer.

Nissim, D., & Penman, S. H. (2003). The association between changes in interest rates, earnings, and equity values. *Contemporary Accounting Research, 20*(4), 775–804.

Nowak, S., & Olbryś, J. (2015). Day-of-the-week effects in liquidity on the Warsaw Stock Exchange. *Dynamic Econometric Models, 15*, 49–69.

Olbryś, J. (2020). *Unexpected returns on bonds. The case of the pandemic period in Poland.* Available at SSRN. https://ssrn.com/abstract=3706654

Olbryś, J., & Oleszczak, A. (2020). Intraday patterns in trading volume. Evidence from high frequency data on the Polish stock market. In K. Saeed & J. Dvorsky (Eds.), *Computer information systems and industrial management. CISIM 2020* (Lecture Notes in Computer Science) (Vol. 12133, pp. 390–401). Springer.

Rebucci, A., Hartley, J. S., & Jiménez, D. (2020). *An event study of COVID-19 central bank quantitative easing in advanced and emerging economies*. NBER Working Paper No. 27339.

Stiglitz, J. E., Shiller, R. J., Gopinath, G., Reinhart, C. M., Posen, A., Prasad, E., Tooze, A., Tyson, L. D. A., & Mahbubani, K. (2020). How the economy will look after the coronavirus pandemic. *Foreign Policy, 4/17/20*.

Chapter 3
Volatility Modelling of Volatility Indices: The Case of Emerging Markets

Nadia de Villiers and Pierre J. Venter

Abstract The purpose of this paper was to examine the stylised facts of volatility and volatility modelling of volatility index returns in the context of emerging markets. The stylised facts of volatility include volatility clustering, mean reversion, a negative relationship with stock market returns and positive relationship with trading volume. By using autoregressive models, linear regression and unit root tests, empirical results indicate that the volatility indices reproduce all the stylised facts of volatility for the following emerging economies: Brazil, India, China, Korea and South Africa. In addition, the volatility modelling of volatility index returns is also considered. In the empirical analysis, the symmetric GARCH, asymmetric GJR-GARCH and EGARCH models were estimated using the volatility indices of emerging economies; the best fitting model was determined using the AIC and SIC. The asymmetric terms of the GJR-GARCH and EGARCH models are statistically significant. The information criterion suggests that the EGARCH model is the best fitting model for all the volatility indices, except Korea. For Korea, the GJR-GARCH model is the best fitting model.

Keywords Volatility indices · Stylised facts · GARCH · Emerging markets

3.1 Introduction

The purpose of a volatility (fear) index is to measure market forecasts of future volatility of an underlying index. The use of volatility indices (hedging and risk management) has become very popular in recent years. The Chicago Board Options Exchange Volatility Index (CBOE VIX) is the most popular volatility index. The CBOE VIX is a benchmark designed to estimate the expected (implied) volatility of the Standard & Poor's 500 (S&P 500) index options and is often referred to as

N. de Villiers · P. J. Venter (✉)
Department of Finance and Investment Management, University of Johannesburg, Auckland Park, South Africa

N. Tsounis, A. Vlachvei (eds.), *Advances in Quantitative Economic Research*, Springer Proceedings in Business and Economics,
https://doi.org/10.1007/978-3-030-98179-2_3

the fear index. This index is used as a benchmark to measure market volatility of expected stock market volatility and financial returns in the future. The analysis on financial returns brought about a set of stylised facts used to explain empirical results that are consistent across a wide range of financial instruments.

Literature shows that stylised facts of financial returns are well documented, but not a lot of research has been done on the stylised facts of volatility indices. Research based on the stylised facts of financial returns dates back to the macroeconomist, Kaldor (1961). The author identifies various statistical facts relating to economic growth for the construction of theoretical models. The method was later adapted by authors like Cont (2001), who identified statistical properties of financial time series that revealed interesting stylised facts, commonly seen in a wide variety of financial markets and instruments. However, authors like Kumar (2010) studied the statistical properties of volatility indices with the overall objective of defining a set of properties, which is common across many volatility indices. The author mainly focused on one developing county, namely India.

In this study, the focus is on stylised facts of volatility indices that apply to emerging markets. Good examples of emerging market economies are Brazil, Russia, India, China and South Africa (BRICS), and emerging and growth-leading economies (EAGLEs) indices. The EAGLEs countries are estimated to contribute more to international economic growth in the next ten years than the G6 economies (France, West Germany, Italy, Japan, the UK and the USA). Countries included in the EAGLEs membership are revised annually dependent on the potential growth of those countries in comparison to developed countries (Umer et al., 2018). The emerging economies include Bangladesh, Brazil, China, Egypt, India and 15 other countries (BBVA, 2016). This study will look at the following emerging economies: Brazil, India, China, Korea and South Africa. The stylised facts provide a more realistic approach when studying the statistical properties of volatility in these emerging economies.

This study also considers the volatility modelling of volatility index returns. Classical models, such as the martingale model and random walk models used to measure risk, assume that volatility is constant over time (Bailey, 2005). However, empirical results show that volatility changes over time (Alexander, 2008). This phenomenon is referred to as volatility clustering and can be tested through generalised autoregressive conditional heteroscedasticity (GARCH) models. By making use of family GARCH models, the degree of asymmetry can be estimated and whether positive and negative shocks affect volatility the same way.

The rest of this paper is structured as follows: the next section presents the literature on stylised facts, mainly focused on the review of a small collection of well-established stylised facts of financial return series, and subsequently mentions a different approach used to reproduce stylised facts for volatility indices. Furthermore, the literature on the use of GARCH models of volatility index returns is used to examine volatility clustering. Section 3.3 examines the methodology, where the stylised facts for volatility indices are explained, including the GARCH modelling of volatility index returns. Section 3.4 investigates the empirical results of the stylised facts and GARCH models of volatility indices, and Sect. 3.7 concludes with a general discussion about the purpose of this study and the benefits and shortcomings of the use of stylised facts and modelling of volatility indices on emerging markets.

3.2 Literature Review

This section is divided into two parts. The first part focuses on the stylised facts of volatility, and the second part focuses on volatility modelling and volatility indices.

3.2.1 Stylised Facts of Volatility

In this section, the recent and relevant literature on the stylised facts of financial returns and volatility is briefly discussed. Statistical properties of prices of commodities and stocks, and market indices have been studied for centuries. The recording of a sequence of numerical data points (prices) is called a time series. The analysis of financial time series is of great importance for making predictions, due to uncertainty in the market. The inherent uncertainty in financial time series makes it very interesting for statisticians, physicist and economists (Tsay, 2005). Different assets are not necessarily influenced by similar information as they exhibit different properties. However, empirical studies of financial time series reveal that asset prices "do share some quite non-trivial statistical properties" (Cont, 2001 [224]). These properties are common across a wide range of instruments, markets and time periods and are revered as stylised empirical facts (Cont, 2001).

Research focusing on the stylised facts of financial returns is well documented in the literature. However, not many studies have focused on the stylised facts of volatility indices. Research based on the stylised facts of financial returns dates back to Kaldor, 1961. The author states that scientists should summarise the facts by starting with a stylised view of the facts (Kaldor (1961). Kaldor (1961) isolates several statistical properties pertaining to long-term macroeconomic growth in several countries and used these properties to construct theoretical models. Kaldor's (1961) concept was later used and adapted to describe statistical facts or regularities that arose from statistical studies of return series of financial markets. Many different lists of these facts can be found in several reviews (e.g. Bollerslev et al. 1994; Pagan 1996; Guillaume et al. 1997; Cont 2001). In this study, a minimum set of facts are presented.

Guillaume et al. (1997) considered a set of stylised facts that describe the foreign exchange (FX) markets and how it functions. The authors identified the following stylised facts: non-stable, fat-tailed distribution, a finite distribution, systematic distribution, a decrease in leptokurtosis, negative first-order autocorrelation of returns and quoted spreads are discrete, and extremely short-term triangular arbitrage, seasonal patterns, short- and long-term memory (autocorrelation of volatility and its clustering), institutional framework, conditional predictability, positive impact of interventions, effect of news (new information) and the high complex system. The authors presented these stylised facts concerning the spot intra-daily FX markets.

Authors like Cont (2001) identified a set of stylised facts that emerged from the statistical analysis of price variations of different financial markets. The author focused mainly on the statistical properties of the S&P 500 index, which can be generalised across many instruments. The following stylised facts were observed: little autocorrelation was shown in return series, significant autocorrelation was detected through squared returns, conditional expectations of return are close to zero, volatility fluctuates over time, return series indicate signs of flat tails or leptokurtosis, and return series shows evidence of volatility clustering. The author later used these stylised facts to exhibit volatility clustering in terms of market participant behaviour to new information (Cont, 2007).

In a similar study done by Einarsson (2013), the stylised facts were used to identify a subset of stylised facts of financial price series. The stylised facts examined by the author were as follows: the absence of autocorrelation in returns, autocorrelation of squared returns, returns are not normally distributed or have flat tails, and the skewness of the returns. The author used various models to replicate or explain these stylised facts. These models showed success in reproducing the stylised facts of financial time series. However, the author pointed out that the results may be a coincidence (the set stylised facts identified) and may not indicate an explanation for some of the regularities seen in financial markets.

Kumar (2010) applied the stylised fact theory to volatility indices, instead of financial returns as seen in studies by Kaldor (1961), Guillaume et al. (1997), Cont (2001) and Einarsson (2013). The author examined the statistical properties of India's volatility index (Ivix) with the overall objective of defining a set of properties, common across many volatility indices. Kumar (2010) concludes with the following list of stylised facts of volatility:

Fact 1: volatility clustering and volatility persistence,
Fact 2: the mean reversion of volatility,
Fact 3: the negative relationship between stock returns and volatility,
Fact 4: the positive relationship between trading volumes and volatility.

The limitation of Kumar's (2010) study was that the author only focused on India as an emerging economy. In this study, Kumar (2010) is used as a basis for the empirical analysis, where the emphasis is on stylised facts of volatility indices for five emerging markets (as mentioned previously). To test for volatility clustering and persistence, the autocorrelation function is considered. An autoregressive model (unit root test) is used for the presence of mean reversion. To indicate the negative relationship between stock markets and volatility, the relationship between volatility indices and stock market returns is considered by making use of regression analysis. The positive relationship between trading volumes and volatility is shown by regressing detrended trading volume on volatility indices. In addition, the study done by Kumar (2010) is also extended to consider the volatility modelling of volatility index returns.

3.2.2 *GARCH Modelling of Volatility Index Returns*

In this section, the recent and relevant literature based on volatility modelling and volatility modelling of volatility indices is outlined. As mentioned in the introduction, research focused on the stylised facts of financial returns is well documented in literature. However, not many studies have considered volatility modelling of volatility index returns. Literature shows that martingales and random walk models assume restrictive assumptions to simplify the testing of returns on assets (Bailey, 2005). These models assume that the rate of return at one point in time is uncorrelated with the rate of return at any later point in time (absence of autocorrelation). However, according to Alexander (2008), empirical evidence shows that autocorrelation is non-zero and volatility of financial asset returns are not constant but changes over time. A study done by Cont (2001) showed results that large price fluctuations are most likely to be followed by large price fluctuations. Stated differently, volatility clustering is the tendency of volatility to occur in bunches.

When it comes to the topic of volatility clustering, there is a large body of empirical evidence that dates back to Mandelbrot (1963). According to Cont (2007), volatility clustering properties are often seen in time series of financial asset returns that result in continued amplification of price changes. Among these properties, the phenomenon of volatility clustering has led to the development of additional stochastic models in finance. Engle (1982) and Bollerslev (1986) introduced the generalised autoregressive conditional heteroscedasticity (GARCH) models, which are designed to capture volatility clustering of returns. These models capture the time variation in volatility and are therefore a more realistic approach to measure risk (Alexander, 2008).

The use of univariate GARCH models is also well documented. Authors like Ahmad and Ping (2014) made use of the standard GARCH, GARCH in mean, threshold GARCH and exponential GARCH (EGARCH) models to model the volatility of gold prices in Malaysia, where the Akaike (AIC) and Schwarz (SIC) information criteria were used to identify the best fitting model. Results indicated that the EGARCH model was the best fit model. Furthermore, the asymmetric GARCH model found that positive shocks lead to a greater increase in volatility than negative shocks.

In a similar study done by Oberholzer and Venter (2015), the standard GARCH, Glosten, Jagannathan and Runkle (GJR-GARCH) and EGARCH models were used to determine the best fitting model for the five indices of the Johannesburg Stock Exchange (JSE), after and leading up to the Global Financial Crises of 2008. The AIC and SIC were used to determine the best fitting GARCH model. Results showed that the GJR-GARCH model was the best fitting model for the JSE. Furthermore, the results showed signs of the leverage effect. According to Black (1976), the leverage effect occurs when negative shocks give rise to even greater volatility when compared to positive shocks.

Huang, Lin and Wang (2019) used four general pricing models to evaluate volatility index option (VXO) prices on the Taiwan stock index (using CBOE VIX as a benchmark due to the unavailability of VXO trading at the time). The models used by the authors consisted of Black-Scholes (BS), square root (SQR), lognormal Ornstein–Uhlenbeck (LOU) and GARCH models. Results showed that the Taiwan Futures Exchange (TAIEX) and VIX move in conflicting directions. The estimated VXOs determined by the different models indicated a descending order of GARCH > BS > SQR > LOU. Thus, when VIX is heteroscedastic, the VXOs could be unevaluated by the BS model. The SQR and LOU models could seriously undervalue the options when VIX has no mean reverting property, especially for the long-term maturity options.

In a recent study, Venter and Maré (2021) tested whether GARCH models can be used for price discovery in the volatility index options market. The authors applied different GARCH models to VIX futures returns. The results indicated that the symmetric GARCH model with skewed Student's t errors was the best performing model. Furthermore, when the GARCH model is applied to the VIX, it provided reasonable price discovery.

Literature shows that volatility modelling of index returns is well documented, as seen above. However, not a lot of research has been done on the volatility modelling of volatility index returns. In this study, the focus is on volatility modelling of volatility indices by making use of the standard GARCH model, the asymmetric GJR-GARCH and EGARCH models. This will give an indication of the degree of asymmetry and whether positive and negative shocks affect volatility the same way.

3.3 Methodology

In this section, the methods applied in this study to illustrate the statistical properties and volatility models applied to volatility indices are discussed. This section is divided into two subsections, the first focuses on the stylised facts of volatility, and the second considers GARCH models applied to volatility index returns.

3.3.1 Stylised Facts of Volatility

This analysis of the stylised facts of volatility is based on the work by Kumar (2010). The empirical analysis applied to test for the presence of each stylised fact is outlined below.

Stylised Fact 1 According to Brooks (2015), volatility clustering is the tendency for volatility to occur in bunches. Hence, high volatility is generally followed by periods of high volatility, and low volatility is followed by periods of low volatility.

To test for the presence of volatility clustering and persistence, the autocorrelation function (ACF) is considered. Mathematically, the ACF is defined as follows:

$$\rho_t = Cor\left(VI_t, VI_{t-1}\right),$$

where VI_t is the volatility index level at time t, and $Cor(\cdot)$ is the correlationv function (Danielsson, 2011).

Stylised Fact 2 As discussed, volatility tends to be mean reverting. Based on the work by Kumar (2010), a formal (Augmented Dickey–Fuller–ADF) test for stationarity is applied. According to Asteriou and Hall (2015), the ADF test takes the following form:

$$\Delta y_t = \gamma y_{t-1} + \sum_{i=1}^{p} \delta_i \Delta y_{t-1} + u_t,$$

where y_t is an arbitrary time series, the optimal lag length p is determined using information criteria, and u_t is a white noise error process. If $\gamma = 0$, it implies that y_t is stationary. This test can be extended to incorporate an intercept and a trend. In addition, the following autoregressive model is estimated:

$$IV_t = \lambda_0 + \lambda_1 IV_{t-1} + \varepsilon_t,$$

where ε_t is a white noise error term. The mean reversion level is calculated as $\frac{1}{1-\lambda_1}$, and this gives an indication of how long the process will take to dissipate half of the mean reversion effect following a shock to the equity market.

Stylised Fact 3 This fact focuses on the relationship between equity returns and volatility. According to Alexander (2008), the negative relationship between equity returns and volatility is referred to as the leverage effect. The following regression model is used to test for the existence of this property,

$$RIV_t = \alpha_0 + \alpha_1 1_{\{R<0\}} R_t + \alpha_2 \alpha_1 1_{\{R>0\}} R_t,$$

where $RIV_t = \ln {}^{IV_t}\!/_{IV_{t-1}}$, and $R_t = \ln {}^{S_t}\!/_{S_{t-1}}$, where S_t denotes the underlying index/ETF level at time t, $1_{\{R<0\}}$ is an indicator function that takes a value of 1 when the market goes up ($R_t > 0$) and 0 otherwise, and the indicator function $1_{\{R>0\}}$ takes a value of one when the market goes down. For the observed relationship to hold, α_0 should be equal to zero, and the expected signs of α_1 and α_2 are negative.

Stylised Fact 4 Regression analysis is also used to test for the presence of a positive relationship between trading volume and volatility. To be consistent with

Kumar (2010), detrended trading volume is used. If trading volume is denoted by v_t, detrended trading volume ($\tilde{v}_t$) is the error term of the following regression equation:

$$v_t = \theta_1 + \theta_2 t + \theta_3 t^2 + \tilde{v}_t.$$

The following regression model is estimated to give an indication of the relationship between equity returns and trading volume:

$$IV_t = \beta_1 + \beta_2 \tilde{v}_t + \beta_3 \tilde{v}_t - 1 + \beta_4 \tilde{v}_t - 4 + \epsilon_t,$$

where ϵ_t is a white noise error term. In this case, positive slope coefficients are expected. GARCH models applied to volatility index returns are discussed in the next subsection.

3.3.2 GARCH Modelling of Volatility Index Returns

The study by Kumar (2010) is extended to consider the GARCH modelling of volatility index returns (*RIV*$_t$). The following mean model is assumed:

$$RIV_t = \mu + \xi_t,$$

where ξ is assumed to be normally distributed with mean zero and conditional variance h_t. For the conditional variance, the following models are considered: GARCH(1,1), GJR-GARCH(1,1) (Glosten et al.) and EGARCH(1,1) (exponential GARCH). According to Asteriou and Hall (2015), the symmetric GARCH model takes the following form:

$$h_t = \omega + a\xi_{t-1}^2 + bh_{t-1},$$

where the coefficients ω, a and b are estimated using maximum-likelihood estimation. To take asymmetric effects into account, the GJR-GARCH model is estimated. Brooks (2015) defines the GJR-GARCH(1,1) model as follows:

$$h_t = \omega + a\xi_{t-1}^2 + bh_{t-1} + c1_{\{\xi_{t-1}<0\}}\xi_{t-1}^2,$$

where the indicator function $1_{\{\xi_{t-1}<0\}}$ takes a value of one when shocks are negative ($\xi_t < 0$) and zero otherwise. A well-known shortcoming of univariate GARCH model estimation is the non-negativity constraints that are required. Therefore, the EGARCH(1,1) model that does not require non-negativity constraints is also considered. The EGARCH(1,1) model takes the following form (Alexander, 2008),

$$\ln h_t = \omega + a \left| \frac{\xi_{t-1}}{\sqrt{h_{t-1}}} \right| + b \ln h_{t-1} + c \frac{\xi_{t-1}}{\sqrt{h_{t-1}}} .$$

The different univariate GARCH models are compared based on the Akaike (AIC) and Schwarz information criterion (SIC) to determine the best fitting model. The empirical results are considered in the next section.

3.4 Empirical Results

3.4.1 Data Specification

Daily data from 2 January 2012 to 31 March 2021 were used for most of the empirical analysis of this study. The underlying index/exchange-traded fund (ETF) and volatility index for each country are listed in the Table 3.1 below.

The data were obtained from the Thomson Reuters Datastream databank. The volatility indices are plotted below.

The volatility indices, Fig. 3.1, seem to be mean reverting. However, this will be tested formally in Sect. 3.5 below. As can be seen from the graph below, there is a substantial increase in volatility in all countries during the COVID-19 pandemic of 2020. This is consistent with expectations. According to a recent study by Baker et al. (2020), the increase in volatility during 2020, can be attributed to the role of new information about infectious diseases. Furthermore, the authors explained that the stock market reaction can be explained by mandatory business hours, restrictions on social activities and social distancing, including the effect of government intervention and policies (Baker et al., 2020). In conjunction with Fig. 3.1, the descriptive statistics of the volatility indices are reported in the Table 3.2 below.

From Table 3.2, it can be noted that Brazil reached a maximum level of 144.42 during the COVID-19 pandemic of 2020, and South Africa reached 49.04%. All the volatility indices are not normally distributed as can be seen from the Jarque–Bera probability. The kurtosis and skewness indicate the volatility indices are positively skewed (skewness>0) and indicate leptokurtosis with fat tails (kurtosis>3). The presence of the stylised facts of volatility in emerging markets is considered in the next subsection.

Table 3.1 Underlying and volatility index data

Country	Underlying	Volatility index
Brazil	iShares MSCI Brazil ETF	CBOE Brazil ETF Volatility Index
India	Nifty	India VIX
China	iShares China Large-Cap ETF	CBOE China ETF Volatility Index
Korea	KOSPI 200	VKOSPI
South Africa	FTSE/JSE Top 40 Index	South African Volatility Index

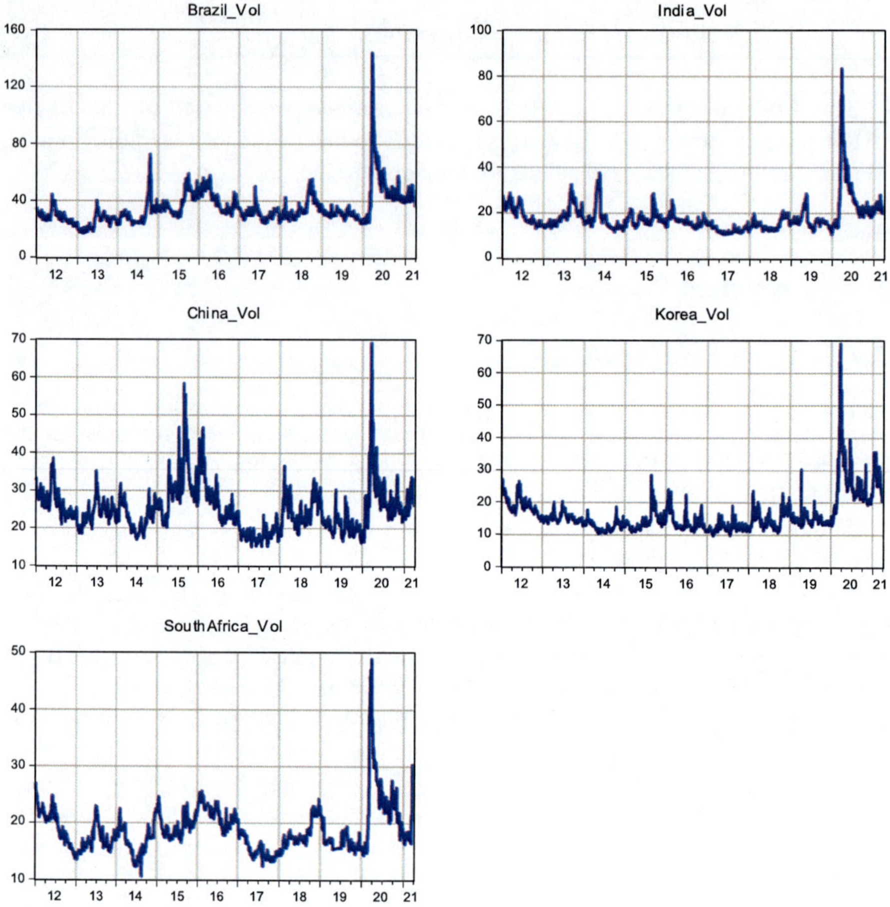

Fig. 3.1 Line graphs of the volatility indices

Table 3.2 Descriptive statistics

	Brazil	India	China	Korea	South Africa
Mean	34.94	18.0486	25.0706	16.3562	18.83686
Median	32.18	16.41	24.21	14.55	17.95
Maximum	144.42	83.61	69.28	69.24	49.04
Minimum	16.67	10.45	15.09	9.72	10.61
Std. Dev.	11.6961	6.6893	5.998	5.9176	4.100167
Skewness	2.9789	3.7526	1.7553	3.1316	2.305241
Kurtosis	21.1234	25.5825	9.3047	18.9777	14.02171
Jarque–Bera	36592.21	56936.55	5235.604	29611.15	14350.79
Probability	0	0	0	0	0
Sum	84310.11	43551.31	60495.27	39467.6	45453.34
Sum Sq. Dev.	329960.1	107927.7	86775.45	84464.04	40549.01
Observations	2413	2413	2413	2413	2413

3.5 Stylised Facts of Volatility

Stylised Fact 1 As mentioned in the methodology section, a graphical representation of the autocorrelation function (ACF) illustrates the correlation between a variable and lagged values of itself. The ACF of the different volatility indices considered in this study is plotted below (Fig. 3.2).

Tsay (2005) defines ACF as the dependence or correlation of a variable and lagged values of that variable. Based on the graph above, the log difference shows no significant autocorrelation and is therefore consistent with stylised fact 1.

Stylised Fact 2 To determine if the mean is reverting, the data need to be tested for stationary through a unit root test. An augmented Dicky–Fuller (ADF) test was used to test for unit roots. The results are shown in Table 3.3 below.

An ADF unit root test done for all countries indicates that all volatility indices considered in this study do not have a unit root, and this confirms the presence of stylised fact 2. Therefore, the volatility mean is reverting.

Next, an attempt is made to compute the mean reversion rate that determines the number of days it takes for the data to revert to the long-term norm (Table 3.4).

The table below shows the number of days required for the mean reversion effect to dissipate after a market shock, for each volatility index. The reversion for each country differs, while the reversion process in China takes roughly one month, it takes more than twice as long in South Africa.

Stylised Fact 3 The negative relationship between stock returns and volatility is tested using the leverage effect. The results are shown in Table 3.5 below.

The constant term, α_0, is close to zero for each volatility index (however, only the constant terms of China and South Africa are statistically insignificant). Furthermore, the α_1 and α_2 are negative and statistically significant, which is consistent with the stylised facts of volatility.

Stylised Fact 4 The positive relationship between trading volumes and volatility is tested by using a regression model as discussed in the methodology. Table 3.6 indicates the results from this regression.

Trading volume date for the FTSE/JSE Top 40 Index was not available, and therefore, South Africa's volatility is excluded from this analysis. The coefficients, β_2, β_3 and β_4, for each country are positive. This shows that there is a positive relationship between volatility and trading volume, which is consistent with stylised fact 4.

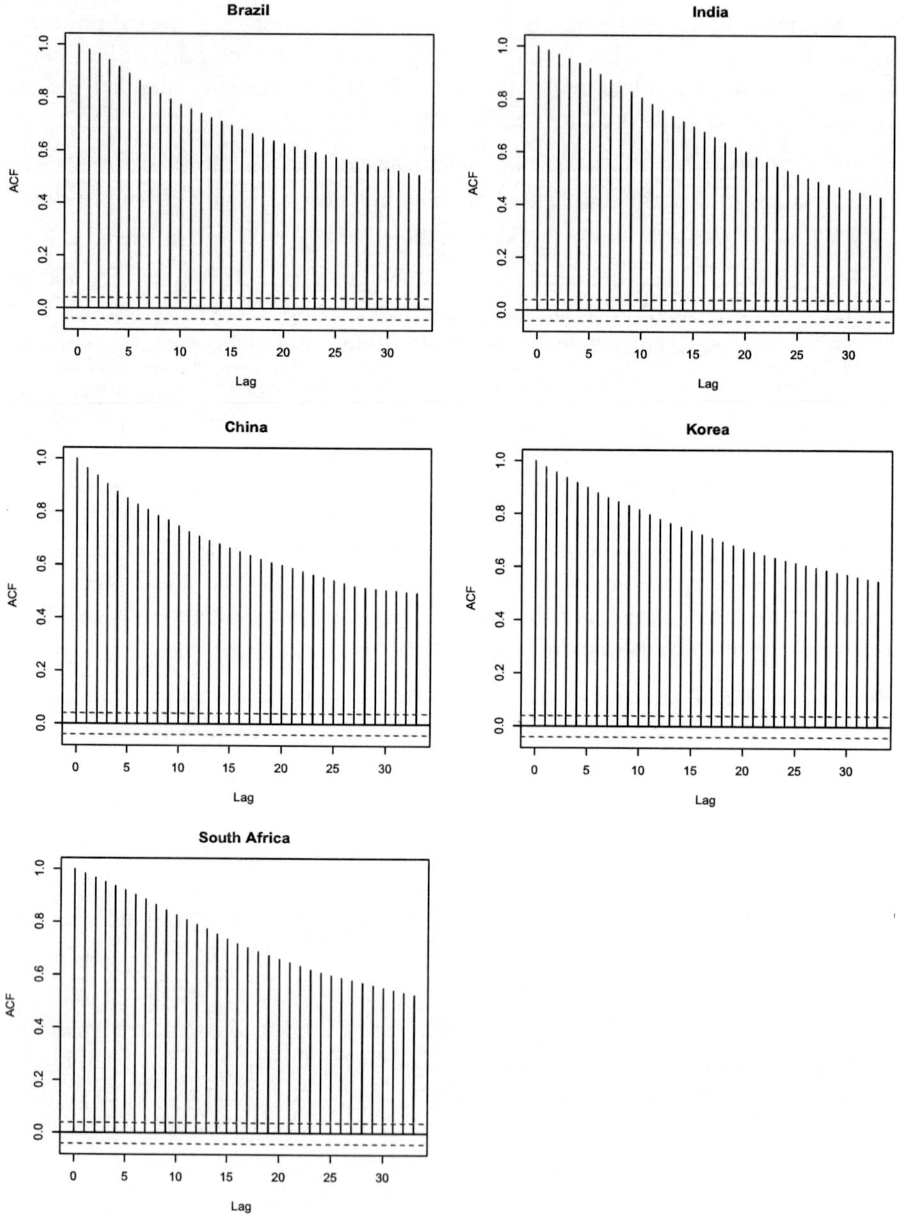

Fig. 3.2 ACF of volatility index levels

Table 3.3 ADF test of volatility indices

Volatility Index	ADF t-stat
Brazil	−4.8566***
India	−5.4864***
China	−6.0959***
Korea	−5.3561***
South Africa	−4.5678***

*(**) [***]: statistically significant at a 10(5)[1] % level

Table 3.4 Estimation of the mean reversion rate

Volatility index	λ_0	λ_1	Mean reversion
Brazil	0.6678***	0.9809***	52.3697
India	0.2641***	0.9852***	67.6133
China	0.9125***	0.9635***	27.3845
Korea	0.3721***	0.9771***	43.6243
South Africa	0.3082***	0.9835***	60.7349

*(**) [***]: statistically significant at a 10(5)[1] % level

Table 3.5 Leverage effect

Volatility index	α_0	α_1	α_2
Brazil	−0.0078***	−1.7365***	−0.7539***
India	−0.0045***	−1.139***	−0.2997***
China	−0.0021	−1.7151***	−0.9418***
Korea	−0.0079***	−4.5324***	−2.003***
South Africa	−0.0015	−1.4599***	−1.0033***

*(**) [***]: statistically significant at a 10(5)[1] % level

Table 3.6 Trading volume and volatility regression coefficients

Volatility index	β_1	β_2	β_3	β_4
Brazil	34.949	0.0002	0.0001	0.0002
India	17.9071	1E-09	1E-09	2E-09
China	25.0528	0.0001	0.0001	0.0001
Korea	16.3945	1.97E-05	1.13E-05	1.83E-05

*(**) [***]: statistically significant at a 10(5)[1] % level

3.6 GARCH Modelling of Volatility Index Returns

The study by Kumar (2010) is extended to consider the GARCH modelling of volatility index returns. As discussed in the methodology, the following models are considered: GARCH(1,1), GJR-GARCH(1,1) and EGARCH(1,1). Before GARCH models can be estimated, it is necessary to establish the presence of autoregressive conditional heteroscedastic (ARCH) effects. The results of the ARCH Lagrange multiplier (LM) test are reported in the Table 3.7 below.

The F-statistic shows evidence of ARCH effects at a 1% level for all the countries except South Africa. Hence, there is volatility clustering present, and the optimal parameters of different GARCH family models for all the variables, except South Africa, can be estimated. The GARCH coefficients and information criteria (AIC and SIC) are reported in the Tables 3.8, 3.9 and 3.10 below.

Table 3.7 ARCH LM results

Volatility Index	F-Statistic
Brazil	15.0106***
India	17.5665***
China	111.6441***
Korea	641.8913***
South Africa	0.0367

*(**) [***]: statistically significant at a 10(5)[1] % level

Table 3.8 GARCH(1,1) optimal parameters

	Brazil	India	China	Korea
μ	−0.0003	0.0001	−0.0001	0.0016
ω	0.0004***	0.0004***	0.0002***	0.001***
a	0.1578***	0.0848***	0.1269***	0.256***
b	0.6706***	0.7591***	0.7875***	0.4598***
AIC	−3.3358	−3.2221	−3.221	−3.0037
SIC	−3.3262	−3.2125	−3.2114	−2.9941

*(**) [***]: statistically significant at a 10(5)[1] % level

Table 3.9 GJR-GARCH(1,1) optimal parameters

	Brazil	India	China	Korea
μ	0.0016*	0.001	0.0022**	0.003***
ω	−0.2214***	−0.1984***	−0.3514***	−0.6219***
a	0.0519***	0.0289***	0.1223***	0.1439***
c	0.1407***	0.0994***	0.1281***	0.126***
b	0.97***	0.9705***	0.9563***	0.9094***
AIC	**−3.3616**	**−3.2453**	**−3.2356**	−3.0196
SIC	**−3.3496**	**−3.2333**	**−3.2236**	−3.0076

*(**) [***]: statistically significant at a 10(5)[1] % level

Table 3.10 EGARCH(1,1) optimal parameters

	Brazil	India	China	Korea
μ	0.0011	0.0008	0.0012	0.0018
ω	0.0001***	0.0003***	0.0002***	0.0002***
a	0.145***	0.1213***	0.1552***	0.1359***
c	−0.1531***	−0.1118***	−0.1343***	−0.2091***
b	0.8711***	0.8258***	0.8364***	0.9071***
AIC	−3.3513	−3.2333	−3.2354	**−3.0494**
SIC	−3.3393	−3.2213	−3.2234	**−3.0374**

*(**) [***]: statistically significant at a 10(5)[1] % level

The asymmetry parameters (c) of the GJR-GARCH and EGARCH models are negative and positive, respectively. This implies that positive shocks lead to a greater rise in volatility when compared to negative shocks. Hence, the volatility indices considered in this study behave more like commodities rather than equities (Alexander, 2008), and this is also consistent with the findings by Venter and Maré (2021). When the information criterion is considered, it is clear that the EGARCH model is the best fitting model for all the volatility indices, except Korea. For Korea, the GJR-GARCH model is the best fitting model.

3.7 Conclusion

The purpose of this chapter is to examine the stylised facts of volatility and volatility modelling of volatility index returns. The stylised facts of volatility were tested by making use of autoregressive models, linear regression and unit root tests. The stylised facts tested included volatility clustering, mean reversion, negative relationship with stock market movements and positive relationship with trading volumes. Empirical results indicated that the volatility indices reproduced all the stylised facts of volatility for the following emerging economies: Brazil, India, China, Korea and South Africa.

In addition to the stylised facts of volatility (based on the work by Kumar, 2010), the volatility modelling of volatility index returns was also considered. The symmetric GARCH and asymmetric GJR-GARCH and EGARCH models were estimated for emerging economies' volatility index returns; the best fitting model was determined using the AIC and SIC. The information criteria suggested that the EGARCH model is the best fitting model for all the volatility indices, except Korea. For Korea, the GJR-GARCH model was the best fitting model. Results showed that volatility indices considered behave more like commodities rather than equities, which implies that positive shocks cause higher volatility when compared to negative shocks.

Areas for future research might include the application of different GARCH processes and error distribution assumptions (e.g. Student's *t* and the generalised error distribution) that incorporate skewness and excess kurtosis to volatility index returns.

References

Ahmad, M. H., & Ping, P. Y. (2014). Modelling Malaysian gold using symmetric and asymmetric GARCH models. *Applied Mathematical Sciences, 8*(17), 817–822.

Alexander, C. (2008). *Market risk analysis: Practical financial econometrics* (Vol. II). Wiley.

Asteriou, D., & Hall, S. G. (2015). *Applied econometrics*. Palgrave Macmillan.

Baker, S. R., Bloom, N., Davis, S. J., Kost, K. J., Sammon, M. C., & Viratyosin, T. (2020). *The unprecedented stock market impact of COVID-19*. (No. w26945). National Bureau of Economic Research.

BBVA. (2016). Emerging and Growth Leading Economies Economic Outlook. Annual Report 2016. https://www.bbvaresearch.com/en/publicaciones/eagles-economicoutlook-annual-report-2016/

Bollerslev, T. (1986). Generalized autoregressive conditional heteroskedasticity. *Journal of Econometrics, 31*(3), 307–327.

Cont, R. (2001). *Empirical properties of asset returns: stylized facts and statistical issues. Quantitative Finance* (Vol. I). Institute of Physics Publication.

Einarsson, R. A. S. M. U. S. (2013). *Reproducing the stylized facts of financial returns.* Chalmers University of Technology.

Guillaume, D. M., Dacorogna, M. M., Davé, R. R., Müller, U. A., Olsen, R. B., & Pictet, O. V. (1997). From the bird's eye to the microscope: A survey of new stylized facts of the intra-daily foreign exchange markets. *Finance and Stochastics, 1*(2), 95–129.

Kaldor, N. (1961). Capital accumulation and economic growth. In *The theory of capital* (pp. 177–222). Palgrave Macmillan.

Kumar, S. S. S. (2010). The behaviour of India's volatility index. *Indore Management Journal,* 2(2), 27–33.

Oberholzer, N., & Venter, P. J. (2015). Univariate GARCH models applied to the JSE/FTSE stock indices. *Procedia Economics and Finance, 24*, 491–500.

Umer, U. M., Coskun, M., & Kiraci, K. (2018). Time-varying return and volatility spillover among eagles stock markets: A multivariate Garch analysis. *Journal of Finance and Economics Research, 3*(1), 23–42.

Venter, P. J., & Maré, E. (2021). *Price discovery in the volatility index option market: A univariate GARCH approach* (p. 102069). Finance Research Letters.

Chapter 4
Quantitative Analysis of Corruption Political Factors

Beáta Mikušová Meričková, Michal Lendvorský, and Nikoleta Jakuš Muthová

Abstract The factors of corrupt behaviour resulting from the political environment have the strongest impact on corruption. The enforceability of political accountability and the transparency of the political system can be considered as the political factors of corruption. The aim of the study is to quantitatively confirm the impact of the degree of political accountability and transparency of the political system on corruption in country. The quantitative testing of relationship between corruption (measured by Corruption Perceptions Index), enforceability of political accountability (measured by Rule of Law Index) and the transparency of the political system determined by freedom of press (measured by Press Freedom Index) and quality of institution (included in Global Competitiveness Index) is realized. The relevance enforceability of political accountability and the transparency of the political system as political factors of corruption are confirmed by statistical methods and discussed in broader socio-political context. Within it, the quality of the institutions, the freedom of the press has the greatest impact on the level of corruption.

Keywords Corruption · Enforceability of political accountability · The transparency of the political system · The rule of law index · Press Freedom Index · Global Competitiveness Index

4.1 Introduction

Corruption is a response to the legal, economic, cultural and political institutions in a country (Schelling, 1960). The causes of corruption thus stem from the economic, political and cultural–social environment. The phenomenon of corruption is most strongly associated with the political environment, and factors of corrupt

B. M. Meričková (✉) · M. Lendvorský · N. J. Muthová
Faculty of Economics, Matej Bel University, Banská Bystrica, Slovakia
e-mail: beata.mikusovamerickova@umb.sk

N. Tsounis, A. Vlachvei (eds.), *Advances in Quantitative Economic Research*, Springer Proceedings in Business and Economics,
https://doi.org/10.1007/978-3-030-98179-2_4

behaviour resulting from the political environment have the strongest influence (; Aidt et al., 2020; Santoro & Kumar, 2018; Statista, 2020). The political factors of corrupt behaviour can be identified as the enforceability of political accountability (OECD, 2017; Wu, 2005) and the transparency of the political system (Hudori & Mustikasari, 2020; Lima & Delen, 2020).

The rule of law, law enforcement and the powers of supervisory authorities (Apergis & Cooray, 2017; Klitgaard, 1998) determine the enforceability of political accountability. Transactions with state representatives, the government or other public officials are marked by a certain asymmetry of information (Kaufmann & Wei, 2000; Klitgaard, 1998; Ondráčka, 2005), which naturally creates a motive to act corruptly (Hudori & Mustikasari, 2020; Vašečka, 2007). From this point of view, increasing the transparency of the political system can reduce the risk of corruption (Holcombe & Boudreaux, 2015; Malagueño et al., 2010; Wroe et al., 2013). The freedom of the press reduces this information asymmetry and increases the transparency of the political system. Political decentralization, perceived as a positive phenomenon, can negatively affect the risk of corruption, mainly in case of low institutional quality (Treisman, 2000; Fan & Lin a Treisman, 2009; Tanzi, 2010; Arikan, 2004; Freille et al., 2008). However, the quantitative analysis of relationship between corruption enforceability of political accountability and the transparency of the political system is missing. The aim of the study is to quantitatively confirm the impact of the degree of political accountability and transparency of the political system on corruption in country. Quantitative analysis of relationship between corruption (measured by Corruption Perceptions Index), enforceability of political accountability (measured by Rule of Law Index) and the transparency of the political system determined by freedom of press (measured by Press Index Freedom) and quality of institution (included in Global Competitiveness Index) is realized to achieve this aim.

4.2 Theoretical Framework

The essence of political responsibility is to justify political decisions and take responsibility for their consequences (Lewis & Hendrawan, 2019). Political responsibility is given by a certain limit of the exercise of state power directly corresponding to guaranteed civil liberties (Duvanova, 2014). Given this, it can be assumed that the enforceability of political responsibility is low in countries where socialist or authoritarian regimes of government predominate. However, the application of the principle of enforcing political accountability is also challenging in countries with democratic regimes (Acemoglu & Verdier, 1998; Lewis & Hendrawan, 2019; OECD, 2016). Political enforcement is thus directly linked to the degree of democracy in the country (Liu, 2010; Malagueño et al., 2010). Many studies confirm that a high level of democracy reduces the risk of corrupt behaviour (Kimbro, 2002; Li et al., 2015; Rose-Ackerman, 1998).

Stable parliamentary democracy and guaranteed political accountability (Rose-Ackerman, 1998; Shleifer & Vishny, 1993) reduce the risk of politicians' own interests and those close to their interest groups taking precedence over the public interest (Amin & Soh, 2020; Anderson, 2015; Apergis & Cooray, 2017; Holcombe & Boudreaux, 2015) and thus the risk of corruption.

The enforceability of political accountability is determined by the rule of law, law enforcement and the powers of supervisory authorities (Apergis & Cooray, 2017; Klitgaard, 1998). From this point of view, the Rule of Law Index is an important indicator for us (Apergis & Cooray, 2017; Carr & Outhwaite, 2011; Kimbro, 2002; Klitgaard, 1998; Ngozi, 2018). It encompasses the nine dimensions of the rule of law: the absence of corruption, order and security, restrictions on government powers, fundamental rights, open governance, regulatory enforcement, access to civil justice, effective criminal justice and informal justice.

There is a certain degree of natural information asymmetry in the political environment, which is necessary from the point of view of maintaining top secret data and security of the country (Houqe & Monem, 2013). On the other hand, the benefits of information asymmetry can be misused for personal gain by public officials. The tool of solving information asymmetry in governance is the transparency of the political system (Hudori & Mustikasari, 2020; Kaufmann & Wei, 2000; Klitgaard, 1998). The transparent functioning of individual levels of government is positively influenced by a free and independent press, which plays an important role in informing society and especially in a situation where society is active and able to put pressure on responsible behaviour of political institutions (Hirsch & Watson, 2010; Ghur, 1998; Malagueño et al., 2010; Wroe et al., 2013; Holcombe & Boudreaux, 2015). A certain indicator of the transparency of the political system is the Press Freedom Index (Chayes, 2016; Kuris, 2014; Szeghyová, 2011). The freedom of the press index identifies the degree of representation of opinions in the media space, the independence of the media (Ngozi, 2018; Schweizer, 2019). Transactions with state representatives, the government or other public officials are marked by a certain asymmetry of information (Ondráčka, 2005), which naturally creates a motive to act corruptly (Vašečka, 2007). The presence of freedom of the press (quantified by Press Freedom Index) reduces this information asymmetry, increasing the transparency of the political system.

As the number of individual levels of government increases, the transparency of the political system decreases. Decentralization as part of the democratization process therefore has a paradoxically negative effect in terms of reducing corruption. Research on the relationship between political decentralization and corruption has concluded that the incidence of accepting and providing bribes increases with increasing levels of government (Apergis & Cooray, 2017; Rose-Ackerman, 1998; Tanzi, 2010; Treisman, 2000; Unger, 2018). Political decentralization, perceived as a positive phenomenon, can therefore negatively affect the risk of corruption. Paradoxically, authoritarian regimes with development-oriented elites reduce the risk of corruption (Glaeser & Saks, 2004; Rose-Ackerman, 1999).

The division of power into different levels of government, reducing the transparency of the political system, increases the risk of corruption, especially in the case of poor-quality institutions. Political systems lack balanced sharing of power and transparent and accountable functioning of institutions (Amundsen, 1999; Niskanen & William, 1971; Vašečka, 2007). The quality of institutions can be assessed as part of the Global Competitiveness Index (Anderson, 2015; Unger, 2018). This index consists of twelve pillars: quality of public institutions, infrastructure, macroeconomic environment, health and primary education, higher education and training, goods market efficiency, labour market efficiency, financial market maturity, technological readiness, market size, business maturity and innovation.

4.3 Methodology

The aim of the study is to quantitatively confirm the impact of the degree of political accountability and transparency of the political system on corruption in country. The subject of the examination with regard to the set goal is the mutual relationship between the level of corruption and the enforcement of political responsibility. The research precondition, the source of which is the theoretical basis of the political factors of corruption, is the existence of a mutual relationship between the level of corruption and the enforcement of political responsibility. The level of political enforceability given by the degree of democracy—the level of the rule of law, freedom of the media and the quality of institutions have an impact on the level of corruption in a given country. We describe the relationship quantitatively by determining the dependence between the Corruption Perceptions Index as a dependent variable and the rule of law, freedom of the press and global competitiveness indices as independent variables.

The Corruption Perceptions Index has been compiled annually since 1995 by the non-governmental organization Transparency International (TI). The index reflects the views of experts on the prevalence of corruption and various expert surveys. The value of the index is in the range < 0–100>, where 100 means an economy without corruption. According to TI, the CPI expresses how corruption is perceived in a given country, while corruption is the abuse of public office for private gain. The calculation of this index is based on thirteen different sources based on ten independent organizations, but not all sources are used in the calculation of the CPI. The minimum for including a country in the assessment of the level of perception of corruption in the country is set at three independent sources. The professional community, entrepreneurs and various analysts answer questions about corruption in the public sector (abuse of power by public officials for their own benefit). The CPI value itself is obtained using the average of the responses. As the data are from different sources and therefore have different rates, they have to be standardized before entering the final index. The final CPI value is thus the average of the transformed values of all sources. Vojtková (2007) points out the different reliability of this index consisting in the "inconsistency of input data, which is caused by the availability of different input indicators for different countries".

The independent variable The Rule of Law Index includes nine dimensions of the rule of law—limitation of government powers, absence of corruption, order and security, fundamental rights, open government, regulatory enforcement, access to civil justice, effective criminal justice and informal justice. Its quantification is based on expert opinions, but also on the experience and opinions of citizens. The score of the index ranges from 0 points to a maximum of 10 points, where 0–4 is authoritarian regimes, 4.01–6 is hybrid regimes, 6.01–8 is flawed democracies, and 8.01–10 is full democracies.

The second independent variable is the press freedom index. The score of the index ranges from 0 to 100, with values towards one hundred representing the low level of the Freedom of the Press Index.

The last independent variable is the global competitiveness index. The index takes values from 0 to 100, where 100 represents the frontier, an ideal state where an issue ceases to be a constraint to productivity growth (Schwab, 2019).

We verify the validity of the research assumption as a null hypothesis in a random set of countries. We obtained a list of countries from the website of the Ministry of Foreign Affairs and European Affairs of the Slovak Republic. We then assigned numbers from 1 to 199 to the individual countries in alphabetical order. Subsequently, we compiled a random sample using a random selection function. A suitable way of selecting countries is random selection, given that each entity has the same chance to get into the sample, other words is in no way excluded from the selection. These countries are as follows: Argentina, Austria, Bangladesh, Belgium, Brazil, Canada, Czech Republic, Denmark, Dominican Republic, Finland, France, Germany, Haiti, Hungary, China, Indonesia, Luxembourg, Mexico, Netherlands, New Zealand, Poland, Russia, Slovakia, Sudan, Switzerland, Turkey, Ukraine, UK, USA and Zimbabwe. Countries are diverse in terms of economic maturity, demography, geography, different cultures, different levels of corruption and different political systems in the countries of the world.

We use the statistical software IBM SPSS Statistics 19 for evaluation, we consider a significance level of 0.05 during testing. From statistical methods, we use Pearson's correlation coefficient and multiple linear regression. Pearson's correlation coefficient takes values from -1 to 1. Dependence between individual characters, resp. degree/degree of how the characters are related to each other, we determined as follows: values of the correlation coefficient (r) in the range from 0 to | 0.3 | we evaluate it as a weak direct, resp. indirect dependence, values in the interval from | 0,3 | after | 0.6 | we evaluate it as a medium direct, resp. indirect dependence and values in the interval from | 0.6 | after | 1 | as a strong direct, resp. indirect dependence.

We use multiple linear regression when looking for the values of a dependent variable from a linear combination of the values of several independent variables. The aim of multiple linear regression is to explain the variance of the dependent variable by statistics R2 and to estimate the effect of each independent variable on the dependent variable by non-standardized regression coefficients b, controlling the action of other independent variables that enter the model. The relative strength of the influence of individual variables on the dependent variable is determined by standardized regression coefficients beta (Vojtková, 2007).

We draw input data for evaluation from databases of international organizations that ensure primary data collection.

4.4 Results and Discussion

We compiled scatter plots of interdependence between the individual independent variables (Rule of Law Index, Freedom of the Press Index and Competitiveness Index) and the dependent variable (Corruption Perceptions Index).

The scatter plot of the dependence of the Rule of Law Index and the Corruption Perceptions Index indicates a slight fragmentation of countries; these countries are not concentrated in one area. Approximately common values are characteristic of Switzerland, Finland and New Zealand, while the Netherlands, Germany and Luxembourg are also approaching these countries in terms of value. Sudan, Zimbabwe, Russia and China are on the periphery, caused by the low values of both indices (the prevalence of corruption in the country is high, and the rule of law is low). Brazil, along with the Dominican Republic (high rule of law and more widespread corruption than other countries), also separated from the group. The pair of countries Czech Republic and Poland are characterized by similar values of both indices, but in the case of the Czech Republic and Poland, these are the inverse values of both indices. While Poland, compared to the Czech Republic, is characterized by a lower prevalence of corruption, the rule of law has become lower. In the case of the Czech Republic, this is the opposite situation—more widespread corruption and a higher rule of law (Fig. 4.1).

Kotera et al. (2010) find that in countries with high democracy levels, an increase in government size can decrease the level of corruption, while it will do the opposite, if democracy is weak. This is precisely because, in countries with functioning democracies, politicians are monitored through the media and free elections. On the contrary, if these institutions are weak, it will cause an increase in the level of corruption (Kotera et al., 2010). The following figure (Fig. 4.2) shows the relationship between the Corruption Perceptions Index and the Press Freedom Index as one of the institutions that has a positive effect on the level of corruption in a functioning democracy. According to Pellegrini (2011), if democracy has existed in a country for at least 10 years but not more than 45 years, it leads to a reduction in the level of corruption in the country. Similar results were obtained by Treisman (2000) and Rock (2009), who state that democracy leads to a reduction in corruption only if it is established in the country for a long time. Our results point out that the level of corruption is higher in the former post-communist countries, because of democratic establishment in these countries has not been established for a long enough time.

The scatter plot of the Corruption Perceptions Index and the Freedom of the Press Index indicates the fragmentation of countries, which means that even in this

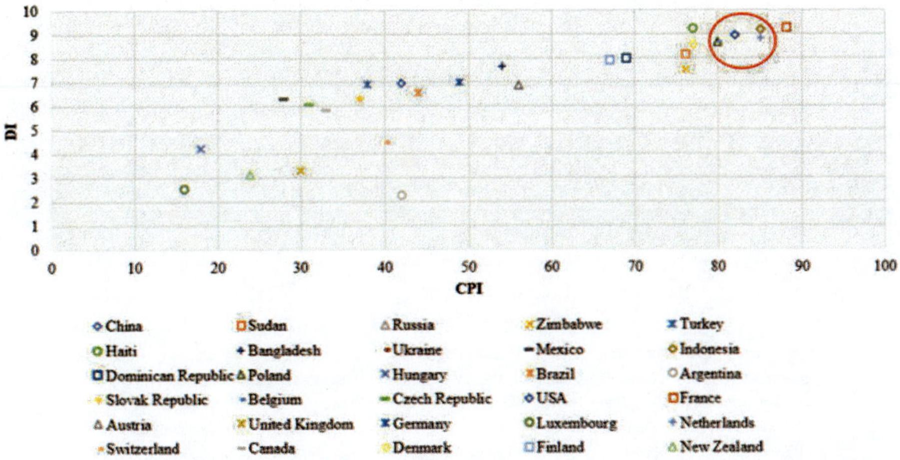

Fig. 4.1 Combinations of corruption perceptions index and rule of law index (2019). (Source: Processing based on Infographics.economist and transparency international data; World Justice Project 2021)

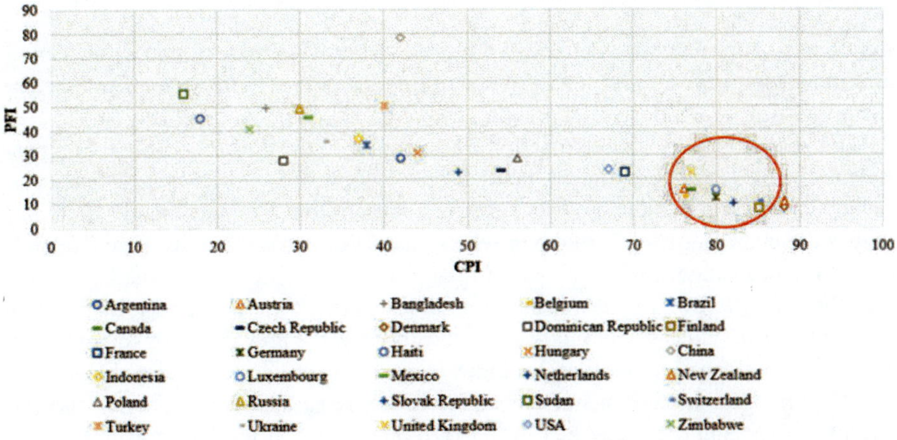

Fig. 4.2 Combinations of corruption perceptions index and press freedom index (2020). (Source: Processing based on Infographics.economist and reporters without borders data; Reporters Without Borders 2021)

case, countries are not concentrated in one area. Approximately common values are characteristic of Switzerland, Finland and Austria. These are countries that have achieved a high level of the rule of law. These countries are at about the same level as in the previous case (Fig. 4.1). Sudan and China are on the periphery, which is due to the low values of both indices (in the country, the prevalence of corruption is high and the freedom of the press is low). Haiti, along with the Dominican Republic and Zimbabwe (a high degree of freedom of the press and more widespread corruption

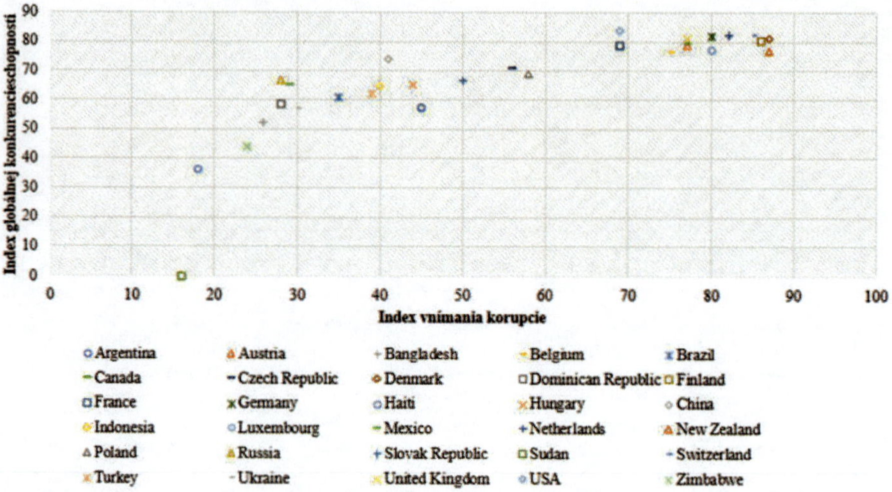

Fig. 4.3 Combinations of corruption perceptions index and global competitiveness index (2019). (Source: Own processing from the obtained flia.org data)

than other countries), also separated from the group. The pair of countries, China and Indonesia, have similar levels of corruption index, but in the case of Indonesia, the promotion of freedom of expression in public is at a better level (Fig. 4.3).

The scatter plot of the Corruption Perceptions Index and the Global Competitiveness Index indicates the fragmentation of countries, which means that even in this case, countries are not concentrated in one area. Approximately common values are characteristic, as in the previous case of countries such as New Zealand, Switzerland, Denmark and Finland. Similar values are achieved in Canada, Austria and the UK. Haiti, Zimbabwe and Bangladesh are on the periphery, which has caused the low values of both indices (in the country, the prevalence of corruption is high and the global competitiveness index is low). According to Enste and Heldman (2017), the same regulations and changes in tax rates adopted in Russia and the Scandinavian countries may also bring differences in the level of corruption due to the historical development of individual countries. Dreher (2009) state that the quality of an institution has a major impact on the level of corruption. This effect can be divided into a direct effect and an indirect effect which works through lowering the scope of the shadow economy. According to Lamsdorff (2006) the economic freedom, the degree of competitiveness in economy is essential for the reduction of corruption. If there is a lower degree of economic freedom in a given country, resp. competitiveness, this results in an increase in the level of corruption. The reason is that more competition there is, the harder is it to hide corrupt payments, because competitors might uncover the corrupt activities and therefore the risk of being detected is higher than in a monopoly market (Enste & Heldman, 2017).

In the next section, we will focus on independent variables that affect the level of corruption. Data are processed by Pearson correlation coefficient and

Table 4.1 Correlations between the dependent variable corruption rate index and the independent variables

Year	Independent variable	Democracy measure index	Freedom of the press index	Global competitiveness index
2012	**r**	0.860	−0.727	0.907
	p	0.000	0.000	0.000
2013	**r**	0.836	−0.762	0.903
	p	0.000	0.000	0.000
2014	**r**	0.862	−0.778	0.900
	p	0.000	0.000	0.000
2015	**r**	0.849	−0.776	0.915
	p	0.000	0.000	0.000
2016	**r**	0.853	−0.749	0.909
	p	0.000	0.000	0.000
2017	**r**	0.874	−0.748	0.901
	p	0.000	0.000	0.000
2018	**r**	0.848	−0.752	0.970
	p	0.000	0.000	0.000
2019	**r**	0.832	−0.782	0.929
	p	0.000	0.000	0.000
2020	**r**	0.841	−0.823	
	p	0.000	0.000	

Source: Own processing

linear regression analysis. The results of the dependence between the independent variable and the dependent variables are given only for those independent variables for which the dependence has been confirmed. The results are processed for the years 2012 to 2020 or from 2019. Due to the different methodology, we use only data for 2019 in the competitiveness rate index. If the relationship between the dependent and independent variables appeared in more than half of the observed periods, we consider this independent variable affecting the level of corruption. The following Tables 4.1 and 4.2 summarize the values of the correlation coefficients and determinations for independent variables for which the existence of interdependence was confirmed within the observed years.

All independent variables in the table can be considered as significant factors influencing the level of corruption in the given countries. Similarly, Enste and Heldman (2017) state that the index of freedom of the press and the quality of institutions—the competitiveness index and the rule of law index are among the strong factors influencing the level of corruption. According to Laderman et al. (2005), Pellegrini (2011) press freedom reduces corruption. On the other hand, there are opinions as stated by Freille et al. (2007), who claim that the media cannot be considered beneficial in general since newspapers might report false information in order to increase the sales. Also, journalist may be involved in corruption themselves leading to false or omitted information (Enste & Heldman, 2017). The

Table 4.2 Coefficients of determination between the dependent variable and the independent variables in %

Independent variable/year	Democracy measure index	Freedom of the press index	Global competitiveness index
2012	73.96	52.85	82.26
2013	69.89	58.06	81.54
2014	74.3	60.53	81.00
2015	72.08	60.22	83.72
2016	72.76	56.1	82.63
2017	76.39	55.95	81.18
2018	71.91	56.55	94.09
2019	69.22	61.15	86.30
2020	70.73	79.92	

Source: Own processing

table shows the extent to which individual independent variables determine the dependent variable.

The global competitiveness index has the most significant impact on the level of corruption. In the following section, we present the results of multiple linear regression for the period from 2012 to 2019 (Table 4.3).

Significant variables in our case are the variables in the column Sig. They have a value less than 0.05. From the data, it is possible to find out whether the given variable influences the index of perception of corruption in a positive or negative sense. A positive relationship can be found, for example, in 2018 between the Global Competitiveness Index and the Perceived Corruption Rate Index—the higher the level of competition, the lower the level of corruption. If the value of this variable increases by 1, it is possible to expect an increase in the perceived corruption rate index by 16,230. On the contrary, there is a negative relationship between the index of perceived corruption and the index of freedom of the press. In this case, however, it should be noted that the Press Freedom Index has the opposite rating; it means 0 is the best possible level. This means that if it is possible to present free speech in a country, the level of corruption in that country is reduced. Changing this variable by 1 would cause the Corruption Perceptions Index to increase by 8939 points in 2019. According to standardized coefficients, the independent variable Global Competitiveness Index has the greatest impact on the Corruption Perceptions Index.

4.5 Conclusion

Several scientific studies declare the impact of the political environment on the level of corruption in the country. However, in the cases known to us, these are claims based on qualitative analysis. Quantitative verification of political factors of

Table 4.3 Linear regression year 2012–2017

		Unstandardized coefficients		Standardized coefficients			Correlations		
Model		B	Std. Error	Beta	t	Sig.	Zero order	Partial	Part
2012	(Constant)	−53.219	9.537		−5.581	0.000			
	GCI 2012	24.679	1.938	0.748	12.736	0.000	0.907	0.928	0.670
	PFI_2012	−0.243	0.040	−0.360	−6.139	0.000	−0.692	−0.769	−0.323
2013	(Constant)	−46.464	11.560		−4.020	0.000			
	GCI 2013	24.874	2.204	0.719	11.288	0.000	0.903	0.911	0.624
	PFI_2013	−0.542	0.093	−0.372	−5.833	0.000	−0.728	−0.753	−0.323
2014	(Constant)	−44.996	10.135		−4.440	0.000			
	GCI 2014	24.782	1.922	0.703	12.891	0.000	0.900	0.930	0.616
	PFI_2014	−0.608	0.081	−0.411	−7.535	0.000	−0.749	−0.828	−0.360
2015	(Constant)	−46.739	8.659		−5.398	0.000			
	GCI 2015	25.470	1.616	0.721	15.761	0.000	0.915	0.951	0.629
	PFI_2015	−0.631	0.072	−0.398	−8.714	0.000	−0.750	−0.863	−0.348
2016	(Constant)	−44.265	9.399		−4.710	0.000			
	GCI 2016	24.555	1.745	0.735	14.071	0.000	0.909	0.940	0.655
	PFI_2016	−0.555	0.075	−0.385	−7.373	0.000	−0.717	−0.822	−0.343
2017	(Constant)	−39.894	10.303		−3.872	0.001			
	GCI 2017	23.450	1.876	0.722	12.501	0.000	0.901	0.926	0.642
	PFI_2017	−0.572	0.085	−0.390	−6.761	0.000	−0.721	−0.798	−0.347
2018	(Constant)	−31.148	7.475		−4.167	0.000			
	GCI 2018	1.525	0.094	0.861	16.230	0.000	0.970	0.954	0.657
	PFI_2018	−0.252	0.079	−0.168	−3.175	0.004	−0.725	−0.529	−0.128
2019	(Constant)	−7.056	5.609		−1.258	0.220			
	GCI 2019	1.253	0.072	0.733	17.383	0.000	0.929	0.960	0.626
	PFI_2019	−0.537	0.060	−0.377	−8.939	0.000	−0.758	−0.869	−0.322
2020	(Constant)	−0,130	7080		−0,018	0,985			
	PFI_2020	8272	1006	0,841	8219	0,000	0,841	0,841	0,841

Source: Own processing

corruption in the context of understanding the problem of corruption is lacking. The presented study is unique in this respect; it quantifies the impact of the level of enforcement of political accountability and transparency of the political system on the level of corruption in the country. The secondary research seeks a relationship between the Corruption Perceptions Index on the one hand and the Rule of Law Index, the Freedom of the Press Index, the Competitiveness Index of Capabilities capturing the rule of law, press freedom and the quality of institutions on the other.

The result is the creation of a unique basic basis for identified political factors conditioning corrupt behaviour, the relevance of which has been confirmed by mathematical and statistical methods. Although we could assume that the enforceability of political responsibility given the degree of democracy is key to maintaining a low level of corruption, quantitative testing of the level of corruption in relation to the quality of the rule of law has not clearly demonstrated this. The reason is the fact that democracy combined with political decentralization can guarantee a reduction in the level of corruption only in the case of transparent operation of the political system and guaranteed quality of institutions.

The quality of institutions, which realistically reflects the very functioning of society, is thus an important factor in corrupt behaviour. This was confirmed by our analysis. When we speak about the protection of property rights, the existence of organized crime and especially in its economic form have the greatest impact on the level of corruption—recently several facts in the Slovak Republic, connected with the murder of investigative journalist Ján Kuciak, have clearly demonstrated this documenting the huge scope and impact the murder of investigative journalist Ján Kuciak. These contexts confirm the results of our analysis, which have shown that, in addition to the quality of the institutions, the freedom of the press also affects the transparency of the political environment and thus the level of corruption.

In addition, other factors expressed in other indicators can be taken into account—the Happy Planet Index (contains inequality), the Human Development Index and the e-Government Development index. In this regard, we see other possibilities of our research, the results of which could be used as a basis for design and implementation of more targeted anti-corruption measures by bodies of the decisive and executive public administration.

Acknowledgement This study was supported by VEGA 1/0029/21 Management of contracting services in public sector.

References

Acemoglu, D., & Verdier, T. (1998). Property rights, corruption and the allocation of talent: A general equilibrium approach. *The Economic Journal., 108*, 1381–1403. https://doi.org/10.1111/1468-0297.00347

Aidt, T. S., Hillman, A. L., & Qijun, L. (2020). *Who takes bribes and how much? Evidence from the China corruption conviction Databank.* World Development.

Amin, M., & Soh, C. (2020). Does greater regulatory burden Lead to more corruption? In *Evidence using firm-level survey data for developing countries* (Policy research working paper 9149). World Bank Group. http://documents1.worldbank.org/curated/en/296861582037503905/pdf/Does-Greater-Regulatory-Burden-Lead-to-More-Corruption-Evidence-Using-Firm-Level-Survey-Data-for-Developing-Countries.pdf. Accessed 2020

Amundsen, I. (1999). *Political corruption: An introduction to the issues*. Chr. Michelsen Institute.

Anderson, B. B. (2015). Corrupting activities and economic development. *World Journal of Entrepreneurship Management and Sustainable Development, 11*(Suppl 1), 64–70.

Apergis, N., & Cooray, A. (2017). Economic freedom and income inequality: Evidence from a panel of global economies – A linear and a nonlinear long-run analysis. *The Manchester School, 85*, 88–105. https://doi.org/10.1111/manc.12137

Arikan, G. G. (2004). Fiscal decentralization: A remedy for corruption? *International Tax and Public Finance, 11*(2), 175–195. https://doi.org/10.1023/B:ITAX.0000011399.00053.a1

Carr, I., & Outhwaite, O. (2011). Controlling corruption through corporate social responsibility and corporate governance: Theory and practice. *Journal of Corporate Law Studies, 11*(Suppl 2), 299–341.

Chayes, S. (2016). *Thieves of state: Why corruption threatens global security*. W. W. Norton & Company.

Dreher, A. (2009). Development aid and international politics: Does membership on the UN Security Council influence World Bank decisions? *Journal of Development Economics, 88*(1), 9–17.

Duvanova, D. (2014). Economic regulations, red tape, and bureaucratic corruption in Post-communist economies. *World Development, 59*, 298–312.

Enste, D., & Heldman, C. (2017). Arbeitsplatz Privathaushalt Minijobs und Schwarzarbeit von Haushaltshilfen. *Institute der deuschen, 6*, 3–17.

Fan, S., Lin, CH., & Treisman, D. (2009). Political decentralization and corruption: Evidence from around the world. Journal of Public Economics, 93(1–2), 14–34. https://doi.org/10.1016/j.jpubeco.2008.09.001.

Freille, S., et al. (2007). A contribution to the empirics of press freedom and corruption. *European Journal of Political Economy, 23*, 840–852.

Freille, S., Haque, M. E., & Kneller, R. (2008). Federalism, Decentralisation and Corruption. Centre for Economic Policy Research. http://www.cepr.org/meets/wkcn/6/6675/papers/FreilleFinal.pdf. Accessed 2012.

Glaeser, E., & Saks, R. (2004). Corruption in America. *Nber Working, 7*, 12–18.

Hirsch, R., & Watson, S. (2010). The link between corporate governance and corruption in New Zealand. *New Zealand Universities Law Review, 24*(Suppl 1), 42–74.

Holcombe, R., & Boudreaux, C. (2015). Regulation and corruption. *Public Choice, 164*(Suppl 1), 75–85.

Houqe, N., & Monem, R. M. (2013). Corruption, political institutions, and accounting environment: A cross-country study. *SSRN Electronic Journal, 17*, 1–35. https://doi.org/10.1016/j.worlddev.2020.104985

Hudori, R., & Mustikasari, E. (2020). The strength of audits, reporting standards and corruption, on tax evasion: A cross-country study. *International Journal of Economics and Business Administration, 8*(Suppl 2), 554–567.

Kaufmann, D., & Wei, S. (2000). *Does 'Grease Money' speed up the wheels of commerce?* (IMF Working Papers 00:64). International Monetary Fund.

Kimbro, M. B. (2002). A cross-country empirical investigation of corruption and its relationship to economic, cultural, and monitoring institutions: An examination of the role of accounting and financial statements quality. *Journal of Accounting, Auditing and Finance, 17*, 325–350.

Klitgaard, R. (1998). *Controlling corruption*. University of California Press.

Kotera, S., et al. (2010). Mental health attitudes, self-criticism, compassion. *British Journal of Social Work, 49*(2), 12–29.

Kuris, G. (2014). *From underdogs to watchdogs*. Princeton University.

Laderman, G., et al. (2005). Bridging the two cultures. *Journal of College Science Teaching, 35*(1), 27–30.
Lamsdorff, J. (2006). Consequences and causes of corruption: What do we know from a cross-section of countries? *Economics of Corruption, 1*, 22–50.
Lewis, B. D., & Hendrawan, A. (2019). The impact of majority coalitions on local government spending, service delivery, and corruption in Indonesia. *European Journal of Political Economy, 58*, 178–191. https://doi.org/10.1016/j.ejpoleco.2018.11.002
Li, H., Xiao, H., & Gong, T. (2015). The impact of economic well-being on perceptions of anti-corruption performance: Evidence from China. *Policy and Society, 34*, 97–109. https://doi.org/10.1016/j.polsoc.2015.05.001
Lima, S. M., & Delen, D. (2020). Predicting and explaining corruption across countries: A machine learning.Approach. *Governemnt Information Quarterly, 37*, 1–25. https://doi.org/10.1016/j.giq.2019.101407
Liu, H. (2010). The criminal enforcement of intellectual property rights in China: Recent developments and implications. *Asian Journal of Criminology, 5*, 137–156.
Malagueño, R., Albrecht, C., Ainge, C., & Stephens, N. (2010). Accounting and corruption: A cross-country analysis. *Journal of Money Laundering Control, 13*, 372–393.
Ngozi, I. (2018). *Fighting corruption is dangerous*. The MIT Press.
Niskanen, A., & William, J. (1971). *Bureaucy and representative government*. Aldine.
OECD. (2016). Corruption in the extractive value chain. In *Typology of risks, mitigation measures and incentives. OECD development policy tools*. OECD Publishing.
OECD. (2017). *Terrorism, corruption and the criminal exploitation of natural resources*. https://www.oecd.org/investment/.Terrorism-corruption-criminal-exploitation-natural-resources-2017.pdf. Accessed 2017.
Ondráčka, D. (2005). *Nedostatky českého systému zadávání veřejných zakázek a rizika korupce*. http://transint.xred.cz/doc/vz_studie_text.pdf. Accessed 12 Oct 2005.
Pellegrini, A. (2011). Causes and consequences of corruption. *Enconstor, 2*, 31–40.
Reporters Without Borders. (2021). *World press freedom index*. https://rsf.org/en/ranking. Accessed 2021.
Rose-Ackerman, S. (1998). Altruism, nonprofits, and economic theory. *Journal of Economic Literature, 34*, 701–728.
Rose-Ackerman, S. (1999). Political corruption and democracy. *Connecticut Journal of International Law, 1*, 363–367.
Santoro, D., & Kumar, M. (2018). *Speaking truth to power – A theory of Whistleblowing*. https://link.springer.com/content/pdf/10.1007%2F978-3-.319-90723-9.pdf. Accessed 2018.
Schelling, T. (1960). *The strategy of conflict*. Harvard University.
Schwab, K. (2019). Global competitiveness report 2019. *World Economic Forum, 1*, 231–302.
Schweizer, P. (2019). *Secret emipres: How the American political class hides corruption and Enriches family and friends*. Harper Paperbacks.
Shleifer, A., & Vishny, R. (1993). Corruption. *Quarterly Journal of Economics, 108*, 599–617. https://doi.org/10.2307/2118402
Statista. (2020). *Ease of doing business (EODB) ranking of Slovakia compared to other worldwide locations in 2019*. Dostupné na. https://www.statista.com/statistics/1012681/slovakia-ease-of-doing-business-ranking/
Szeghyová, B. (2011). *Korupcia v stredoveku a ranom novoveku*. Internete. https://www.academia.edu/34671627/Korupcia_v_stredoveku_a_ranom_novoveku. Accessed 25 Sept 2011.
Tanzi, V. (2010). *Corruption around the World: Causes, consequences, scope and cures*. http://www.imf.org/external/pubs/ft/wp/wp9863.pdf. Accessed 17 Nov 2010.
Treisman, D. (2000). The causes of corruption: A cross-national study. *Journal of Public Economics, Los Angeles*.
Unger, C. (2018). *House of Trump, House of Putin*. Dutton.
Vašečka, M. (2007). *Sociologické aspekty korupcie*. ADIN.
Vojtková, M. (2007). *Viacrozmerné štatistické metódy s aplikáciami*. Iura Edition.

World Justice Project. (2021). *WJP rule of law index*. https://worldjusticeproject.org/rule-of-law-index/. Accessed 2021.

Wroe, A., Allen, N., & Birch, S. (2013). The role of political trust in conditioning perceptions of corruption. *European Political Science Review, 5*, 175–195.

Wu, X. (2005). Firm accounting practices, accounting reform and corruption in Asia. *Policy and Society, 24*, 53–78.

Chapter 5
Impact of COVID-19 Pandemic on Financial Health of SMEs

Lenka Papíková, Mário Papík, and Jana Kajanová

Abstract European governments, in order to limit the spread of the COVID-19 pandemic, adopted restrictive measures in the early 2020. These measures were aimed at restricting business operations and the free movement of individuals. These restrictions significantly worsened business situation of thousands of small- and medium-sized enterprises. Compared to large companies, small- and medium-sized enterprises generally possess limited human and financial capital and it is more difficult for them to survive longer periods of lockdown or partial lockdown with limited or no income. The aim of this manuscript is to analyse the impact of the COVID-19 pandemic on the financial health of small- and medium-sized enterprises in Slovakia. Analysis was performed on a sample of 109,340 small- and medium-sized enterprises from Slovakia by comparison of selected financial indicators for the pre-COVID year 2019 and the COVID year 2020 on a sector level. The identification of statistically significant differences was performed by the Kruskal–Wallis test (nonparametric ANOVA). Results indicate that the most COVID-affected sectors were construction, food processing industry, law, consulting and accounting, retail, services and tourism and gastronomy. Impact of COVID restrictions was observed by worsened indicators of debt and profitability, while the liquidity indicators did not worsen compared to the 2019 levels.

Keywords COVID-19 · Pandemic · SMEs · Financial health · Bankruptcy

5.1 Introduction

As the COVID-19 started spreading across Europe at the beginning of 2020, European countries adopted protective measures and professional circles began to discuss the start of currently ongoing financial crisis. Prevention of free individual

L. Papíková (✉) · M. Papík · J. Kajanová
Comenius University, Bratislava, Slovakia
e-mail: lenka.papikova@fm.uniba.sk

N. Tsounis, A. Vlachvei (eds.), *Advances in Quantitative Economic Research*, Springer Proceedings in Business and Economics,
https://doi.org/10.1007/978-3-030-98179-2_5

movement, cancellation of flights and transportation links among countries, closure of production halls or reduction of business hours of shops all directly affected small- and medium-sized enterprises (SMEs) across Europe.

Small- and medium-sized enterprises are defined, as per the European Union recommendation 2003/361, as companies with less than 250 employees, and annual sales turnover below 50 million Euro or total asset value below 43 million Euro as reported on company balance sheet. Unlike large enterprises or multi-national corporations, SMEs might not have adequate human and financial capital to face long-term shortage of employees due to health reasons, decrease in sales or shortages of supply and material flow.

During the first COVID wave, which dates in Slovakia from the end of March to May/June 2020, Slovakia experienced one of the worst economic downturns in the European Union. Eurostat (2020) states that GDP of Slovakia decreased by more than 5%. This decrease was caused by the production shutdown of all four major car manufacturers (Volkswagen Slovakia, Groupe PSA Slovakia, Kia Motors Slovakia and Jaguar Land Rover Slovakia) and followed by restriction of related supply chain, as well as by situation on foreign markets, on which Slovak industry is highly dependent (Bečka, 2020). According to the Statistical Office of the Slovak Republic (2020), industrial production decreased by 7.3% year on year in the first quarter of 2020, while in April 2020 industrial production reached an all-time low, experiencing a record year-on-year decline of 42%. According to the Slovak Business Agency (SBA) (2020), the automotive industry production recorded only 21.1% of the volume compared to the same month of the previous year. Due to the introduced lockdown and limited human movement, sales revenues decreased also in other sectors, such as accommodation services and gastronomy. Revenues in accommodation services recorded a year-on-year decline of more than 80% in April and May 2020. The decline in sales of gastronomy services companies was 42.10% in April 2020 and 32.70% in May 2020 (National Bank of Slovakia, 2021).

During the second pandemic wave (October to December 2020), the partial lockdown no longer affected industrial operations and these sectors continued to operate. This continual operation contributed to a modest 2.0% increase of GDP during the fourth 2020 quarter, leading to overall 2.7% GDP decline in Slovakia in 2020 (National Bank of Slovakia, 2020). The second COVID wave and its restrictive measures impacted mainly services and retail sector as the movement of individuals was restricted and curfew was implemented. Decline in sales revenues of these two sectors was higher than during the first wave. At the end of the fourth quarter of 2020, this decline was 90% in accommodation services sector and 70% in catering services (National Bank of Slovakia, 2021).

According to the SBA, the most affected sectors by restrictive measures, such as accommodation and catering, are mainly created by small- and medium-sized enterprises. SMEs operating in these two sectors represent up 8.9% of the total number of SMEs in Slovakia (Slovak Business Agency, 2020). According to a survey conducted by the Entrepreneurs Association of Slovakia on a sample of 1109 respondents from SMEs, 25% of entrepreneurs experienced a decline in sales revenues of 31% to 50%, followed by 20% of entrepreneurs experiencing 51%

to 80% decline in revenues, and 30% of small- and medium-sized enterprises experienced revenue decline by more than 80% (Entrepreneurs Association of Slovakia, 2020).

The aim of this manuscript is to analyse the impact of the COVID-19 pandemic on financial health of SMEs in Slovakia. This analysis was conducted on a sample of 109,340 small- and medium-sized enterprises from Slovakia whose financial statements were already available in May 2021. Financial position of Slovak SMEs was tested by the Kruskal–Wallis test (nonparametric ANOVA). Results of the analysis confirm the assumption that the most affected sectors include accommodation and gastronomy services and retail. This finding can also be of benefit to authors in other small open economies (e.g. other countries in Central and Eastern Europe), for which the COVID-19 pandemic had a similar course and impact.

This manuscript is divided into six sections. The first section is the introduction, and the second section includes literature review. Methodology is included in the third section, and the fourth section includes the results of analysis. The last section describes concluding remarks of this manuscript.

5.2 Literature Review

Impact of the COVID-19 pandemic on company financial health can be analysed from several perspectives. During the first wave (Spring 2020), authors such as Sergi et al. (2020), Wang et al. (2020), Baker et al. (2020) and Harjoto and Rossi (2021) focused mainly on COVID impact on the stock market responses. Sergei et al. (2020) showed that the global equity market across 76 countries reacted negatively to the global pandemic. The decline in GDP, increasing unemployment, inflation and long-term interest rates contributed to volatility of stock markets. Similar findings, for Chinese economy, were observed by Wang et al. (2020) who estimated the impact of COVID-19 on Chinese GDP at 4.8 trillion Yuan in the first quarter of 2020. This decline represented year-on-year decline of 15.60%. Baker et al. (2020) pointed out that responses in stock markets could be explained not only by the lethality of the virus, but also by the government restrictions on mobility and business activities, which mainly affected developed service-oriented economies. Harjoto and Rossi (2021) identified significant differences in cumulative abnormal returns on stock markets in developed and developing economies during the first wave of COVID-19 pandemic.

Another view to analyse impact of COVID restrictions is through the analysis of financial health of SMEs through various financial and non-financial variables. Ciampi et al. (2021), for example, argued that the chances of SMEs to survive the COVID-19 pandemic increased with the ability to innovate and adapt to new market and human capital requirements. Carletti et al. (2020) analysed COVID-related decrease in profits and equity ratios on a sample of 80,972 Italian companies. Analysis of individual sectors conducted by Carletti et al. (2020) indicates that bankruptcy occurred in SMEs with high levels of pre-pandemic debt or in SMEs from manufacturing, wholesale and trading sectors. Study of Gourinchas et al. (2021) indicates that the least affected sector in 2020 was health and social work, while the most affected sectors were mining, accommodation and catering. According to a survey of more than 5800 US small enterprises conducted by Bartik et al. (2020), the following sectors were affected the most: personal services, tourism and lodging and restaurant/bar/catering. These sectors experienced the lowest probability of reopening if the restrictions lasted 6 months. Efforts of these companies to stay in business depended on availability of loans and other economic policies to help bridge the lockdown period. Harjoto and Rossi (2021) concluded that in emerging and developed markets the COVID-19 pandemic had negative effects on sectors such as energy and financial services, but it also had positive impact on other sectors like telecommunications and health care. He et al. (2020) studied positive impact of the pandemic on high-tech industries, such as manufacturing, information technology, education and health care, based on stock prices on the Shanghai Stock Exchange and the Shenzhen Stock Exchange. The negative impact was observed, like in other countries, mainly in transportation, mining, electric and heating, and environmental sectors. This study showed a heterogeneous reaction of industries to major emergencies to COVID-19 pandemic.

COVID impact on SMEs therefore depends on the economic sector and the development level of an economy. Most existing studies focused mainly on SMEs from developed economies such as the USA or Western European countries. So far, only several studies analysed the impact of the pandemic on small open economies such as Slovakia, other CEE or Balkan countries. Based on this gap in existing literature, framework of this manuscript focuses on small- and medium-sized enterprises operating in Slovakia. This manuscript compares pre-COVID and COVID levels of liquidity, debt and profitability. Based on the results of this study, governments of small open economies would be able to take steps to help SMEs survive periods of reduced liquidity and keep them alive through state loans and grants.

5.3 Research Methodology

5.3.1 Data Sample

Financial statements of 120,485 companies for the fiscal years 2019 and 2020 were collected to fulfil the aim of this manuscript. These financial statements were already published in May 2021. The Finstat database, which contains the financial statements of companies operating in Slovakia, was used as a data source. All companies that were not classified as SMEs did not have published financial statements for analysed years or did not contain some of the items required to calculate financial ratios were removed from the data sample. The final data sample, after this adjustment, therefore consisted of 109,340 financial statements. The number of companies and their division into individual sectors is shown in Table 5.1. Companies were divided into individual categories according to the NACE classification. The largest representation of companies in the data sample was from construction (11%), law, consulting and accounting (9%), retail (8%) and real estate (7%) sectors.

Financial indicators of companies included in the data sample were calculated. These indicators were divided into liquidity, debt and profitability ratios—ratios for which the impact of the COVID-19 pandemic was expected the most. The list of all financial ratios and their calculation is provided in Table 5.2. These indicators were chosen as they are the most commonly used financial ratios in assessing financial health of companies (Farooq & Qamar, 2019; Xiao et al., 2012; Xie et al., 2011) and also because the pandemic affected mainly liquidity, profit and level of debt of companies.

5.3.2 *Statistical Methods*

The Kruskal–Wallis test, also called a nonparametric one-way ANOVA (analysis of variance), was used to verify the hypothesis that the medians of two company groups were identical. In this study, the two groups were the pre-pandemic year 2019 and the COVID year 2020 and their respective selected financial indicators.

The assumption of this test is the independence of the sample and the continuity of random variable X_i, $i = 1, \ldots, n$, where n represents the number of companies in the data sample. As financial indicators calculated for years 2019 and 2020 were based on independent financial statements, both measurements were considered as independent. Also, the calculated financial indicators were expressed as real numbers and therefore were be considered as continuous random variables—fulfilling the second assumption of the Kruskal–Wallis test. (Gibbons, 1993).

Tested hypothesis (5.1) of the Kruskal–Wallis test has the following form:

$$H_0 : M_{j,2019} = M_{j,2020} \tag{5.1}$$

and alternative hypothesis (5.2) for the Kruskal–Wallis test has the following form:

$$H_1 : M_{j,2019} \neq M_{j,2020} \tag{5.2}$$

where j equals index for particular sector, $M_{j,\,2019}$ represents median of financial indicator for sector j in pre-pandemic year 2019, and $M_{j,\,2020}$ represents median of financial indicator for sector j in pandemic year 2020. All calculations were performed in RStudio version 1.3.959.

Table 5.1 Sample distribution

Sector	Number	%	Sector	Number	%
Advertising	2384	2.18	Intermediary activity	4266	3.90
Agriculture and forestry	2782	2.54	Law, consulting and accounting	9735	8.90
Automobile industry	151	0.14	Media, publishing and culture	1955	1.79
Clothing and footwear	569	0.52	Metalworking and metallurgy	2335	2.14
Construction	12,169	11.13	Production—Other	415	0.38
Development and civil engineering	4268	3.90	Real estate	8125	7.43
Education	1375	1.26	Research and development	1675	1.53
Electrical engineering	835	0.76	Retail	8525	7.80
Energy and mining	674	0.62	Sales and maintenance of vehicles	2013	1.84
Engineering	1090	1.00	Service	7410	6.78
Finance	2332	2.13	Telecommunications	292	0.27
Food processing industry	1091	1.00	Tourism and gastronomy	5568	5.09
Gambling	118	0.11	Transportation and logistics	4132	3.78
Health care	6470	5.92	Waste management	454	0.42
Chemistry and plastics	598	0.55	Wholesale	7754	7.09
Information technology	6615	6.05	Wood and paper	1165	1.07
Total	**109,340**				

Source: own calculation based on Finstat database

Table 5.2 Financial ratios

Type	Ratio	Formula
Liquidity	Cash ratio	Cash and cash equivalents/current liabilities
	Quick ratio	(Cash and cash equivalents + marketable securities + accounts receivables)/current liabilities
	Current ratio	Current assets/current liabilities
Leverage	Total debt-to-asset ratio	Total debt/total assets
	Long-term debt-to-asset ratio	Long-term debt/total assets
	Financial leverage ratio	Total assets/total shareholders' equity
Profitability	Return on equity	Net income/total shareholders' equity
	Return on assets	Net income/total assets
	Return on sales	Operating profit/net sales

Source: own source

5.4 Results of Analysis

The results of analysis were divided into three separate parts depending on financial indicators used—liquidity, debt and profitability ratios. Table 5.3 contains calculated median for liquidity ratios for the pre-pandemic year 2019 and the COVID year 2020 along with the significance levels determined by the Kruskal–Wallis test. Based on the results, the only statistically significant change in quick and current ratios is observed only for two sectors: health care, and law, consulting and accounting. This change in values of the two sectors may be explained by increased proportion of invoices (services provided on account) with longer payment periods than direct cash or card payments. Values of cash ratio in Table 5.3 are the same for all sectors as the differences are only in the fourth and further decimal points.

No statistically significant differences in liquidity ratios between the pre-pandemic and the COVID year were observed for companies from other sectors. If companies had any liquidity problems, they probably occurred only temporarily during the first wave of the pandemic. These problems were then overcome by the time the financial statements were prepared and published and therefore did not result in changes in the liquidity ratios.

Table 5.4 contains the median values of the debt ratios for the pre-pandemic year 2019 and the COVID year 2020 along with the significance levels determined by the Kruskal–Wallis test. Results indicate that the total debt or long-term debt of companies increased statistically significantly for the construction, food processing, law, consulting and accounting, retail, service and tourism and gastronomy sectors. These sectors did not show any liquidity problems as described in Table 5.3—this can be explained by increased volume of loans and outstanding invoices which provided much-needed cash for companies. On the other hand, there are sectors such as development and civil engineering, education, information technology and media, publishing and culture which all increased their shareholders' equity statistically significantly meaning the company owners invested additional capital into their businesses to overcome difficult COVID period.

Table 5.5 includes the median values of selected profitability ratios for the pre-pandemic year 2019 and the COVID year 2020 along with the significance levels as determined by the Kruskal—Wallis test. As shown in Table 5.5, the COVID pandemic most severely affected profit of companies. This decrease in profitability was caused by temporary closure of many business activities and decrease in individual consumption. Return on assets of companies from tourism and gastronomy sector during the COVID year even reached negative numbers. There was also significant decrease in return on sales, apart from only a few sectors (advertising, development and civil engineering, education, gambling, intermediary activity, real estate, and research and development). It can be concluded that the COVID pandemic hit the economy widely, especially in company sales revenues.

Table 5.3 Liquidity ratios and Kruskal–Wallis test

	Cash ratio			Quick ratio			Current ratio		
Sector	2019	2020	Sign.	2019	2020	Sign.	2019	2020	Sign.
Advertising	0.000	0.000		0.295	0.283		0.367	0.367	
Agriculture and forestry	0.000	0.000		0.344	0.287		0.720	0.687	
Automobile industry	0.000	0.000		0.503	0.571		1.000	0.986	
Clothing and footwear	0.000	0.000		0.285	0.249		0.705	0.563	
Construction	0.000	0.000		0.384	0.363		0.563	0.552	
Development and civil engineering	0.000	0.000		0.516	0.472		0.572	0.557	
Education	0.000	0.000		0.161	0.130		0.190	0.164	
Electrical engineering	0.000	0.000		0.580	0.560		0.966	0.917	
Energy and mining	0.000	0.000		0.726	0.725		0.820	0.838	
Engineering	0.000	0.000		0.600	0.565		0.922	0.954	
Finance	0.000	0.000		0.217	0.265		0.279	0.340	
Food processing industry	0.000	0.000		0.148	0.154		0.424	0.412	
Gambling	0.000	0.000		0.607	0.307		0.743	0.343	
Health care	0.000	0.000		0.704	0.814	***	0.905	1.000	***
Chemistry and plastics	0.000	0.000		0.565	0.452		1.037	0.953	
Information technology	0.000	0.000		0.648	0.647		0.713	0.719	
Intermediary activity	0.000	0.000		0.203	0.177		0.357	0.364	
Law, consulting and accounting	0.000	0.000		0.411	0.431	*	0.467	0.489	*
Media, publishing and culture	0.000	0.000		0.345	0.290		0.446	0.398	
Metalworking and metallurgy	0.000	0.000		0.582	0.545		0.803	0.801	
Production—Other	0.000	0.000		0.237	0.233		0.653	0.576	
Real estate	0.000	0.000		0.086	0.087		0.124	0.128	
Research and development	0.000	0.000		0.488	0.482		0.556	0.568	

(continued)

Table 5.3 (continued)

	Cash ratio			Quick ratio			Current ratio		
Sector	2019	2020	Sign.	2019	2020	Sign.	2019	2020	Sign.
Retail	0.000	0.000		0.087	0.087		0.588	0.583	
Sales and maintenance of vehicles	0.000	0.000		0.159	0.160		0.623	0.635	
Service	0.000	0.000		0.143	0.152		0.241	0.268	
Telecommunications	0.000	0.000		0.622	0.498		0.785	0.618	
Tourism and gastronomy	0.000	0.000		0.069	0.077		0.164	0.150	
Transportation and logistics	0.000	0.000		0.567	0.568		0.615	0.631	
Waste management	0.000	0.000		0.528	0.544		0.690	0.760	
Wholesale	0.000	0.000		0.445	0.432		0.915	0.915	
Wood and paper	0.000	0.000		0.302	0.294		0.575	0.553	

Significance codes: 0 '***' 0.001 '**' 0.01 '*' 0.05 '.' 0.1 ' ' 1

Table 5.4 Leverage ratios and Kruskal–Wallis test

	Total debt-to-asset ratio			Long-term debt-to-asset ratio			Financial leverage ratio		
Sector	2019	2020	Sign.	2019	2020	Sign.	2019	2020	Sign.
Advertising	0.336	0.334		0.000	0.000		1.184	1.159	
Agriculture and forestry	0.501	0.489		0.001	0.002		1.575	1.548	
Automobile industry	0.569	0.596		0.003	0.003		1.673	1.639	
Clothing and footwear	0.508	0.487		0.001	0.001		1.378	1.306	
Construction	0.535	0.559	**	0.000	0.000	***	1.454	1.449	
Development and civil engineering	0.326	0.311		0.000	0.000		1.286	1.241	*
Education	0.279	0.289		0.000	0.000		1.167	1.119	*
Electrical engineering	0.384	0.363		0.001	0.001		1.341	1.312	
Energy and mining	0.694	0.675		0.002	0.003		2.216	2.049	
Engineering	0.483	0.495		0.002	0.003		1.523	1.445	
Finance	0.366	0.385		0.000	0.000		1.192	1.168	

(continued)

Table 5.4 (Continued)

	Total debt-to-asset ratio			Long-term debt-to-asset ratio			Financial leverage ratio		
Sector	2019	2020	Sign.	2019	2020	Sign.	2019	2020	Sign.
Food processing industry	0.571	0.638	*	0.001	0.001		1.372	1.349	
Gambling	0.204	0.202		0.001	0.000		1.159	1.120	
Health care	0.371	0.350		0.003	0.003		1.402	1.368	
Chemistry and plastics	0.503	0.481		0.002	0.002		1.533	1.506	
Information technology	0.225	0.215		0.000	0.000		1.203	1.174	**
Intermediary activity	0.375	0.370		0.000	0.000		1.147	1.134	
Law, consulting and accounting	0.266	0.261		0.000	0.000	*	1.186	1.169	
Media, publishing and culture	0.358	0.348		0.000	0.000		1.234	1.162	**
Metalworking and metallurgy	0.510	0.505		0.002	0.002		1.592	1.544	
Production—Other	0.478	0.544		0.000	0.000		1.249	1.243	
Real estate	0.585	0.576		0.000	0.000		1.316	1.287	
Research and development	0.257	0.259		0.000	0.000		1.180	1.178	
Retail	0.605	0.612		0.000	0.000	*	1.249	1.239	
Sales and maintenance of vehicles	0.689	0.699		0.000	0.001		1.449	1.458	
Service	0.304	0.334	**	0.000	0.000	**	1.135	1.133	
Tele commu-nications	0.338	0.324		0.000	0.000		1.367	1.320	
Tourism and gastronomy	0.649	0.722	***	0.000	0.001	**	1.098	1.055	
Transportation and logistics	0.599	0.606		0.001	0.002		1.650	1.603	
Waste management	0.522	0.508		0.001	0.001		1.511	1.513	
Wholesale	0.559	0.548		0.000	0.000		1.470	1.425	
Wood and paper	0.637	0.661		0.001	0.002		1.551	1.544	

Significance codes: 0 '***' 0.001 '**' 0.01 '*' 0.05 '.' 0.1 ' ' 1

Table 5.5 Profitability ratios and Kruskal–Wallis test

	Return on equity			Return on assets			Return on sales		
Sector	2019	2020	Sign.	2019	2020	Sign.	2019	2020	Sign.
Advertising	0.060	0.050		0.014	0.005	**	0.008	0.010	
Agriculture and forestry	0.018	0.018		0.005	0.004		0.721	0.016	***
Automobile industry	0.098	0.062		0.019	0.017		0.086	0.018	**
Clothing and footwear	0.034	0.035		0.004	0.002		0.028	0.008	***
Construction	0.058	0.047	***	0.017	0.009	***	0.026	0.013	***
Development and civil engineering	0.104	0.092	**	0.053	0.043	***	0.037	0.055	
Education	0.049	0.045		0.017	0.004	*	0.006	0.013	
Electrical engineering	0.105	0.077	*	0.046	0.029	**	0.100	0.028	***
Energy and mining	0.092	0.104		0.031	0.040		1.234	0.078	***
Engineering	0.092	0.077	*	0.041	0.026	***	0.212	0.029	***
Finance	0.042	0.059		0.011	0.013		0.005	0.012	**
Food processing industry	0.034	0.030		0.000	0.000		0.001	0.000	***
Gambling	0.017	0.000	*	0.010	0.000	**	0.010	0.000	
Health care	0.235	0.218	*	0.159	0.146	**	0.199	0.113	***
Chemistry and plastics	0.049	0.049		0.011	0.015		0.105	0.019	***
Information technology	0.154	0.167		0.085	0.096		0.056	0.092	*
Intermediary activity	0.028	0.024		0.000	0.000	**	0.000	0.000	
Law, consulting and accounting	0.071	0.079		0.030	0.030		0.014	0.042	***
Media, publishing and culture	0.070	0.041	***	0.029	0.006	***	0.020	0.013	***
Metalworking and metallurgy	0.085	0.060	***	0.029	0.018	***	0.151	0.020	***
Production—Other	0.031	0.023		0.001	0.000		0.008	0.000	**
Real estate	0.027	0.022		0.002	0.001	*	0.007	0.006	

(continued)

Table 5.5 (continued)

Sector	Return on equity			Return on assets			Return on sales		
	2019	2020	Sign.	2019	2020	Sign.	2019	2020	Sign.
Research and development	0.103	0.083	**	0.055	0.035	*	0.031	0.049	
Retail	0.039	0.037		0.000	0.000		0.003	0.000	***
Sales and maintenance of vehicles	0.058	0.057		0.005	0.003		0.013	0.007	***
Service	0.029	0.027		0.001	0.000		0.001	0.001	***
Tele commu-nications	0.069	0.072		0.043	0.044		0.055	0.042	*
Tourism and gastronomy	0.033	0.007	***	0.000	−0.026	***	0.000	0.000	***
Transportation and logistics	0.042	0.059	*	0.005	0.007		0.019	0.015	***
Waste management	0.032	0.076	*	0.005	0.015		0.023	0.022	*
Wholesale	0.061	0.053	**	0.013	0.010	**	0.046	0.011	***
Wood and paper	0.040	0.039		0.007	0.004		0.049	0.009	***

Significance codes: 0 '***' 0.001 '**' 0.01 '*' 0.05 '.' 0.1 ' ' 1

5.5 Conclusions

The aim of this manuscript was to analyse the impact of the COVID-19 pandemic on the financial health of SMEs in Slovakia. This analysis was performed on a sample of 109,340 SMEs from Slovakia by comparison of selected financial indicators for the pre-pandemic year 2019 and the COVID year 2020 on a sector basis. The results of this manuscript show that the most significant impact was on profitability indicators, which decreased significantly in the majority of sectors. Impact of the COVID restrictions was less significant for debt indicators, which only increased in the most affected sectors. The lowest impact of the pandemic was observed for the liquidity indicators, where only two sectors experienced statistically significant decrease. Unlike profitability and debt indicators, it can be assumed that companies managed to overcome their liquidity problems by the time their financial statements were prepared, and therefore no significant changes in the liquidity indicators were observed in this manuscript.

The most affected sectors, in terms of both debt and profitability, were construction, food processing industry, law, consulting and accounting, retail, service, and tourism and gastronomy. This finding is in line with findings of other authors like Bartik et al. (2020). Bartik identified the most significant COVID impact on the tourism and gastronomy sector. Compared to other studies, however, this manuscript showed also significant decrease in profitability ratios (especially return on sales) across majority of the sectors. Year on year, though, even increase in the return on assets or return on equity was observed in some sectors (e.g. transportation and logistics, waste management), and this increase was statistically significant for return on assets. Nevertheless, these sectors cannot be considered as those purely benefiting from the ongoing COVID-19 pandemic.

Possible limitation of this study is that its data sample does not include financial reports of all SMEs operating in Slovakia, but only those that published their financial statements by May 2021 (in regular deadline). It is highly likely that these companies are among those with better financial health and have not requested the Financial Administration of Slovakia for extension of their tax return deadline. The financial situation of companies that ceased business activities in 2020 was not considered in this research. If these companies were considered in this manuscript, its results might have been more unfavourable.

Suggestion for future research is to conduct similar analysis on the sectors basis; however, further comparison among various countries might provide also interesting results.

Acknowledgments This manuscript was funded by VEGA 1/0393/21 titled Impact Analysis of Restrictive Measures and Government Aid Associated with Coronavirus on Financial Health of Small and Medium-Sized Enterprises in Slovakia. The support of the Faculty of Management, Comenius University in Bratislava, Slovakia, is acknowledged, as well.

References

Baker, S. R., Bloom, N., Davis, S. J., Kost, K., Sammon, M., & Viratyosin, T. (2020). The unprecedented stock market reaction to COVID-19. *The Review of Asset Pricing Studies, 10*(4), 742–758. https://doi.org/10.1093/rapstu/raaa008

Bartik, A., Bertrand, M., Cullen, Z. B., Glaeser, E. L., Luca, M., & Stanton, C. H. (2020). The Impact of COVID-19 on small business outcomes and expectations. *Proceedings of the National Academy of Sciences, 117*(30), 17656–17666.

Bečka, M. (2020). The Impact of the current global pandemic of SARS-CoV-2 on employment in the Slovak economy. *Economic Review, 49*(2).

Carletti, E., Oliviero, T., Pagano, M., Pelizzon, L., & Subrahmanyam, M. (2020). The COVID-19 shock and equity shortfall: Firm-level evidence from Italy. *The Review of Corporate Finance Studies, 9*(3), 534–568. https://doi.org/10.1093/rcfs/cfaa014

Ciampi, F., Giannozzi, A., Marzi, G., & Altman, E. (2021). I: Rethinking SME default prediction: A systematic literature review and future perspectives. *Scientometrics, 126*, 2141–2188. https://doi.org/10.1007/s11192-020-03856-0

Entrepreneurs Association of Slovakia: Názory podnikateľov na dopady druhej vlny korona krízy, (2020). available at: https://www.zps.sk/novinky/2020/vysledky-prieskumu-nazory-podnikatelov-druha-vlna. Accessed 24 May 2021.

Eurostat: Newsrelease Euroindicators 91/2020. (2020). Available at: https://ec.europa.eu/eurostat/documents/2995521/10294996/2-09062020-AP-EN.pdf/8a68ea5e-5189-5b09-24de-ea057adeee15. Accessed 21 May 2021.

Farooq, U., & Qamar, M. A. J. (2019). Predicting multistage financial distress: Reflections on sampling, feature and model selection criteria. *Journal of Forecasting, 38*(7), 632–648. https://doi.org/10.1002/for.2588

Gibbons, J. D. (1993). *Nonparametric statistics – An introduction*. SAGE Publications Ltd..

Gourinchas, P.O., Kalemli-Özcan, S., Penciakova, V. and Sander, N: COVID-19 and SME Failures, (2021). Working paper no. 27877, available at: http://www.nber.org/papers/w27877

Harjoto, M.A., & Rossi, F. (2021). Market reaction to the COVID-19 pandemic: Evidence from emerging markets. *International Journal of Emerging Markets*, Vol. ahead-of-print No. ahead-of-print. https://doi.org/10.1108/IJOEM-05-2020-0545.

He, P., Sun, Y., Zhang, Y., & Li, T. (2020). COVID–19's impact on stock prices across different sectors—An event study based on the Chinese stock market. *Emerging Markets Finance and Trade, 56*(10), 2198–2212. https://doi.org/10.1080/1540496X.2020.1785865

National Bank of Slovakia: Ekonomický a menový vývoj – jar 2021. (2021). Available at: https://www.nbs.sk/_img/Documents/_Publikacie/ekonomicky_menovy_vyvoj/2021/protected/emv_jar-2021.pdf. Accessed 24 May 2021.

National Bank of Slovakia: Flash odhad HDP a zamestnanosti: Druhá vlna pandémie zastavila rýchle dobiehanie strát. (2020). Available at: https://www.nbs.sk/_img/Documents/_komentare/2021/1225_rk_fHDP_20210216_4q20.pdf. Accessed 24 May 2021.

Sergi, B., Harjoto, M. A., Rossi, F., & Lee, R. (2020). Do stock markets love misery? Evidence from the COVID-19. *Finance Research Letters*, 101923. https://doi.org/10.1016/j.frl.2021.101923

Slovak Business Agency: Analýza malých a stredných podnikov pôsobiacich v odvetviach najviac zasiahnutých karanténnymi opatreniami. (2020). Available at: http://www.sbagency.sk/sites/default/files/analyza_msp_posobiacich_v_odvetviach_najviac_zasiahnutych_karantennymi_opatreniami.pdf. Accessed 24 May 2021.

Slovak Business Agency: Podpora zamestnanosti v období koronakrízy v SR a v okolitých krajiných. (2020). Available at: http://monitoringmsp.sk/wp-content/uploads/2020/08/Podpora-zamestnanosti-v-obdob%C3%AD-koronakr%C3%ADzy-v-SR-a-v-okolit%C3%BDch-krajin%C3%A1ch.pdf. Accessed 24 May 2021.

Statistical Office of the Slovak republic: Štatistická správa o základných vývojových tendenciách v hospodárstve SR – 1. štvrťrok. (2020). Accessed 24 May 2021.

Wang, Y., Fang, Z., & Gao, W. (2020). COVID-19's impact on China's economy based on data of Spring Festival travel rush. Working paper, available at: https://papers.ssrn.com/sol3/papers.cfm?abstract_id53554638. Accessed 22 May 2021.

Xiao, Z., Yang, X., Pang, Y., & Dang, X. (2012). The prediction for listed companies' financial distress by using multiple prediction methods with rough set and Dempster–Shafer evidence theory. *Knowledge-Based Systems, 26*, 196–206. https://doi.org/10.1016/j.knosys.2011.08.001

Xie, C., Luo, C., & Yu, X. (2011). Financial distress prediction based on SVM and MDA methods: The case of Chinese listed companies. *Quality & Quantity, 45*(3), 671–686. https://doi.org/10.1007/s11135-010-9376-y

Chapter 6
Preference Reversal and Impulsivity in Discounting of Monetary Losses

Bartlomiej Wisnicki and Adam Karbowski

Abstract We investigate delay discounting of monetary losses using the experimental data ($N = 203$). Based on the titration algorithm, we estimate the individual delay discounting rates of monetary losses. We further compare the fit of exponential, hyperbolic, and q-exponential models to the experimental data. The obtained results suggest that the hyperbolic model fits better than the classical exponential one. Hence, the preference reversal effect in delay discounting of monetary losses is observed in our experiment. Moreover, the best fit for the data is obtained through the q-exponential model. Also, participants would strongly like to postpone the immediate loss, even for a month, while the difference between further postponement comes with a much lower discount.

Keywords Monetary losses · Preference reversal · Exponential and hyperbolic discounting

6.1 Introduction

The human economic behavior can be described with the use of three dimensions (Hendrikse, 2003; Karbowski, 2016)—degree of rationality (full or bounded), behavioral motivation (egoistic, altruistic, among others), and degree of self-control (unbounded or bounded willpower). This chapter focuses on the third dimension of human economic behavior—the degree of self-control.

This paper was supported by funds from the National Science Centre, Poland through grant number 2018/31/D/HS4/00203.

B. Wisnicki (✉) · A. Karbowski
Department of Business Economics, SGH Warsaw School of Economics, Warsaw, Poland
e-mail: bwisni@sgh.waw.pl

N. Tsounis, A. Vlachvei (eds.), *Advances in Quantitative Economic Research*,
Springer Proceedings in Business and Economics,
https://doi.org/10.1007/978-3-030-98179-2_6

In the economics literature, human self-control is measured using discounting procedures, i.e., individual delay discounting rates are computed based on experimental data (Holt et al., 2003; Myerson et al., 2017). In the domain of monetary gains, decision-makers usually choose a smaller and less delayed gain compared with a larger but more delayed one, but moving both gains by the same period promotes self-control, i.e., a choice of a larger and more delayed gain. This is a well-known preference reversal effect (cf., e.g., Ainslie & Herrnstein, 1981; Loewenstein & Prelec, 1992; Cubitt et al., 2004). The latter effect has been observed in the domain of monetary gains. The natural question arises whether a similar effect can be discovered in the area of monetary losses. In the COVID-19 times, the area of monetary losses seems particularly interesting due to a very serious threat of a prolonged economic downturn.

A decent number of behavioral economics articles find evidence that the delay discounting of monetary gains is hyperbolic rather than exogenous (cf. Ainslie, 1975; Azfar, 1999; Kirby & Maraković, 1995; Laibson, 1997; Estle et al., 2006). Following (Takahashi, 2013), we compare the fit of exponential, hyperbolic, and q-exponential models to the same experimental data on discounting monetary losses. We do that to first test the ongoing hypothesis that hyperbolic discounting serves as a better fit than exponential discounting when describing the delay discounting of monetary losses. This procedure allows us to test whether the preference reversal effect is present in the area of time discounting of monetary losses. Holt et al. (2003) show that the preference reversal effect occurs. However, their sample is limited to less than 50 participants. Similar procedures were performed in Ostaszewski & Karzel (2002); Estle et al. (2006), however, as well on much smaller samples. Therefore, we can treat our research as a replication of existing research with a sample that provides generalization on the general population.

Second, we also use the q-exponential discounting function and check how it fits the data (controlling for an increase in the number of estimated parameters) comparatively to the previous two functions. We do that also to obtain the value of an individual's impulsivity: it provides us with evidence over how persons change their relative preferences over losses with different time frames. To our knowledge, such research has not been performed for monetary losses but only gains (cf. Takahashi, 2013).

The article proceeds as follows. First, we present the materials and methods. Next, we present the obtained results. The discussion follows and closes the paper.

6.2 Method

6.2.1 Survey

We collected data through the online experiment on delay discounting of monetary losses. The experiment was conducted in the autumn semester 2020/2021 among

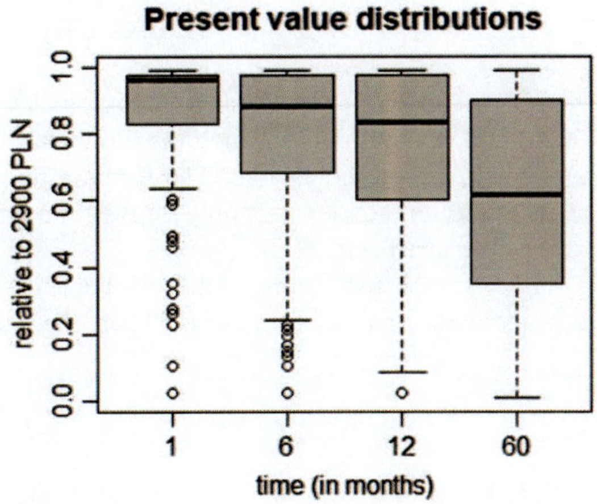

Fig. 6.1 Boxplots of the present value of the loss of 2900 in the time periods presented on the x-axis. The losses are normalized to a unit interval

the Polish University students—SGH Warsaw School of Economics. In total, 203 participants constituted a sample (86 males—average age: 24.5, 117 females—average age: 23.4). An in-depth description of the sample is in Karbowski & Wiśnicki (2021).

In the experimental task, we used the titration algorithm by Holt et al. (2003). In the first choice between two monetary losses (loss of 1450 PLN (about 320 EUR) now—option A—or 2900 PLN (640 EUR) in some fixed time period (1, 6, 12, and 60 months)—option B), option A was half the amount in option B. In the further choices, option A increased or decreased depending on the previous choices. The amount in option A after the sixth choice constituted the estimated equivalent amount in option B. This equivalent can be treated as the respondent's present value of a loss in a specific period.

We can plot the present value points, rescaled to a unit interval, for the corresponding time delay on the X-Y plot, which will show us the coordinates of one's discounting function. Figure 6.1 depicts the distributions of the present values for different time periods the loss is due. In line with the intuition, as the loss is due increases, the instant equivalent goes down. Moreover, the variance of the money equivalents increases with the analyzed time period. It is also in line with theory: we observe more variance in results since small differences in subjective discounting rates result in larger gaps between money equivalents as time comparison goes up.

6.2.2 Models of Discounting

Using the behavioral data, we estimate three models of intertemporal choice between losses. The first one is the classical exponential discounting following the rational paradigm of dynamic decision-making. In that sense, an individual should evaluate the losses in the following manner:

$$V(0) = V(t)e^{-k_e t}, \tag{6.1}$$

where $V(0)$ is an amount of instant loss, and $V(t)$ is the loss to be paid in time t (measured in months) for which the individual is indifferent.[1] The parameter k_e is the individual's discount rate. The formula represents time-consistent preferences as the discount rate depends only on the time difference between losses, not on the time of the loss itself.

An approach more consistent with behavioral decision-making is to adopt the hyperbolic discounting framework. Then, the indifference between losses would be

$$V(0) = \frac{V(t)}{1 + k_h t}, \tag{6.2}$$

with k_h being the parameter of the discount rate. This model shows that preferences are time inconsistent as individuals overvalue the loss if it is close to present. An alternative, more general measure is to apply the q-exponential discounting, cf. Cajueiro (2006) or Rambaud & Torrecillas (2013), of the following form:

$$V(0) = \frac{V(t)}{(1 + (1 - q)k_q t)^{\frac{1}{1-q}}}. \tag{6.3}$$

Here, apart from the discount rate k_q, we have a second parameter q that canonically puts weights between exponential and hyperbolic discounting (with $q \in [0, 1]$, the higher the q the discounting becomes more exponential). However, as (Takahashi, 2007) points out, q may take values outside of unit interval and has a broader interpretation. The value of q represents the rate of impulsivity that the decision-maker exhibits. Impulsivity here is defined by a strong will to delay the instant loss, manifested by hyperbolic and absent in exponential discounting. The rate of impulsivity decreases for $q < 1$, so the decision-maker chooses a higher discount rate (in exponential terms) for losses comparisons with a closer due date. A specific case of $q = 0$ represents the classic hyperbolic discounting. For $q > 1$ the individual exhibits increasing impulsivity, while for $q \to 1$ the formula (6.3) converges to exponential discounting presented in (6.1).

6.2.3 Data Analysis

We conduct statistical procedures to estimate the parameters for each of the presented discounting models. First, we find parameters by fitting curves through the indifference revealed in the survey. Hence, we find the estimated discount rates by

[1] We decided to switch the values of $V(0)$ and $V(t)$ from the canonical approach as we describe preferences over losses.

regressing the relative present values against the discounting functions of equations (1)–(3), presented in the previous subsection. As the functions are nonlinear, the estimated parameters are obtained via nonlinear regression using the Gauss–Newton algorithm.

The independent variable is the time the loss is due. We pool all the observations from different time comparisons, which benefits the number of degrees of freedom (811 or 800 for q-exponential discounting).

Thus, this study differs from the existing ones, as we use all the data from the sample, not only median data, to estimate parameters, cf. Takahashi (2007, 2013). As we obtained a fairly large and representative sample, we believe our results may, to some extent, be generalized.

Apart from the parameter estimates, we calculate the two information criterion for each model: the Akaike information criterion (AIC) and Bayesian information criterion (BIC), to help determine the model's quality. We employ the information criteria method rather than the standard R^2 criterion of fitness (with adjusted R^2 to penalize for loss in the degrees of freedom) for two reasons: first, it does not have the same interpretation in the nonlinear models as in the linear case and hence should not be universally applied (c.f. Spiess & Neumeyer, 2010); second, the values of the determination coefficient are usually very low and hence meaningless. Furthermore, to resolve the problem of heteroskedasticity of residuals, we employ the Eickert–White technique of estimating the covariance matrix (cf. Zeileis, 2006). All of the procedures were performed in R statistical language using the statistical packages.

6.3 Results

Figure 6.2 shows the fitted discounting curves for the three models along with the averages of indifference points obtained from the study. As we can see from the indifference points, the participants would strongly like to postpone the immediate loss, even for a month. At the same time, the difference between further

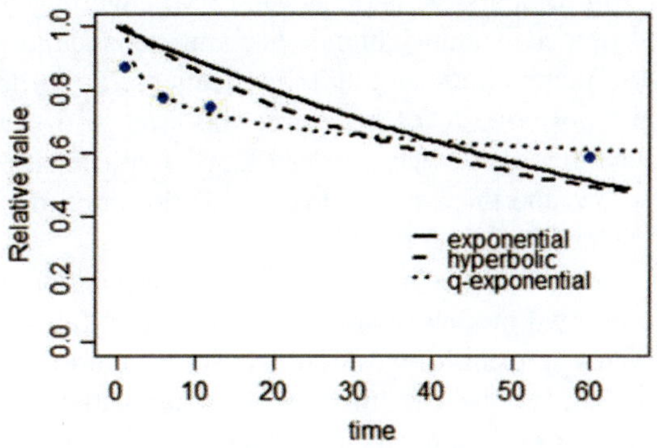

Fig. 6.2 Fitted discounting curves of exponential (solid line), hyperbolic (dashed line), and q-exponential (dotted line) to the indifference points (the averages are plotted as blue points)

Table 6.1 Estimated parameters of discounting models with information criteria regarding the model fitness

	Exponential	Hyperbolic	q-exponential
k	0.0112	0.017	0.2
q			−8.57
AIC	254.53	212.86	88.16
BIC	263.93	222.26	102.25

postponement comes with a much lower discount. This behavior is highly consistent with decreasing impulsivity connected to hyperbolic discounting.

As we can see from Table 6.1, the discount rates for exponential and hyperbolic discounting are close. Objectively, these values are rather substantial: over 1% monthly discount rate leads to about 14% annual rate. Such a high discounting rate shows a significant loss aversion of individuals: the postponement of a loss is desirable, even with a substantial interest.

In addition, we can see that the preference reversal effect occurs in the context of monetary losses. This phenomenon is indicated by the fact that the drop rate in the monetary equivalents decreases. It can also be seen due to the fact that hyperbolic discounting serves as a better fit to the data than the exponential one, as we can see from the information criteria values (note that lower values of AIC and BIC indicate a better model quality).

However, while showing an improvement over exponential discounting, the classic hyperbolic discounting model fails to fit completely into the data as it does not represent the scope of the impulsivity rate associated with losses. Instead, that scope is captured by the q-exponential discounting model, which generally fits well with the data.

Objectively, these values are rather substantial: over 1% monthly discount rate leads to over 14% annual rate. However, both of these values do not seem to capture the true magnitude of losses discount. The individuals seem to have a much higher discount rate at $t = 0$ than at subsequent periods. As the q-exponential model suggests, the initial discount rate is extremely high and is equal to about 20% monthly, but it shrinks with $q = -8.57$. This characterization shows a very rapid decrease in the impulsivity of delayed losses.

In comparison to Takahashi (2007), who studies gains, we can see that losses are attributed to a much higher discount rate and more severe decrease of that rate. These two factors indicate that individuals prefer not to be faced with a loss immediately and postpone it for a short period, even if the amount would increase sharply. On the other hand, when comparing two losses with distant due dates, the discount rate is low, and the time the loss is due does not make much difference to the decision-maker.

As we can see in Fig. 6.2, the q-exponential model fits very well compared to the other two models. Naturally, as a general framework, we expect it to fit data better than the specific ones. Therefore, to determine how well the data fit the specific model, we use the information criteria that balance the model's quality with the number of parameters used. Nevertheless, as both AIC and BIC are much lower for the q-exponential discounting model, we must declare it the best method to identify the intertemporal preferences over losses.

6.4 Discussion

The above results allow us to conclude that hyperbolic discounting serves as a better fit than the exponential one to describe the time discounting of monetary losses. The preference reversal effect occurs in the delay discounting of monetary losses. In the choice between two losses borne relatively soon, the participants prefer the more delayed loss, but postponing those two losses by the same period promotes the choice of a less delayed one. These results are a confirmation of already established results. Holt et al. (2008) confirm the preference reversal effect for a small sample of students. Our results indicate that a similar procedure performed on a larger sample also provides similar insight.

Further, the hyperbolic model constitutes a good fit to the experimental data, but an even better fit is achieved by the q-exponential model proposed by Takahashi (2007, 2013). Hence, while providing a better fit than the exponential one, the hyperbolic discounting framework does not fully represent an individual's preferences over losses incurred in different time periods. Hence, while a simpler framework of hyperbolic discounting might be sufficient to describe the decisions over gains (cf. Ostaszewski & Karzel, 2002; Estle et al., 2006), a richer one is necessary to represent the choices over losses.

Interestingly, the observed behavioral pattern of delay discounting of monetary losses reveals a very rapid decrease in impulsivity. It differs highly from the one observed in gains (cf. Takahashi, 2013). It means that decision-makers are very averse to immediate financial losses, and even a small postponing is highly preferred. However, when it comes to already significantly postponed losses, the subjective valuation of those losses is to a great extent similar. This finding might provide a potential insight into the optimal decision-making of financial institutions. Prolonging a loss repay (i.e., a bank loan) can be accepted with a significant postponement fee might be a desirable option when the loss is due. However, it might not be in the individual's consideration when the money is borrowed.

The observed results can be partly biased since our participants were students who might not be "liquid" enough. Thus they avoid immediate financial losses dramatically. Therefore, a natural extension of the above study would be to test more affluent experimental groups. Also, the use of real instead of hypothetical losses would greatly enhance the research's validity. However, it is very difficult to recruit people to participate in the experiment in which they lose real money. Therefore, some compensation would be needed.

Finally, we believe that a relationship of delay discounting with other forms of discounting of monetary losses is worth investigating. Thus, the correlations between delay discounting and social or probability discounting of financial losses need to be studied.

References

Ainslie, G. (1975). Specious reward: a behavioral theory of impulsiveness and impulse control. *Psychological bulletin, 82*(4), 463.

Ainslie, G., & Herrnstein, R. J. (1981). Preference reversal and delayed reinforcement. *Animal Learning & Behavior, 9*(4), 476–482.

Azfar, O. (1999). Rationalizing hyperbolic discounting. *Journal of Economic Behavior & Organization, 38*(2), 245–252.

Cajueiro, D. O. (2006). A note on the relevance of the q-exponential function in the context of intertemporal choices. *Physica A: Statistical Mechanics and its Applications, 364*, 385–388.

Cubitt, R. P., Munro, A., & Starmer, C. (2004). Testing explanations of preference reversal. *The Economic Journal, 114*(497), 709–726.

Estle, S. J., Green, L., Myerson, J., & Holt, D. D. (2006). Differential effects of amount on temporal and probability discounting of gains and losses. *Memory & cognition, 34*(4), 914–928.

Hendrikse, G. (2003). *Economics and management of organizations: co-ordination, motivation and strategy*. New York: McGraw-Hill.

Holt, D. D., Green, L., & Myerson, J. (2003). Is discounting impulsive?: Evidence from temporal and probability discounting in gambling and non-gambling college students. *Behavioural processes, 64*(3), 355–367.

Holt, D. D., Green, L., Myerson, J., & Estle, S. J. (2008). Preference reversals with losses. *Psychonomic bulletin & review, 15*(1), 89–95.

Karbowski, A. (2016). Discussion on the social rate of discount: From Sen to behavioural economics. *Economics and Sociology, 9*(2), 46–60.

Karbowski, A., & Wiśnicki, B. (2021). Are there gender differences in delay discounting of monetary losses?. *Kwartalnik Nauk o Przedsiębiorstwie, 59*(2), 18–26.

Kirby, K. N., & Maraković, N. N. (1995). Modeling myopic decisions: Evidence for hyperbolic delay-discounting within subjects and amounts. *Organizational Behavior and Human decision processes, 64*(1), 22–30.

Laibson, D. (1997). Golden eggs and hyperbolic discounting. *The Quarterly Journal of Economics, 112*(2), 443–478.

Loewenstein, G., & Prelec, D. (1992). Anomalies in intertemporal choice: Evidence and an interpretation. *The Quarterly Journal of Economics, 107*(2), 573–597.

Myerson, J., Baumann, A. A., & Green, L. (2017). Individual differences in delay discounting: Differences are quantitative with gains, but qualitative with losses. *Journal of Behavioral Decision Making, 30*(2), 359–372.

Ostaszewski, P., & Karzel, K. (2002). Discounting of delayed and probabilistic losses of different amounts. *European Psychologist, 7*(4), 295.

Rambaud, S. C., & Torrecillas, M. J. M. (2013). A generalization of the q-exponential discounting function. *Physica A: Statistical Mechanics and its Applications, 392*(14), 3045–3050.

Spiess, A.-N., & Neumeyer, N. (2010). An evaluation of r 2 as an inadequate measure for nonlinear models in pharmacological and biochemical research: A Monte Carlo approach. *BMC pharmacology, 10*(1), 1–11.

Takahashi, T. (2007). A comparison of intertemporal choices for oneself versus someone else based on Tsallis statistics. *Physica A: Statistical Mechanics and Its Applications, 385*(2), 637–644.

Takahashi, T. (2013). The q-exponential social discounting functions of gain and loss. *Applied Mathematics, 4*, 445–448.

Zeileis, A. (2006). Object-oriented computation of sandwich estimators. *Journal of Statistical Software, 16*(1), 1–16.

Chapter 7
Loss Sharing and Social Distance: An Experimental Study

Bartłomiej Wiśnicki and Adam Karbowski

Abstract We investigate the prosocial behaviour of decision-makers in the context of financial losses. We find that in the dictator game, the loss transferred to other people occupying subsequent positions on the social distance scale behaves non-monotonically (it initially drops and then rises). Further, those effects tend to be smaller when the dictator game is replaced by the ultimatum game. Finally, we find that for the 20th ranked person and higher, decision-makers are prone to transfer a higher amount of loss to that person than willing to receive it from her. It means that egoistic motive dominates the altruistic one starting from a place no. 20 on a social distance scale.

Keywords Prosocial behaviour · Monetary losses · Social discounting · Economic games

7.1 Introduction

Yi et al. (2011) distinguish intertemporal and interpersonal dimensions of human behaviour. While the first dimension describes choices between 'present self' and 'future self', the second dimension describes choices between 'self' and 'another person' (Karbowski, 2018).

The above dimensions help researchers gain insights into the mechanisms of human self-control (intertemporal dimension) and prosocial (interpersonal dimension) behaviour (cf., Henrich et al., 2006; Hopkins, 2014; Schnall et al., 2010; Karbowski, 2018).

Prosocial behaviour plays an important role in today's business (Benabou & Tirole, 2006; Taylor & Curtis, 2018). It is also the underlying force behind corporate social responsibility or corporate sustainability policies (Choi & Yu,

B. Wiśnicki (✉) · A. Karbowski
Department of Business Economics, SGH Warsaw of Economics, Warsaw, Poland
e-mail: bwisni@sgh.waw.pl

N. Tsounis, A. Vlachvei (eds.), *Advances in Quantitative Economic Research*, Springer Proceedings in Business and Economics,
https://doi.org/10.1007/978-3-030-98179-2_7

2014; Pellegrini et al., 2018). Furthermore, prosocial behaviour towards future generations is the rationale for global sustainable development and managerial education oriented at responsible global leadership. Also, prosocial behaviour has very practical implications—it promotes human cooperation, which is the core idea of modern business policies.

In the scientific literature, there are different methods to measure the prosocial behaviour of decision-makers. To our best knowledge, social discounting procedures (Jones & Rachlin, 2006) or economic games—dictator or ultimatum (Kovarik, 2009)—can be used for that purpose. In this paper, we merge those two approaches and set out to investigate (with the use of both discounting procedures and economic games) human prosocial behaviour in the context of monetary losses. We think that during the COVID-19 pandemic, the exploration of human behaviour in the domain of financial losses constitutes an important research topic. The knowledge of human motivations and decisions in the context of losses can help us better understand social responses to COVID-19 economic challenges.

The experimental psychological or game-theoretic research on monetary losses gained a decent interest in recent years. For example, Neumann et al. (2018) show that people behave differently in the context of gains and losses—subjects are less generous in dictator and ultimatum games in the domain of losses compared with gains' domain. The differences in behaviour under losses and gains were also found by Kahneman and Tversky (1979) in their seminal paper on foundations of prospect theory—people, in general, are risk-seekers in the domain of losses but are risk-averse in the context of gains.

In this piece of research, we decided to formulate the following hypotheses. The hypotheses are inspired by the social discounting and game theory literature (see, e.g., Jones & Rachlin, 2006; Kovarik, 2009; Osiński et al., 2015).

Hypothesis 1: In the dictator game with loss sharing, the share of monetary loss moved to another player increases with the social distance.

Comment on Hypothesis 1: It is expected that a smaller part of the monetary loss will be moved to a socially close player, say a parent, and a larger part will be moved to a socially distant player, say a stranger.

This hypothesis is an initial step of analysing the behaviour of individuals in terms of losses. As we get further on the social distance scale, we suspect that individuals are more likely to transfer a significant loss as the psychological connection diminishes.

Hypothesis 2: The monetary losses moved to another player are smaller when another player can reject the division of losses (ultimatum game with loss sharing) than when another player cannot reject the division of losses (dictator game with loss sharing).

We suspect that individuals refrain from shifting a similar loss to their relative if the loss can be denied. Thus, if the loss can be denied, it makes the individual withhold the amount from rising. Moreover, although it is not stated in the hypothesis, we reckon that the addition of possible loss decline impacts the stated in Hypothesis

1 monotonic relationship between social distance and money transferred. Mainly, for people further down the social scale, individuals might suspect that they would not accept a high loss shift. Hence, we might not observe an increase in the amount transferred in the ultimatum game with the social distance.

Hypothesis 3: The financial loss moved to another player is always larger than the maximal loss accepted by the proposer if another player would move the loss to the proposer.

We presume that the amount of loss shifted in the ultimatum game would be higher than the one accepted, controlling for the time the loss is due and social distance. The above hypotheses mean that, in general, we expect a decline in the extent of prosocial behaviour along the social distance scale. This expectation is based on the literature—see, e.g., Maner and Gailliot (2007) and references therein. Also, we conjecture that the extent of prosocial behaviour expected from others is always greater than our prosocial behaviour executed to others. The latter claim is inspired by the elegant study by Branas-Garza and others (2017). The above expectations will be tested empirically in the present paper.

The paper proceeds as follows. The next section briefly presents the materials and methods used in the study. The subsequent section is devoted to the presentation of experimental results. Discussion follows and ends the article.

7.2 Materials and Methods

The online experiment has been conducted in the fall semester 2020/2021 among students of SGH Warsaw School of Economics, Poland (the link to the experiment is as follows: https://web.sgh.waw.pl/~akarbo1/Badania/5lfddn3x91f688s2b/Badanie1/Eksperyment_AK1_ZL.html; translated experimental procedure constitutes an appendix to this study). 203 persons (86 males, 117 females; the average age for men was 24.5, the average age for women was 23.4) participated in the study (a detailed description of the sample is present in Karbowski & Wiśnicki, 2021).

The first part of the study regarded the social discounting of monetary losses over time. We asked the participants three types of questions regarding the social discounting of losses. We asked them to imagine losing a fixed amount of money—5000 PLN (about 1100 EUR) in some period t. First, the participants were told that they could transfer some part of this loss to a person they find socially close. Namely, they were asked to think about a person they find k-closest to them ($k = 1$ means the socially closest person to a participant, e.g. a parent, where $k = 5$ means the fifth closest person to a participant, e.g. a cousin or a friend) and decide on the amount of loss transferred to that person. The amount of money was fixed, but the time the loss ought to be paid changed: the loss could occur instantly or in 1, 6, 12 and 50 months. The loss could be transferred to the persons ranked 1, 5, 20, 50 and 100 on a social distance scale. Each participant was asked about each combination of t and k.

Then, participants were asked two more rounds of structurally similar questions regarding the amount of loss, time of the loss and the person upon which it can be transferred. However, in the second round, the participants were told that the person receiving the loss could decline the transfer (ultimatum game, hence UG). In the case of loss decline, the whole loss would need to be incurred by the respondent. Hence, the game is parallel to the classic ultimatum game on losses: if the transfer is not accepted, the game results in the worst-case scenario from the perspective of the person proposing the loss—the whole loss would be covered by the respondent.[1]

Finally, in the third round, we asked the participants about the reverse situation: What would be the maximal accepted loss, given that it was transferred from person k and is due in time t (reversed UG)?

The procedure provided us with 75 answers per participant: three rounds, five time periods and five different persons socially close to the participant. Thus, it gives us both insight into the time discounting of transferring losses, but most importantly, it provides us with information on the social discounting of monetary losses. Furthermore, the order inside the procedures was randomized: for each of the games, the order of t and k was random.[2]

After this set of problems, we also asked participants questions regarding their attitude towards temporal discounting of losses. This last exercise was timed, and we also excluded all the answers from the respondents that provided answers in higher or lower than three standard deviations from mean time.

7.3 Results

All the hypotheses are investigated with a significance level of $\alpha = 0.05$.

First of all, we analyse how the time of the loss being due affects participants' choices in all three experiment stages. We establish no statistically significant differences between any choices in which the loss does not have to be paid immediately. That is, for any given k, as long as $t > 0$, the difference between choices for different time periods is insignificant (for the significance level 0.05). Therefore, we treat the decisions with $t > 0$ as one group with the average value across time periods for a given participant. Thus, we are left with two options concerning the time of loss repayment in our analysis: it is either immediate ($t = 0$) or delayed ($t > 0$).

Figure 7.1 shows the mean of transferred losses in the first round of questions: the dictator game (hence DG). The lines represent different periods that plot the

[1] In the standard ultimatum game, if the transfer is not accepted, both proposer and recipient are worst off: they both end up with nothing. In our setting, if the sum is not agreed upon only the respondent has the objectively worst outcome: she would need to incur the total amount of loss.

[2] First, the time of the loss was given to the participant and then for a given period the respondent answered questions concerning people on different social distance scale.

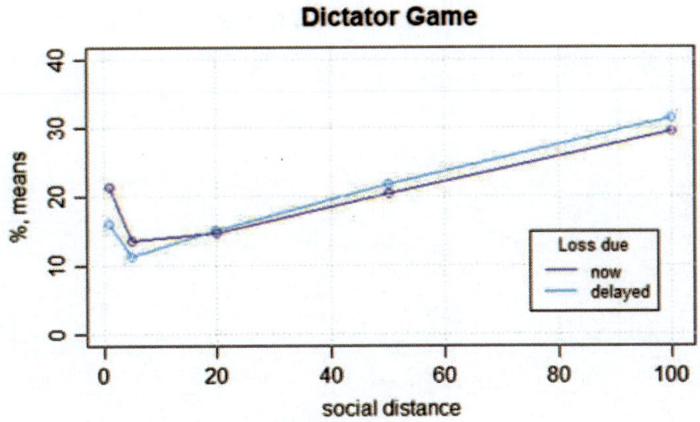

Fig. 7.1 Mean losses transferred in the dictator game

Table 7.1 Student's t-test for the loss transfers in the adjacent social distances in the dictator game

Group (k) comparison	Time period (t)	t-test statistic	p-value
1 vs 5	Now	3.15	0.0018
	Delayed	2.36	0.0190
5 vs 20	Now	−0.49	0.3108
	Delayed	−1.84	0.0330
20 vs 50	Now	−1.98	0.0243
	Delayed	−2.45	0.0074
50 vs 100	Now	−2.52	0.0061
	Delayed	−2.69	0.0037

The null hypothesis is that the loss transfers are equal. The alternative hypothesis is that the money transfers are not equal (for 1 vs 5) and that the transfer is higher for greater social distance (for the other cases)

relationship between social distance (x-axis) and the mean percentage of money transferred (y-axis).

We can analyse the data in Fig. 7.1 from several angles. We can see that the relationship between social distance and money transferred is not monotonic. Table 7.1 presents the Student's t-test outcomes analysing the differences between money transfers to adjacent social distance groups for immediate and delayed loss.

The average amount assigned to the first person is about 15–20% of the loss, depending on the time the loss is due. This sum goes down to about 10–15% assigned to the 5-th closest person. Then, money passed on to the further ranked people increases to about 15% for the 20th ranked person, 20% for the 50th ranked person and about 30% for the 100th ranked person. The increase in the amount of money transferred with the social distance is intuitive: the further the person is in our social ranking, the less connection we feel towards her, so we transfer her more loss.

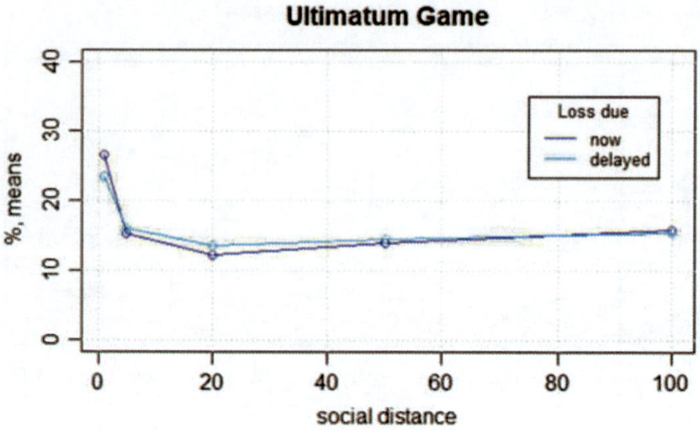

Fig. 7.2 Mean losses transferred in the ultimatum game

A first-glance anomaly is a drop from 1-st to 5-th person ranked. However, as our participants are mainly students, we believe that their closest person would be their parent, who supports them financially. Therefore, it might be easier for them to shift a significant sum of money to them.

The time aspect of the data is also important. We also can notice some inconsistencies between the assigned losses in Fig. 7.1. For example, for the first closest person, the necessity of instant payment of the loss increases the amount of money transferred to that person (the difference is statistically significant with $t = 2.06$, $p = 0.04$). On the other hand, for people further on the social distance scale, the contingency of instant loss makes subjects elect less money to be assigned to those persons than the delayed payment. However, these differences are not statistically significant (the lowest p-value is 0.2). Hence, the time effect only affects the closest person when it comes to the forced loss transfer, and it does so in an unintuitive manner.

7.3.1 *Ultimatum Game*

The second round of social distance questions regarded the same situation as previously but with an option of decline from the receiving party. Figure 7.2 shows the relationship between money transferred and social distance for different loss deadline levels.

The introduction of the possibility of rejection into the transferred sum changes the assigned loss amounts. First of all, we observe a similar but rather moderate relationship of money transferred to the social distance, compared to the previous analysis. Thus, participants believe that further related persons would most likely reject covering vast amounts of money and offer statistically similar loss shares.

Table 7.2 Student's t-test for the dictator game vs ultimatum game

Group (k)	Time period (t)	t-test statistic	p-value
1	Now	−1.79	0.007
	Delayed	−3.05	0.002
5	Now	−0.81	0.416
	Delayed	−2.48	0.014
20	Now	1.04	0.30
	Delayed	0.62	0.53
50	Now	2.18	0.03
	Delayed	2.53	0.01
100	Now	3.82	<0.01
	Delayed	4.56	<0.01

The null hypothesis is that the loss transfers are equal. The alternative hypothesis is that the money transfers are not equal. Positive and significant results show that the amount transferred in the dictator game is greater than in the ultimatum game and vice versa

Moreover, we observe an analogous relationship of instant to delayed loss. For close relationships (here for the closest person), the instant loss transfer is greater than the delayed ones. However, for more further related people, it is lower than the delayed loss or insignificantly different.

There is a significant quantitative difference between assigned money losses with and without the possible rejection. Table 7.2 provides statistical evidence of these differences. For high social distance, the amount of money transferred is significantly lower with rejection than without it. This difference is extremely significant in the very far social distance case: the loss transfer is halved if the rejection is possible. It means that the participants think that far related people would rather reject covering high losses.

On the other hand, for very close persons (the most and 5-th closest), the participants elected, on average, a higher amount of loss to be transferred. One may think of the following explanation of this phenomenon: an idea of shifting a loss to a very close person might be more psychologically tolerable if it can be denied. Note that the differences between Dictator and ultimatum game are enhanced by the loss delay (a lone exception is $k = 20$).

7.3.2 *Reversed Ultimatum Game*

In the third and final round of the social discounting questions, we asked participants to reverse the roles in an ultimatum game. Now, the question is, what would be the maximal part of a 5000 PLN loss that a person would be willing to accept after being offered one by a kth ranked person. Figure 7.3 depicts the averages of a maximal loss that participants would accept from the k-ranked person. We can see that the

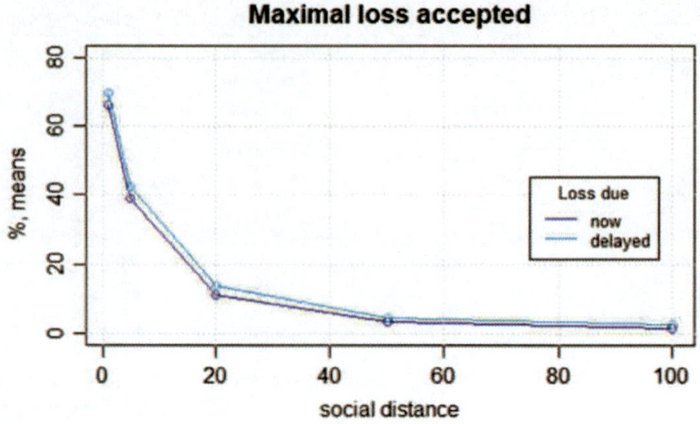

Fig. 7.3 Averages of maximally accepted financial losses

further the person is ranked, the lower loss the participants will accept to be placed on them (for the far-ranked comparisons, the difference is insignificant). Thus, while from the highest-ranked person, there is a willingness to accept about 65–70% of the loss, and the amount goes down exponentially with a bit more than zero accepted on average for the 100th ranked person.

There is not much considerable difference between maximal accepted loss and time delay of the loss. Respondents would accept a delayed loss; however, this is not a significant difference.

One of the interesting results of the experiment comes from comparing the decisions made in the dictator game and the one of the maximal loss accepted in the ultimatum game. In both of these decisions, individuals end up with a definite decision about the amount of loss he or she will incur. In the dictator game, the individual ends up with 5000PLN minus the amount shifted to the other person. In the reversed ultimatum game, he or she incurs a loss of maximally the amount accepted. Hence, intuitively, these amounts should be similar. However, as is depicted in Fig. 7.4, there is a substantial difference between these two answers. The differences are statistically significant, with the p-value of the Student's t-test less than 0.001 for every examined pair. These results show two things about the dictator and ultimatum game in the area of losses and about the loss sharing itself. First of all, framing is important for individuals. There is a difference between being the one who needs to decide how much loss to shift to another person and accepting the loss of the other individual. Second, the difference can also be explained by the fact that there is a previous step to accepting or rejecting a loss in the ultimatum game made by a close person. This dichotomy means that the individuals do not expect high amounts to be transferred to them or find that action inappropriate.

Noting the above results, the comparison of maximal accepted loss with the loss shift examined in the UG section might be significant. We can see the difference between accepted loss and the shift of the loss as some prosocial behaviour index.

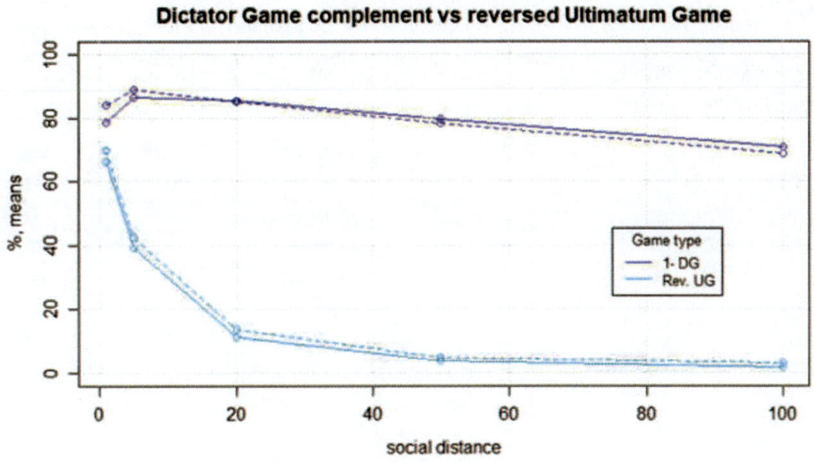

Fig. 7.4 Complement of the dictator game and maximal loss accepted for ultimatum game averages. The dotted lines represent choices where loss is delayed

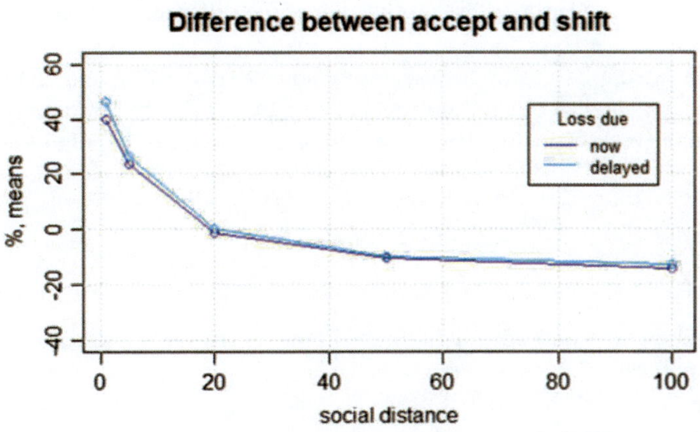

Fig. 7.5 Difference between maximal accepted loss and loss shift (averages)

For example, a perfectly altruistic person would not shift any loss and pay up to a total loss. On the other hand, a full egoist would not pay up any loss and shift it to somebody else. As it is situated in the same framework of the ultimatum game, we think this difference allows for that comparison to be made. Figure 7.5 shows the differences between averages from these two questions for different combinations of time that the loss is due and social distance.

We can see that altruism diminishes with the level of social distance. That is, we tend to care less about people that we are less related to. The decrease is exponential, as was the one in Fig. 7.3. For people further than 20th ranked person, we are more, on average, prone to transfer a higher amount of loss to that person than willing to

Table 7.3 Student's t-test for the difference between maximal accepted transfer and amount proposed in the ultimatum game

Group (k)	Time period (t)	t-test statistic	p-value
1	Now	12.29	<0.01
	Delayed	15.6	<0.01
5	Now	8.82	<0.01
	Delayed	10.06	<0.01
20	Now	0.55	0.583
	Delayed	0.02	0.986
50	Now	−5.17	<0.01
	Delayed	−4.96	<0.01
100	Now	−6.46	<0.01
	Delayed	−5.77	<0.01

The null hypothesis is that the loss transfers are equal. The alternative hypothesis is that the money transfers are not equal. Positive and significant results show that the maximal accepted transfer is greater than the one proposed and vice versa

receive it from her. A proper test for the sign of the difference is presented in Table 7.3.

The presented relationship also seems, to some extent, to depend on the time the loss is due. We tend to be more altruistic if the loss is due in the future. However, this difference is statistically insignificant to be a predictor of population behaviour.

7.4 Discussion

We rejected the first and third hypotheses in the above study and did not reject the second hypothesis.

As regards the first hypothesis, it means that the expectation that, in the dictator game with loss sharing, the part of monetary loss moved to another player increases with the social distance to another player turned out to be false. The observed relationship was not monotonic. The moved loss initially declined and further increased. The former is an interesting finding of our study. The subjects prefer to move a larger part of the financial loss to the closest person (say a parent) compared with the fifth closest person (say a cousin or a good friend). For more distant persons, the transferred loss increases monotonically. We can interpret those results in the following way. The first five persons on the social distance scale constitute a so-called extended self group, so people are very close to the decision-maker. Decision-makers prefer the 'extended self' group compared with other people, so the loss moved to the 'extended self' group is smaller compared with the loss moved to other people. Also, the socially closest person is special, so we can share with her all our problems and costs (not only financial). Thus, the transfer to the closest person is significantly higher compared with the transfer to the fifth closest person.

As regards the second hypothesis, we did not find the evidence to reject this hypothesis. The observed behavioural pattern is consistent with the second hypothesis, so the mechanism of rejection lowers the losses transferred to another player. The result is quite intuitive, and the rejection mechanism plays a disciplinary role.

Regarding the third hypothesis, it turned out that for relatively close persons (up to no. 20 in the social distance scale), the participants were eager to accept a higher loss than they transferred. This observation allows us to reject the third hypothesis. So, the altruism turned out to be local (places 1–20 on the social distance scale). On the other hand, for the 20th ranked person and higher, we are prone to transfer a higher amount of loss to that person than willing to receive it from her. This relationship depends on the time the loss is due. We tend to be more altruistic if the loss is due in a long time. The latter constitutes an interesting preference reversal effect in social discounting.

The methods used to examine the above hypotheses were simple statistical parametric tests. One could think about employing more sophisticated ones, such as regression models. However, while regression seems a more comprehensive method, it also has certain limitations. For instance, consider regressing the money transfers of the dictator game against the social distance might give insight concerning the first hypothesis. However, apart from the various limiting assumption of regression models, we need to assume a certain functional form. From Fig. 7.1, we see that the relationship is not linear, so a nonlinear form seems necessary. A more general approach would be to either regress the transfer values against each other. This approach would lose the functional form, but a collinearity problem arises. One way to solve that would be to employ a panel model. Nevertheless, there are limits to this approach as the number of degrees of freedom would be low. Hence, the simple approach that we took seems plausible given the limitations of more advanced methods.

When it comes to comparisons of obtained results to those present in the literature, we can say that we confirm the existence of different behavioural patterns in dictator and ultimatum games (Neumann et al., 2018; Bechler et al., 2015). As Bechler et al. (2015) observe, the proportion of gains offered in the ultimatum game is higher than in a dictator game. We observe the reversed outcome; i.e., the proportion of amount (loss) offered in the ultimatum game is lower than in a dictator game. This result is rather intuitive. Under losses, the social control (or fairness motive, see Kim et al., 2013) works oppositely than under gain sharing. A similar result is obtained quite recently by Vravosinos and Konstantinou (2019). Our results are also in line with Charness and Gneezy (2008) findings, who report increased altruism (revealed in dictator and ultimatum games) towards socially closer persons.

The above study has certain limitations. First, the payoffs were only hypothetical (due to budget constraints). Therefore, the natural step would be to replicate the study with the use of real money. Second, the tested group consisted of students. Thus, it would be interesting to extend this research to other social groups regarding age and occupation. Finally, a deeper analysis of the relationship between social and delay discounting of monetary losses can be executed. Such an exercise would complete the intertemporal and interpersonal picture of human behaviour sketched out by Yi et al. (2011). In addition, to indicate how the findings are affected by examining monetary losses, we would need to perform a similar experiment in gains. However, we feel that since there is a rich literature concerning dilemma in gains (apart from the examples mentioned above, consider Engel (2011)) such research would not be substantially beneficial.

Moreover, although the sample we used is relatively large, it is fairly homogeneous as it contains mostly students. Hence, it has its limitations in generalizing its results. Nevertheless, considering that most of the research is performed on students and the sample size, we are confident we can, to an extent, compare our results to the existing research.

Funding This paper was supported by funds from the National Science Centre, Poland, through grant number 2018/31/D/HS4/00203.

Appendix. Experimental Procedure (Translated)

Thank you for agreeing to participate in this study.

Please give reliable answers.

Gender:

- - Select - -

Age:

Major:

Start the experiment

Please read out the following instructions carefully.

The study is on the evaluation of the value of monetary losses. You will be asked to make a series of choices about different amounts of losses. The choices are hypothetical—you will not lose those amounts, but we ask you to indicate your preferences as if you were to really lose those amounts. We are interested in your preferences. There are no right or wrong answers. We have no expectations of you, except that you choose according to your preferences.

Imagine that you made a list of 100 people you know, sorted by social proximity. The first position on the list is the person you consider socially closest to you. In the last position is a person you know only by sight. You do not have to create this list physically; just imagine it.

Imagine you have a financial loss of PLN 5000. You can cover this loss entirely by yourself, or you can transfer the part of the loss to another person occupying a specific position on your list. In the following, we will ask you to make a series of choices considering different people on the list and different delays. Remember that the decision is entirely yours.

Monetary losses in 5 years [immediately, in a month, in 6 months, in a year].

Choose how much of a monetary loss you will shift to person number 1 [5, 20, 50, 100].

Imagine you have a loss of PLN 5000. You can cover this loss entirely by yourself, or you can transfer a part of the loss to another person occupying a specific position on your list. However, if that person does not accept your decision, you will have to cover the entire loss by yourself. In the following, we will ask you to make a series of choices considering different people on the list and different delays.

Monetary losses in 5 years [immediately, in a month, in 6 months, in a year].

Choose how much of a monetary loss you will shift to person number 1 [5, 20, 50, 100].

This time the roles were reversed. Another person on your list suffered a loss of PLN 5000. She can either cover that loss entirely by herself or pass on to your part of the loss. However, if you do not accept her decision, the loss will be covered in full by another person on your list. In the following, we will ask you for the minimum acceptable (for you) loss shifted by another person, considering different people on the list and different delays.

Monetary losses in 5 years [immediately, in a month, in 6 months, in a year].

Choose how much of a monetary loss you will shift to person number 1 [5, 20, 50, 100].

In the following, we will ask you to make hypothetical choices between monetary losses just for you. Option A will be equal to the lower loss immediately incurred and Option B to the greater and delayed loss.

[here standard delay discounting task with titration algorithm, option B is 2900 PLN].

Thank you very much for your participation!

References

Bechler, C., Green, L., & Myerson, J. (2015). Proportion offered in the dictator and ultimatum games decreases with amount and social distance. *Behavioural Processes, 115*, 149–155.

Benabou, R., & Tirole, J. (2006). Incentives and prosocial behavior. *American Economic Review, 96*, 1652–1678.

Branas-Garza, P., Rodriguez-Lara, I., & Sanchez, A. (2017). Humans expect generosity. *Scientific Reports, 7*, 42446.

Charness, G., & Gneezy, U. (2008). What's in a name? Anonymity and social distance in dictator and ultimatum games. *Journal of Economic Behavior & Organization, 68*, 29–35.

Choi, Y., & Yu, Y. (2014). The influence of perceived corporate sustainability practices on employees and organizational performance. *Sustainability, 6*(1), 348–364.

Engel, C. (2011). Dictator games: A meta study. *Experimental Economics, 14*(4), 583–610.

Henrich, J., McElreath, R., Barr, A., Ensminger, J., Barrett, C., Bolyanatz, A., Cardenas, J. C., Gurven, M., Gwako, E., Henrich, N., Lesorogol, C., Marlowe, F., Tracer, D., & Ziker, J. (2006). Costly punishment across human societies. *Science, 312*(5781), 1767–1770.

Hopkins, E. (2014). Competitive altruism, Mentalizing, and signaling. *American Economic Journal: Microeconomics, 6*, 272–292.

Jones, B., & Rachlin, H. (2006). Social discounting. *Psychological Science, 17*, 283–286.

Kahneman, D., & Tversky, A. (1979). Prospect theory: An analysis of decision under risk. *Econometrica, XLVII*, 263–291.

Karbowski, A. (2018). *Delay and social discounting of losses*. Mimeo.

Karbowski, A., & Wiśnicki, B. (2021). *Are there gender differences in delay discounting of monetary losses?* Mimeo.

Kim, H., Schnall, S., Yi, D., & White, M. (2013). Social distance decreases responders' sensitivity to fairness in the ultimatum game. *Judgment and Decision making, 8*, 632–638.

Kovarik, J. (2009). Giving it now or later: Altruism and discounting. *Economics Letters, 102*, 152–154.

Maner, J., & Gailliot, M. (2007). Altruism and egoism: Prosocial motivations for helping depend on relationship context. *European Journal of Social Psychology, 37*, 347–358.

Neumann, T., Kierspel, S., Windrich, I., Berger, R., & Vogt, B. (2018). How to split gains and losses? Experimental evidence of dictator and ultimatum games. *Games, 9*(4), 78.

Osiński, J., Karbowski, A., & Ostaszewski, P. (2015). Social discounting: Choice between rewards for other people. *Behavioural Processes, 115*, 61–63.

Pellegrini, C., Rizzi, F., & Frey, M. (2018). The role of sustainable human resource practices in influencing employee behavior for corporate sustainability. *Business Strategy and the Environment, 27*, 1221–1232.

Schnall, S., Roper, J., & Fessler, D. M. T. (2010). Elevation leads to altruistic behavior. *Psychological Science, 21*, 315–320.

Taylor, E. Z., & Curtis, M. B. (2018). Mentoring: A path to prosocial behavior. *Journal of Business Ethics, 152*, 1133–1148.

Vravosinos, O., & Konstantinou, K. (2019). Asymmetric social distance in the ultimatum game. *Review of Behavioral Economics, 6*, 159–192.

Yi, R., Charlton, S., Porter, C., Carter, A. E., & Bickel, W. K. (2011). Future altruism: Social discounting of delayed rewards. *Behavioural Processes, 86*, 160–163.

Chapter 8
Impatience and Altruism Over Hypothetical Monetary Losses

Adam Karbowski, Bartłomiej Wiśnicki, and Jerzy Osiński

Abstract In the following paper, the relationship between impatience (measured with delay discounting procedures) and altruism (measured with social discounting procedures and behaviour of subjects in the dictator game) in the context of hypothetical monetary losses was investigated. The experiment results (sample size—164) show that contrary to our expectations, there is no significant relationship between impatience and altruistic behaviour. We, however, discovered that both immediate altruism and delayed altruism in the context of financial losses are negatively correlated with age. This inspiring result shows that older people are probably less likely to accept financial losses or participate in the social costs generated by others. The latter result needs to be carefully investigated using broader and more heterogeneous samples (especially in terms of the age of respondents).

Keywords Impatience · Altruism · Monetary losses · Behavioral economics

8.1 Introduction

This article focuses on the relationship between social discounting and delay discounting of monetary amounts but in the context of monetary losses. The literature review shows that the relationship between social discounting and delay discounting of monetary amounts was investigated in the context of monetary gains. Therefore, the present analysis of the above relationship in losses constitutes a value-added to the current state of knowledge.

Rachlin and Jones (2007) show that both social discounting and delay discounting of monetary gains can be effectively modelled by a hyperbolic function, and hence, both types of discounting exhibit a similar behavioural pattern. The same thesis can be deduced from Jones and Rachlin (2009). As Karbowski (2018)

A. Karbowski (✉) · B. Wiśnicki · J. Osiński
SGH Warsaw School of Economics, Warsaw, Poland
e-mail: akarbo1@sgh.waw.pl

N. Tsounis, A. Vlachvei (eds.), *Advances in Quantitative Economic Research*,
Springer Proceedings in Business and Economics,
https://doi.org/10.1007/978-3-030-98179-2_8

stresses, both delay discounting and social discounting are based on similar cognitive/neurobiological mechanisms, e.g. fluid intelligence and perception abilities (see Charlton et al., 2013; Hill et al., 2017; Locey et al., 2011; Yi et al., 2011, 2012, for a wider discussion). Osiński et al. (2017) claim that delay discounting and social discounting are interrelated behavioural patterns, and observed temporal self-control and altruism are not separate phenomena (in this context, see also Curry et al., 2008 or Harris & Madden, 2002).

Nevertheless, social and delay discounting are not always similar in their manifestations. For example, beyond monetary amounts' domain, Igaki et al. (2019) observed that using smartphones while walking can be explained (at least to a significant extent) by delay discounting by individuals but not social discounting. Also, for participants with autism spectrum disorder (ASD), social and delay discounting patterns do not have to be necessarily correlated (cf., Warnell et al., 2019).

Individual social discounting patterns play a role in selfish/altruistic behaviour in Dictator or Ultimatum Games (subjects depending on their individual social discounting rates can behave more or less altruistically)—cf., Kovarik (2009), Yi et al. (2011) or Karbowski (2018). Based on the experimental results of the games mentioned above (usually, it is observed that subjects behave less altruistically in such games if the delay increases), we decided to formulate the following hypothesis (cf., Karbowski, 2018): delaying monetary losses promotes selfish behaviour (observed in a dictator game) to a greater extent for participants who discount in time at a higher rate compared with subjects who exhibit lower delay discounting rates. We also expect that an increase in delay, in general, leads to more selfish behaviour in the experimental dictator game. In broad terms, this paper focuses on investigating the relationship between impatience (measured by delay discounting procedures) and egoism or selfishness (measured by social discounting procedures) in the context of hypothetical monetary losses.

The paper proceeds as follows. The next section is devoted to the presentation of materials and methods. Next, we report on the obtained results. Discussion follows and closes the article.

8.2 Materials and Methods

8.2.1 *Sample*

A detailed description of the experimental sample (as well as experimental procedure) is given in Karbowski and Wiśnicki (2021a; see also Karbowski & Wiśnicki, 2021b). Below is the summary of the sample characteristics (as well as executed procedure).

The experiment was run online. All participants expressed consent to participate in the study. The experiment was run in the Fall semester 2021/2021 among graduate students of SGH Warsaw School of Economics, Poland. The raw experimental data are available online under DOI number 10.13140/RG.2.2.35480.21760.207 students participated in the study. The study was anonymous.

Due to very rapid responses in the experimental task (less than three standard derivations from the mean), we decided to exclude four observations from the analysis. We found those observations unreliable.

In the sample, 86 participants identified themselves as males, 117 as females. It is worth mentioning that the sample is quite homogenous; therefore, future research should test the obtained results with the use of more heterogeneous groups (in terms of age, educational level or occupation).

8.2.2 Procedure

In the delay discounting task, the participants were asked to choose between a monetary loss of 1450 PLN (Polish national currency) now or 2900 PLN in a given period of delay. The procedure followed the algorithm by Holt, Green and Myerson (2003)—in the first choice, the "now option" was half the amount in "delayed option"; in further choices, the "now option" changed depending on the previous choices by participants. Finally, the amount in the "now option" following the sixth choice was treated as the equivalent of the amount in the "delayed option". This procedure was run for financial losses of 2900 PLN in 1, 6, 12 and 60 months for the same initial monetary amounts.

In the social discounting task, we asked the participants questions regarding the social discounting of financial losses. We asked them to imagine losing a fixed amount—5000 PLN in some period t. The subjects were told that they could transfer some part of this financial loss to a person they find socially k-close ($k = 1$ means the socially closest person to a participant, e.g. a father, where $k = 5$ means the fifth closest person to a participant, e.g. a friend)—the procedure worked as a variety of a dictator game.

In order to capture the scope of intertemporal and social discounting, we use a method of the area under the curve (AUC), cf. Myerson et al., 2001. Namely, for each individual, we plot the relationship between the time of the delay or social distance and the monetary amount chosen, both normalized to unit intervals. We plot the money equivalents of the delayed financial loss corresponding to different time periods for intertemporal choice. For social discounting, we plot the monetary choices of loss shared for people placed at the corresponding social distance scale. Observations where the participants chose 0 in the social discounting task were removed from the further regression model since the individual discounting rates cannot be found if AUC is zero. Thus, the final sample used in the analysis consisted of 164 observations.

8.2.3 Methods

The AUC method allows us to obtain a single index of social and time discounting that does not depend on any specific functional form of the discounting function. However, existing research shows that capturing intertemporal discounting (see, e.g., Luhmann, 2013; Takahashi, 2007; Zauberman et al., 2009) as well as social discounting (see, e.g., Jones & Rachlin, 2009; Takahashi, 2013) by an exponential or even general hyperbolic functions might not be sufficient. Therefore, instead of obtaining an explicit discounting factor, the AUC approach provides a non-parametric measure of one's attitude towards discounting either time or social interactions.

Before examining the relationship between time and social discounting, we analyse the specific characteristics regarding time and social discounting of losses.

8.2.4 Methods—Time Discounting and Patience

Figure 8.1 depicts the experimental results concerning the time discounting of losses. Figure 8.1a depicts the distribution of perceived instant equivalents to the loss of 2900 PLN in the time periods presented on the horizontal axis. Intuitively, the more the loss is delayed, the less value it has in absolute terms. Moreover, the variance of answers increases with the delay of the loss, which is also in line with discounting theory: persons have different individual discounting rates, diverging over time. It shall be noted that there are some outliers in the data, especially concerning the short-term relation between money losses. Some respondents wish to incur higher loss now than in the future. Green et al. (2014) and Lipman and Attema

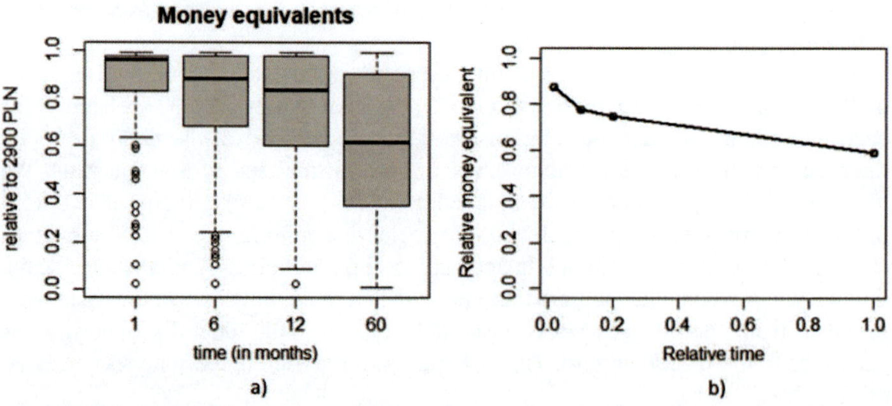

Fig. 8.1 Time discounting and discounting curve (**a**) Distribution of money equivalents (**b**) Time discounting distribution and discounting curve

Fig. 8.2 Distribution of time AUC

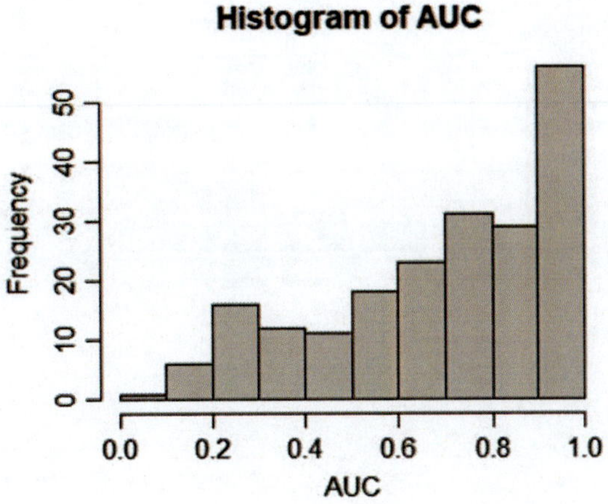

(2020), among others, also found this negative discounting rate due to disutility from future loss anticipation.

For each individual, we can calculate the corresponding relationship of money equivalents over time, normalized to the unit square, as presented in Fig. 8.1b for mean responses. We can see that the discount rate seems to follow a pattern more related to hyperbolic than exponential discounting, with a sharp decline for the small delay and lower discount rate when the time to repay the loss is more distant. Calculating the area under the curve for each individual provides us with their measure of discounting of losses. This procedure gives us an indicator of one's intertemporal patience: low AUC corresponds to a high discounting rate, indicating a more patient person (he or she is more likely to shift the loss in time).

Figure 8.2 depicts the distribution of AUC among participants. We can see that the majority of participants tend to be highly impatient. Therefore, the distribution is highly negatively skewed. The average value of AUC observed in the sample is 0.69.

8.2.5 *Methods—Social Discounting and Altruism*

In order to capture the altruistic behaviour of individuals, we take the results of the dictator games played by the respondents, specifically examining what proportion of the loss was shifted towards a certain person on their social discount scale. Furthermore, we asked the respondents to determine their shifts regarding different people on the social distance scale and the time of the loss. However, as the amount of money shifted did not change with the time, the loss is due as long as it is not immediate. Thus, we distinguish between the shifts when the loss is due now or when it is delayed, with the latter being the average over all the delayed loss answers.

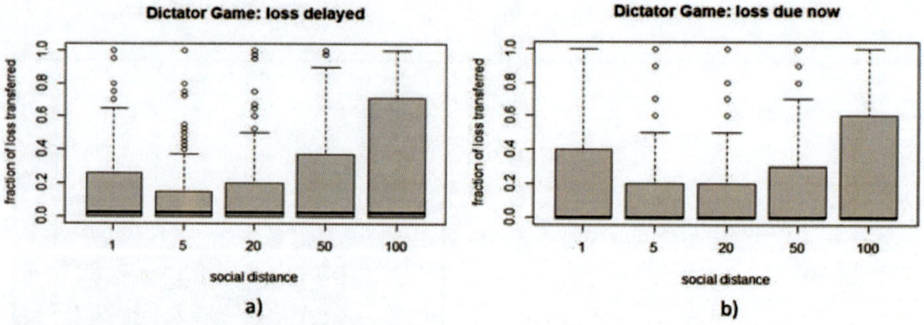

Fig. 8.3 Mean social discounting curve (**a**) loss due now (**b**) loss delayed

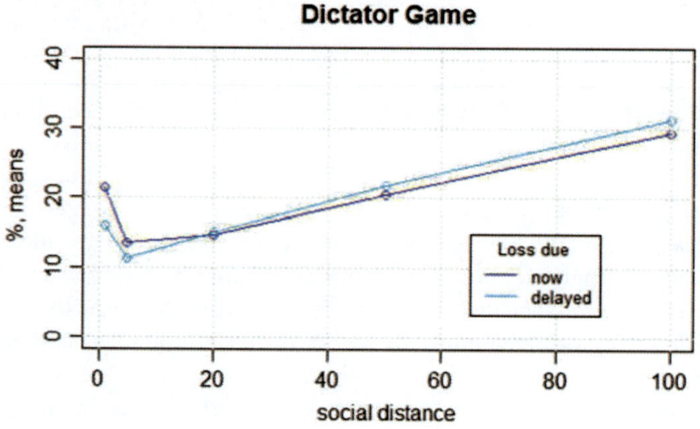

Fig. 8.4 Mean social discounting curve

Figure 8.3a, b show the distribution of loss transferred in the dictator game when the loss is due now, and in the case, it is delayed. The corresponding social discounting curve is depicted in Fig. 8.4. Generally, the amount of money shifted increases with the social distance, which is in line with intuition. However, the amount of loss transferred for the closest person is higher than that for the fifth closest. This intriguing result can be explained in the following fashion. For many participants, the closest person is their parent or partner with whom they share the household budget. Therefore, the shifted amount does not make the participant less due.

The difference between the money transferred if the loss is due now or is delayed is quite similar: for the closely related persons ($k = 1$ and $k = 5$), participants shifted more loss if it is due now. However, for people further on the social scale, this difference is smaller and insignificant for $k \geq 20$.

The social discounting curve provides us with information on the level of altruism of individuals.

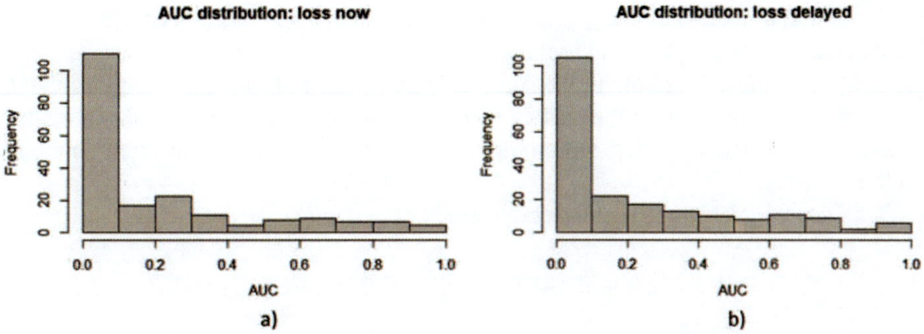

Fig. 8.5 Distribution of AUC for the dictator game (**a**) Loss due now (**b**) Loss delayed

A highly egoistic person would shift almost all of his or her loss to other people. To extract a single measure of a person's altruism, we use the same method of calculating AUC as we did for the temporal discounting. The AUC equal one would indicate a fully egoistic person, whereas it being equal to 0 is a sign of a perfect altruist. The AUC for the average participant was 0.21 for the loss now and 0.22 for the delayed loss.

Figure 8.5a, b present the distribution of AUC for the dictator game. As we can see, there is a solid mode for being overly altruistic: over half of the respondents are characterized with AUC less than 0.1. This result indicates very high altruism compared to the similar research done in the domain of gains (e.g. Jones and Rachlin (2009)) as over 20% of respondents did not shift any positive amount of loss to any person on the social distance scale. In addition, the two distributions (for a loss paid now and delayed) are quite similar, with the average AUC for transfer delayed exceeding by about 3% the one made immediately. Hence, the time aspect of the loss does not seem significantly important. However, we retain the two indicators separately as it might bring consequences to the egoism versus impatience relationship.

8.3 Results

In order to investigate the relationship between individual egoism and impatience in the dimension of losses, we develop a simple regression model. This method helps us quantitatively establish whether more impatient persons are also more egoistic.

We analyse the relationship between egoism and impatience through standard linear regression using ordinary least squares (OLS). As both discounting (temporal and social) measures are quantitatively measured, and we have a significantly large sample of responses, we believe that we can formulate informative statements about the relationship in the population. In our setting, we arbitrary decide that the egoism indicator (AUC from the dictator game) is the dependent variable and the impatience indicator (AUC from the time discounting problem) is the independent variable. We also include sex (encoded as SEX = 1 for males) and age as control variables. As both of the AUC distributions are skewed, we also extend the analysis to models where the variables are logarithmically transformed. To fix for potential heteroskedasticity, we employ the heteroskedasticity-consistent standard errors (HC1).

The model itself has the following form:

$$\text{AUC\_DG\_}i = \beta 0 + \beta 1\text{AUC\_TIME}i + \beta 2\text{SEX}i + \beta_3\text{AGE}i + \varepsilon_i,$$

for the levels of AUCs and

$$\log(\text{AUC\_DG}i) = \gamma 0 + \gamma 1\log(\text{AUC\_TIME}i) + \gamma 2\text{SEX}i + \gamma 3\text{AGE}i + \nu_i,$$

if we use the logarithms for AUC variables instead.

Table 8.1 depicts the coefficient estimates for the regression model where the AUC values for the dictator game with immediate loss are the dependent variable, and one of the regressors is the value of AUC from the intertemporal decision problem. When we analyse the model with the values of AUC not transformed, we find no significant relationship between the answers in both temporal and dictator (assume $\alpha = 0.01$ significance level). Note that only the age variable is significant for the significance level of 0.05 in the model with logarithmic transformation of AUC variables. The t-test statistic for the significance of the coefficient is 2.24 with a corresponding 0.027 p-value (Table 8.2).

If we consider the dictator game with a delayed loss instead of an immediate one, the relationship between one's egoism and impatience is less strong. We can see that the more impatient the person is, the more egoistic it seems. However, this relationship is smaller and statistically insignificant both in terms of the levels of AUC and their relative changes. Hence, with a delayed loss, the egoistic behaviour seems to be less connected to one's impatience and probably other factors account for the amount of loss transfer.

One peculiar result from the research is that both indicators of egoism (amount of money transferred due to the loss now and delayed) are positively related to an individual's age. Considering that the sample mostly consisted of students, thus the age distribution was not vast, the fact of more egoistic behaviour with age may still come as a surprise. The existing literature mostly finds that the level of egoism weakens with age as the material situation of individuals gets better (see, e.g., Kirchler, 1997). Our result contradicts it, which may conclude that the indicators of one's egoism are not fully explained by now.

Table 8.1 Ordinary least squares model for AUC value of the dictator game with an immediate loss

Dependent variable	AUC_TIME	log(AUC_TIME)	Sex	Age	Const	$\overline{R}^2$	AIC
AUC_DG	0.1(0.082)				0.199(0.058)	0.002	50.77
AUC_DG	0.096(0.081)		0.028(0.045)	0.011(0.005)	−0.078(0.13)	0.01	51.13
log(AUC_DG)		0.386(0.17)			−1.85(<0.001)	0.02	547.72
log(AUC_DG)		0.367(0.17)	0.27(0.21)	0.054(0.024)	−3.25(<0.001)	0.04	546.2

The values in brackets are the standard deviations of the estimates. $\overline{R}^2$ represents the determination coefficient adjusted for the loss in the degrees of freedom. AIC is the value of the Akaike information criterion. $n = 164$

Table 8.2 Ordinary least squares model for AUC value of the dictator game with a delayed loss

Dependent variable	AUC_TIME	log(AUC_TIME)	Sex	Age	Const	$\overline{R}^2$	AIC
AUC_DG	0.06(0.075)				0.23(<0.001)	−0.002	40.73
AUC_DG	0.06(0.073)		0.021(0.044)	0.011(0.005)	−0.05(0.13)	0.008	40.98
log(AUC_DG)		0.27(0.18)			−1.96(0.15)	0.004	594
log(AUC_DG)		0.26(0.17)	0.32(0.21)	0.06(0.03)	−3.51(0.68)	0.03	592

The values in brackets are the standard deviations of the estimates. $\overline{R}^2$ represents the determination coefficient adjusted for the loss in the degrees of freedom. AIC is the value of the Akaike information criterion. $n = 164$

8.4 Discussion

In the present paper, we set out to investigate the relationship between impatience and egoism in the context of hypothetical monetary losses. We expected the positive relationship between observed selfishness (based on the choices made in the dictator game with loss sharing) and impatience (measured with the delay discounting procedures). Instead, inspired by the related works (see Karbowski, 2018, for a review) on egoism and impatience (but these works operated in the context of monetary gains), we decided to look into the relationship between selfishness and impatience in the context of hypothetical monetary losses. Differently from our expectations based on Kovarik (2009) or Yi et al. (2011)—see also Karbowski (2018), we did not find plausible evidence for the existence of the positive link between egoism and impatience in the context of monetary losses.

There are at least two possible explanations for this fact. First, decision-making in the context of losses constitutes a distinct cognitive mechanism compared with decision-making in the context of gains, and as a result, different behavioural patterns are observed for these two types of reasoning. In the literature, there is some evidence that discounting of losses and discounting of gains are different phenomena—see, e.g., Thaler (1981), Loewenstein (1987) and Xu et al. (2009). The second explanation lies in the limitations of the current study. We ran the experiment on the relatively homogenous group of graduate students of SGH Warsaw School of Economics (COVID-19 restrictions made it difficult to reach other subjects). Also, the experiment, due to budget reasons, was run with hypothetical and not real payoffs. Thus the incentives to engage in the decision problems by respondents could be suboptimal.

Interestingly, in our experiment, we discovered that both immediate altruism and delayed altruism in the context of losses are negatively correlated with age. This inspiring result shows that older people are less likely to accept financial losses or participate in the social costs generated by others. On the other hand, younger people are more open to participating in such monetary loss sharing. This finding could be possibly attributed to the greater need for financial security or material comfort with age. Also, older people could think that they already have suffered financial losses/costs in the past, so they are unwilling to accept them in future.

The possible extensions of the study are as follows. First, it is advisable to extend the analysis to non-student groups. We run the experiment on the student group due to convenience and COVID-19 restriction reasons. Richer view on the relationship between egoism and impatience in the context of monetary losses would be attained if other social groups were included in the study. Second, the analysis could be made with different values of a loss to be shared. We decided to select the hypothetical amount of 5000 PLN (this is a significant amount for Polish students), but it is interesting how the behavioural patterns will look if the smaller and larger losses were included. Third, the natural extension of the study is to add some real money incentives to increase the validity of the experiment. Finally, it is worth investigating the relationship between egoism and impatience in the context of the ultimatum and not the dictator game. The different structure of the ultimatum game compared with the dictator game can bring significantly different results and shed new light on the link between observed selfishness and temporal self-control.

Acknowledgement We cordially thank JS for his great patience and technical support.

Funding This research was supported by funds from the National Science Centre, Poland, through grant number 2018/31/D/HS4/00203.

References

Charlton, S. R., Yi, R., Porter, C., Carter, A., Bickel, W., & Rachlin, H. (2013). Now for me, later for us? Effects of group context on temporal discounting. *Journal of Behavioral Decision Making, 26*, 118–127.

Curry, O. S., Price, M. E., & Price, G. J. (2008). Patience is a virtue: Cooperative people have lower discount rates. *Personality and Individual Differences, 44*, 778–783.

Green, L., Myerson, J., Oliveira, L., & Chang, S. (2014). Discounting of delayed and probabilistic losses over a wide range of amounts. *Journal of the Experimental Analysis of Behavior, 101*, 186–200.

Harris, A. C., & Madden, G. J. (2002). Delay discounting and performance on the prisoner's dilemma game. *The Psychological Record, 52*, 429–440.

Hill, P., Yi, R., Spreng, R., & Diana, R. (2017). Neural congruence between intertemporal and interpersonal self-control: Evidence from delay and social discounting. *NeuroImage, 162*, 186–198.

Holt, D. D., Green, L., & Myerson, J. (2003). Is discounting impulsive? Evidence from temporal and probability discounting in gambling and non-gambling college students. *Behavioural Processes, 64*, 355–367.

Igaki, T., Romanowich, P., & Yamagishi, N. (2019). Using smartphones while walking is associated with delay but not social discounting. *The Psychological Record, 69*, 513–524.

Jones, B., & Rachlin, H. (2009). Delay, probability, and social discounting in a public goods game. *Journal of the Experimental Analysis of Behavior, 91*, 61–73.

Karbowski, A. (2018). *Delay and social discounting of losses*. Mimeo.

Karbowski, A., & Wiśnicki, B. (2021a). *Are there gender differences in delay discounting of monetary losses?* Submitted to Kwartalnik Nauk o Przedsiębiorstwie, SGH Warsaw School of Economics.

Karbowski, A., & Wiśnicki, B. (2021b). *Behavioral economics of monetary loss sharing*. Mimeo.

Kirchler, E. (1997). The burden of new taxes: Acceptance of taxes as a function of affectedness and egoistic versus altruistic orientation. *The Journal of Socio-Economics, 26*, 421–437.

Kovarik, J. (2009). Giving it now or later: Altruism and discounting. *Economics Letters, 102*, 152–154.

Lipman, S., & Attema, A. (2020). Good things come to those who wait – Decreasing impatience for health gains and losses. *PLoS One, 15*(3), e0229784.

Locey, M. L., Jones, B. A., & Rachlin, H. (2011). Real and hypothetical rewards in social discounting. *Judgment and Decision making, 6*, 552–564.

Loewenstein, G. (1987). Anticipation and the valuation of delayed consumption. *Economic Journal, 97*, 666–684.

Luhmann, C. (2013). Discounting of delayed rewards is not hyperbolic. *Journal of Experimental Psychology: Learning, Memory, and Cognition, 39*, 1274–1279.

Myerson, J., Green, L., & Warusawitharana, M. (2001). Area under the curve as a measure of discounting. *Journal of the Experimental Analysis of Behavior, 76*, 235–243.

Osiński, J., Karbowski, A., & Rusek, J. (2017). The relationship between self-control and altruism in the light of discounting literature. *Polish Psychological Bulletin, 48*, 433–439.

Rachlin, H., & Jones, B. (2007). Social discounting and delay discounting. *Journal of Behavioral Decision Making, 20*, 1–15.

Takahashi, T. (2007). A comparison of intertemporal choices for oneself versus someone else based on Tsallis' statistics. *Physica A: Statistical Mechanics and its Applications, 385*, 637–644.

Takahashi, T. (2013). The q-exponential social discounting functions of gain and loss. *Applied Mathematics, 4*, 445–448.

Thaler, R. (1981). Some empirical evidence on dynamic inconsistency. *Economics Letters, 8*, 201–207.

Warnell, K., Maniscalco, S., Baker, S., Yi, R., & Redcay, E. (2019). Social and delay discounting in autism spectrum disorder. *Autism Research, 12*, 870–877.

Xu, L., Liang, Z., Wang, K., Li, S., & Jiang, T. (2009). Neural mechanism of intertemporal choice: From discounting future gains to future losses. *Brain Research, 1261*, 65–74.

Yi, R., Charlton, S., Porter, C., Carter, A. E., & Bickel, W. K. (2011). Future altruism: Social discounting of delayed rewards. *Behavioural Processes, 86*, 160–163.

Yi, R., Carter, A. E., & Landes, R. D. (2012). Restricted psychological horizon in active methamphetamine users: Future, past, probability, and social discounting. *Behavioural Pharmacology, 23*, 358–366.

Zauberman, G., Kim, K., Malkoc, S., & Bettman, J. (2009). Discounting time and time discounting: Subjective time perception and intertemporal preferences. *Journal of Marketing Research, 46*, 543–556.

Chapter 9
Comparative Study of Static and Dynamic ARIMA Models in Forecasting of Seasonally Headline Inflation

Melina Dritsaki and Chaido Dritsaki

Abstract Consumer Price Index (CPI) is a common indicator of headline inflation. CPI measures the market value of a fixed basket of goods in order to define the inflation of a country's economy. Headline inflation is the measure of the whole inflation in an economy, which consists of all goods, such a price of consumables and energy, which are volatile and prone to inflationary spikes. Headline inflation is usually related to the shift of living cost, which provides useful information to market consumers. The current paper aims at modelling and forecasting the headline inflation in the case of Greece using the Box–Jenkins methodology for the period 2009:1–2020:12. For this purpose, the ARIMA (6,1,6) model was applied. We estimated the ARIMA (6,1,6) model following the maximum-likelihood approach. We maximized the likelihood by iterating the Marquardt and Berndt–Hall-Hall–Hausman algorithms while using numeric derivatives, the optimum step scale and a convergence criterion for the change in the norm of the parameter vector from one iteration to the next. Finally, in order to forecast the headline inflation through the ARIMA(6,1,6) model, a dynamic process and a static process have been applied. The results of the forecasting process suggest that the static process provides a better forecast comparing to the dynamic one.

Keywords Headline inflation · ARIMA model · Box · Jenkins methodology · Forecasting · Greece

---

M. Dritsaki (✉)
University of Oxford, Oxford, UK

Department of Economics & Laboratory of Applied Economics, University of Western Macedonia, Kastoria, Greece
e-mail: mdritsaki@uowm.gr

C. Dritsaki
Department of Accounting and Finance, University of Western Macedonia, Kozani, Greece

Laboratory of Applied Economics, University of Western Macedonia, Kastoria, Greece

N. Tsounis, A. Vlachvei (eds.), *Advances in Quantitative Economic Research*, Springer Proceedings in Business and Economics,
https://doi.org/10.1007/978-3-030-98179-2_9

9.1 Introduction

According to Friedman (1968), "*inflation is a steady and sustained increase in the general price level*". The constant increase of inflation follows a steady pace when inflation is derived from economic or other fluctuations.

Similarly, Laidler and Parkin (1975) defined inflation as "*a process of continuously rising prices, or, equivalently, of a continuously falling value of money*". Nevertheless, the definition of core inflation as a component reflects the trend, which characterizes inflation as a measuring trend of headline inflation.

Headline inflation is a measure of the whole inflation in an economy, which consists of all goods, such a price of consumables and energy, which are volatile and prone to inflationary spikes. The headline inflation movements are a combination of the movements of the underlying trend inflation percentage as well as the transitory price movements. On the other hand, "core inflation" or else "underlying inflation" is calculated from the consumer price index excluding the prices of food and energy (oil and energy). The various measures of core inflation (less food and energy) represent the different approaches to stripping the transitory price movements. The degree to which a core measurement successfully reflects the underlying inflation trend is usually assessed by its ability to forecast the headline inflation in the mid-term horizon of 1–2 years (Stardev, 2010).

Headline inflation is the raw inflation figure, which refers to the consumer price index (CPI) and is being published monthly. CPI measures the market value of a fixed basket of goods in order to determine the inflation of each country. CPI uses a year as a basis and calculates the value of the current year according to the value of the basis one. There are a number of indices that can be used for the calculation of CPI. All indices use the information on prices and quantities and collect them in various ways. A price index can accumulate prices and quantities of the basis period, as well as information on prices and quantities of the later period. The values of the price indices can be defined either in terms of real or hypothetical expenses or as weighted averages. The total inflation could present an accurate picture of the inflation trend of an economy, while the sector-specific inflation spikes are unlikely to persist.

If a measure of core inflation includes information, which is useful for the percentage of headline inflation in a future date, it necessarily follows that when there is a difference between headline and core inflation at the current period, then headline inflation, to some extent, reverts back to the core inflation (Gamber et al., 2015).

Core inflation is not adjusted to seasonality or to the frequently unstable elements of food or energy prices, which are removed in the core of the CPI. Headline inflation is usually presented on a yearly basis, which means that a monthly headline inflation of 4% refers to the monthly rate, which if repeated for 12 months will generate 4% inflation for the whole year. Comparisons of headline inflation usually occur monthly, known as top-line inflation. As core inflation includes all aspects in an economy, which experience inflation, it is not adjusted to exclude very unstable figures including those which could shift regardless of the economic conditions. Headline inflation is often related to the shifts of the cost of living, which provide useful information to the market consumers.

The rest of the paper is organized as follows: Sect. 9.2 describes the literature review, while in Sect. 9.3 the theoretical background is given. Data are provided in Sect. 9.4. In Sect. 9.5, the empirical results are presented. Section 9.6 is the forecasting and finally. Summary and conclusions are provided in Sect. 9.7.

9.2 Literature Review

9.2.1 Literature Theoretical Survey

Otto Eckstein (1981) developed the concept of core inflation as the rise in the trend of household living cost due to the aggregate demand pressure in the economy.

Quah and Vahey (1995) defined core inflation as a persistent measure of headline inflation, presenting it as a medium- to long-term trend towards the headline inflation, regardless of production. The definition by Quah and Vahey has a temporary effect on price level and a non-lasting impact on the percentage of inflation.

Roger (1998) defined core inflation as a persistent and generalized component of headline inflation.

Various statistic measures such as the weighted median, the moving average, the exponential smoothing, Hodrick–Prescott filter and wavelet filter have been used in the past in order to calculate core inflation. All aforementioned measures are flexible so as to exclude the monthly differences of the data based on the extreme price movement at the specific point of time.

9.2.2 Empirical Studies of the Inflation Dynamics

Bhattacharya (2014) analysed the dynamics of inflation and monetary politics in the case of Vietnam. The study considered CPI headline inflation to be weighed against the price variations of tradable and non-tradable goods. Using VAR technique, the study estimated the inflation model.

The study by Ekong and Effiong (2015) analysed the impact of oil price shocks on Nigeria economy for the period 1986–2011. Using a two-stage approach, the study investigated the effects of variation in the supply and demand of crude oil using SVAR techniques. The results of the study suggest that the variation in aggregate supply and demand of oil goods in the local market have significant impact on macroeconomic measures such as inflation.

Gamber et al. (2015) investigated the dynamic relationship between headline and core inflation, in monetary politics for the case of CPI as well as the personal consumption expenditure deflator. More specifically, they investigated the relationship when the headline and core inflations differ and study to which extent the headline moves back to the core one and vice versa and how quickly these adjustments happen. Finally, they conclude that the dynamic relationship between the weighted median off CPI and the respective headline inflation is highly consistent across monetary policy regimes.

In her study, Priyanka Sahu (2019) compares headline and core inflation in the case of macroeconomic variables in India. The study estimates the core inflation using the conventional exclusion measure (excluding food and energy), statistic measurement of weighted median and exponential smoothing applied to monthly CPI data between January 2012 and June 2018. The findings suggest that trimming 20% of the highly volatile components from the overall inflation can serve as a better proxy for the underlying medium and long-term trend in the headline inflation.

9.3 Theoretical Background

9.3.1 *ARIMA Models and the Box–Jenkins Methodology*

An ARIMA model can be comprehensible by describing each of its elements as below:

Autoregression (AR): it refers to a model that presents a changing variable, which regresses to its own values with lags.

Integrated (I): it represents the difference of previous observations to allow time series to become stationary.

Moving Average (MA): it incorporates the dependence between an observation and a residual error of a moving average model, which is applied to observations with a lag.

The models of an integrated model of moving average (ARIMA) are a form of Box–Jenkins model (see Dritsaki & Dritsaki, 2020).

The ARIMA(p,d,q,) can be expressed as follows:

$$y_t = c + \phi_1 y_{t-1} + \cdots + \phi_p y_{t-p} + \vartheta_1 \varepsilon_{t-1} + \cdots + \vartheta_q \varepsilon_{t-q} + \varepsilon_t \tag{9.1}$$

where

y_t is the series differentiation (first, second).

The right side of the equation above consists of the time lags of series y_t as well as the time lagged errors. This model is called the ARIMA (p,d,q) model, where.

p = are the autoregression lags.

d = the level of differentiation.

q = are the moving average lags.

9.3.2 *The Box–Jenkins Methodology*

Box and Jenkins (1976) is a forecasting methodology, which applies regression studies to time series data. The methodology is based on the hypothesis that previous events affect the future ones. The models of autoregressive moving average (ARIMA) are forms of Box–Jenkins model. The Box–Jenkins approach includes the following steps:

- **Stationarity.**

The first step to develop a Box–Jenkins model is to define if the time series is stationary. Detecting stationarity is achieved through time charts, autoregression graphs as well as unit root testing.

- **Order of ARMA Model.**

Once stationarity has been dealt with, the next step is to determine the parameters of the autoregressive and moving averages, p and q, respectively. In order to determine p and q parameters, many authors are using the autocorrelation and partial autocorrelation graphs, while others are using the corrected Akaike criterion.

- **Estimating the Model's Parameters.**

The parameter estimation for Box–Jenkins models includes the arithmetic solution approach of nonlinear equations. For that reason, the econometric software EViews is being used, which has been designed to handle this approach. The estimation methods of the Box–Jenkins models are the nonlinear minimum squares and the maximum likelihood. Maximum-likelihood estimation is preferred.

- **Diagnostic Checks.**

Diagnostic tests for the Box–Jenkins models are similar to the model validation for the nonlinear adjustment of minimum squares. In other words, the error term should follow the hypothesis of a stationary process. The residuals should be a white noise or be independent (when their distributions are normal), with a constant mean and standard deviation (Ljung and Box (1978) test). Model acceptance is done with the Ramsey (1969) test.

- **Post-Sample Forecasting Accuracy.**

One use of Box–Jenkins model analysis is the forecasting. ARIMA models are based on the hypothesis that previous values of the residuals have some effect on the current or future values (Dritsaki, 2015). Once ensuring that one model is stationary and there is no problem with the diagnostic tests, we could move on with the forecasting. Forecasting estimates the return of a model in relation to real data. There is a choice to split the time series in two parts, using the first one to fit it the model and the second part to test the returns of the model. The forecasting accuracy depends on the forecasting error. The mean absolute percentage error, the square

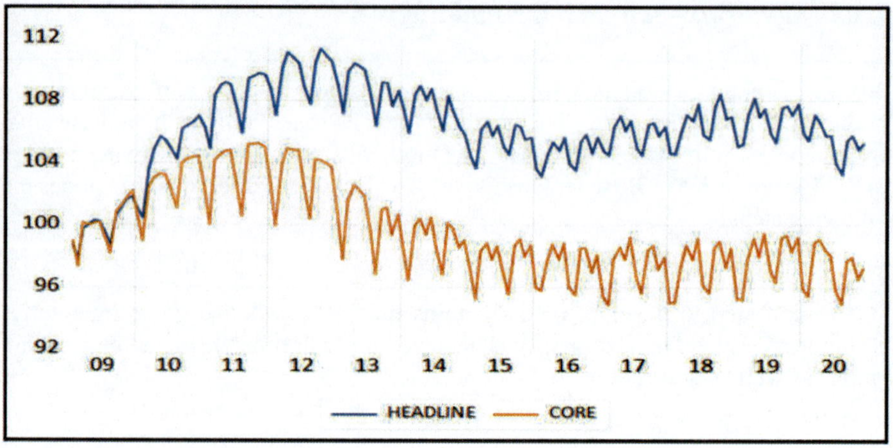

Fig. 9.1 Headline inflation vs core inflation

root of the mean-squared error and the Theil statistics are measures of accuracy whose minimum value provides us with the best fit of the model.

9.4 Data

Data used were extracted from the Hellenic Statistical Authority database source from 2009:1–2020:12. In order to smoothen out the series, data were seasonally using EViews to remove issues of seasonality.

In the following diagram, the monthly indices of headline inflation and core inflation are presented and the base year is 2009 (Fig. 9.1).

From the following diagram, we can see that headline inflation is larger than core inflation throughout the examined period showing the larger convergence after 2011 and up to 2020.

9.5 Empirical Results

9.5.1 Testing for Stationarity

- Time plots.

In the following diagram, the exponential diagram of headline inflation of Greece is presented (Fig. 9.2).

From Fig. 9.2, we can see that the log headline inflation shows an extended period of upward trend (2009–2012) followed by a fall (2012–2016) and during the period

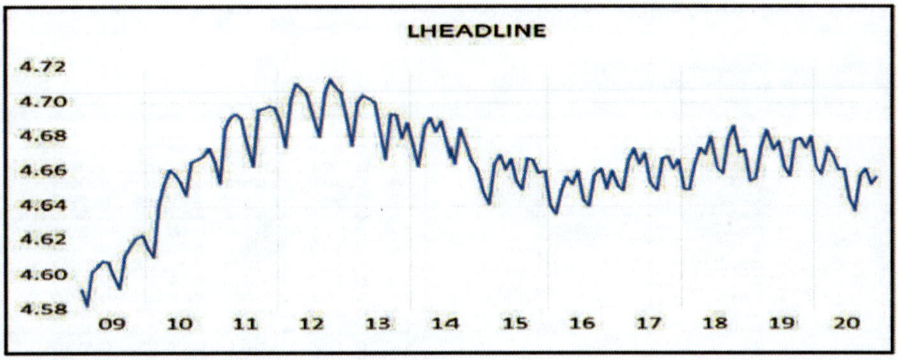

Fig. 9.2 Time series plot of log headline inflation

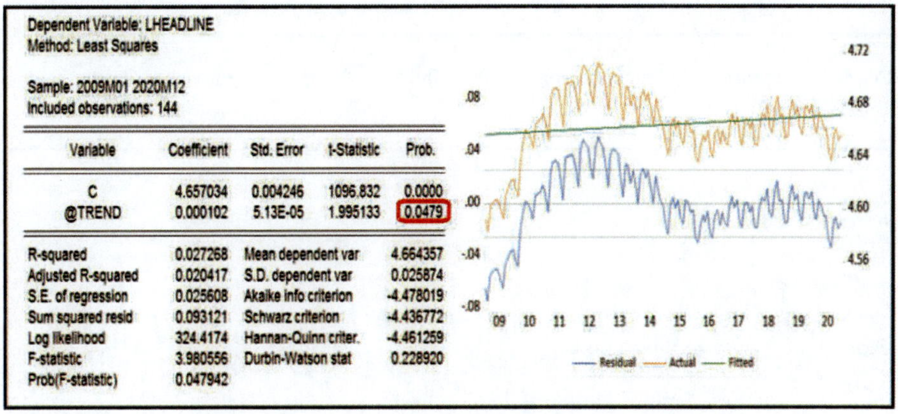

Dependent Variable: LHEADLINE
Method: Least Squares

Sample: 2009M01 2020M12
Included observations: 144

Variable	Coefficient	Std. Error	t-Statistic	Prob.
C	4.657034	0.004246	1096.832	0.0000
@TREND	0.000102	5.13E-05	1.995133	0.0479

R-squared	0.027268	Mean dependent var	4.664357
Adjusted R-squared	0.020417	S.D. dependent var	0.025874
S.E. of regression	0.025608	Akaike info criterion	-4.478019
Sum squared resid	0.093121	Schwarz criterion	-4.436772
Log likelihood	324.4174	Hannan-Quinn criter.	-4.461259
F-statistic	3.980556	Durbin-Watson stat	0.228920
Prob(F-statistic)	0.047942		

Fig. 9.3 Exponential trend model and trend analysis plot log headline inflation

2016–2020 shows a slight upward trend again. In other words, this is considered a random walk model.

- Estimation of exponential trend of series.

In the following figure, the estimation of exponential trend of log headline inflation together with the diagram is presented (Fig. 9.3).

The results show that there is an exponential trend of log headline inflation. Thus, we can regard the log headline inflation as a random walk model.

- Correlograms of autocorrelation coefficients.

Below on the diagram, the correlograms of autocorrelation coefficients of log headline inflation are presented (Fig. 9.4).

We can see from the above diagrams that autocorrelation coefficients decline slowly, denoting that log headline inflation is a non-stationary series.

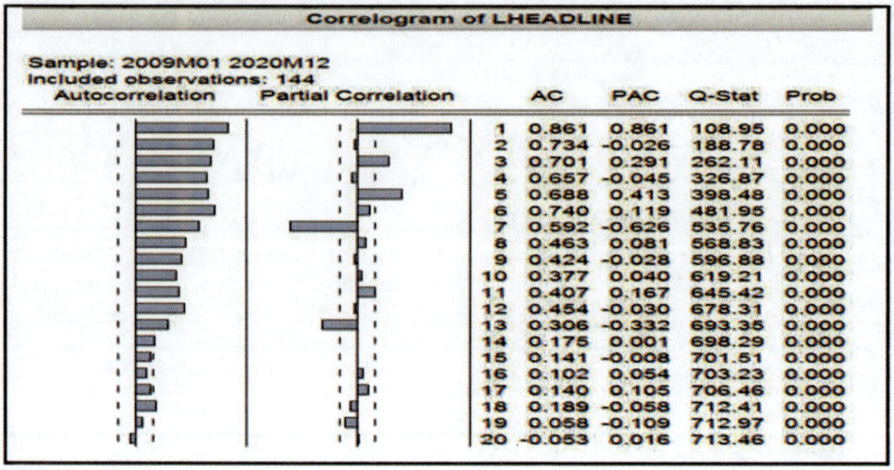

	AC	PAC	Q-Stat	Prob
1	0.861	0.861	108.95	0.000
2	0.734	-0.026	188.78	0.000
3	0.701	0.291	262.11	0.000
4	0.657	-0.045	326.87	0.000
5	0.688	0.413	398.48	0.000
6	0.740	0.119	481.95	0.000
7	0.592	-0.626	535.76	0.000
8	0.463	0.081	568.83	0.000
9	0.424	-0.028	596.88	0.000
10	0.377	0.040	619.21	0.000
11	0.407	0.167	645.42	0.000
12	0.454	-0.030	678.31	0.000
13	0.306	-0.332	693.35	0.000
14	0.175	0.001	698.29	0.000
15	0.141	-0.008	701.51	0.000
16	0.102	0.054	703.23	0.000
17	0.140	0.105	706.46	0.000
18	0.189	-0.058	712.41	0.000
19	0.058	-0.109	712.97	0.000
20	-0.053	0.016	713.46	0.000

Fig. 9.4 Autocorrelation function log headline inflation (with 5% significance limits for the autocorrelations)

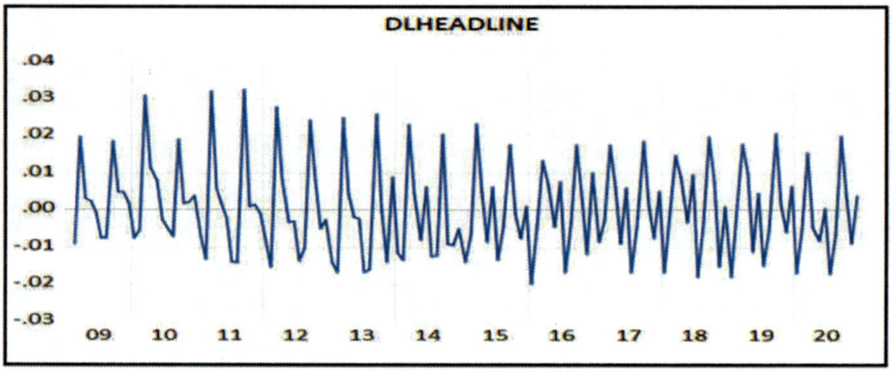

Fig. 9.5 Time series plot of log headline inflation (first differences)

- First and second differences of series.

Afterwards, we apply anew the previous tests finding the existence of stationarity in first and second differences (Fig. 9.5).

From Fig. 9.5, we notice that the course of log headline inflation on first differences features intense fluctuations. This course is a possible evidence of mean stationarity.

In the following diagram, the estimation of exponential trend of log headline inflation in first differences is shown (Fig. 9.6).

The results of Fig. 9.6 and the table on the same figure present that there is no trend (prob. > 5%), whereas the line on the graph is horizontal in the estimated model. Thus, we conclude that the examined series is stationary.

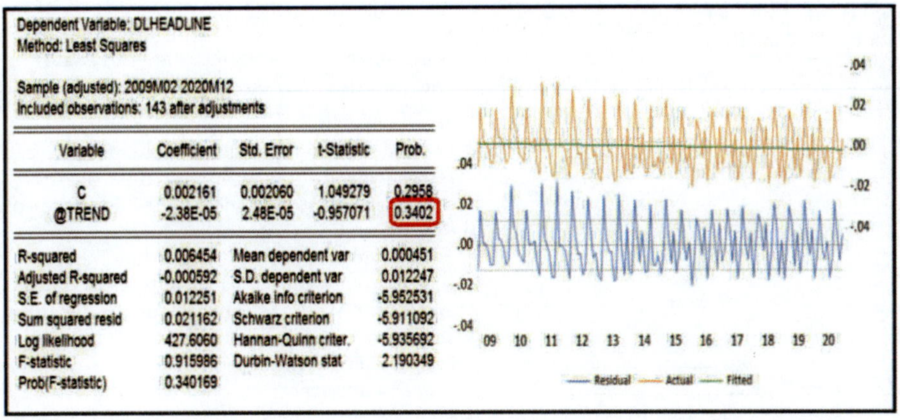

Dependent Variable: DLHEADLINE
Method: Least Squares

Sample (adjusted): 2009M02 2020M12
Included observations: 143 after adjustments

Variable	Coefficient	Std. Error	t-Statistic	Prob.
C	0.002161	0.002060	1.049279	0.2958
@TREND	-2.38E-05	2.48E-05	-0.957071	0.3402

R-squared	0.006454	Mean dependent var	0.000451
Adjusted R-squared	-0.000592	S.D. dependent var	0.012247
S.E. of regression	0.012251	Akaike info criterion	-5.952531
Sum squared resid	0.021162	Schwarz criterion	-5.911092
Log likelihood	427.6060	Hannan-Quinn criter.	-5.935692
F-statistic	0.915986	Durbin-Watson stat	2.190349
Prob(F-statistic)	0.340169		

Fig. 9.6 Exponential trend model and trend analysis plot log headline inflation (first differences)

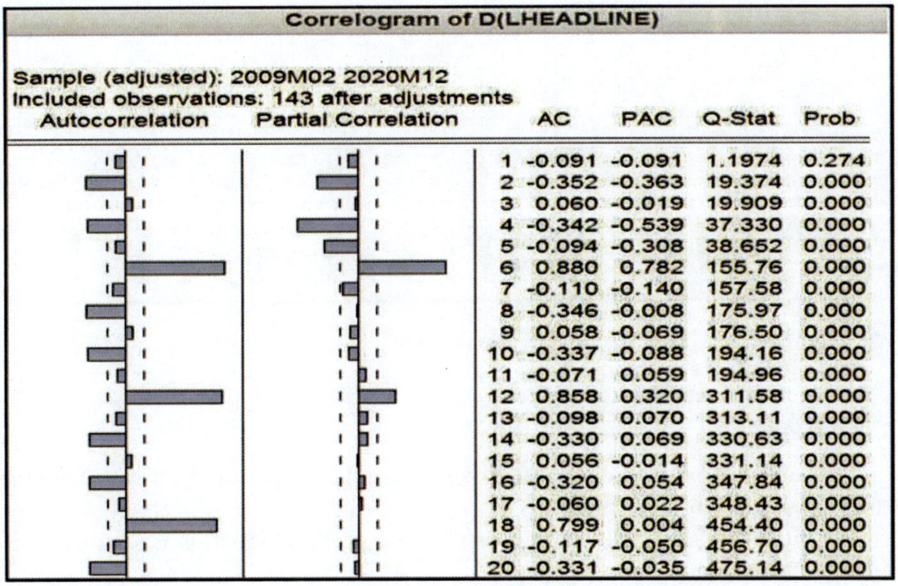

Correlogram of D(LHEADLINE)

Sample (adjusted): 2009M02 2020M12
Included observations: 143 after adjustments

Autocorrelation	Partial Correlation		AC	PAC	Q-Stat	Prob
		1	-0.091	-0.091	1.1974	0.274
		2	-0.352	-0.363	19.374	0.000
		3	0.060	-0.019	19.909	0.000
		4	-0.342	-0.539	37.330	0.000
		5	-0.094	-0.308	38.652	0.000
		6	0.880	0.782	155.76	0.000
		7	-0.110	-0.140	157.58	0.000
		8	-0.346	-0.008	175.97	0.000
		9	0.058	-0.069	176.50	0.000
		10	-0.337	-0.088	194.16	0.000
		11	-0.071	0.059	194.96	0.000
		12	0.858	0.320	311.58	0.000
		13	-0.098	0.070	313.11	0.000
		14	-0.330	0.069	330.63	0.000
		15	0.056	-0.014	331.14	0.000
		16	-0.320	0.054	347.84	0.000
		17	-0.060	0.022	348.43	0.000
		18	0.799	0.004	454.40	0.000
		19	-0.117	-0.050	456.70	0.000
		20	-0.331	-0.035	475.14	0.000

Fig. 9.7 Autocorrelation and partial autocorrelation correlograms of log headline inflation in first differences

Afterwards, we test the stationarity using the autocorrelation correlogram in first differences (Fig. 9.7).

From Fig. 9.7, we can see that the coefficients of autocorrelations decline quickly, meaning that the series is stationary.

Table 9.1 Unit root result for headline inflation

	C	C,T
L Headline	−3.239[69]**	−3.041[55]
DL Headline	−13.923[25]*	−15.505[24]*

Notes
1. * and ** show significant at 1% and 5% levels, respectively
4. Mackinnon (1996) critical value for rejection of hypothesis of unit root applied
5. The numbers within brackets followed by PP statistics represent the bandwidth selected based on Newey West (1994) method using Bartlett kernel
6. *C* constant, *T* trend
7. *D* first differences

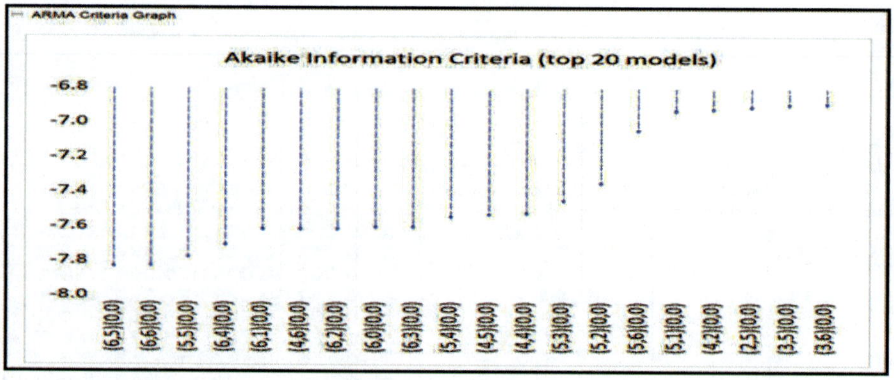

Fig. 9.8 Automatic ARIMA model estimation choice

- Unit root tests.

The confirmation of stationarity of headline inflation is employed with Phillips and Perron unit root test (1998).

The results of Table 9.1 confirm that the log headline inflation is stationary in first differences.

9.5.2 *Identification of the Model*

Using the automatic forecasting ARIMA procedure using EViews, we can find all automatic model estimations. Using the above values, we select the optimal ARMA (*p*,*q*) model among the smallest values of AIC criterion. ARMA (6,5) (0,0) model is the most suitable (Fig. 9.8).

9.5.3 Estimation and Diagnostic Tests of the Models

From the moment that the most suitable model is ARIMA (6,1,5), the estimation will be employed with maximum-likelihood approach. We maximize the likelihood by iterating Marquardt and Berndt–Hall–Hall–Hausman algorithms using derivatives, optimal step ahead and a convergence criterion for the change in the norm of the parameter vector from one iteration to the next.

The following table provides with the estimation results of ARIMA (6,1,5) model.

The results of Table 9.2 show that there is a problem in the significance of MA(5). Thus, we proceed with the ARIMA (6,1,6) model.

The results of Table 9.3 show that there is no problem in the significance of coefficients. Moreover, the estimation coefficient of error variance (volatility) $\rho_s = 1.88\text{E-}05$ is also statistical significant. So, we can use the ARIMA (6,1,6) model for diagnostic testing (Table 9.4).

The test both on F distribution and also LR likelihood show that ARIMA (6,1,6) model is specified correctly (prob>5%) (Fig. 9.9).

The dotted lines in correlograms of autocorrelation and partial autocorrelations of the above diagram are approximately two standard errors, which are calculated as $\pm\frac{2}{\sqrt{n}} = \pm\frac{2}{\sqrt{144}} = \pm 0.166$. As the autocorrelation and partial autocorrelation coefficients are within these limits, we can conclude that there is independence among residuals of ARIMA (6,1,6) model in 5% level of significance (there is no correlation) (Fig. 9.10).

Autocorrelation and partial autocorrelations coefficients of squared residuals are within the ±0.166 limits; thus, we can ascertain that there is no autoregression conditional heteroscedasticity on the residuals of the ARIMA (6,1,6) model on 5% level of significance (there is no ARCH effect).

Table 9.2 Estimation of ARIMA (6,1,5) model

Dependent Variable: DLHEADLINE
Method: ARMA Maximum Likelihood (OPG - BHHH)

Sample: 2009M02 2020M12
Included observations: 143
Convergence achieved after 15 iterations
Coefficient covariance computed using outer product of gradients

Variable	Coefficient	Std. Error	t-Statistic	Prob.
AR(6)	0.902222	0.035501	25.41390	0.0000
MA(5)	-0.148584	0.093178	-1.594634	0.1130
SIGMASQ	2.54E-05	3.00E-06	8.452534	0.0000
R-squared	0.829680	Mean dependent var		0.000451
Adjusted R-squared	0.827247	S.D. dependent var		0.012247
S.E. of regression	0.005090	Akaike info criterion		-7.630789
Sum squared resid	0.003628	Schwarz criterion		-7.568632
Log likelihood	548.6014	Hannan-Quinn criter.		-7.605531
Durbin-Watson stat	1.855988			
Inverted AR Roots	.98	.49-.85i	.49+.85i	-.49-.85i
	-.49+.85i	-.98		
Inverted MA Roots	.68	.21+.65i	.21-.65i	-.55-.40i
	-.55+.40i			

Table 9.3 Estimation of ARIMA (6,1,6) model

Dependent Variable: DLHEADLINE
Method: ARMA Maximum Likelihood (OPG - BHHH)

Sample: 2009M02 2020M12
Included observations: 143
Convergence achieved after 20 iterations
Coefficient covariance computed using outer product of gradients

Variable	Coefficient	Std. Error	t-Statistic	Prob.
AR(6)	0.985747	0.010183	96.80122	0.0000
MA(6)	-0.570597	0.081607	-6.992004	0.0000
SIGMASQ	1.88E-05	2.13E-06	8.840959	0.0000

R-squared	0.873696	Mean dependent var	0.000451
Adjusted R-squared	0.871892	S.D. dependent var	0.012247
S.E. of regression	0.004384	Akaike info criterion	-7.904403
Sum squared resid	0.002690	Schwarz criterion	-7.842246
Log likelihood	568.1648	Hannan-Quinn criter.	-7.879145
Durbin-Watson stat	1.894575		

Inverted AR Roots	1.00	.50+.86i	.50-.86i	-.50+.86i
	-.50-.86i	-1.00		
Inverted MA Roots	.91	.46-.79i	.46+.79i	-.46-.79i
	-.46+.79i	-.91		

Table 9.4 Ramsey RESET test

Ramsey RESET Test
Equation: UNTITLED
Omitted Variables: Squares of fitted values
Specification: DLHEADLINE AR(6) MA(6)

	Value	df	Probability
t-statistic	0.240351	139	0.8104
F-statistic	0.057769	(1, 139)	0.8104
Likelihood ratio	0.199429	1	0.6552

WARNING: the MA backcasts differ for the original and test equation. Under the null hypothesis, the impact of this difference vanishes asymptotically.

9.6 Forecasting

When the selected ARIMA model follows the diagnostic tests of a stationary univariate procedure, then we can use the model for forecasting.

On the following table, we present the indices of log headline inflation for the forecasting assessment of ARIMA (6,1,6) model both on dynamic and static methodologies (Table 9.5).

The results of the above table indicate that all statistical measures converge that the static forecast has the best forecast than the dynamic forecast for the ARIMA (6,1,6) model.

On the following diagram, the course of actual and forecasted values of log headline inflation of dynamic forecasting is presented (Fig. 9.11).

On the following diagram, the course of actual and forecasted values of log headline inflation of static forecasting is presented (Fig. 9.12).

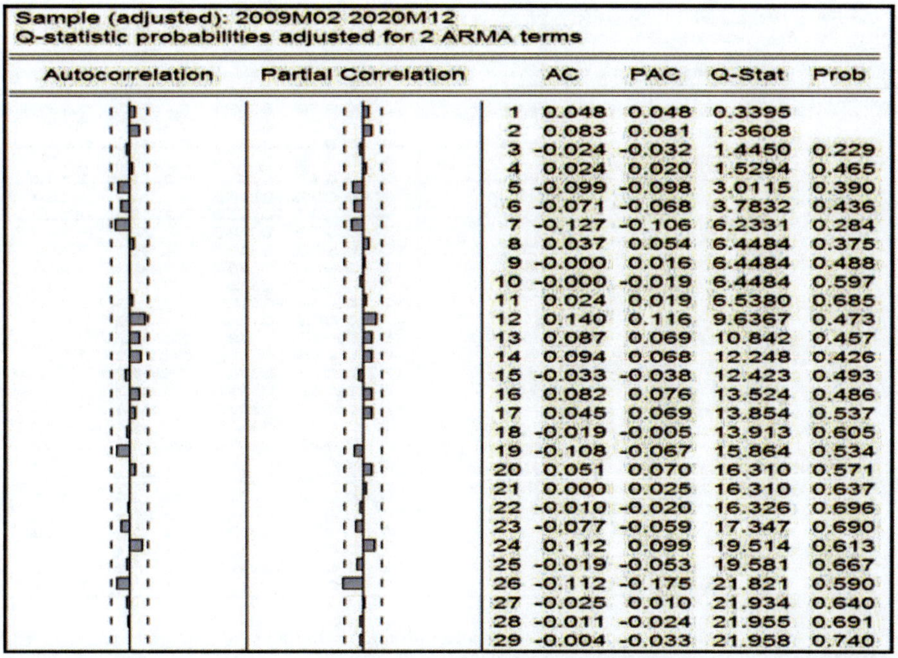
Sample (adjusted): 2009M02 2020M12
Q-statistic probabilities adjusted for 2 ARMA terms

	AC	PAC	Q-Stat	Prob
1	0.048	0.048	0.3395	
2	0.083	0.081	1.3608	
3	-0.024	-0.032	1.4450	0.229
4	0.024	0.020	1.5294	0.465
5	-0.099	-0.098	3.0115	0.390
6	-0.071	-0.068	3.7832	0.436
7	-0.127	-0.106	6.2331	0.284
8	0.037	0.054	6.4484	0.375
9	-0.000	0.016	6.4484	0.488
10	-0.000	-0.019	6.4484	0.597
11	0.024	0.019	6.5380	0.685
12	0.140	0.116	9.6367	0.473
13	0.087	0.069	10.842	0.457
14	0.094	0.068	12.248	0.426
15	-0.033	-0.038	12.423	0.493
16	0.082	0.076	13.524	0.486
17	0.045	0.069	13.854	0.537
18	-0.019	-0.005	13.913	0.605
19	-0.108	-0.067	15.864	0.534
20	0.051	0.070	16.310	0.571
21	0.000	0.025	16.310	0.637
22	-0.010	-0.020	16.326	0.696
23	-0.077	-0.059	17.347	0.690
24	0.112	0.099	19.514	0.613
25	-0.019	-0.053	19.581	0.667
26	-0.112	-0.175	21.821	0.590
27	-0.025	0.010	21.934	0.640
28	-0.011	-0.024	21.955	0.691
29	-0.004	-0.033	21.958	0.740

Fig. 9.9 Autocorrelation and partial autocorrelation correlograms of residuals for ARIMA (6,1,6)

Table 9.5 Assessment criteria of the forecasting of ARIMA (6,1,6)

	Dynamic forecast	Static forecast
RMSE	0.0071	0.0043
MAE	0.0058	0.0034
MAPE	86.919	83.775
Theil	0.3597	**0.1858**
Bias Proportion	0.0084	0.0028
Var. Proportion	0.4843	0.0542
Cov. Proportion	0.5072	0.9428
Theil U2 coef.	0.6494	0.3144
Symmetric MAPE	102.32	62.333

9.7 Summary and Conclusion

Central Banks worldwide are mandated to maintain a stable price level for the economy. That price level is being used by each government towards the designing of monetary policies. Most of central banks make use of headline inflation towards achieving this goal. The reason is that headline inflation is a measure representing the basket of goods and services consumed by most households. However, headline inflation that is more volatile cannot be used to estimate inflation trends, hence being replaced by core inflation. Many economists suggest that whilst designing monetary

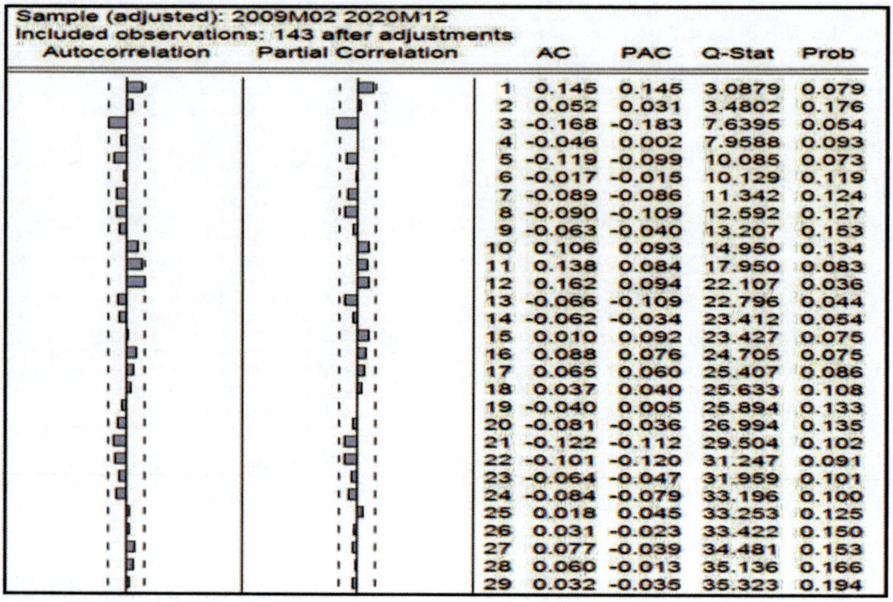

Sample (adjusted): 2009M02 2020M12
Included observations: 143 after adjustments

	AC	PAC	Q-Stat	Prob
1	0.145	0.145	3.0879	0.079
2	0.052	0.031	3.4802	0.176
3	-0.168	-0.183	7.6395	0.054
4	-0.046	0.002	7.9588	0.093
5	-0.119	-0.099	10.085	0.073
6	-0.017	-0.015	10.129	0.119
7	-0.089	-0.086	11.342	0.124
8	-0.090	-0.109	12.592	0.127
9	-0.063	-0.040	13.207	0.153
10	0.106	0.093	14.950	0.134
11	0.138	0.084	17.950	0.083
12	0.162	0.094	22.107	0.036
13	-0.066	-0.109	22.796	0.044
14	-0.062	-0.034	23.412	0.054
15	0.010	0.092	23.427	0.075
16	0.088	0.076	24.705	0.075
17	0.065	0.060	25.407	0.086
18	0.037	0.040	25.633	0.108
19	-0.040	0.005	25.894	0.133
20	-0.081	-0.036	26.994	0.135
21	-0.122	-0.112	29.504	0.102
22	-0.101	-0.120	31.247	0.091
23	-0.064	-0.047	31.959	0.101
24	-0.084	-0.079	33.196	0.100
25	0.018	0.045	33.253	0.125
26	0.031	-0.023	33.422	0.150
27	0.077	-0.039	34.481	0.153
28	0.060	-0.013	35.136	0.166
29	0.032	-0.035	35.323	0.194

Fig. 9.10 Autocorrelation and partial autocorrelation correlograms of squared residuals for ARIMA (6,1,6)

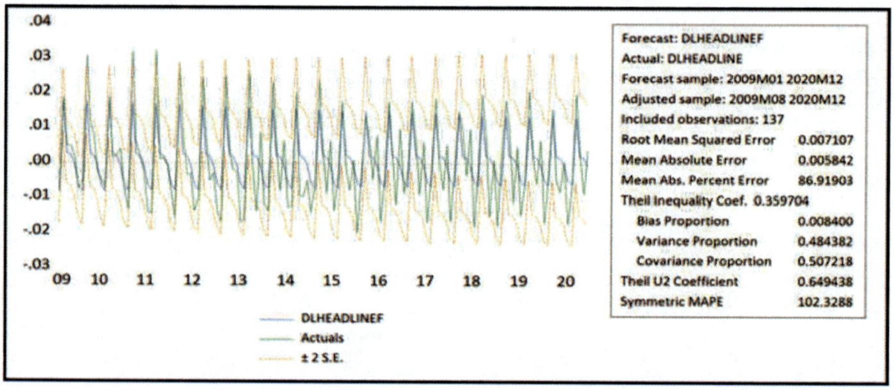

Fig. 9.11 Actual and estimated values of log headline inflation of dynamic forecasting

policies, the core inflation should be used. Their main argument is that food and energy price fluctuations and usually reported in the short run.

Despite the advantages of core inflation, their use as means of exercising monetary politics has been criticized. The measure of core inflation attempts to reduce the most volatile or transitory components of the inflation measures. But because the nature of the fluctuations can change over time, measure that has been highly volatile in the past could change in the future, to the extent that

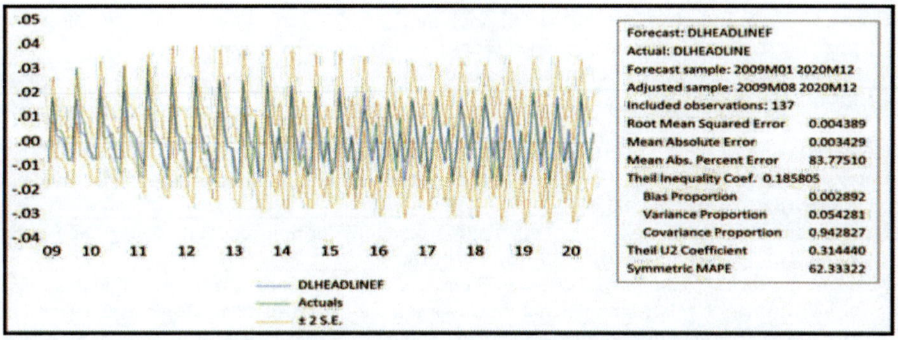

Fig. 9.12 Actual and estimated values of log headline inflation of static forecasting

any core measure could face transitory shocks. As a result, central Banks do not focus exclusively on core inflations but rather devote considerable resources into understanding the evolutions of inflation to distinguish signal from noise in the incoming data (Mishkin, 2007).

The European Central Bank has adopted the aims of inflation based on headline inflation. In contrast, USA focuses on core inflation or else the CPI. However, after the 2008 crisis, the Federal Reserve Bank considers both types of inflation when forecasting inflation.

After adopting the aims of the European Central Bank, we use headline inflation in order to forecast the inflation for Greece using monthly data from 2009:1–2020:12 and applying the Box–Jenkins methodology. The automatic model forecasting process via the Akaike criterion shows that the ARIMA(6,1,6) model is the most suitable one. The estimation of ARIMA (6,1,6) model has been achieved through the maximum-likelihood approach by iterating Marquardt και Berndt–Hall–Hall–Hausman algorithms. Moreover, in order to forecast the headline inflation on the ARIMA(6,1,6) model, both the dynamic and the static processes have been applied. The forecasting results show that static process provides better forecasting in comparison to the dynamic one.

References

Bhattacharya, R. (2014). Inflation dynamics and monetary policy transmission in Vietnam and emerging Asia. *Journal of Asian Economics, 34*, 16–26.

Box, G. E. P., & Jenkins, G. M. (1976). *Time series analysis. Forecasting and control*. Holden-Day.

Dritsaki, C. (2015). Box-Jenkins modeling of Greek stock prices data. *International Journal of Economics and Financial Issues, 5*(3), 740–747.

Dritsaki, M., & Dritsaki, C. (2020). Forecasting European Union CO_2 emissions using autoregressive integrated moving average-autoregressive conditional heteroscedasticity models. *International Journal of Energy Economics and Policy, 10*(4), 411–423.

Eckstein, O. (1981). *Core inflation*. Prentice-Hall.

Ekong, C. N., & Effiong, E. L. (2015). Oil price shocks and Nigeria's macroeconomy: Disentangling the dynamics of crude oil market shocks. *Global Business Review, 16*(6), 920–935.

Friedman, M. (1968). The role of monetary policy. *The American Economic Review, 58*(1), 1–19.

Gamber, E. N., Smith, J. K., & Eftimoiu, R. (2015). The dynamic relationship between core and headline inflation. *Journal of Economics and Business, 81*, 38–53.

Laidler, D., & Parkin, M. (1975). Inflation: A survey. *The Economic Journal, 85*(340), 741–809.

Ljung, G. M., & Box, G. E. P. (1978). On a measure of a lack of fit in time series models. *Biometrika, 65*(2), 297–303.

MacKinnon, J. G. (1996). Numerical distribution functions for unit root and cointegration tests. *Journal of Applied Econometrics, 11*(6), 601–618.

Mishkin, F. (2007). *Headline versus core inflation in the conduct of monetary policy*. A speech at the Business Cycles, International Transmission and Macroeconomic Policies Conference, HEC Montreal, Montreal, Canada, October 20, 2007 (No. 332). Board of Governors of the Federal Reserve System.

Newey, W. K., & West, K. D. (1994). Automatic lag selection in covariance matrix estimation. *Review of Economic Studies, 61*(4), 631–653.

Phillips, P. C. B., & Perron, P. (1998). Testing for a unit root in time series regression. *Biometrika, 75*(2), 335–346.

Priyanka, S. (2019). A study on the dynamic behaviour of headline versus core inflation: Evidence from India. *Global Business Review, 22*(6), 1574–1593.

Quah, D., & Vahey, S. P. (1995). Measuring core inflation. *The Economic Journal, 105*(432), 1130–1144.

Ramsey, J. B. (1969). Tests for specification errors in classical linear least-squares regression analysis. *Journal of the Royal Statistical Society: Series B (Methodological), 31*(2), 350–371.

Roger, S. (1998). *Core inflation: Concepts, uses and measurement*. Reserve Bank of New Zealand Discussion Paper, (G98/9).

Stardev, E. (2010). Measures of underlying inflation in the euro area: Assessment and role for informing monetary policy. *Empirical Economics, 38*, 217–239.

Chapter 10
The Destabilizing Effects of Political Budget Cycles: The Case of Greece

George Petrakos, Konstantinos Rontos, Chara Vavoura, and Ioannis Vavouras

Abstract During the Third Hellenic Republic (Metapolitefsi), that is over the last four decades, Greece has been characterized by severe political fiscal cycles. Regardless of how we measure political fiscal cycles, via the actual budget balance as percent of GDP or via the primary budget balance as percent of GDP, we consistently observe that, in the years of general (parliamentary) elections, the budget deficit jumps to rates unprecedented for a developed economy. This phenomenon has contributed significantly to the recent Greek public debt crisis. In this paper, we have two main objectives. Firstly, we aim to confirm the emergence of political fiscal cycles in Greece during the period known as the Third Hellenic Republic (Metapolitefsi) beginning at 1974. Secondly, we investigate whether general elections affect not only public finances, but also the total output of the economy and try to characterize this effect as stabilizing or destabilizing. Two are the main findings of our analysis: the Greek economy is indeed characterized by very sharp political fiscal cycles during the period of the Third Hellenic Republic and that these cycles have a destabilizing effect on the total output of the economy.

Keywords Political budget cycles · Electoral fiscal cycles · Budget balance · Economic growth · Greek economy · Economic destabilization

---

G. Petrakos
Department of Public Administration, Panteion University of Social and Political Sciences, Athens, Greece
e-mail: petrakos@panteion.gr

K. Rontos
Department of Sociology, University of the Aegean, Mytilene, Greece
e-mail: K.Rontos@soc.aegean.gr

C. Vavoura
Department of Economics, University of Athens, Athens, Greece
e-mail: cvavoura@econ.uoa.gr

I. Vavouras (✉)
Panteion University of Social and Political Sciences, Athens, Greece
e-mail: vavouras@panteion.gr

N. Tsounis, A. Vlachvei (eds.), *Advances in Quantitative Economic Research*, Springer Proceedings in Business and Economics,
https://doi.org/10.1007/978-3-030-98179-2_10

JEL Classification D72, E62, H62

10.1 Introduction

Simply stated, political budget cycles or electoral fiscal cycles occur when governments in the preelection period pursue an expansionary fiscal policy (public spending increases, tax cuts, budget deficit increases) that is followed in the postelection period by a contractionary or restrictive fiscal policy (public spending reductions, tax increases, budget deficit reductions). These budget cycles are deliberately created in the context of governments' opportunistic efforts to maximize their chances of re-election in order to give the electorate the impression that the political party (or parties) in power follows an effective economic policy. As a result, voters acquire the illusion that their economic welfare has improved, either because they have a myopic perspective or because the politicians in power exploit their temporary information advantage.[1]

Regarding the effectiveness of political budget cycles in increasing the prospects of re-election, it appears to be questionable. According to a strand of the empirical literature, the phenomenon increases the re-election chances of incumbents (Aidt et al., 2011; de Haan and Klomp, 2013), while according to other researchers, it has no effect, especially in countries of high social and political levels, where voters decipher the motives of governments that resort to this opportunistic behavior and "punish" them at the ballot box (Brender and Drazen, 2008).[2]

The phenomenon of political budget cycles has been the subject of extensive empirical research, which shows that, in general, the ability of governments to create politico-economic cycles becomes limited as the level of economic and social development of the country increases (Block, 2002; Shi and Svensson, 2006); as the quality of its institutions improves and the transparency of its political process increases (de Haan and Klomp, 2013; Persson and Tabellini, 2005), as well as when the quality and the duration or maturity of democracy in that country increase (Brender and Drazen, 2005; Shi and Svensson, 2003). The quality of institutions and especially the existence of effective mechanisms for controlling the financial decisions of governments (checks and balances) seem to be the most important means of limiting the extent of the phenomenon of political budget cycles, as institutions shape the choices of the electorate and determine the incentives as well as the opportunities for incumbents to resort to these cycles (Chang, 2008; Streb and Torrens, 2013).

[1] See mainly Downs (1957), Nordhaus (1975), Rogoff and Sibert (1988), Rogoff (1990); and Persson and Tabellini (2000).

[2] What's more, political budget cycles occur mainly in conditions of uncertainty regarding the election outcomes, given that if governments are very confident of their re-election, they have little or no incentive to resort to them (Alt and Rose, 2007; Hanusch and Magleby, 2014; Schultz, 1995).

The main conclusion of the existing empirical work is that the phenomenon of political budget cycles is more evident in developing economies (Brender and Drazen, 2005; Shi and Svensson, 2006), while in developed economies, it is either nonexistent or very limited (Andrikopoulos et al., 2004; Mandon and Cazals, 2019). Our analysis focuses on Greece which is a remarkable deviation from the aforementioned rule. In our recent works, we have estimated that the political budget cycles in Greece are enormous (Petrakos et al., 2021a; Vavoura et al., 2019). This fact can be attributed mainly to the limited quality of the country's institutions (Afonso et al., 2015; Trantidis, 2016), as well as to the fact that its governments often pursue clientelist policies and resort to populism (Christodoulakis, 2019; Mitsopoulos and Pelagidis, 2011).

The first objective of this paper is to reaffirm the existence of the phenomenon of political budget cycles in Greece during the period of the Third Hellenic Republic (Metapolitefsi), that is throughout the period 1974–2020. For this purpose, we specify empirical models in which the actual budget balance and the primary budget balance are used as dependent variables, expressed as percentages of GDP. Our aim is to quantify the effects of the electoral cycle on the formation of budget balances in Greece. The second, and in our opinion the most important objective of the present empirical work is to examine whether general (or parliamentary) elections affect the country's GDP and whether their effects are stabilizing or destabilizing. More specifically, the question is whether general elections have statistically significant stabilizing or destabilizing effects on GDP.

The structure of the paper is organized as follows. In Sect. 10.2, we present our data and methodology and discuss our findings. In Sect. 10.3, we present our basic conclusions. The paper is followed by an Appendix where we present the residual plots of the models specified and estimated.

10.2 Data, Methodology, and Results

As it has already been noted, our empirical analysis has two main objectives: First, to reaffirm the existence of the phenomenon of political economic cycles and in particular of political budget cycles throughout the period of the Third Hellenic Republic (Metapolitefsi) using as dependent variables the actual budget balance and the primary budget balance. We must point out that in earlier empirical analysis, we established the existence of this phenomenon in Greece during the period 1980–2017 (Petrakos et al., 2021a; Vavoura et al., 2019).[3] Secondly, to ascertain the possible existence of a statistically significant relationship between election years and real GDP.

[3] It should be noted that we have revealed the existence of the phenomenon of political budget cycles in Greece in the previous ICOAE 2020 Conference paper where we use as a dependent variable the total general government expenditure as a percentage of GDP and which referred to the period 1980–2018 (Petrakos et al., 2021b).

To achieve the first objective, we constructed four empirical models using the following dependent and explanatory variables:

1. *The actual budget balance (ABBN) of general government as percent of GDP*, as it is defined and measured by Eurostat.[4] We consider the actual budget balance as percent of GDP and not in absolute monetary terms for three main reasons: First, because the percentage expression provides a more reliable indicator of the relative magnitude of the actual budget balance. Second, because the percentage term removes the long-term effect of inflation on fiscal aggregates. Third, because the main fiscal policy condition of the EU member states in order to avoid entering the Excessive Deficit Procedure (EDP) of the Stability and Growth Pact is not to breach the fiscal criterion that their actual budget deficit does not exceed the 3% of their GDP.
2. *The one-year lag of actual budget balance (ABBN-1) of general government as percent of GDP*, since the public balance is "compounded" in the sense that the budget deficit of the previous year affects, to some extent of course, the deficit of the current year. In effect, the 1 year lag of the dependent variable is used to allow for any existing slow adjustment process and persistence of actual budget balance, capturing the autoregressive, AR(1), component of the actual budget balance of the series (Petrakos et al., 2021a).
3. *The primary budget balance (PBB) of general government as percent of GDP*, as it is defined and measured by the Greek National Accounts. We consider the primary budget balance as percent of GDP, because it provides the best measure of the "discretionary" fiscal policy, since it differs from ABBN in that it does not include the interest on public debt.
4. *The one-year lag of primary budget balance (PBB-1) of general government as percent of GDP.* We have included this variable for the same reasons we included the variable ABBN-1.
5. *The growth rate of real total GDP (TYGR1)* as it is estimated by the World Bank.
6. *The change in the growth rate of total real GDP (DTYGR1)*, i.e., the difference between the growth rate of total real GDP of the current year and the previous one, i.e., $DTYGR1_i = TYGR1_i - TYGR1_{i-1}$. This variable is introduced as it might not be so much the rates of change in total real GDP that cause pressures for expansionary fiscal policy, as the variations or fluctuations of these rates from year to year.
7. *The unemployment rate (UNR)* as it is measured by the Hellenic Statistical Authority (ELSTAT).
8. *Election (ELE)*, a binary variable taking the value of 1 in the years of the Third Hellenic Republic in which parliamentary (general) elections were held in Greece and 0 otherwise.

[4] The minus (−) sign corresponds to deficit while the plus (+) sign to surplus.

10.2.1 Econometric Regressions

We have specified four models presented in Table 10.1. In Models 1 and 2, the dependent variable is ABBN, while in Models 3 and 4 the dependent variable is PBB.

The four models are presented and analyzed below in the order in which they appear in Table 10.1. In Tables 10.2, 10.5, 10.8 and 10.11, we present the summaries of the four models, while in Tables 10.3, 10.6, 10.9, and 10.12, we present respectively the regression coefficients of these models. Moreover, in Tables 10.4, 10.7, 10.10, and 10.13, we present the analysis of variance of the respective models.

Table 10.1 List of models used in our empirical analysis

No. of model	Dependent variable	Independent variables
1	ABBN	ABBN-1, UNR, ELE
2	ABBN	ABBN-1, UNR, TYGR1, ELE
3	PBB	PBB-1, UNR, ELE
4	PBB	PBB-1, UNR, TYGR1, ELE

Table 10.2 Summary of Model 1

ELE				
0	ABBN	$= -1.801 + 0.8234$ ABBN-1 $+ 0.1155$ UNR		
1	ABBN	$= -3.82 + 0.8234$ ABBN-1 $+ 0.1155$ UNR		
S		**R-sq**	**R-sq(adj)**	**D-W statistic**
2.38908		70.60%	68.45%	2.55572

Table 10.3 Regression coefficients of Model 1

Term/variable	Coefficient	Standard error	*T*-Value	*P*-Value	VIF
Constant	−1.801	0.915	−1.97	0.056	
ABBN-1	0.8234	0.0872	9.44	0.000	1.00
UNR	0.1155	0.0526	2.19	0.034	1.00
ELE	−2.022	0.769	−2.63	0.012	1.00

All independent variables are significant at $\alpha = 0.05$

Table 10.4 Analysis of variance of Model 1

Source	DF	Adj SS	Adj MS	F-Value	P-Value
Regression	3	561.957	187.319	32.82	0.000
ABBN-1	1	509.007	509.007	89.18	0.000
UNR	1	27.483	27.483	4.82	0.034
ELE	1	39.401	39.401	6.90	0.012
Error	41	234.015	5.708		
Lack-of-Fit	40	233.770	5.844	23.85	0.161
Pure error	1	0.245	0.245		
Total	44	795.972			

Table 10.5 Summary of Model 2

ELE				
0	ABBN	= −3.18 + 0.7514 ABBN-1 + 0.221 TYGR1 + 0.1619 UNR		
1	ABBN	= −5.02 + 0.7514 ABBN-1 + 0.221 TYGR1 + 0.1619 UNR		
S		**R-sq**	**R-sq(adj)**	**D-W statistic**
2.32538		72.83%	70.11%	2.54920

Table 10.6 Regression coefficients of Model 2

Term/variable	Coefficient	Standard error	*T*-Value	*P*-Value	VIF
Constant	−3.18	1.17	−2.71	0.010	
ABBN-1	0.7514	0.0937	8.02	0.000	1.22
TYGR1	0.221	0.122	1.81	0.078	1.52
UNR	0.1619	0.0573	2.83	0.007	1.26
ELE	−1.843	0.755	−2.44	0.019	1.02

All independent variables are significant at $\alpha = 0.05$ except TYGR1 that is significant at $\alpha = 0.1$

Table 10.7 Analysis of variance of Model 2

Source	DF	Adj SS	Adj MS	*F*-Value	*P*-Value
Regression	4	579.68	144.919	26.80	0.000
ABBN-1	1	347.51	347.508	64.27	0.000
TYGR1	1	17.72	17.720	3.28	0.078
UNR	1	43.20	43.204	7.99	0.007
ELE	1	32.16	32.164	5.95	0.019
Error	40	216.30	5.407		
Total	44	795.97			

Table 10.8 Summary of Model 3

ELE				
0	PBB	= −0.905 + 0.726 PBB-1 + 0.0902 UNR		
1	PBB	= −2.850 + 0.726 PBB-1 + 0.0902 UNR		
S		**R-sq**	**R-sq(adj)**	**D-W statistic**
2.42271		57.81%	54.72%	2.27451

Table 10.9 Regression coefficients of Model 3

Term/variable	Coefficient	Standard error	*T*-Value	*P*-Value	VIF
Constant	−0.905	0.775	−1.17	0.250	
PBB-1	0.726	0.106	6.86	0.000	1.01
UNR	0.0902	0.0534	1.69	0.099	1.01
ELE	−1.945	0.782	−2.49	0.017	1.00

All independent variables are significant at $\alpha = 0.05$ except UNR that is significant at $\alpha = 0.1$

Table 10.10 Analysis of variance of Model 3

Source	DF	Adj SS	Adj MS	F-Value	P-Value
Regression	3	329.71	109.902	18.72	0.000
PBB-1	1	276.37	276.371	47.09	0.000
UNR	1	16.75	16.752	2.85	0.099
ELE	1	36.33	36.332	6.19	0.017
Error	41	240.65	5.870		
Total	44	570.36			

Table 10.11 Summary of Model 4

ELE				
0	PBB	= −2.10 + 0.619 PBB-1 + 0.1427 UNR + 0.216 TYGR1		
1	PBB	= −3.82 + 0.619 PBB-1 + 0.1427 UNR + 0.216 TYGR1		
S		**R-sq**	**R-sq(adj)**	**D-W statistic**
2.37661		60.39%	56.43%	2.20761

Table 10.12 Regression coefficients of Model 4

Term/variable	Coefficient	Standard error	T-Value	P-Value	VIF
Constant	−2.10	1.06	−1.98	0.055	
PBB-1	0.619	0.123	5.01	0.000	1.43
UNR	0.1427	0.0617	2.31	0.026	1.39
TYGR1	0.216	0.134	1.61	0.114	1.77
ELE	−1.721	0.779	−2.21	0.033	1.04

All independent variables are significant at $\alpha = 0.05$ except TYGR1 that is marginally significant at $\alpha = 0.1$

Table 10.13 Analysis of variance of Model 4

Source	DF	Adj SS	Adj MS	F-Value	P-Value
Regression	4	344.43	86.106	15.24	0.000
PBB-1	1	142.00	142.003	25.14	0.000
UNR	1	30.26	30.262	5.36	0.026
TYGR1	1	14.72	14.719	2.61	0.114
ELE	1	27.56	27.562	4.88	0.033
Error	40	225.93	5.648		
Total	44	570.36			

10.2.2 Analysis of Means for DTYGR1

In order to investigate possible differences in the mean of DTYGR1 between the two ELE groups, we test the hypothesis H_0: $\mu_1 - \mu_2 = 0$ against H_1: $\mu_1 - \mu_2 \neq 0$, where $\mu_1 = \mathsf{E}(\text{DTYGR}|\text{ELEC} = 0)$ και $\mu_2 = \mathsf{E}(\text{DTYGR}|\text{ELEC} = 1)$. H_0 is rejected at $\alpha = 0.05$ and the differences in the means of TYGR1 are presented in Table 10.14.

Table 10.14 Analysis of means

ELE	N	Mean	StDev	95% CI
0	31	0.823	3.620	(−0.338; 1.983)
1	14	−1.229	1.929	(−2.956; 0.499)

Pooled StDev = 3.20437

10.2.3 Discussion of Results

All four models presented above have an overall good fit, especially those having ABBN as dependent variable, as R^2 vary between 72.83% (Model 2) and 70.6% (Model 1). In models having PBB as the dependent variable, the value of R^2 is lower varying between 60.39% (Model 4) and 57.81% (Model 3). Moreover, the F-tests indicate overall statistical significance in all four models. In all the estimated models, public deficits (actual or primary) appear to be strongly correlated to their 1-year lagged value.

More importantly, in all four models we specified and estimated above, it turns out that ELE is a statistically significant dummy variable. That is, and in those cases where we use ABBN as a dependent variable and in those where we use PBB, the binary variable ELE seems to be statistically significant. In other words, the political cycle (general elections) in Greece significantly affects the actual budget balance and the primary budget balance. In all models, the coefficient of ELE is much higher than −1.5. That is, in the years of general or national elections, the budget deficit increases by more than 1.5% of GDP, namely by 2.022% according to Model 1, by 1.843% of GDP according to Model 2, by 1.945% according to Model 3, and by 1.721% according to Model 4. This effect is disproportionately higher in relation to other developed economies where the effects of budget cycles are from well below 1% of GDP to insignificant.

As it has already been stated, the second objective of the paper was to investigate the possible effects of the political cycle to total output. To comply with this objective, we investigate the relationship between general elections (ELE) and the change in the growth rate of total real GDP (DTYGR1) throughout the period 1974–2019. The analysis of means indicates that when there are no parliamentary elections in the country, the economic growth rate (DTYGR1) changes from year to year increasing by an average of 0.823%. On the contrary, when there are parliamentary elections, the economic growth rate decreases compared to the previous year by an average of 1.229%. It is therefore obvious that the electoral cycle in Greece has serious destabilizing effects on total real output. The descriptive and inductive measures of the variables DTYGR1 | ELE = 0 and DTYGR1 | ELE = 1 (separately) are given in Table 10.14, while in Fig. 10.1, we present the corresponding confidence intervals (CI) at 95%.

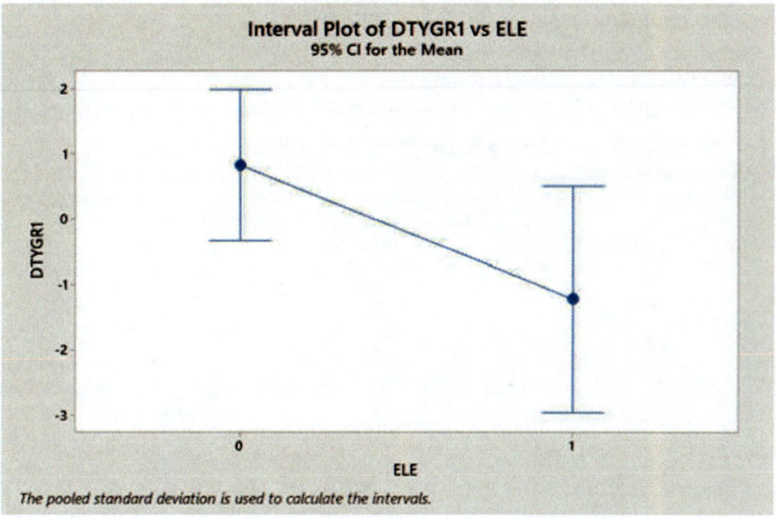

Fig. 10.1 Interval Plot of DTYGR1 vs. ELE

10.3 Conclusions

According to the analysis presented above, Greece is characterized by the existence of large political budget cycles that are in fact of unprecedented size for an economically developed country. The large political budget or fiscal cycles are destabilizing in terms of the budget deficit and consequently in terms of the country's public debt stimulating its upward trend. Moreover, the political budget cycles in Greece are also destabilizing in terms of real GDP. This is mainly due to the fact that during the election years in Greece, the "unproductive" public expenditures increase, especially social transfers. It is therefore crucial to restrict political budget cycles for two reasons. Not only so as to improve the country's public finances, but also in order to stabilize its economy in general.

In addition, the existence of large political budget cycles in Greece is a strong indication that the country has certain socio-political characteristics that are more in line with those of developing countries, such as low-quality political institutions and insufficient control mechanisms or ineffective checks and balances. These are basically the results of low-quality governance. Consequently, the effects of the electoral cycles cannot be ignored by any systematic scrutiny of the reforms needed to boost economic growth and to reduce budget deficits and public debt. These issues seem to be two of the most serious structural problems of the country and the most prominent topics for future research.

Appendix (Figs. 10.2, 10.3, 10.4 and 10.5)

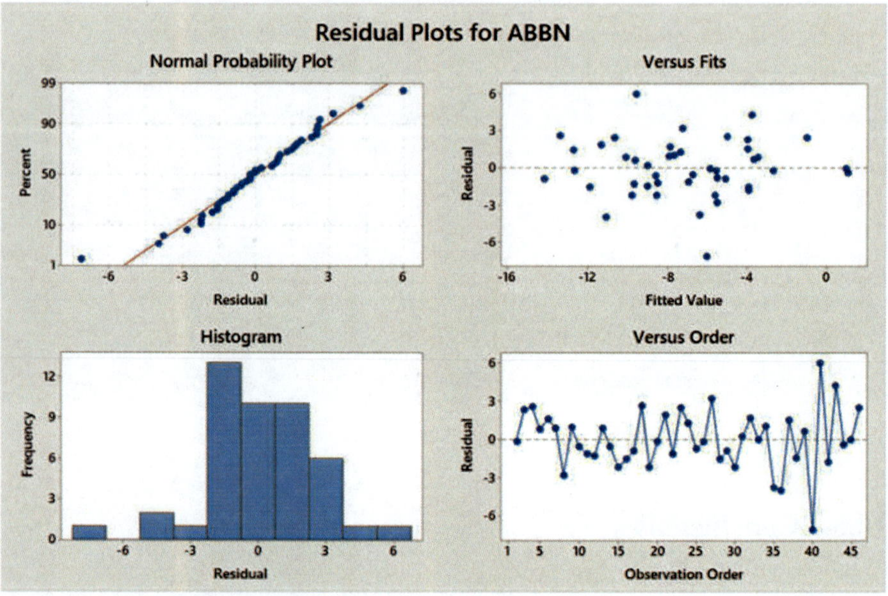

Fig. 10.2 Residual plots of Model 1

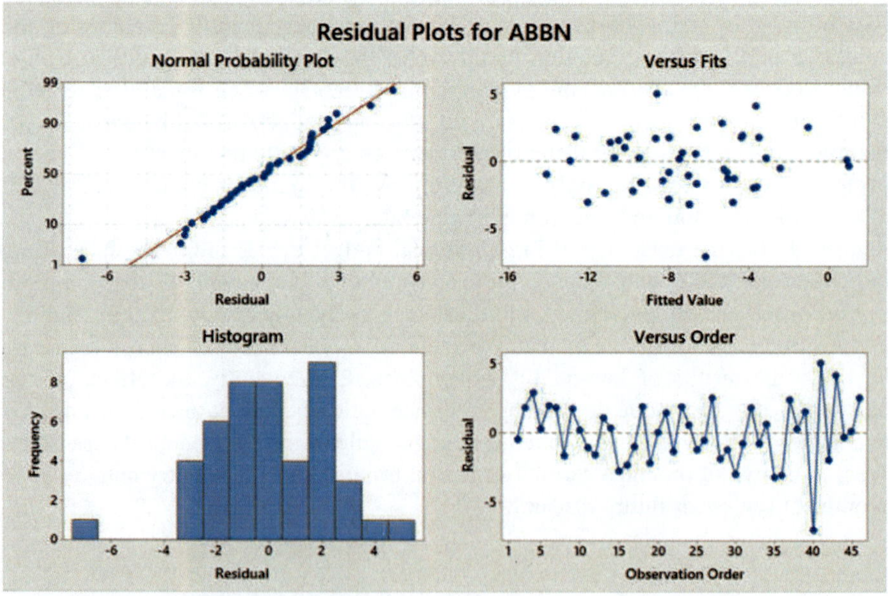

Fig. 10.3 Residual plots of Model 2

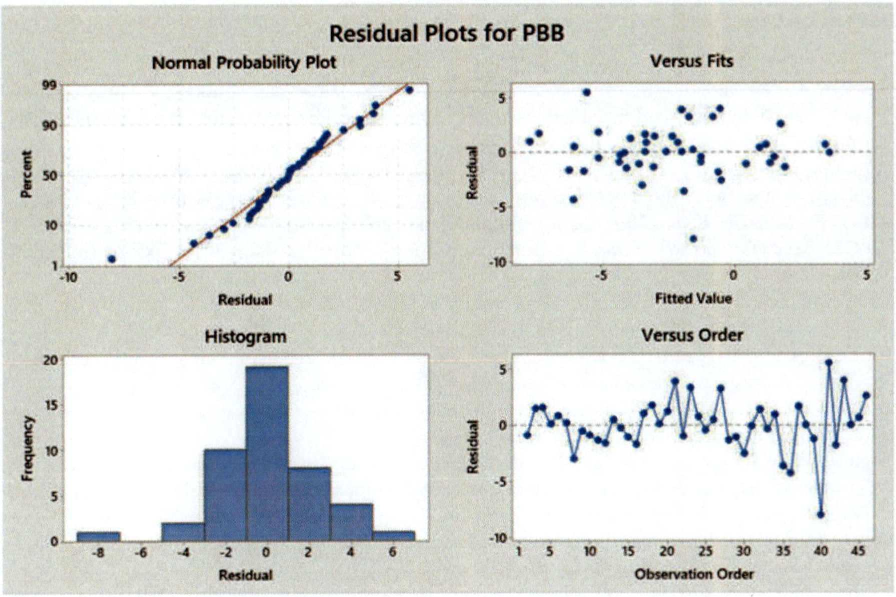

Fig. 10.4 Residual plots of Model 3

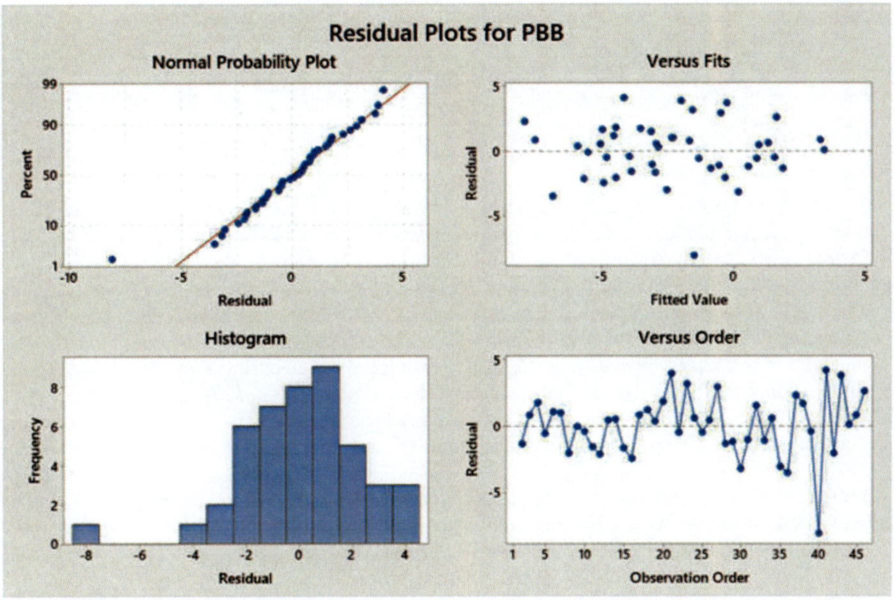

Fig. 10.5 Residual plots of Model 4

References

Afonso, A., Zartaloudis, S., & Papadopoulos, Y. (2015). How party linkages shape austerity politics: Clientelism and fiscal adjustment in Greece and Portugal during the eurozone crisis. *Journal of European Public Policy, 22*(3), 315–334.

Aidt, T. S., Veiga, F. J., & Gonçalves Veiga, L. (2011). Election results and opportunistic policies: A new test of the rational political business cycle model. *Public Choice, 148*(1–2), 21–44.

Alt, J. E., & Rose, S. S. (2007). Context-conditional political business cycles. In C. Boix & S. C. Stokes (Eds.), *Oxford handbook of comparative politics* (pp. 845–867). Oxford University Press.

Andrikopoulos, A., Loizides, I., & Prodromidis, K. (2004). Fiscal policy and political business cycles in the EU. *European Journal of Political Economy, 20*(1), 125–152.

Block, S. A. (2002). Political business cycles, democratization, and economic reform: The case of Africa. *Journal of Development Economics, 67*(1), 205–228.

Brender, A., & Drazen, A. (2005). Political budget cycles in new versus established democracies. *Journal of Monetary Economics, 52*(7), 1271–1295.

Brender, A., & Drazen, A. (2008). How do budget deficits and economic growth affect reelection prospects? Evidence from a large panel of countries. *American Economic Review, 98*(5), 2203–2220.

Chang, C. C. (2008). Electoral incentives and budgetary spending: Rethinking the role of political institutions. *The Journal of Politics, 70*(4), 1086–1097.

Christodoulakis, N. (2019, May). *Greece and the euro area: The cost of weak institutions* (CGK working paper no. 2019-05). Tufts University, The Fletcher School.

de Haan, J., & Klomp, J. (2013). Political budget cycles and election outcomes. *Public Choice, 157*(1/2), 245–267.

Downs, A. (1957). *An economic theory of democracy*. Harper & Row.

Hanusch, M., & Magleby, D. B. (2014). Popularity, polarization, and political budget cycles. *Public Choice, 159*(3–4), 457–467.

Mandon, P., & Cazals, A. (2019). Political budget cycles: Manipulation by leaders versus manipulation by researchers? Evidence from a meta-regression analysis. *Journal of Economic Surveys, 33*(1), 274–308.

Mitsopoulos, M., & Pelagidis, T. (2011). *Understanding the crisis in Greece: From boom to bust*. Palgrave Macmillan.

Nordhaus, W. D. (1975). The political business cycle. *Review of Economic Studies, 42*(2), 169–190.

Persson, T., & Tabellini, G. (2000). *Political economics: Explaining economic policy*. The MIT Press.

Persson, T., & Tabellini, G. (2005). *The economic effects of constitutions*. The MIT Press.

Petrakos, G., Rontos, K., Vavoura, C., & Vavouras, I. (2021a). The mechanism of political budget cycles in Greece. In N. Tsounis & A. Vlachei (Eds.), *Advances in longitudinal data methods in applied economic research* (Springer proceedings in business and economics, 2020 international conference on applied economics (ICOAE 2020)) (pp. 123–133). Springer.

Petrakos, G., Rontos, K., Vavoura, C., Salvati, L., & Vavouras, I. (2021b). Political budget cycles and the effects of the excessive deficit procedure: The case of Greece. *Regional Statistics, 11*(2), 1–20.

Rogoff, K. (1990). Equilibrium political budget cycles. *American Economic Review, 80*(1), 21–36.

Rogoff, K., & Sibert, A. (1988). Elections and macro-economic policy cycles. *Review of Economic Studies, 55*(1), 1–16.

Schultz, K. A. (1995). The politics of the political business cycle. *British Journal of Political Science, 25*(1), 79–99.

Shi, M., & Svensson, J. (2003). Political budget cycles: A review of recent developments. *Nordic Journal of Political Economy, 29*(1), 69–76.

Shi, M., & Svensson, J. (2006). Political budget cycles: Do they differ across countries and why? *Journal of Public Economics, 90*(8–9), 1367–1389.

Streb, J. M., & Torrens, G. (2013). Making rules credible: Divided government and political budget cycles. *Public Choice, 156*(3–4), 703–722.

Trantidis, A. (2016). *Clientelism and economic policy: Greece and the crisis* (Advances in European politics (book 126)). Routledge.

Vavoura, C., Vavouras, I., Rontos, K., & Petrakos, G. (2019). Electoral cycles and public deficits in Greece. *Social sciences today: Dilemmas and perspectives beyond the crisis.* Conference Proceedings, scientific edition N. Nagopoulos, Mytilene (pp. 730–741) (in Greek).

Chapter 11
Beautification for Tourism! Economics and Marketing of the Italian Cultural Foundation During and After Pandemic Times

Angela Besana and Annamaria Esposito

Abstract Foundations are not-for-profit organizations, whose main business is to supply *merit goods* like culture and creativity and to deliver grants for the welfare of communities. Operating and grant-making foundations support the Welfare State of public administrations, and they commit for legacy and resilience in a community and a destination, whose both creative assets and tourism can be positively impacted.

Beautification is the consequence of supply and grants in a landscape where tangible and intangible heritages are given back to communities after disruptive events, from failing memories to pandemic. Beautification is granted both by the Public Welfare State and the Private Welfare State of foundations.

The resource allocation can afford funds for restoration and valorization of legacies and lost memories. Relationship marketing can shape community engagement, both as regards fundraising in order to maximize endowments and as regards grant-making to the best projects.

With a strong advocacy for community betterment and beautification in Italy, these foundations include FAI (Fondo Ambiente Italiano).

The aim of this paper is to highlight the role of FAI for beautification and resilience of heritages from the North to the South of Italy.

The methodology includes regression analysis of 2014–2019 FAI data, together with a qualitative analysis of strategies during pandemic. The Welfare Role of FAI will be highlighted as a benchmark for resilience for both communities and tourists.

Keywords Foundation · Economics · Marketing · Culture · Creativity

Many thanks to our students of Workshop "Analytical Skills for Tourism and Arts". Their analysis was very inspiring.

A. Besana (✉) · A. Esposito
Department Business, Law, Economics and Consumer Behaviour "Carlo A. Ricciardi", IULM, Milan, Italy
e-mail: angela.besana@iulm.it; annamaria.esposito@iulm.it

N. Tsounis, A. Vlachvei (eds.), *Advances in Quantitative Economic Research*, Springer Proceedings in Business and Economics,
https://doi.org/10.1007/978-3-030-98179-2_11

11.1 When Beauty Is Facing the Pandemic Beast, Will One Rose Be Enough?

Before pandemic times, culture and creativity flourished in Italy thanks to operating and grant-making foundations, both of them collecting and pooling resources, efforts and strategies with public administrations of the so-called Public Welfare State. Different thorns affected this flourishing rose. Marketing and management of tangible and intangible heritages, they were not easy, as bureaucracy affected performances of Welfare States matching. Project management was not always flexible and efficient, when multiple boards had to decide for multiple issues, agendas, and resources.

The beautification was enhanced by different stakeholders, who were getting on into different frames of partnershiping (Esposito & Besana, 2016, 2018; Ma & Konrath, 2018; Besana, 2017). Beautification was the consequence of supply and grants in a landscape where cultural and creative assets were given back to communities after disruptive events, from failing memories to relaxing commitments. Beautification was granted both by the most proactive and sustainable Public Welfare State and the Private Welfare State of far-sighted and visionary foundations (Vecco & Srakar, 2020; Zurbuchen, 2017; Essig, 2014). The cultural and creative supply was gaining appreciation of citizens and tourists, as it was investigated in several reports and international conferences, where Italy was mentioned as the main European destination for cultural tourism (Fondazione Symbola, *Io Sono Cultura*, 2020).

If "once upon a time" had been waiting for a happy end, the end was the beginning of a tragedy. With pandemic, culture, creativity, and tourism, they all suffered for no demand and no supply. The market was declining apart of spot virtual events and online transactions.

In the meanwhile, foundations stopped *and stabilized* partnerships for post-pandemic. After the fear, boards and governances had to focus on management of key relations and allocation of scarce resources in order not to collapse and to plan the recovery. Relationship marketing was pivotal in order to maintain connections and media, from websites to social media granted this "crisis communication". If partnerships were meant by a high level of engagement, deep interaction, bidirectional exchange of interdependencies, and sharing of resources, risks, revenues, and benefits, they had to be postponed in such frames (Meyrick & Barnett, 2021; Hyunjung et al., 2021; Hoellen et al., 2020; Hadida, 2015; Shea & Hamilton, 2015). Some partnerships were revised for addressing deep-rooted, new and complex social issues like the unemployment of cultural professionals or the emergence of online creative supplies, as long as new segments and their willingness-to-pay could be detected. Some partnerships were meant to enable organizations to take on larger social agendas, tougher issues, revenue maximization and diversification, and longer-term challenges, as a master plan during and after pandemic (Hoellen et al., 2020; Berrett & Holliday, 2018; Kim, 2017; Besana, 2017).

In Italy, one of the most prominent cultural foundations is Fondo Ambiente Italiano. Since its founding in 1975, FAI has drawn inspiration from the National Trust for England, Wales, and Northern Ireland, as Fai: takes care of places, heritages, parks in Italy for the benefit of present and future generations, promotes education, appreciation, awareness, and enjoyment of the Nation's environmental, natural, historic, and artistic heritage, and monitors the protection of Italy's natural and cultural assets, according to the article 9 of the Italian Constitution. FAI has always implemented partnerships within the framework of the Public and Private Welfare State.

The aim of this paper is to highlight the role of FAI for beautification and resilience of heritages from the North to the South of Italy, before and soon after the pandemic.

The methodology includes regression analysis of 2014–2019 FAI accounting data, together with a qualitative analysis of strategies during the pandemic times. The Welfare Role of FAI will be highlighted as a benchmark for resilience for both communities and tourists.

11.2 Relationship Marketing of Italian Cultural Foundations Before and During Pandemic

Relationship marketing aims at establishing, maintaining, and enhancing mutually successful relationships, where value is created for all parties (Gummesson, 2011) involved with profit or nonprofit organizations. As a theoretical construct, it is a process of communication and interaction that leads to value creation (Abeza et al., 2020; Grönroos, 2012, 2004). In fact, the essentials for maintaining and enhancing trustworthy long-term relationships rely in an ongoing dialogue with relevant stakeholders, aimed at acknowledging the value of stakeholder relationships and widening communications efforts beyond standard activities, taking necessarily into account social media (Abeza et al., 2020; Besana & Esposito, 2018).

The above leads to consider relationship marketing as a crucial lever to support nonprofit organizations in building up, and proactively maintaining, relational assets consisting of long-term relationships/partnerships with key stakeholders (Esposito & Besana, 2018).

Stakeholder relationships allow cultural foundations for a continuous exchange of information and provide the opportunity to know their stakeholders and their needs and thereby to encourage mutual concern, trust, and commitment (Esposito & Besana, 2018; Bennet, 2019; Hussain et al., 2014).

In this context, relationship marketing encompasses a diverse range of topics: fundraising, of course, but also image and reputation management, attraction of volunteers, and the measurement of levels of satisfaction beneficiaries and users. Still, the acquisition of funds remains the main and final objective of relationship marketing, as well as all forms of nonprofit marketing activities aimed at stimulating public interest and support, and retaining and satisfying existing donors.

As mentioned above, effective relationships depend on effective communication and for this reason cultural foundations need to develop communication strategies consistent with their mission and core activities. Indeed, communication priorities must be clearly identified and aimed toward spreading and increasing knowledge of cultural foundations among key stakeholders to engage them.

Over time, relationship marketing has reinforced its power. Alongside traditional institutional communications with traditional media, most Italian cultural foundations convey both corporate and project communications through their website and online communication, such as social media accounts.

Italian cultural foundations convey corporate communications, annual reports, and product/service communications through their website, which represent the first touch point for stakeholders (individual donors, partners, sponsors, volunteers), whilst online communication, aims at broadening the interactions with users and more in general with people, inspiring them to be involved. Still, online and social media communications are aimed at strengthening the offline traditional media (brochures, posters, and press releases) and the usage on stakeholder relationships is below potential due to the lack of a full understanding of the tool properties and capabilities on the side of nonprofit organizations (Nah & Saxton, 2013).

As an example, social media are used primarily for organizational one-way communication despite the interactive opportunities that this online channel offers its followers. Indeed, social media may enable and strengthen people's effective engagement, especially with heritage.

Social media are useful both for foundations and users to quickly create and share contents such as photo-sharing (Instagram, Flickr); video and audio sharing (YouTube); short written message sharing (Facebook, Twitter) (Esposito & Besana, 2016; Liang et al., 2021), but in Italian experience, foundations remain leader of contents limiting the participatory level of their online community.

Furthermore, compared with offline communication, online one is totally geo-free, thus, it can promote mutual understandings between people with different cultural backgrounds (Shaw et al., 2017), enabling people to access cultural heritage from all over the world. This has been, and still is, important during pandemic.

However, even if in the last decades, digital transformation affected the cultural organizations (Fondazione Symbola, 2020) – enabling them to experiment new ways to getting in touch with stakeholders –, digital experience and social media have been overrated but still underutilized by cultural foundations (Esposito et al., 2021) before the pandemic.

During pandemic, experiences have demonstrated what benefits can be brought to the management and enhancement of cultural foundations, by innovation and a targeted use of digital technology in order to remain in touch with stakeholders, improve the quality of services, and expand the audience of users. The use of digital tools allows reaching a wider and more diversified audience at any time, also reaching people physically distant.

Pandemic forced cultural institutions to rethink products, formats, and sources of income. They have looked for other channels and communication tools in the attempt to retain sponsors and grant-makers, who had to face a dramatic economic crisis and could change their minds and sensibility on cultural issues, as well as to find new sources of funding, and reorient the way to establish relationships with the different stakeholders (e.g., to raise funds and find support for projects through crowdfunding campaigns or cross-sector collaborations).

Digitization and social media brought the need of new investments in technologies, and the raising of new issues concerning personnel skills, knowledge, and expertize (Esposito et al., 2021; Booth et al., 2020). And times of uncertainty might also encourage conservative management styles and reduce innovation.

Although one of the challenges of the implementation of two-way communication is the loss of information control, the hope is that post-pandemic communication actually is able to boost digital strategies valuing the role played by two-way interaction and reciprocity. This will result in even more positive relationships between cultural foundations and their stakeholders.

11.3 Performances of FAI Open Heritages, from Maintenance to Beautification

Multiple data of Fondo Ambiente Italiano were collected from 2014 to 2019: visitors, subscribers, delegations (committed boards in local communities), open heritages, events, maintenance cost, beautification cost (for betterment of heritages), personnel cost, advertising cost, program service revenue, grants, subscriptions, and rents. The growth of the biggest cultural foundation in Italy can be given evidence in Fig. 11.1, with the polynomial correlation between visitors and subscribers. Having been visitor, it is a stimulus for heritages to collect friends and subscribers, who fall in love with landscapes and reveal a strong advocacy for their beautification with the renewal of subscriptions year-by-year.

At the same time, the number of open heritages grew from 160 in 2014 to 1100 in 2019. The commitments of the private and public Welfare States can be appreciated for the extraordinary growth together with program service revenues in the Fig. 11.2.

The impressive growth of events and attendance at FAI heritages was, as a consequence, well-funded by revenue diversification. While Program Service revenue has been growing with Grants since 2014, other revenues like subscriptions have doubled from 2.9 million euros to 6.0 million euros. Rents for exclusive locations have doubled from 1.8 to 4.0 million euros, too. While stakeholders were increasing, revenues' diversification was optimized thanks to the FAI Team, from marketing officers to fundraisers, from public relations to the exploitation of willingness-to-pay and willingness-to-give. Relationship marketing was a crucial lever to support FAI in building up, and proactively maintaining, relational assets consisting of long-term

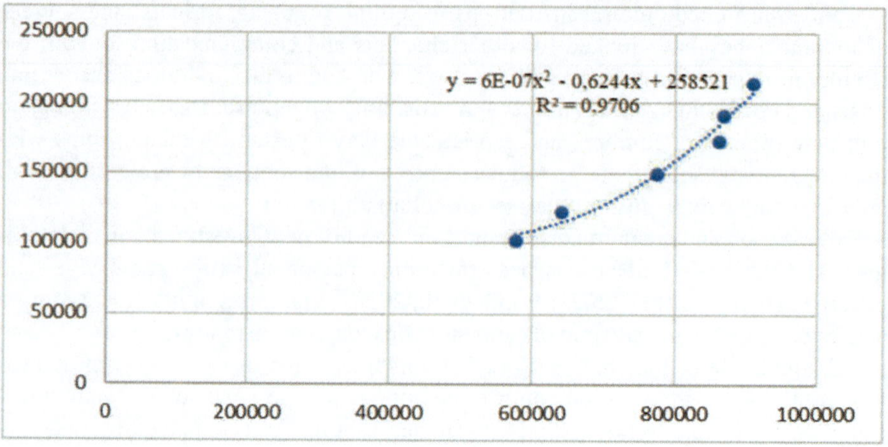

Fig. 11.1 The growth of visitors and subscribers – FAI, 2014–2019. (Source: FAI data (numbers) in Reports at www.fondoambiente.it)

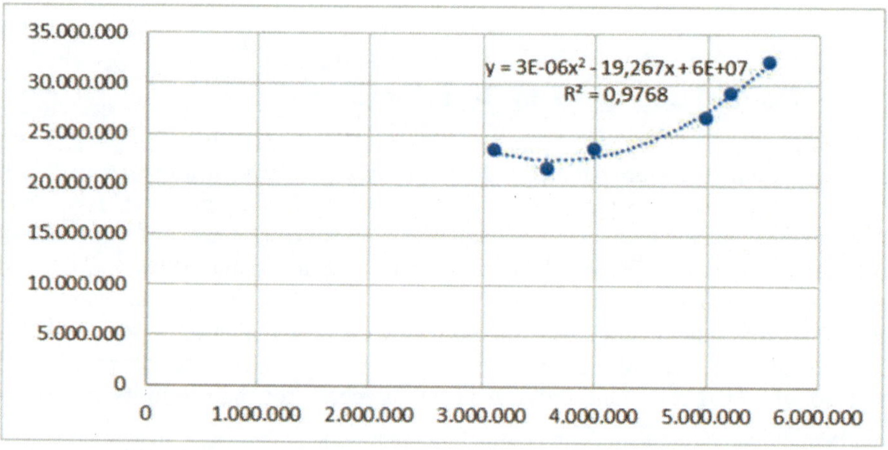

Fig. 11.2 The growth of program service revenue and grants – FAI, 2014–2019. (Source: FAI data (euros) in Reports at www.fondoambiente.it)

relationships/partnerships with key stakeholders: big donors, international friends, corporate supporters, local grant-makers, public administrations, and communities.

Multiple regression was implemented for evidence that beautification is enabled by costs: more than day-by-day maintenance, by the beautification cost which is consistent of betterment and restoration of tangible heritages and advertising cost. The opening of more than 1000 heritages in 2019 is a target of a constant and efficient care for the well-being of communities and tourists. Open heritages were here calculated as function of beautification, personnel, and advertising expenses. As a matter of fact, beautification is not possible unless project managers,

Table 11.1 Some results of multiple regression

Summary of fit				
R	0.982			
R Square	0.964			
R Square Adj.	0.910			
Analysis of variance				
Source	DF	SS	Mean square	F Ratio
Model	3	90704.263	30234.754	17.895
Error	2	3379.070	1689.535	Sign.
Total	5	94083.333		0.053

Open Heritages= f(advertising, personnel, beautification costs)
Open Heritages = +0.327Advertising +0.621Personnel +0.006Beautification
Source: Elaboration with SPSS Statistics Software

fundraisers, marketing officers, and the whole FAI personnel, they are not fully committed. Beautification is useless if it is not promoted and signaled to all available audiences and stakeholders. The advertising expense is therefore a pivotal strategy.

Table 11.1 gives some details of the multiple regression. Though collinearity is relevant for the personnel cost, ANOVA is significant for all items and the multiple regression shows that the number of open heritages grow with advertising, personnel, and beautification costs. Some of these costs include restoration with original components, story-telling of families, legacies, tangible, and intangible heritages like craftsmanship and creative supplies, locally and typically confined.

From the donor perspective, when FAI is collecting resources from different Welfare States and stakeholders, means, motives, and rewards of donors are in the enabled heritages and the restitution process. From the organizational perspective, important issues relating to the leadership, power, and governance of projects refer to FAI as leader, who is pooling strategies and resources. From the beneficiary perspective, the changing appeal of particular philanthropic causes has different impacts on communities and tourists. As a consequence of FAI highlighted commitments, citizens reveal the advocacy for reactivated both tangible and intangible legacies and FAI delegations support the long-term appeal of heritages for communities and tourists. These ones are planning for different formats, from school trips to holidays with one-day stops in FAI beauties.

Over time, relationship marketing has reinforced its added value in partnerships. Alongside traditional institutional communications with traditional media, FAI optimized both corporate and project communications through website and online communication, such as social media accounts. As a consequence, FAI was able to develop long-term relationships with grant-makers, sponsors, public administrations, local individuals, and communities; to work more closely with all stakeholders on development and implementation of projects; to generate ground-level experience and insights important for benchmarking for next-generations project management. Beautification was achieved with advertising and promotion through different media and the official website as the main tool.

During the pandemic, activities were stopped and partially implemented online. Online was the crucial lever, where efforts were maximized in order to stress the co-leadership of FAI and stakeholders: FAI called for a comprehensive engagement as the success of the recovery would not be possible, if multiple stakeholders did not participate. FAI developed two main virtual strategies: call for advocacy for environment and landscape, asking for attention, suggestions, consideration, on one side; online events like exhibitions, conferences, and meetings, on the other side. When stringency was alleviated, some events might have taken place. For sure, restoration and beautification were not fully stopped, as the number of heritages collected new items in 2021. Events like Spring Day in FAI heritages were inevitably converted to an opportunity for story-telling, virtual meetings for delegations, subscribers, and visitors. In Spring 2021, FAI regularly opened heritages and, according to laws and rules of meetings during and soon after pandemic, the advocacy was fully recovered in sites, locations, and any legacies of FAI. Online platforms and media still remain both for events and for relationship marketing with stakeholders.

11.4 Conclusion

Before, during, and after pandemic, Italian foundations are involved in the strategic *stabilization*, recovery, and development of culture and heritage.

From a marketing and communication point of view, relationship marketing is a key strategy in order to develop multiple relations with fund-givers, sponsors, artists, community administrations, and promote initiatives, thanks to social media, too.

Before pandemic, the biggest Italian cultural foundations like FAI profited by a growing availability of resources. As the analysis highlighted, the growth of open heritages was matched by the growth of stakeholders, revenues, and grants. FAI was leader of the valorization of tangible and intangible heritages and the communication was focused on this leadership, mainly with the website.

Pandemic forced foundations to rethink products, formats, and sources of income. They optimized other channels, communication media, and contents in the attempt to retain sponsors and grant-makers, who had to face a dramatic economic crisis and could change their sensibility on cultural issues, as well as to find new sources of funding, and reorient the way to establish and co-implement relationships with the different stakeholders.

During the pandemic, FAI profited by a geo-free and pervasive online communication, which could promote mutual understandings between people with different cultural backgrounds, enabling people to access cultural heritage from all over the world. FAI developed the advocacy and the sensibility for co-leadership as it was in the middle of June (18th) with the call for action to roundabouts ("circondari") and districts with their communities, exactly in the nearby of FAI heritages. Before and after pandemic, the growth did not only concern the amount of resources and stakeholders but also the new vision "from leadership to co-leadership".

Further research will investigate how much Italian foundations take part to the international scenario as they can be partners for European recovery projects and fundraisers for European creative issues. This research mainly confirmed their role in Italy. Nevertheless, it is for sure that FAI has got international friends and international visitors, as this foundation together with other operating Italian Foundations, they are multipliers of resources, assets, projects, and they are *shaping* the post-pandemic of cultural and creative industries.

References

Abeza, G., O'Reilly, N., Finch, D., Séguin, B., & Nadeau, J. (2020). The role of social media in the co-creation of value in relationship marketing: A multi-domain study. *Journal of Strategic Marketing, 28*(6), 472–493.

Bennet, R. (Ed.). (2019). *Nonprofit marketing and fundraising*. Routledge.

Berrett, J. L., & Holliday, B. S. (2018). The effect of revenue diversification on output creation in nonprofit organizations: A resource dependence perspective. *Voluntas, 29*, 1190–1201.

Besana, A. (2017). Animal Spirits or Engaging Spirits? The importance of the not-for-profit economy, coopetitiveness and grant-making foundations. In A. Vlachvei (Ed.), *Factors affecting firm competitiveness and performance in the Modern Business World, 2017*. IGI Global.

Booth, P., Ogundipe, A., & Røyseng, S. (2020). Museum leaders' perspectives on social media. *Museum Management and Curatorship, 35*(4), 373–391.

Esposito, A., & Besana, A. (2016). Sense and sensibility in the contemporary generous society: Economics and social media communication of the biggest grant-making foundations. *Social Business*.

Esposito, A., & Besana, A. (2018). US community foundations: Building a generous society in challenging times. *Journal of Nonprofit & Public Sector Marketing.*

Esposito, A., Besana, A., Fisichella, C., & Vannini, M. C. (2021). *COVID-19 effects in museum management. Insight about the Italian context*. Proceedings of the International Conference Marketing Trends, Venice 14–16 January 2021.

Essig, L. (2014). Arts incubators: A typology. *The Journal of Arts Management, Law, and Society, 44*, 169–180.

Fondazione Symbola. (2020). *IoSonoCultura, Annual Report*. Available at https://www.symbola.net/rubrica/io-sono-cultura-2020/

Grönroos, C. (2004). The relationship marketing process: Communication, interaction, dialogue, value. *Journal of Business and Industrial Marketing, 19*(2), 99–113.

Grönroos, C. (2012). Conceptualising value co-creation: A journey to the 1970s and back to the future. *Journal of Marketing Management, 28*(13–14), 1520–1534.

Gummesson, E. (2011). *Total relationship marketing*. Routledge.

Hadida, A. (2015). Performance in the creative industries. In C. Jones, M. Lorenzen, & J. Sapsed (Eds.), *The Oxford handbook of creative industries* (pp. 219–249). Oxford University Press.

Hoellen, M., Lengfeld, C., & Konrad, E. D. (2020). Business success for creative and cultural entrepreneurs: Influences of individual- and firm-related factors on revenue and satisfaction. *International Journal of Arts Management, 22*(2), 52–65.

Hussain, S. B., Rawjee, V. P., & Penceliah, S. (2014). The applicability of relationship marketing at non-profit organizations: A developing country perspective. *Problems and Perspectives in Management, 12*(4), 155–160.

Hyunjung, L., Youngseon, K., & Ranucci, R. (2021). Stability and compatibility in the receptivity of US arts and culture organizations to corporate support. *International Journal of Arts Management, 23*(2), 43–55.

Kim, M. (2017). The relationship of nonprofits' financial health to program outcomes: Empirical evidence from nonprofit arts organizations. *Nonprofit and Voluntary Sector Quarterly, 46*(3), 1–24.

Liang, X., Lu, Y., & Martin, J. A. (2021). Review of the role of social media for the cultural heritage sustainability. *Sustainability, 13*(3), 1–17.

Ma, J., & Konrath, S. (2018). A century of nonprofit studies: Scaling the knowledge of the field. *Voluntas, 29*, 1139–1158.

Meyrick, J., & Barnett, T. (2021). From public good to public value: Arts and culture in a time of crisis. *Cultural Trends, 30*(1), 75–90.

Nah, S., & Saxton, G. (2013). Modeling the adoption and use of social media by nonprofit organisations. *New Media and Society, 15*(2), 294–313.

Shaw, B. J., Draux, H., García Martín, M., Martin, J., & Bieling, C. (2017). Contributions of citizen science to landscape democracy: Potentials and challenges of current approaches. *Landscape Research, 42*(8), 831–844.

Shea, M., & Hamilton, R. D. (2015). Who determines how nonprofits confront uncertainty? *Nonprofit Management & Leadership, 25*(4), 383–401.

Vecco, M., & Srakar, A. (2020). Direct, indirect and cross-lagged: The effects of cultural policy on nascent cultural entrepreneurship. *International Journal of Arts Management, 22*(2), 66–82.

Zurbuchen, M. S. (2017). Legacies of cultural philanthropy in Asia. *Austrian Journal of South-East Asian Studies, 10*(2), 165–184.

Chapter 12
For Heritage Memory and Survival, Though Pandemic Times! Philanthropy of Leading Trust and Foundation in Italy and UK

Angela Besana and Maria Cristina Vannini

Abstract Cultural not-for-profit organizations can be split into operating and grant-making foundations. Both of them support restoration, recovery, and resilience of culture and creativity. For this goal, they can mix the operating and the grant-making roles.

Big organizations like National Trust (NT) in UK and FAI (Fondo Ambiente Italiano) in Italy collect memory of tangible and intangible heritages, which are restored, renovated, and given back to communities after disruptive events, from death of the founder to pandemic emergency. Their fundraising gets on into grant-making to heritages, whose management is fully operating thanks to NT and FAI managers.

Their philanthropy, their leading roles, and their reputation are founded on virtuous underlying vision, strategy, or set of principles, grassroots approach, dedication, and professionalism. This is empowered by the communication, traditional, and online, where the former contributes to the capillary dissemination and gathering of information.

The aim of this paper is to compare performances of NT and FAI. These performances concern the range of revenues and costs of these big and leading organizations, together with the growth of visitors and members.

The methodology includes regression analysis of 2014–2019 NT and FAI data, together with a qualitative analysis of strategies during pandemic times. The magnitude of the philanthropy of these foundations will be highlighted with a

Many thanks to our students of Workshop "Analytical Skills for Tourism and Arts". Their analysis was very challenging.

A. Besana (✉) · M. C. Vannini
Department Business, Law, Economics and Consumer Behaviour 'Carlo A. Ricciardi', IULM, Milan, Italy
e-mail: angela.besana@iulm.it; cristina.vannini@soluzionimuseali.com

N. Tsounis, A. Vlachvei (eds.), *Advances in Quantitative Economic Research*, Springer Proceedings in Business and Economics,
https://doi.org/10.1007/978-3-030-98179-2_12

multiple regression for total revenues being function of operating and fundraising costs.

Keywords Philanthropy · Heritage · Memory · Foundation · Economics

12.1 Recovery of Memories, Resilience of Heritages: The Philanthropy of NT and FAI in Turbulent Times

Cultural not-for-profit organizations can be split into operating and grant-making foundations. Both of them support restoration, recovery, and resilience of culture and creativity. The operating foundation is managing the heritages and their cultural contents. For this goal, the operating foundation needs money and in-kind resources. The grant-making foundation is supporting the operating one with grants (money and in-kind). These foundations usually work as separate organizations.

In contemporary and turbulent times, they can mix the operating and the grant-making roles. They have been matching roles both in Europe and North America for decades (Besana, 2017; Esposito & Besana, 2016, 2018). Some of them have grown as for resources, reputation, and leading roles.

Among them, big organizations like National Trust (NT) in UK and FAI (Fondo Ambiente Italiano) in Italy collect memory of tangible and intangible heritages, which are restored, renovated, and given back to communities after disruptive events, from death of the founder to pandemic contingency. The National Trust is 125 years old. FAI is more than 45 years old. Their fundraising is at a stage of maturity: events, membership programs, big donors, and big campaigns are all and at the best implemented. Their philanthropy is regularly getting on into grant-making to heritages, whose management is fully operating thanks to FAI and NT managers.

With different frames of partnershiping (Esposito & Besana, 2016, 2018; Ma & Konrath, 2018; Besana, 2017), both NT and FAI are connecting with communities, local and national constituencies, grant-makers, sponsors, and public administrations. One of the most consistent legacies of their long history and mature experience is the building of strong relationships between them being senior leaders and any other organizations at start-up or growing stage, above all if partners are corporations and public administrations (Hyunjung et al., 2021; Vecco & Srakar, 2020; Ma & Konrath, 2018; Zurbuchen, 2017; Kim, 2017). Including their operational staffs, their volunteers, and their members, together with monitoring and keeping cooperation, training, and communication in any projects they lead, it results into a benchmark so that they are looked for main partners by cultural project managers.

In the meanwhile, their philanthropy is impacted by social media marketing. Above all, during pandemic, virtual relationships and partnerships grew. The crisis committed them to much more communication than in the past, with a diversified and multifaceted strategy (Meyrick & Barnett, 2021; Daniels, 2021; Jaskyte et al., 2018; Topaloglu et al., 2018; Faulk et al., 2016).

And they mutually take inspiration. Since its founding in 1975, FAI has drawn advocacy and benchmark from the National Trust for England, Wales, and Northern Ireland, as Fai: takes care of places, heritages, parks in Italy for the benefit of present and future generations, promotes education, appreciation, awareness, and enjoyment of the Nation's environmental, natural, historic, and artistic heritage, and monitors the protection of Italy's natural and cultural assets, according to the article 9 of the Italian Constitution. FAI has always implemented partnerships within the framework of the Public and Private Welfare State of grant-makers like foundation of banking origin and corporate philanthropy.

The aim of this paper is to compare performances of NT and FAI. These performances concern the range of revenues and costs of these big and leading organizations, together with the growth of visitors and members.

The methodology includes regression analysis of 2014–2019 NT and FAI data, together with a qualitative analysis of strategies during pandemic. The magnitude of the philanthropy of these foundations will be highlighted with a multiple regression for total revenues being function of operating and fundraising costs.

12.2 Philanthropy Between Innovating Strategies and Best Practices

While philanthropy has been at the basis of the British culture since the schism from the Church of Rome (Davies, 2016) and the introduction of the Statues of Charitable Uses in 1601, philanthropic practices have been entered the Italian habits relatively recently (Barbetta, 2012) and their operational sector has not been fully organized yet (Campedelli, 2018).

Nevertheless, FAI has been a guiding light in the sector since its foundation in 1975, due to the close filiation with the NT, started out in 1895.

Differences in the number of assets between FAI and NT are relevant although proportionally comparable considering the corporate composition and the management costs.

The most part of the FAI heritage sites is concentrated in Northern Italy, area where the original founders belonged to, the first legacies and assets stemmed from, and where a "radius of trust" (Fukuyama, 1999) initiated in a pristine circle of people and developed in time and through institutional communication, public relations and work-of-mouth in reputational leadership and relevance.

Assets owned and managed by FAI represent one-tenth of the NT patrimony in line with the other figures related to their organizations.

As Mitchell has reported (Mitchell, 2015), virtuous underlying vision, strategy, or set of principles, grassroots approach, dedication, and professionalism are the pillars at the basis of reputation.

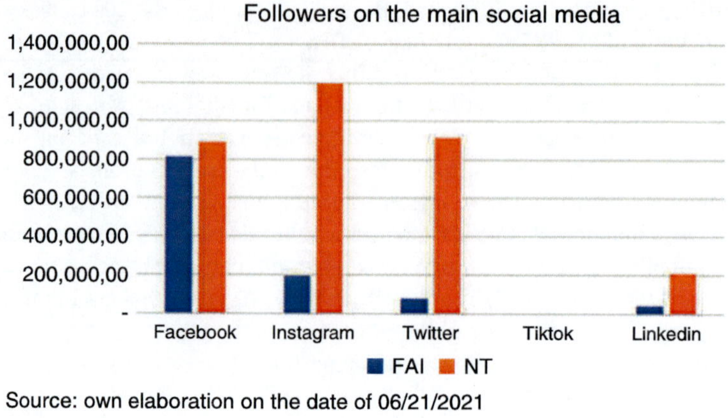

Fig. 12.1 The social media in FAI and NT. (Source: Own elaboration on the date of 06/21/2021)

Both the Trust and the Foundation rely on their strong mission to foster and preserve national and identity heritage of their country and pursue it by solid social interactions and in cooperation with several stakeholders. Their activities are established in a recognizable grassroots approach, but on the other hand their outcomes aim at suggesting environmental and cultural policies.

In both cases, the champions have been criticized for being elite and popular and due to this dichotomy, their actions sometimes have been controversial but actually it witnesses the NT's and FAI's ability in catching the most relevant issues in contemporary world (environmental and climatic sustainability, attention to the rural areas, accessibility to and democratization of culture to all category of people, social inclusion, education, and training . . .).

This ability of theirs enhances their visibility and reputation and makes them a good partner for CSR actions. This is empowered by the communication, traditional and online, where the former contributes to the capillary dissemination and gathering of information (Fig. 12.1).

The main differences between FAI and NT concern the dimension of the noncore activities and in the status of Independent Research Organization.

In the first in case, NT gave birth to some five subsidiary companies to manage and develop business on top of the core activity of fostering and preserving national heritage. One of them, National Trust (Renewable Energy) Limited, is a company wholly owned by the NT, that carries out the electricity trading to the National Grid, generated by the NT Renewable Energy Investment Program.

Commercialization, including ecommerce, of products grown by tenants of the sites goes along with the promotion of the sites themselves as shooting and gathering venues summoning partners or sponsors interested in linking their names to those, providing various kind of resources, but and above all enlarging the number of visitors and of the audience. Travels both for tourism and cultural purposes are a top for both champions, and by comparison it seems that holiday sales could represent an interesting offer since, NT even in a year of pandemic saw the grew of it by 9% year-on-year.

12.3 Performances of FAI and NT: Parallel Success and Merit Growth

Multiple data of FAI and NT were collected from 2014 to 2019: visitors, subscribers or members, delegations (committed boards in local communities for FAI heritages), open heritages, events, maintenance cost, beautification cost (for betterment of heritages), property operating costs, personnel cost, advertising and fundraising cost, expenditures on property projects, program service revenue, grants, subscriptions, and rents. The growth of community engagement in both NT and FAI in Italy can be appreciated in Figs. 12.2 and 12.3, with the polynomial trend for both visitors and members. Once visited, the heritages have been inspiring commitments of people, who fall in love with them and support them according to different membership programs from individual memberships to donors' clubs of different engagement and amounts for subscriptions. For both FAI and NT, it is not only a matter of donations and memberships of citizens, friends, international friends, and supporters during their life. When they write their will, the donors commit their legacies to FAI and NT: money, in-kind, buildings, parks, gardens, paintings, and works of art, so that the collection is constantly growing for both FAI and NT.

At the same time, both FAI and NT collect enough resources in order to cope with maintenance and projects for heritages they support. Figures 12.4 and 12.5 show the growth of operating costs and grants. Grants are quite enough for operating and extraordinary costs, for specific projects and restoration, first of all.

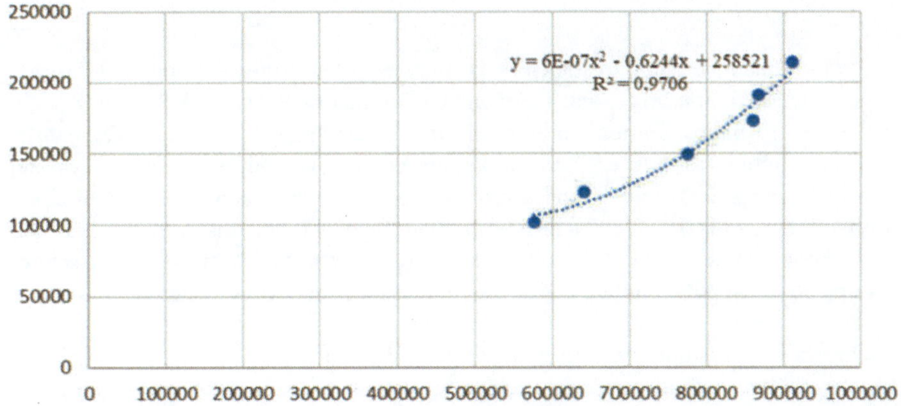

Fig. 12.2 The growth of visitors and members – FAI, 2014–2019

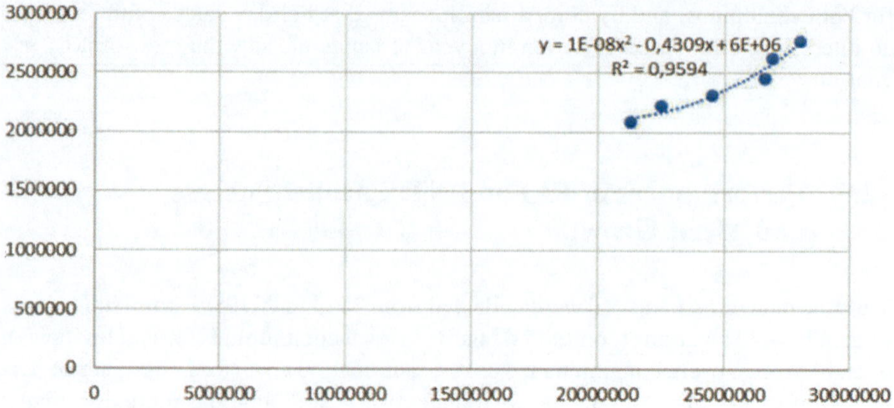

Fig. 12.3 The growth of visitors and members – NT, 2014–2019. (Source: Own elaboration of FAI (euros) and NT (pounds) data at their own websites)

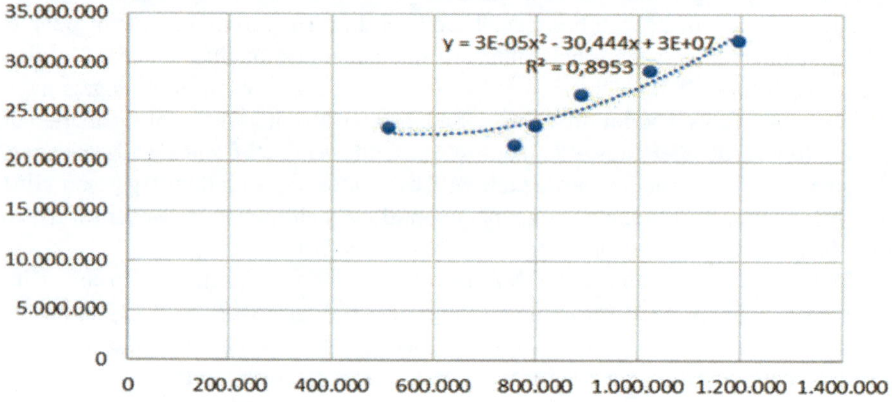

Fig. 12.4 The growth of operating costs and grants in FAI – 2014–2019

Grant-makers are next to sponsors, corporate philanthropy, national and international friends, community, and independent foundations. The stakeholders' range is constantly paid attention, monitored, and investigated by NT and FAI staffs, who can include fundraisers and marketing experts with different specialties and relationship spheres: some fundraisers connect with foundations; some of them with affluent citizens and friends with their legacy to be inspired for NT and FAI; some marketing staff is allocating efforts for young visitors, from school groups to university students, friends, and volunteers; other marketing staff is organizing events for their heritages being opened to several targets: from business managers to contemporary artists with artists' in residence projects, from families to corporations, whose managers are interested in locations for a wide range of purposes: movie sets, weddings, concerts, exhibitions, congresses, conferences, meetings, holiday packages, etc. Governances of both FAI and NT are complex,

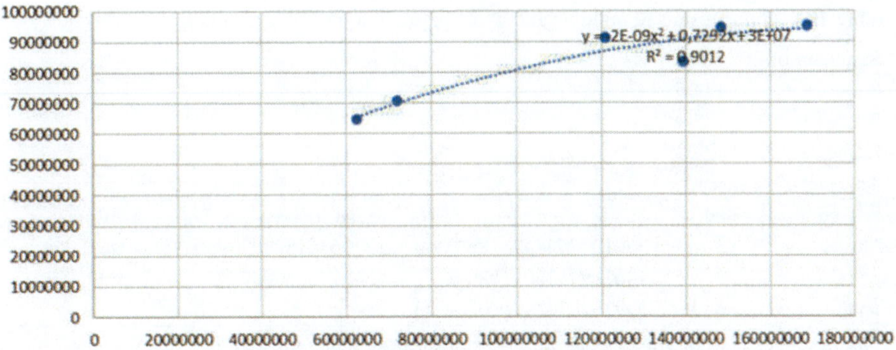

Fig. 12.5 The growth of operating costs and grants in NT – 2014–2019. (Source: Own elaboration of FAI (euros) and NT (pounds) data at their own websites)

multifaceted, and separated in different roles for different targets, with segmentation and sub-division of segments.

Grants are part of their revenue diversification. Program service revenue, grants, memberships, and rents are their main revenues. Ancillary revenues stem from their staff being consultants, experts, and editors, in addition to a huge amount of volunteers' staff who calls for small and big donations. Being the biggest share of revenues, grants grew for FAI from more than 23 million euros in 2014 to more than 32 million euros in 2019. Being the biggest share of revenues, the membership income grew for NT from more than 150 million pounds in 2014 to more than 269 million pounds in 2019.

Multiple regression was implemented in order to show how much their total revenues are being enabled by operating and communication costs. As a matter of fact, memory and resilience, they cannot be supported and empowered, unless project managers, fundraisers, marketing officers, and the whole personnel of both organizations are not fully committed to their different roles: on one side, the operating role of things-making (restorations, events, maintenance, etc.) and, on the other side, the grant-raising and the grant-making thanks to their advertising and fundraising. If FAI and NT are both operating and grant-making organizations, this double face of their being not-for-profit organizations can be appreciated with the growth of revenues depending on the main costs.

The revenue diversification is given evidence in the multiple regression for growth depending on both the operating and maintenance costs and the communication ones, advertising and fundraising being pivotal strategies.

Table 12.1 gives some details of the multiple regression for NT performances. ANOVA is significant for all items and the multiple regression shows how much revenues grow with signaling and operating costs. Some of these costs include restoration with original components, story-telling of families, legacies, tangible, and intangible heritages comprehensive of landscapes, parks, gardens, literature, and history-telling. The equation $\text{Revenues} = +0.181\text{Fundraising} + 0.314\text{OperatingCost}$

Table 12.1 Some results of multiple and linear regression for NT performances

Summary of fit				
R	1.000			
R Square	1.000			
R Square Adj.	0.999			
Analysis of variance				
Source	DF	SS	Mean square	F Ratio
Model	3	39919085484239880.000	13306361828079960.000	1820.054
Error	2	14621945260118.426	7310972630059.213	Sign. 0.001
Total	5	39933707429500000.000		

Total Revenues = f(fundraising, operating cost, expenditure on projects)
Revenues = +0.181Fundraising +0.314OperatingCost +0.560ExpOnProjects
Source: Elaboration with SPSS Statistics Software

Table 12.2 Some results of multiple and linear regression for FAI performances

Summary of fit				
R	.996			
R Square	.992			
R Square Adj.	.980			
Analysis of variance				
Source	DF	SS	Mean square	F Ratio
Model	3	236624932488640.660	78874977496213.550	84.568
Error	2	1865362911896.682	932681455948.341	Sign. 0.012
Total	5	238490295400537.340		

Total Revenues = f(advertising, maintenance cost, beautification cost)
Revenues = +0.479Advertising +0.480MaintenanceCost −0.157BeautificationCost
Source: Elaboration with SPSS Statistics Software

+0.560ExpOnProjects shows positive correlations, expenditure on specific projects being the most compelling and absorbing issue, most of grants are collected and delivered to.

Table 12.2 gives some details of the multiple regression for FAI performances. ANOVA is significant for all items and the multiple regression shows how much revenues grow with advertising and costs for ordinary maintenance and special projects as concerns betterment of heritages (beautification). Some of these costs include restoration with original contents, materials, fabrics and, at the same time, training of volunteers and delegations in local communities, who are fully empowered and engaged with the recovery and resilience of local amenities with the goal of tourism growth. The equation Revenues = +0.479Advertising +0.480MaintenanceCost −0.157BeautificationCost shows a negative correlation for beautification, as long as some projects are particularly engaging and their complexity means that revenues can increase, if their costs are diminishing as well as their difficulties (long-term project management and master planning) are solved.

As regards NT and FAI during pandemic, they were in stand-by as for events and open heritages, though both of them implemented their virtual activity. NT inaugurated the new strategy Nature, Beauty, History for a green renewal and integration both with culture and history. With a foreseen loss of 200 million £ during the pandemic time, NT was anyway committed to the planned restoration of some of heritages and, above all the embellishment of the vision. With the main issue of the climate crisis, the new NT strategy concerns six major themes: the sustainable future by increasing opportunities for people to be involved with, stimulated in their advocacy and benefit from the comprehensive NT heritage of landscapes, buildings, and objects in care; the state of nature in the UK by making the land project management, by restoring degraded landscapes and by improving the delivery of nature-friendly farming; experiencing in wonder, beauty, understanding, or a sense of connection and the accessibility for all people; access to beauty matched with history by working with others to increase access to parks and green spaces in, around, and near urban areas; support with more many events for community engagement and empowerment; the inclusion with the goal of the diversity of boards, people, and supporters. After pandemic times, the six themes are the prevailing objectives.

During the pandemic, FAI activities were stopped and partially implemented online. FAI developed two main virtual strategies: call for advocacy with online events for boards, subscribers, friends, and clubs, on one side; online events like exhibitions, conferences, and meetings for visitors and stakeholders like corporations, on the other side. For sure, restoration and beautification were not fully stopped as the number of heritages collected new items in 2021. Events like Spring Day in FAI heritages were inevitably converted to an opportunity for virtual storytelling. Only in spring 2021, FAI regularly re-opened heritages and, according to laws and rules of meetings during and soon after pandemic times, the advocacy was fully recovered in sites, locations, and any legacies of FAI. Online platforms and media still remain both for virtual events and for relationship marketing with stakeholders.

12.4 Conclusion

Combining efforts for old and contemporary heritages, tangible and intangible legacies, NT and FAI develop a project management which is at least in three steps: approval of different stakeholders' in public and open meetings, where participatory roles are granted at any different engagement, both of them being leaders; collection of resources with a constant and continuant monitoring for their being used thanks to different media and social media; redemption to all stakeholders with selection of benchmarks and well-done projects, in order to inspire the next project management.

Inclusion and diversity are now priorities both for FAI and NT, though differences in governance, asset dimensions, noncore activities, and performances can shape dissimilar approaches and best practices.

A long-term vision constantly supports their project management with boards, whose roles are well-defined and separated from staff, volunteers, and communities.

Grant-makers and sponsors might be foreseen, selected, and matched for different projects and roles, in order not to crowd-out any one of them on a long-term perspective and in order to enhance co-leadership.

Media and social media can be efficient tools in order to provide information, support visions, values, and promote, without the annoying overload of useless data. At the same time, media and social media echo the best projects and benchmarks for the reputation of all partners in national and international scenarios, where reputation can further grant new resources.

The multiple regression confirmed that revenues of both organizations are increasing with their efforts (and costs) on conservation and projects, though the master planning and long-term perspective of some project management for beautification can be inverse correlated with revenues. The multiple regression was, otherwise, related to performances before pandemic times. Pandemic was a full stop to offline activities, though it was a stimulus and "provocation" to create a new strategy and a comprehensive and different supply of events and projects.

Further research will also investigate how much NT and FAI take part to the international scenario, as they can be partners for European recovery projects and fundraisers for European creative issues, apart from Brexit implications.

References

Barbetta, G. (2012). Le fondazioni. In G. C. Gori (Ed.), *L'alternativa al pubblico?* (pp. 145–160). Le forme organizzate di finanziamento privato nel welfare sociale, Franco Angeli, Milano.

Besana, A. (2017). Animal Spirits or Engaging Spirits? The importance of the not-for-profit economy, competitiveness and grant-making foundations. In A. Vlachvei (Ed.), *Factors affecting firm competitiveness and performance in the Modern Business World, 2017*. IGI Global.

Campedelli, M. (2018). Due anni dopo. L'implementazione della riforma del Terzo settore. *Politiche Sociali, Social Policies., 2*, 281–286.

Daniels, A. (2021). Foundation helps nonprofits boost online giving. *Chronicle of Philanthropy, 33*(6), 35.

Davies, R. (2016). *Public Good by Private Means: How philanthropy shapes Britain*. Alliance Publishing Trust.

Esposito, A., & Besana, A. (2016). Sense and sensibility in the contemporary generous society: Economics and social media communication of the biggest grant-making foundations. *Social Business*.

Esposito, A., & Besana, A. (2018). US community foundations: Building a generous society in challenging times. *Journal of Nonprofit & Public Sector Marketing*.

Faulk, L., Willems, J., McGinnis Johnson, J., & Stewart, A. J. (2016). Network connections and competitively awarded funding: The impacts of board network structures and status interlocks on nonprofit organizations' foundation grant acquisition. *Public Management Review, 18*(10), 1425–1455.

Fukuyama, F. (1999). *Social capital and civil society*. The Institute of Public Policy George Mason University.

Hyunjung, L., Youngseon, K., & Ranucci, R. (2021). Stability and compatibility in the receptivity of US arts and culture organizations to corporate support. *International Journal of Arts Management, 23*(2), 43–55.

Jaskyte, K., Amato, O., & Sperber, R. (2018). Foundations and innovation in the nonprofit sector. *Nonprofit Management & Leadership, 29*(1), 47–64.

Kim, M. (2017). The relationship of nonprofits' financial health to program outcomes: Empirical evidence from nonprofit arts organizations. *Nonprofit and Voluntary Sector Quarterly, 46*(3), 1–24.

Ma, J., & Konrath, S. (2018). A century of nonprofit studies: Scaling the knowledge of the field. *Voluntas, 29*, 1139–1158.

Meyrick, J., & Barnett, T. (2021). From public good to public value: Arts and culture in a time of crisis. *Cultural Trends, 30*(1), 75–90.

Mitchell, G. E. (2015). The attributes of effective NGOs and the leadership values associated with a reputation for organizational effectiveness. *Nonprofit Management & Leadership, 26*(1), 39–57.

Topaloglu, O., McDonald, R. E., & Hunt, S. D. (2018). The theoretical foundations of nonprofit competition: A resource-advantage theory approach. *Journal of Nonprofit & Public Sector Marketing, 30*(3), 229–250.

Vecco, M., & Srakar, A. (2020). Direct, indirect and cross-lagged: The effects of cultural policy on nascent cultural entrepreneurship. *International Journal of Arts Management, 22*(2), 66–82.

Zurbuchen, M. S. (2017). Legacies of cultural philanthropy in Asia. *Austrian Journal of South-East Asian Studies, 10*(2), 165–184.

Chapter 13
Sectoral and Occupational Employment Analysis in Greece: Evidence From Labor Market

Kostas Karamanis and Georgios Kolias

Abstract This study employs a flexible econometric framework using a panel data set to model employment trends and behavior by sector and occupation in the Greek labor market. By applying mixed fixed and random coefficient techniques, this paper analyzes the impact of certain variables on employment by occupational category across the sectors of economic activities, projecting occupational trends. Using annual data from 2000 to 2018, we examine the effects of compensation, gross value added, unemployment, and a proxy for participation rate on workers' share by sector and occupation. Research findings reveal that the explanatory variables' elasticities vary widely across sectors and occupational categories. Our model can be used to identify occupations in current and future shortages across sectors as well as for employment needs assessment and anticipation.

Keywords Occupation · Employment · Labor market · Random coefficient modeling · Greece

13.1 Introduction

Labor market participants require the development of employment forecasting models enabling them to design their policies. These models can provide information to the main social partners and stakeholders in the labor market (employers, employees, trade unions, and policymakers) to reduce the social and economic problems arising from market deficiencies, reduce adjustment costs, and ultimately increase the labor market's productivity and efficiency. In particular, in terms of productivity and efficiency, forecasting models ensure that employees are employed

K. Karamanis (✉) · G. Kolias
Department of Accounting and Finance, Institute of Economic Analysis and Solidarity Economy, University of Ioannina, Ioannina, Greece

Hellenic Open University Greece, Patras, Greece
e-mail: kkaraman@uoi.gr

N. Tsounis, A. Vlachvei (eds.), *Advances in Quantitative Economic Research*, Springer Proceedings in Business and Economics,
https://doi.org/10.1007/978-3-030-98179-2_13

in jobs that correspond to their skill level resulting in a significant improvement of these features. For forecasting, simple extrapolative approaches or shift-share techniques are used in most studies (Briscoe & Wilson, 2003). However, recently the increasing availability in many countries of data on the occupational category within sectors allows the development of longitudinal and panel data econometric techniques for modeling and analyzing employment in these groups (see, e.g., Briscoe & Wilson, 2003; Cörvers & Dupuy, 2010; Weber & Zika, 2016; Bresson et al., 2006; Frees & Miller, 2004).

In this paper, we use random coefficient modeling on panel data to analyze and investigate sectoral and occupational employment as well as to assess the impact of important determinants on employment behavior across sectors of economic activity and their respective occupational structures. We exploit the flexibility provided by random coefficient panel data modeling for estimating employment shares (the number of employees) on the sectoral and occupational level. These models can capture the data's characteristics and allow specification for the dynamic nature through the correlation structure of subject-specific error terms (Frees & Miller, 2004). More specifically, using annual data for employment over the period from 2000 to 2018 for six main sectors and ten occupational categories of the Greek labor market, we apply mixed fixed and random coefficient techniques (see, e.g., Goldstein, 1995; Rabe-Hesketh & Skrondal, 2008; Hsiao, 2014) to analyze the impact of certain variables on the employment by occupational category across the main sectors of the economy. Linear mixed models containing both fixed and random effects allow for the inclusion of random deviations (effects) other than those associated with the overall error term. The econometric modeling considers six explanatory variables; unemployment, gross value added, employee compensation; two variables, one for the total population size of citizens aged between 15 and 19 years old and another for the number of people aged 65 and above; and the time trend.

This study's main contribution is the provision of a flexible and innovative econometric tool, with minimal data requirements, for investigating and assessing employment across economic activities over time. Moreover, in conjunction with other forecasting, macroeconomic models can offer accurate forecasts for employment future levels and trends.

The paper's structure is as follows: Section two presents a literature review, while section three provides a discussion of the data and their sources. Section four outlines the methodology of the research and summarizes the results. The last section concludes.

13.2 Literature Review

The first attempts for the labor demand forecasts' applications were based on input-output models and directly linked economic growth to skills requirements without approaching the level of occupations (Wilson, 2001; Maier et al., 2017; Maier et al., 2015). Internationally, early works for forecasting labor demand can be found in the mid-1950s (Hughes, 1993). Spalletti (2008) lists nine different methodological approaches applied to address the issue of future human resource requirements. They range from simple employer surveys to econometric approaches.

In many countries today, such applications for forecasting and projection purposes are employed. In the US, the Bureau of Labor Statistics estimates models for hundreds of detailed industries aggregated into subsectors and sectors. Macroeconomic factors like labor force, GDP, and labor productivity influence total employment. The behavior of these macrovariables and projection models for each sector determine the final projections of employment and production in the industry (Lacey et al., 2017). In Canada, The Canadian Occupational Projection System (COPS) for nearly 30 years has produced analytical outputs and Labor Market Information. Using a system of models, provide, among others, projections of occupational trends for policy analysts and labor market information users (Ignaczak, 2017).

Toossi (2011) states that according to the Bureau of Labor Statistics model, the job supply is a product of many demographic features, such as the size and growth of the population, by age, sex, race, and nationality. Bishop and Carter (1991) and Bishop (1997) analyzed occupational employment trends for 13 general occupational categories in the US. They state that the evolution in occupational employment shares follows a logistic growth path. In their model, the dependent variable is the log of the ratio of the occupation's share of employment by category each year. Briscoe and Wilson (2003) use annual data from UK Labor Force Surveys to model occupational trends from 1981 to 1999. In particular, they use data for 17 standard industries for nine occupations. Using panel data models, they analyze the trends in occupational employment shares across industries and occupational categories over the above period. Foster-McGregor and Pöschl (2009) evaluate labor mobility's importance at the cross-sectional level for employment flows and reveal that labor mobility has beneficial effects on industry productivity. Maier et al. (2017) argue that employers respond to job shortages by raising wages to attract employees who can, to some extent, adapt their behavior to mobility. Cörvers and Dupuy (2010) present several examples suggesting the importance of employment dynamics across occupations and sectors. They investigate these dynamics by estimating labor demand equations by sector and occupation using multiple cointegrating models (Stock & Watson, 1993; Mark et al., 2005).

The available evidence indicates that independent academic studies and government agencies' programs are part of the complex task of making forecasts for employment in sectors and professions of the economies. The projection and employment forecasts require the specification and estimation with longitudinal or panel data techniques concerning econometric models. In most models, the regressors necessarily represent the economy's macroeconomic characteristics such as unemployment, value-added, wages, and demographic population changes.

13.3 Data Analysis and Model Specification

For the study's purposes, we use employment data for six industry sectors and ten occupations. Table 13.1 presents the Greek economy's main sectors, while Table 13.2 shows the occupation by category analyzed in this study.

As shown in Table 13.3, the evolution of the percentage of employees per sector of activity as a percentage of the total number of employees in the economy displays mixed trends. The employees' percentage in the sector "Agriculture, forestry, fisheries" decreased from 17.28% of the total number of employees in 2000 to 12.27% in 2018. The "Industry, energy" sector also decreased by almost four percentage points, from 15.42% in 2000 to 11.29% in 2018. The "Construction" sector also recorded a similar decrease of four percentage points from 7.34% in 2000 to 3.96% in 2018. On the contrary, an increase in the percentage of employees presented in the sectors of economic activity "Trade, hotels, catering, transport, and communications", "Financial, business activities", and "Other services". The "Other services" sector recorded the largest increase from 22.60% in 2000 to 27.37% in 2018. The "Trade, hotels, catering, transport and communications" sector increased about four percentage points, from 29.82% in 2000 to 33.92% in 2018. The sector "Financial, business activities" followed the same rising trend in which the percentage of employees increased from 7.55% in 2000 to 11.20% in 2018.

Figure 13.1 displays the evolution of the professions' categories from 2000 to 2018 in percentages of total workers, and records no significant fluctuations during the decade 2000–2010. Figure 13.2 presents the time trends by profession category.

Table 13.1 Sectors classification

#	Sectors
1	*Agriculture, forestry, and fishing*
2	*Industry including energy*
3	*Construction*
4	*Trade, hotels and restaurants, transport and communication*
5	*Financial, real estate, renting, and business activities*
6	*Other service activities*

Table 13.2 Occupational classification

#	Occupational categories
1	*Managers*
2	*Professionals*
3	*Technicians and associate professionals*
4	*Clerical support workers*
5	*Service and sales workers*
6	*Skilled agricultural, forestry, and fishery workers*
7	*Craft and related trades workers*
8	*Plant and machine operators and assemblers*
9	*Elementary occupations*
10	*Occupations not possible to classify*

Table 13.3 Time series of employment share by sectors

Year	Agriculture, forestry, and fishing	Industry including energy	Construction	Trade, hotels and restaurants, transport and communication	Financial, real estate, renting, and business activities	Other service activities
2000	17.28%	15.42%	7.34%	29.82%	7.55%	22.60%
2001	15.86%	15.54%	7.50%	30.22%	8.08%	22.80%
2002	15.31%	15.20%	7.65%	30.07%	8.38%	23.40%
2003	15.09%	14.53%	8.10%	30.38%	8.42%	23.48%
2004	12.38%	14.26%	8.14%	30.25%	9.23%	25.74%
2005	12.16%	14.12%	8.27%	30.98%	9.25%	25.22%
2006	11.72%	13.91%	8.11%	30.95%	9.18%	26.13%
2007	11.33%	13.73%	8.72%	30.72%	9.21%	26.29%
2008	11.14%	13.60%	8.62%	31.11%	10.11%	25.43%
2009	11.69%	13.00%	8.13%	31.36%	10.04%	25.77%
2010	12.40%	12.31%	7.28%	31.44%	9.97%	26.60%
2011	12.35%	11.63%	6.07%	32.02%	10.66%	27.28%
2012	13.01%	11.10%	5.44%	31.48%	11.50%	27.47%
2013	13.69%	10.94%	4.62%	31.72%	11.22%	27.81%
2014	13.57%	10.69%	4.28%	32.43%	11.32%	27.71%
2015	12.90%	10.91%	4.02%	33.41%	11.35%	27.41%
2016	12.37%	11.24%	4.00%	33.72%	11.32%	27.34%
2017	12.08%	11.43%	3.98%	33.99%	11.23%	27.30%
2018	12.27%	11.29%	3.96%	33.92%	11.20%	27.37%

Source: Data research

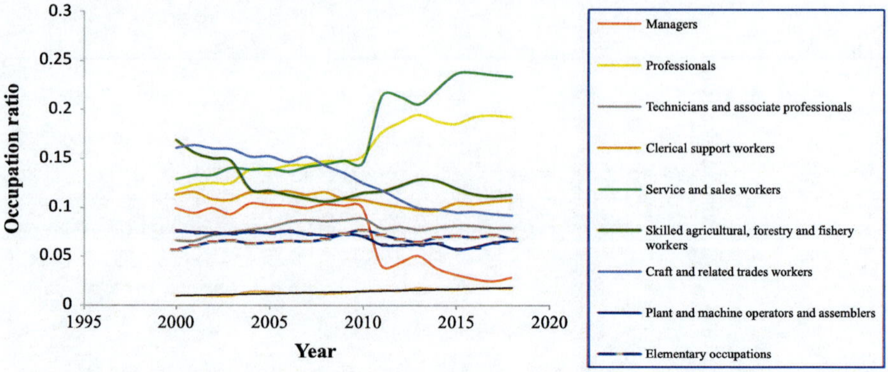

Fig. 13.1 Share of employees per occupation category over the period 2000–2018. (Source: Data research)

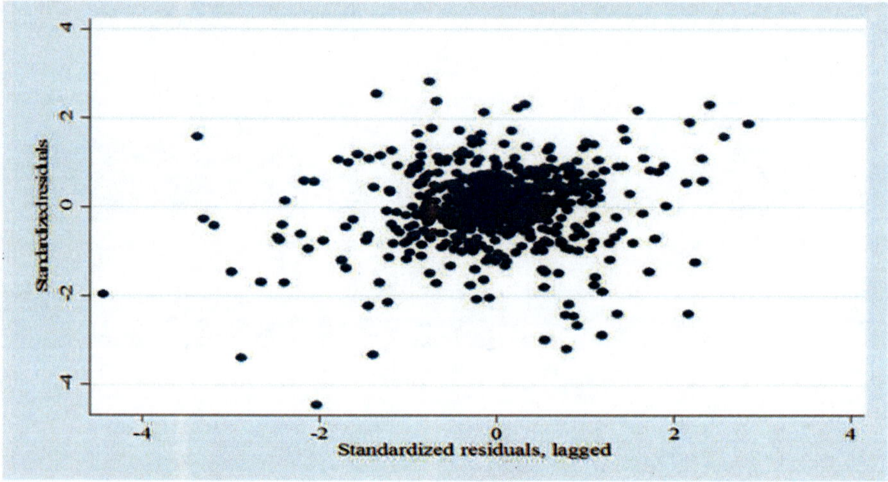

Fig. 13.2 Scatter plot of residuals versus lagged residuals. (Source: Data research)

There is a clear upward trend for the categories "Professionals" and "Service and sales workers". In particular, "Professionals" increased by about eight percentage points, from 11.82% in 2000 to 19.26% in 2018. The largest increase recorded in the profession category "Technicians and associate professionals" reaching 23.38% in 2018, from 12.96% in 2000. The category "Craft and related trades workers" had a marginal increase from 6.63% in 2000 to 7.96% in 2018, while the category "Elementary occupations" from 5.70% in 2000 to 6.84% in 2018. On the contrary, a downward trend for the same period over seven percentage points was presented by the category "Managers", especially, from 9.93% in 2000 on the total number of employees reached 2.83% in 2018. The profession category "Craft and related trades workers" had a similar decrease, reaching in 2018 at a rate of 9.25% from

16.12% in 2000. Occupation category “Skilled agricultural, forestry and fishery workers“ decreased by about 5%, from 16.93% in 2000 to 11.34% in 2018. This percentage reveals a marginal decrease in the categories of occupations “Clerical support workers” and “Plant and machine operators and assemblers”, for less than one percent for “Clerical support workers“, from 11.32% in 2000 to 10.80% in 2018 and for “Plant and machine operators and assemblers“, from 7.62 in 2000 to 6.67% in 2018.

Table 13.4 below presents descriptive statistics of the variables of interesting determined by the discussion in the literature review section.

Table 13.5 shows the Pearson correlation matrix between the variables that represent the employment per sector.

A preliminary conclusion drawn from the correlation table concerns the Construction and Industry sector. Both sectors show a high and statistically significant negative correlation with the sectors of *Trade, hotels and restaurants, transport and communication (4)* , *Financial, real estate, renting, and business activities* (5), and *Other service activities (6)*. The lowest degree of correlation with other sectors of the economy is presented for the employment in the *Agriculture, forestry, and fishing* sector.

13.4 Model Specification and Forecasting Procedure

After investigating and presenting the relationships between the share of employees in the main sectors of the economy, we will present the econometric model development that will be used to predict the number of employees per category per industry.

13.4.1 Model Specification

The process is integrated into two stages: The first specifies the econometric model is used to estimate the relationship's parameters between the dependent variable and the variables that potentially affect the employment behavior per occupational category in each economic sector. The second includes the forecast of the explanatory variables' values in the period under consideration, i.e., from 2017 to 2025. Although the available data are until the year 2018, data up to 2015 used to estimate model parameters, while the period 2016–2018 constitutes the validation period to testing the model on actual data. Using the estimates of the explanatory variables and having available the estimates of the model's parameters, the forecasts for the number of employees for the period 2017–2025 are generated.

According to the preceded analysis, Table 13.6 includes the variables affecting the number of employees by occupational category in each sector.

Table 13.4 Descriptive statistics of the variables

Sector	Variable	Obs	Mean	Std. Dev.	Min	Max
Agriculture, forestry, and fishing	Number of persons employed by occupation by industry	95	106660.00	204424.40	900.00	688100.00
	Compensation of employees by industry	19	89.34	11.19	64.86	106.40
	Gross value added by industry	19	7067.25	897.90	5794.10	8944.86
	Unemployment rate by industry	19	1.47	0.21	1.03	1.80
	Population aged between 15 and 19 years	19	599.29	60.51	525.50	720.54
	Population aged 65 years or over	19	2099.93	156.46	1793.88	2319.05
	Year	19	2009	5.51	2000	2018
Industry including energy	Number of persons employed by occupation by industry	152	66712.50	69612.52	10500.00	328800.00
	Compensation of employees by industry	19	131.99	27.98	94.80	176.90
	Gross value added by industry	19	39556.07	3944.33	31049.00	47755.00
	Unemployment rate by industry	19	11.06	1.04	8.60	12.97
	Population aged between 15 and 19 years	19	599.29	60.39	525.50	720.54
	Population aged 65 years or over	19	2099.93	156.14	1793.88	2319.05
	Year	19	2009	5.50	2000	2018

(continued)

Table 13.4 (continued)

Sector	Variable	Obs	Mean	Std. Dev.	Min	Max
Construction	Number of persons employed by occupation by industry	133	39222.56	74788.58	1800.00	310500.00
	Compensation of employees by industry	19	135.50	25.51	99.10	180.80
	Gross value added by industry	19	8905.59	4516.71	3313.80	18085.79
	Unemployment rate by industry	19	6.06	2.88	2.87	10.75
	Population aged between 15 and 19 years	19	599.29	60.42	525.50	720.54
	Population aged 65 years or over	19	2099.93	156.22	1793.88	2319.05
	Year	19	2009	5.50	2000	2018
Trade, hotels and restaurants, transport and communication	Number of persons employed by occupation by industry	152	161665.80	157523.60	24500.00	666100.00
	Compensation of employees by industry	19	108.64	10.44	86.50	126.00
	Gross value added by industry	19	48714.87	7530.40	39716.00	64978.00
	Unemployment rate by industry	19	25.52	2.73	20.55	28.82
	Population aged between 15 and 19 years	19	599.29	60.39	525.50	720.54
	Population aged 65 years or over	19	2099.93	156.14	1793.88	2319.05
	Year	19	2009	5.50	2000	2018

(continued)

Table 13.4 (continued)

Sector	Variable	Obs	Mean	Std. Dev.	Min	Max
Financial, real estate, renting, and business activities	Number of persons employed by occupation by industry	152	50648.03	52184.69	1500.00	182400.00
	Compensation of employees by industry	19	136.83	26.13	105.20	182.30
	Gross value added by industry	19	7722.27	1410.97	5317.82	9774.65
	Unemployment rate by industry	19	5.49	1.34	2.52	7.12
	Population aged between 15 and 19 years	19	599.29	60.39	525.50	720.54
	Population aged 65 years or over	19	2099.93	156.14	1793.88	2319.05
	Year	19	2009	5.50	2000	2018
Other service activities	Number of persons employed by occupation by industry	190	106285.30	115110.70	1000.00	434800.00
	Compensation of employees by industry	19	118.54	20.85	87.05	148.90
	Gross value added by industry	19	75408.90	14074.50	46525.00	99591.00
	Unemployment rate by industry	19	12.61	2.26	7.97	15.57
	Population aged between 15 and 19 years	19	599.29	60.35	525.50	720.54
	Population aged 65 years or over	19	2099.93	156.04	1793.88	2319.05
	Year	19	2009	5.49	2000	2018

Source: Data research

Table 13.5 Correlations of employment share between sectors

		1	2	3	4	5	6
1	*Agriculture, forestry, and fishing*	1.000					
2	*Industry including energy*	0.458	1.000				
3	*Construction*	0.023	0.828	1.000			
4	*Trade, hotels and restaurants, transport and communication*	−0.441	−0.843	−0.857	1.000		
5	*Financial, real estate, renting, and business activities*	−0.558	−0.975	−0.786	0.851	1.000	
6	*Other service activities*	−0.685	−0.936	−0.660	0.765	0.937	1.000

Table 13.6 Variable definition

Variables	Description	Variable name
1	Number of persons employed by occupation by industry	*logpro*
2	Compensation of employees by industry	*logcoben*
3	Gross value added by industry	*logaddedvalue*
4	Unemployment rate by industry	*logunempl*
5	Population aged between 15 and 19 years	*logunder*
6	Population aged 65 years or over	*logabove*
7	Time trend	*year*

For the study's purposes, the following model is used :

$$y_{ijt} = b_0 + h_i + \delta t + x'_{kit}\beta_i + \varepsilon_{it} \tag{13.1}$$

We define the dependent variable ***logpro***$_{ijt}$ as the *log* of the number of persons employed in occupation *i* in sector *j* at time *t*.

Where ***i***=*(1,2,..,10)* the categories of professions,***j***=*(1,2,..,6)* the main sectors of the economy, ***k***=*(1,2,3)* the explanatory variables, ***and t*** =(2000, 2001,. . . ,2017) the time period of the data. Therefore, occupation-sector combinations are 60.

The error term (disturbances) ε_{it} covers the effect of random factors that change both over time and from category to category of a profession.

We assume the presence of unobserved effects at the occupational category across sectors level and, allowing for the inclusion of random deviations (effects) other than those associated with the overall error, we estimate these parameters (the coefficients of the variables), treating them as random variables different for each occupational category. The first step is to determine the model that best fits the data. Our work aims to take advantage of each of the explanatory variables' contribution in determining employment for each category of occupation in each economic sector. This contribution is represented by the coefficients, b_{ki}*'s*, in the model. However, the variables included in the model representing the conditional effects, together with the error terms, cannot fully describe the systematic differences between employment levels in each occupational category across sectors. The possibility of including additional variables is not an option since our goal is to keep the model as simple as possible, given the difficulty of finding relevant data. There were a few alternatives for deriving the coefficients' estimates; mixed fixed and random coefficient modeling was considered the best practice. Another alternative could be to consider the b_{ki}*'s* as fixed and different for each occupation category by sector. In this case, the pattern coincides with that of Zellner's seemingly unrelated regression framework (Zellner, 1962). However, to conclude about the characteristics of the number of occupation categories and sectors, we consider each category's different coefficients to represent a random effect for the specific population. The coefficients (as random variables) are unrelated to the explanatory variables. Therefore, the mixed fixed and random coefficient model is the most appropriate for the study's purposes.

Conclusively, we allow the coefficients b_{ki}*'s* to vary between occupational categories by treating them as random variables consisting of two parts. The first part is the common mean of the specific category's coefficients, while the second part is represented by random factors with constant variation and an expected value of zero.

Therefore the coefficients b_{ki} will have the following form:

$$\boldsymbol{\beta_{ki}} = \boldsymbol{b_k} + \boldsymbol{\alpha_{ki}} \tag{13.2}$$

Where $\boldsymbol{b_k}$: the coefficient of the $\boldsymbol{k}$ explanatory variable common within sectors and occupations.

$\boldsymbol{\alpha_{ki}}$: the variable part of the coefficient as a random variable with zero mean, constant variance, and covariance unrelated to the explanatory variables.

The model should have the following form (model 5):

$$\begin{aligned} logpro_{ijt} =& b_0 + \delta t + \left(b_1 logcoben_{it} + b_2 logaddedvalue_{it} + b_3 logunempl_{it}\right. \\ & \left. + b_4 logaddedvalue_{it} + b_5 logunempl_{it}\right) + \left(h_i + \alpha_{1,\iota} logcoben_{it}\right. \\ & + \alpha_{2,\iota} logaddedvalue_{it} + \alpha_{3,\iota} logunempl_{it} + \alpha_{4,\iota} logaddedvalue_{it} \\ & \left. + \alpha_{5,\iota} logunempl_{it} + u_{sit}\right) \end{aligned} \tag{13.3}$$

Along with the estimation of model 5, we will estimate the corresponding simpler model that does not allow heterogeneity in the effects of explanatory variables using the maximum likelihood estimation method. Then we apply the appropriate test for heterogeneity in the effects:

$$\begin{aligned} logpro_{ijt} = & b_0 + \delta t + b_1 logcoben_{it} + b_2 logaddedvalue_{it} + b_3 logunempl_{it} \\ & + b_4 logaddedvalue_{it} + b_5 logunempl_{it} + u_{sit} \end{aligned} \tag{13.4}$$

As mentioned above, the estimation period was initially for the years 2000–2016. The period 2017–2018 will be the period of testing the model's forecast performance. We notice that the limited availability of data does not allow for further increases in the validation period. Then we will get the estimates of independent variables with the methods that we will describe in the next section. Having these estimates available, we will then proceed to the last stage of our work regarding the forecast (out of sample) of employment per occupation category per sector of activity. In detail, Table 13.7 presents the estimates of models 5 and 6.

From the two models, comparison based on the Loglikelihood statistic's value, we found that model 5 is appropriate for testing our hypotheses. More specifically, the difference *−2Loglikelihood (6) −2Loglikelihood (5)* = *−2 (−363.03) − 2(−237.24)* = *251.26* that follows a χ^2 distribution with 6 degrees of freedom,

Table 13.7 Estimations of models 5 and 6

Depended variable: ***logpro****$_{ijt}$*, *the natural logarithm of the number of employees in occupationiin sectorjat timet*

	Model 5				*Model 6*			
Panel A	*Coef.*	*Std.Err.*	*z*	*P>|z|*	*Coef.*	*Std.Err.*	*z*	*P>|z|*
logcoben	0.388	0.129	3.000	0.003	0.361	0.092	3.910	0.000
logaddval	0.266	0.111	2.400	0.017	0.357	0.055	6.510	0.000
logunempl	0.334	0.101	3.320	0.001	0.366	0.059	6.260	0.000
logunder	−1.421	0.718	−1.980	0.048	−1.454	1.158	−1.260	0.209
logabove	−0.603	0.569	−1.060	0.290	−0.330	0.928	−0.360	0.722
year	−0.006	0.008	−0.780	0.437	−0.003	0.013	−0.200	0.838
constant	46.628	22.587	2.060	0.039	35.286	37.256	0.950	0.344
Panel BRandom-effects Parameters	***Estimate***	***Std. Err***			***Estimate***	***Std. Err***		
var (logcoben)	0.460	0.136						
var (logaddval)	0.288	0.110						
var (logunempl)	0.183	0.075						
var (logunder)	1.400	0.364						
var (logabove)	1.015	0.278						
var(year)	0.000	0.000						
var(Residual)	0.034	0.002			0.325	0.008		
Loglikelihood :	−237.24				−363.03			
AIC	443.62				742.01			
BIC	508.89				783.97			

Notes: Panel A presents estimations of the fixed part of the model, while Panel B estimations of the random parameters

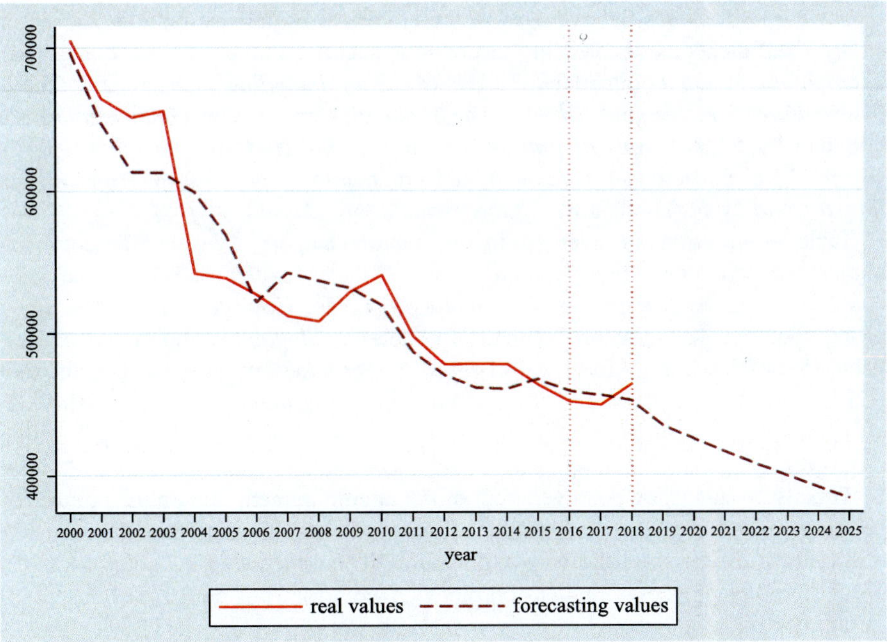

Fig. 13.3 Agriculture, forestry, and fishing

which are the additional parameters for the model (5), i.e., variances of the coefficients, is statistically significant that leads us to the conclusion that model (5) fits better our data. Additionally, the other two model selection criteria, AIC and BIC, also indicate that model (5) provides an improved fit compared to model (6). The proportion of variance between occupation and sector-specific depended variable explained by the variability in coefficients can be computed by comparing the two models' residual variances. The residual variance for models (6) and (5) is 0.325 and 0.034, respectively. The residual variance explained by introducing random effects in slopes at the firm level is *89.5% (= (0.325–0.034)/0.325).*

Based on the estimates of the fixed part of the model, we conclude that the coefficients of the variables *logcoben, logaddval, logunempl,* and *logunder* are found statistically significant at CI 95%. The *trend*, as well as the *logabove* coefficients, are found statistically insignificant. When we refit the model excluding the two variables with insignificant z-statistic, we did not receive substantially better performance in terms of overall model fit statistics, e.g., BIC and AIC.

To ensure reliable results, we examine the behavior of the error terms plotting current versus lagged residuals (Fig. 13.3). The plot did not display correlation patterns. Hence, we do not consider the autocorrelation structure of the error terms.

Table 13.8 includes the averages of the empirical Bayes[1] estimations by sector of b_{kj}, coefficients as denoted in the previous section. The elasticities concerning unemployment are bounded by 19.1% (*Industry including energy*) and 55.6% (*Agriculture, forestry, and fishing*). The elasticities concerning *compensation* are bounded by 52.0% (*construction sector*) and 16.3% (*Industry including energy sector*). The elasticities for *value added* are bounded by −13.3% (*Agriculture, forestry, and fishing*) and 58.6% (*Industry including energy*).

Table 13.9 presents the averages by occupation category of $b_{k,i}$, coefficients. The highest elasticity concerning *logunder* (−21.4%) is estimated for *Service and sales workers* while the lowest for *Managers* (−314.0%). However, in the *Managers* profession, the elasticity of occupation concerning *logabove* shows the highest value (58.4%), while in *Service and sales workers,* the lowest value is estimated (−147.3%). The elasticities of occupation concerning *logaddvalue* are positive in all occupation categories though in *Service and sales workers* category negative (−6.0%).

The results suggest a positive effect of the unemployment rate on the number of people employed in all sectors of the economy. Using the term "Greek paradox", this study provides the following explanation. The undeclared economy includes unregistered employees without a contract who work for a business, for a household, as family members, private tutors, or as farm workers. They may be Greek citizens, legal immigrants, or immigrants with irregular status, and the movement from undeclared to registered employment is a "gray area" that influences statistical analysis. Moreover, according to the Diagnostic report on undeclared work in Greece (ILO, 2016), there are problems with the estimates of the undeclared economy in Greece; there are very few data sources, leading to inconsistent estimates about the undeclared work rates. Hence, the shift from undeclared to registered employment along with the inconsistency of the estimates about real undeclared employment, add bias to statistical inference.

According to the study's analysis, and in line with CEDEFOP (2020), employment in the Greek agricultural sector is expected to decline significantly in recent years. Moreover, our results indicate a negative correlation between value-added and the number of employees in the agricultural sector. The relationship can be interpreted as follows: The family nature of the agricultural sector in Greece also determines the employment structure for the self-employed and employees. Besides, employment in the Greek agricultural sector remains directly linked to the population's retention in rural areas, especially in mountainous and disadvantaged areas. Also, increasing industrial wages attract low-paid or underemployed labor from agriculture into manufacturing while nonagricultural productivity increases

[1] The Bayes predictor of sector and category-specific slopes is a weighted average between the least square estimators of $b_{k,s}$ and the overall mean b_k ($k = 1, \ldots, 5$) and is different from the classical sampling approach predictors (least square estimators). Moreover, in the Bayesian approach, prior probability distributions are introduced for the parameters as a part of the model (see, Hsiao & Pesaran, 2004).

Table 13.8 Averages of the estimations of employment elasticities across sectors

Sector	Coefficients				
	Logunempl	Logaddval	Logcoben	Logunder	Logabove
Agriculture, forestry, and fishing	55.6%	−13.3%	47.5%	−147.5%	−35.6%
Industry including energy	19.1%	58.6%	16.3%	−165.2%	−49.1%
Construction	36.6%	38.8%	52.0%	−157.3%	−61.1%
Trade, hotels and restaurants, transport and communication	33.3%	37.1%	40.6%	−143.5%	−62.4%
Financial, real estate, renting, and business activities	37.2%	9.1%	25.0%	−79.4%	−111.7%
Other service activities	28.8%	17.9%	52.9%	−159.3%	−38.0%

Source: Data research

Table 13.9 Averages of the estimations of employment elasticities across occupation categories

Occupation	Coefficients				
	Logunempl	Logaddvalue	Logcoben	Logunder	Logabove
Managers	33.3%	82.0%	112.0%	−314.0%	58.4%
Professionals	49.2%	17.8%	2.1%	−56.7%	−134.0%
Technicians and associate professionals	39.6%	37.9%	53.4%	−150.4%	−66.5%
Clerical support workers	29.6%	40.3%	25.7%	−151.3%	−51.5%
Service and sales workers	47.6%	−6.0%	−28.0%	−21.4%	−147.3%
Skilled agricultural, forestry, and fishery workers	6.7%	5.9%	110.5%	−222.6%	25.0%
Craft and related trades workers	21.8%	26.6%	35.8%	−164.2%	−31.6%
Plant and machine operators and assemblers	23.7%	0.4%	25.8%	−136.4%	−46.9%
Elementary occupations	33.0%	18.0%	47.6%	−96.4%	−105.3%
Occupations not possible to classify	45.1%	23.9%	7.1%	−89.7%	−105.4%

Source: Data research

played a larger role than agricultural productivity in overall reallocations of labor out of agriculture (Alvarez-Cuadrado & Poschke, 2011). Internal migration to urban centers in search of employment in combination with the predominance of only large agricultural firms may lead on the one hand to higher value-added due to intensification and modernization of agricultural production and, on the other hand, to a reduction of self-employed and employees.

13.4.2 Out of Sample Forecasting

Since the purpose is to make future predictions for the dependent variable, estimates for the five dependent variables' future values for the six sectors should be provided. These values are then used in the estimated regression model, and the predicted values of the dependent variable are obtained. The model to forecast the explanatory variables' future values is the following (Holt's linear exponential smoothing method, see e.g., Gardner, 2006; Hyndman & Athanasopoulos, 2018). This method assumes two smoothing constants a and b (lie in the interval 0 and 1), and three equations:

$$\hat{y}_{it} = L_{i,t-1} + T_{i,t-1}$$

$$L_{i,t} = \alpha . y_{it} + (1 - a) . \left(L_{i,t-1} + T_{i,t-1}\right)$$

$$T_{i,t} = \beta . \left(L_{it} - L_{i,t-1}\right) + (1 - \beta) . T_{i,t-1}$$

Where L_t denotes the estimate of the level of the series at time t and T_t denotes an estimate of the slope of the series at time t. $\hat{y}_{it}$ is the forecast value at time t and is point forecast of the explanatory variables. Holt's linear method does not permit the calculation of prediction intervals. However, prediction intervals can be obtained from the equivalent ARIMA (0,2,2) method (Makridakis et al., 1998). An iterative process chooses the values of α and β constants to minimize the in-sample sum-of-squared prediction errors. As mentioned above, values for the last two years of the data held out for validation, while the data used to estimate the model's parameters are for 15 years. To evaluate the model's forecasting performance, we compare the mean absolute error (MAE) of the forecast errors in the validation period with those in the estimation period. The formula of MAE and the results are:

$$MAE = \frac{1}{jn} \sum_{1}^{j} \sum_{1}^{n} \left| \log \hat{pro}_{jn} - \log pro_{jn} \right|$$

Where n denotes the years within the validation and estimation period.

Table 13.10 Comparison of the mean absolute error (MAE) for the validation and estimation period

Period	MAE
Estimation period	0.1160
Validation period	0.1483

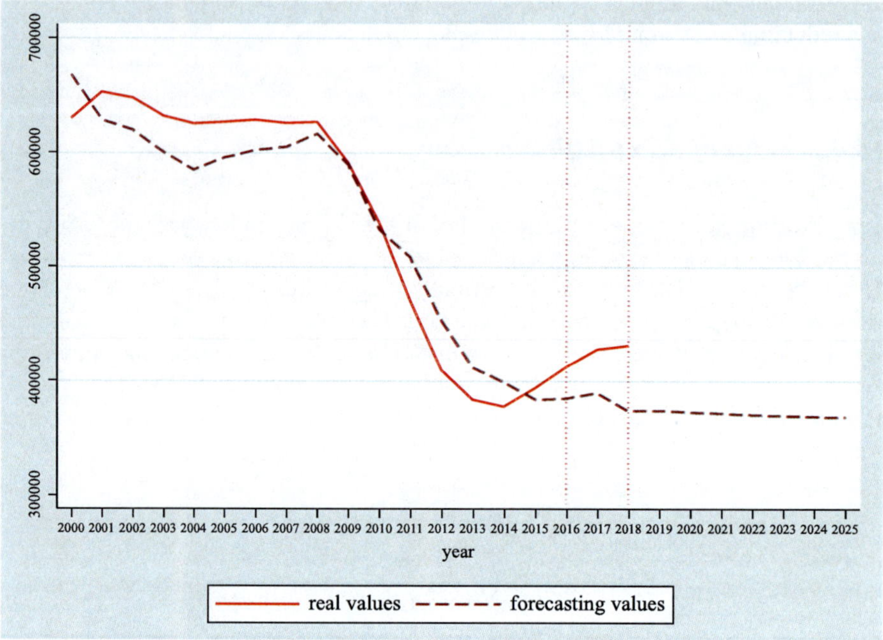

Fig. 13.4 Industry including energy

According to the results presented in Table 13.10, MAE for the validation period, although higher, is not alarming. Hence, our model provides a satisfactory fit to the data. However, as we already noticed, running separate models to obtain a more accurate forecast for independent variables will improve model performance.

Figures 13.3, 13.4, 13.5, 13.6, 13.7 and 13.8 below depict plots of the number of employees by sector over the estimation period (2000–2015). For comparison, at the same figures, the forecasts of the number of employees by sector are plotted.

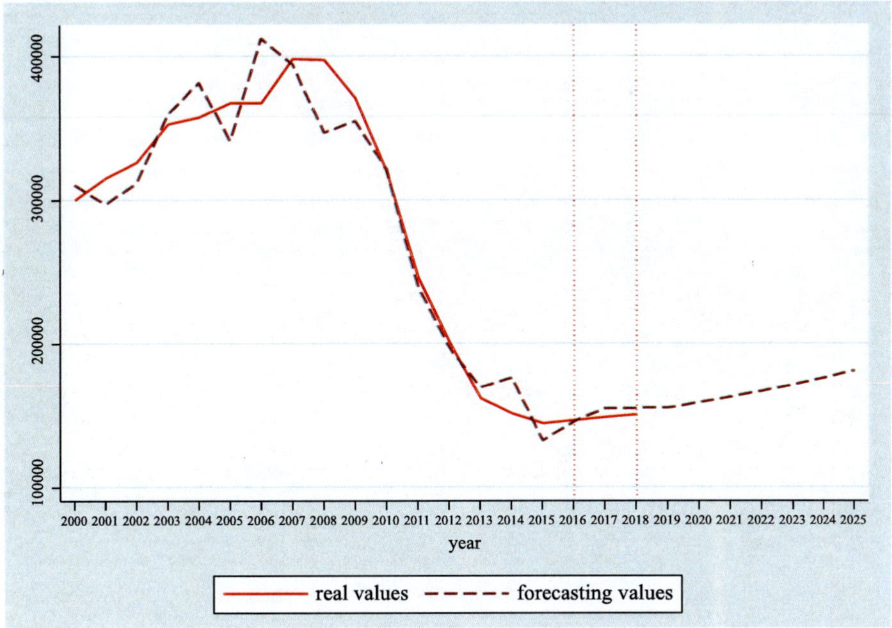

Fig. 13.5 Construction

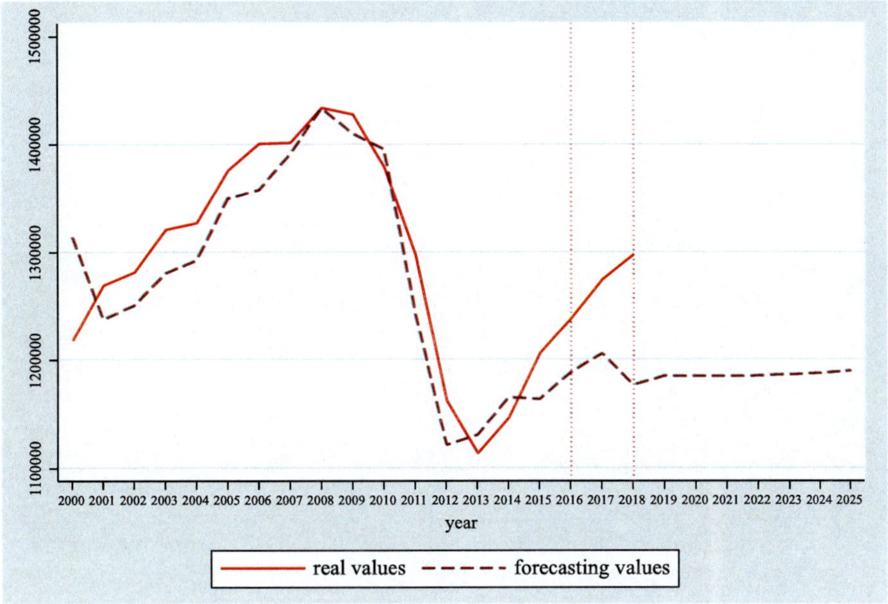

Fig. 13.6 Trade, hotels and restaurants, transport and communication

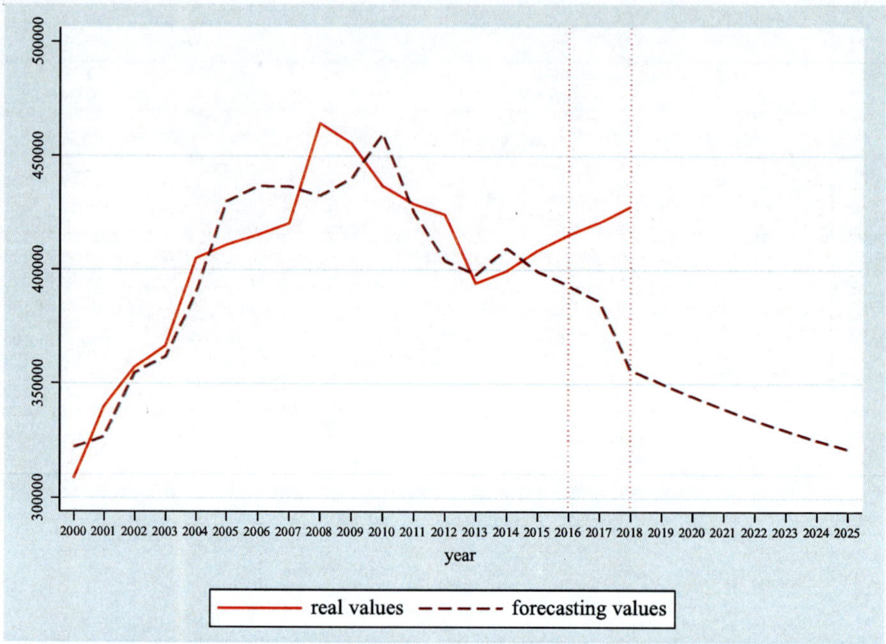

Fig. 13.7 Financial, real estate, renting, and business activities

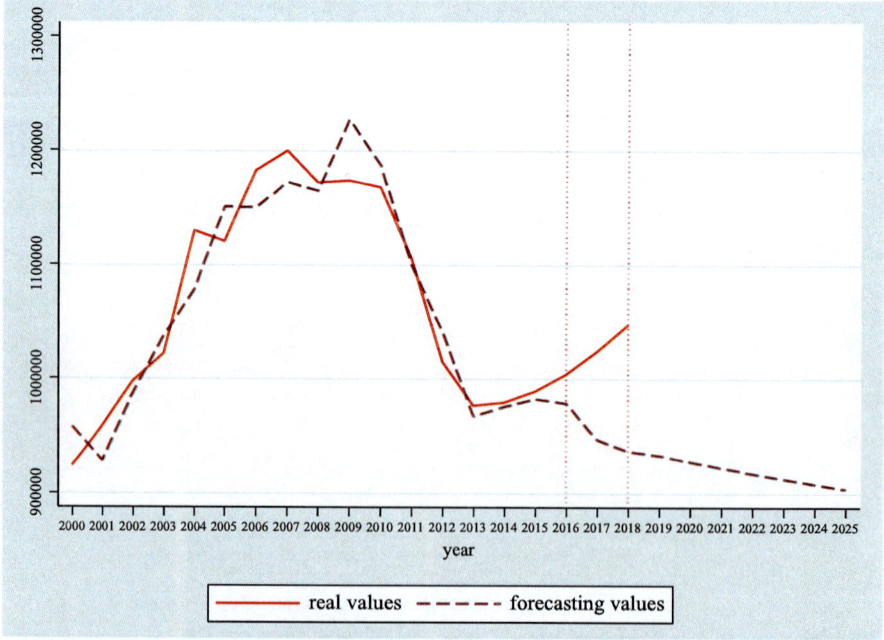

Fig. 13.8 Other service activities

13.5 Conclusion

In this paper, we use random coefficient modeling on panel data to analyze and investigate sectoral and occupational employment as well as to assess the impact of important determinants on employment behavior across sectors of economic activity and their respective occupational structures. More specifically, using annual data for employment over the period from 2000 to 2018 for six main sectors and ten occupational categories of the Greek labor market, we apply mixed fixed and random coefficient techniques to analyze the impact of certain variables on the employment by occupational category across the main sectors of the economy. The econometric modeling considers six explanatory variables; unemployment, gross value added, employee compensation; two variables, one for the total population size of citizens aged between 15 and 19 years old and another for the number of people aged 65 and above; and the time trend.

Our results confirm that the random coefficient panel data framework's estimations outperform the estimators that consider common slopes, avoid heterogeneity bias, and correctly estimate the dependent variable and the heteroscedastic variances of the random effects' main sectors of the economy and also by profession category. We find that the elasticity of the number of employees in the Greek economy's main sectors concerning unemployment, gross value added, compensation, and participation rate varies widely across sectors and occupational categories. Regarding the sign of the explanatory variables and especially of the unemployment variable, the following unexpected relationship was found: The impact of the unemployment rate on the number of employees in all sectors of the economy is positive. A possible explanation for this paradox may be the recorded shift of undeclared to registered employment in the Greek labor market, along with the inconsistency of competent authorities and bodies' estimates about real undeclared employment.

Testing the forecasting performance of the model, we perceive reasonable prediction accuracy. However, our model's forecasting ability may be improved if the exploratory variables' future values are derived using separate econometric models.

References

Alvarez-Cuadrado, F., & Poschke, M. (2011). Structural change out of agriculture: Labor push versus labor pull. *American Economic Journal: Macroeconomics, 3*(3), 127–158.

Bishop, J. (1997). *Is an oversupply of college graduates coming?* NCPI – National Center for Postsecondary Improvement (508 CERAS).

Bishop, J., & Carter, S. (1991). The worsening shortage of college-graduate workers. *Educational Evaluation and Policy Analysis, 13*, 221–246.

Bresson, G., Hsiao, C., & Pirotte, A. (2006). *Heteroskedasticity and random coefficient model on panel data* (No. 0601)..

Briscoe, G., & Wilson, R. (2003). Modelling UK occupational employment. *International Journal of Manpower, 24*(5), 568–589.

Cedefop. (2020). Future employment growth in *Greece* in 2020–2030 across sectors. https://skillspanorama.cedefop.europa.eu/en/sources#cedefop

Cörvers, F., & Dupuy, A. (2010). Estimating employment dynamics across occupations and sectors of industry. *Journal of Macroeconomics, 32*(1), 17–27.

Foster-McGregor, N., & Pöschl, J. (2009). *The importance of labour mobility for spillovers across industries* (No. 58). wiiw Working Paper.

Frees, E. W., & Miller, T. W. (2004). Sales forecasting using longitudinal data models. *International Journal of Forecasting, 20*(1), 99–114.

Gardner, E. S., Jr. (2006). Exponential smoothing: The state of the art—Part II. *International journal of forecasting, 22*(4), 637–666.

Goldstein, H. (1995). Hierarchical data modeling in the social sciences. *Journal of Educational and Behavioral Statistics, 20*(2), 201–204.

Hsiao, C. (2014). *Analysis of panel data* (No. 54). Cambridge University Press.

Hsiao, C., & Pesaran, M. H. (2004). *Random coefficient panel data models*. CESifo Working Paper Series No. 1233; IZA Discussion Paper No. 1236; IEPR Working Paper No. 04.2.

Hughes, G. (1993). *Projecting the occupational structure of employment in OECD countries* (No. 10). OECD Publishing.

Hyndman, R. J., & Athanasopoulos, G. (2018). *Forecasting: principles and practice*. OTexts.

Ignaczak, L. (2017). Projecting labour market needs in Canada: The COPS national model after 30 years. *Human Resources and Skills Development Canada, Ottawa, viewed, 27.*

International Labour Office (ILO), *World Employment and Social Outlook: Trends* 2016. Geneva.

Lacey, T. A., Toossi, M., Dubina, K. S., & Gensler, A. B. (2017). Projections overview and highlights, 2016–26. *Monthly Labor Review, 140*, 1.

Maier, T., Mönnig, A., & Zika, G. (2015). Labour demand in GERMANY by industrial sector, occupational field and qualification until 2025 – Model calculations using the IAB/INFORGE model. *Economic Systems Research, 27*(1), 19–42. https://doi.org/10.1080/09535314.2014.997678

Maier, T., Neuber-Pohl, C., Mönnig, A., Zika, G., & Kalinowski, M. (2017). Modelling reallocation processes in long-term labour market projections. *Journal for Labour Market Research, 50*(1), 67–90.

Makridakis, S., Wheelwright, S. C., & Hyndman, R. J. (1998). *Forecasting methods and applications* (3rd ed.). John wiley & sons.

Mark, N. C., Ogaki, M., & Sul, D. (2005). Dynamic seemingly unrelated cointegrating regressions. *The Review of Economic Studies, 72*(3), 797–820.

Rabe-Hesketh, S., & Skrondal, A. (2008). *Multilevel and longitudinal modeling using Stata.* STATA press.

Spalletti, S., 2008, *The history of manpower forecasting in modelling labour market*, Working Papers, 18–2008, Macerata University, Department of Studies on Economic Development (DiSSE)

Stock, J. H., & Watson, M. W. (1993). A simple estimator of cointegrating vectors in higher order integrated systems. *Econometrica: Journal of the Econometric Society*, 783–820.

Toossi, M. (2011). A behavioral model for projecting the labor force participation rate. *Monthly Lab. Rev., 134*, 25.

Weber, E., & Zika, G. (2016). Labour market forecasting in Germany: Is disaggregation useful? *Applied Economics, 48*(23), 2183–2198.

Wilson, R. A. (2001). *Projections of occupations and qualifications, 2000/2001*. Department of Education and Skills, IER, University of Warwick, Coventry.

Zellner, A. (1962). An efficient method of estimating seemingly unrelated regressions and tests for aggregation bias. *Journal of the American Statistical Association, 57*(298), 348–368.

Chapter 14
Cognitive/Emotional Errors and Financial Education

Anastasios D. Konstantinidis, Spinthiropoulos Konstantinos, Garefalakis Alexandros, and Hara Haritaki

Abstract Behavioral Finance has already become the new theoretical financial paradigm. Based on other disciplines, such as psychology, sociology, and philosophy, it comes to fill in the gaps of the Efficient Market theory by studying and interpreting the behavior of people who are involved in the stock market, and, thus, discover the reasons for wrong investment choices and financial anomalies resulting from such activities.

The research carried out on a sample of students attending additional degree upgrading courses demonstrates that the subjects, who are also going to be prospective investors and stock market professionals, are vulnerable to cognitive and emotional errors.

Keywords Cognitive errors · Emotional errors · Behavioral finance · Efficient market theory

A. D. Konstantinidis (✉)
School of Economic Sciences, Department of Accounting and Finance, University of Western Macedonia, Kozani, Greece
e-mail: ankonstantinidis@uowm.gr

S. Konstantinos
School of Economic Sciences, Department of Management Science and Technology, University of West Macedonia, Kozani, Greece
e-mail: kspinthiropoulos@uowm.gr

G. Alexandros
School of Economic Sciences, School of Management and Economics Sciences, Department of Business Administration and Tourism, Kozani, Greece
e-mail: agarefalakis@hmu.gr

H. Haritaki
School of Economic Sciences, School of Management and Economics Sciences, Department of Accounting and Finance, Kozani, Greece
e-mail: haritaki@hmu.gr

N. Tsounis, A. Vlachvei (eds.), *Advances in Quantitative Economic Research*, Springer Proceedings in Business and Economics,
https://doi.org/10.1007/978-3-030-98179-2_14

14.1 Introduction

Behavioral Finance is the new comprehensive financial investment paradigm, which combines financial analysis with other disciplines, such as statistics, psychology, anthropology, and sociology. It aims at understanding and predicting the impact of human psychology on the market and on business decision making (Alexakis, & Xanthakis, 2008). Shefrin (2001) states that "Behavioral Finance is the study of how psychology affects financial decision making and financial markets", and Thaler (1993) defines it as "simply 'open-minded finance'".

Until the early 1990s, the dominant financial theory was the Efficient Market theory, according to which stock market investors are consistent and rational, aiming at maximizing investment utility. Rational investors are not inhibited by irrational behavior, failure, ingratitude or fear. Information is accessible to everyone, and is, in effect, integrated into securities price; it is readily available to everyone, objective and accurate. This leads to stock market equilibrium and creates a context, in which surplus value and, thus, extreme securities prices are not feasible.

By exploiting the weaknesses and gaps of the one-dimensional Efficient Market model, the Financial Behavior theory has managed to maintain a significant place in interpreting activity methods and decision-making processes in a broader financial framework, and more specifically, in the stock market.

Investors, considerably affected by emotions and biases, which hinder investment rationality and maximum gains, possess special individual traits that distinguish them from rational robots that never suffer a loss.

On the other hand, information is not always integrated in securities prices, which can be significantly incompatible with actual prices. Thus, it is not accessible to everyone and similarly interpreted, and, accordingly, not efficiently used. Investment failure is established by occasional long-standing stock market bubbles.

Accordingly, the advanced behavioral theory, relying on rather than rejecting the Efficient Market theory, offers new dimensions and perspectives within the volatile context of the stock market, and keeps it away from utopian, ideal conditions, and processes.

14.2 Heuristics and Cognitive and Emotional Errors

Contrary to the assumption of the rationality of preferences, individuals seem to acquire and process information using a limited number of intuitive or heuristic rules.

Heuristics in psychology are the simple effective rules, which are used for quick and efficient decision-making processes. Despite reducing intricacy, they may cause systematic and significant errors (Kahneman & Tversky, 1984).

Cognitive biases/errors imply cognitive errors occurring during information processing and interpretation. They are rules-of-thumb, employed to enable understanding of the world and quick decision making, which is mostly wrong. Psychology research has demonstrated that cognitive biases are related to memory, rationality, and decision making.

Emotional biases/errors are defined as distortion of cognitive function and decision making due to emotional reasons. They are part of a heuristic that affects the way events or situations are evaluated.

Evaluations are commonly affected by emotions and perceptions. Decision-making processes (either significant or not) made under emotional stress, are deprived of rationality and rely on intuitive and impulsive thinking and, ultimately, choice and decision-making errors.

Emotional errors and biases affect investment attitudes, and, consequently, financial choices. Irrational investment choices upset market efficiency.

14.3 Biases and Errors

14.3.1 Representativeness

Representativeness is a cognitive bias which involves classifying situations on the basis of previous experience or belief patterns, thus, affecting decision making.

In an attempt to integrate a new and unknown situation into an existing one, and if something does not exactly fit into a category, it is approached by employing the nearest category available.

In the context of the stock market and investments, representativeness is the investors' tendency to rely on previous experiences. When investment experience is irrationally assessed, investors assume that success and gains will be long-lasting.

Predictable gains rely on interpreting recent previously made gains, by employing representativeness (Shleife, 2000).

In this framework, the conjunction fallacy is also a stereotype and representativeness fallacy (Tversky & Kahneman, 1983), which takes place when two events occurring together or separately are more likely to occur together, as, in case people are asked to compare, they believe that conjunction is more probable (Tversky & Kahneman, 1983). It is substantially a reasoning fallacy, diverging from rationality and wise rational investment choices generated by impulsive rather than deliberate thinking.

14.3.2 Herd Behavior

Herd behavior or herd psychology is typical of acting and behaving without much deliberation or plan, like a herd, imitating other people's behavior.

It is a most interesting phenomenon in economics describing people's psychological propensity to herd rather than follow their own beliefs or perceptions, particularly, when threatened (Tariq et al., 2013). It is also an adaptive, protective mechanism, an integral part of human nature (Alexakis & Xanthakis, 2008), also described as an emulating behavior arising from specific factors frequently leading to ineffective situations (Bikhchandani & Sharma, 1992).

The two major reasons accounting for compliance with a group's beliefs and choices involve, first, people's wish to be accepted by a group with different views or opinions and, second, a commonly accepted conviction that the majority cannot be wrong.

Herding in investing processes can also be defined as the behavior of a group of investors following the same investment plan/pattern over a period of time (Nofsinger & Sias, 1998), especially under uncertainty.

This causes a stock market contagion (Cipriani & Guarino, 2008) and is considered a threat to stock market functions, likely to lead to stock imbalance or stock bubbles and bankruptcy (Boortz et al., 2013).

14.3.3 *Overconfidence*

Overconfidence involves people's tendency to overestimate their skills and abilities. According to Cheng (2007), it is a typical behavior reflecting overestimation of abilities, chances, and control for success and outcomes, as well as knowledge accuracy.

Overconfidence is a common bias in capital market investing processes. Barben and Odean (2001) maintain that investors are as overconfident about their abilities as about forecasts (Shefrin, 2001).

Although they believe they are knowledgeable, well-informed and capable, they are unable to make further improvements and correct assessments. In addition, in case of failure, they do not seem to learn from wrong, irrational behavior, as they consider that always other people make irrational decisions and choices, not themselves.

Overconfident investors consider that their qualifications, knowledge, and skills are superior to those of other people's. By being arrogant and overestimating themselves, they become conceited and contemptuous; this often leads to irrational behavior and investment failure.

14.3.4 *Loss Aversion*

Loss aversion is people's tendency to strongly prefer avoiding losses to gains. People hate loss more than they enjoy success and they make decisions and plan strategies accordingly.

The fundamental principle of loss aversion, which can explain why penalties are sometimes more effective than rewards in motivating individuals (Gächter et al., 2009), has been applied to behavioral change strategies.

In the context of the stock market, loss averse investors either make investments based on previous returns, or follow a conservative riskless investment plan. In addition, they take greater risks to balance them with higher expected returns (Thaler et al., 1997).

On the other hand, stock market investors commonly sell profitable securities very soon and hold loss-making ones longer. Fearing for a new failure, they follow a more conventional investment policy of investment uncertainty, and hold portfolios until loss-making securities recover. Thus, they miss opportunities for a fast and greatest recovery, by restructuring current portfolios.

Fear for a new loss overrides investment rational behavior perceived in neutral attitudes toward emotion and bias.

14.3.5 Framing

Framing includes a set of concepts and theoretical perspectives in terms of how individuals and societies organize, perceive, and communicate reality. Perceptions, decision making, and investing processes are framed.

The term "frame" implies that the way people behave is affected by the way the problems they are called upon to decide are framed – presented (Shefrin, 2001; Zhen et al., 2020). It also encompasses the context, perspectives, and received information.

Framing defies the traditional financial theory of rational choice, which assumes independence of the problem frame of reference (frame independence).

In terms of investments, especially in periods of uncertainty and time pressure, under which investors are called to make investment decisions, framing is employed to facilitate event understanding and management.

In addition, investors manage events with a view to deriving the greatest pleasure and satisfaction rather than gains, thus, seeking maximum personal happiness rather than utility.

A major problem with regard to framing is information-based manipulation. Information processing based on individual perceptions can result in varied investment options. Investors are commonly misled by half-truth and by constantly highlighting and suppressing or underestimating negative outcomes.

14.4 Criticism of Behavioral Finance

Criticism has been focused on the fact that the effects of behavior are empirical (Hirshleifer, 2001; Giannarakis et al., 2011; Lemonakis et al., 2016).

Major criticism is leveled at the fact that the new theory is impossible to rely on psychological factors and biases characterized by instability and unable to be verified in scientific-economic terms.

However, empirical research in behavioral finance takes place under conditions very similar to or identical with real life, which asserts its higher validity based on randomized group control and testing (Thaler, 1999a, b; Huddart & Abdullah, 2018; Nofsinger et al., 2020).

According to Shiller (2003), price fluctuations cannot be explained only by the fundamental magnitudes of the market, but must be also interpreted in terms of other considerations, such as investor psychology and mood.

In addition, the empirical findings of behavioral finance have been established both in longitudinal and cross-sectional surveys (investment behavior of different investor profiles over a period of time) in a number of countries (Subrahmanyam, 2008; Gupta & Bhduri, 2019; Giannarakis et al., 2017a, b).

Proponents of the new theory have frequently highlighted the fact that research may not absolutely comply with scientific findings, as psychology, emotion, and bias may not always conform to scientific principles. They are indicators, or short-term trends, as emotions are changeable and differently shaped at times. However, they enable demonstrating and validating current trends in the market at a specific time.

14.5 The Research

Research sampling was based on the answers given by Accounting and Finance students of the former TEI of Western Macedonia, who wished to upgrade their awarded degree, by attending six additional courses, among which a course in Behavioral Finance.

Notably, the participating students, who had been taught about stock market issues, but never before about the new financial behavioral theory, will be future investors or market professionals, and those who will affect customers' decisions and market equilibrium.

The research took place during the first week of course sessions, after the first introductory session and more specifically, from 23/2/2021 to 1/3/2021. Of the total number of 106 students who had registered in the new degree upgrading course, 67 (i.e., 63%) answered the survey questionnaire.

In detail, of the 67 participating students, 38 were female aged 23–30 (74.5%). Overall, the subjects' background in stock market issues was fairly good (52%), and good (19.4%); 40% of the subjects stated that they were likely to work in the stock market, whereas 38% of them definitely wished to work there.

The questionnaire includes closed-ended questions, drawn from previous research in behavioral finance. Apart from personal detail and framing questions, the questionnaire includes questions on a scale from one to nine. Large nine- and ten-item scales have been frequently applied by a variety of scholars (Derek & Tanniru, 2000; Vavra, 1997; Bachmann, 2018; Calma, 2018; Grezo, 2020).

In addition, it is characterized by high content validity, as it includes the various dimensions of each concept or measured variables. It consists of problem–/test-like questions, indirectly attempting to approach a specific behavior; straightforward questions were avoided for fear of deriving negative answers.

The questions are tailored to the participating students' profile, course content, and interests of the specific age group to which they belong. They also include common concepts so as not to influence the subjects' choices.

Regarding the questionnaire reliability (Cronbach alpha >0.7 reliable research), it is demonstrated that the specific index can be applied to research questionnaires employing factor analysis. In the present research, no further analysis of the data is possible, as there is no factor correlation.

14.6 Research Results

14.6.1 Representativeness and Conjunction Fallacy

Representativeness is a heuristic rule, according to which people try to find common elements between the projected perspectives and those they can recall, or they consider that random possibilities are representative of specific situations. The conjunction fallacy is a fallacy of stereotypes and representativeness (Tversky and Kahneman, 1983), when two concurrent or separate events are more likely to occur together than separately.

The subjects were asked to answer the question:

> *Linda is 31 years old, single, outspoken and bright. She majored in philosophy, and as a student she was deeply concerned with racial discrimination and social justice, and also participated in anti-nuclear demonstrations.*
>
> *Which is more probable? Linda is a bank teller and is active in the feminist movement, or Linda is a bank teller?*
>
> *On a scale from 1 to 9, where 9 is "Linda is more probable to be a bank teller and active in the feminist movement rather than just a bank teller", and 1 "it is more probable for Linda to be just a bank teller", state your opinion.*

The question was drawn from Tversky and Kahneman's (1983) work, "Extensional versus intuitive reasoning: The conjunction fallacy in probability judgment".

The analysis demonstrated that the majority of subjects (above 49%, if percentages for items 7, 8, and 9, and 19.4% opting for "I am absolutely sure" are added), answered that Linda is more probable to be a bank teller and active in the feminist movement.

In mathematics, the probability of two events occurring together is always less than or equal to the probability of one occurring alone. Therefore, the answers given were not irrational due to poor knowledge of mathematics, but as a result of a spontaneous, impulsive response.

The fallacy in this case is not the result of ignorance, but an impulsive decision, which, in case of investment decision making, will generate irrational outcomes.

Only 10.4% of the students were absolutely certain that Linda is just a bank teller, and 22.4% of them (total sum of percentages for options 1,2,3) gave rational rather than impulsive and calculated answers.

Even 14.9% of the students who chose option 5, the equilibrium point, made an irrational choice, as neutrality in decision-making processes is considered irrational.

14.6.2 Herding

Herding is described as people's need to join groups (herds) and be influenced in their own decision making. They tend to match the majority of decision-makers under the same circumstances (Banerjee, 1992).

The question students were asked to answer was drawn from Shiller's (2000) survey on Irrational Exuberance.

> *Suppose in the same street there are two equally nice-looking restaurants and as it is early in the afternoon, they are empty. A couple chooses to dine in Restaurant A, completely by chance. Suppose you, too, wish to dine. You walk down the same street and the two restaurants – which are unknown to you – look just as attractive. When you see in Restaurant A there are customers dining, in contrast to Restaurant B, would you choose to dine in Restaurant A?*

A percentage of 28.4% were absolutely certain that they would choose restaurant A. If options 7 and 8 are added, the percentage reaches 55%, whereas if the positive trend of the sixth option (11.9%) is also included, the percentage accounts for 67.2%.

The key words in this question are that both restaurants are unknown and just as attractive. Restaurant A is chosen, because it has already been chosen by other customers. The subjects' decisions were influenced by the decisions other people have made. Their choice, being rather impulsive than rational, is influenced by other people's decisions and demonstrates that the subjects wish to be part of a group and act accordingly.

Only 18% of the subjects chose the equilibrium point (option 5), which is the only rational answer showing no clear preference for the two restaurants. Even 15% of those who chose restaurant B make an irrational choice for no particular reason. We cannot interpret these motives (possibly agoraphobia), which also lead to an irrational decision.

In terms of investment, when decision making is based on others' decisions, then personal achievement and gains are not possible. Poor personal qualities and investment incompetence are counselors of irrationality, and in the short run, counselors of personal frustration and investment failure.

Herding is one of the most serious reasons why stock market and everyday life efficiency can be upset.

14.6.3 Overconfidence and the Above-average Effect

People's propensity to overestimate their abilities and skills is typical of overconfidence. Overconfident individuals evaluate themselves more favorably than others. This is called the above-average effect.

Based on the extant literature, a free question to investigate over-confidence rates' competencies in comparison with their average:

> *On a scale from 1 to 9, where 9 is "I absolutely believe I am above average" and 1 is "I am sure I am below average", rate your answer.*

The question is taken from Kahneman and Riepe's "Aspects of Investor Psychology" (1998).

Based on the answers, a great majority (50%, sum of percentages for options 7, 8, and 9, of which 10.4% account for the answer "I absolutely believe I am above average") consider themselves superior to others. Their abilities are overestimated compared to their fellow students, so they take their success for granted, and, obviously, they do not feel they should try harder to improve further.

Rationality concerning skills and abilities compared to those of other students accounts for 21%, and involves answers including option 5, the equilibrium point. In addition, 7% of the answers (sum of percentages for options 1, 2, and 3) demonstrate irrational underestimation of skills and abilities, as people who do not believe in themselves, cannot make the best choice, unless this reveals modesty; in this case, it is acceptable since it implies greater efforts and, therefore, success.

On the other hand, in case of arrogance, and, thus, irrational behavior, wrong choices and decisions will lead to failure.

14.6.4 Loss Aversion

It is people's tendency to prefer avoiding losses to gains. "Losses loom larger than gains" (Kahneman & Tversky, 1984). Previous gains reduce risk, whereas previous losses do not.

The question the survey subjects were asked was: *You have just lost a lot of money on gambling. Would you keep gambling in order to recover any damage or would you give up? On a scale from 1 to 9, where 9 is "I would definitely go on" and 1 is "No, I would definitely give up", rate your answer.*

The question is focused on people's choice to keep taking risks after a loss, in order to achieve a gain. It was drawn from Kahneman and Tversky's "Choice,

Values and Frames" (1983) and Bernoulli's scientific research, "Exposition of a New Theory on the Measurement of Risk" (1954).

The subjects, at first, make a decision based on an event that has already happened. About 40.3% of the answers demonstrated students' tendency to quit if they lost a large amount. The specific ratio is increased to 67.2%, if options 2 (20.9%) and 3 (6%) are summed up.

The results do not comply with those in Kahneman and Tversky (1979) and Thaler et al (1997) research, according to which past losses force investors to take greater risks.

Despite the fact that risky choices are not likely to be taken after a loss, investors tend to give up any effort rather than simply be more conservative, which demonstrates greater rationality. This results in no change, and reveals no attempt to reverse a condition; in contrast, it deteriorates it dramatically.

Neutrality, which demonstrates rational behavior, is preferred by 11.8% of the subjects, who display a neutral attitude toward a loss and, thus, toward future choices. Only 7.5% (sections 9 (1.5%), 8 (1.5%), and 7 (4.5%)), affected by a previous loss, decide to keep on taking risks to recover losses, which reveals rationally walking along dangerous paths to no avail.

Loss aversion and fear for loss or taking new risks to recover losses imply irrational investments and a new loss.

14.6.5 Framing

Framing is the most common cognitive bias, according to which, depending on how an event or perspective is presented, investment decisions are significantly affected.

The students were presented with two choices to demonstrate their attitudes toward an event:

(i) *In the European Union, two alternative programs are going to be implemented to fight the outbreak of an Asian epidemic, which is expected to cause the death of 600 people: In case of program A, 200 people will be saved, whereas in case of program B, there is a 33.3% probability that all 600 people will be saved and a 66.6% probability that no one will be saved. Which of the two programs is better to implement?*

(ii) *In the European Union, two alternative programs are going to be implemented to fight the outbreak of an Asian epidemic, which is expected to cause the death of 600 people: In case of program C, 400 people will die, whereas in case of program D, there is a 33.3% probability that no one will die and a 66.6% probability that 600 people will die. Which of the two programs is better to implement?*

The questions are adapted from Kahneman and Tversky's "Choices, Values, and Frames" (1984).

The two options are identical in both questions. In the first question, option B gives exactly the same number of people who will be saved {(33.3% ×600 + 66.6% ×0) = 200}, similar to program A, and program D (33, 3% ×0 + 66.6% ×600 = 400) is similar to program C.

Thus, opting either for program A or program B in the first case is irrational. About 80.6% of the students (46.3% chose program A and 34.3% chose program B), gave an irrational answer and only 19.4% made a rational decision by choosing "no preference".

As regards the first question, the results demonstrated that 46.3% of the respondents who chose program A were seriously affected by the phrase "will be saved". In terms of psychology, placing emphasis on those to be saved worked positively, in contrast to the phrase "no one will be saved" which worked as a deterrent. The way the problem was phrased caused a change in the subjects' decision.

As regards the second question, rational behavior, demonstrated in making no preference, accounts for 28.4%, in contrast to 71.7%, which accounts for the answers given by the subjects who, by opting for program C (44.8%) and D (26.9%), displayed irrational behavior and were emotionally affected.

Remarkably, the researched students violate the theory of utility, on which the Efficient Market theory was based. A vast majority of the subjects (80%, first question and 70%, second question) are motivated by how perspectives and data are presented rather than utility.

It is also worth noting that there was no significant change in the percentage of students who opted for program A (46%), and, subsequently, opted for C (45%), since it generated a similar result (2OO people will survive). The phrase "they will die" did not seem to have affected them in choosing answer C.

14.7 Conclusion

The present research demonstrated the weaknesses and gaps of the Efficient Market theory and the emergence of the theory of behavior as a comprehensive theoretical paradigm.

Notably, the conclusions drawn by a simple percentage analysis cannot be fully consistent as measurement of emotions – which are variable and volatile – cannot be achieved via sophisticated scientific approaches (Fama, 1998); however, it can reveal a major trend.

The analysis demonstrated that the students, who had already been familiar with financial theories and stock market issues and are expected to become stock market executives in the future, developed an irrational behavior, which was affected by psychological errors and biases. They were misled and perceived that the probability that two events occurring together is always less than or equal to the probability that either event will occur separately. Although their knowledge of mathematics and probability theories was not poor, they answered impulsively, without making informed and rational decisions. They wished to be part of a group and, thus, in order to become acceptable, they made decisions similar to others'; they are subject to irrational Herding behavior. By overestimating their abilities and skills, they believe they are superior to others. Their arrogant overconfidence does not allow them to improve and learn from errors.

They prefer to avoid losses, and, fearing for a new loss, they opt for casual and static investment policies, which are subject to neutral and irrational behaviors.

In effect, they defy the theory of utility, which was the basis of the theory of effective markets, as they make impulsive rather than utility-based choices that maximize gains.

The above discussed biases are five errors which lead to irrational behavior and prevent maximizing utility and successful efforts. When investors become aware of their import, they are likely to avoid such behavior in the future and, thus, make rational decisions.

In addition, by recognizing the significance of psychology and its effect on irrational behavior, they will be able to apply rational and effective choices.

Finally, future research carried out on a sample consisting of students previously researched, but later employed in stock market jobs, would derive interesting findings about whether the subjects could meet new requirements and conditions.

To conclude, the research demonstrated the inherent weaknesses of the Efficient Market theory, on which the model of behavioral finance is considered to be based. The behavioral paradigm emerged as complementary to already existing theoretical approaches, and, finally, became the new dominant financial paradigm.

The major research findings, drawn from a sample comprising students in a transitional stage of their studies, which involve upgrading their awarded degree (an institutionalized opportunity offered to Technological Education Institution TEI graduates after the recent TEI mergers with universities), cannot be compared with similar research, as TEI mergers took place the previous year.

Remarkably, similar research could be carried out in the near future, when interesting findings and comparisons could be more easily available. In addition, a similar research repeated in the near future using the same sample could obtain new findings as regards the subjects' decisions made in a new context.

It is worth noting that emotional and cognitive errors can change any time, depending on the individuals' psychological state, the pressure under which they have to make decisions, the overall socio-political-economic context as well as on any improvement or new method to address them, affected by new knowledge, awareness, and experience gained.

References

Books

Alexakis, C., & Xanthakis, M. (2008). *Behavioral finance*. Stamoulis Publications.

Derek, A., & Tanniru, R. (2000). *Analysis of customer satisfaction data: a comprehensive guide to multivariate statistical analysis in customer satisfaction, loyalty, and service quality research.* ASQ Quality Press, U.K.

Shiller, R. (2000). *Irrational exuberance.* Princeton University Press.

Shleifer, A. (2000). *Inefficient markets: An introduction to behavioral finance.* Clarendon Lectures in Economics.

Thaler, R. H. (1993). *Advances in behavioral finance.* New York: Russell Sage Foundation.

Vavra, T. G. (1997). *Improving your measurement of customer satisfaction: A guide to creating, conducting, analyzing, and reporting customer satisfaction measurement programs.* ASQ Quality Press.

Papers

Bachmann, K. (2018). Can advisors eliminate the outcome bias in judgements and outcome-based emotions? *Review of Behavioral Finance, 10*(4), 336–352.

Banerjee, A. (1992). A simple model of herd behavior. *Quarterly Journal of Economics, 107*(3), 797–817.

Barber, B., & Odean, T. (2001). Boys will be boys: Gender overconfidence and common stock investment. *Quarterly Journal of Economics, 116*(1), 261–292.

Bikhchandani, S., & Sharma, S. (1992). Herd behavior in financial markets: A review. *IMF Staff Papers, 47*(3), 279–310.

Boortz, C., Kremer, S., Jurkatis, S., & Nautz, D. (2013). *Herding in financial markets: Bridging the gap between theory and evidence* (SFB 649 discussion paper, No 36) (pp. 1–34).

Calma, A. (2018). A review of its publications as a case in behavioral finance. *Journal of Behavioral Finance in retrospect, 11*(4), 468–476.

Cheng, K. (2007). The trader interaction effect on the impact of overconfidence on trading performance: An empirical study. *Journal of Behavioral Finance, 8*(2), 59–69.

Cipriani, M., & Guarino, A. (2008). *Herd behavior in financial markets: An experiment with financial market professionals* (IMF working paper) (pp. 1–30).

Fama, E. (1998). Market efficiency, long-term returns, and behavioral finance. *Journal of Financial Economics, 49*(3), 283–306.

Gächter, S., Orzen, H., Renner, E., & Starmer, C. (2009). Are experimental economists prone to framing effects? A natural field experiment. *Journal of Economic Behavior & Organization, 70*, 443–446.

Giannarakis, G., Garefalakis, A., Lemonakis, C., & Konteos, G. (2017a). The drivers of social responsible stock index: The case of Dow Jones sustainability index world. *Corporate Ownership and Control, 14*(2-1), 173–180.

Giannarakis, G., Garefalakis, A., Lemonakis, C., & Sariannidis, N. (2017b). The impact of Dow Jones sustainability index on US dollar value. *International Journal of Economics and Financial Issues, 7*(2), 556–561.

Giannarakis, G., Sariannidis, N., & Garefalakis, A. (2011). The content of corporate social responsibility information: The case of Greek telecommunication sector. *International Business Research, 4*(3), 33–44.

Grezo, M. (2020). Overconfidence and financial decision-making: A meta-analysis. *Review of Behavioral Finance, 13*(3, 2021), 276–296.

Gupta, S., & Bhaduri, S. (2019). Skin in the game – Investor behavior in asset pricing, the Indian context. *Review of Behavioral Finance, 11*(4), 373–392.

Hirshleifer, D. (2001). Investor psychology and asset pricing. *Journal of Finance, 56*(4), 1533–1597.

Huddart, S., & Abdullah, A. (2018). The efficiency of stock-based incentives: Experimental evidence. *Journal of Behavioral Finance, 18*(3), 281–303.

Kahneman, D., & Riepe, M. (1998). Aspects of investor psychology. *Journal of Portfolio Management, 24*(4), 1–22.
Kahneman, D., & Tversky, A. (1979). Prospect theory: An analysis of decision making under risk. *Econometrica, 47*(2), 263–291.
Kahneman, D., & Tversky, A. (1984). Choices, values, and frames. *American Psychologist, 39*(4), 341–350.
Lemonakis, C., Garefalakis, A., Giannarakis, G., & Adamou, A (2016). Exporting activity using manufacturing firms' financial data: The case of clothing and footwear (CFW) sector, *European Journal of Economics, Finance and Administrative Sciences*, Issue 91.
Nofsinger, J., & Sias, R. (1998). *Herding and feedback trading by institutional and individual investors* (Working paper) (pp. 1–41). Marquette University.
Nofsinger, J., Patterson, F., & Corey, S. (2020). On the physiology of investment biases: The role of cortisol and testosterone. *Journal of Behavioral Finance, 22*(3), 338–349.
Shefrin, H. (2001). Behavioral corporate finance. *National Bureau of Economic Research, 14*(3), 21–33.
Shiller, R. (2003). From efficient markets theory to behavioral finance. *Journal of Economic Perspectives, 17*(1), 83–104.
Tariq, J., Nousheen, Z., & Hafeez, B. (2013). Herding behavior in Karachi stock exchange. *International Journal of Management Sciences and Business Research, 2*(2), 1–28.
Thaler, R. (1999a). Mental accounting matters. *Journal of Behavioral Decision Making, 12*, 183–206.
Thaler, R. (1999b). The end of behavioral finance. *Financial Analysts Journal, 56*(6), 12–17.
Thaler, R., Tversky, A., Kahneman, D., & Schwartz, A. (1997). The effect of myopia and loss aversion on risk taking: An experimental test. *Quarterly Journal of Economics, 112*(2), 647–661.
Tversky, A., & Kahneman, D. (1983). Extensional versus intuitive reasoning: The conjunction fallacy in probability judgments. *Psychological Review, 90*, 293–315.
Subrahmanyam, A. (2008). Behavioural finance: A review and synthesis. *European Financial Management, 14*(1), 12–29.
Zhen, C., Ki, O., & Xuewu, W. (2020). Investor attention, divergence of opinions, and stock returns. *Journal of Behavioral Finance, 22*(3), 265–279.

Chapter 15
Application of the Experiential Value Scale in Online Booking Conditions: Are There Consumer Demographic Characteristic Differences?

Aikaterini Stavrianea, Irene (Eirini) Kamenidou, Spyridon Mamalis, and Ifigeneia Mylona

Abstract Purchasing goods online constitute an ever-increasing trend in consumer behavior. In this way, the experience that a business offers its customers when they want to acquire services or products through an online platform is of particular interest to them. Experiential value is regarded as a precondition for customer loyalty and buyer satisfaction when considering the circumstances in which goods or services are purchased. The present study introduces research findings that explore whether there is consumer characteristics (education level and area of residence) differentiation with respect to the elements of experiential values when it comes to booking accommodation online. A sample ($N = 1540$) of individuals between the ages of 18–68 – all users of online booking sites – were obtained using quantitative research through a method of nonprobability sampling. Data were examined by descriptive statistics, factor, reliability analysis, One-way ANOVA test for hypothesis testing, as well as multiple comparisons of means. On the basis of the outcomes of the study, specific marketing proposals relating to e-booking websites are submitted as part of this paper.

Keywords Experiential Values · Tourism · Online Booking · Marketing · Demographic Differences · Digital Communication

JEL codes M30, M31, M37, M39

A. Stavrianea (✉)
Dept. of Communication and Media Studies, National and Kapodistrian University of Athens, Athens, Greece
e-mail: aikstavria@media.uoa.gr

I. (Eirini) Kamenidou · S. Mamalis · I. Mylona
Dept. of Management Science and Technology, School of Business and Economics, International Hellenic University, Kavala, Greece
e-mail: rkam@mst.ihu.gr; mamalis@mst.ihu.gr; imylona@mst.ihu.gr

N. Tsounis, A. Vlachvei (eds.), *Advances in Quantitative Economic Research*,
Springer Proceedings in Business and Economics,
https://doi.org/10.1007/978-3-030-98179-2_15

15.1 Introduction

Adopting new technologies has affected all traditional business areas, with an evident trend toward gradually being supplanted by digital outlets (Hallikainen et al., 2018). According to researchers in the field, technology in the tourism industry has had a substantial impact because the sector is based on a variety of services (Kyriakou et al., 2015). All of these services strive to attain a sense of differentiation as well as reduce costs (Vaško & Abrahám, 2015). A large number of studies have been carried out on the subject of technology adoption (Fernandes & Oliveira, 2021; Janssen et al., 2020; Taherdoost, 2018; Srinivasan et al., 2002; Thong and Yap, 1995), with a particular focus on the tourism sector and its technology adoption and digital transformation (Vijayabanu & Karthikeyan, 2021; Stavrianea et al., 2019, 2021; Nuryyev et al., 2020; Valeri, 2020; Lee, 2016; Wang & Qualls, 2007).

A significant increase in competition is evident in the tourism industry due to digitalization, which has also meant many new prospects in the sector. At the same time, as Vendrell-Herrero et al. (2017) argue, the fact that buyers now feel a certain familiarity with new technologies has resulted in them being more readily drawn toward – and willing to use – digital platforms to acquire services and goods. To be exact, digital platforms are now widely used by the vast majority of consumers in order to obtain relevant information relating to planning trips and making bookings (Turban et al., 2008). The subject of making bookings on the Internet has not only been the focus of past studies (Li et al., 2017; Zhao et al., 2015; Dickinger & Mazanec, 2008). It is also an area of study that continues to attract an ever-increasing amount of academic research and scholarly interest (Foris et al., 2020; Wen et al., 2020; Zeng et al., 2020).

Research suggests that the concepts of digital technologies and user experience are the two central elements that the idea of digital transformation encompasses (Henriette et al., 2016). Gentile et al. (2007) explain how consumer experience is the result of an interaction between the "object" and the user. Customer value is generated as a result of such interactions (Holbrook, 2006).

Despite the fact that some research has been carried out exploring the experience that customers have had online (Stavrianea et al., 2019, 2021; Hoyer et al., 2020; McLean & Wilson, 2016; Rose et al., 2012; Novak et al., 2000) as well as the concept of experiential value (EV) relating to Internet usage (e.g., Zhang et al., 2020; Rezaei and Valaei, 2017; Jeong et al., 2009), there is only a relatively limited number of studies which place focus on the dual concept of combining consumer EV directly with online Booking (OB) (Stavrianea et al., 2019, 2021; Choi, 2015; Sigala, 2004).

Furthermore, few studies examine statistical differences between socioeconomic and demographic characteristics of users and EV in an OB setting (Stavrianea et al., 2019, 2021). The latter centered exclusively on the issues around generational cohorts, with reference to the generation Z population.

Therefore, further research relating to users' socioeconomic and demographic variables with specific references to EV in OB is necessary. Taking into account the above notions, the present research seeks to examine the concept of experiential customer values exhibited in the process of searching for and purchasing services on the Internet. Specifically, this study aims to explore if consumers' EV from an OB setting differs upon their socioeconomic and demographic variables and specifically refers to their education level and area of residence.

The study presented here is significant because it concentrates on the concepts of EV and OB, both of which have so far not been adequately studied. It also offers perspectives into how developers of online platforms could potentially use consumer differences to attract and retain new customers.

15.2 Literature Review

The concept of value has long been considered by researchers to be central to academic research on the subject of consumer assessment and evaluation of services rendered and this relates in particular to work done in the field of tourism (Stavrianea et al., 2019, 2021; Kavoura & Stavrianea, 2016; Tsai & Wang, 2017). It can be stated with complete confidence and certainty that a company's survival in a fiercely competitive market depend entirely on the type of value which they offer and deliver to customers. Those who are able to deliver high standard of service will effectively be successful.

The question of what the customer could potentially experience, as well as the question of the quality of experiential value, has been the subject of a number of recent studies in the area of tourism (Pine & Gilmore, 1999; Wu & Liangm, 2009; Kim, 2014; Tsai & Wang, 2017). Some discuss how consumers feel a sense of reward and satisfaction through the purchase of a service or a product. In particular, there is an inherent correlation between this gratifying experience and the concept of the EV. The pleasing encounters that customers have with the provider represent an added experiential reward for the customer (Shobeiri et al., 2018). As a result, brands are presented with a chance to serve contemporary consumers more effectively by ensuring that they offer unparalleled value and an overall outstanding experience (Stavrianea et al., 2019, 2021; Brakus et al., 2009; Kavoura & Stavrianea, 2016; Shobeiri et al., 2018).

Holbrook has suggested that there are two levels of EV (1994). The first level represents the extrinsic rather than the intrinsic value of experience. The other level which Holbrook identifies is what he refers to as the sources of value, and in particular, what can be described as the active versus the reactive aspects of value. The core of the so-called intrinsic value lies within the emotional reaction which arises from the experience of consuming the actual product. On the other hand, there are clear links between the extrinsic value and the effectiveness of the transaction (Mano & Oliver, 1993; Holbrook, 1994; Tsai & Wang, 2017). The second dimension that Holbrook describes corresponds to the active and reactive value elements (Holbrook, 1994; Hanif et al., 2017). Within this framework, the active value dimension refers to the concept of the customer's own involvement, interaction, and engagement with the company that provides the service, whereas the reactive value relates to the perception, appreciation, and assessment in which the individual has taken part in through these experiences (Holbrook, 1994; Hanif et al., 2017).

Tsai and Wang (2017) explain that similarly to Holbrook's concept of a two-dimensional model, four EV-related axes have been identified and proposed by Mathwick et al. (2001). The customer experiences a set of four dimensions relating to the idea of playfulness (PL), to the notion of aesthetics (AES), to excellence in service (SE), as well as the notion of customer return on investment, i.e., CROI (Mathwick et al., 2001). The notion of AES incorporates the elements of physical attraction in terms of appearance, presentation through beautiful colors, interesting photography, as well as an interesting form and design (Mathwick et al., 2001; Tsai & Wang, 2017). Excellence in terms of service is obtained by the consumer's assessment of the actual product. It includes the level of quality in the knowledge that it is being offered to the client, and the specialist's knowledge, which is made available to them (Mathwick et al. 2001). This notion of SE is inextricably connected to the concepts of extrinsic and intrinsic values. PL is linked to the customer's quintessential understanding of what constitutes satisfaction and pleasure; what is more, these stem from an engagement with experiences that can function as an alternate route of escape from the ordinary and prosaic commitments of a daily routine (Mathwick et al., 2001). Finally, as regards to CROI, the notion of utility is directly associated with the issue of whether the customer experiences a return on investment, a feeling of satisfaction felt by the consumer relating to any particular experience.

The financial and behavioral aspects as well as the temporal and psychological factors involved in the investment which the consumer has made in the product, all link into the experience itself (Mathwick et al., 2001; Tsai & Wang, 2017). Recent research has pointed out how EV can be positively impacted by a sense of consumer satisfaction (Lee & Overby, 2004) as well as commitment (Shobeiri et al., 2014) and an intention to show loyalty. However, as previously stated, the notion and the process of EV as encountered in its web-based format, have not, as of yet, been studied sufficiently.

Very few studies deal with experiential values in OB and their association with users' socioeconomic and demographic characteristics. Specifically, according to Shobeiri (2018), EV has a beneficial effect on how the consumer perceives the advantages they will receive. Nevertheless, the stimulus, which is related to the cognition of potential benefits, is interpreted in a different way by women (Liang et al., 2013). According to research, the way in which consumers manage information throughout the cognitive problem process, is greatly influenced by gender, resulting in potentially divergent patterns in terms of purchasing (Chang, 2007; Liang et al., 2013). Likewise, there is a very limited number of studies on the subject of EV and consumer's socioeconomic and demographic differences whilst purchasing goods online (Stavrianea et al., 2019, 2021; Hasan, 2010; Andrews et al., 2007). Furthermore, Leong et al. (2019) observe that there is an absence of studies referring to the role of demographic variables on intention to book a hotel room.

Leong et al. (2019) examined the socioeconomic and demographic effects (age, gender, education, and income) on hotel patron's intention to book. Qi et al. (2013) explored differences between online and offline consumers' purchase of hotel rooms and the impact of their socioeconomic and demographic variables. They found statistically significant differences in terms of gender, educational level, income, and region. They found that subjects that booked online were females, young participants, and had a college degree. All the more, a handful of studies refer to the EV during an online accommodation booking encounter and consumers' socioeconomic and demographic characteristics. In this setting, only two studies have been found (Stavrianea et al., 2019, 2021) both referring to gender differences. Stavrianea et al. (2021) explored gender differences (general population) in EV components from OB platforms. They found that significant differences were observed in one case, the PL dimension of EV and gender. Additionally, Stavrianea et al. (2019) focused on the generation Z cohort and observed gender differences in EV in OB. Through t-tests, they found gender differences in two out of four EV components, i.e., for the CROI and SE components.

The present research draws from this previous work, and on the basis of that work, it additionally proposes that differences indeed exist between user's demographic variables, and especially education level and area of residence and EV in an e-accommodation booking environment. The research hypotheses for this work are as follows:

- H1: Statistically significant differences exist between subjects' education and EV from an accommodation e-booking platform.
- H2: Statistically significant differences exist between subjects' area of residence and EV from an accommodation e-booking platform.

Since EV consists of four dimensions, i.e., AES, PL, CROI, and SE, the above hypotheses are extended to the four dimensions of EV.

15.3 Materials and Methods

The study employed a quantitative survey, since the construct is understood, valid measures exist, and the hypothesis testing requires quantitative data (Edmondson & McManus, 2007). The research has made use of an online questionnaire and the scale proposed by Mathwick et al. (2001) was applied when investigating the items related to EV; the same scale was also used by Shobeiri et al. (2018) as well as Stavrianea et al. (2019, 2021). The scale which was used by Shobeiri et al. (2018) was within the framework of shopping online, and the four elements of EV were employed for the analysis, i.e., the aesthetic component (AES), the customer return on investment (CROI), the component of playfulness (Pl), and finally the element of service excellence (SE). Stavrianea et al. (2019, 2021) also employed the same components to evaluate the concept of EV with reference to accommodation bookings made online. For this study, users' EV from the OB platform was rated on a 7-point Likert scale, which was used to present the scale's answers. Specifically, referring to the answer scale, 1 = completely disagree up to 7 = completely agree for each statement.

The research targeted Greek adults who use OB platforms. The questionnaire was pilot tested into a smaller group of individuals and subsequently, the quantitative research was carried out from July 2019 to December 2019. Data were collected via the Internet and a nonprobability sampling method (including criteria, convenience, and snowball sampling) was applied. The criterion to participate in the research was that participants had to use OB platforms. The link of the questionnaire was distributed through social media and emails and respondents were asked to forward the link to friends and acquaintancies that met the research criterion. Finally, a total of 1540 valid questionnaires were gathered for analysis. Data were analyzed with the SPSS ver.25 software and included descriptive statistics, reliability analysis, One-way ANOVA, and multiple comparisons of means. All tests were preset at $a = 0.05$.

15.4 Results

15.4.1 Sample Profile

The samples' profile has as follows: in addition to males being overrepresented (55.7%), subjects belonging to the 18–25 age group were also disproportionately represented (43.8%). Furthermore, the number of respondents who belonged to each age group decreased as the age group increased. The overwhelming majority (60.6%) of respondents were single individuals with a background of secondary-level education, i.e., gymnasium or lyceum (48.3%), while the participants who were highly educated were also a significant percent (39.1%). Subjects were dependent on other individuals, i.e., students, homemakers, or unemployed (42.9%), or monthly salaried (36.9%), residents in an urban area (74.9%), and in possession of a family net monthly income of between 1000.01 and 2000.00€ (37.1%).

15.4.2 Online Booking Platforms

Participants were asked to report the OB platform that they usually use (one answer) when booking an accommodation. Twelve booking platforms were presented, including international (e.g., Booking.Com, Trivago, Airbnb, and Expedia) as well as domestic sites (e.g., Greekhotels.com, Hotelscombined.gr, and Discount sale - platforms). Results revealed that the most used OB platforms are Booking.com (45.8%), Trivago (25.3%), and Airbnb (10.0%), the Hotel's/ house/ room site (5.5%) and ebooking.com (4.4%). All these sum up to 90% of the total responses, while the rest, 10%, was formed by additional seven booking platforms, each enjoying a small percentage.

15.4.3 Components of Experiential Values – Hypothesis Testing

Factor analysis with varimax rotation offered EV dimensions, providing the initial four dimensions (AES, PL, CROI, and SE) and explaining 79.3% of the total variance (TV). Additionally, the indices of factor analysis were calculated, revealing a good fit for the factor model (KMO = 0.932; BTS = 18985.823; df = 105; $p = 0.000$). The first factor was the PL factor, interpreting 31.4% of TV and having a mean factor score (MFS), MFS = 3.82 (StD = 1.52). The reliability of the factor lies on $\alpha = 0.919$. The second dimension was the AES dimension, which interpreted 21.3% of TV and had MFS = 4.68 (StD = 1.30). The reliability of the factor was $\alpha = 0.887$. The third factor, i.e., CROI, interpreted 16.9% of TV, having an MFS = 4.53(StD = 1.52), and $\alpha = 0.890$. Lastly, the fourth factor interpreted 9.6% of TV, had MFS = 4.56 (StD = 1.51), and $\alpha = 0.800$. These dimensions were continuously used for further analysis, i.e., in the hypotheses testing.

15.4.3.1 Hypothesis No.1

H1 = Statistically significant differences exist between subjects' education and EV from an accommodation e-booking platform.

In order to examine the four sub-hypotheses stemming from this general hypothesis, each experiential component (by their MFS) was tested, i.e., AES, PL, CROI, and SE (Tables 15.1 and 15.2). One-Way ANOVA tests ($a = 0.05$) were implemented and tested each dimension amongst the educational level groups ($N = 3$). More precisely, Table 15.1 offers the outcome of One-Way ANOVA tests for these sub-hypotheses. In the ANOVA model, the educational level and its subgroups form the independent variable, while the attitude toward the four dimensions of EV (based on their MS) creates the dependent variables. The ANOVA results revealed that in two cases, EV differed significantly between users' educational levels (one on borderline). Thus, in these cases, the null hypothesis is rejected (Table 15.1).

For those results that provided with statistical differences, multiple comparisons of means were executed to undercover the between groups'/subsets' specific differences using the posthoc Tukey's HSD (Honesty Significant Difference) test, comparisons measures (Table 15.2). Table 15.2 portrays the outcomes of the posthoc Tukey HSD tests. The a and b letters reveal if each mean score is significantly different from the rest in the same row. Thus, in each row, mean scores with different letters are significantly different. The letter "a" is the starting point for all cases and carries the highest mean score per row.

From Table 15.2, it is revealed that in both cases (AES and CROI component), the highest MS, thus the highest experiential values observed, refers to the graduate and postgraduate participants, followed by the participants with secondary education. The participants with the least experiential values obtained and with the lowest

Table 15.1 ANOVA statistics and components of experiential values

Dimensions of EV		Sum of squares	df	Mean square	F	Sig.
MFSQ2_AES	Between groups	31.272	2	15.636	8.697	.000*
	Within groups	2763.164	1537	1.798		
	Total	2794.436	1539			
MFSQ2_PL	Between groups	5.556	2	2.778	1.196	.303
	Within groups	3569.258	1537	2.322		
	Total	3574.814	1539			
MFSQ2_CROI	Between groups	13.222	2	6.611	2.887	.056*
	Within groups	3520.002	1537	2.290		
	Total	3533.224	1539			
MFSQ2_SE	Between groups	6.537	2	3.269	1.425	.241
	Within groups	3524.725	1537	2.293		
	Total	3531.262	1539			

Source: The authors
*One-Way ANOVA tests ($a = 0.05$)

Table 15.2 Multiple comparisons of means through the posthoc Tukey's HSD

Dimensions of EV	Secondary	Postsecondary	Graduate/postgraduate
AES	4.86a	4.47b	4.92a
PL	3.87a	3.84a	3.74a
CROI	4.51ab	4.32b	4.62a
SE	4.63a	4.55a	4.49a

Source: The authors

MS are the participants with postsecondary education. Table 15.2 also reveals that as to the AES component, statistically significant differences exhibit both graduate/postgraduate participants and secondary education participants with the participants with postsecondary education. Moreover, the first two groups (graduate/postgraduate participants and secondary education participants) compared do not exhibit statistically significant differences. Regarding the CROI component, statistically significant differences demonstrate the graduate/postgraduate participants with the participants with postsecondary education, while no other statistically significant differences are found.

15.4.3.2 Hypothesis No.2

H2 = Statistically significant differences exist between subjects' area of residence and EV from an accommodation e-booking platform.

To examine the four sub-hypotheses stemming from this general hypothesis, also, each experiential component (by their MFS) was tested, i.e., AES, PL, CROI, and SE (Tables 15.3 and 15.4). One-Way ANOVA tests ($a = 0.05$) were implemented and tested each dimension amongst the area of residence groups ($N = 3$). More

Table 15.3 ANOVA statistics and components of experiential values

Dimensions of EV		Sum of squares	df	Mean square	F	Sig.
MFSQ2_AES	Between groups	28.394	2	14.197	7.889	.000*
	Within groups	2766.041	1537	1.800		
	Total	2794.436	1539			
MFSQ2_PL	Between groups	3.902	2	1.951	.840	.432
	Within groups	3570.912	1537	2.323		
	Total	3574.814	1539			
MFSQ2_CROI	Between groups	18.626	2	9.313	4.073	.017*
	Within groups	3514.598	1537	2.287		
	Total	3533.224	1539			
MFSQ2_SE	Between groups	14.333	2	7.167	3.132	.044*
	Within groups	3516.929	1537	2.288		
	Total	3531.262	1539			

Source: The authors
*One-Way ANOVA tests ($a = 0.05$)

Table 15.4 Multiple comparisons of means through the posthoc Tukey's HSD test

	Dimensions of EV	Urban	Semirural	Rural
1	AES	4.85a	4.53b	5.07a
2	PL	3.84a	3.69a	3.78a
3	CROI	4.52ab	4.29b	4.73a
4	SE	4.57ab	4.35b	4.74a

Source: The authors

precisely, Table 15.3 offers the outcome of One-Way ANOVA tests for these sub-hypotheses. In the ANOVA model, the area of residence and its subgroups form the independent variable, while the attitude toward the four dimensions of EV (based on their MS) creates the dependent variables. The ANOVA results revealed that in three cases (AES, CROI, and SE), EV differed significantly between users' areas of residence. Thus, in these cases, the null hypothesis is rejected (Table 15.3).

For the cases that the results provided with statistically significant differences, multiple comparisons of means were executed to undercover the between groups'/subsets' specific differences through the posthoc Tukey's HSD comparisons measures (Table 15.4). Table 15.4 portrays the outcome of the tests. The a and b letters reveal if each mean score is significantly different from the rest in the same row. Thus, in each row, mean scores with different letters are significantly different. The letter "a" is the starting point for all cases and carries the highest mean score per row.

Table 15.4 shows that in all cases where statistically significant differences were found (AES, CROI, and SE components), the highest MS, thus the highest experiential values observed, refers to people residing in rural areas, followed by the participants living in urban areas. The participants with the least experiential values obtained and with the lowest MS are the participants living in the semirural areas. Table 15.4 also exposes that as to the AES component, statistically significant differences exhibit both participants who live in the rural and urban areas with the participants residing in semirural areas. On the other hand, the first two groups compared (living in rural areas and urban areas) do not exhibit statistically significant differences. Regarding both the CROI and the SE components of experiential value, statistically significant differences demonstrate the participants residing in rural areas with the participants residing in the semirural areas, while no other statistically significant differences are found.

15.5 Discussion – Conclusions

The current paper concluded that Greeks with different education levels differ concerning two out of four dimensions of the EV construct: the AES component and the CROI component. This conclusion cannot be directly compared with previous studies since no study has examined EV in an online booking setting and educational level differences. Compared indirectly, previous studies state that consumers with higher education levels tend to buy more online than the lower education consumers (Monsuwe' et al., 2004; Li et al., 1999). Likewise, Qi et al. (2013) found significant differences among online and off-online five-star hotel booking in terms of education level. Though, booking intention was not examined. Leong et al. (2019) found that consumers' educational level was a significant predictor of hotel booking intention, though having a negative relationship (the higher the education level, the less the intention to book a hotel room). It must be pointed out that Leong et al. (2019) did not measure experiential values in an online booking setting. Räsänen et al. (2020) in their study which examined online information seeking patterns found that educational differences exist and specifically, they found a significant gap between those who had studied after the second degree and those who had not.

In the same vein, consumers' area of residence in the context of EV in an online accommodation booking situation has not been studied either. For so comparison of these findings cannot be made directly. Indirectly though, Räsänen et al. (2020) in their study found that "the residential differences exist mainly through other background variables, as we did not find significant differences between areas after the standardization of the background variables". This study found that people from rural areas experienced the highest EV in the dimensions where statistically differences were found. One explanation for this outcome could be that OB platforms provide them simultaneously with information that a tourist operator in the area (if there is one) cannot provide, such as room, hotel, and price comparisons. Very few tourism operators function in many rural areas- mainly in the nearest city, thus being a monopoly in information diffusion. In the recent past, the exceptionally low internet adoption in small villages due to the internet providers' technical problems led people to address tourism operators in the area and been provided with selective information. Though, in the last few years, there has been improvement and extension of lines for internet in even remote areas. Thus, people can search for information on their own very quickly and gain reliable feedback; this could be the reason for the highest EV of these consumers.

Having the abovementioned results of the study, OB providers should pay attention to their platform design to offer higher experiential values in all dimensions of the OB platform EV scale tested.

15.5.1 Limitations and Directions for Future Research

It would be advisable for future work to consider the limitations of the present research and be informed by it. The limitations are primarily evident within the sampling method (application of nonprobability sampling) and the method of collecting data (i.e., using online platforms for collection) and as a final point, through the fact that the research was restricted to a single country: Greece. It is therefore clear that we cannot use the findings for generalized purposes. However, they provide with data relevant to tendencies and glean insights into differences based on education and area of residence when it comes to EV from online booking platforms. In addition, we borrowed the elements and items included in this study from the questionnaire, which assessed the experiential values of an online shopping condition and was devised by Shobeiri et al. (2018). Therefore, it is possible that further elements measuring EV in online booking conditions may be available but have not been incorporated into this work. The limitations of this study just mentioned above notwithstanding, the study's implications on the provision of relevant information on the subject of tourism behavior are crucial as it provides new perspectives on a topic that has so far remained under-researched.

References

Andrews, L., Kiel, G., Drennan, J., Boyle, M. V., & Weerawardena, J. (2007). Gendered perceptions of experiential value in using web-based retail channels. *European Journal of Marketing, 41*(5), 640–658.

Brakus, J. J., Schmitt, B. H., & Zarantonello, L. (2009). Brand experience: What is it? How is it measured? Does it affect loyalty? *Journal of Marketing, 73*(3), 52–68.

Chang, C. (2007). The relative effectiveness of comparative and noncomparative advertising: Evidence for gender differences in information-processing strategies. *Journal of Advertising, 36*(1), 21–35.

Choi, S. (2015). *Understanding roles of experiential value and perceived switching drivers on travelers' loyalty: An empirical study of third-party travel websites*. Doctoral dissertation, Kansas State University.

Dickinger, A., & Mazanec, J. (2008). *Consumers' preferred criteria for hotel online booking*. In P. O'Connor, W. Höpken, & U. Gretzel (Eds.), *Information and communication technologies in tourism 2008*. Springer.

Edmondson, A. C., & McManus, S. E. (2007). Methodological fit in management field research. *Academy of Management Review, 32*(4), 1246–1264.

Fernandes, T., & Oliveira, E. (2021). Understanding consumers' acceptance of automated technologies in service encounters: Drivers of digital voice assistants adoption. *Journal of Business Research, 122*, 180–191.

Foris, D., Tecau, A. S., Hartescu, M., & Foris, T. (2020). Relevance of the features regarding the performance of booking websites. *Tourism Economics, 26*(6), 1021–1041.

Gentile, C., Spiller, N., & Noci, G. (2007). How to sustain the customer experience: an overview of experience components that co-create value with the customer. *European Management Journal, 25*(5), 395–410.

Hallikainen, H., Alamäki, A., & Laukkanen, T. (2018). Individual preferences of digital touchpoints: A latent class analysis. *Journal of Retailing and Consumer Services, 50*, 386–393.

Hanif, H., Wan Khairuzzaman, W., & Norshidah, M. (2017). *Acceptance of hedonic technology: The case of mobile-game application towards industry excellence: the application of technology and innovation.* Universiti Teknologi Malaysia.

Hasan, B. (2010). Exploring gender differences in online shopping attitude. *Computers in Human Behavior, 26*(4), 597–601.

Henriette, E., Feki, M. & Boughzala, I. (2016, September). *Digital transformation challenges*. In MCIS (p. 33). https://aisel.aisnet.org/cgi/viewcontent.cgi?article=1033&context=mcis2016

Holbrook, M. B. (2006). Consumption experience, customer value, and subjective personal introspection: An illustrative photographic essay. *Journal of business Research, 59*(6), 714–725.

Holbrook, M. B. (1994). The nature of customer value: an axiology of services in the consumption experience. *Service quality: New directions in theory and practice, 21*, 21–71.

Hoyer, W. D., Kroschke, M., Schmitt, B., Kraume, K., & Shankar, V. (2020). Transforming the customer experience through new technologies. *Journal of Interactive Marketing, 51*, 57–71.

Janssen, M., Weerakkody, V., Ismagilova, E., Sivarajah, U., & Irani, Z. (2020). A framework for analysing blockchain technology adoption: Integrating institutional, market and technical factors. *International Journal of Information Management, 50*, 302–309.

Jeong, S. W., Fiore, A. M., Niehm, L. S., & Lorenz, F. O. (2009). The role of experiential value in online shopping. *Internet Research, 19*, 105–124.

Kavoura, A., & Stavrianea, A. (2016). A brand experiences' conceptual model for visitors' attitudinal loyalty. *TOURISMOS: An International Multidisciplinary Refereed Journal of Tourism, 11*(4), 1–21.

Kim, J. H. (2014). The antecedents of memorable tourism experiences: The development of a scale to measure the destination attributes associated with memorable experiences. *Tourism Management, 44*, 34–45.

Kyriakou, D., Mpregkou, M., Grigoriou, I., Blanas, N., Belias, D., & Koustelios, A. (2015). Rethinking of experiential tourism through Social Media: Could Greece keep up the pace?. Proceedings of the 10th MIBES Conference – Larisa, Greece, 15–17 October 2015, 281–293. URL: http://mibes.teilar.gr/proceedings/2015/19.%20Kyriakou%20D,%20Mpregkou%20M,%20Blanas%20N,%20Belias%20D,%20Koustelios%20%20A.pdf (Accessed on 15.1.2019).

Lee, E. J., & Overby, J. W. (2004). Creating value for online shoppers: Implications for satisfaction and loyalty. *Journal of Consumer Satisfaction, Dissatisfaction and Complaining Behavior, 17*, 54–67.

Lee, L. Y. S. (2016). Hospitality industry web-based self-service technology adoption model: A cross-cultural perspective. *Journal of Hospitality & Tourism Research, 40*(2), 162–197.

Leong, L. Y., Hew, T. S., Ooi, K. B., & Lin, B. (2019). Do electronic word-of-mouth and elaboration likelihood model influence hotel booking? *Journal of Computer Information Systems, 59*(2), 146–160.

Li, H., Kuo, C., & Russell, M. G. (1999). The impact of perceived channel utilities, shopping orientations, and demographics on the consumer's online buying behavior. *Journal of Computer-Mediated Communication, 5*(2), JCMC521.

Li, L., Peng, M., Jiang, N., & Law, R. (2017). An empirical study on the influence of economy hotel website quality on online booking intentions. *International Journal of Hospitality Management, 63*, 1–10.
Liang, J.-L., Chen, Y.-Y., Duan, Y.-S., & Ni, J.-J. (2013). Gender differences in the relationship between experiential marketing and purchase intention. *Journal of International Management Studies, 8*(1), 10–19.
Mano, H., & Oliver, R. L. (1993). Assessing the Dimensionality and Structure of the Consumption Experience: Evaluation, Feeling, and Satisfaction. *Journal of Consumer Research, 20*(3), 451.
Mathwick, C., Malhotra, N., & Rigdon, E. (2001). Experiential value: Conceptualization, measurement, and application in the catalog and internet shopping environment. *Journal of Retailing, 77*(1), 39–56.
McLean, G., & Wilson, A. (2016). Evolving the online customer experience... is there a role for online customer support? *Computers in Human Behavior, 60*, 602–610.
Monsuwe´, P., Dellaert, B.G.C. & Ruyter, K. (2004). What drives consumers to shop online? A literature review. *International Journal of Service Industry Management, 15*(1), 102–121.
Novak, T. P., Hoffman, D. L., & Yung, Y. F. (2000). Measuring the customer experience in online environments: A structural modeling approach. *Marketing Science, 19*(1), 22–42.
Nuryyev, G., Wang, Y. P., Achyldurdyyeva, J., Jaw, B. S., Yeh, Y. S., Lin, H. T., & Wu, L. F. (2020). Blockchain technology adoption behavior and sustainability of the business in tourism and hospitality SMEs: an empirical study. *Sustainability, 12*(3), 1256.
Pine, B. J., & Gilmore, J. H. (1999). *The Experience Economy*. Harvard Business School Press.
Qi, S., Law, R., & Buhalis, D. (2013). Who booked five-star hotels in Macau? A study of hotel guests' online booking intention. *Journal of Hospitality and Tourism Management, 20*, 76–83.
Räsänen, P., Koivula, A., & Keipi, T. (2020). Online information seeking patterns and social inequality in a digital economy. *The International Review of Retail, Distribution and Consumer Research, 31*(2), 1–18.
Rezaei, S., & Valaei, N. (2017). Crafting experiential value via smartphone apps channel. *Marketing Intelligence & Planning.*
Rose, S., Clark, M., Samouel, P., & Hair, N. (2012). Online customer experience in e-retailing: An empirical model of antecedents and outcomes. *Journal of Retailing, 88*(2), 308–322.
Shobeiri, S., Mazaheri, E., & Laroche, M. (2014). Improving customer website involvement through experiential marketing. *The Service Industries Journal, 34*(11), 885–900.
Shobeiri, S., Mazaheri, E., & Laroche, M. (2018). Creating the right customer experience online: The influence of culture. *Journal of Marketing Communications, 24*(3), 270–290.
Sigala, M. (2004). *Designing experiential websites in tourism and hospitality: A customer centric value approach*. In Information and Communication Technologies in Tourism 2004 (pp. 161–171). Springer.
Srinivasan, R., Lilien, G. L., & Rangaswamy, A. (2002). Technological opportunism and radical technology adoption: An application to e-business. *Journal of marketing, 66*(3), 47–60.
Stavrianea, A., Kamenidou, I., & Bara, E. Z. (2019). Gender differences in experiential values components in an online booking condition: Insights from generation Z. In *12th Annual Conference of the EuroMed Academy of Business* (pp. 1233–1244).
Stavrianea, A. & Kamenidou, I., Conference: SIBR 2021 (Tokyo) Conference on Interdisciplinary Business and Economics Research At: Tokyo, Japan Volume: PROCEEDINGS Volume 10 (2021) Issue 1 (January) ISSN: 2223-5078.
Taherdoost, H. (2018). A review of technology acceptance and adoption models and theories. *Procedia manufacturing, 22*, 960–967.
Thong, J. Y., & Yap, C. S. (1995). CEO characteristics, organizational characteristics and information technology adoption in small businesses. *Omega, 23*(4), 429–442.
Tsai, C.-T. (Simon) & Wang, Y.-C. (2017). Experiential value in branding food tourism. *Journal of Destination Marketing & Management, 6*(1), 56–65.
Turban, E., King, D., McKay, J., Marshall, P., Lee, J., & Viehland, D. (2008). *Electronic commerce 2008: A managerial perspective* (5th ed.). Pearson Prentice Hall.

Vaško, M., & Abrhám, J. (2015). Issues of secure and sustainable e-tourism: Case of the Czech Republic. *Journal of Security & Sustainability Issues, 5*(2), 137–148.

Valeri, M. (2020). Blockchain technology: adoption perspectives in tourism. In *Entrepreneurship and Organizational Change* (pp. 27–35). Springer.

Vendrell-Herrero, F., Bustinza, O. F., Parry, G., & Georgantzis, N. (2017). Servitization, digitization and supply chain interdependency. *Industrial Marketing Management, 60*, 69–81.

Vijayabanu, C., & Karthikeyan, S. (2021). *Digital transformation and the competitive advantage of global tourism*. In M. Dinis, L. Bonixe, S. Lamy, & Z. Breda (Eds.), *Impact of new media in tourism* (pp. 308–326). IGI Global.

Wang, Y., & Qualls, W. (2007). Towards a theoretical model of technology adoption in hospitality organizations. *International Journal of Hospitality Management, 26*(3), 560–573.

Wen, J., Lin, Z., Liu, X., Xiao, S. H., & Li, Y. (2020). The interaction effects of online reviews, brand, and price on consumer hotel booking decision making. *Journal of Travel Research*, 0047287520912330.

Wu, C. H. J., & Liang, R. D. (2009). Effect of experiential value on customer satisfaction with service encounters in luxury-hotel restaurants. *International Journal of Hospitality Management, 28*(4), 586–593.

Zeng, G., Cao, X., Lin, Z., & Xiao, S. H. (2020). When online reviews meet virtual reality: Effects on consumer hotel booking. *Annals of Tourism Research, 81*, 102860.

Zhang, Y., Fiore, A. M., Zhang, L., & Liu, X. (2020). *Impact of website design features on experiential value and patronage intention toward online mass customization sites. An International Journal.*

Zhao, X., Wang, L., Guo, X., & Law, R. (2015). The influence of online reviews to online hotel booking intentions. *International Journal of Contemporary Hospitality Management, 27*(6), 1343–1364.

Chapter 16
Firm Conduct in a Duopolistic Industry with Product Innovation

Jacek Prokop

Abstract The objective of this paper is to investigate the firm conduct in a model of duopolistic industry with product innovation and price competition. Three different scenarios (industry-wide competition, R&D cooperation, and industry-wide cartel) are compared in a two stage game of firms. It is shown that independent of the extent of research spillovers and the level of product differentiation, the duopolists have strong incentives to form a full industry cartel that results in the highest level of R&D investments (in comparison to research cooperation and industry-wide competition) as long as the extent of research spillovers is not too low.

Keywords R&D investments · Product innovation · Price competition · Coopetition · Industry cartel

JEL Classification L13, O32

16.1 Introduction

R&D activities of firms are crucial for their market success. However, research investments of one firm generate positive spillovers to other industry participants. This encourages firms to consider coordination of R&D decisions to save the costs of supplying the final product and to reduce the free riding (e.g., Martin, 2002; Pippel, 2014). In addition, oligopolistic market structure may create an opportunity for the firms to form a collusive agreement to raise prices of final output and achieve higher profits (Lipczynski et al., 2017, pp. 195–215).

Firm conduct and performance in oligopolistic industries has been an important topic of theoretical and empirical analysis. In particular, the research has focused

J. Prokop (✉)
Department of Business Economics, SGH Warsaw School of Economics, Warsaw, Poland
e-mail: jacek.prokop@sgh.waw.pl

N. Tsounis, A. Vlachvei (eds.), *Advances in Quantitative Economic Research*, Springer Proceedings in Business and Economics,
https://doi.org/10.1007/978-3-030-98179-2_16

on the relationship between the R&D activities undertaken by firms and their behavior in the final product market. Various combinations of cooperative and noncooperative conduct of firms in research investments and final product market have been considered to predict the dynamics of innovative industries (e.g., Cellini & Lambertini, 2009; Kamien & Zang, 2000).

The literature distinguishes between process and product innovations. A process innovation involves the introduction of cost-saving technological changes in manufacturing of the final product. A product innovation involves the introduction of an improved or more attractive product and contributes to the increase in the market demand. It should be noticed that the distinction between product and process innovation may not always be easy. Improved products may require new piece of technology and vice versa (Lipczynski et al., 2017, p. 508).

Most works on firms conduct and performance highlight process innovations (e.g., Amir et al., 2003; Kamien et al., 1992; Karbowski & Prokop, 2019). However, Ramsza and Karbowski (2020) point out that a vast share of R&D investments is actually linked to product innovation. The importance of product innovation becomes more and more recognized by researchers.

Recently, Karbowski (2019) studied the impact of cooperative and noncooperative R&D strategies on product innovation and firm performance. A market with differentiated goods and simultaneous price and quality competition has been considered. It was shown that profit-maximizing firms prefer to pursue cooperative strategies, rather than industry-wide competition. Such choice would lead to a lower level of investments in product innovation compared to the noncooperative case.

The objective of this paper is to investigate the firm conduct in a modified model of duopolistic industry with product innovation and price competition. We consider the product development investments that increase the size of the market, similarly to Ramsza and Karbowski (2020), but in our model, the decision variable of firms in the final product market is price rather than quantity, which is similar to Karbowski (2019). However, in contrast to Karbowski (2019), we assume a sequential (two-stage) decision making similarly to, e.g., Symeonidis (2003), i.e., first, the firms decide about product innovation and next, they choose the prices of the final product. Additionally, we take into account various degrees of exogenous product differentiation and research spillovers.

Three different scenarios are compared: industry-wide competition, R&D cooperation (coopetition), and industry-wide cartel. It is shown that independent of the extent of research spillovers and the level of product differentiation, the duopolists have strong incentives to form a full industry cartel that results in the highest level of R&D investments (in comparison to research cooperation and industry-wide competition) as long as the extent of research spillovers is not too low. It has been shown that the duopolists have strong incentives to engage in some degree of cooperative behavior which leads to a reduced research investment.

The paper is organized as follows. In Sect. 16.2, the model is presented. The basic market setup is given in subsection 16.2.1. Subsection 16.2.2 describes the noncooperative behavior of firms in a duopolistic industry that is followed by the model of a firms cooperating in research investments, but competing in the final product market (coopetition). In subsection 16.2.4, a fully cartelized industry is considered. The results are discussed in Sect. 16.3. The last section contains the conclusions.

16.2 The Model

16.2.1 Market Setup

Consider a two-stage game in a duopolistic industry with the firms labeled 1 and 2. In the first stage, each firm decides about the size of R&D investments in product innovation. In the second stage, firms operate in the final product market by supplying a differentiated product.

The costs of the R&D investments x_i undertaken by firm i ($i = 1, 2$) are modeled by the following function:

$$\gamma \frac{x_i^2}{2}, \tag{16.1}$$

where γ ($\gamma > 0$) is a constant parameter. Observe that the quadratic cost function captures the decreasing marginal returns from R&D investments (see, e.g., Dasgupta, 1986).

In the final product market, firm i ($i = 1, 2$) faces the following inverse demand function:

$$p_i = a - q_i - sq_j, \tag{16.2}$$

where p_i and q_i are the price and output of firm i, q_j is the output of firm j, parameter a denotes the initial market size, and parameter s ($0 < s < 1$) measures the level of product substitutability.

Marginal production costs for both firms are assumed to be identical and constant. Without loss of generality, we normalize them to zero. Entry barriers are assumed to be high enough to prevent entry.

Product R&D investments positively affect the size of the final product market according to the function:

$$p_i = a + \left(x_i + \beta x_j\right) - q_i - sq_j. \tag{16.3}$$

where $i \neq j$, and parameter β ($0 \leq \beta \leq 1$) captures the extent of R&D spillovers, i.e., the market benefit of a given firm due to research investments made by the competitor. Higher level of parameter β increases the market size of the competitor.

In order to capture the price-setting behavior of duopolists, we invert (16.3) and obtain the direct demand function:

$$q_i = \frac{a + x_i + \beta x_j - s\left(a + x_j + \beta x_i\right)}{1 - s^2} - \frac{p_i}{1 - s^2} + \frac{s p_j}{1 - s^2}. \tag{16.4}$$

The profit of firm i is given by:

$$\pi_i = p_i q_i - \gamma \frac{x_i^2}{2}. \tag{16.5}$$

Substituting (16.4) into (16.5) we obtain the profit of firm i as a function of prices and R&D investments:

$$\pi_i = p_i \left(\frac{a + x_i + \beta x_j - s\left(a + x_j + \beta x_i\right)}{1 - s^2} - \frac{p_i}{1 - s^2} + \frac{s p_j}{1 - s^2} \right) - \gamma \frac{x_i^2}{2}, \tag{16.6}$$

or

$$\pi_i = -\frac{p_i^2}{1 - s^2} + \frac{a + x_i + \beta x_j - s\left(a + x_j + \beta x_i\right) + s p_j}{1 - s^2} p_i - \gamma \frac{x_i^2}{2}. \tag{16.7}$$

16.2.2 *Industry-Wide Competition*

First, let us consider the noncooperative behavior of firms at both stages of the game. We assume the price competition between firms in the final product market. From the first order conditions (optimization with respect to p_i), we obtain the profit maximizing price of firm i (Bertrand-Nash equilibrium):

$$p_i\left(x_i, x_j\right) = \frac{\left(2 - s - s^2\right) a + \left(2 - s^2 - s\beta\right) x_i - \left(s - 2\beta + s^2\beta\right) x_j}{4 - s^2}. \tag{16.8}$$

Substituting (16.8) into the profit function (16.7), we have the profit of firm i expressed as a function of research investments of both firms:

$$\pi_i\left(x_i, x_j\right) = \frac{\left(2(2 - s(s + \beta))^2 - \left(4 - s^2\right)^2 \left(1 - s^2\right)\gamma\right) x_i^2 - 4\left(2 - s(s + \beta)\right) x_i \left(a\left(2 - s - s^2\right)\left(\left(2 - s^2\right)\beta - s\right) x_j\right)}{2\left(4 - s^2\right)^2 \left(1 - s^2\right)}$$

$$+ \frac{2\left(a\left(2 - s - s^2\right) + \left(\left(2 - s^2\right)\beta - s\right) x_j\right)^2}{2\left(4 - s^2\right)^2 \left(1 - s^2\right)}. \tag{16.9}$$

Now, we may find the optimal decisions of firms at the R&D stage by solving the following system of two equations in two unknowns:

$$\frac{\partial \pi_i}{\partial x_i} = 0 \quad (i = 1, 2). \tag{16.10}$$

We arrive at the noncooperative Nash equilibrium at the first stage of our game:

$$x_i^{rdcom} = \frac{2a\left(2 - s^2 - s\beta\right)}{s^4\gamma 2s^2\left(1 + \beta - 3\gamma\right) - s^3\gamma + 2s\left(\beta + \beta^2 + 2\gamma\right) - 4\left(1 + \beta - 2\gamma\right)}. \tag{16.11}$$

Expression (16.11) gives the optimal levels of investment in product innovation. Using (16.7), (16.8), and (16.11), we obtain the optimal levels of each duopolist profit:

$$\pi_i^{rdcom} = \frac{a^2\gamma\left(-8 + 8s\beta - 4s^3\beta - s^4\left(2 - 9\gamma\right) + 16\gamma - s^6\gamma + 2s^2\left(4 - \beta^2 - 12\gamma\right)\right)}{\left(2s^2\left(1 + \beta - 3\gamma\right) - 4\left(1 + \beta - 2\gamma\right) - s^3\gamma + s^4\gamma + 2s\left(\beta + \beta^2 + 2\gamma\right)\right)^2}. \tag{16.12}$$

The equilibrium prices of goods offered in the final product market are:

$$p_i^{rdcom} = \frac{a\left(4 - s^2\right)\left(1 - s^2\right)\gamma}{2s^2\left(1 + \beta - 3\gamma\right) - 4\left(1 + \beta - 2\gamma\right) - s^3\gamma + s^4\gamma + 2s\left(\beta + \beta^2 + 2\gamma\right)}, \tag{16.13}$$

and the equilibrium supply of the final product by each firm is:

$$q_i^{rdcom} = \frac{a\left(4 - s^2\right)\gamma}{2s^2\left(1 + \beta - 3\gamma\right) - 4\left(1 + \beta - 2\gamma\right) - s^3\gamma + s^4\gamma + 2s\left(\beta + \beta^2 + 2\gamma\right)}. \tag{16.14}$$

The results of numerical analysis for this variant of market behavior (assuming the following values of parameters: $a = 100$, $s = 0.5$, $\gamma = 20$, $\beta \in [0, 1]$) are shown in Table 16.1.

Table 16.1 shows that with the larger extent of research spillovers (β), the R&D investments are falling, but the market prices, quantities supplied, and profits of duopolists are increasing in the case of industry-wide competition.

Table 16.1 Noncooperative equilibrium for $a = 100$, $s = 0.5$, $\gamma = 20$, $\beta \in [0, 1]$

β	x_i^{rdcom}	p_i^{rdcom}	q_i^{rdcom}	π_i^{rdcom}
0.0	2.11800	34.0393	45.3858	1500.04
0.1	2.06048	34.0888	45.4518	1506.94
0.2	2.00255	34.1344	45.5125	1513.44
0.3	1.94423	34.1758	45.5678	1519.52
0.4	1.88553	34.2132	45.6177	1525.18
0.5	1.82648	34.2466	45.6621	1530.41
0.6	1.76711	34.2758	45.7011	1535.21
0.7	1.70742	34.3009	45.7345	1539.58
0.8	1.64745	34.3218	45.7624	1543.51
0.9	1.58720	34.3386	45.7848	1546.99
1.0	1.52672	34.3511	45.8015	1550.03

Source: own calculations

16.2.3 R&D Cooperation (Coopetition)

In this section, we consider the case of R&D cooperation and price competition in the final product market.

The analysis of the firms' behavior in the final product market will be the same as in the case of full competition in the industry, i.e., the competitors will be setting prices simultaneously and independently. Thus, the optimal price levels as functions of R&D investments will be set according to (16.8), and the profit of each firm will be given by (16.9).

At the R&D stage, firms decide about the level of research investments to maximize a joint profit, i.e.,

$$\pi\left(x_1, x_2\right) = \pi_1\left(x_1, x_2\right) + \pi_2\left(x_2, x_1\right). \tag{16.15}$$

To find the optimal level of research investments, we substitute (16.9) into (16.15), and formulate the first order conditions as:

$$\frac{d\pi}{dx_i} = 0. \tag{16.16}$$

Since we focus on the symmetric equilibrium, i.e., $x_1 = x_2$, expression (16.16) takes the form:

$$\frac{d\pi}{dx_i} = \frac{2a\left(1-s\right)\left(1+\beta\right) + \left(2\left(1-s\right)\left(1+\beta\right)^2 - \left(2-s\right)^2\left(1+s\right)\gamma\right)x_i}{\left(2-s\right)^2\left(1+s\right)} = 0. \tag{16.17}$$

As a solution to (16.17), we obtain optimal levels of research investments undertaken by firms at the first stage of the game:

$$x_i^{rdcar} = \frac{2a\,(1-s)\,(1+\beta)}{2s(1+\beta)^2 + (2-s)^2\,(1+s)\,\gamma - 2\left(1+2\beta+\beta^2\right)}. \tag{16.18}$$

The optimal price level set by the firms will be equal:

$$p_i^{rdcar} = \frac{a\,(2-s)\left(1-s^2\right)\gamma}{2s(1+\beta)^2 + (2-s)^2\,(1+s)\,\gamma - 2(1+\beta)^2}. \tag{16.19}$$

Each firm's supply of the final product will be:

$$q_i^{rdcar} = \frac{a\,(2-s)\,\gamma}{2s(1+\beta)^2 + (2-s)^2\,(1+s)\,\gamma - 2(1+\beta)^2}, \tag{16.20}$$

and the profit will amount to:

$$\pi_i^{rdcar} = \frac{a^2\,(1-s)\,\gamma}{2s(1+\beta)^2 + (2-s)^2\,(1+s)\,\gamma - 2(1+\beta)^2}. \tag{16.21}$$

Table 16.2 gives the results of numerical analysis for this variant of the model (assuming the same values of parameters as in the previous section. Since we consider cooperation in the first stage of the game and competition in the second stage, such situation may be labeled coopetition.

Table 16.2 demonstrates that in the case of coopetition, together with the increase in the scale of R&D externalities (β), there is also an increase in research investments of individual firms aimed at the final product innovation. At the same time, we observe an increase of the market price and the supply of the final product as well the profits of each firm when the extent of R&D externalities is growing.

Table 16.2 Coopetitive equilibrium for $a = 100$, $s = 0.5$, $\gamma = 20$, $\beta \in [0, 1]$

β	x_i^{rdcar}	p_i^{rdcar}	q_i^{rdcar}	π_i^{rdcar}
0.0	1.50376	33.8346	45.1128	1503.76
0.1	1.65938	33.9418	45.2557	1508.52
0.2	1.81653	34.0599	45.4133	1513.78
0.3	1.97538	34.1893	45.5858	1519.53
0.4	2.13610	34.3302	45.7736	1525.79
0.5	2.29885	34.4828	45.9770	1532.57
0.6	2.46381	34.6474	46.1965	1539.88
0.7	2.63117	34.8243	46.4324	1547.75
0.8	2.80112	35.0140	46.6853	1556.18
0.9	2.97386	35.2168	46.9557	1565.19
1.0	3.14961	35.4331	47.2441	1574.80

Source: own calculations

16.2.4 Industry-Wide Cooperation

Finally we consider the case of fully cartelized industry by the duopolists, i.e., cooperation at the R&D stage as well as in the final product market.

In the final product market, firms choose prices to maximize joint profit, i.e.,

$$\pi = \pi_1 + \pi_2. \tag{16.22}$$

where π_i is given by (16.7).

Since we consider a symmetric equilibrium, R&D investments as well as the prices of both firms are identical, i.e., $x_1 = x_2 = x$ and $p = p_1 = p_2$, where p is the solution to first order condition for joint profit maximization $\left(\frac{\partial \pi}{\partial p} = \frac{2(a-2p+(1+\beta)x)}{1+s} = 0\right)$. Thus given the size of R&D investments, the price charged in the cartelized industry equals:

$$p(x) = \frac{a + (1+\beta)\,x}{2}. \tag{16.23}$$

Substituting (16.23) into (16.22), we calculate the joint profit as a function of research investments of both firms:

$$\pi = \frac{a^2 + 2a\,(1+\beta)\,x + \left((1+\beta)^2 - 2\,(1+s)\,\gamma\right)x^2}{2\,(1+s)}. \tag{16.24}$$

The optimal level of R&D investments is found as a solution to:

$$\frac{\partial \pi}{\partial x} = \frac{a\,(1+\beta) + \left((1+\beta)^2 - 2\,(1+s)\,\gamma\right)x}{1+s} = 0. \tag{16.25}$$

The optimal level of R&D investment in a fully cartelized industry is the solution to (16.25):

$$x^{fcar} = x_1^{fcar} = x_2^{fcar} = \frac{a\,(1+\beta)}{2\,(1+s)\,\gamma - (1+2\beta)^2}. \tag{16.26}$$

The optimal price in the cartelized industry is obtained by substituting (16.26) into (16.23). Thus:

Table 16.3 Cooperative equilibrium for $a = 100$, $s = 0.5$, $\gamma = 20$, $\beta \in [0, 1]$

β	x_i^{fcar}	p_i^{fcar}	q_i^{fcar}	π_i^{fcar}
0.0	1.69492	50.8475	33.8983	1694.92
0.1	1.87107	51.0291	34.0194	1700.97
0.2	2.04918	51.2295	34.1530	1707.65
0.3	2.22946	51.4492	34.2994	1714.97
0.4	2.41213	51.6885	34.4590	1722.95
0.5	2.59740	51.9481	34.6320	1731.60
0.6	2.78552	52.2284	34.8189	1740.95
0.7	297,671	52.5302	35.0201	1751.01
0.8	3.17125	52.8541	35.2361	1761.80
0.9	3.36939	53.2009	35.4673	1773.36
1.0	3.57143	53.5714	35.7143	1785.71

Source: own calculations

$$p^{fcar} = p_1^{fcar} = p_2^{fcar} = \frac{a\,(1+s)\,\gamma}{2\,(1+s)\,\gamma - (1+\beta)^2}. \tag{16.27}$$

The optimal production level of each firm is calculated by substituting (16.26) and (16.23) into (16.4):

$$q^{fcar} = q_1^{fcar} = q_2^{fcar} = \frac{a\gamma}{2\,(1+s)\,\gamma - (1+\beta)^2}. \tag{16.28}$$

The equilibrium profit of each cartel member is:

$$\pi_1^{fcar} = \pi_2^{fcar} = \frac{\pi^{fcar}}{2} = -\frac{a^2\gamma}{2\left(1+2\beta+\beta^2-2\,(1+s)\,\gamma\right)}. \tag{16.29}$$

The results of numerical analysis in the case of fully cartelized industry for the previously selected set of parameters are given in Table 16.3.

Table 16.3 shows that in the case of full cartelization of the industry, together with the increase in the size of R&D externalities (β), there is also an increase of research investments, the supply of the final product, and the market price as well as the profits of each firm.

16.3 The Results and Discussion

The algebraic form of equilibria obtained in the three cases make the analytical comparison slightly tedious. Therefore, we use numerical analysis to compare the equilibrium behavior of firms in each of the above settings.

First, we consider the prices of the final product set by each firm. Based on the numerical analysis, the following property can be formulated.

Property 1

(a) The price of the final product is the largest in the fully cartelized industry, i.e., $p_i^{fcar} > p_i^{rdcar}$ and $p_i^{fcar} > p_i^{rdcom}$.

(b) When the extent of research spillovers is large enough, the price of the final product is lower in the fully competitive industry than in the case of coopetitive behavior, i.e., $p_i^{rdcar} > p_i^{rdcom}$.

(c) When the extent of research spillovers is not too large, the price of the final product is higher in the fully competitive industry than in the case of coopetitive behavior, i.e.,$p_i^{rdcom} > p_i^{rdcar}$.

Next, let us compare the size of R&D investments in product innovation of firms. Property 2 summarizes observations based on our numerical analysis.

Property 2

(a) When the size of research spillovers is large enough, the level of R&D investments is the highest in the fully cartelized industry and the lowest in the case of full competition, i.e., $x_i^{fcar} > x_i^{rdcar} > x_i^{rdcom}$.

(b) When the size of research spillovers is not too large, the level of R&D investments is the highest in the fully competitive industry and the lowest in the case of coopetition, i.e., $x_i^{rdcom} > x_i^{fcar} > x_i^{rdcar}$.

Finally, we compare the profits of firms in each of the three cases. The results are given as the following property.

Property 3

For any size of research spillovers, the profit of duopolists is the highest in the fully cartelized industry and the lowest in the case of full competition, i.e., $\pi_i^{fcar} > \pi_i^{rdcar} > \pi_i^{rdcom}$.

Based on Property 3, we may conclude that independent of the extent of research spillovers and the level of product differentiation, the duopolists have strong incentives to form a full industry cartel. According to Property 3, that would result in the highest level of R&D investments (in comparison to coopetition and industry-wide competition) as long as the size of spillovers is not very low.

When the firms follow the law and do not create a cartel in the final product market, they would prefer to cooperate at the R&D stage rather than engage in the industry-wide competition. In this situation, when the extent of spillovers is relatively low, the R&D investments will be lower than in the cases of industry-wide competition or full industry cartel. However, in this case, it follows from our numerical analysis that the consumers would enjoy the lowest prices.

16.4 Conclusions

In this paper, we considered the price competition of firms in a duopolistic industry with product differentiation and R&D spillovers. The duopolists were assumed to operate in two stages. In the first stage, they made decisions regarding the research investments aimed at product innovation. In the second stage, they decided about the price in the final product market.

We analyzed three cases of firms' behavior: industry-wide competition, coopetition, and full industry cartel. We found that the profits of firms that compete freely are never bigger than their coopetitive profits or the profits in the fully cartelized industry no matter the extent of research spillovers. Hence, it can never be expected that the duopolist will give up on some level of cooperation at product R&D and, quite probably, also on the final product market.

The industry-wide cooperation of firms generates the highest profits for duopolists, but at the same time the prices to consumers of the final product are the highest in comparison to noncartelized markets. However, the relationship between prices in the fully competitive industry and in the case of coopetitive behavior depends on the size of R&D spillovers. When the extent of research externalities is relatively low, the price of the final product is higher in the fully competitive industry than in the case of coopetitive behavior, but this relationship is reversed when the level of R&D spillovers is relatively high.

The relationship between the levels of R&D investments in the three cases under consideration varies depending on the size of research spillovers. When the extent of externalities is relatively low, the amount of R&D investments is the highest in the fully competitive industry and the lowest in the case of coopetition. However, when the size of R&D spillovers is relatively large, the investments in product innovation are the highest in the fully cartelized industry and the lowest in the case of full competition.

Clearly, further research is required to explore other types of firm behavior in oligopolistic markets. Additional analysis should be conducted by varying the level of product differentiation. Also, endogenization of product differentiation and the control of research spillovers could be considered. We will leave the analysis of these ideas for future papers.

Acknowledgments This work was supported by National Science Center, Poland under Grant Number UMO-2017/25/B/HS4/01632.

References

Amir, R., Evstigneev, I., & Wooders, J. (2003). Noncooperative versus cooperative R&D with endogenous spillover rates. *Games and Economic Behavior, 42*(2), 183–207.

Cellini, R., & Lambertini, L. (2009). Dynamic R&D with spillovers: Competition vs. Cooperation. *Journal of Economic Dynamics and Control, 33*(3), 568–582.

Dasgupta, P. (1986). The theory of technological competition. In J. Stiglitz & F. Mathewson (Eds.), *New developments in the analysis of market structures*. MIT Press.

Kamien, M., & Zang, I. (2000). Meet me halfway: Research joint ventures and absorptive capacity. *International Journal of Industrial Organization, 18*, 995–1012.

Kamien, M., Muller, E., & Zang, I. (1992). Research joint ventures and R&D cartels. *American Economic Review, 82*, 1293–1306.

Karbowski, A. (2019). Greed and fear in downstream R&D games. *Decyzje, 32*, 63–76.

Karbowski, A., & Prokop, J. (2019). The impact of vertical R&D cooperation on market performance of firms. *Entrepreneurial Business and Economics Review, 7*, 73–89.

Lipczynski, J., Wilson, J. O. S., & Goddard, J. (2017). *Industrial organization: Competition, strategy and policy*. Pearson.

Martin, S. (2002). Spillovers, appropriability, and R&D. *Journal of Economics, 75*(1), 1–32.

Pippel, G. (2014). R&D cooperation for non-technological innovations. *Economics of Innovation and New Technology, 23*(7), 611–630.

Ramsza, M., & Karbowski, A. (2020). Product R&D coopetition and firm performance. The B.E. *Journal of Theoretical Economics, 20*(2), 1–9.

Symeonidis, G. (2003). Comparing Cournot and Bertrand equilibria in a differentiated duopoly with product R&D. *International Journal of Industrial Organization, 21*(1), 39–55.

Chapter 17
Gender Equality Issues in Labor Markets: Lessons for COVID-19 Era

Nihal Bayraktar

Abstract Contributions of women to labor force participation and gender equality have been considered as one of the important aspects of economic growth. After decades-long struggles, many countries had ultimately accomplished some improvements in terms of gender equality in their labor markets. All this hard work makes sense if gender equality is protected. Unfortunately, the times of economic crisis may reverse the trend in a quick pace. The aim of this chapter was to show the severe negative impacts of the 2008 global crisis on female labor force, especially in some middle-income countries. The study of the effects of this earlier global crisis can provide us with some valuable lessons on how to ease negative consequences experienced by female labor force in the presence of severe economic and financial problems associated with the COVID-19 pandemic crisis. The dataset covers 187 countries from different regions of the world and from different income groups between 2008 and 2019. The findings of the probit regression analysis identify some country characteristics associated with improving gender equality, such as governance quality, access to financial markets by women, and higher female human capital index. During the times of economic crisis, governments tend to spend more money, but sometimes such spending may not target the groups in most needs. However, given that females in the labor market tend to be more negatively affected by economic problems, governments instead may target businesses by women or female workers and training of females to support gender equality in labor markets.

Keywords Gender equality · Labor market · Economic crisis · Determinants of gender equality

JEL Codes J16, D63, E24, J08

N. Bayraktar (✉)
Penn State University, Harrisburg, PA, USA
e-mail: nxb23@psu.edu

N. Tsounis, A. Vlachvei (eds.), *Advances in Quantitative Economic Research*, Springer Proceedings in Business and Economics,
https://doi.org/10.1007/978-3-030-98179-2_17

17.1 Introduction

Gender equality in economic activities has been considered one of the important determinants of economic development, but there are many issues observed in this area (Duflo, 2012). Female labor force participation rates in the long run tend to increase on average, but the rates are not at the desired levels yet; there are ups and downs (Fernandez, 2013). Furthermore, the status of women in the labor market becomes more vulnerable during economic crisis periods because women still earn less on average and have less accumulated wealth to support themselves during difficult times (DiCecio et al., 2008). It was not different after the 2018 global crisis (Cho & Newhouse, 2013). Indeed, this study shows that global female labor force participation declined after the 2008 crisis, but this drop was interestingly temporary on average in the low-income and high-income countries. Gender equality improved quickly in these groups of countries with their economic recovery. However, the problem became alarming in middle-income countries with continuously declining female labor force participation since 2008. After this global crisis, the situation got even worse with the COVID-19 pandemic crisis, which erased year-long gains (see, for example, Yu et al. (2020) for initial findings). The share of females in labor force tremendously declined with increasing female unemployment rates.

The labor force participation of women has declined, but their share in business owners and managers has been negatively affected too. As studied extensively in the literature, the share of women in business ownership or in management positions was already low in almost all countries, even before the crisis. Given that the share of women owners and managers is largest in small-sized businesses and this size of businesses has been affected most negatively with the pandemic crisis, the negative trend is expected to continue for a while. These accumulating problems require special government targeted support to protect gender equality in the labor market. If governments target such vulnerable groups in their spending plans, funds could be spent for more productive causes in a way to protect year-long investments to achieve better gender equality in their workforce.

Why is it important to support females in labor force participation? There are many studies in the literature showing the importance of gender equality in labor markets. In addition to boosting growth and shared-prosperity objectives, particularly through productivity and labor-intensive employment channels, greater gender equality can improve other development outcomes, including prospects for the next generation and for the quality of societal policies and institutions (Albanesi, 2019; Duflo, 2012; Klasen & Lamanna, 2009; OECD, 2012; Teignier & Cuberes, 2015; World Bank, 2012). Higher gender equality in economies can also improve income equality (Gonzales et al., 2015).

The role of women in labor force participation has been increasing in many advanced economies, especially after the Second World War. Females initially had started to work to replace declining male labor force, but they continued to contribute more and more after the war with the changing structure of labor markets (Acemoglu et al., 2004; Goldin, 2010; Goldin & Olivetti, 2013). Despite all improvements in gender equality, there are many studies in the literature pointing out how job losses during economic crises have long-lasting, negative impacts on future income and job securities of women (Davis & von Wachter, 2011; Doepke & Tertilt, 2016). What makes women more vulnerable during economic crises is that they already earn lower incomes and own less wealth, and their poverty rates are higher too (OECD, 2020; Schneebaum, 2018; Sierminska et al., 2010). Therefore, when women lose their jobs, the negative impact would be stronger because they have less resource to rely on in the absence of regular income. The effect of the 2008 global financial and economic crisis on women had been relatively less serious in some countries, mainly developed ones, because the crisis had affected the male-dominant and cyclical industries more (OECD, 2012; Rubery & Rafferty, 2013; Sahin et al., 2012). However, when the impact is investigated in a systematic and detailed way in this paper, the outcomes show that women were indeed affected negatively and their share was declining in the labor market after 2008, especially in middle-income countries.

The impact of the recent pandemic crisis has been worse for women in many countries. The first edition of International Labor Organization's (ILO) report after the crisis (2020c) indicated that the problem was expected to be more significant on women in the labor market with quickly deteriorating economic conditions. As new unemployment data were announced, it became clearer that the negative impact on women was indeed stronger when compared to the position of males (He & Torres, 2020; Kochhar, 2020). Alon et al. (2020) indicate that economic closings due to COVID-19 affected women in the labor market disproportionally worse in the United States. Women experienced more job losses, especially because they had to spend more time for childcare needs during school closures. Queisser et al. (2020) report that COVID-19 crisis caused disproportionately more damage to jobs and incomes of females because the negative impact and consequent job losses were stronger in several female-dominated industries, including food and beverage services, retail, and accommodation services.

This paper tries to investigate the status of females in labor force participation in different countries and how it has changed after the 2008 crisis to better understand the possible impacts of the current pandemic crisis. The paper also tries to identify different country characteristics that would determine gender equality in females' labor force participation. Country characteristics include such variables as the size of government spending, geographical location of countries, governance quality, income levels, growth performance, female education level, and female human capital index. Binary probit regression models are estimated to identify the relevant characteristics. The dataset covers 187 countries and focuses on the years after the 2008 global crisis up to 2019 to predict what the impact of the current pandemic crisis would be on gender equality in labor markets. The results based on probit estimations show that middle-income countries and countries with lower financial market access for females are on average less likely to have gender equality in their labor markets, where gender equality is captured by the share of female labor force in female adult population and the ratio of female to male labor force participation.

Similarly, higher human capital and health indicators of females can improve their positions in labor markets.

The next section gives information about data. Section 17.3 explains the regression specification and the methodology. Section 17.4 presents the results, while Sect. 17.5 concludes.

17.2 Data Information

The main data sources are the World Bank's World Development Indicators (WDI) and gender databases and ILO databases. The data cover the period between 1990 and 2019, but the focus is between 2008 and 2019. There are 187 countries. 31 of them are low-income countries; 98 of them are middle-income countries; and 58 of them are high-income countries. The definitions of the main variables are (taken from WDI (2020) and ILO (2020a, b, c)) given as follows.

Labor Force Participation Rate, Female (% of Female Population Ages 15+): Labor force participation rate is the proportion of the population ages 15 and older that is economically active: all people who supply labor for the production of goods and services during a specified period.

Labor Force Participation Rate, Male (% of Male Population Ages 15+): Labor force participation rate is the proportion of the population ages 15 and older that is economically active: all people who supply labor for the production of goods and services during a specified period.

Ratio of Female to Male Labor Force Participation Rate (%): Labor force participation rate is the proportion of the population ages 15 and older that is economically active: all people who supply labor for the production of goods and services during a specified period. Ratio of female to male labor force participation rate is calculated by dividing female labor force participation rate by male labor force participation rate and multiplying by 100.

Unemployment, Female (% of Female Labor Force): Unemployment refers to the share of the labor force that is without work but available for and seeking employment.

Unemployment, Male (% of Male Labor Force): Unemployment refers to the share of the labor force that is without work but available for and seeking employment.

Figure 17.1 reports the labor force participation rates for females and males in different income groups. In the upper left panel, the labor force participation rate is reported for females as a percent of female adult population (15+ years of age). As it can be seen in the panel, while the participation rate of females has been increasing in high-income countries, unfortunately it has a downward trend in the low- and middle-income countries. Especially, starting right after the 2008 global economic crisis, these declining trends became more obvious. In low-income countries, this downward trend slowed down around 2012, and a small improvement was observed

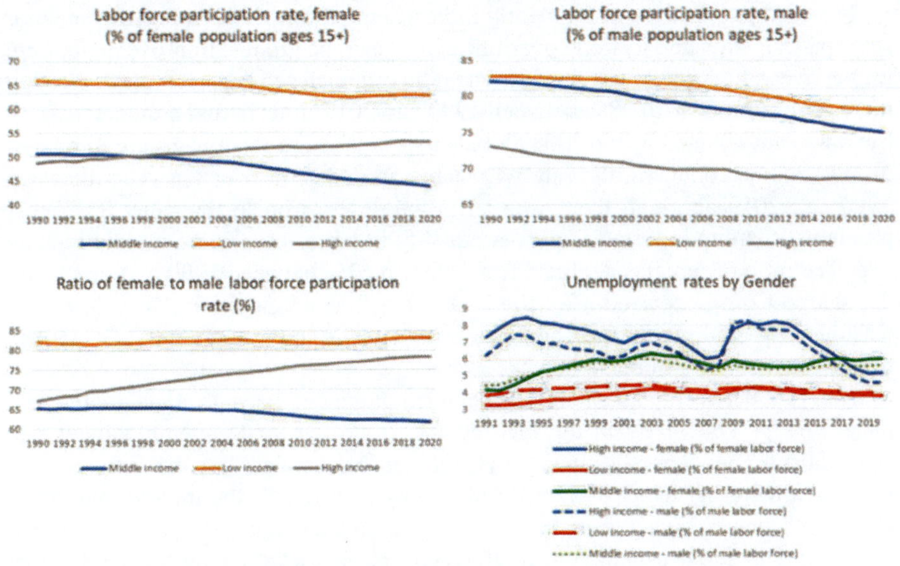

Fig. 17.1 Labor force participation and unemployment by gender (1990–2019). (Source: The author's calculations based on World Development Indicators and ILO databases)

in gender equality. However, the declining trend has still been continuing in the middle-income group up to most recent years.

When we compare the income groups, Fig. 17.1 shows that the female participation rate is highest in the low-income countries and lowest in the middle-income countries on average. Female labor force participation was relatively high at the beginning of the 1990s in the middle-income group too, but it declined along the years from 51% to 44% between 1990 and 2019. On the other hand, the female labor participation rate was increasing from 49% to 53% in the high-income group until 2019, mostly thanks to the widespread promotion of diversity in labor markets. It is expected that these rates sharply dropped with the pandemic crisis. Labor market reports indicate that women disproportionally lost their jobs. For example, the ILO (2020a, b) estimates that women were over-represented in high-risk sectors in terms of the impact of the crisis, especially in the lower-middle and upper-middle-income countries. The impact is expected to be relatively lower in the low-income group, but still women were negatively affected in this process. Therefore, it is important to consider how governments should target women specifically in their economic stimulus efforts.

The second panel of Fig. 17.1 shows that the share of male labor force in percent of male adult population has been declining in all income groups, but its values are still higher compared to female labor force participation. For example, while the female participation rate in the low-income countries is around 63% (a higher value compared to the middle-income and high-income groups), it is 78% for male labor force participation for the same group.

The third panel of Fig. 17.1 clearly indicates the lower share of females in labor force participation and its trend overtime across income groups. Improvements were impressive in high-income countries. The ratio of females in labor force was steadily increasing from 67% to 78% between 1990 and 2019. Interestingly, this increasing trend was not affected by the 2008 global crisis in the high-income group. Similarly, in low-income countries, the rate was stable around 83% over the years between 1990 and 2019 although there was an initial slight drop in the ratio. The most problematic group in terms of gender equality in labor force is the middle-income one. The ratio of females declined from 66% to 62% between 1990 and 2019, and the sharpest drop occurred after the 2008 global economic crisis. Therefore, this was the only group with deteriorating gender equality on average in labor markets before the COVID-19 crisis.

The gap between male and female unemployment rates is wide in the last panel of Fig. 17.1. Only in the low-income group, the male unemployment rate is slightly higher than the unemployment rate of females, but the difference is small. On the other hand, the female unemployment rate in the middle- and high-income groups is higher than the male unemployment rate. The size of the gap was getting larger, especially during the recovery period following the 2008 global crisis. The difference is expected to get larger with the COVID-19 crisis (see, for example, Karageorge, 2020). This larger gap can be taken as an indicator of a higher vulnerability of females in labor markets.

Another negative observation for gender equality during crisis periods is related to the types of firms where generally females work as workers or top managers and own a business. Gender inequality is high in almost all countries when female top managers and business ownership are considered (Bayraktar, 2021b). However, the share of female ownership, top management, and workers is commonly largest in small-sized businesses (Ali, 2018; Amin, 2010; Mijid, 2017).

The issue during economic crises is that small businesses tend to be more fragile and more likely to be closed because of the lack of funds to support such small businesses even for a short time period (Sahin et al., 2011). The situation was not different during the COVID-19 pandemic crisis (Bartik et al., 2020; Nicola et al., 2020). Small business closures were more common, and they were financially more fragile. Therefore, it is essential to consider the distribution of females across different firm sizes and industries to better evaluate the possible impacts of the COVID-19 crisis.[1]

Table 17.1 presents the average values of the share of firms with female top managers, owners, and the share of women in total employees of firms. The data source is Enterprise Surveys of the World Bank. This database classifies firm sizes as follows: micro firms (less than 5 workers); small (5–19 workers); medium (20–99

[1] It should be noted that the empirical findings of this paper do not cover the COVID period because the data are not complete yet for cross-country comparisons. But still, they can be helpful to understand the role of females in labor markets and its determinants in different income groups before the latest economic issues caused by the COVID-19 pandemic.

Table 17.1 Gender differences in management, ownership, and workers across sector and firm size, 2008–19

			High-income	Upper middle-income	Lower middle-income	Low-income
Sector	Core	Share of firms with female owners	0.343	0.312	0.286	0.206
		Share of female workers in firms	0.275	0.248	0.224	0.118
		Share of firms with female top managers	0.131	0.131	0.122	0.078
	Manufacturing	Share of firms with female owners	0.380	0.474	0.433	0.167
		Share of female workers in firms	0.198	0.207	0.182	0.107
		Share of firms with female top managers	0.136	0.140	0.112	0.070
	Services	Share of firms with female owners	0.432	0.353	0.324	0.218
		Share of female workers in firms	0.477	0.363	0.294	0.161
		Share of firms with female top managers	0.214	0.186	0.181	0.122
Size	Large	Share of firms with female owners	0.342	0.342	0.329	0.257
		Share of female workers in firms	0.307	0.264	0.234	0.165
		Share of firms with female top managers	0.104	0.117	0.100	0.066
	Medium	Share of firms with female owners	0.353	0.330	0.315	0.222
		Share of female workers in firms	0.313	0.263	0.232	0.166
		Share of firms with female top managers	0.137	0.146	0.119	0.080

(continued)

Table 17.1 (continued)

		High-income	Upper middle-income	Lower middle-income	Low-income
Small	Share of firms with female owners	0.391	0.329	0.308	0.205
	Share of female workers in firms	0.320	0.279	0.248	0.178
	Share of firms with female top managers	0.192	0.171	0.157	0.110
Micro	Share of firms with female owners	0.379	0.314	0.232	0.245
	Share of female workers in firms	0.340	0.282	0.242	0.213
	Share of firms with female top managers	0.245	0.223	0.224	0.198

Source: the author's calculations based on WDI and Enterprise Surveys Database. The core sector includes coal, crude oil, natural gas, refinery products, fertilizers, steel, cement, and electricity. 154 developing and developed countries are included

workers); and large (100+ employees). The data cover 2008–2019. As can be seen in Table 17.1, males are heavily dominant across all firm classifications and income groups. The share of females is larger in high-income countries in all categories. Consistently rising female labor force participation for this group of countries, at least before the COVID-19 crisis, supports this conclusion, as was presented in Fig. 17.1. The service industry provides most opportunities for females. The share of female workers and the share of firms with female top manager are highest in the service industry in each income group. For example, in the services sector of middle-income countries, almost 33% of firms were owned by females, 34% of workers were females, and 18% of firms had a female top manager. In each income group, the share of females is larger in micro- and small-size firms. In each size category, the share is largest in high-income countries. The share of females in the upper-middle-income group is 28.2% in micro- and small-size firms. The share is 26% in medium and large firms. The differences across firm sizes are even more sticking when the share of firms with female ownership is considered. In middle-income countries, 22% of micro-firms were managed by females. This share was 16%, 12%, and 10%, successively, in small, medium, and large size firms. The table clearly shows that women contribute more to micro- and small-sized firms. The share of female involvement was lowest in the low-income group because the data cover only formal sectors. The labor force participation rate for females was higher in low-income countries, as presented in Fig. 17.1, but this figure covers both formal and informal sectors. Because females mostly take place in informal sectors in low-income countries (Bayraktar & Fofack, 2018), a survey study based on formal sectors cannot successfully capture the role of females in labor markets. The share of female workers was around 21% in micro firms, 18% in small firms, and 16% in medium and large firms in low-income countries. In this group, 20% of micro-firms' top managers was female, 11% in small firms, 8% in medium-size firms, and 6% in large-sized firms.

Table 17.2 presents the share of countries with declining female labor force between 1990 and 2019 as well as between 2008 and 2019, following the 2008 global crisis. Gender equality in labor force is calculated with the help of two variables: female labor force participation (in % of female adult population) and the ratio of female to male labor force participation. The time trend of these variables is presented in Fig. 17.1. Table 17.2 gives more detailed information on countries in terms of gender equality. In each group, there are countries with declining female labor contributions. Female labor force participation declined more rapidly after 2008 in a high number of countries, except the low-income group. For example, the change in female labor force between 1990 and 2019 was negative in 40%, 30%, and 19% of countries in lower-middle, upper-middle, and high-income countries, successively. On the other hand, between 2008 and 2019, the share of countries with dropping female labor force was 45%, 32%, and 31% in lower-middle, upper-middle, and high-income countries, successively. Table 17.2 shows that not only female labor force participation, but the ratio of female to male labor force participation was also declining in many countries. This means that male labor force was getting more dominant. The dropping share of female-to-male labor force participation was relatively low in the high-income group. Only 6.90% of countries in this group had a negative rate between 2008 and 2019. However, this drop was more problematic in low- and middle-income countries. Also, the share of countries with negative rates was much higher after the 2008 crisis. During this period, in 38.71% of low-income countries, we observe a declining role of females in labor force relative to males. The share of countries was 42% and 38% in the lower-middle and upper-middle groups, respectively. These values were much higher than what was observed in the high-income group. Therefore, we can conclude that gender inequality increased in the labor market of many low-income and middle-income countries. Even though the share of countries with increasing gender inequality was higher in the low-income group, we have seen a relatively flat or slightly increasing share of females in labor force in Fig. 17.1 at the aggregate level. The reason for these conflicting aggregate results is that aggregate averages were calculated as weighted averages based on the populations of countries. Therefore, even if gender inequality was increasing at the country levels, it was improving at the aggregate level because gender equality was improving in more populated low-income countries, which dominate the calculation of aggregate values. On the other hand, in the middle-income group, gender inequality was rising both at the aggregate and country levels. Not only less women were participating in the labor market relative to the size of the female adult population, but they were also participating less relative to males, which led to an increasing gender gap in the labor market. Oppositely, the high-income group provided better opportunities for females in their labor market both at the aggregate and country levels, especially after the 2008

Table 17.2 Share of countries with declining female labor force (%)

	Low income		Lower-middle income		Upper-middle income		High income	
	Change from 1990 to 2019	Change from 2008 to 2019	Change from 1990 to 2019	Change from 2008 to 2019	Change from 1990 to 2019	Change from 2008 to 2019	Change from 1990 to 2019	Change from 2008 to 2019
Share of countries with negative change in labor force participation rate, female (% of female population ages 15+)	61.29%	48.39%	40.00%	44.44%	30.19%	32.08%	18.97%	31.03%
Share of countries with negative change in ratio of female to male labor force participation rate (%)	41.94%	38.71%	35.56%	42.22%	18.87%	37.74%	8.62%	6.90%

Source: The author's calculations based on gender database of the World Bank and ILO database crisis. This success was partially due to measures taken to promote diversity and inclusiveness in businesses. Given that females are affected more negatively with the COVID-19 crisis, the share of countries with widening gender gaps in labor markets is expected to increase (see, for example, Bateman & Ross, 2020).

Table 17.3 reports the list of countries with changes in their female labor force participation as a share of female adult population and also relative to male labor force participation. The years cover 2008–19 to understand the impact of the economic crisis on the gender gap. Countries are sorted out based on their population in each income group to give better idea on the changes in highly populated countries, which heavily dominate aggregate measures reported in Fig. 17.1. Table 17.3 is also useful to see in which countries the gender gap was getting wider even before the COVID-19 crisis so that government policies can be set accordingly to improve their positions. The high-income group presented the narrowest and most improving gender gap. The most populated country in the high-income group is the USA. In 2019, the ratio of females to males was 82% in the labor market. This ratio improved by 1%age point between 2008 and 2019. In Japan, the ratio of females to males in labor force was relatively low at 74%, but there was a big improvement at 8% points. The gender gap improved with the highest percentages in Spain, Malta, Luxembourg, U.A.E., Chile, and Singapore in the high-income group.

Table 17.3 shows that middle-income countries had serious issues with widening gender gaps in their labor markets even before the COVID-19 crisis. The upper-middle-income group was in a relatively better shape, compared with the lower-income group, meaning that there were more countries with improving gender equality, but still increasing gender inequality after the 2008 crisis was problematic in some countries. China is the most crowded country in the upper-middle-income group, and the ratio of females to male was one of the highest in 2019 at 80%, but the ratio declined by 3% points between 2008 and 2019, indicating lower gender equality. Because of its large size, declining gender equality in China led to lower gender equality in the upper-middle-income group at the aggregate level. In this group, Brazil is the second most populous country, and we can see a 3-percentage point improvement in this country between 2008 and 2019. The ratio of females to males in labor force reached 73% in 2019. In this group, Russia Thailand, Venezuela, Romania, and Georgia were some of the countries with declining shares of females. On the other hand, Dominican Republic, Turkey, and Guyana achieved the highest improvements. In the labor market of Turkey (the fifth most populous county in the group), the ratio of females to males increased to 47% in 2019 by a 13-percentage point rise from 2008. Big improvements before the COVID-19 crisis were encouraging. South Africa, Colombia, Argentina, Azerbaijan, Paraguay, Namibia, Mauritius, and Belize were some of the countries that experienced improvements in gender gaps after the 2008 crisis. However, the impact of the COVID-19 crisis was fairly negative for females in many countries, as studied by Djankov et al. (2021). Therefore, targeted government policies can be essential to improve the gender gap back to its pre-crisis levels.

Table 17.3 Income groups: ratio of female-to-male labor force participation rate (%)

High income	Ratio 2019	Δ in ratio (2008–19)	Upper-middle income	Ratio 2019	Δ in ratio (2008–19)	Lower-middle income	Ratio 2019	Δ in ratio (2008–19)	Low income	Ratio 2019	in ratio (2008–19)
USA	82	1	China	80	−3	India	27	−9	Ethiopia	86	3
Japan	74	8	Brazil	73	3	Indonesia	65	5	Congo, D.R.	92	−4
Germany	83	5	Russia	78	−3	Pakistan	27	3	Tanzania	91	−5
France	85	4	Mexico	56	4	Nigeria	83	−3	Uganda	91	5
UK	85	5	Turkey	47	13	Bangladesh	45	11	Afghanistan	29	10
Italy	69	7	Iran	25	0	Philippines	63	0	Mozambique	98	−5
Korea Rep.	72	4	Thailand	78	−2	Egypt	31	0	Yemen	8	−10
Spain	82	11	South Africa	79	5	Vietnam	88	0	Nepal	97	7
Poland	74	0	Colombia	71	7	Myanmar	61	−5	Madagascar	94	−1
Canada	88	2	Argentina	70	4	Kenya	93	6	Korea, D.R.	84	−1
Saudi Arabia	28	4	Algeria	22	3	Ukraine	74	−3	Niger	72	−3
Australia	85	5	Iraq	16	−1	Sudan	43	4	Burkina Faso	78	7
Chile	70	12	Peru	83	1	Morocco	31	−4	Mali	76	2
Netherlands	84	5	Malaysia	66	9	Uzbekistan	67	−2	Malawi	90	−2
Belgium	83	7	Venezuela	61	−2	Angola	96	1	Syria	19	0
Greece	74	8	Sri Lanka	48	0	Ghana	89	−5	Chad	82	3
Czech Rep.	77	5	Romania	70	−6	Cameroon	88	−4	Somalia	30	2

Portugal	85	4	Kazakhstan	83	−4	Cote d'Ivoire	73	10	Guinea	104	7
Sweden	91	3	Guatemala	46	−2	Zambia	89	3	Rwanda	101	2
Hungary	74	1	Ecuador	68	5	Cambodia	86	0	Benin	94	4
UAE	56	13	Cuba	61	0	Senegal	61	11	Burundi	103	0
Israel	87	7	DominicanR.	66	13	Zimbabwe	88	1	Haiti	85	0
Austria	83	5	Jordan	23	0	Tunisia	34	−2	South Sudan	96	4
Switzerland	85	6	Azerbaijan	91	5	Bolivia	78	4	Tajikistan	59	5
HK (China)	80	5	Belarus	80	−2	Honduras	61	14	Togo	97	−3
Denmark	88	2	Bulgaria	79	−1	Papua N. G.	96	1	Sierra Leone	98	1
Singapore	79	10	Serbia	75	3	Lao PDR	96	−2	Liberia	89	3
Finland	88	1	Paraguay	70	6	Nicaragua	59	3	CAR	81	0
Slovak Rep.	77	3	Lebanon	32	2	El Salvador	60	2	Eritrea	84	−3
Norway	90	2	Libya	52	−1	Kyrgyz Rep.	59	−11	Gambia	75	4
Ireland	82	7	Turkmeni.	66	−2	Congo, Rep.	95	0	Guinea-Bissau	84	2
New Zealand	86	5	Costa Rica	63	7	W.Bank&Ga.	25	2			
Oman	34	2	Georgia	71	−3	Mauritania	46	3			
Panama	67	8	Bos&Herz.	61	7	Mongolia	80	−3			
Kuwait	57	5	Armenia	71	−1	Moldova	88	−1			
Croatia	79	6	Jamaica	82	6	Lesotho	79	−2			
Uruguay	76	6	Albania	72	0	Timor-Leste	85	0			
Puerto Rico	66	1	Namibia	89	8	Eswatini	85	7			
Lithuania	83	2	Botswana	85	6	Djibouti	74	8			
Qatar	60	7	Gabon	70	3	Comoros	73	6			

(continued)

Table 17.3 (continued)

High income			Upper-middle income			Lower-middle income			Low income		
	Ratio	Δ in ratio		Ratio	Δ in ratio		Ratio	Δ in ratio		Ratio	in ratio
	2019	(2008–19)		2019	(2008–19)		2019	(2008–19)		2019	(2008–19)
Slovenia	84	4	N.Macedo.	64	−1	Bhutan	80	−8			
Latvia	81	5	Equ. Guinea	82	2	Solomon Isl.	96	0			
Bahrain	52	5	Mauritius	63	9	Cabo Verde	79	15			
Trin. & Tob.	71	3	Fiji	50	2	Vanuatu	77	0			
Estonia	80	1	Guyana	64	15	SaoTome&P.	56	2			
Cyprus	85	8	Montenegro	74	−1						
Macao (China)	85	2	Suriname	61	3						
Luxembourg	86	13	Maldives	49	−7						
Malta	69	21	Belize	62	6						
Bru. Darus.	81	8	Samoa	56	−1						
Bahamas	83	−2	St. Lucia	79	3						
Iceland	89	2	St. Vin.&Gre.	71	3						
Barbados	89	4	Tonga	62	1						
New Cal.	84	−1									
French Po.	79	6									
Channel I.	77	3									
Guam	69	−2									
Virgin Isl.(U.S.)	93	6									

Source: The author's calculations based on gender database of the World Bank and ILO database

When the lower-middle-income group is considered in Table 17.3, the most populous country, India, experienced widening gender inequality by 9% points. Nigeria, Myanmar, Ukraine, Ghana, Cameroon, Kyrgyz Republic, Mongolia, and Bhutan were some other countries experiencing lower participations of the females in labor markets relative to the males after the 2008 economic crisis. The impact of the COVID-19 crisis on the labor gender gap would be expected to be more severe in these countries. Some countries were able to improve gender equality, such as Indonesia, Bangladesh, Kenya, Sudan, Cote d'Ivoire, Senegal, Honduras, and Cabo Verde. Because these countries are relatively small, their impacts on the weighted average at the aggregate level were limited in terms of improvements in gender equality.

The low-income group in Table 17.3 presents some improvements and drops in their gender equality in labor markets. The most crowded country in the group is Ethiopia. This country was able to improve the gender gap by 3% points, reaching to 86% for the ratio of females to males in the labor force. This rate corresponds to one of the highest values in the world. Some countries experienced declining gender equality, but overall, the share of females in labor force was pretty large in this group. Even, there were countries where the share of females was larger than males, such as Guinea, Rwanda, and Burundi. Given that these countries are low-income countries, male and female members of households are expected to work to be able to earn enough income to make ends meet. Despite such encouraging improvements, some countries had declining gender equality, such as Congo Democratic Republic, Tanzania, Yemen, and Niger. Because these countries are relatively small, they cannot dominate the average values for the low-income countries. Therefore, at the aggregate level, gender equality slightly improved for this group (see Fig. 17.1).

Table 17.3 shows that each country's experience is different in terms of where they stand in gender equality and whether it has been improving or deteriorating. The countries experiencing declining gender equality after the 2008 economic crisis may need to be more careful to protect the position of their female labor with the COVID-19 crisis. Internationally comparable data have not been reported yet to analyze the case of females in the labor market in a systematic way following the COVID-19 crisis, but initial data reports indicate that females have been disproportionally negatively affected. For example, in the USA, the unemployment rate increased more for females. Given that the sectors in which female participation is traditionally higher suffered more with the current crisis, gender equality, which took decades to improve, went downhill, especially in countries where it was already deteriorating after the 2008 crisis. In this process, government supports can be essential to help businesses owned and/or managed by females or to protect female workers directly.

17.3 Specification and Methodology—Probit Analysis

To identify the country characteristics, which can be helpful to improve gender equality in labor markets in terms of higher female labor force participation as a share of female population or higher share of females to males in labor force, a set of probit specifications are estimated. More specifically, we try to understand which country characteristics can promote gender equality, such as income levels, regions, female education, governance indicators, female health indicators, female financial indicators, trade, and economic growth. By assigning probabilities to different country characteristics with probit regressions, we can better understand the types of changes countries may need to introduce to improve or protect their gender equality. In the analysis, we consider changes in gender equality after the 2008 economic crisis to have a better opinion on what is expected following the COVID-19 crisis. The dataset is cross-sectional. Country averages are calculated for all variables between 2008 and 2019, except the gender gap measures (the dependent variable of the regression model).

Dependent variable: The aim of this analysis is to understand the determinants of improved gender equality following the global economic crisis of 2008. In the regression specification, we label the countries with improving gender equality between 2008 and 2019 as successful (equal to 1). The methodologies used to identify successful participants are adopted from the gender literature and modified slightly (see, for example, Hansen & Rand, 2014; Bigsten et al., 2003; Nwosu et al., 2014; Wellalage & Locke, 2017).

The first dependent variable is defined as follows: If the change in the ratio of females to males in labor force participation between 2008 and 2019 is greater or equal to 0, GENDER EQUALITY_LABOR_1 = 1; 0 otherwise.

We also consider an alternative definition of gender equality in the labor market: If the change in the share of female labor force in percent of female adult population between 2008 and 2019 is equal or greater than 0, we mark this country as successful, meaning GENDER EQUALITY_LABOR_2 = 1; 0 otherwise.

Explanatory Variables The regression specification is based on the literature on possible determinants of gender equality in the labor market. Female participation in financial markets, female education, cultural differences, differences in income levels, macroeconomic conditions, female health indicators, governance quality, human capital quality are some of the factors that can determine gender equality in the labor market. Culture is approximated by the location of countries (geographic regions) and included as indicator variables in the analysis. Table 17.4 introduces the definitions of the variables used in the regression analysis. While defining the binary variables, the change for each variable is calculated by subtracting the value of the variables in 2008 from their value in 2019 for each country. Therefore, each country ends up with one data point after the calculation of the binary variables.

Based on these dependent and independent variables, the regression equation takes the following form:

Table 17.4 Definition and measurement of variables included in regressions

Variables	Definition	Measurement
GENDER_EQUALITY_LABOR_1	Is the change in the ratio of females to males labor force participation between 2008 and 2019 is greater than zero? "Yes" indicates improved gender equality in the labor market.	1 = yes; 0 = otherwise
GENDER_EQUALITY_LABOR_2	Is the change in the share of female labor force in adult female population between 2008 and 2019 is greater than zero? "Yes" answer indicates improved gender equality in the labor market.	1 = yes; 0 = otherwise
LOW	Is the country a low-income country?	1 = yes; 0 = otherwise
LOWER_MIDDLE	Is the country a lower-middle income country?	1 = yes; 0 = otherwise
UPPER_MIDDLE	Is the country a upper-middle income country?	1 = yes; 0 = otherwise
HIGH	Is the country a high-income country?	1 = yes; 0 = otherwise
SOUTH_ASIA	Is the country a South Asian country?	1 = yes; 0 = otherwise
SSA	Is the country a Sub-Saharan African country?	1 = yes; 0 = otherwise
LA	Is the country a Latin American and Caribbean country?	1 = yes; 0 = otherwise
EAST_ASIA_PAC	Is the country an East Asia & Pacific country?	1 = yes; 0 = otherwise
MENA	Is the country a Middle East & North African country?	1 = yes; 0 = otherwise
EUROPE_CA	Is the country a European & Central Asian country?	1 = yes; 0 = otherwise
NA	Is the country a North American country?	1 = yes; 0 = otherwise
WOMEN_HEALTH	Is the life expectancy for females at birth in a country higher than the median value of the world?	1 = yes; 0 = otherwise
WOMEN_EDU	Is the women education for females in a country higher than the median value of the world? Indicator: School enrollment, primary and secondary (gross), gender parity index (GPI)	1 = yes; 0 = otherwise

(continued)

Table 17.4 (continued)

Variables	Definition	Measurement
GOVERNANCE_Quality	Is the value of Government Effectiveness Index in a country higher than the median value of the world? Alternative: Rule of Law Indicator	1 = yes; 0 = otherwise
Gender_equality_Finance	Is the gap between female and male financial indicator in a country lower than the median value of the world? "Yes" answer indicates gender equality in financial markets. Indicators: Financial institution account,female(% age 15+) or Account ownership at a financial institution or with a mobile-money-service provider, female (% of population ages 15+)	1 = yes; 0 = otherwise
Macroeconomic_stab	Is the measure of inflation in a country is lower than the median value of the world? "Yes" answer indicates macroeconomic stability.	1 = yes; 0 = otherwise
Size_Gov	Is the size of government spending in % of GDP is higher than the median value of the world? (General government final consumption expenditure (% of GDP))	1 = yes; 0 = otherwise
HCI_FEMALE	Is the size of female HCI in a country lower than the median value of the world?	1 = yes; 0 = otherwise

Source: The author's calculations based on gender database of the World Bank and ILO database

```
GENDER_EQUALITY_LABOR = f(GENDER_EQUALITY_FINANCE, WOMEN_EDU,
CULTURE, INCOME, MACROECONOMIC_STAB, WOMEN_HEALTH,
GOVERNANCE_QUAL, SIZE_GOV, HCI)
```

Methodology The aim of the regression specification is to examine gender equality in labor markets and country characteristics affecting the labor gender gap. Because of the dichotomous nature of the definition of the success for the countries in closing their gender gaps, a qualitative response model is introduced in the analysis. In general, qualitative response models link the likelihood of an event for different explanatory variables (Amemiya, 1981). Qualitative models are more useful, especially when assessing country characteristics that are related to their success or failure in different considerations. More specifically, a discrete choice probit model is introduced to determine country characteristics. The variables in the regression specification are identified as binary choices (yes (1), no (0)) based on whether a country has accomplished to improve gender equality in their labor markets, as defined above. In binary outcome regression analysis, it is generally assumed that the estimated value of a binary outcome of y (unobservable variable y_hat) is defined in an equation as follows: $y\_hat = x'\beta + e$, where x is the explanatory variables, β is estimated coefficients for marginal effects of explanatory variables, and e is the error term. Although y_hat is unobservable, it could be classified as 1 or 0 based on the probabilities calculated from estimated coefficients. The probability of y_hat = 1, given x, is determined by comparing the probability of $x'\beta$ to a threshold probability, such as 50%. If the estimated probability is lower than the threshold probability, then y_hat = 0. All variables are binary in the regression specifications.

17.4 Results

Table 17.5 gives information on the descriptive statistics. The probability of success, as defined in Table 17.4, is 71% and 63% for the positive changes in the ratio of females to males and changes in the share of female labor force in female adult population, successively, between 2008 and 2019. These values give the share of countries with success. These two variables are going to be the alternative dependent variables of the regression model. The descriptive statistics of explanatory variables are also reported in Table 17.5. They show the probability of success for each variable, as defined in Table 17.4. There are 187 countries. 8 of them are from South Asia; 29 of them from East Asia and Pacific; 49 of them are from Europe and Central Asia; 47 from sub-Saharan Africa; 21 from MENA; and 31 from Latin America. 31 countries are low-income countries; 45 are lower-middle-income countries; 53 are upper-middle-income countries; and 58 are high-income countries.

The probit estimation outcomes for improvements in gender equality are reported in Table 17.6. In each column, different variables and country groups are introduced for robustness checks of the results. The findings show that one of the consistently most significant variables in determining gender equality after the 2008 economic crisis is human capital index (HCI). Countries that accomplished better HCI improvements are also more likely to improve gender equality in their labor markets. It is positively and significantly correlated with improved gender equality in labor markets. For example, as shown in column 1 of Table 17.6, countries with higher HCI for females are on average 27% more likely to improve gender equality; everything else remains constant.[2] This result indicates that governments should continue to invest in education and training of females to support gender equality. Similar results are observed for female education in the regression results.

[2] It should be noted that the estimated coefficients can be interpreted as marginal effects because all variables are binary in the regression equation.

Table 17.5 Descriptive statistics

Variables	Mean	Standard Dev	Min	Max	Sum	Count
GENDER_EQUALITY_LABOR_1	0.71	0.45	0	1	133	187
GENDER_EQUALITY_LABOR_2	0.63	0.48	0	1	118	187
WOMEN_EDU1	0.56	0.50	0	1	104	187
WOMEN_HEALTH	0.50	0.50	0	1	93	187
WOMEN_EDU2	0.40	0.49	0	1	75	187
HCI_FEMALE	0.34	0.47	0	1	63	187
Macroeconomic_stab	0.53	0.50	0	1	100	187
Gender_equality _Finance1	0.42	0.49	0	1	78	187
Gender_equality _Finance2	0.42	0.49	0	1	78	187
Size_Gov	0.45	0.50	0	1	84	187
GOVERNANCE_Quality1	0.51	0.50	0	1	95	187
GOVERNANCE_Quality2	0.51	0.50	0	1	95	187
LOW	0.17	0.37	0	1	31	187
LOWER_MIDDLE	0.24	0.43	0	1	45	187
UPPER_MIDDLE	0.28	0.45	0	1	53	187
HIGH	0.31	0.46	0	1	58	187
SOUTH_ASIA	0.04	0.20	0	1	8	187
SSA	0.25	0.43	0	1	47	187
LA	0.17	0.37	0	1	31	187
EAST_ASIA_PAC	0.16	0.36	0	1	29	187
MENA	0.11	0.32	0	1	21	187
EUROPE_CA	0.26	0.44	0	1	49	187
NA	0.01	0.10	0	1	2	187

However, its impact is limited on labor market gender equality. It even has an unexpected negative sign in some cases. Therefore, not only education but also other improvements are needed to promote gender quality. Improved health indicators for females help them contribute more to the labor market. As they live longer, they participate more in the labor market, maybe because the returns from working would be larger when one lives longer. Therefore, governments should pay special attention for female health to make them continue to contribute to labor force.

Columns 1, 3, 4, and 6 indicate that lower-middle-income countries are negatively correlated with improvements in gender equality. More specifically, for the lower middle-income group, the probability of improved gender equality is lower by around 30% on average. Further, as shown in columns 2 and 5, some regions are also associated with lower probability of gender equality in the labor market. For example, South Asian countries and East Asian countries are on average 7–85% less likely to improve gender equality in the labor market. This may be due to economic issues in the region, which would affect job creation for females. This can be also caused by cultural factors. Some of the countries in these regions traditionally have low female labor participation. Another possibility is that the findings may indicate that females in these regions are not qualified enough to find jobs in markets. The

Table 17.6 Estimation results

Dependent variables	GENDER_ EQUALITY _LABOR_1	GENDER_ EQUALITY _LABOR_1	GENDER_ EQUALITY _LABOR_1	GENDER_ EQUALITY _LABOR_2	GENDER_ EQUALITY _LABOR_2	GENDER_ EQUALITY _LABOR_2
WOMEN_EDU1	0.04*	0.06*	..	−0.136	−0.143	..
WOMEN_HEALTH	0.107*	0.188*	0.140	−0.016	0.146*	0.081*
WOMEN_EDU2	–	–	0.12**	–	–	0.051*
HCI_FEMALE	0.27**	0.639**	0.319*	0.239*	0.267**	0.221*
Macroeconomic_stab	0.420	0.446	0.351	0.427	0.348*	0.291*
Gender_equality _Finance1	0.262**	0.239**	–	0.327*	0.364**	–
Gender_equality _Finance2	–	–	0.281*	–	–	0.154**
Size_Gov	0.153*	0.137	0.081	0.023	0.037	0.121*
GOVERNANCE_Quality1	0.284*	0.461**	–	−0.247	−0.207	–
GOVERNANCE_Quality2	–	–	0.312*	–	–	−0.181
LOW	−0.113***	–	−0.085***	−0.184**	–	−0.121**
LOWER_MIDDLE	−0.345**	–	−0.451***	−0.232**	–	−0.234**
UPPER_MIDDLE	0.182**	–	0.213*	0.318*	–	0.327*
HIGH	–	–	–	–	–	–
SOUTH_ASIA	–	−0.345***	–	–	−0.076***	–
SSA	–	0.191**	–	–	0.188**	–
LA	–	–	–	–	–	–
EAST_ASIA_PAC	–	−0.852*	–	–	−0.338**	–
MENA	–	0.158*	–	–	0.267*	–
EUROPE_CA	–	−0.027**	–	–	−0.006	–
NA	–	–	–	–	–	–
No of obs.	187	187	187	187	187	187
Pseudo-R squared	0.449722	0.435464	0.482314	0.479028	0.4828	0.5123
Log likelihood	−102.6933	−97.7001	−117.7201	−117.2605	−117 -	−127.1234

Note: Definitions of variables are given in Table 17.4. Regression methodology is probit binary regression method. The dataset covers 187 countries, and the period is 2008–19. *, **, and *** stand for significance at 10%, 5%, and 1% levels, successively existence of large informal sectors can be another explanation for lower gender equality. Given these findings, countries in the lower-middle-income group and in some Asian countries with the COVID-19 crisis should take additional steps, such as special job trainings for females, to protect already low female participation in the labor market.

The indicator measuring the governance quality in countries is significantly and positively linked to gender equality when the gender equality is measured by the ratio of female to male participation rates. This result suggests that countries with better governance indicators could make a substantial difference in gender equality in their labor markets. It might be challenging to improve the quality of governance in the middle of economic crisis, but still governments should do their best to stimulate their economies in an effective way. In columns 1, 2, and 3, the probit results show that countries with better governance indicators on average 28% to 46% more likely to improve gender equality than the countries with less effective governance. Protection of rights of females is essential to promote gender equality in labor markets. They are more vulnerable compared to males on average. Given that females are relatively more negatively affected in the labor market with the COVID-19 crisis, protection of women by government policies would be important for the continuation of their participations in labor force. Furthermore, Table 17.6 presents that an increasing size of government in terms of pending increases the probability of improvements in gender equality by 10% on average. Therefore, governments play an important role in promoting gender equality.

Interestingly, macroeconomic stability, captured by declining inflation rates between 2008 and 2019, has positive but not significant effects in most specifications. Although it is expected that more stable economies can create more jobs for both males and females, the estimations in columns 1, 2, 3, and 4 of Table 17.6 reveal that macroeconomic stability has no significant effect on promoting gender equality in labor markets. A possible explanation for this finding is that the positive of negative value of change in inflation between 2008 and 2019 may not capture macroeconomic stability well. Therefore, alternative measures might be included. It should be noted that even though it is not highly significant, the marginal effect of the dummy variable capturing macroeconomic stability is high around 30%. In the last two columns of Table 17.6, this variable is actually significant at 10%. Therefore, we can conclude that there are cases where improved macroeconomic stability can increase the success rate of achieving higher gender equality. This result supports the observation that during economic crises, the likelihood of gender inequality tends to rise.

The results in Table 17.6 also present that gender equality in the labor market requires gender equality in financial markets and in their access to funds, which has been also shown by (Bayraktar, 2021b). Firms owned and managed by females may have difficult times to finance their firms' activities in the presence of constraints in financial markets, especially during economic downturns. Small-sized businesses are mostly owned and/or managed by females, and such firms might be affected more severely during economic crises, including the economic crisis caused by the current pandemic crisis. Therefore, governments may support such female-owned/managed businesses to simulate gender equality in the labor market. If not, as we witnessed during the COVID-19 crisis, improvements in gender equality can quickly start going downhill in the presence of unstable economic and financial markets. It may not be easy to reverse the negative trend when losses are extensive.

17.5 Conclusions and Policy Recommendations

Many segments of economic systems have been negatively affected by economic closures due to the COVID-19 pandemic crisis. However, the undesirable impact on the female population is expected to be stronger and more persistent because of their financial fragility and job insecurity. It took long years to improve and promote gender equality in labor markets. Even before the COVID-19 crisis, gender equality was not close to the desired point. For example, in the middle-income countries, the share of females in labor force has been already declining since the global crisis of 2008. With the COVID-19 crisis, it is not hard to imagine that women's situation in labor markets will get worse. Not only the share of females relative to males in labor force is low, but the labor force participation rate of females in percent of female population is also at the lowest point in many countries.

Given the fragility of women in labor markets, there are important policy implications of the findings of this paper. Governments spend large amounts of funds during economic crises to stimulate the economy. It was not different with the COVID-19 health crisis. Governments introduced large stimulus packages to support the economy (see, for example, Bayraktar, 2021a). Policy responses to the COVID-19 pandemic crisis should continue to take specifically women into account to protect gender equality in the economic structure. It is understandable that governments might have many challenges to overcome to manage effectively the pandemic crisis or other economic crises and support people and businesses in need, but still they would carefully consider that some groups of people, such as females, can be more vulnerable due to their historically weaker positions. The downward moving trend in gender equality in labor force participation can be corrected by protecting females in labor markets through carefully targeting government spending. Targeted government spending can be one important solution. Governments may support businesses owned by females or managed by females or businesses where the share of female employees is higher.

The findings show that countries with lower female human capital index and female education rates may need to take more urgent actions to protect gender equality, based on their experiences after the 2008 global crisis. Based on the regression results, training and education of females, better health services for them, improved governance quality, and easier access to financial resources for women can all improve gender equality. Such policy actions can also increase the overall economic well-being more quickly in a sustainable way because gender equality is important for development. Governments of such countries can support female workers, managers, and business owners by targeted government spending plans if they do not want to witness further drops in the share of women in labor force participation, which would affect economic growth in a negative way.

The initial studies show that the negative impact of the COVID-19 crisis on female labor force participation has been extensive. However, this paper covers the period before 2020; therefore, it does not address the exact changes observed with the recent economic crisis in a systematic way. The paper gives information on the trends in female employment and its determinants right before the COVID-19 crisis era to state the weak and strong points in the process. Therefore, the findings of the paper should be judged keeping this in mind. The analyses in the paper can be extended in the future to better evaluate the exact effects of the recent economic recession on female employment when data across countries are available.

References

Acemoglu, D., Autor, D., & Lyle, D. (2004). Women, war, and wages: The effect of female labor supply on the wage structure at midcentury. *Journal of Political Economy, 112*(3), 497–551.

Albanesi, S. (2019). *Changing business cycles: The role of women's employment* (Vol. No. w25655). National Bureau of Economic Research.

Ali, R. S. (2018). Determinants of female entrepreneurs growth intentions: A case of female-owned small businesses in Ghana's tourism sector. *Journal of Small Business and Enterprise Development, 25*(3), 387–404.

Alon, T., Doepke, M., Olmstead-Rumsey, J., & Michèle, T. (2020, April 19). *The impact of the coronavirus pandemic on gender equality*. VOX.

Amemiya, T. (1981). Qualitative response models: A survey. *Journal of Economic Literature, 19*(4), 1483–1536.

Amin, M. (2010). Gender and firm-size: Evidence from Africa. *Economics Bulletin, 30*(1), 663–668.

Bartik, A. W., Bertrand, M., Cullen, Z. B., Glaeser, E. L., Luca, M., & Stanton, C. T. (2020). *How are small businesses adjusting to covid-19? Early evidence from a survey* (Vol. No. w26989). National Bureau of Economic Research.

Bateman, N., & Ross, M. (2020). *Why has COVID-19 been especially harmful for working women*. The brookings gender equality series (No. 19, October). The Brookings Institution.

Bayraktar, N. (2021a). Does government spending cause investment?: A panel data analysis. In *Advances in longitudinal data methods in applied economic research* (2020 International Conference on Applied Economics (ICOAE)) (p. 169). Springer Nature.

Bayraktar, N. (2021b, June 26). *Financial inclusion of females and gender inequality in businesses*. Work-in-progress.

Bayraktar, N., & Fofack, H. (2018). A model for gender analysis with informal production and financial sectors. *Journal of African Development, 20*(2), 1–20.

Bigsten, A. P., Collie, S., Dercon, M., Fafchamps, B., Gauthier, J., & Gunning, W. (2003). Credit constraints in manufacturing enterprises in Africa. *Journal of African Economies, 12*(1), 104–125.

Cho, Y., & Newhouse, D. (2013). How did the great recession affect different types of workers? Evidence from 17 middle-income countries. *World Development, 41*, 31–50.

Davis, S., & von Wachter, T. (2011). Recessions and the costs of job loss. *Brookings Papers on Economic Activity, 2*, 1–72.

DiCecio, R., Engemann, K. M., Owyang, M. T., & Wheeler, C. H. (2008). Changing trends in the labor force: A survey. *Review-Federal Reserve Bank of Saint Louis, 90*(1), 47.

Djankov, S., Zhang, E. Y., Goldberg, P. K., & Hyland, M. (2021). *The evolving gender gap in labor force participation during COVID-19* (No. 21-8, April). Peterson Institute for International Economics.

Doepke, M., & Tertilt, M. (2016). *Families in macroeconomics*. Handbook of Macroeconomics, vol. 2. North Holland.

Duflo, E. (2012). Women Empowerment and Economic Development. *Journal of Economic Literature, 50*(4), 1051–1079.

Fernandez, R. (2013). Cultural change as learning: The evolution of female labor force participation over a century. *American Economic Review, 103*(1), 472–500.

Goldin, C. (2010). *How to achieve gender equality*. The Milken Institute Review.

Goldin, C., & Olivetti, C. (2013). Shocking labor supply: A re-assessment of the role of World War II on women's labor supply. *American Economic Review, 103*(3), 257–262.

Gonzales, C., et al. (2015). *Catalyst for Change: Empowering Women and Tackling Income Inequality*. IMF.

Hansen, H., & Rand, J. (2014). Estimates of gender differences in firm's access to credit in Sub-Saharan Africa. *Economics Letters, 123*(3), 374–377.

He, E., & Torres, N. (2020, May 8). *Women are bearing the brunt of the Covid-19 economic pain*. Bloomberg.

ILO. (2020a, April 29). *ILO Monitor: COVID-19 and the world of work* (3rd ed.). Updated estimates and analysis. The International Labour Organization.

ILO. (2020b, May 27). *ILO Monitor: COVID-19 and the world of work* (4th ed.). Updated estimates and analysis. The International Labour Organization.

ILO. (2020c, March 18). *ILO Monitor: COVID-19 and the world of work: Impact and policy responses* (1st ed.). The International Labour Organization.

Karageorge, E. (2020, September). *COVID-19 recession is tougher on women. Monthly labor review*. Bureau of Labor Statistics.

Klasen, S., & Lamanna, F. (2009). The impact of gender inequality in education and employment on economic growth: New evidence for a panel of countries. *Feminist Economics, 15*(3), 91–132.

Kochhar, R. (2020, June 11). *Unemployment rose higher in three months of COVID-19 than it did in two years of the Great Recession*. Pew Research Center.

Mijid, N. (2017). Dynamics of female-owned smallest businesses in the USA. *International Journal of Gender and Entrepreneurship, 9*(2). https://doi.org/10.1108/IJGE-10-2016-0041

Nicola, M., Alsafi, Z., Sohrabi, C., Kerwan, A., Al-Jabir, A., Iosifidis, C., Agha, M., & Agha, R. (2020). The socio-economic implications of the coronavirus and COVID-19 pandemic: a review. *International Journal of Surgery, 78*, 185–193.

Nwosu, E. O., Orji, A., & Nwangwu, C. (2014). *Is there discrimination against women entrepreneurs in formal credit markets in Nigeria?* Working paper: 2014-08.

OECD. (2012). *Closing the gender gap: Act now*. OECD Publishing.

OECD. (2020). *OECD Income Distribution Database (IDD)*. OECD.

Queisser, M., Adema, W., & Clarke, C. (2020, April 22). *COVID-19, employment and women in OECD countries*. VOX.

Rubery, J., & Rafferty, A. (2013). Women and recession revisited. *Work, Employment and Society, 27*(3), 414–432.

Sahin, A., Kitao, S., Cororaton, A., & Laiu, S. (2011). Why small businesses were hit harder by the recent recession. *Current Issues in Economics and Finance, 17*(4), 1–7.

Sahin, A., Song, J., & Hobijn, B. (2012). The unemployment gender gap during the 2007 recession. *SSRN Electronic Journal, 17*(42011), 1–7.

Schneebaum, A. (2018). The gender wealth gap across European countries. *Review of Income and Wealth, 64*, 295–331.

Sierminska, E., Frick, J., & Grabka, M. (2010). Examining the gender wealth gap. *Oxford Economic Papers, 62*(4), 669–690.

Teignier, M., & Cuberes, D. (2015). Aggregate costs of gender gaps in the labor market: A quantitative exercise. *Journal of Human Capital, 10*(1), 2016, pp. 1–32.

WDI (2020) World Development Indicators Database. The World Bank group. Retrieved on July 1, 20220. https://databank.worldbank.org/source/world-development-indicators

Wellalage, N., & Locke, S. (2017). Access to credit by SMEs in South Asia: do women entrepreneurs face discrimination. *Research in International Business and Finance, 41*, 336–346.

World Bank. (2012). *Accelerating progress on gender mainstreaming and gender-related MDGs: A progress report* (IDA 16 mid-term review (Washington)). World Bank.

Yu, Z., Xiao, Y., & Li, Y. (2020). The response of the labor force participation rate to an epidemic: Evidence from a cross-country analysis. *Emerging Markets Finance and Trade, 56*(10), 2390–2407.

Chapter 18
Interrelation Between Reinsurance and Financial Performance in Slovak Insurance Companies

Janka Grofčíková, Katarína Izáková, and Dagmar Škvareninová

Abstract In addition to floods, which have been considered a priority risk factor in the context of global warming and thus more research has been focused on this issue, there are still a number of other risks that require more attention. A significant risk factor that has recently occurred is the coronavirus SARS COV-2 and that is why its management has been implemented in the risk management of insurance companies. Due to its high infectivity and rapid spread across the planet, this virus has resulted in a pandemic situation. Hence, countries all over the world have had to take plenty of unpopular measures in order to mitigate the spread and the consequent adverse socioeconomic situation. Obviously, this situation has gradually affected various economic subjects at many levels. Insurance companies, as profit-oriented business entities, have the option to transfer the risks they undergo to reinsurance companies in accordance with reinsurance contracts. Reinsurance can thus affect the financial performance of insurance companies. The aim of our study was to examine and quantify the relationship between reinsurance and selected indicators of financial performance of insurance companies in Slovakia. We quantify these relationships through regression coefficients, which are the output of regression analysis.

Keywords Financial performance · Reinsurance · Insurance companies

J. Grofčíková (✉) · K. Izáková
Faculty of Economics, Department of Finance and Accounting, Matej Bel University in Banská Bystrica, Banská Bystrica, Slovakia
e-mail: janka.grofcikova@umb.sk; katarina.izakova@umb.sk

D. Škvareninová
Faculty of Economics, Department of Language Communication in Business, Matej Bel University in Banská Bystrica, Banská Bystrica, Slovakia
e-mail: dagmar.skvareninova@umb.sk

N. Tsounis, A. Vlachvei (eds.), *Advances in Quantitative Economic Research*, Springer Proceedings in Business and Economics,
https://doi.org/10.1007/978-3-030-98179-2_18

18.1 Introduction

Undoubtedly, insurance plays an important role in the modern society, so as insurers, who are an inevitable part of economies since their role is to manage various risks, such as the risk of epidemics, war, climate change, floods, and risks related to individuals, companies, and countries. A significant risk that has manifested itself at the global level and that still affects insurance companies is the COVID-19 pandemic, which began to spread at the end of 2019. As of June 14, 2021, there were 175,966,000 infected persons and 3,804,217 people died in this pandemic, according to a report by Johns Hopkins University (2021). In Slovakia, a total of 391,026 people were infected and 12,439 people died. Hence, the governments of individual countries all over the world have had to take action that has affected their economies deeply in order to prevent the virus from spreading. Due to these state measures, many companies have closed down, or their operations and activities have been temporarily suspended. In order to mitigate the effects of coronavirus for employees, and self-employed, or for small- and medium-sized companies, the Ministry of Finance of the Slovak Republic elaborated measures, which were released under the official name Lex Korona. With regard to this, the Ministry of Labor, Social Affairs, and Family of the Slovak Republic has already paid 1850 million Euros under more than 200,000 aid agreements. These measures enable employers and self-employed to defer social contributions until May 2021, and at the same time, the deadline was postponed until the end of September 2023, by which they are obliged to pay deferred contributions. Measures related to loan repayments and further mitigation of the negative consequences of the pandemic are comprehensively covered in Act No. 67/2020 Collection of Laws on certain emergency financial measures in connection with the spread of the dangerous contagious human disease COVID-19 with effect from April 4, 2020.

With regard to a pandemic, insurance companies in the Slovak Republic have also had to adapt to the conditions and take a stand. These conditions have been mainly reflected in particular products that are directly related to the pandemic. Concerning this, i.e., the product of life insurance that is provided by Allianz—Slovenská poisťovňa (Allianz—the Slovak Insurance Company), ČSOB Poisťovňa (the Czechoslovak Trade Bank Insurance Company), insurance companies Generali, UNIQA, NN, and Poštová poisťovňa (the Post Insurance Company), and Wüstenrot Insurance Company cover also insurance events related to the coronavirus. It is also the case of the insurance company Kooperativa, which ended hundreds of COVID-19 claims since March 2020 and paid out more than 2 million Euros.

Apparently, the tourism sector is that one which has been significantly affected by the coronavirus pandemic. Due to this, insurance companies had to reflect these changes mainly in the case of travel insurance products. The coverage conditions for the product remained unchanged, but only if the destination was not declared risky at the time of departure. Only the AXA Insurance Company pays for the costs of coronavirus treatment even if their clients travel to an area where the disease has already been confirmed.

The global economy remains below pre-pandemic growth, and in many OECD countries, living standards will not return to pre-pandemic levels by the end of 2022, according to the OECD economic outlook (OECD, 2021).

The world is currently facing the effects of the COVID-19 crisis, not least because the pandemic is still ongoing, creating many uncertainties and consequently also new risks. While standard insurance companies must anticipate risks in all areas where they enter into contracts with their clients, reinsurance companies should be able to take into account not only individual and local but also global risks, processes, and trends. The importance of reinsurance companies is growing, especially in situations where it is necessary to spread the risk coverage so that the stability of individual insurance institutions is not endangered in the event of large insurance claims. An important part of assessing the quality of an insurance company is its financial stability, solvency, and sufficient insurance capacity. Reinsurers, who are part of the reinsurance program of particular insurance companies, significantly help to meet the requirements of solvency and financial strength. An important area that needs to be taken into account when interpreting financial indicators is the rating, which is expressed by the rating of particular agencies. S&P Global Ratings since 1971. Regarding the insurance industry, the rating is also performed by the world famous agencies such as Moody's Investors Service, Fitch, and others.

18.1.1 Reinsurance in Insurance Companies in the Slovak Republic

Reinsurance, as a risk management tool, protects the insurance company's clients, its shareholders, and the insurance company from unexpected damage events of an individual or catastrophic nature and represents an important stabilizing factor of the insurance company. At the European level, Directive 2005/68/EC of the European Parliament and of the Council on Reinsurance defines reinsurance under Paragraph 4 as a significant financial activity, which, by broadening the global risk distribution, makes it possible to increase the ability of primary insurers to engage in insurance and provide insurance cover, as well as to decrease their capital costs. In addition, reinsurance also plays a crucial role in financial stability, as it is an important element in ensuring the soundness and stability of direct insurance markets, as well as the financial system as a whole, through its role as a major financial intermediary and institutional investor. In Slovakia, reinsurance activities are regulated by Act No. 39/2015 Collection of Laws on Insurance, Section 4, Paragraph 14. In accordance with this act, reinsurance activities are defined as the acceptance of risks ceded by an insurance company, or an insurance company from another member state, or a foreign insurance company.

Reinsurance activity in the territory of the Slovak Republic may be performed only on the basis of a permit for the performance of reinsurance activity, which is granted by the National Bank of Slovakia (NBS). Insurance companies may carry out reinsurance business, but only for the types of insurance specified in the insurance business license. There are currently no reinsurance companies domiciled in Slovakia, and the National Bank of Slovakia authorizes the authorization of reinsurance activities for non-life insurance as of June 12, 2021, to all insurance companies except Poštová poisťovňa (the Post Insurance Company), NOVIS poisťovňa (the NOVIS Insurance Company), and from May 11, 2021, to a new Partners Insurance Company as well. All in all, this is a total of nine insurance companies domiciled in Slovakia.

Under the Insurance Act, an authorization to conduct reinsurance business granted to an insurance or reinsurance company is valid for all member states and entitles an insurance or reinsurance company to conduct reinsurance business in another member state through a branch established in another member state or under the freedom to provide services (Act on Insurance No. 39/2015 of Collection of Laws and on Amendments to Certain Acts). In the case of non-life insurance, the given permit is met by 6 branches of insurance companies from another member state and 11 foreign insurance companies freely providing cross-border services in the territory of the Slovak Republic. Reinsurance in both life and non-life insurance is provided by Groupama alone, a branch of an insurance company from another member state. Under the consent of the National Bank of Slovakia, reinsurance only for life insurance is provided by two foreign insurance companies freely providing cross-border services in the Slovak Republic (BNP Paribas Cardif Pojišťovna a.s. and VIG RE zajišťovna a.s.).

The insurance market in the Slovak Republic has recently undergone an intensified process of acquisitions and mergers. In 2020, UNIQA Insurance Company bought AXA Insurance Company. At the same time, Poštová poisťovňa (the Post Insurance Company) was bought by the Union poisťovňa (the Union Insurance Company). In the year 2021, another takeover is expected, since one hundred percent of the shares from the current shareholders of Poštová banka a.s. (the Post Bank) and Slovenská pošta a.s. (the Slovak Post Office) will be transferred to the company Union poisťovňa a.s. (the Union Insurance Company). This transaction will make Poštová poisťovňa (the Post Insurance) part of the Dutch insurance group Achmea.

The reinsurance system is not coordinated, and reinsurance companies are independent financial organizations from which insurance companies choose reinsurance partners according to their own criteria. Not all insurance companies publish their reinsurance partners on their websites or in their annual and financial stability reports.

Insurance companies in Slovakia, which provide this information at least in part, prefer reinsurance coverage provided by renowned global reinsurance companies or their own parent companies. For example, ČSOB Insurance Company cooperates with the parent company KBC and the reinsurance company KBC Group Re. The primary reinsurer for UNIQA is a sister company of UNIQA Re AG, Switzerland, and in selected cases other external reinsurers, whose risk transfer is defined depending on the planning of Solvency Capital Requirements, which are targeted in the risk strategy. The main obligatory partner of the insurance company Kooperativa poisťovňa (the Kooperativa Insurance Company) and KOMUNÁLNA poisťovna (the Communal Insurance Company) is the group reinsurance company VIG Re Zaisťovňa a.s. and VIG Holding. Kooperativa and KOMUNÁLNA insurance companies are governed by the document binding on the entire Austrian VIG Group, which is known as VIG Reinsurance Security Guidelines. This document is updated on a quarterly basis.

The most important non-life insurance reinsurers of Generali Insurance Company are mainly GP Reinsurance EAD, Sofia, which also operates within its Generali Group. Its history dates back to 1831, when the Assicurazioni Generali Company was founded in Trieste, Italy.

The Union Insurance Company uses reinsurance contracts with the main reinsurers—the parent company Achmea and Kooperativa Insurance Company, mainly to mitigate losses in insurance against fire and other property damage.

Allianz—Slovenská poisťovňa (Allianz—the Slovak Insurance Company) reinsurers as part of its reinsurance program, which is based on a combination of reinsurance contracts with priority within the Allianz Group and reinsurance contracts with external reinsurers, in order to reduce the risk of financial loss and protect its own capital resources.

Allianz—Slovenská poisťovňa (Allianz—the Slovak Insurance Company) and ČSOB Poisťovňa (the Czechoslovak Trade Bank Insurance Company) cooperate with such reinsurers who have achieved a rating of A and higher according to S&P Global Ratings (2019), which is in accordance with their internal guidelines. Similarly, the ratings of reinsurers Kooperativa Insurance Company and KOMUNÁLNA poisťovňa (communal insurance company) are updated on the basis of valid ratings of rating agencies, in particular S&P Global Ratings (2019) and A.M. Best Company (2019).

The reinsurance program of ČSOB Poisťovňa (the Czechoslovak Trade Bank Insurance Company) is also placed through reinsurance brokers Aon Benfield and Guy Carpenter. The most important reinsurers participating in the main compulsory non-life insurance reinsurance contracts from ČSOB Poisťovňa, KOMUNÁLNA poisťovňa, and Kooperativa poisťovňa are the reinsurance companies such as SCOR Global P&C (France) and Swiss Re (Germany). Wüstenrot poisťovňa (insurance company) also cooperates with Swiss Re Europa S.A. In addition, Wüstenrot also cooperates with the reinsurance company Hannover Rückversicherungs AG (Germany). ČSOB Poisťovňa also cooperates with this reinsurance company. It is high-quality reinsurance that enables ČSOB Poisťovna to participate in the insurance of companies with a large asset value, which significantly contributes to the reliable and quick settlement of the insurance company's liabilities to clients in the event of an insured event and guarantees safe insurance coverage for clients of ČSOB Poisťovňa even in catastrophic events. Kooperativa poisťovňa states also its other reinsurers such as Hannover Re (Germany). Together with KOMUNÁLNA poisťovňa, they also cooperate with Sirius International (Sweden), whose financial strength and rating provide a sufficient guarantee of the fulfillment of their obligations. The above mentioned European reinsurance companies such as Hannover Re, SCOR SE, and Swiss Re are among the top five global reinsurers in the world according to the insurance premium written for reinsurance premium written according to several rating agencies, e.g., A.M. Best Company (2019).

The reinsurance programs of the abovementioned insurance companies within the years 2020–2021 related to the pandemic are adequate for the accepted risks and are also in accordance with the underwriting capacity of the insurance companies, as well as with the business plan and strategy of the companies. Through the specific terms of reinsurance contracts that are set, reinsurance sufficiently fulfills the function of mitigating financial losses due to the occurrence of potentially high claims and is consistent with the risk appetite of companies and the underwriting concept.

18.2 Literature Review

Reinsurance is one of the practical means that are adopted by insurance companies to transfer insurance risk, which consequently increases the financial stability of the insurance company. The efficiency and capacity of the reinsurance market are directly regulated by insurance markets. Flood insurance risks have become a recognized priority across the continent of Europe, so statistical analyses of Munich Re's NatCatSERVICE database explain the reasons for growing trends in flood losses. The purpose of the authors Deelstra and Plantin (2014) is also to provide application procedures for reinsurance. The studies by Kron et al. (2019) deal with the taxonomy of floods, and at the same time, they examine the reduction in flood risks with a focus on various aspects of flood insurance as a means of risk transfer. Powers and Shubik (2001) discuss the possibility of an optimal number of reinsurance levels. The optimal reinsurance strategy is also discussed by the author Meng et al. (2016). Similarly, Anthropelos and Boonen (2020) pay attention to the optimal reinsurance and strategic behavior of the insurer and reinsurer. The issue of reinsurance optimization is discussed in the literature on risk theory, but mainly from the point of view of actuarial mathematics. The optimal reinsurance and investment policies are also published in studies by Luo et al. (2008) and Chen and Yang (2020).

Since 2019, the pandemic has significantly affected health and the economy worldwide. The epidemic is spreading rapidly in various ways. With regard to this highly infectious virus, it was inevitable to categorize the risk factors and rank them in terms of infection. In their study, Ghorui et al. (2021) pay attention to the risk factors involved in the spread of COVID-19 and simultaneously these factors were ranked. Ecer and Pamucar (2021) evaluate insurance companies during the COVID-19 pandemic, focusing mainly on health care on the basis of several criteria.

Doumpos et al. (2012) also contributed to the discussions focused on the financial performance of insurance companies. In their studies, they state that contributions related to the financial performance of insurance companies can be divided into the following groups: (a) contributions that take into account individual financial circumstances, (b) documents examining companies' credit ratings, (c) the functionality of default forecasts, and (d) studies on the efficiency of insurance companies.

The performance of insurance companies was studied by Tone et al. (2019). In their study, they pay attention to the practical implications for insurance companies and policymakers in terms of resource and investment management, with respect to investments and relevant performance ratios. Subsequently, Grofčíková and Izáková (2019) examine the performance of insurance companies in the Slovak and Czech Republic and compare insurance companies through several indicators of financial performance. Úradníček et al. (2016) and Boďa and Úradníček (2016) also contribute to a comprehensive view of this specific issue with the use of alternative methods of predicting the financial health of companies in the conditions of a dynamic economic environment.

18.3 Methodology

As mentioned above, reinsurance is an important risk management tool for insurance companies. Its application in practice is also reflected in the achieved financial performance of insurance companies. The aim of this study was to examine and evaluate the relationship between reinsurance and selected indicators of financial performance of insurance companies. The monitored period includes the accounting periods from 2008 to 2020. Data are obtained from the Statement of Financial Position and the Statement of Comprehensive Income, which are part of the financial statements of individual insurance companies prepared in accordance with International Financial Reporting Standards as adopted by the European Union, and which are publicly available for the period under review in the Register of Financial Statements or on the websites of individual insurance companies. The obtained data are always as of December 31 for the relevant period and are on an annual basis.

The relationship of reinsurance with selected indicators of financial performance of insurance companies will be quantified with the use of regression analysis. We will examine the performance of individual insurance companies through return on assets (ROA) and return on revenue (ROR) indicators. Reinsurance will be calculated through the ratio of gross premium earned ceded to reinsurers on gross premium earned. From the variables listed in Table 18.1, we compile a regression model, the general form of which is as follows:

$$y = \beta_0 + \beta_1 x_1 + \beta_2 x_2 + \cdots + \beta_n x_n + \varepsilon, \quad (18.1)$$

where y = an explained, dependent variable, β = a regression coefficient, x = a selected independent, explanatory variable, ε = a random error, and n = a number of explanatory variables.

With regard to the selection of the indicators entering the regression model, the criterion that has been taken into consideration is their ability to describe the processes of managing the financial performance of insurance companies in relation

Table 18.1 Research variables

Ratio description	Abbrev.	Measurement
Return on assets	ROA	Profit before taxes/total assets
Return on revenues	ROR	Profit before taxes/revenues
Reinsurance	REINS	Gross premium earned ceded to reinsurers/gross premium earned
Firm size	FS	Natural logarithm of assets
Insurance leverage	IL	Gross premium written/profit after taxes
Financial leverage	FL	Total liabilities/total assets
Reinsurance price	RP	(Gross earned premium ceded to reinsurers − reinsurance commissions − insurance claims and benefits ceded to reinsurers)/gross written premium
Insurance risk	IR	Insurance claims and benefits/gross premium written
Growth rate of gross premiums written	GRPW	$(GPW_1/GPW_0) - 1$
Return on investment	ROI	Profit after taxes/average investment
Member of the holding	H	1/0 (yes/no)
Active reinsurance	AR	1/0 (yes/no)

to reinsurance. Reinsurance (REINS) is the main variable examined in our research, and we calculate it with respect to the available data as the ratio of the premium ceded to the reinsurer to the gross premium. The exact calculation of individual indicators is shown in Table 18.1.

ROA and ROR are among the basic indicators, as they indicate the company's ability to generate the required outputs, which will then be reflected in the amount of their revenues and assets. ROI is another indicator that can measure the contribution of insurance companies' investments to profit generation. The size of the insurance company (FS) can affect the efficiency of operating costs, and regarding, this many studies point to a positive correlation between the size of the company and its performance. Insurance companies must have sufficient underwriting capacity and reinsurance enables them to expand this capacity. In addition, some studies point to a positive correlation between insurance leverage (IL) and reinsurance demand. Although financial leverage (FL) reduces operating costs, high leverage is usually associated with the likelihood of bankruptcy. The price of reinsurance (RP), insurance risk (IR), and the year-on-year change in the amount of written premium (GRPW) can affect both the demand for reinsurance and the financial benefits resulting from reinsurance. The binary variables whose impact on the explanatory variables we examine are (H)—which determines whether an insurance company is part of a holding company, and (AR)—which indicates whether an insurance company provides active reinsurance.

The explaining ability of the regression model is verified by F test ANOVA (H_0: $\mu_0 = \mu_1 = ... = \mu_n$; H_1: $\mu_0 \neq \mu_1 \neq ... \neq \mu_n$). Adequacy of the respective explanatory variables included in the model is evaluated with T test (H_0: $\mu_0 = \mu_1$;

H_1: $\mu_0 \neq \mu_1$). To assess the multicollinearity of the explanatory variables entering the regression model, we use the variance inflation factor (VIF) indicator with the maximum reference value of 10. Variables with VIF < 10 can be assessed as weakly, insignificantly linearly interdependent. By means of the Durbin–Watson test, we assess residues ε_i independence (H_0: residues ε_i are independent; H_1: residues ε_i are interdependent). If required, this might be complemented with a test of statistical relevance of the autocorrelation coefficient of the first degree.

For the purpose of assessment of the used statistical methods, we use significance level $\alpha = 0.05$. The SPSS program will be used for the calculations.

In the research, we use the information for all insurance companies based in the Slovak Republic (20 entities) and branches of insurance companies of another member state (7 entities), which operated in the Slovak Republic in the period under review and which were entered in the Commercial Register of the Slovak Republic, and data from their financial statements were publicly available. The data file contains a total of 245 accounting periods of individual entities. During the period under review, there were on average 24 branches of insurance companies in another member state and on average 16 insurance companies domiciled in the Slovak Republic. As of June 20, 2021, there were 20 branches and 13 insurance companies. Due to the fact that we work with all data published in the financial statements for the period under review and that the file contains data for all key players in the insurance market in the Slovak Republic, we consider our data set to be a basic (i.e., representative) file.

18.4 Empirical Results and Discussion

18.4.1 Descriptive Statistics of Variables

Descriptive statistics of the examined variables are shown in Table 18.2. The statistics provide information on the minimum, maximum, and average value of the surveyed indicator, about their standard deviation, variance, skewness, kurtosis, and percentiles. "N" expresses the total number of variable values in the base data file.

In this paper, we focus on examining the relationship between ROA, ROR, and reinsurance. ROA correlates profit with total assets, regardless of the sources from which these assets were financed. It measures the productive power of insurance companies. The median value of ROA of insurance companies in the Slovak Republic is 2.25% in the observed period. Despite the fact that the average ROA is −0.7%, we found a higher number of concentrations of higher ROA values (skewness = −8.9). The results in Table 18.2 also indicate that in a quarter of the period under review (i.e., 61 accounting periods), insurance companies reported ROA higher than 3.86%.

Table 18.2 Descriptive statistic of variables

Ratio description	N	Minimum	Maximum	Mean	Std. Dev.	Variance	Skew.	Kurtos.	Percentiles 25	50	75
Return on assets (ROA)	244	−2.609	0.283	−0.007	0.211	0.044	−8.893	.310	.00412	.02249	.03857
Return on revenues (ROR)	243	−57.1	4.526	−0.168	3.713	13.789	−15.002	.311	.01412	.08259	.151592
Reinsurance (REINS)	243	−0.922	0.996	0.137	0.202	0.041	1.578	.311	.02183	.06937	.19274
Firm size (FS)	245	12.823	21.606	18.534	1.778	3.163	−.429	.310	17.0279	18.8019	19.8424
Insurance leverage (IL)	245	−405.361	7307.622	56.464	492.776	242828.26	13.518	.310	4.7940	10.527	21.4905
Financial leverage (FL)	244	0.038	13.748	0.866	1.192	1.421	.464	.310	0.00	0.00	1.00
Reinsurance price (RP)	243	−1291.29	4966.967	15.169	329.552	108604.5	13.875	.311	.0075	.0237	.0635
Insurance risk (IR)	243	−1.586	134168.2	1063.203	11699.05	136867885	10.980	.311	.2372	.4858	.6839
Growth rate of gross premiums written (GRPW)	217	−1	165722.7	764.625	11249.93	126561016	14.731	.329	−.014245	.03446	.117485
Return on investment (ROI)	213	−2.040	1.547	0.037	0.253	0.064	−.199	.332	.008595	.02393	.03913
Member of the holding (H)	245	0	1	0.79	0.407	0.166	−1.447	.310	1.00	1.00	1.00
Active reinsurance (AR)	245	0	1	0.39	0.488	0.238	0.464	0.31	0	0	1
Valid N (list wise)	211	x	x	x	x	x	x	x	x	x	x

Return on revenues informs about the ability of insurance companies to generate income, and the median value of ROR is 8.2%. In the data set, ROR tended to concentrate on higher values (skew. = −15). We measured ROR values at least 15.16% for a quarter of the period under review.

Insurance companies assign an average of 13.7% of their earned premiums to the reinsurer. The median of reinsurance is 6.94%. We found a higher concentration of lower shares of assigned premiums (skew. = 1.6). However, in the quarter of the examined accounting periods, the ratio of reinsurance (REINS) was at least 19.27%.

18.4.2 Regression Analysis

We use linear regression analysis to analyze the relationships between the performance of insurance companies and reinsurance. We examine these relationships in two steps.

In the first step, we quantify the relationship between ROR and REINS. We formulate models that contain the variables listed in Table 18.1 exempt ROA. In model 1, the dependent variable is ROR, and the other variables, including REINS, are independent variables. In model 2, the dependent variable is REINS and ROR has been included as an independent variable. Individual models can be written in the form:

$$\begin{aligned}\text{Model Nr 1}: \text{ROR} = \beta_0 + \beta_1 H + \beta_2\text{AR} + \beta_3\text{REINS} + \beta_4\text{FS} + \beta_5\text{IL} + \beta_6\text{FL}\\ +\beta_7\text{RP} + \beta_8\text{ROI} + \beta_9\text{IR} + \varepsilon,\end{aligned} \tag{18.2}$$

$$\begin{aligned}\text{Model Nr 2}: \text{REINS} = \beta_0 + \beta_1\text{H} + \beta_2\text{AR} + \beta_3\text{FS} + \beta_4\text{IL} + \beta_5\text{FL} + \beta_6\text{RP}\\ +\beta_7\text{ROI} + \beta_8\text{IR} + \beta_9\text{ROR} + \varepsilon.\end{aligned} \tag{18.3}$$

The outputs of the regression analysis are summarized in Table 18.3.

From the outputs for model 1 in Table 18.3, we can see that ROR is moderately strongly influenced by REINS ($B = 0.529$). This finding does not support the claims of some authors (Lee & Lee, 2012) that insurance companies with a higher ratio of premiums written show lower performance. The results of our research point to the opposite fact. Insurance companies in Slovakia achieve a higher ROR in the case of a higher reinsurance ratio (REINS). Increasing the reinsurance by 1 unit will increase the ROR by 0.529 units. In addition to REINS, the ROR of insurance companies is also significantly affected by ROI ($B = 1.44$), FS ($B = 0.04$).

The opposite relation is quantified in model 2. The dependent variable in this case is REINS, and ROR has become an independent variable. The other independent variables remained the same as in model 1. Compared to model 1, we have a higher number of significant explanatory variables in model 2. We are primarily interested

Table 18.3 Coefficients

		Unstandardized coefficients		Standardized coefficients			Collinearity statistics	
		B	Std. error	Beta	t	Sig.	Tolerance	VIF
Model Nr 1: dependent variable ROR								
Independent variables	(Constant)	−.78132	.331		−2.361	.019**		
	H	−.09160	.066	−.069	−1.378	.170	.862	1.160
	AR	.00827	.062	.007	.134	.894	.695	1.439
	REINS	.52892	*.157*	*.190*	*3.363*	*.001****	*.667*	*1.499*
	FS	.03972	.018	.117	2.219	.028**	.767	1.305
	IL	.00034	.000	.057	1.175	.241	.917	1.090
	FL	.06646	.029	.109	2.328	.021**	.969	1.032
	RP	−1.353E-06	.000	−.001	−.016	.987	.769	1.301
	ROI	1.44004	.110	.662	13.042	.000***	.831	1.203
	IR	−1.153E-07	.000	−.003	−.050	.960	.773	1.293
Model Nr 2: dependent variable REINS								
Independent variables	(Constant)	.54096	.141		3.837	.000***		
	H	.11831	.028	.246	4.248	.000***	.930	1.075
	AR	.11596	.026	.289	4.522	.000***	.765	1.306
	FS	−.02937	.008	−.241	−3.859	.000***	.803	1.245
	IL	−.00052	.000	−.239	−4.267	.000***	.993	1.007
	FL	−.00197	.013	−.009	−.156	.876	.944	1.059
	RP	−1.372E−05	.000	−.024	−.383	.702	.769	1.300
	ROI	.08443	.065	.108	1.300	.195	.455	2.198
	IR	7.855E-08	.000	.005	.078	.938	.773	1.293
	ROR	.10025	*.030*	*.278*	*3.363*	*.001****	*.456*	*2.191*

* Correlation is significant at the 0.1 level (2-tailed). ** Correlation is significant at the 0.05 level (2-tailed). *** Correlation is significant at the 0.01 level (2-tailed)

Table 18.4 Model summary

	Model summary				ANOVA		
Model Nr	R	R square	Adj. R square	SE of the Est.	F	Sig.	Durbin–Watson
1	.754	.568	.549	.37034812	29.493	.000***	1.733
2	.607	.368	.340	.16122993	13.090	.000***	1.253

in the impact of ROR on REINS. ROR affects REINS weakly ($B = 0.1$), but its effect is significant. Other variables that significantly affect ROR are H ($B = 0.118$), AR ($B = 0.116$), FS ($B = -0.029$), and IL ($B = -0.001$).

In Table 18.4, we see that in both models there is a moderately strong correlation between the dependent variable (ROR or REINS) and the explanatory variables. This is indicated by the multiple correlation coefficient R, which in model 1 has the value $R = 75.4\%$ and in model 2 $R = 60.7\%$. R square indicates the proportion of variability of the dependent variable, which we can explain by this model. Adjusted R square revises the estimate of the ratio of variability of the dependent variable, which we can explain by the included number of explanatory variables in the model. The VIF values of all variables are less than the reference value (see Table 18.3).

The value of the Durbin–Watson (DW) test of residuals independence in model 1 is 1.733. This value is situated within the interval in which we cannot decide on residual independence. Therefore, we have decided based on the results of the test of statistical significance of the 1st-degree autocorrelation coefficient, for standardized residuals. On the grounds of comparison of autocorrelation coefficients with the critical value of cyclical autocorrelation coefficient for $\alpha = 0.05$ and $n = 27$, we can accept the null hypothesis of residual independence. On the ground of DW values for model 2, we cannot accept the null hypothesis of residual independence.

In the second step, we quantify the relationship between ROA and REINS. We reformulate the models that contain the variables listed in Table 18.1, but in this case ROR is not included. In model 3, the dependent variable is ROA and the other variables, including REINS, are independent variables. In model 4, the dependent variable is REINS and ROA was included among the independent variables. The models are in the following form:

$$\text{Model Nr 3}: \text{ROA} = \beta_0 + \beta_1\text{H} + \beta_2\text{AR} + \beta_3\text{REINS} + \beta_4\text{FS} + \beta_5\text{IL} + \beta_6\text{FL} + \beta_7\text{RP} + \beta_8\text{ROI} + \beta_9\text{IR} + \varepsilon, \tag{18.4}$$

$$\text{Model Nr 4}: \text{REINS} = \beta_0 + \beta_1\text{H} + \beta_2\text{AR} + \beta_4\text{FS} + \beta_4\text{IL} + \beta_5\text{FL} + \beta_6\text{RP} + \beta_7\text{ROI} + \beta_8\text{IR} + \beta_9\text{ROA} + \varepsilon. \tag{18.5}$$

The outputs of the regression analysis are summarized in Table 18.5.

Table 18.5 Coefficients

		Unstandardized coefficients		Standardized coefficients			Collinearity statistics	
		B	Std. error	Beta	t	Sig.	Tolerance	VIF
Model Nr 3: dependent variable ROA								
Independent variables	(Constant)	−.23462	.043		−5.508	.000***		
	H	−.01332	.009	−.060	−1.557	.121	.862	1.160
	AR	−.00686	.008	−.037	−.863	.389	.695	1.439
	REINS	*−.05471*	*.020*	*−.119*	*−2.703*	*.007***	*.667*	*1.499*
	FS	.01456	.002	.259	6.318	.000***	.767	1.305
	IL	−6.074E-06	.000	−.006	−.164	.870	.917	1.090
	FL	−.01556	.004	−.154	−4.233	.000***	.969	1.032
	RP	3.594E-06	.000	.014	.339	.735	.769	1.301
	ROI	.30220	.014	.837	21.264	.000***	.831	1.203
	IR	−2.484E-08	.000	−.003	−.083	.934	.773	1.293
Model Nr 4: dependent variable REINS								
Independent variables	(Constant)	.32182	.154		2.085	.038**		
	H	.10272	.028	.214	3.607	.000***	.907	1.103
	AR	.11464	.026	.286	4.410	.000***	.759	1.317
	FS	−.01659	.009	−.136	−1.945	.053*	.652	1.534
	IL	−.00049	.000	−.230	−4.052	.000***	.992	1.008
	FL	−.00514	.013	−.023	−.393	.695	.891	1.122
	RP	−1.183E-05	.000	−.021	−.327	.744	.769	1.301
	ROI	.426	.082	.544	5.193	.000***	.291	3.438
	IR	5.242E-08	.000	.003	.052	.959	.773	1.293
	ROA	−.63788	.236	−.294	−2.703	.007**	.270	3.708

* Correlation is significant at the 0.1 level (2-tailed). ** Correlation is significant at the 0.05 level (2-tailed). *** Correlation is significant at the 0.01 level (2-tailed)

Table 18.6 Model summary

	Model summary				ANOVA		
Model Nr	R	R square	Adj. R square	SE of the Est.	F	Sig.	Durbin–Watson
3	.860	.740	.728	.04766935	63.793	.000***	1.708
4	.597	.356	.328	.16276527	12.422	.000***	1.272

We identify the negative impact of reinsurance (REINS) on return on assets (ROA). Based on the results of model 3, we can expect a decrease in ROA of 0.055 units when increasing reinsurance by 1 unit. Another indicator that has a statistically significant effect on ROA is ROI ($B = 0.302$). ROA is also weakly affected by FS ($B = 0.014$) and FL ($B = -0.016$).

We summarize the results of the analysis of the impact of ROA on REINS in model 4. We found a moderately strong negative statistically significant effect of ROA on reinsurance ($B = -0.638$), which we measured by the ratio of gross premium earned ceded to reinsurers on gross premium earned. When increasing the ROA by 1 unit, we can expect a decrease in reinsurance by 0.638 units. The above findings on the negative impact of ROA on REINS and also REINS on ROA also confirm the results of the findings of Lee and Lee (2012), who also identified mutually negative effects. We can therefore argue that ROA growth reduces insurance companies' interest in reinsurance purchase and also that higher reinsurance tends to decrease ROA. We assume that this indicates lower efficiency of using insurance companies' assets in the case when risk is transferred to a reinsurance company.

Table 18.6 indicates that in both models there is a moderate correlation between the dependent variables (ROA, REINS) and the explanatory variables. This is indicated by the multiple correlation coefficient R, which in model 3 has the value $R = 86\%$ and in model 4 $R = 59.7\%$. R square indicates the proportion of variability of the dependent variable, which we can explain by the given model. Adjusted R square revises the estimate of the share of variability of the dependent variable, which we can explain by the included number of explanatory variables in the model. The VIF values of all variables are less than the reference value.

The value of the Durbin–Watson (DW) test of residual independence in model 3 is 1.708. This value is situated within the interval in which we cannot decide on residual independence. Therefore, we have decided, based on the results of the test of statistical significance of the 1st-degree autocorrelation coefficient, for standardized residuals. On the grounds of comparison of autocorrelation coefficients with the critical value of cyclical autocorrelation coefficient for $\alpha = 0.05$ and $n = 27$, we can accept the null hypothesis of residual independence. On the ground of DW values for model 4, we cannot accept the null hypothesis of residual independence.

Given the lower DW value, the regression coefficients of models 2 and 4 may be skewed to some extent, but still provide valuable information about the relationships that have been studied.

18.5 Conclusion

The objective of our research was to use regression analysis to evaluate the mutual relations between selected indicators of financial performance of insurance companies (ROR, ROA) and the ratio of premiums that the insurance company transfers to its reinsurance partner. We conducted the research in two steps with the use of regression analysis. The analysis indicates the following outcomes:

1. In models 1 and 2, we identified a positive relationship between REINS and return on revenues. The regression coefficient quantifying the effect of REINS on the dependent variable ROR turned out stronger ($B = 0.52890$), and the regression coefficient quantifying the effect of ROR on reinsurance showed lower ($B = 0.10025$). This means that a change in the share of premiums ceded to a reinsurance company has a more significant effect on the insurance of a company that is able to generate revenues, as is the case when the change in ROR results in a change in the share of ceded premiums, but to a lesser extent. This is related to the process and relevant costs that the insurance company incurs in underwriting insurance risks. The quantification of risks in the process of their underwriting directly affects the amount of written premiums. In the case of using the services of a reinsurance company, the insurance company incurs lower costs in this respect, compared to the situation where it would bear the entire risk itself, which also directly affects the amount of its profit and ROR;
2. In models 3 and 4, a negative relationship between REINS and return on assets was identified. The regression coefficient quantifying the effect of REINS on the dependent variable ROA turned out weaker ($B = -0.05741$) and the regression coefficient quantifying the effect of ROA on reinsurance turned out stronger ($B = -0.63788$). This means that the change in ROA has a more significant effect on the ratio of premiums ceded to the reinsurer than is otherwise. We can explain this by the fact that the profits of insurance companies are directly affected by the amount of written premiums, which is consequently reflected in the volume of the insurance company's assets. Transfer of the risk to the reinsurance company may result in lower prudence of insurance companies with regard to managing their own assets. Furthermore, this may subsequently be reflected in a decline in ROA. Conversely, the decline in the ratio of reinsured insurance contracts puts more pressure on the management of insurance companies, and thus, it forces them to manage their assets more efficiently.

More precise interpretations of our findings and their more specific targeting of problem areas presuppose a deeper analysis of the influencing factors, which creates more opportunities for further scientific research. We assume that this paper contributes to the specific issues of insurance policies through the application of financial analysis procedures in insurance companies, since their prior focus is to evaluate insurance risks. Taking this into consideration, our scientific approach brings a new perspective of research in the insurance sector.

Acknowledgement This paper has been supported by the Scientific Grant Agency of Slovak Republic under project VEGA No. 1/0579/21 "Research on Determinants and Paradigms of Financial Management in the context of the COVID-19 Pandemic." The authors would like to express their gratitude to the Scientific Grant Agency of the Ministry of Education, Science, Research, and Sport of the Slovak Republic for financial support of this research and publication.

References

Act No. 39/2015 on Insurance

Act No. 67/2020 on certain emergency financial measures

A.M. Best Company, Inc. (2019). *Best's review. Best's rankings. Top 50 world's largest reinsurance groups.* [cit. 2021-06-20]. Available on: http://www.ambest.com/review/displaychart.aspx?Record_Code=274409

Anthropelos, M., & Boonen, T. J. (2020). Nash equilibria in optimal reinsurance bargaining. *Insurance: Mathematics and Economics, 93*(2020), 196–205. https://doi.org/10.1016/j.insmatheco.2020.05.001

Boďa, M., & Úradníček, V. (2016). Inclusion of weights and their uncertainty into quantification within a pyramid decomposition of a financial indicator. *Ekonomicky casopis, 64*(1), 70–92. ISSN 0013-3035.

Chen, Z., & Yang, P. (2020). Robust optimal reinsurance–investment strategy with price jumps and correlated claims. *Insurance: Mathematics and Economics, 92*(2020), 27–46. https://doi.org/10.1016/j.insmatheco.2020.03.001

Deelstra, G., & Plantin, G. (2014). Reinsurance market practices. In *Risk theory and reinsurance* (EAA series). Springer.https://doi.org/10.1007/978-1-4471-5568-3_2

Directive 2005/68/EC of the European Parliament and of the Council of 16 November 2005 on reinsurance. Available on: https://eur-lex.europa.eu/legal-content/SK/TXT/PDF/?uri=CELEX:32005L0068&from=sk

Doumpos, M., Gaganis, C., & Pasiouras, F. (2012). Estimating and explaining the financial performance of property and casualty insurers: A two-stage analysis. *The Business and Economics Research Journal, 5*(2), 155–170.

Ecer, F., & Pamucar, D. (2021). MARCOS technique under intuitionistic fuzzy environment for determining the COVID-19 pandemic performance of insurance companies in terms of healthcare services. *Applied Soft Computing, 104*, 107199. https://doi.org/10.1016/j.asoc.2021.107199

Ghorui, N., Ghosh, A., Mondal, S. P., Bajuri, M. Y., Ahmadian, A., Salahshour, S., & Ferrara, M. (2021). Identification of dominant risk factor involved in spread of COVID-19 using hesitant fuzzy MCDM methodology. *Results in Physics, 21*, 103811. https://doi.org/10.1016/j.rinp.2020.103811

Grofčíková, J., & Izáková, K. (2019). Impact of the CG on the financial performance of insurance companies in the Slovak and Czech Republics. In N. Tsounis & A. Vlachvei (Eds.), *Advances in cross-section data methods in applied economic research. ICOAE 2019* (pp. 1–21). Springer Proceedings in Business and Economics. https://doi.org/10.1007/978-3-030-38253-7

Johns Hopkins University & Medicine. Corona Virus Resource Center. (2021). Available online: https://coronavirus.jhu.edu/map.html. Accessed June 2021

Kron, W., Eichner, J., & Kundzewicz, W. (2019). Reduction of flood risk in Europe – Reflections from a reinsurance perspective. *Journal of Hydrology, 576*, 197–209. https://doi.org/10.1016/j.jhydrol.2019.06.050

Lee, H. H., & Lee, C. Y. (2012). An analysis of reinsurance and firm performance: Evidence from the Taiwan property-liability insurance industry. *The Geneva Papers, The International Association for the Study of Insurance Economics, 37*, 467–484. https://doi.org/10.1057/gpp.2012.9

Luo, S. Z., Taksar, M., & Tsoi, A. (2008). On reinsurance and investment for large insurance portfolios. *Insurance: Mathematics and Economics, 42*(1), 434–444. https://doi.org/10.1016/j.insmatheco.2007.04.002

Meng, H., et al. (2016). Optimal insurance risk control with multiple reinsurers. *Journal of Computational and Applied Mathematics, 306*, 40–52. https://doi.org/10.1016/j.cam.2016.04.005

Munich Re's NatCatSERVICE. https://www.munichre.com/en/solutions/for-industry-clients/natcatservice.html

OECD Economic Outlook May 2021. [cit. 2021-06-24]. https://www.oecd.org/economic-outlook/

Powers, M. R., & Shubik, M. (2001). Toward a theory of reinsurance and retrocession. *Insurance: Mathematics and Economics, 29*(2), 271–290. https://doi.org/10.1016/S0167-6687(01)00087-7

Register of Financial Statements (Register účtovných závierok). [cit. 2021-05-15]. Available on: https://www.registeruz.sk/cruz-public/domain/accountingentity/simplesearch

S&P Global Ratings. (2019). Insurers Rating Methodology. [cit. 2021-06-23]. Available on: https://www.spglobal.com/ratings/en/

Tone, K., Kweh, Q. L., Lu, W. M., & Ting, I. W. K. (2019). Modeling investments in the dynamic network performance of insurance companies. *Omega, 88*(October 2019), 237–247. https://doi.org/10.1016/j.omega.2018.09.005

Úradníček, V., et al. (2016). *Variantné metódy predikcie finančného zdravia podnikov v podmienkach dynamického ekonomického prostredia*. Belianum. 136 s. ISBN 978-80-557-1172-0.

Chapter 19
Trends in the Use of Social Media in Cultural Centres in Developing Audiences

Tatiana Corejova, Andrea Pilatikova, Maria Rostasova, and Alexandra Valicova

Abstract New emerging technologies strengthen the perception of companies' activities in several levels of sustainability – economic, environmental and social. Decisions on the implementation of the latest technologies, innovations and new business models determine the application of new technologies and business models in scale and time. They change the demand and supply side, affect the structure of the market, interrupt the market borders, etc. These changes do not bypass culture either. They raise questions about the possibility of implementing new technological solutions, their sustainability, impact on visitors and overall attendance on the one hand, on the other hand on the change in the offer of individual entities in the cultural and creative industries. The purpose of the paper is to present a case study focussed on the proposal of the use of new technologies in a selected area of cultural and creative industries. The case study is based on the theoretical definition of the culture and creative industry and its components, the identification of bottlenecks and the design of solutions using technologies that support audience development. On the example of cultural centres within a selected region of Slovakia, the possibilities of using social media in relation to increasing the efficiency and intensity of communication with target segments in audience development are identified.

Keywords Cultural centre · Culture and creative industry · Audience development

JEL Codes O18, O33

T. Corejova (✉) · A. Pilatikova · M. Rostasova · A. Valicova
University of Zilina, Zilina, Slovakia
e-mail: tatiana.corejova@uniza.sk

N. Tsounis, A. Vlachvei (eds.), *Advances in Quantitative Economic Research*, Springer Proceedings in Business and Economics,
https://doi.org/10.1007/978-3-030-98179-2_19

19.1 Introduction

Significant changes in technological development and the growth of interconnectedness of individual countries and entities are reflected in all areas of society. These changes are not bypassed by the cultural and creative industries. Several studies point to the interrelationship between the level of companies' investments in new technologies and the financial return on technological investments, which, however, are influenced by other, especially environmental, factors. Currently used technologies generate extensive data and cause or enable the transformation of business models within individual industries or institutions.

New emerging technologies enhance the perception of companies' activities in various levels of sustainability – economic, environmental and social. Decisions on the implementation of the latest technologies and innovations determine the application of new business models in scope and time. They change the demand and supply side, affect the very structure of the market, the size and sustainability of ecosystems, the ability of entities to generate and use network effects. These changes do not bypass culture either.

They raise questions about the possibility of implementing new technological solutions, their sustainability, impact on visitors and overall attendance on the one hand, on the other hand on the change in the offer of individual entities in the cultural and creative industries. The individual processes become part of strategic documents at various levels of public administration. Within the Slovak Republic, new strategic documents are currently being formulated at the regional and local level for the cultural and creative industries, focussing on smart solutions and smart strategies. In particular, they also concern the promotion of marketing by building the image of the region, the development of cultural and creative industries, links with tourism, international cooperation within the Euroregion and audience development. Smart solutions and smart strategies are generally based on the use of new technologies. The pandemic in 2020 clearly pointed out and emphasised the need to use new technologies in communication with the audience, addressing it but also by providing the required services by cultural institutions. It was not possible to apply traditional methods of communication and the activity of cultural and creative institutions would thus be significantly limited or even impossible without the application of new procedures. Here it is possible to identify a gap that needs to be bridged in the communication of cultural and creative institutions with the audience. The solution can be found in changing the ways of communication and delivery of required services or offered services to the audience.

The purpose of the paper is to present a case study focussed on the proposal of the use of new technologies especially social media in a selected area of cultural and creative industries. The study is based on the theoretical definition of the culture and creative industry and its components, the identification of bottlenecks and the design of solutions using technologies that support audience development.

19.2 Theoretical Background

The cultural and creative industries include several areas. Although the term industry is currently understood more as a characteristic of production, in this context it must be seen as an exploitative chain, which is created by creating the conditions for creative activity. Creative activity, production, reproduction, representation, preservation, archiving and restoration are an essential part of this industry by the Ministry of Culture of Slovak Republic (2020a). The cultural and creative industries are particularly specific in that they create a bridge between art, culture, business and technology. The jobs it creates are linked to specific cultural and historical skills and are also linked to the territory and traditions that define them. Therefore, these jobs cannot be relocated abroad. The influence of the cultural and creative industries (Ministry of Culture of The Slovak Republic, 2020b) is not limited exclusively to the field of culture and creativity; it also extends to many sectors of the economy. They play an important role in the field of innovation, where they act as their catalyst and disseminator. Bagnasco (2020) states that increasing the number of people regularly going to the cinema, it is necessary to strengthen supply in the summer and keep diversifying our product. The above conclusion in relation to the offer and regular visitors also applies to other areas of the cultural and creative industries. Seasonality must be considered in each of its parts.

A characteristic feature of cultural and creative industries is a high proportion of creative workers who work in them, respectively perform the so-called creative professions. Firms in the creative industries are significantly smaller in terms of number of employees compared to other industries (Buček et al., 2014). A substantial part of their work is individual and the way they are produced does not allow for scale savings. Unlike traditional industries, companies in the creative industries do not form large value chains, but organise themselves around projects. The cultural and creative industries are very close and intersect. Currently, the common term cultural and creative industry is used. The hierarchy of terms is illustrated by the so-called The Singapore model of cultural and creative industries (Balog et al., 2014).

The cultural sector includes the field of traditional art (fine and theatrical arts, cultural heritage) and the field of cultural industry (film, audio-visual, television and radio broadcasting, computer games, music, publishing). The creative sector includes design, architecture and advertising, as well as related areas, e.g. software development, hardware production, players and telephones. Both sectors are made up of a number of entities and together form a specific ecosystem. Within the Slovak Republic, the regional self-government, which is the founder of cultural institutions such as theatres, galleries, libraries, museums, observatories and cultural centres, also has an important position in the cultural sector. It is the cultural centres within the region that are an interesting bridge between the cultural and creative industries.

Scope and activities of the cultural centres are defined by Act no. 189/2015 Coll. on cultural and educational activities (2020). According to § 2 of this Act, cultural and educational activities mean activities which contribute to respect for human rights and diversity of cultural expressions, to the formation of cultural way of life, to increase the cultural and educational level of the Slovak population and to develop creativity as the basic cultural value of society. The mission of cultural centres is to preserve, promote and develop the values of local culture and traditions in their territorial scope and to develop hobby-artistic activities, lifelong learning of the population and leisure activities. Their significant contribution can also be observed in the field of prevention of anti-social phenomena and various addictions. Cultural centres cooperate with local and regional institutions; prepare progressive competitions in hobby-artistic activities, education centres and events (regional, national competitions, educational events, festivals, shows, exhibitions).

Cultural centres as well as other institutions belonging to the cultural and creative industries are interested in gaining and growing audiences. But how can this be ensured or implemented? What measures to take and what technologies to use? The Covid 19 pandemic in the years 2020–2021 significantly affected the activities of cultural institutions and closed the physical gates and cultural centres. In many cases, communication has moved to virtual space. Social media occupies an important position here (Corejova et al., 2020). Social media enables the sharing of information, thoughts and ideas, the building of virtual networks and communities through information and communication technologies (Dollarhide, 2021). Social networks are part of a broader category of social media. They are based on the mutual interaction of users, who through them connect into groups and establish relationships, thus creating a network of relationships between them (Lukačovičová & Vargová, 2015). The functions provided by social networks for marketing purposes represent an important communication channel through which marketing activities can be targeted very precisely. The social network profile page is a place that allows you to communicate all relevant activities very effectively and operatively (Hollá-Bachanová & Garbárová, 2019).

19.3 Goal and Methodology

The aim of the paper is to identify the possibilities of using social media in the work of selected institutions of the cultural and creative industries in the Slovak Republic. After extensive analytical work, a regional cultural centre was selected as a suitable institution to fulfil the goal. Within the Slovak Republic, it is possible to identify eight regions – territorial administrative units. In each region, there are several cultural centres, which are interconnected. The Žilina self-governing region (further ŽSK) was chosen for the case study that is based on the smart concept of cultural development of the Žilina self-governing region (2021). There are five cultural centres in ŽSK. The case study of the cultural centre (further CC) includes:

- Analysis of the activities of the CC and its internal and external environments
- Analysis of the current state of use of social networks for more intensive and effective communication with visitors
- Proposal for the use of other functionalities and procedures to improve the communication policy of the centre in order to expand the audience and increase attendance

In the case study, we address the answers to four research questions, namely:

- RQ1 – how do cultural centres currently use social networks and which of them are the most used from the point of view of the audience?
- RQ2 – what contributions are most often shared on social network Facebook within the profiles of cultural centres?
- RQ3 – which sources of information are most used by the audience of cultural centres?
- RQ4 – what are the decisive strengths and weaknesses, opportunities and threats of cultural centres in terms of communication with the audience and audience development?

In answering these questions, several procedures were used, from the analysis of information from individual statuses on social networks and their visitors, a survey aimed at participants in cultural centre events, as well as visitors and a processed SWOT analysis. The analytical work used publicly available materials on the activities of cultural centres and a survey was also conducted on the use of social networks in the centres. The decisive period was set for September – December 2020, i.e. for the period of the second wave of the pandemic.

19.4 Case Study

The Regional Cultural Centre in Žilina has been operating in the field of regional culture since 1953. Its main mission is to create conditions for the activities of individuals and groups strengthening national and cultural identity, bringing values in local culture, folklore, traditional folk art and education (SMART concept of culture development of the Žilina self-governing region, 2021). It is possible to identify five CCs within the region, of which one central and four regional centres (Garbarova et al., 2017). The answers on the first research question (RQ1) are shown in the Table 19.1. All of CC currently use several social networks for communication with visitors and especially for their promotion.

The Regional Cultural Centre shared a total of 112 posts on Facebook in the analysed period. Most of them were in September, when they published 41 articles.

Table 19.1 Use of social networks by cultural centres (CCs)

Name of the CC	Facebook	Pinterest	YouTube	Instagram	Use of Facebook	
					Followers	The number of page likes
Regional CC	x		x	x	1296	1108
CC of Kysuca	x		x	x	1260	1230
CC of Liptov	x		x	x	2017	1892
CC of Orava	x	x	x	x	1745	1635
Turčianske CC	x		x	x	717	671

Source: Pilatikova (2021)

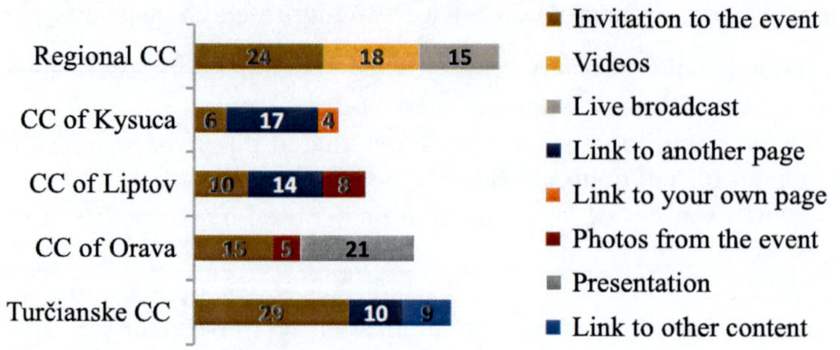

Fig. 19.1 The most common types of contributions shared by CCs within the scope of the Žilina self-governing region. (Source: Pilatikova, 2021)

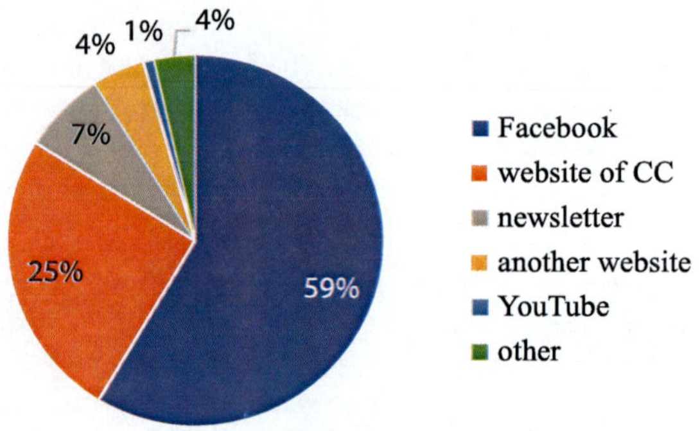

Fig. 19.2 Preferred information source about events. (Source: Pilatikova, 2021)

It shared 32 posts in October and 39 in December. The CC used the social network mainly to inform the audience about organised events, to share photos and videos from events and to broadcast live events (Madleňák, 2017). It regularly published its own videos with a cultural and educational focus, as well as external links to videos, pages and articles from its field of activity. It also used the social network to inform the public about new competitions, the conditions of competitions and their winners. The best rated contribution concerned the live broadcast of the opening of the exhibition. The most common types of contributions shared by individual cultural centres on the social network Facebook are shown in Fig. 19.1. This is also the answer on the research question RQ2.

As part of a survey related to research question RQ3 between users about information sources on CC events, social networks (Facebook, YouTube and Instagram), a newsletter and the cultural centre's website with a published program of events were most frequently mentioned. For the majority of respondents (59%), Facebook was the preferred source of information; on the contrary, not a single respondent indicated the option Instagram (Fig. 19.2).

Cultural centres are generally little-known institutions for the public. They organise or participate in a large number of cultural events in cooperation with various other entities and the public.

An important part is also their club activity and preservation of intangible cultural heritage of the regional regions. Due to the nature of their activities, we are currently unable to measure the attendance of their events, activities and the like with sufficient accuracy. The number of participants in cultural and educational events increased by 83.67% in 2015–2019, the number of participants in art events by 15.72% and the number of visitors to the event also increased by 24.74%. CCs are contributory organisations. Their revenues include contributions from public administration entities, cooperating institutions for individual events and income from admission. It is the share of the entrance fee in the total income that expresses the self-sufficiency of the CC. The self-sufficiency of CCs is low (3.81%), as they offer services mostly for free or for a symbolic fee. In the analysed period of 2015–2019, the costs of CCs increased by 21.95%, revenues by 17.32% and subsidies from public sources increased by 15.33%.

The SWOT analysis of CCs in the region at the end of 2020 (RQ4) as part of the formulation of a broader smart strategy for the cultural and creative industries, lists the following aspects as key:

- The strengths of CCs include the intensity and diversity of events, educational and children's activities, documentation and preservation of cultural values, cooperation and project activities.
- Weaknesses include the number of activities for seniors and disadvantaged groups, ICT equipment and twenty-first-century staff competencies, data handling, marketing and financial evaluation of employees and also some insufficient space.
- Opportunities can be considered calls for projects from the EU and MC structural funds, support from the state, local government and the founder, the development of tourism in the regions, the trend of digital transformation, the advantage of location and the interest of schools.
- Threats include, in particular, the impact of the Covid 19 pandemic, cultural legislation, the shortage of skilled workers in the labour market and climate change.

Based on the evaluation of the SWOT analysis while ensuring the effective direction of the future activities of CCs in the region, it is possible to recommend the adoption of an offensive strategy (SO strategy). The resulting strategy is based primarily on even greater use of strengths (S) and use of opportunities (O), with the strengths with the highest weight of their importance coming to the fore, as well as those opportunities that were evaluated by the evaluators of individual aspects with the highest strength. The global trend and the associated offer of ready-made solutions in the field of digital transformation and smart solutions are assessed by CCs as an opportunity with a weight of 4. At the same time, the use of online marketing is a weakness. As part of the offensive strategy, it is possible to further increase the intensity and diversity of regional, county and national events, including the educational activities of CCs, precisely through the use of modern information and communication technologies.

It is also possible in this way to intensify cooperation with the documentary digitisation centre and through this cooperation to preserve documentation and traditional cultural values. The use of digitisation and smart solutions can help even more intensively in organizing club and exhibition activities in cooperation with other cultural institutions in the region and evaluate their attractiveness and quality through feedback from visitors to CC events (online applications, social networks, QR codes, etc.).

19.5 Discussion and Conclusions

The results of the analysis show that CCs are relatively little known institutions in the region with weak online marketing. To increase their visibility and thus gain a higher number of visitors, it is possible to use social media. As part of the activities of the CC itself, it is a matter of increasing interactions and gaining new followers of their sites, or increase in the number of visitors, as well as the development of new services with the aim of an extended service for existing visitors. Thus, three primary objectives are set:

- Increase of interactions on the Facebook page (to restore the attention and interest of the followers of the FB page of the Regional CC)
- Increase in the number of Facebook page followers (increase awareness of the FB page of the Regional CC)
- Extension of services for all, i.e. current and future visitors/followers

Increasing the number of active followers of the FB site should contribute to the fulfilment of the business goal, which is to increase the overall (physical and virtual) attendance of the CC.

Based on the analysis of the activities of CCs and their ways of using social networks, the following proposals were formulated for the gradual fulfilment of the above three tasks:

- Linking a Facebook page to an Instagram account, allowing the centre to share all its posts and stories on both social networks at the same time. Synchronisation of both accounts will also be reflected in the change of data, which only needs to be edited on one of the social networks. The advantage is also the possibility to use the Creator studio tool on Facebook when planning posts for the Facebook page and Instagram account. At present, however, only post-planning works, it is not possible to plan stories. After linking the accounts, it is possible to reply to Instagram messages simultaneously in the received messages on the Facebook page, without unnecessary switching between social networks.
- Adding social networking links to the CC's Facebook page, as only the link to the website is currently visible. Users who view the Facebook page of the CC will be able to easily click on the profiles of other social networks and start following them.

- Using stories on social networks that expand services and features for followers. Stories are usually displayed in a visible place at the top of the bulletin board or by clicking on the profile photo of the page. The advantage of stories is the ability to share more often without the page being too crowded with posts. Through the stories, the CC can constantly reach its followers. Stories also have an impact on the so-called passive audiences who do not view the posts on the bulletin board, or only view them occasionally. If anyone in the audience misses a shared post, they can still see the same content in the story, which is also displayed in a visible place. Stories, as well as any other user who views them, can reply to or respond to the stories, giving the site administrator room to connect with their fans. The features of the stories include the ability to add various effects, stickers, or frames for editing photos and videos. As a result, the content in the stories is more personalised compared to classic posts. Story statistics are also available for Facebook pages. This option must first be turned on, in the statistics section, by clicking on the stories option. You can then track the number of unique story openings, the total number of responses, interactions and responses to all stories shared in the last 28 days. In addition, demographic statistics such as age, gender and location of the story's viewers can be seen. Stories can also be shared across two platforms.
- Increasing site interactions or engagement is a form of feedback. Followers like, comment, share, tag in other users' comments, click on links and add responses to posts in a variety of emotions. If a page follower interacts with a post, that post will also appear on their friends' bulletin board. In this way, the content, as well as the page that originally shared it, is spread among social network users. It is an organic process that works without the need to pay for advertising. An effective way to involve fans on the site is comments, which also stimulate discussion. The paper may include a direct invitation to the discussion, for example by asking for an opinion, asking a question that followers should answer, or by launching a competition. The cultural centre can invite its followers to show their interest in culture and share their own photo in traditional costume, video with a folk song, folk dance, or any other cultural content in the commentary below the post. Not only would the result increase the number of interactions on the site, the followers would become part of the community in which they engage and spread the culture with other users. However, interactions on the site should not be one-sided. Trackers usually want to communicate with organisations they like. Social users are commenting on posts and waiting for a response. This response should come as soon as possible, in the form of a direct response to the comment. Only then will users be motivated to continue to get involved. Through comments, you can find out what the site's fans like or, conversely, what they are dissatisfied with, i.e. their feedback. It is therefore important to regularly check the comments and subsequent feedback from the administrator of the Facebook page.

The use of new technologies in institutions that are more connected with culture and creativity finds new dimensions. It is no longer just a matter of simply addressing visitors and informing them. It is technologies that make it possible to make the activities of institutions more efficient. There is also a gradual digital transformation, associated with the digitisation of documents, digitisation of processes and change in the management of these institutions. Extensive changes brought about by the application of new digital technologies are one of the key determinants of the overall performance of companies and the economy. Other equally important determinants are the business model and the environment in which companies operate. All three determinants simultaneously affect performance and interact at the same time. The performance of cultural institutions is associated with their attendance and their impact on society as a whole. It is the increase in awareness of the activities of cultural institutions through the use of social networks, the provision of new products and services in the digital environment and their availability that leads to the desired trend in attendance and thus to increased performance.

Acknowledgement This contribution was undertaken as a part of the research project VEGA 1/0011/21 Research on the interactions among new emerging technologies, the performance of enterprises and industries based on network technology infrastructure, the application of new business models and the institutional regulatory, environmental and social environment.

References

Act no. 189/2015 Coll. on cultural and educational activities (Zákon č. 189/2015 Z. z. o kultúrno-osvetovej činnosti). Retrieved from https://www.zakonypreludi.sk/zz/2015-189

Bagnasco, A. M. (2020). Trends in the Italian Movie sector: evidence from Box office performances. In N. Tsounis & A. Vlachei (Eds.), *Advances in cross-section data methods in applied economic research* (ICOAE 2019, Springer Proceedings in Business and Economics) (pp. 523–530). Springer. ISBN 978-3-030-38252-0.

Balog, M., et al. (2014). *Možnosti rozvoja kreatívneho priemyslu.* Slovenská inovačná a energetická agentúra SEIA, ISBN 978-80-88823-56-8 Retrieved 2020-11-10 from https://www.researchgate.net/publication/260876895_Moznosti_rozvoja_kreativneho_priemyslu_na_Slovensku

Buček, M., Rehák, Š., & Hudec, O. (2014). *Kreatívna ekonomika – národohospodárske a regionálne podmienky a stimuly.* [online]. Bratislava: Vydavateľstvo EKONÓM, 2014. ISBN 978-80-225-3954-8. Retrieved 2020-11-10 from https://www.researchgate.net/profile/Oto_Hudec/publication/317208243_Kreativna_ekonomika__narodohospodarske_a_regionalne_podmienky_a_stimuly/links/592c329ca6fdcc44435fd914/Kreativna-ekonomika-narodohospodarske-a-regionalne-podmienky-a-stimuly.pdf

Corejova, T., Rostasova, M., & Valicova, A. (2020). Remarks on the evaluation of the strategic focus of the social network. In *Economic and social development. 53rd international scientific conference on Economic and social development: Book of abstracts.* – ISSN 1849-7535 (1st ed., pp. 47–48). Varazdin Development and Entrepreneurship Agency.

Dollarhide, M. (2021) *Social Media Definition.* [online]. Retrieved 2021-06-22 from https://www.investopedia.com/terms/s/social-media.asp

Garbarova, M., Holla-Bachanova, P., & Vartiak, L. (2017). Current policy and support in the advertising industry in the Zilina region. In *SGEM 2017: International multidisciplinary scientific conference on social sciences & arts: conference proceedings: Urban planning, architecture & design Book 5* (Vol. II: Urban studies, planning & development architecture and design. ISSN 2367-5659, ISBN 978-619-7408-25-6) (pp. 97–104). STEF92 Technology.

Hollá-Bachanová, P., & Garbárová, M. (2019). Instagram as an effective marketing communication tool of higher education institution. In *Vision 2025: Education excellence and management of innovations through sustainable economic competitive advantage: Proceedings of the 34th international business information management association conference* (1st ed., pp. 4830–4840). International Business Information Management Association, ISBN 978-0-9998551-3-3. - s.

Lukačovičová, Z., & Vargová, D. (2015). Využitie sociálnych sietí v marketingu firiem. In *Studia commercialia Bratislavensia*. [online]. 2015, vol. 8, no. 30. Retrieved. 2020-10-30 from https://of.euba.sk/www_write/files/veda-vyskum/scb/vydane-cisla/2015-02/scb0215_Lukacovicova-Vargova.pdf. ISSN 1339-3081.

Madleňák, R. (2017). The study of the advertising perception on the customer's segment of mobile operators in Slovak Republic. In: *Marketing Identity. Conference Proceedings from International scientific conference: 7th – 8th November 2017.* – ISSN 1339-5726. 1st ed. Trnava: Fakulta masmediálnej komunikácie, 2017. – ISBN 978-80-8105-918-6. – pp. 146–153.

Ministry of Culture of The Slovak Republic. (2020a). Kreatívny priemysel. Retrieved 2020-11-11 from https://www.slovensko.sk/sk/agendy/agenda/_kreativny-priemysel/

Ministry of Culture of The Slovak Republic. (2020b). *Kultúrny a kreatívny priemysel.* Retrieved 2020-10-30 from http://www.mksr.sk/posobnost-ministerstva/kreativny-priemysel-165.html

Pilatikova, A. (2021). Návrh reklamnej kampane vo vybranom kultúrnom a kreatívnom odvetví prostredníctvom sociálnej siete Facebook – kultúrne strediská. Diploma thesis Tutor: Valicova, A. 28330420212029. Žilinska univerzita v Ziline

SMART concept of cultural development of the Žilina self-governing region/SMART koncepcia rozvoja kultúry Žilinského samosprávneho kraja (2021). Analytická časť. ŽSK Žilina

Chapter 20
Investigation of the Redesigning Process of the Development Identity of a Local Government Regional Unit (City): A Case Study of Kozani Regional Unit in Greece

Stavros Kalogiannidis, Stamatis Kontsas, George Konteos, and Fotios Chatzitheodoridis

Abstract This paper investigates the redesigning process of the development identity of a Local Government Regional Unit (City), a case study of Kozani City, Greece. This paper considers Kozani as a potential competitive tourist, investment, and cultural heritage destination that can contribute greatly to place and regional development once redesigned to meet the local and international customer needs. This study utilized data collected from 50 residents of Kozani city who were majorly local authorities to understand the process of city redesigning, the importance of such redesign, and the challenges involved in the process. The study established that a successful city redesigning process encompasses three phases: having a better understanding of the Community, appreciating the city's identity, and implementing the principles of city redesign. Factors such as proper strategic planning processes, availability of resources, and strategic leadership are also essential for a successful city redesigning process, which further helps achieve city redesigning objectives.

Keywords City redesigning · Repositioning · Place marketing · Kozani city

S. Kalogiannidis (✉) · S. Kontsas
Department of Business Administration, University of Western Macedonia, Kozani, Greece
e-mail: aff00056@uowm.gr; skontsas@uowm.gr

G. Konteos
Department of Business Administration, University of Western Macedonia, Grevena, Greece
e-mail: gkonteos@uowm.gr

F. Chatzitheodoridis
Department of Regional and Cross Border Development, University of Western Macedonia, Kozani, Greece
e-mail: fxtheodoridis@uowm.gr

N. Tsounis, A. Vlachvei (eds.), *Advances in Quantitative Economic Research*, Springer Proceedings in Business and Economics,
https://doi.org/10.1007/978-3-030-98179-2_20

20.1 Introduction

20.1.1 Background to the Study

Cities or region across the world have in recent past decades focused on redefining their visions, constructing their identity, and shaping their cultural outlook to cope with the highly globalized world. Dril et al. (2016) indicate that redefining a country's vision and shaping its image help the country become attractive and competitive on the global market or economy, thereby fostering desired economic growth or development.

To achieve the desired level of transformation, competitive advantage, and repositioning, most cities have continued to implement several competitive policies, majorly through different aspects of place marketing, the launch of prestigious projects, and civic boosterism. Some cities have also decided to utilize different strategic plans to attract potential target markets that fall in new investments, tourism, new residents, and specialized human resources (Ifezue, 2019). According to Borsekova (2017), building a highly attractive investment, cultural or tourism image for a particular culture or place requires total regeneration of the place's or city's economy.

Most cities worldwide are facing the changes associated with increased globalization, climate change, and high domestic or foreign competition. Most of these cities have experienced an unstable market share in the recent decades which has resulted in significant fluctuations, thereby affecting their competitive advantage and the ability to maintain quality human potential, double as major driving forces of development (Khattab, 2015).

Dril et al. (2016) indicate that the difficult situations faced by most cities have forced the latter to search for new innovative and creative approaches that are effective enough to aid in the repositioning or development and general economic transformation of the population. Place marketing is considered the strategic and highly effective method essential in the city and regional development.

In theory and practice, the different approaches associated with city repositioning are much different. Nevertheless, strategic development of a city or place and the rising welfare of the general population require a market-oriented approach concerning the management of the place development, which is normally expressed through place marketing (Khattab, 2015). In the frame of city redesigning toward achieving more growth, this paper uses Kozani, Greece, as the case study.

20.1.2 Problem Statement

City marketing has greatly evolved into a highly powerful repositioning and image-building technique or strategy with significant relevance to the different functions of the contemporary city and its specific socioeconomic characteristics for city development. Most cities fail to meet the demands of the rapidly changing global market due to lack of the capacity to rebrand, innovate, and attract local and international investors. Kozani's situation is not unique, but it is unique in that it is both a tourism destination and a strategic city for investment (Hasan et al., 2020; Seukindo, 2017). Even though Kozani is a globally recognized tourist destination, there is a need to redesign and promote its image policy to meet new trends and challenges in the global investment market and consequently improve the city's competitive advantage. However, there is limited research concerning the general redesign of cities or regional units to improve their development identity. This justifies the need to clearly understand the redesigning process of the development identity of a Local Government Regional Unit or City.

20.1.3 Objectives of the Study

The study was majorly aimed at investigating the redesigning process of the development identity of a Local Government Regional Unit or City while using Kozani regional unit in Greece as the case study.

The study was also based on different specific objectives that are listed below;

- To establish the importance of city redesigning
- To investigate the role of local government authorities in city redesigning processes
- To determine the factors that influence the success of city redesigning
- To establish the challenges involved in the city or regional unit redesigning process

20.1.4 Research Questions

1. What is the importance of city redesigning?
2. What is the role of local government authorities in city redesigning processes?
3. What are the factors that influence the success of city redesigning?
4. What are the challenges involved in the city or regional unit redesigning process?

20.1.5 Significance

The study contributes to the existing knowledge concerning place or city redesigning and how this influences place repositioning and image building and enhances the town's identity.

The study findings will be essential in repositioning Kozani city into a highly competitive tourism destination with several opportunities for investment by both local and foreign investors.

20.2 Literature Review

20.2.1 Framework for City Redevelopment to Improve the City's Development Identity

The urban design framework helps local governments and property redesign city elements to highlight the city's cultural identity through appropriate sustainability and enhancement work and promote a vibrant and evolving community that balances heritage and development (Teles, 2012). The quality of the built environment is improved by a stronger development identity, which ensures that shared public areas are accessible, pleasant, and welcome to all. By expanding our understanding of the past and ourselves, heritage can improve our quality of life. By preserving history and appropriate new construction, city redesign gives a chance to enhance the local Community's sense of identity and urban character. To maintain a long-term future, all historical assets require cyclical upkeep. Nonheritage artifacts, too, require regular care. Cultural assets, on the other hand, may necessitate a different or more cautious approach to maintenance and restoration. If this is not taken, major implications in terms of heritage value, local identity, and character might result (Mohga, 2015).

As indicated in Fig. 20.1, three urban design phases influence the enhancement of local identity throughout city development.

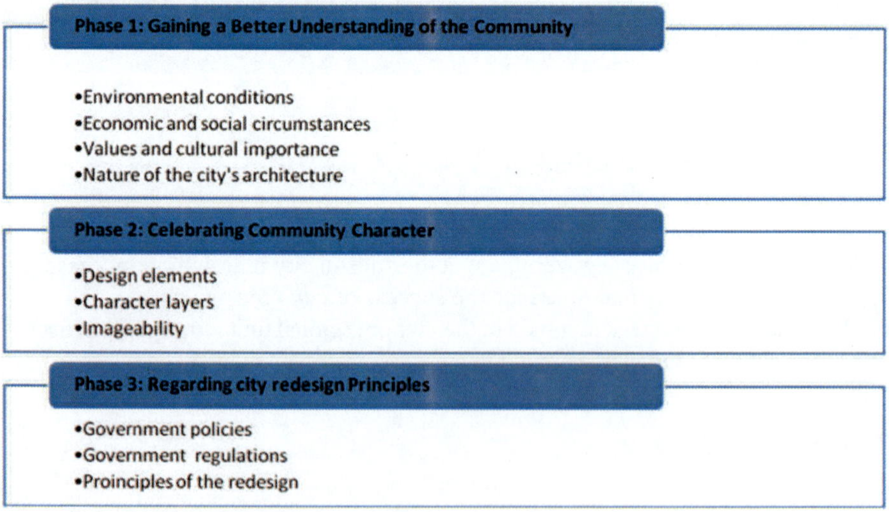

Fig. 20.1 Phases of city redesigning. (Source: Mohga, 2015)

20.2.1.1 Phase 1: Gaining a Better Understanding of the Community

It is the first and most important step of cityscape redesign plans, in which extensive information about the urban setting is examined. It aids a community's understanding of its historical, cultural, economic, and social context, laying the groundwork for developing and maintaining a sense of place. A matrix of needed research may be established on the level of architectural and urban circumstances, socioeconomic, cultural value, and ecological. The study and recording of all aspects that impact the revival vision, policies, and intervention projects are included in the site research and analysis of existing circumstances. Population, demographic, and language skills; physical and natural facilities; social heritage; climate; customs; natural scenery; design and structural elements; local government establishments; and temporary art and creative exhibits, events, and spaces are all part of this context. Ecological circumstances, economic status, cultural importance and significance, and urban landscape circumstances are the four basic categories in which the community context components and circumstances can be characterized (Teles, 2012).

20.2.1.2 Phase 2: Celebrating Character of the Community

While an inventory of place offers the first framework for developing a sense of place and generating community identity, it combines context and reinforcement of a place's contemporary environment and culture that gives it character or identity. Character is something that comes naturally to a community, not something that can be added, like cosmetics. Reinforcing a sense of place requires, first, a thorough understanding of a community's historical, cultural, economic, and social context, and, second, a vision for the future that evolves and embraces new ideas while balancing the inherent conflicts of past, present, and future community values and culture. This step necessitates a careful approach to documenting the architectural and urban components of the city or regional unit environment and the detailed recording of city character layers and aspects. City imageability studies can help to strengthen a city's distinct character and feeling of identity (Mohga, 2015).

20.2.1.3 Phase 3: Regarding Principles City Redesign

Using city redesign to keep and improve a community's cultural identity, uniqueness, and arts and culture assets requires that local decision-making, planning procedures, laws, and laws reflect and promote this regional identity.

Local government programs, rules, and laws that embrace a community's core philosophy or identity can be the basis for city redesign, which aims to encourage place-based development and strengthen a community's cultural goals and vision (Metaxas, 2015). By supporting the work of civic leaders and community activists, this framework can help bring new partners, skills, and ideas into the process of remaking a city. If different steps are taken, all work on historic assets and remaking a city works well. These include realizing how important it is, making policies that are good for the environment and can be kept up, and following the rules by making any repairs that are needed and doing regular maintenance.

20.2.2 City Redesign and Development Identity

Local governments and others concerned in the healthy development of cities have established policies and launched programs to mitigate the negative impacts of cultural globalization while increasing a feeling of uniqueness and individuality (Teles, 2012). The implementation of marketing initiatives that highlight unique assets and local identity has ranged from refurbishing architectural heritage and revamping urban areas to make impressive architectural styles, implement better city designs, support events or festivals, and introduce distinctive city signs. It is important to understand cultural heritage in an urban setting. Knowing cultural identity in the modern world and the city redesign's effectiveness in enhancing and promoting cultural identity help analyze practices that promote cultural identity at the urban levels (Dril et al., 2016).

20.2.2.1 Cultural Identity Revitalization

Culture has been described as "a whole society's way of existence" (Mohga, 2015, p. 12). It encompasses etiquette, dress, language, religion, rituals, and behavioral conventions such as law and morality and belief systems. The culture was considered to contain coherence and order, allowing it to operate as the basis for constructing stable identities. According to Mohga (2015), the cultural approach to the city has several key effects, including making public areas safer and encouraging localism or a feeling of identity in the face of homogenizing globalization. This interpretation necessitates a thorough and complete knowledge of culture, which is supplied in the World Culture Report, which defines culture as "individual and communal ways of life." This perspective on culture places it in a broader context, implying that "cultural identity" is linked to the unique ways individuals live individually and collectively. A cultural network encompasses the architectural preservation of cultural assets and a wide variety of cultural concerns such as art, literature, tradition, rituals, and more subjective themes of identity, belonging, and feeling of the place. Cultural identification refers to a person's sense of belonging to a specific culture or community, which plays a vital role in people's well-being. Learning about and adopting a culture's customs, heritage, language, religion, lineage, esthetics, thinking habits, and social systems are all part of this process. People usually assimilate their culture's views, values, customs, and social customs and identify themselves.

Mohga (2015) indicates that identification with a specific culture provides people with a sense of belonging and security. According to some scholars, cultural identity refers to values as guiding principles, significant symbols, and lifestyles that people share with others, but not always within recognized groupings. Cultural regeneration is the process of validating and developing people's individual and communal cultural identities, and it is essential for keeping a culture alive for future generations. Many cultures will be lost to us if we do not have them. The different culture revival initiatives aid in revealing and enhancing the underlying identity of a community's social and physical form and its distinct value and character. The character or feeling of a place of the Community reflects this identity. The feeling of place in a city is not a static idea; rather, it changes and develops throughout time, reflecting the range of social values found inside and surrounding the area. In this sense, a city's local identity may be viewed as a tale or narrative about a place.

20.2.3 Place Marketing as a Tool of Regional Development

Place marketing is considered a continuous social process that accelerates sustainable development of a city or region majorly by enhancing competitive advantage levels and creating a favorable environment for investment. Strategic city or place marketing plays a crucial role in reducing the risks associated with repositioning and consequently helps to maximize benefits derived from entering a new market (Borsekova, 2017).

The modern age has increased the recruitment of several marketing techniques to aid in the regeneration of different industrial cities, especially in European countries (Kalogiannidis & Mavratzas, 2020). Successful urban or city development is much dependent on a highly strategic marketing plan. This, therefore, indicates that city marketing should be incorporated into the different aspects of the city's actual development and sustainability.

Dril et al. (2016) indicate that city marketing plays a key role influencing the different social benefits of the city. Maximizing the social benefits of a place helps to attain the desired level of area or regional development. However, the social benefits of a city can be perceived differently by different individuals or subjects; hence an effective place marketing strategy is required to harmonize all the needs of a placer with those of the market. According to Vuignier (2016), city repositioning through place marketing is associated with several benefits that involve profits or financial stability and involve welfare growth and growth of social benefits of the town following the city's short-term, long-term strategic objectives. These objectives may also apply the different moral and ethical values of the place or city. Metaxas (2015) also indicates that place marketing considers the market of places a major basis for establishing the best repositioning strategy.

20.3 Methodology

20.3.1 *Research Design*

The study adopted a case study research design, which is considered very important in investigating a particular phenomenon within its real-life context. Case studies are always based on an in-depth investigation of a single individual, group, area or event to explore the dynamics of different underlying principles. For this particular study, the case study research design helped investigate the redesign process of a city, particularly Kozani, Greece.

20.3.2 *Sample Size*

The sample size was 50 respondents who included residents and local authorities from Kozani city in Greece. It is assumed that the city authorities have the best knowledge concerning the marketing dynamics and challenges of Kozani city that can be addressed to reposition the city into a highly competitive tourism and investment destination.

20.3.3 *Data Collection*

A survey questionnaire was emailed to the different selected participants to collect data concerning the redesigning process of the development identity of a regional unit or city with focus on Kozani city.

20.3.4 *Data Analysis*

Data collected using the questionnaire were analyzed using SPSS. The obtained results were presented using tables and graphs as well as pie charts. The interpretation of the results was made based on the received frequencies and percentages.

20.4 Results

20.4.1 *Demographic Characteristics*

The results about the different attributes or demographic characteristics of the study participants are presented in Table 20.1.

Table 20.1 Showing demographic characteristics of participants

Item	Frequency	Percentage (%)
Sex		
Male	37	74
Female	13	26
Age		
20–30	4	8
31–40	20	40
41–50	17	34
Above 50	9	18
Position in the city		
Administrator	21	42
Resident	29	58
Years spent in the city		
1–10	3	6
11–20	11	22
21–30	28	56
Above 30	8	16
Total	**50**	**100**

Source: Survey (2021)

The results in Table 20.1 show that more than half of the participants (74%) were male and only 26% were female. The largest portion of the participants (40%) were in the age bracket of 31–40 years, and only 8% were 20–30 years. Most of the respondents (58%) were merely residents of the city and only 42% were administrators with positions of responsibility in the city.

20.4.2 Descriptive Analysis

The results about the different factors that influence the redesigning process of the city are presented in Fig. 20.2.

From Fig. 20.2, majority of the respondents (31.6%) identified financial capital as the major factor that influences successful city redesigning, followed by human capital (17.5%), strategic planning tactics (15.5%), robust place management strategies (14.9%), advanced technologies (11.3%), and the least number of participants (9.2%) identified infrastructure plan and design. The results clearly show that financial capital plays a crucial role in the successful redesigning of the city or regional unit and this helps to achieve the different objectives of the redesigning process of the city. The results concerning objectives that influence city redesign are presented in Fig. 20.3.

From Fig. 20.3, majority of the local authority personnel (54.4%) indicated that the objectives of city redesigning are normally tactical, followed by 23.8% who indicated that the objectives are operational, and only 21.8% participants

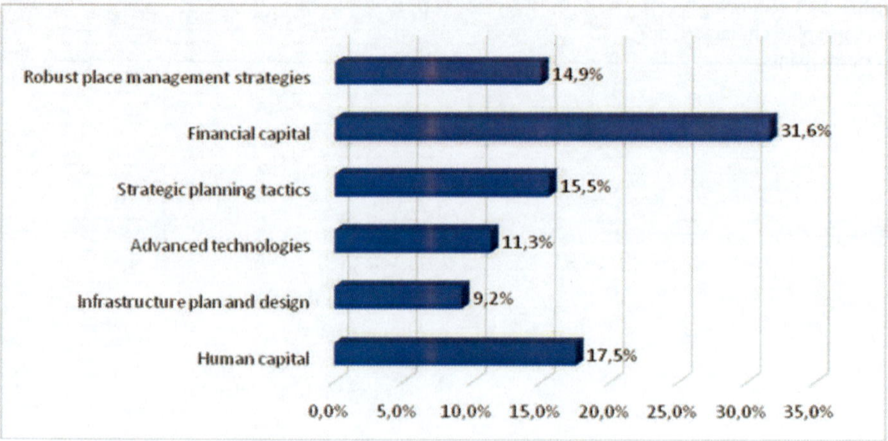

Fig. 20.2 Key factors that influence successful city redesigning. (Source: Survey, 2021)

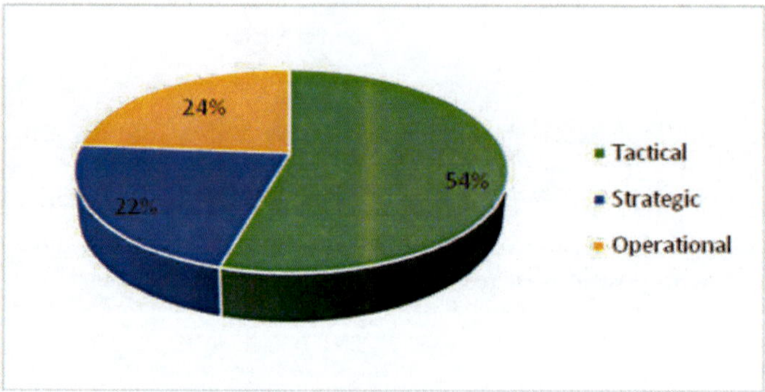

Fig. 20.3 Objectives that influence city redesign. (Source: Survey, 2021)

indicated that the objectives are strategic. The results clearly show that most cities are redesigned to achieve different tactical objectives that are normally long-term in nature and take about 3–5 years to be achieved. On the other hand, operational objectives are short-term and take about 1 year to be achieved. Past studies indicate that the combination of the tactical, strategic, and operational objectives helps to achieve the long-term vision of the city.

The study also sought to establish the role played by local authorities in the redesigning process of a city and the results are presented in Fig. 20.4.

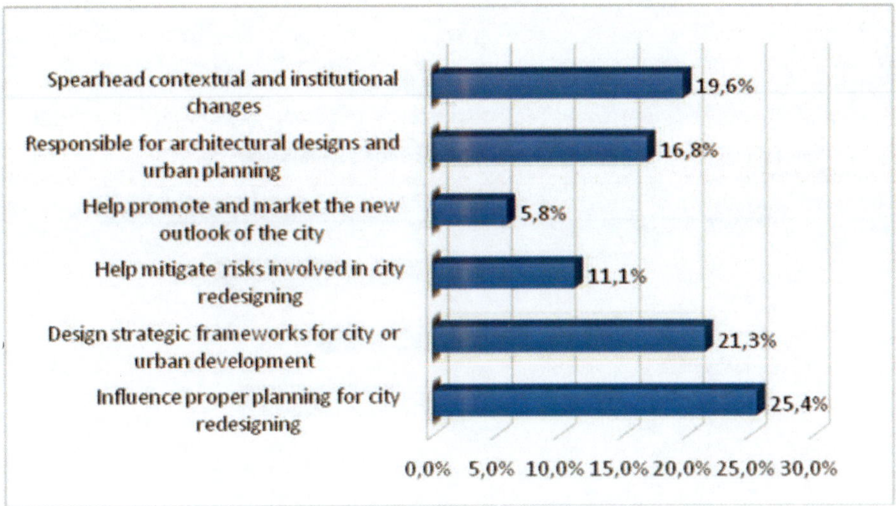

Fig. 20.4 Role of local authorities in city redesigning. (Source: Survey, 2021)

Majority of the participants (25.4%) indicated that local authorities influence proper planning for city redesigning, followed by design strategic frameworks for city or urban development (21.3%), spearhead contextual and institutional changes (19.6%), responsible for architectural designs and urban planning (16.8%), and the least number of participants (5.8%) indicated that the authorities help promote and market the new outlook of the city.

Majority of the participants in Fig. 20.5 below (28.3%) indicated that city redesigning attracts local and foreign investors, followed by fosters tourism growth and development (19.4%), improves revenue growth for the city (18%), preserves existing historic scale and character (17.8%), and the least number of participants (4.9%) gave other opinions concerning the relevance of city redesigning and some of these included, combating crime rates, eradicating poverty among citizens, and improves standards of living of the people especially the city residents. Enjoying the benefits of city redesigning can be difficult due to different challenges as presented in Fig. 20.6.

From Fig. 20.6, majority of the participants (27.1%) indicated that limited funds and other resources are the major challenges that face the process of city redesigning, followed by corruption and embezzlement of funds (21.4)%, resistance from the locals or citizens (15.3%), incompetent technical personnel (11.2%), and the least number of participants (7.3%) identified natural hazards as a challenge affecting city redesigning.

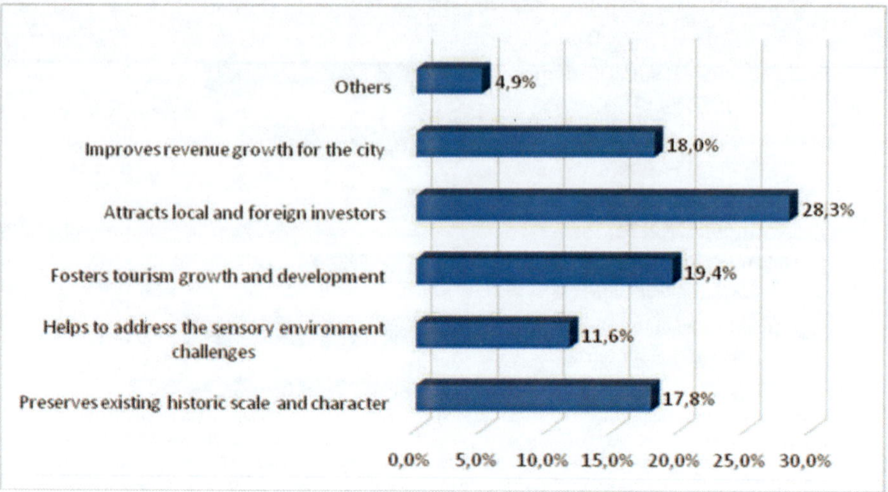

Fig. 20.5 Importance of redesigning a regional unit or city. (Source: Survey, 2021)

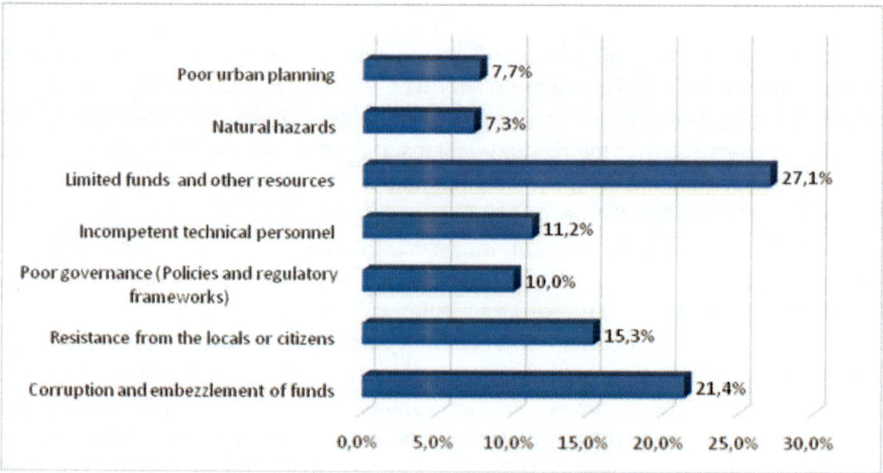

Fig. 20.6 Challenges in redesigning a city. (Source: Survey, 2021)

20.5 Discussion

This study focused on investigating the redesigning process of the development identity of a Local Government Regional Unit or City particularly Kozani in Greece. The study revealed that to achieve positive outcomes from city redesigning, three key phases have to be considered and these include; having a better understanding of the community, appreciating the identity of the city, and implementing the principles of city redesign. The study confirms the relevance of several factors such human capital, financial capital, and other resources in the redesigning of a city. Strategic planning was also identified as an essential factor in the city redesign process (Mohga, 2015). Strategic planning for city redesigning or repositioning is normally identified as a mere process of establishing the need for a redesign, the available market opportunities associated with the redesign, and the level of availability of the resources to support the redesigning process (Metaxas, 2015). This therefore indicates that strategic planning is a very important factor in the city redesigning process. It is important to note that absence of factors such as capital and proper leadership and the objectives of a city redesign cannot be met.

20.6 Conclusion

The study clearly covered the importance of city redesigning most particularly in regard to maintaining the cultural and development identity of a city or regional unit. Several, socioeconomic, environmental, ecological, and cultural as well as government-based factors are essential in the redesigning of a city. Character components, layers, and imageability along cities must be stressed to emphasize community character, which is linked to key values and identity. The city redesign principles concentrate on identifying the most important intervention tools for enhancing a city's community character and identity (Teles, 2012). These concepts range from the elimination of incompatible parts and activities to the design of infill structures and expansions. It explains how to build and rejuvenate old streets using theoretical criteria. When these principles are used, there are significant variances in the actual urban circumstances on the street; therefore each of these principles has its own significance and efficacy. The main difficulty in the redesign process of a city is determining how to apply appropriate different city redesign ideas based on the city's unique characteristics. Finally, historic cities worldwide must make significant efforts to preserve and restore their specific development character to preserve local heritage, customs, and identities.

20.7 Recommendations

The results clearly show that poor leadership affects the success of any redesign process of a city. Therefore, city authorities need to cooperate to ensure that the objectives of the city redesign are achieved.

It is also essential to engage all the stakeholders of their city, most notably the residents, since they also play a vital role in the success of the redesigning process of the town. In this case, the government can decide to compensate any residents affected by the redesign process, which helps avoid resistance.

References

Borsekova, K. (2017). *Place marketing Ekonomická fakulta Univerzity Mateja Bela v Banskej Bystrici* (Issue November).

Dril, N., Galkin, A., & Bibik, N. (2016). Applying city marketing as a tool to support sustainable development in small cities: Case study in Ukraine. *Transportation Research Procedia, 16*(March), 46–53. https://doi.org/10.1016/j.trpro.2016.11.006

Hasan, M., Komaladewi, R., & Huda, M. (2020). Review article marketing mix performance and customer relationship in improving trust of indihome customer: A case from west java indonesia. *Journal of Critical Reviews, 7*(2), 275–282.

Ifezue, A. N. (2019). *"The role of marketing in economic development of developing countries". The Role of Marketing in Economic Development of Developing Countries.*

Kalogiannidis, S., & Mavratzas, S. (2020). *Impact of marketing mix strategies effective product development issues in MNCs/Retail. 5*(December), 118–125.

Khattab, S. A. (2015, January). *E-Integrated marketing communication and its impact on customers ' E-Integrated marketing communication and its impact on customers' attitudes.* https://doi.org/10.4236/ajibm.2015.58053

Metaxas, T. (2015, March). *Place marketing, strategic planning and competitiveness: The case of Malta.* https://doi.org/10.1080/09654310903053539

Mohga, E. E. (2015). Promoting Cultural Identity along Streetscape Redesign "Case studies in Cairo and Luxor Cities, Egypt". *International Journal of Engineering Research and Technology (IJERT), 4*(5), 1248–1261. www.ijert.org

Seukindo, N. O. (2017). *Effect of marketing communication mix on sales performance of soft drink companies in dar es salaam, tanzania neema omary seukindo d58ea/cty/pt/20917/2012 a thesis submitted to the school of business in partial fulfilment of the requirements for.*

Teles, F. (2012). Local governance, identity and social capital: A framework for administrative reform. *Theoretical and Empirical Researches in Urban Management, 7*(4), 20–34.

Vuignier, R. (2016). *Place marketing and place branding: A systematic (and tentatively exhaustive) literature review To cite this version : HAL Id : hal-01340352 Renaud Vuignier Vuignier Renaud marketing and Working paper paper de de l ' IDHEAP.*

Chapter 21
Role of Management in Optimising the Quality of Education in Educational Organisations

Stavros Kalogiannidis, Stavroula Savvidou, Olympia Papaevangelou, and Fotini Pakaki

Abstract Education management has long been critical in improving students' academic performance in schools in any country with Greece inclusive. Education management entails overseeing all educational procedures and techniques utilised in the learning process to enhance students' learning environment. The goal of school improvement is to ensure that students have the best possible learning environment, which has an impact in both the student's performance and quality of education in the long run, though the latter has received little attention from research scholars. The primary purpose of this research was to assess the role of management in optimising the quality of education in educational organisations. Data was collected using an online survey questionnaire from 170 participants of the education sector of Kozani, Greece. The results confirmed when education is well managed, and schools get upgraded in a country, student performance improves, and the education offered is relevant and of high quality. According to the study's findings, vital parts of educational administration include proper planning, improving the school environment, effective leadership and teacher rewards and appreciation. The study has highlighted that management plays a key role in optimising the quality of teaching and learning in the different education institutions thereby enhancing the quality of education.

S. Kalogiannidis (✉)
Department of Business Administration, University of Western Macedonia, Kozani, Greece
e-mail: aff00056@uowm.gr

S. Savvidou
Department of Business Administration, University of Western Macedonia, Kozani, Greece
Educator, Ministry of Education, Kozani, Greece

O. Papaevangelou
Secondary & Postsecondary Educator, Ministry of Education, Kozani, Greece

F. Pakaki
Postsecondary Educator, Researcher, Kozani, Greece

N. Tsounis, A. Vlachvei (eds.), *Advances in Quantitative Economic Research*, Springer Proceedings in Business and Economics,
https://doi.org/10.1007/978-3-030-98179-2_21

Keywords Educational management · Quality education · Education organisations

21.1 Introduction

21.1.1 Background to the Study

Education management is a method through which managers influence other educational organisations to correctly implement the organisation's strategies at the appropriate times and with the right inputs. The relevant inputs continuously improve adaptation, resulting in increased production, profitability and quality (Latorre-Medina & Blanco-Encomienda, 2013). Education nowadays is more important than it has ever been in the growth of any country. It is a reality that no civilisation can flourish without first receiving a good education. Education is the gateway to a developed society, making it a valuable instrument for human growth. Students get the information and skills they need to live a complete, meaningful and productive life at school. School administrators and heads play an essential role in overseeing and providing the necessary leadership to ensure that students receive a high-quality education. In this case, excellent education is impossible to attain without the involvement of school principals (Njiru, 2014).

Every citizen understands that a good education is essential for our country's overall prosperity. Quality education positively affects the political climate and economic, social and cultural endeavours. If accessible, human resources play an essential role in utilising material resources in an education institution. As a result, low academic performance arises from a lack of teaching and learning resources, a teacher shortage and an unfriendly school climate (Hénard & Roseveare, 2012).

However, Ibrahim et al. (2017) suggest that low performance in developing countries depends on the cooperation between the different stakeholders in the education institutions or sector. Therefore, there is an essential link between management and educational outcomes since management influences the level of collaborations by different school stakeholders. Therefore, weak leadership cannot provide good results. However, if management is competent but the other variables lack, successful performance is not guaranteed (Ozmusul, 2015). In this case, excellent management necessitates additional resources or elements to provide good school results. This research focuses on the importance of management in improving education quality at educational institutions worldwide.

21.1.2 Problem Statement

Because of bad educational management and a lack of proper school reforms, students in many nations such as Greece have failed to have high-quality education.

Therefore, many governments have concentrated heavily on correctly managing education and upgrading schools to establish a suitable atmosphere for students to study to offer high-quality education (Saiti, 2012). Furthermore, countries with well-managed education can generate specialists and professionals who can compete fiercely in the global market because nations that lack enough education specialists spend a significant amount of money hiring specialists from other countries (Hénard & Roseveare, 2012). In this context, managing education entails ensuring that students get the necessary skills and information. Generally, most past studies have focused on the role of management on students' performance, and limited focus is on management's influence on the quality of education (Alexopoulos, 2019; Díez et al., 2020). Therefore, this study focused on establishing the role of management on the quality of education in different educational institutions.

21.1.3 Objectives of the Study

The study's primary aim is to assess the role of management in enhancing the quality of education in educational institutions. The study also had different specific objectives that include the following:

1. To establish the relationship between strategic management and quality of education in educational institutions
2. To establish the factors that influence the quality of education in educational organisations
3. To explore the barriers to improved quality education in educational institutions
4. To suggest possible solutions to barriers to improved quality education in educational institutions

21.1.4 Research Questions

1. What are the factors that influence the quality of education in educational organisations?
2. What are the barriers to improved quality education in educational institutions?
3. What are the possible solutions to barriers to improved quality education in educational institutions?

21.1.5 Hypothesis

H_O1: There is no significant relationship between educational management and quality of education

21.1.6 Significance of the Study

The findings of the study will render an outstanding contribution to the existing knowledge concerning the role of management in optimising the quality of education in different educational institutions. Furthermore, scholars researching the same field of study can use these study findings as a reference point.

The study findings will also benefit different policymakers and managers in the education sector by providing details about the effective ways of improving organisational management and the quality of education in the long run.

21.2 Literature Review

21.2.1 Management and Quality of Education

The quality standards of an educational system are developed and defined at numerous stages on both the inputs and process sides in anticipation of desired outputs and impacts expressed or documented by stakeholders in a specific context. On the process side, the essential elements are students entering schools, teachers, infrastructure, equipment and educational or school facilities that act as inputs and internal efficiency factors (Ibrahim et al., 2017).

Hatwal (2020) indicates that educational quality should not focus solely on academic inputs but also on different scholarly outputs, such as learning achievement, and the general acquisition of essential life skills. In this sense, educational professionals, learning methods and materials and education institutions are the three main academic input categories that help boost the relationship between management and the general quality of education.

Quality education relates to the amount of information and skills that society seeks to teach to kids. In teaching and learning, the development of knowledge and abilities should adhere to a competency-based approach. However, quality relates to an educational environment that supports skills and knowledge in a teaching and learning process. Some of the critical features of a learning environment include the number of employees, the availability of learning resources, the condition of the classrooms, the restrooms and the playgrounds (Akkaya, 2021).

Overall, there is no single definition of quality education. Instead, every culture defines quality education in terms of society's specific demands, and this definition changes throughout time. However, in traditional contexts, where secondary school is considered a stepping stone to higher learning institutions, a description of "quality" stresses academic accomplishment. Consequently, parents, instructors and students believe that higher-quality secondary schools, such as those found in private and seminary secondary schools, will attract more children than public and community secondary schools (Njiru, 2014).

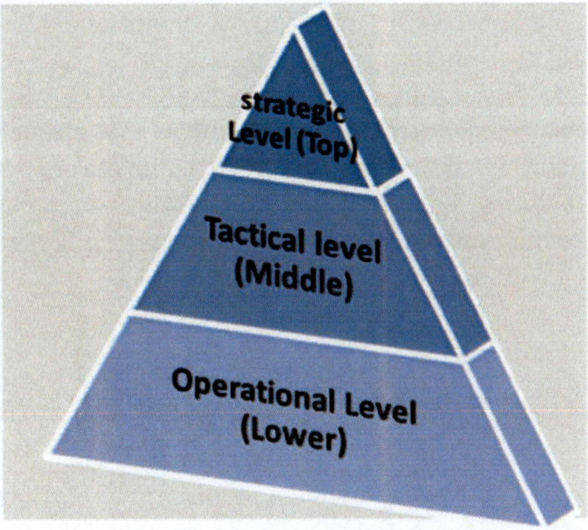

Fig. 21.1 Levels of organisational management. (Source: Rudhumbu, 2015)

Effective management of institutions requires collaboration among the different levels of control that include the strategic, tactical and operational levels of management, as shown in Fig. 21.1.

All of the organisation's highest positions participate in the planning and staffing process at the top management level. Ministers, commissioners and executive secretaries make up this management level, comprising chief executives who formulate the organisation's strategic plans. Departmental heads (HoD), the different branch managers and the junior executives make up the middle-level management. These aid in interpreting, explaining and monitoring top management policies and compiling and issuing comprehensive operational instructions. The foremen and supervisors make up the lower-level management and are selected by the management at the intermediate level. These aid in planning daily output within the goals set by higher authorities, assigning roles to employees and planning their training and development.

21.3 Educational Management Factors That Influence Education Quality

21.3.1 Educational Planning

Various scholars have identified educational planning as a component of efficacy and school improvement (Alexopoulos, 2019; Hénard & Roseveare, 2012). Short-term planning has risen in the last two decades since school planning consists of target-setting plans to enhance previously defined standards. However, short-term planning must get integrated within a longer-term planning framework. Given the goal of school development, most research studies suggest that educational planning focuses on creating organisational structures that support educational change, notably improving student learning outcomes while also developing a school's ability to manage change (Hatwal, 2020; Njiru, 2014). Establishing management structures or facilities that can help sustain the capacity building and educational transformation starts with the analysis of organisational atmosphere and facilities. The investigation focuses on corporate culture, circumstances, methods, teaching and learning methods and a school's decision-making and problem-solving capabilities (Ozmusul, 2015).

21.4 Effective Management Communication

If quality development in schools is to be accomplished, relationships and communication are essential aspects. Interpersonal relationships are one of four variables that leaders should provide to create a school environment that facilitates changes. First and foremost, there must be a commitment to collaborative planning. Second, school rules and decisions must include input from staff, students and the community. Finally, efficient coordinating mechanisms must be developed (OECD, 2017).

Kalogiannidis and Papaevangelou (2020) indicate that to build coordination, communication and human encounters are essential. In the setting of a school, good interpersonal interactions have a significant impact on attaining goals. A good work environment is appreciated, with coordinators who understand how to communicate with co-workers and build abilities to assist working teams in developing new projects. A well-designed and regulated communication system makes it easier to talk about teaching, agree on shared goals and share best practices and knowledge (Ozmusul, 2015). As a result, cooperative structures have a favourable impact on performance and provide a learning-rich environment in the classroom. As a result, efforts in the four areas below ensure strategic coordination structures for improvement: establishing skilled coordinators, leveraging task groups to get things done, establishing different reliable communication networks and promoting practice discussion (Alexopoulos, 2019).

21.4.1 Rewards and Management Support for Teachers

A study by Alexopoulos (2019) indicates that most teachers who feel appreciated have a favourable attitude toward their profession, possess strong self-esteem and self-confidence, accept leadership roles and are driven to offer quality work hard. They are more engaged in the company and have a more positive outlook. Teachers and other professionals in the education sector are at the core of any educational community; therefore, their support and professional development are very important in improving the general quality of education (Hatwal, 2020).

Several scholars believe that promoting capacity growth among professionals and educational institutions is essential for education quality enhancement (Goldberg & Cole, 2002; Kalogiannidis, 2021). In this case, capacity building is much concerned with the different capabilities, resources and motivation of educators on a personal level. Individuals and groups have significant abilities, which may be developed by participating in knowledge and skill development programs. More so, most teachers and other employees in the education sector, who are committed to working together regularly, build their abilities as the institution's capacity grows. Professional educators who participate in building capacity face new challenges and have the chance to try new things, develop new skills and enhance their teaching to become more effective.

21.5 Teaching and Learning Processes

Latorre-Medina and Blanco-Encomienda (2013) indicate that educational centres provide the settings that encourage instructors to participate in the learning process. Staff development programs are usually designed to help educators in their efforts to improve their teaching abilities and in analysing students' learning. Schools create a classroom-focused policy for staff development based on these clear goals. Furthermore, they make organisations serve as professional learning centres.

Furthermore, professional development programs tend to be tailored to specific needs, which normally results in a well-trusted operational environment and framework (Akkaya, 2021). Ozmusul (2015) indicates that teachers normally feel safe and motivated to challenge and share their knowledge and practices. A policy's goal is to create a thriving learning community to improve pedagogy and student progress. Staff development programs target classroom practices, allow the opportunity to model instructional techniques and help teachers gain in-depth knowledge about some subject regions (Saiti, 2012).

21.6 Methodology

21.6.1 Research Design

A quantitative methodology based on the cross-sectional survey design was used in this study. The cross-sectional helps examine data on variables gathered simultaneously across a sample population or a pre-defined subset of the people.

21.6.2 Sample Size

A sample of 170 participants from the education sector of Kozani was selected for the study, but only 150 managed to successfully respond to the question representing a response rate of 88.2%.

21.6.3 Data Collection

The study utilised an online survey questionnaire to collect data from the selected participants. The questionnaire encompassed different categorical questions about educational management and quality of education in educational institutions or organisations.

21.6.4 Data Analysis

Data collected were carefully sorted, coded and consequently analysed using SPSS. Results were presented in tables and graphs, and interpretation was based on frequencies and percentages. Chi-square test was used to test the hypothesis and establish the relationship between the study variables based on the formula below:

$$\chi^2 = \sum_{i=1}^{r} \sum_{j=1}^{c} \frac{\left(O_{ij} - E_{ij}\right)^2}{E_{ij}} \tag{21.1}$$

where:
χ^2 is the chi-square test
$\mathbf{O_{ij}}$ represents total number of observed frequencies
$\mathbf{E_{ij}}$ represents number of expected frequencies
r is the number of rows
c is the number of columns

The dependent variable was cross-tabulated with the chi-square test's independent variables to establish the relationship between study variables. The relationship between management and quality of education is based at a 95% confidence interval which is equivalent to 0.05 level of significance.

21.6.5 Ethical Considerations

Ethical requirements help ensure that the study is free from any harm and bias. First and foremost, informed consent was obtained from the prospective study participants, and the study's purpose or objective was explained to the participants before collecting data. Participants had the freedom to share their opinions about the different questions presented in the questionnaire.

21.7 Results

This section presents results and their interpretation concerning the research questions and objectives of the study.

21.7.1 Demographic Characteristics (Table 21.1)

More than half of the participants (65.3%) were male, and only 34.7% were female. The majority of participants (44.7%) were in the age bracket of 26–35 years, followed by 38.7% with 36–45 years, and only 7.3% were below 25. Concerning the level of education, the majority of the participants (44.87%) had master's degrees, and only 2.7 had certificates. Concerning the level of organisational management, majority of the participants (75.3%) were in the top level, and only 6.7% were in the lower level of educational management.

21.7.2 Descriptive Statistics

This section presents the different descriptive statistics that helped in answering the research questions of the study. The results concerning the components of effective management in educational organisations are presented in Table 21.2.

From Table 21.2, the majority of the participants (39.3%) identified proper planning and policymaking as the component of educational management, followed by controlling and collaborative working (32.7%) and adequate evaluation and reporting (15.3%), and the least number of participants (12.7%) selected budget formulation as the component of education management.

The study also established the quality of education in educational institutions in Kozani, Greece, and the results are in Table 21.3.

From Table 21.3, more than half of the participants (57.3%) indicated that the quality of education is high in their educational institutions, and 30% indicated that the quality of education is moderate. Only 12.7% stated that it is low.

The study further explored the importance of management in educational organisations, and the results are in Table 21.4.

Table 21.1 Showing demographic characteristics of participants

Item	Frequency	Percentage (%)
Sex		
Male	98	65.3
Female	52	34.7
Age bracket		
Below 25	11	7.3
26 to 35	67	44.7
36 to 45	58	38.7
46 years and above	14	9.3
Level of education		
Certificate	4	2.7
Diploma	34	22.7
Bachelor's degree	38	25.3
Master's degree	67	44.7
PhD	7	4.6
Level of educational management		
Top level	113	75.3
Middle level	27	18.0
Lower level	10	6.7
Years spent in the education sector		
0 to 5	16	10.7
6 to 9	36	24.0
10–15	79	52.7
16 years and above	19	12.6
Total	**150**	**100**

Source: Survey (2021)

Table 21.2 Components of effective management in educational organisations

Item	Frequency	Percentage (%)
Budget formulation	19	12.7
Controlling and collaborative working	49	32.7
Proper evaluation and reporting	23	15.3
Proper planning and policymaking	59	39.3
Total	**150**	**100**

Source: Survey (2021)

Table 21.3 Level of education quality in educational institutions

Item	Frequency	Percentage (%)
High	86	57.3
Moderate	45	30.0
Low	19	12.7
Total	**150**	**100**

Source: Survey (2021)

Table 21.4 Importance of management in educational organisations

Item	Frequency	Percentage (%)
Improves the quality of education	54	36.0
Improves professionalism and competence in the education sector	13	8.7
Enhances quality of student's academic performance	24	16.0
Improves learning experiences of students	11	7.3
Promotes effective teaching and learning	17	11.3
Creates favourable operational environment within educational institutions	31	20.7
Total	**150**	**100**

Source: Survey (2021)

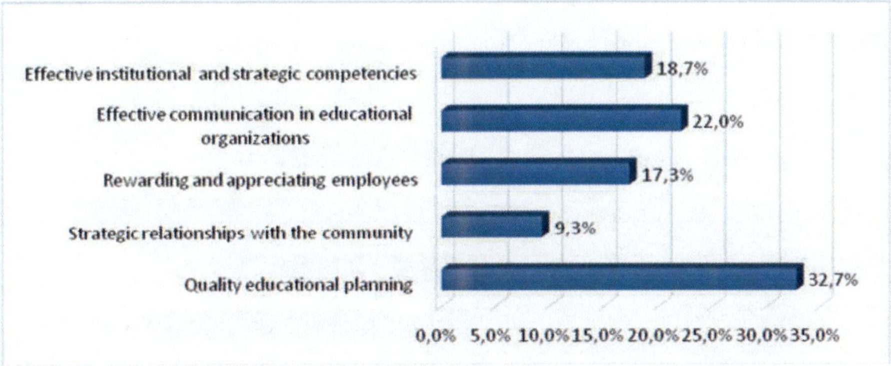

Fig. 21.2 Factors that enhance the quality of education. (Source: Survey, 2021)

From Table 21.4, the majority of the participants (36%) indicated that educational management improves the quality of education, followed by creates favourable operational environments within educational institutions (20.7%), enhances the quality of student's academic performance (16%) and promotes effective teaching and learning (11.3%), and the least number of participants (7.3%) indicated that management improves learning experiences of students.

The results concerning the different factors that help improve the quality of education in educational organisations are presented in Fig. 21.2.

From Fig. 21.2, the majority of the participants (32.7%) indicated quality educational planning as a major factor that enhances the quality of education, followed by 22% for effective communication in educational organisations, 18.7% for practical institutional and strategic competencies and 17.3% for rewarding and appreciating employees, and the least number of participants (9.3%) indicated that strategic relationships with the community are also a significant factor in enhancing the quality of education. These results confirm the relevance of educational planning in influencing the quality of education majorly because it properly helps managers achieve the different goals and objectives of other educational organisations.

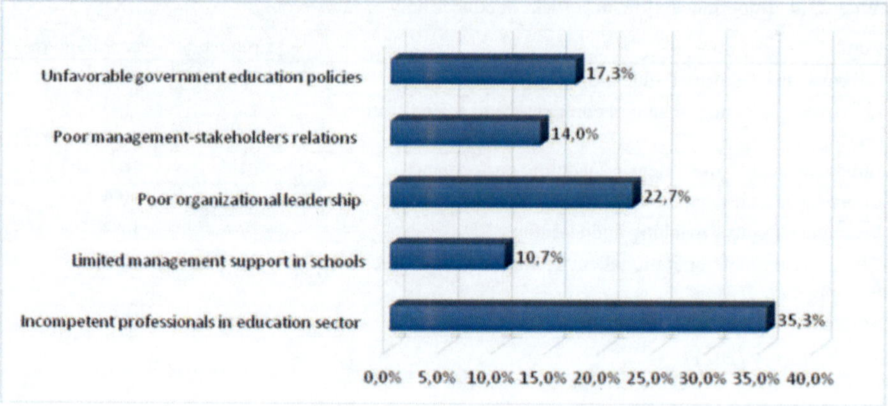

Fig. 21.3 Barriers to improved quality of education. (Source: Survey, 2021)

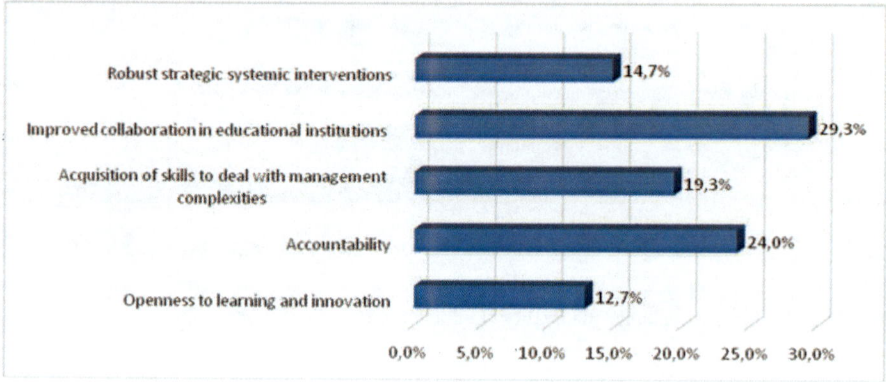

Fig. 21.4 Solutions to barriers of quality education in education institutions. (Source: Survey, 2021)

The study also sought to establish the barriers to improved quality of education, and the results obtained after analysis are presented in Fig. 21.3.

Concerning barriers to improved quality education in Fig. 21.3, the majority of the study participants (35.3%) selected incompetent professionals in the education sector, followed by poor organisational leadership (22.7%), unfavourable government education policies (17.3%) and poor relationships between management and educational stakeholders (14%), and only 10.7% selected limited management support as a barrier to improved quality education. These results confirm the impact of incompetent and unskilled professionals on the performance of the educational sector. In this case, the quality of education is influenced by highly skilled teachers and education policymakers. The possible solutions to the barriers to quality education in educational institutions are presented in Fig. 21.4.

Table 21.5 Relationship between management and quality of education in education organisations

	Components of management				
Quality of education	Budget formulation	Controlling and collaborative working	Proper evaluation and reporting	Adequate planning and policy-making	Total
High	5	10	16	55	86
Moderate	13	21	7	4	45
Low	1	18	0	0	19
Total	19	49	23	59	150
$\chi^2 = 4.952$		df = 3	$p = 0.023$		$\alpha = 0.05$

Source: Survey (2021)

From Fig. 21.4, the majority of the participants (29.3%) indicated improved collaboration in educational institutions as a solution to barriers of quality education in educational institutions, followed by accountability (24%), acquisition of skills to deal with management complexities (19.3%) and robust strategic, systemic interventions (14.7%), and the least number of participants (2.7%) selected openness to learn and innovations the strategy to address barriers to quality education in educational organisations.

21.7.3 Hypothesis Testing (Table 21.5)

Since the calculated $x^2 = 4.952$ is greater than the tabulated $x^2 = 3.841$ and $p = 0.023 < 0.005$, we reject the null hypothesis and conclude that there is a statistically significant relationship between management and quality of education in education organisations.

21.8 Discussion

This research emphasises the need to combine accountability measures with other tactics to advance quality education, which is the primary goal of educational systems. In any company and education, implementing a high-quality design is a top priority. Educational institutions must recognise their pedagogical purpose to set themselves apart from other schools and consequently promote the most appropriate teaching and learning processes in a highly dynamic environment (Alexopoulos, 2019; Latorre-Medina & Blanco-Encomienda, 2013; Njiru, 2014). Some elements of this quality procedure can be highlighted as a result of this research. The findings confirm that proper educational planning and effective management communication are among the highly valued factors that help managers improve the quality of education in Greek-based educational institutions. Schools may make genuine attempts to promote these essential elements inside their organisation and the community. Scholars indicate that educational institutions engaged in improvement planning procedures attempt to encourage students' learning via excellent teaching and leadership (Ibrahim et al., 2017; Saiti, 2012). Another area of this research emphasised as necessary for improving educational centre quality is closely tied to leadership, the work being done to strengthen interpersonal communication, particularly among school employees and students and their families (Díez et al., 2020; Kalogiannidis & Papaevangelou, 2020). Collaborative and collegial working methods in educational communities encourage educators to produce, exchange and critique their teaching techniques.

Furthermore, the study findings confirm that support and incentive structures for instructors are aspects that the participants regard the least. Recognition is an external process influenced by various circumstances; it might come from models that are supported and even funded by government agencies, or it can come from a single accrediting institution. Regardless of the model's additional value, this has a more negligible social impact. This indicates that when a centre achieves model accreditation, the impression of the recognition changes depending on the level of assistance obtained by the responsible public administration (Latorre-Medina & Blanco-Encomienda, 2013). The findings show that educational organisations can only enhance teaching and learning quality by establishing proper professional development and incentive systems that encourage personnel to get involved in change processes. As a result, school administrators and education policymakers should agree on an improvement strategy that considers how to improve the quality of teaching and learning. Furthermore, professional learning opportunities become available to provide instructors with the necessary technological capabilities (Alexopoulos, 2019).

21.9 Conclusion

The study has highlighted that management plays a key role in optimising the quality of teaching and learning in the different education institutions thereby enhancing the quality of education. Evidence indicates that creating external and internal assessment procedures significantly impacts school development, particularly in classes with poor teaching quality. Self-evaluation techniques aid educational institutions in identifying development objectives, analysing opportunities for change and fostering responsibility. Furthermore, several authors have emphasised the potential advantages of data, especially when staff participate in inquiry and reflection activities that strengthen school planning and teaching methods. As a result, more study into quality-control systems in educational organisations should offer light on the factors that need to be reviewed to foster educational transformation, which will enhance learning professionals' and organisations' teaching practices.

21.10 Recommendations

Several components stand out as important for sustainable educational change under and among all the efforts toward school improvement. Therefore, active learning, honest assessment, community, choice, new technology, lifelong learning and character education should be emphasised to bring meaningful change in educational organisations.

Strategic planning for an educational institution is fundamentally a question of constructing a bridge or creating a path between the observed current condition and the intended future condition and hence should be emphasised in educational organisations across Greece.

Principles should take care of the resources available to their institutions and maximise their usage by taking care of the planning and process factors because human resource development is a long-term goal.

Government should also implement favourable policies that support the different activities of the educational sector so as to achieve and maintain quality teaching and learning in educational organisations.

References

Akkaya, A. (2021). Theories of educational management and leadership. *Educational Review, 73*(April), 1–2.

Alexopoulos, N. (2019). Resolving school staffing problems in Greece: A strategic management approach. *Frontiers in Education, 4*(November), 1–11.

Díez, F., Villa, A., López, A. L., & Iraurgi, I. (2020). Impact of quality management systems in the performance of educational centers: Educational policies and management processes. *Heliyon, 6*(4), e03824.

Goldberg, J. S., & Cole, B. R. (2002). Quality management in education: Building excellence and equity in student performance. *Quality Management Journal, 9*(4), 8–22.

Hatwal, V. (2020). *A study of performance management system in Higher Education Institution with Special Reference to Academicians*. (June 2018): 3–7.

Hénard, F., & Roseveare, D.. (2012, September). *Fostering quality teaching in higher education: Policies and practices* (p. 54).

Ibrahim, I. A., Ali, I. A. A., & Abdalla, M. S. (2017, December). *Educational management, educational administration and educational leadership: Definitions and general concepts thyroid hormones view project normal values of Hemoglobin A1c (Hb A1c) and HbA1c Level in Diabetes View Project SAS Journal of Medicine (SASJM)*. http://sassociety.com/sasjm/

Kalogiannidis, S. I. (2021). The effects of total quality management practices and marketing on performance of SMEs. A case of selected manufacturing industries, Greece. *Business Management and Strategy, 12*(1), 48.

Kalogiannidis, S., & Papaevangelou, O. (2020). Impact of business communication on the performance of adult trainees. *International Journal of Academic Research in Progressive Education and Development, 9*(3), 213–222.

Latorre-Medina, M. J., & Blanco-Encomienda, F. J. (2013). Strategic management as key to improve the quality of education. *Procedia – Social and Behavioral Sciences, 81*, 270–274.

Njiru, L. M. (2014). Job satisfaction and motivation among teachers of Kiharu district in Kenya. *Mediterranean Journal of Social Sciences, 5*(5 SPEC. ISSUE), 135–152.

OECD. (2017). *Education policy in Greece: A preliminary assessment*. OECD Publishing: 92. chrome-extension://oemmndcbldboiebfnladdacbdfmadadm/, http://www.oecd.org/education/Education-Policy-in-Greece-Preliminary-Assessment-2017.pdf

Ozmusul, M. (2015). The unblocking leadership for effectiveness of teachers as knowledge staff: A theoretical framework for School management. *Universal Journal of Educational Research, 3*(10), 757–773.

Rudhumbu, N. (2015). Managing curriculum change from the middle: How academic middle managers enact their role in higher education. *International Journal of Higher Education, 4*(1), 106–119.

Saiti, A. (2012). Leadership and quality management: An analysis of three key features of the Greek Education System. *Quality Assurance in Education, 20*(2), 110–138.

Chapter 22
Simple and Transparent: A Positive Correlation for Virtuous Public Administrations

Anna Maria Bagnasco and Tiziana Alti

Abstract The health emergency which started in 2020 has set off a new request for the understanding of public decision-making and underlying information.

During the emergency phase, governments encouraged the use of simplified purchasing procedures to ensure the acceleration of public action and to attempt to stem the pandemic. As considerable amounts of public money have been rightly used during the emergency in the interest of public health, our goal is to investigate the level of transparency ensured by the procedures utilized for purchasing goods and services.

To this end, we have considered data regarding all the expenses related to the health emergency through public administration calls for tenders between January 01, 2020, and April 30, 2021. The data analyzed suggests speed, simplification, and transparency are not always strictly correlated, and this could be a critical issue in order to guarantee virtuous public policies.

Keywords Government transparency · Procurement · Government expenditure · Public sector accounting

JEL Codes H51, H57, H83, I18

22.1 Introduction

The quality of a country's public administration is a key determining factor in both economic productivity and the well-being of a society. There is ample evidence

A. M. Bagnasco (✉)
IULM University, Milan, Italy
e-mail: annamaria.bagnasco@iulm.it

T. Alti
G. Romagnosi Foundation, Pavia, Italy

N. Tsounis, A. Vlachvei (eds.), *Advances in Quantitative Economic Research*, Springer Proceedings in Business and Economics,
https://doi.org/10.1007/978-3-030-98179-2_22

that high per capita income economies have the most effective and efficient public institutions (Jütting, 2003; Rodrik et al., 2002).

To achieve this, the country's governing institutions must ensure that economic and social interactions take place in an environment free of corruption, with effective competition policies and an efficient judicial system.

Since governance is based on trust, public administrations need to apply and share fundamental principles such as legality, integrity, and impartiality and demonstrate flexibility, efficiency, and administrative responsibility: the goal of a such behavior and attitude is gaining, and maintaining over time, the trust of stakeholders, from voters to investors to other administrations (EC, 2017).

In order to ensure good governance, in high-income countries, strategies have been developed to combat the phenomenon of corruption.

Systematic corruption imposes economic costs and discourages enterprise, investments, and innovation; it distorts decision-making and diverts funds that governments can ill-afford to lose;[1] it is costly and unhealthy for long-term economic prosperity and sound public finances.

Corruption is a complex phenomenon. There is no single set of causes, and the risk of corruption tends to be higher in the presence of opportunities to exercise it: risk factors are represented by secrecy, opacity, and the absence of constraints relating to compliance with legality, such as laws and regulations, social conventions, controls, verifications, sanctions, or control by public opinion (Mungiu-Pippidi, 2014).

Each EU Member State has its own framework for promoting public conduct inspired by correctness and respect for legality: there is no standard package of measures that can be applied in every circumstance, while the most effective policy response depends on local conditions and includes its own strategies, regulations, and institutions (EC, 2017).

Among the solutions envisaged in the context of anti-corruption preventive measures, administrative transparency represents a lever of contrast of great interest and effectiveness.

Given that corruption usually relies on secrecy, a very powerful antidote is open government, enabling citizens to exercise their democratic right to oversee the executive and the judiciary branches of government, by ensuring they have access to information and enabling citizens' representatives to verify administrative performance. Transparency acts to deter and detect corruptive practices, providing a safeguard against potential abuses of power, and shining a light on transgressions when they arise.

Today, the public sector is more open than ever in history, and many public administrations have embraced that reality by adopting legislation permitting freedom of information. ICT is both a driver and an enabler of this openness: digital-

[1] Analysis by the EU-financed ANTICORRP program shows a strong correlation between corruption and government overspending, under-collection of taxes, and fiscal deficits. See https://anticorrp.eu/project/overview/.

ization now allows the public to monitor the extent to which public administrations meet their obligations on transparency and access to information and hold them accountable for public spending and integrity, inter alia, opening a window, for example, on the use of resources, encouraging civic involvement in performance monitoring, enticing media interest, and supporting participation, and protecting against corruption and misuse of public funds.

It is down to individual governments to decide how ambitious they wish to be when extending the boundaries on that openness.[2]

It is in this context that in Italy the legislation on administrative transparency is inserted, with the most recent law on the right of generalized access, or FOIA (Freedom of Information Act).

In terms of access to information, the pandemic has most likely constituted a "watershed." The health sector is currently at the center of public policy in the global crisis: it has become clear to everyone that the availability of information and data and their free circulation are an essential condition for making concrete the possibility of evaluating and verifying adopted policies.

The health sector is more than others, characterized by situations of conflicts of interest, as well as by a marked asymmetric distribution of relevant information and skills between users and public and private operators. In the health sector, many know little, while few know a lot, and can take advantage of this situation for undue enrichment from that information. It follows that in this area, perhaps even more than in others, transparency is essential, as a means by which to allow greater control at all levels and make criminal infiltration more difficult.

Taking into account all these considerations, our goal is to analyze the level of public-sector transparency, interpreted as key factor both to guarantee sound governance and to ensure the efficient use of available funds. Even if the relationship between transparency and various dimensions of the quality of government is complex, we don't enter in questions on the value of transparency and its ability to improve the quality of government (Etzioni, 2014; Fukuyama, 2015), while we focus on assessing how transparency works.

The paper is organized as follows: in Sect. 22.2, we present the context and the law framework on transparency in Italy; in Sect. 22.3, we describe dataset; and, finally, we discuss the findings and the limitations of the analysis, and we conclude.

[2] All Member States are signatories to the 2017 Tallin and 2009 Malmö Ministerial Declaration on eGovernment, and many are part of the Open Government Partnership. Transparency is integral to the vision and principles of the eGovernment Action Plan 2016–2020, measured by the eGovernment Benchmark and the Digital Economy and Society Index (DESI), and subject to several projects under Horizon 2020 (EU, 2017).

22.2 The Transparency of Public Procurement in the Italian Context

In the wide debate around public policy choices in reaction to COVID-19 pandemic crises, it is interesting to concentrate on administrative transparency, intended as the right to know all information emerging along the decision-making process, including its effects.

This thinking affects at least three areas of significance: the effectiveness of the government in using public resources, the respect of existing laws in public action, and the possibility for participation on the part of citizens in decision-making process.

Although the topic of administrative transparency and open government has been the object of many studies and investigation for decades (see Cucciniello et al., 2016), the health emergency which started in 2020 kicked off a new request for the understanding of public decisions and underlying information, especially in relation to the enactment of decrees with heavy impact on personal freedoms.

It is easy to discover in the news, or learning from ad hoc analysis,[3] that an actual call for transparency is emerging, and beyond the media effect, it imposes a technical approach to the topic, pondering pros and cons already shown in literature (Etzioni, 2010, 2014).

If it is true that the expression "transparency" can assume many suggestive meanings and different definitions, it is only in the observation of its operative implementation that its essential functions emerge and, at the same time, reveals the possible gap between the principles of transparency and its effective application.

If, among the different definitions of transparency, we consider "the effective availability of information related to public administration," this particular meaning, in the Italian legal framework, leads to a quite recent piece of legislation, developed in the last three decades, to grant citizens an increasing level of access to government information.

Briefly, the initial appearance of transparency in the Italian legal framework coincides with the so-called access to documents and concerns the citizens' right to participate to an administrative process, only in cases where a citizen was directly involved (Law n. 241/1990).

Many years later (Decree n. 33/2013), in accordance with the national anti-corruption strategy (Law 190/2012), the notion of "civic access" was introduced, with the intention to provide citizens a lever of control, in case they would claim the information specified by the legislator as a real duty of transparency imposed to public administrations, through the publication on their website.

Finally, to complete the process toward the affirmation of a right to transparency, a proper Freedom of Information Act was introduced in the Italian legal framework (Decree 97/2016) to guarantee general access to all information concerning public

[3] See Open polis survey at https://www.openpolis.it/il-ruolo-del-foia-per-la-tutela-della-salute/

administration, with the exemption of particular cases, when the disclosure could seriously affect some public or private interests.

If it is therefore certainly true that today, in Italy, anybody can have access to any kind of information concerning public administration, nowadays, the increasing request for transparency imposes the need to consider the right to transparency in its real enforceability.

In the Italian case, it is possible to detect internal opposition – by the administrative apparatus – to the construction of a real system of transparency, due to the Italian delay in the adoption of a free information legislation which, in turn, can be traced back to specific traits of the cultural model of Italian bureaucracy, such as a strong attachment to the principles of State secret and professional secrecy.

Once again, on the side of "transparency production," some uncertainties in correctly interpreting how to deal with the abovementioned exceptions to transparency represent a real weight on the shoulders of officials, and make the process of evaluation, judging, and deciding about the boundaries of disclosure quite arduous.

However, the real sore point concerns the actual usability of information by citizens, both in quantity and in quality.

As a paradox, the vast amount of information which transparency laws make available could provoke the adverse effect of "opacity by confusion."[4]

Besides, even if requested data is easily available, it is not unusual to come across very technical texts, quite unclear propositions, or illogical distribution of the main information in different sections of the website.

In short, the suspicion arises as to whether the big effort and meaning of transparency is likely to be ineffective, since information, definitely published somewhere, and in any case available by request as a right, does not reach its natural recipients.

This possibility should represent a real concern, if we consider the essential role played by administrative transparency in terms of legality, legitimation, and participation, and even a bigger alarm in consideration of the necessity of these ingredients in the ongoing process of policymaking for recovery, through the investment of enormous amounts of resources.

In fact, among the categories of dataset subjected to administrative transparency, the area of public procurement is a particularly sensitive field, in consideration of its financial weight and, accordingly, its exposure to the risk of corruption.

In this perspective, in implementation of the European Directives (2014/23/UE, 2014/24/UE, 2014/25/UE), public procurement is well guarded by the Italian Code (Decree 50/2016) even if this legislation is continually reconsidered in order to balance different requirements: assurance as to the legality of procedures, rationality of business operations, and availability of goods and services pursuing public interests.

---

[4] As pronounced in the decision n. 20/2019 of the Italian Constitutional Court

The common point of these different requirements seems to consist precisely of the disclosure regime requested all along the process of procurement, as clearly indicated by the Italian Code and affirmed in the national anti-corruption Law.

In fact, in addition to account for the use of public resources, the access to public procurement information prevents the wider phenomenon of "maladministration," enables the wider participation of economic agents, promotes competition, and represents a deterrent for the distorted use of public finances.

The respect of high standard of transparency in public procurement is a precise recommendation by the European Union, and even OCSE (2015) has pointed to transparency as a fundamental principle for integrity, inviting governments to provide economic agents with all the needed information to make the procurement process fair and competitive.

The inter-relations between the disclosure requirements provided by Italian legislation on transparency form a solid basis for the public information assets, completed by the presence of institutional data base (National Database of Public Contracts of the Anti-Corruption Authority).

If citizens have the keys to access and effectively use these assets, this is still a hypothesis to test, as described in following pages.

22.3 Dataset Description

With the aim to analyze the expenses related to the epidemiological emergency of COVID-19 through the public administration's calls for tenders, we used data downloaded from the website *openpolis.it* on 15/05/2021. It refers to all calls for tenders published between 01 January 2020 and 30 April 2021.[5]

The original dataset contains 15,418 rows, each corresponding to a different public purchasing lot.[6]

Each row is uniquely identified by a Tender Identification Code[7] (CIG) and is also described by the following information:

- Contracting authority, in detail and aggregated (e.g., central national health service, local health authority)

[5] Data is mainly from ANAC (national anti-corruption authority) source through the National Public Contracts Database which only provides lots with a starting price of more than 40,000 euros. Openpolis has selected some keywords for the search in the subject of the lots. Another source is the data on the contracts made available by the Civil Protection. Furthermore, various data were obtained from the sites of some contracting stations. See https://bandicovid.openpolis.it

[6] A call for tenders is divided into one or more lots which may relate to different supplies, services, and works. Consequently, lots of the same tender can have different amounts and be awarded to different companies.

[7] In Italian CIG (codice identificativo di gara): it is a code adopted in Italy to identify a public contract stipulated following a tender or entrusted with one of the other methods permitted by the public contracts code.

- Region of the contracting authority
- Object of the lot in tender, in detail and aggregate (i.e., surgical masks and other protections, products and services used in analysis)
- Framework agreement (yes/no)
- Procedure (e.g., direct awarding, open procedure)
- Lot status (e.g., published, awarded, revoked)
- Starting price and awarded price
- Publication date and award date[8]

In a preliminary control phase, some missing or incorrect data was identified:

- 30 tenders with publication date 2018 or 2019, but certainly subsequent (e.g., "FUNCTIONAL REQUALIFICATION OF THE EX OBI DEL PS AREA – INTENSIVE CARE COVID 19/BUILDING WORKS"), have been eliminated (starting price amount eliminated is € 11.5 million, no award).
- 236 tenders with an award amount greater than the starting price were corrected where possible; alternatively, they were corrected by setting the award amount equal to the starting price.

Final dataset under analysis contains 15,388 lots in tender.

In the 16 months considered, tenders for more than 23 billion euros were issued and approximately 7,5 billion were awarded. The difference between starting price and what was awarded may depend on discounts during the award phase or on the fact that the lot has not yet been awarded or the final amount is not yet available. In Fig. 22.1, we can see the lots' status.

The distribution by product category (Fig. 22.2) shows that 51% of the total expenditure is attributable to the purchase of masks and other personal protective

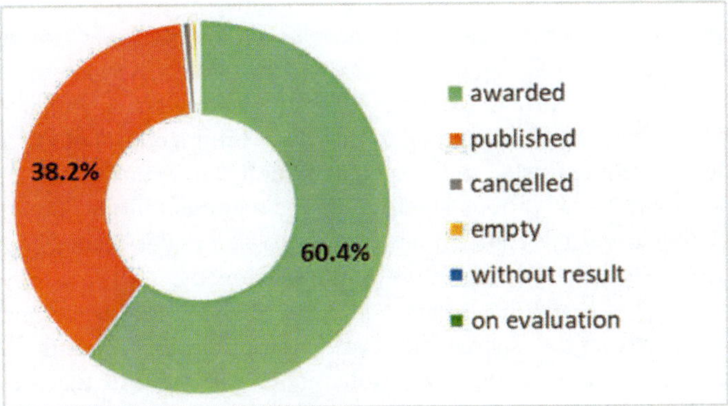

Source: Authors' calculations

Fig. 22.1 The status of the lots. (Source: Authors' calculations)

[8] Other detailed information on the contract and on the winners have not been used in our analysis.

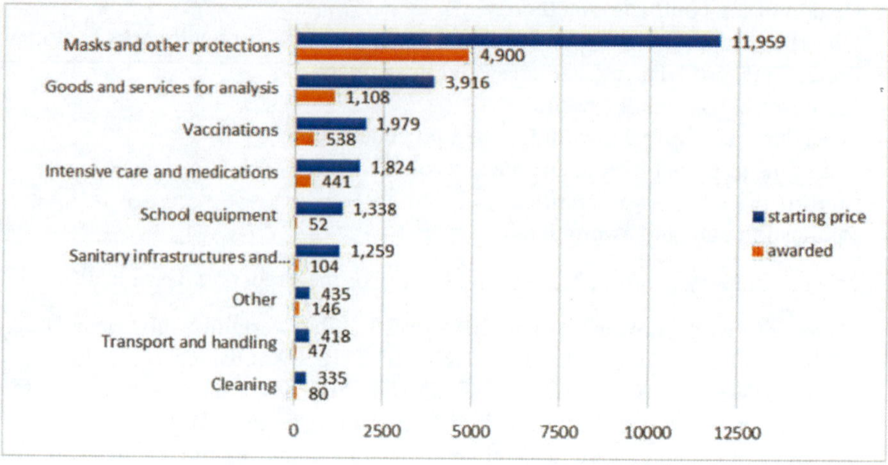

Fig. 22.2 Starting price and awarded by product category (MIL €). (Source: Authors' calculations)

equipment: it amounts to almost 12 billion euros, of which 4.9 results awarded. 16.7% of the amounts relate to products and services useful for screening or diagnostics, such as the swabs necessary for the virus detection.

Spending categories have followed the evolution of the health emergency: in the course of months, the weight of the category vaccination has grown, while at the beginning of the emergency, categories relating to school infrastructures and furniture as well as those products relating to ICU and medications were greater.

The following figure shows the distribution of expenditure by type of contracting authority.

Over the course of months, the role of the special commissioner[9] for the COVID-19 emergency has dramatically increased: the commissioner structure has become the main protagonist in the management of the emergency. The amounts tendered by this institution represent 44.5% (equal to over 10.4 billion euros) of the amount put up for tender or were entrusted to the special commissioner during the emergency.

Figure 22.3 shows the various levels of public administrations (among the 1358 considered) that have tendered amounts equal to or greater than 1% of the total starting price since the beginning of the health emergency.

Among the subjects that have launched more tendered lots, there are also three regional public entities that specifically deal with purchasing in Lombardy, Veneto, and Tuscany, in addition to the civil protection department of the presidency of the council of ministers and the public company Consip S.p.A. Nevertheless, as is

[9] On March 17, 2020, in our healthcare system, a Special Commissioner was introduced for the implementation and coordination of the measures necessary for the containment and contrast of the epidemiological emergency COVID-19.

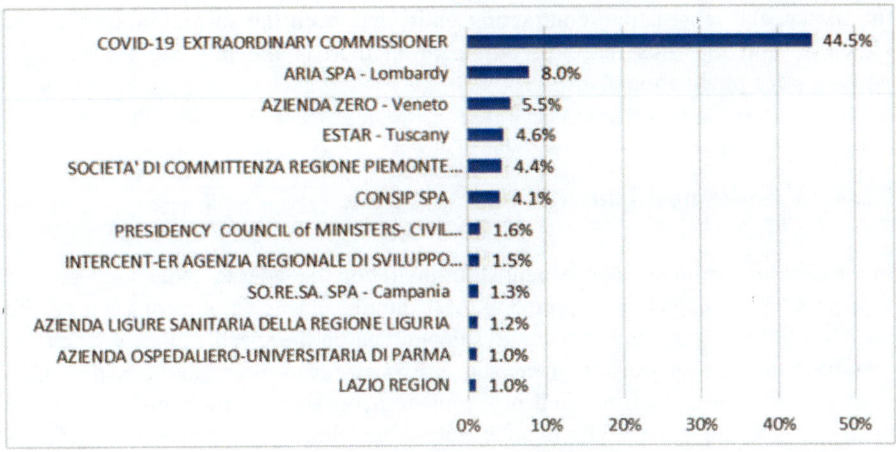

Fig. 22.3 Starting price by contracting authority (% of total). (Source: Authors' calculations)

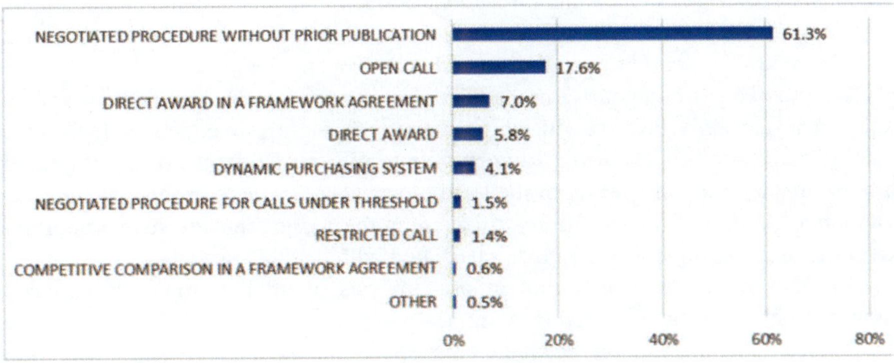

Fig. 22.4 Starting price by procedure (% of total). (Source: Authors' calculations)

evident from the graph, the extraordinary commissioner clearly remains the first contracting entity.

In Fig. 22.4, we can see the main procedures followed in the assignment of the tender notices.

The prevailing method, considering both the tender and the award amounts, is the negotiated procedure without prior publication of a contract notice:[10] this procedure regards 14.4 billion Euros of auctioned tenders and 4.5 billion of awards.

From data, therefore, the trends that have characterized these months regarding public expenditure for the health emergency emerge: the most purchased goods are

[10] It is a type of negotiated procedure with which the contracting authority awards a public contract without completing the ordinary preliminary phase of publication of the tender notice. See public contract code, art. 59.

the masks, the most active contracting entity has been the special commissioner structure, and the most used procurement method is the procedure negotiated without prior publication.

22.4 Results and Conclusions

We used information on the procedures for invitation to tender to understand how far transparency policy is being applied in these circumstances. Public contracts can be awarded following different procedures depending on the specific circumstance.[11]

Observing the procedures (see Fig. 22.4), we can note that the non-open ones prevail: these are simplified procedures encouraged by the legislation in the emergency phase, with the aim of accelerating lead times.[12] In fact, 74% of the total amounts tendered were awarded with simplified procedures: negotiated procedure without prior publication of a contract notice (61%), direct award in adherence to a framework agreement (7%), and direct award (6%).

We note a big proportion of simplified procedures, less transparent, against a small share of transparent procedures (such as the open ones).

The use of a less competitive procedure is not in and of itself a damaging practice: there may certainly be cases in which the use of these procedures is legitimate and indeed desirable. However, in aggregate terms, the frequent use of simplified procedures leads to a lowering of the level of transparency both in the management of public funds and in the ability to monitor the assignment of such important services as those regarding the costs associated with healthcare.

To date, what emerges is that in our analysis, there is a trade-off between transparency and simplification (Fig. 22.5).

The positive correlation between emergency and opacity emerges from the following transmission channel:

Emergency→ Speed → Simplification → Extraordinary measures → Opacity

This correlation suggests some considerations: Day-to-day common law is not able to ensure speed and simplification; speed and simplification are not linked to transparency.

But if in an emergency situation, such as the one in which we have been in for over a year, it is vital to ensure the speed of purchases to accelerate public action and stem the pandemic; on the other hand, it is also necessary to ensure adequate

[11] Contractor selection procedures are how contracting authorities decide how to award a contract. They are governed by the procurement code which establishes the situations and ways in which they can be used.

[12] The emergency legislation has greatly simplified the use of extraordinary procedures.

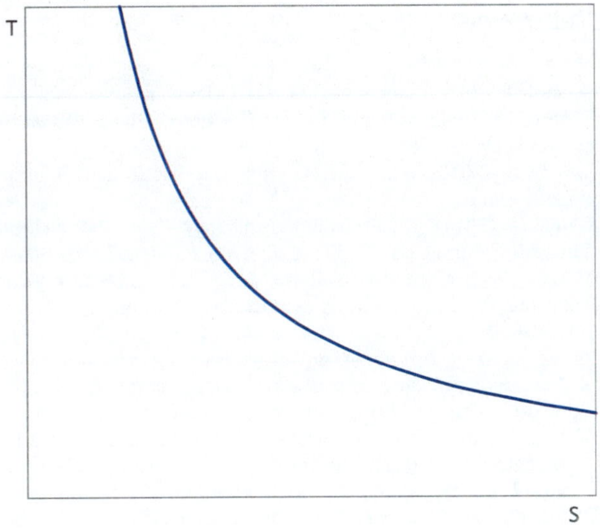

Fig. 22.5 The transparency function. (Source: Authors' calculations)

transparency in the procedures for purchasing goods and services, as these are important sums of resources. Besides, public contracts are the tangible expression of the good use of our tax money: they provide schools, hospitals, and infrastructure and all other services on which our well-being depends.

Simplification and emergency, together, must not sacrifice transparency. The issue is particularly important and current in the perspective of the European funds associated with the NGEU. In the meantime, in Italy, a debate has begun on the need to make simplifications in the Italian legal framework that allows for the spending of European money within the tight deadlines provided for in the EU agreements.

22.5 Limitations and Future Research

This work represents the first step in a broader research project on the economics of administrative transparency. The emergency linked to the pandemic, although representing an extreme case, and although data is still too fresh and incomplete to offer a global perspective, has allowed us to highlight the trade-off between transparency and simplification. Our future goal is to build a transparency index that allows us to focus on the essential elements of public contracts which cannot be ignored in order to guarantee a minimum level of transparency necessary to a proper functioning of our societies.

References

Cucciniello, M., Porumbescu, G., & Grimmelikhuijsen, S. (2016). 25 years of transparency research: Evidence and future directions. *Public Administration Review*. https://doi.org/10.1111/puar.12685

Etzioni, A. (2010). Is transparency the best disinfectant? *Journal of Political Philosophy, 18*(4), 389–404.

Etzioni, A. (2014). The limits of transparency. *Public Administration Review, 74*(6), 687–688.

European Commission. (2017). *Quality of Public administration – A Toolbox for Practitioners*. https://ec.europa.eu/esf/main.jsp?catId=3&langId=en&keywords=&langSel=&pubType=434

Fukuyama, F. (2015). Why is democracy performing so poorly? *Journal of Democracy, 26*(1), 11–20.

Jütting, J. (2003). *Institutions and development: A critical review* (Working Paper No. 210). OECD Development Centre. https://www.oecd.org/dev/4536968.pdf

Mungiu-Pippidi, A. (2014). Why control of corruption works – When it does. In A. Mungiu-Pippidi, A. Bozzini, M. Fazekas, J. Chvalkovská, L. Khatib, L. King, et al. (Authors) & A. Mungiu-Pippidi (Ed.), *The Anticorruption Frontline: The Anticorruption Report, volume 2* (pp. 90–123). Verlag Barbara Budrich. https://doi.org/10.2307/j.ctvddzrb6.9

OCSE. (2015). *Recommendation of the Council on Public Procurement*. Directorate for Public Governance and Territorial Development. https://www.oecd.org/gov/public-procurement/OECD-Recommendation-on-Public-Procurement.pdf

Rodrik, D., Subramanian, A., & Trebbi, F. (2002). *Institutions rule: The primacy of Institutions over integration and geography in economic development*. IMF Working Paper https://www.imf.org/external/pubs/ft/wp/2002/wp02189.pdf

Chapter 23
Circular Economy and the Clothing Industry

E. Pitoska, A. Kataraxia, and I. Araviadi

Abstract The present chapter includes a brief discussion of circular economy, a new economic growth model aiming at reducing waste and decreasing the need for new resources, the economic and environmental cost of which is high. Circular economy is a new product and consumer model, which enables longer use of materials while minimizing the use of natural resources. It requires the transition from a vertical model of production, consumption, and disposal to a closed circular model, based on recovery and reuse of products, which are minimally processed.

The survey focuses on the textile industry, particularly the clothing industry, which, due to overproduction and overconsumption, produces excessive waste, thus, affecting societies, economies, and the environment in various ways. The chapter includes a discussion about clothing life span, the five Rs of clothes recycling, the best practices already applied, and an empirical survey investigating Greek people's recycling awareness and practices as well as their intention to recycle clothes. Finally, conclusions are drawn that demonstrate that in recent years, the serious efforts in Greece as regards clothing and footwear recycling display a growing and positive trend.

Keywords Circular economy · Recycling · Reuse · Clothing life cycle · Clothing · Sustainable fashion · Business recycling practices

23.1 Circular Economy

A necessary condition for development and natural resource adequacy, sustainability, and life span is the application of a new economic growth model that will reduce waste and the need for new resources, the economic and environmental cost

E. Pitoska (✉) · A. Kataraxia · I. Araviadi
Department of Accounting & Finance, School of Economic Sciences, University of Western Macedonia, Kozani, Greece
e-mail: ipitoska@uowm.gr; akatarachia@uowm.gr

N. Tsounis, A. Vlachvei (eds.), *Advances in Quantitative Economic Research*, Springer Proceedings in Business and Economics,
https://doi.org/10.1007/978-3-030-98179-2_23

of which is high. Sustainable development implies upgrading living standards, by making a more intelligent use of resources and applying modern economic models that contribute to people's well-being (Hellenic Documentation Center, 2019). In terms of circular economy, industrial systems operation should apply methods implemented by organizations, namely, materials reprocessing and recovery. In a circular economy, the use of resources and waste will be minimized.

Recycling is one of the key components of circular economy and involves treating end products as potential waste material. Despite the fact that production cycles require that products and product quality of the next cycles (secondary) be equal to those of the first cycle (primary), in practice, secondary products are generally of lower quality than primary ones, which implies poor rather than complete recycling.

According to the VDI (VereinDeutscherIngenieure, the Association of German Engineers), recycling, defined as the reuse or repurposing of products or their components in a new production system, is distinguished in:

1. Recycling of old materials (the most important form of recycling): Used products or old materials are restored in production cycles as secondary materials.
2. Recycling of product residues: Waste as well as supplementary or functional materials in production processes is directly used or reprocessed.
3. Product recycling: Used products have a different use before the end of their first cycle (Veneti, 2019).

Circular economy is a new regenerative and consumer model, which enables longer use of materials while minimizing the use of natural resources. It requires the transition from a vertical model of production, consumption, and disposal to a closed circular model, based on recovery and reuse of products, which are minimally processed. In effect, circular economy entails "sustainable development," as product, material, and resources value life span is longer, and, thus, waste and pollutants are significantly reduced. It is based on the appropriate use of resources, the concept of recycling and reuse, as well as the model of industrial symbiosis. In addition, it prompts production renovation and restructuring and is characterized for its regional dimension.

The transition to a circular economy, including circular bio-economy, is a huge opportunity to create a competitive advantage in terms of sustainability. According to the European Commission's Reflection Paper, "Towards a Sustainable Europe by 2030," the application of the circular economy principles in all sectors and industries enables generating a net economic benefit of 1.8 trillion by 2030, creating more than 1 million new jobs in the EU and playing a central role in reducing greenhouse gas emissions (Hellenic Documentation Center, 2019).

In Greece, circular economy applications can also encompass construction and recyclable packaging materials, food waste, clothing, as well as in the tourism industry, where water use and management can create new recycled products to be used in tourist accommodation units. To address materials recycling in Greece, a competent body has been established, the Hellenic Recovery Recycling Corporation (HRRCO), which is a legal nonprofit entity under private law, administratively and financially fully independent, operating under the supervision and control of the Ministry of the Environment and Energy (RIS). HRRCO aims at implementing policies for the prevention and alternative management of products and waste via alternative management programs and proposing relevant measures and programs to the Minister of the Environment and Energy.

23.2 The Transition from Linear to Circular Economy

The transition from a linear to a circular growth model is a leap in quality and development, which involves creating local jobs and opportunities for social inclusion as well as added value for investments through cost-effective measures. In addition, it aims at reducing greenhouse gas emissions and dependence on imported raw materials. The transition is closely linked to the EU's key priorities for employment and development, social economy, and industrial innovation and, in parallel, generates new knowledge, technologies, and professional skills, thus, improving competitiveness.

The four additional benefits of circular economy applications include:

- Small- and medium-sized start-ups, trading mainly in materials preparation for reuse, restoration, and recovery
- New jobs based on the specific structural reforms
- Dissemination, maturation, and diffusion of relevant technologies and implementation of such technologies by young professionals and employees, which is an additional benefit for Greece
- Social economy, which would promote the employment of a significant number of human resources, thus, producing wealth and additional fund allocation for setting up social cooperative enterprises linked to production units (Hellenic Documentation Center, 2019)

Similar to some EU countries (e.g., England, the Netherlands, Germany), the rational design and implementation of Circular Economy in Greece could encourage business innovation and extroversion as well as the creation of new jobs, by exploiting relevant European funds.

In addition, the transition to a circular economy offers comparative competitive advantages and is friendlier to the current structure of Greek production units comprising mostly small-sized enterprises. It enhances long-term sustainability and competitiveness, as it enables addressing future price increases for finite raw materials and helps reduce industrial costs. It also facilitates preserving finite raw materials for a longer period of time and contributes to creating new jobs and consumer attitudes toward environmentally friendly products. Innovative forms of consumption can encourage new business opportunities during the transition to a circular economy, e.g., infrastructure sharing (sharing economy) and increased use of digital platforms (Ministry of Environment & Energy, 2019, Electronic Waste Register).

In recent years, there have been serious efforts in Greece in relation to clothing and footwear recycling. Such practices involve using recycled clothing and footwear for making cleaning cloths in industry, car insulation materials, mattress and furniture padding, and reusable cotton and wool fibers of lower quality and nonreusable in textile manufacturing.

23.3 Clothes Life Span and Its Impact on the Environment

According to the "texcycle" (textile-cycle) organization, clothes life span and its impact on the environment involve clothing items which are (Organization "GIVE SECOND LIFE TO YOUR CLOTHES," 2020):

Produced It takes on average between 10,000 and 20,000 liters of water to produce a kilogram of cotton equal to the weight of a shirt and pair of jeans. 25% of all insecticides used are applied by cotton producers, and energy consumption during the clothes life cycle in the EU generates 195 million CO_2 tons per year.

Sold In the EU, where fast fashion is a dominant business model, people typically buy 6.4 million tons of clothes per year. The vast majority of purchases include new clothes and only 6% second-hand clothes.

Used An average person buys 60 percent more clothing items and keeps them for about half as long as 15 years ago. The active life of clothing in the EU varies between 3 and 4 years, and doubling it from 1 year to 2 years reduces CO_2 emissions by 24% over the year.

Dropped off in clothing bins As clothes collection and recovery methods are easily available, alternative clothes disposal methods enable dropping off clothes in special bins and allow the textile cycle to loop forward.

Sorted The collected textile waste is sorted at recovery facilities depending on its next best possible utilization. Each item is evaluated according to international waste management hierarchy.

Recycled After properly treated, sorted clothing can be reused as second-hand clothes, wiping cloths, insulation materials, and fillings textured or burned for energy recovery.

23.4 The Five Rs for clothing

Recycle
According to the Textile Recycling Council, textile waste includes clothing, textiles, and fabrics that are no longer used and are disposed of. As fabrics are almost 100% recyclable, they should not end up in landfills (Hawley, 2009a, b).

Textile recycling is a reuse or remanufacturing method during the production process. Solid textile waste is found mainly in discarded clothing, furniture fabrics, carpets, shoes, sheets, and towels (Gunther, 2014). By recycling worn clothes, fillings for car seats, work uniforms, and materials for sound and thermal insulation are made. For example, recycled old jeans can be used as insulating material in buildings (http://www.Eoan.Gr/el/content/164).

Textile recycling is a complicated process involving reconstructing complex and heterogeneous materials, such as cellulose, synthetic fabrics, and various chemical substances (Laitalla & Klepp, 2011). It is a cost-effective method with multiple social, economic, and environmental implications.

Rewear
Another method of clothes recycling is rewear. This method of recycling, also applied in Greece, implies that clothes are reworn, given away to family members, or sold in "second-hand" clothing stores rather than reprocessed or recovered clothes.

Reuse
Reuse means rewearing used clothes. This method of recycling is not very popular nowadays, as it requires effort, time, and sewing skills. There are many sites on the web with tips and information about how to renew clothes.

Repurpose (Upcycling)
"Repurpose" means giving clothes a new or different life. More specifically, clothes that can no longer be worn are turned into something new and useful, such as wiping cloths, rags, etc.

Reduce
Clothing volume on the market has significantly increased nowadays, thus, requiring new transportation, storage, and waste methods, and causing serious environmental problems (Laitalla & Klepp, 2011).

23.5 Best Practices in Recycling Business

For the last 8 years, companies, mainly large ready-made clothing chains, have applied circular economy practices and promoted clothes recycling for various uses. Examples of such international chains, also operating in Greece, are:

- H&M and Zara stores in 2017, which offer in-store recycling initiatives, enabling customers to throw away their old/junk clothes in bins inside the store. The concept/goal involves increasing textile collection and recycling rates and reducing waste in landfills. Since 2013, H&M has collected approximately 40,000 tons of clothing, which is transported to a partner recycling plant in Berlin. What cannot be reused is made wiping cloths or insulation fibers. H&M aims to increase clothes collection at 25,000 tons annually. Zara started clothes collection in bins in 2016 in its stores across Europe. The collected clothes are given away to charities, including the Red Cross. Zara belongs to the "Inditex" group, which is the largest fashion group in the world, with 7200 stores in 93 different markets worldwide.
- Worn Again, founded by Cyndi Rhoades in 2005, a recycling company, which aims at changing people's attitudes toward textiles. Current engineering recycling methods for natural fibers, such as cotton and wool, produce small, lower-quality textile fibers that cannot be reused for clothing. In contrast, they are used for lower-value products, such as wiping cloths, which are finally burnt or dumped in landfills (Levi's jeans, 2017).
- Levi's, which started recycling plastic bottles and food trays in 2013. Each Levi's® Waste <LessTM product will contain a minimum of 20% recyclable material, or, on average, eight bottles per one pair of jeans (12 to 20 ounces/bottle, i.e., 350 to 500 ml). Levi's brand partners collect PET plastic bottles, including brown beer bottles, green soda bottles, clear water bottles, and black plastic food trays, all to be used in Municipal Recycling Programs in all US states. Food bottles and trays are separated by color, crushed into small pieces, and turned into polyester fibers, which are then mixed with cotton fibers, finally woven with traditional Cone Denim cotton yarn to create the denim, from which Levi's® Waste <Lessjeans and trucker jackets are made. Bottle color produces a beautiful shade of denim and creates a unique finish in the final product. Levi's runs programs in five countries (the USA, Canada, Japan, the UK, and Germany), which offer customers a 15% discount for clothes recycling. In an effort to create sustainable business opportunities, Levi's also plans to expand Levi's Tailor' Shops, where customers can have their clothes repaired, changed, or tailored. In the USA only, 13.1 million tons of textile waste are produced annually, of which 11 million end up in landfills. About 30% of the recycled cotton is used for the end product.
- The German company Nuuwai, which manufactures 100% vegan bags, uses materials made from apple fibers and fruit peels collected from juice companies. The founder of the company, Svenia Deto, has stated that apples are a sustainable raw material which replace 50% of the polyurethane to be used. This implies that instead of ending up in the trash, apple peels re-enter the life cycle.
- Based in Munich, Nat _2, a shoe company, which manufactures highly priced shoes (120–1000 Euros) from milk, straw, mushrooms, and other natural products. "We make handmade shoes in Italy, from moss, recycled bottles, glass, organic cotton, cork, rubber, 100% vegan. We have also made a model from rose

petals. We have veneer shoes and recycled Swarovski stones on grass from an Austrian meadow," says Sebastian Ties, the company founder (Drouga, 2019).

23.6 The Empirical Survey

In order to investigate circular economy in the clothing industry, a convenience sampling research was carried out. The specific sampling method was applied because of the emergency measures and the special conditions due to the coronavirus pandemic, as it was the only possible method of data collection.

The research was based on the answers of a structured Google Form questionnaire, sent via social media (Facebook, e-mails, etc.). The questionnaire includes 24 questions and is structured in three sections. The first section contains the participants' demographic information, the second investigates recycling applications and practices, and the third section discusses clothing reuse and people's relationship with fashion.

The survey took place from October 20, 2020, to January 31, 2021. The corpus of data includes 4526 completed questionnaires.

In detail, the vast majority of survey participants were female (91%), and only a small percentage (9%) were male. Ages ranged from 18 to over 56. The majority included those aged 36–45 (37.3%), followed by 26–35 (25.80%) and 46–55 (23.20%), whereas those aged 18–25 and 56 and over were 7.90% and 5.80%, respectively.

In terms of educational status, the highest percentage of subjects comprised higher education graduates (49.10%), followed by secondary education certificate holders (34.40%). A smaller number of participants were postgraduate/doctoral degree holders (12.60%), and only 3.80% of the subjects have graduated primary school.

As regards professional status, the participants were private sector employees (35.50%), civil servants (15.70%), unemployed (14.40%), housewives (10.90%), freelancers (9.50%), and students (4.10%). In addition, 3.10% of the sample was pensioners, army officers, teachers, sailors, hotel employees, salesmen, nurses, and truck drivers. Finally, freelance scientists were 2.80%, entrepreneurs 2.10%, and farmers 2.90%.

In terms of average monthly income, 23.8% earned 601–900 Euros, 23.6% had a very low income (0–300 Euros), and 20.2% an average income of 901–1200 Euros. Similarly, 19.2% earned an average monthly income of 301–600 Euros and only 13.2% more than 1200 Euros.

Almost all participants (98.60%) were in favor of recycling. They apply recycling systematically (48.3%), sometimes (29.8%), rarely (11.90%), and never/not at all (10%).

In addition, the vast majority (95.70%) were aware that paper, glass, and plastic are recyclable materials. Only 3.40% were ignorant and 0.90% did not answer the

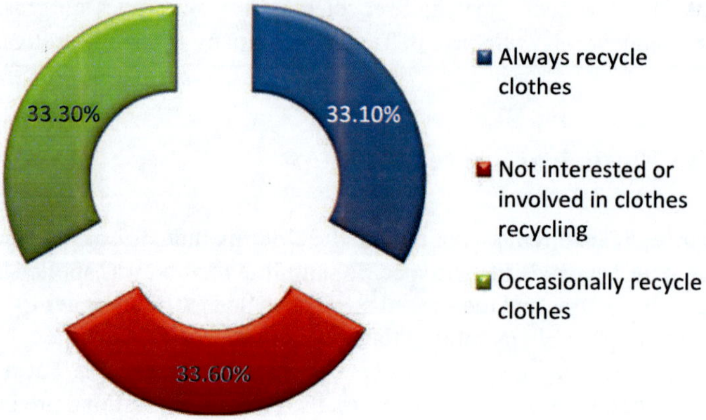

Fig. 23.1 Recycling rates

question. The greatest majorities (80%) were aware of clothes recycling, and only 17% were not, whereas 2.2% did not answer.

In relation to which sectors benefit from recycling, most subjects answered mainly the environment (91%), economy (4.90%), and personal economy (1%), while 3.10% answered "all the above." Overall, the analysis demonstrated that 33.6% of the respondents are not interested or involved in clothes recycling, and, similarly, 33.3% of them answered that they occasionally recycle clothes, whereas 33.1% answered that they always recycle clothes (Fig. 23.1).

A large number of the respondents (48.2%) were unaware that discarded "non-recyclable clothing" has an impact on the environment, whereas 30.7% were aware and 0.6% of them were not interested. In addition, the research finding reveled that discounts or incentives offered by clothing stores affect participants' intention to recycle clothes (Fig. 23.2).

Most subjects (64.90%) were not informed about ready-made clothing stores using recycling, whereas 31.90% do. Of those, the majority recycle clothes at H&M (50%), Zara (30%), Intimissimi (10%), and Calzedonia (10%).

A great number of the research participants were interested in fashion (75%), and 25% were not. The highest percentage includes those who buy clothes using criteria such as their personal shopping style (54.70%), clothes budget (22%), quality (17%), fashion trends (3.30%), brand (1.30%), web influencers (1.20%), friends' choices (0.30%), and recyclability (0.30%).

As regards the clothes that they do not use, the vast majority of the researched subjects (84.60%) stated that they give them away to people in need, such as relatives, neighbors, or charities. On the contrary, a small number of subjects keep clothes in closets (6.10%), whereas the rest recycle them (5%) and throw them away (2.90%), and 1.40% sell them (Fig. 23.3).

The highest percentage of the subjects who answered the question "Do you buy clothes that you do not need?" answered "No-never" (40.80%), sometimes (35%), not always (19.70%), and Yes (4.50%).

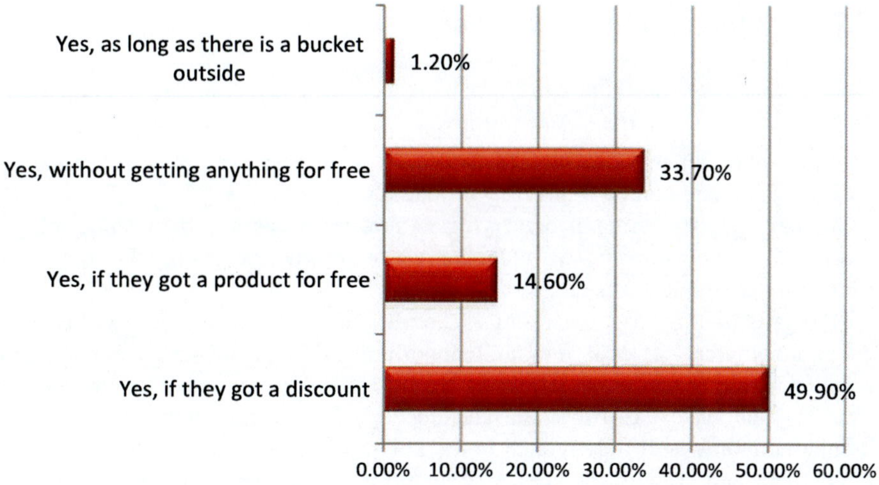

Fig. 23.2 Intention to recycle

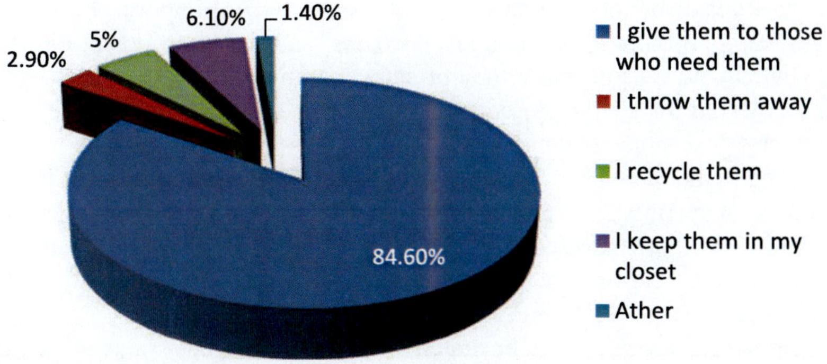

Fig. 23.3 Disposal of non-usable clothing

Half of the participants (50.90%) consider that fashion is a personal way of expression. The rest (28.20%) answered that it sometimes is (28.20%), not always (18.10%), and No (2.80%). As regards whether clothes reveal one's own personality, they answered Yes (37.40%), sometimes (37.30%), not always (21.50%), and No (3.80%).

In addition, as regards whether clothing reflects one's self-image, most subjects answered Yes (40%) and sometimes (37.20%), whereas the rest not always (18.90%) and No (4%). In addition, as regards their perceptions about whether clothes reveal a person's financial status, they answered not always (39%), sometimes (39%), Yes (15%), and No (7%).

23.7 Summary and Conclusions

Circular economy, which involves reducing waste of resources, is a compelling concept applied to products with a life span and implies product recovery, reuse, recycling, and remanufacturing. Recycling is a principle of circular economy causing a drastic reduction in primary production.

Circular economy aims at preserving natural materials and their value longer within the economy cycle, by reducing waste, promoting energy savings, and eliminating greenhouse gas emissions.

The transition from a linear to a circular model is a leap in quality and development creating local jobs and opportunities for social inclusion as well as added value for investments through cost-effective measures. In addition, it reduces greenhouse gas emissions and dependence on imported raw materials. Circular economy is closely related to the key priorities of the EU and Greece for employment and growth, social economy, and industrial innovation and generates new knowledge, technology, and professional skills to improve competitiveness.

Textile recycling is a very interesting issue worldwide. Clothes, once valued and usable, as a result of their increased supply and overconsumption, have become an aggravating problem for economies, societies, and the environment on account of the volume and type of waste they produce. Clothing life cycle and the various prospects offered for a circular economy have been a global academic, legislative, political, and governmental concern.

In recent years, there have been serious efforts in Greece in relation to clothing and footwear recycling. Such practices involve using recycled clothing and footwear for making wiping cloths used in industry, car insulation materials, mattress and furniture padding, and reusable cotton and wool fibers, of lower quality and non-reusable in textile manufacturing.

The empirical research demonstrated that Greek citizens are well aware of recycling and circular economy. They usually recycle glass, plastic, and plastic bags and are also aware of the prospects for clothes recycling, although most of them do not apply such practices. Obviously, however, the best practices and incentives offered by a number of clothing chains contribute to clothes recycling in Greece.

Finally, the research analysis emphasized that a large number of people do not buy clothes they do not need, and, in case they do not use them, they give them away.

References

Association of German Engineers, Wie gelingt die ‚Rohstoffwende“am Beispiel Kunststoffe? 16.10.2019, dbb forum Berlin

Drouga, N. (2019). "Fashion" the sustainable fashion, at *euronews* 03/07/2019

European Commission's Reflection Paper, "Towards a Sustainable Europe by 2030"

Gunther, M. (2014). Clothing bin wars: The battle over your charitable used donations. *The Guardian*. ISSN 0261-3077.

Hawley, J. (2009a). *Economic impact of textile recycling*. Fairchild Books.

Hawley, J. M. (2009b). Understanding and improving textile recycling: A systems perspective. In R. S. Blackburn (Ed.), *8 – Understanding and improving textile recycling: A systems perspective* (Sustainable Textiles. Woodhead Publishing Series in Textiles) (pp. 179–199). Woodhead Publishing. https://doi.org/10.1533/9781845696948.1.179. ISBN 9781845694531. Retrieved 2019-11-08.

Hellenic Documentation Center. (2019). *Circular Economy: A new economic model of sustainable development*. Tribute | Issue 115 March – May 2019

Laitalla & Klepp (2011). Potential for environmental improvements in laundering. *International IJC, 35*(2), 254–264. https://doi.org/10.1111/j.1470-6431.2010.00968.x

Ministry of Environment & Energy, 2019, Electronic Waste Register

Organization "GIVE SECOND LIFE TO YOUR CLOTHES, 2020 στο https://texcycle.com/

Veneti, M. (2019). The vision of an ideal economy where nothing is lost. *Liberal Free View, 12*(10), 2019.

Chapter 24
Working Capital Management in Relation to the Size and Profitability of Companies in the Czech Republic

Markéta Šeligová

Abstract The aim of this article is to find out how working capital and its management affect the size of companies and the profitability of companies operating in the manufacturing industry and wholesale and retail trade sector in the Czech Republic. In order to fulfill the aim of the article, the method of comparison and the generalized method of moments (GMM method) will be used. The data sample will include data for the period 2009 to 2019. The analysis will include companies operating according to the CZ-NACE classification in the manufacturing industry, wholesale, and retail trade sector in the Czech Republic. The data sample contained 3645 companies operating in the manufacturing industry and 5257 companies operating in the wholesale and retail trade sector. Using the comparison method and the GMM method a statistically significant relationship was found between working capital management and profitability and size of companies. It was found that variables such as cash conversion cycle, current assets ratio, current liabilities ratio, and working capital ratio affect the profitability of companies and the size of companies in the manufacturing industry and the wholesale and retail trade sector in the Czech Republic.

Keywords Cash conversion cycle · GMM method · Inventory · Liabilities · Profitability of companies · Receivables · Size of companies · Working capital

24.1 Introduction

The business sector is the backbone of the whole economy. Businesses contribute to job creation and also to economic growth. Businesses are the main provider of job opportunities. In particular, small- and medium-sized enterprises contribute

M. Šeligová (✉)
Department of Finance and Accounting, School of Business Administration, Silesian University, Karviná, Czech Republic
e-mail: seligova@opf.slu.cz

N. Tsounis, A. Vlachvei (eds.), *Advances in Quantitative Economic Research*, Springer Proceedings in Business and Economics,
https://doi.org/10.1007/978-3-030-98179-2_24

to promoting the social and economic cohesion of regions and are particularly important for regions facing high unemployment or lower economic development. Businesses stimulate competition in the economy and a healthy business environment. Businesses increase competitive pressure and thus force other companies to increase their productivity, increase quality, introduce innovations, or reduce costs. Increasing efficiency and introducing innovations in companies also lead to an increase in the competitive strength of the whole economy. Of course, consumers can also benefit from this, as this means that they can choose from a wider and higher-quality range or lower prices. The manufacturing industry is one of the key sources of gross domestic product in advanced economies. After services, the manufacturing industry is the second most important sector of the national economy, which is a decisive source of gross domestic product. The great competitive advantage of the Czech Republic is its strategic position in Central Europe, membership in the EU and NATO and thus easy access to the European Union market, developed transport and telecommunications infrastructure, developed technological base, high level of education and skills of the workforce, strong innovation potential of workers, great potential for research and development projects, as well as investment support.

Retail in the Czech Republic is one of the most advanced in Europe, using all modern technologies and introducing many new trends. There is a high degree of competition between individual traders, which benefits mainly the consumer, who ultimately obtains the most advantageous price. In terms of added value, the wholesale, retail, and repair of motor vehicles sector is one of the second largest sectors in the Czech Republic. In order for companies to prosper and expand their production, they must generate a certain level of profit. The goal of every company is primarily to generate profit over a longer period of time. To do this, they need a certain amount of working capital. This is capital that is constantly circulating in the company and therefore works. Every company should have as many current assets (stocks of raw materials, materials, cash, receivables) as the economical operation of the company requires. If it is lacking, the operation of the company is slowed down. Excess working capital, in turn, causes unnecessary costs. The company should try to optimize it there. However, it is not generally possible to determine the optimal amount of working capital. This depends on many factors, where, for example, manufacturing companies need much more inventory than service companies. Another factor may be, for example, production technology, which affects the amount of supplies or materials, etc. Higher volumes of working capital in the company mean easier operation for the company, but there are unnecessarily high costs of holding capital.

For this reason, the aim of this article is to find out how working capital and its management affect the size of companies and the profitability of companies operating in the manufacturing industry, wholesale, and retail in the Czech Republic.

In order to fulfill the aim of the article, it was necessary to define the following research questions:

- How do working capital and its management affect the size of companies operating in the manufacturing industry in the Czech Republic?
- How do working capital and its management affect the profitability of companies operating in the manufacturing industry in the Czech Republic?
- How do working capital and its management affect the size of companies operating in the wholesale and retail in the Czech Republic?
- How do working capital and its management affect the profitability of companies operating in the wholesale and retail in the Czech Republic?

The article is divided into several parts. The first part contains an overview of relevant literature dealing with a similar topic. The next part of the article is focused on the description of data and the methodology used. The third part focuses on the results of the research and the subsequent discussion of the results.

24.2 Literature Review

There are a number of studies in which the authors examined working capital and its management in relation to the profitability and size of companies. Lazaridis and Tryfonidis (2006) examined the relationship between working capital and the profitability of companies listed on the Athens Stock Exchange for the period 2001 to 2004. The data sample included 131 companies. They examined the relationship between profitability and cash conversion cycle (CCC) using correlation analysis and regression analysis. The results of our research showed that there is statistical significance between profitability, measured through gross operating profit, and the cash conversion cycle. Moreover, managers can create profits for their companies by handling correctly the cash conversion cycle and keeping each different component (accounts receivables, accounts payables, inventory) to an optimum level.

Uyar (2009) examined the relationship between the length of the CCC and the size of the firms and the length of the CCC and profitability. The author collected data of this study from the financial statements of the corporations listed on the Istanbul Stock Exchange (ISE) for the year 2007. The author utilized ANOVA and Pearson correlation analyses for empirical investigation. The major findings of the study are as follows. The lowest mean value of the CCC is found in the retail/wholesale industry, with an average of 34.58 days, and the highest mean value of the CCC is found in the textile industry, with an average of 164.89 days. There is a significant negative correlation between the CCC and the variables: the firm size and the profitability. The sample comprises merchandising and manufacturing companies. Therefore, the results are valid for those industries.

Rehn (2012) concluded that the efficiency of working capital management can be determined by the cash conversion cycle and the net trade cycle. By testing the two variables with corporate profitability, it can see that Finnish and Swedish corporations can increase their gross operating profitability by reducing the cash conversion cycle and net trade cycle. The various components of the cash transfer cycle were also studied. There is significant evidence that by effectively managing each portion of working capital, a company can increase its net present value, cash flows, thereby increasing shareholder value.

Huynh (2012) examined the impact of working capital management on the liquidity and profitability of non-financial corporations in the Netherlands. The research was conducted on 62 companies operating in the manufacturing and services sectors for the period 2006–2010. Pearson's correlation analysis and regression method (OLS method) were used to determine the relationship between working capital management and company profitability. Fixed effect regressions indicate that company profitability in both sectors is all negatively influenced by number of days accounts receivable. In the meantime, ordinary least square regressions result in positive impacts of firm size and sales growth on company profitability. In addition, some other results are found specifically to each sector. Number of days inventory and cash conversion cycle are shown to negatively affect the profitability of companies operating in the manufacturing area that they have positive influences on profitability of service companies. In addition, manufacturing and service sectors respectively witness negative influences of number of days accounts payable and aggressive financing policy on their company profitability.

Baveld (2012) investigated how public listed firms in The Netherlands manage their working capital. A sample of 37 firms is used, which are among the 50 largest companies in The Netherlands. The working capital policies during the non-crisis period of 2004–2006 and during the financial crisis of 2008 and 2009 are compared. This comparison investigates whether companies have to change their non-crisis working capital policies when the economy is into a recession. The results of this study indicate that, in crisis periods, firms don't need to change their working capital policy concerning accounts payables and inventory, if their goal is to enhance profit. For the working capital policy managing accounts receivables, this is not the case. This is because during a crisis, accounts receivables have a positive effect on a firm's profitability of the next year. These results are on a short-term basis. On the long term, benefits of aiding customers during crisis periods are likely to grow, because future sales will still be there. Also, the risks taken by these aiding firms are relatively low, and for large reputable firms, it is also relatively cheap.

Enqvista et al. (2014) examined the role of business cycles on the working capital and profitability relationship using a sample of Finnish listed companies over an 18-year period. They found the impact of business cycle on the working capital and profitability relationship is more pronounced in economic downturns relative to economic booms. They further showed that the significance of efficient inventory management and accounts receivables conversion periods increase during periods of economic downturns. Their results demonstrated that active working capital management matters and, thus, should be included in firms' financial planning.

24.3 Data and Methodology

The method of comparison and the generalized method of moments (GMM method) will be used to evaluate how working capital has developed in relation to the size of companies and the profitability of companies operating in the manufacturing industry and wholesale and retail trade sector in the Czech Republic for the period 2009–2019. The analysis will include companies operating according to the CZ-NACE classification in manufacturing industry and wholesale and retail trade sector in the Czech Republic. We used 3645 companies operating in the manufacturing industry and 5257 companies operating in the wholesale and retail trade sector in the Czech Republic.

The data used in this research were drawn from the Orbis database. It is a database that includes annual reports of companies around the world. Annual data from companies operating in the manufacturing industry and in wholesale and retail trade in the Czech Republic from 2009 to 2019 were used for this research. The econometric software Eviews 10 was used to find out how working capital affects the size of companies and the profitability of companies.

Table 24.1 includes all variables used, including their calculation. These variables were used in the comparison method and the GMM method. Operating profit, total assets, and total sales are dependent variables (i.e., endogenous variables). Operating profit, total assets, and total sales are very important indicators for the company for the future operation. In order for a company to be able to operate for a longer period of time and achieve a positive economic result (i.e., profit), it needs to have an appropriate amount of working capital, including all items of current assets such as inventories, receivables, and financial assets. A variable such as operating profit is a dependent variable in research and represents the profitability of companies operating in the manufacturing industry and the wholesale and retail

Table 24.1 Description of used variables for comparison method and GMM method

Variables	Calculation	Expected relationship
Operating profit (OP)	(Operating revenue – operating expenses) divided by total assets	Dependent variable
Total sales (TS)	lnTotal sales (total sales growth rate)	Dependent variable
Total assets (TA)	lnTotal assets (total assets growth rate)	Dependent variable
Cash conversion cycle (CCC)	(Number of days inventory + number of days accounts receivables – number of days account payables)	+−
Current assets ratio (CAR)	Current assets divided by total assets	+−
Current liabilities ratio (CLR)	Current liabilities divided by total assets	+−
Working capital ratio (WCR)	Current assets divided by current liabilities	+−

Source: Own processing

trade sector in the Czech Republic. Variables such as total assets and total sales are also dependent variables. These variables represent the size of companies operating in the manufacturing industry and the wholesale and retail trade sector in the Czech Republic.

Cash conversion cycle (CCC) shows how many days you need to sell inventory and then how many days you need to collect debts and how many days the company needs to pay on average payables. To put it simply, cash conversion cycle means the time needed to convert short-term assets into cash and pay short-term liabilities. In a cash flow management context, the more the longer the cash conversion cycle is, the more resources are needed to finance short-term assets, and as a rule, funding is more expensive and vice versa. If the cash conversion cycle is positive, it means that the conversion cycle is greater than the maturity of payables. A positive cash conversion cycle expresses the time period in which the firm has to finance operating activities from sources other than personal liabilities (working capital, other short-term liabilities). If the cash conversion cycle is balanced, it means that the conversion cycle equals the maturity of payables. A balanced cash conversion cycle occurs when the maturity of liabilities is equal to the conversion cycle. If the cash conversion cycle is negative, it means that the conversion cycle is less than the maturity of payables. A negative cash conversion cycle expresses the condition when the maturity of liabilities is shorter than the conversion cycle. A negative cash cycle often arises when a company finances negative working capital or problematic current assets, etc. from trade payables.

Current assets are used primarily to settle liabilities. They are constantly in motion, one form passes into another. The money is used to buy material that is in the production of work, it is used to create finished products after delivery to customers, receivables arise, and after their payment we have money again. Turnover of current assets is in the order of days (in the store) to weeks (in production). The faster current assets are turned under the same conditions, the greater the profit. Therefore, the important indicators of the use of current assets are the speed of their turnover. Current assets represent the working capital of the company. Working capital consists of inventories, receivables, and financial assets. If we deduct short-term liabilities from current assets, we get net working capital.

Current liabilities represent short-term capital due within 1 year. No organization can do without short-term commitments. They naturally result from the normal operation of the organization and repeated business dealings. Typically, they finance current assets or other operating needs. Short-term debt is all liabilities (debts) that the organization has to repay to third parties, but for some reason has not yet done so. This is not a bad thing; short-term liabilities are a natural phenomenon. These include invoices that have not yet been paid, short-term bank loans, wages not yet paid, or taxes that have not yet been paid. Current assets are used to settle liabilities, primarily money. If the company does not have money, it must also use other current assets. The volume of short-term capital affects the volume of working capital (current assets minus current liabilities) and current liquidity.

The working capital ratio (WCR) determines whether a firm has sufficient short-term borrowings to cover short-term assets. The working capital ratio is used by the company's management, e.g., in the management of working capital. The financial manager manages the individual maids of working capital, defines its optimal amount with respect to the volume and nature of sales, monitors the recoverability of receivables, and evaluates its individual components. From his position, the financial manager cannot influence individual items of working capital, and his role is to encourage others to look for better solutions. It shows how many times the current assets cover the short-term liabilities of the company, i.e., how many times the company is able to satisfy the creditor if it converts all current assets into cash at a given moment. The main purpose of this measurement is for the company to pay short-term liabilities from those components of assets that are intended for this purpose and not, for example, by selling tangible fixed assets. The stated optimum is between 1.8 and 2.5. The higher the value, the lower the risk of insolvency.

All these variables will be used to determine how working capital affects the profitability and size of companies operating in the manufacturing industry and the wholesale and retail trade sector in the Czech Republic. The comparative method and the GMM method will be used for this finding. These methods will work with a time series including annual data for the period from 2009 to 2019. According to Prucha (2014), panel data are suitable when it is not possible to use the OLS method, mainly due to the shorter time series. When working with panel data, it is advisable to use the generalized method of moments (GMM method). Assumptions of the OLS method such as heteroskedasticity, autocorrelation, multicollinearity, normality, and stationarity cannot be tested within this method. All variables and observed links will be verified at 1%, 5%, and 10% statistical significance to ensure that the results are meaningful. The robustness of the model will be verified using the Sargan/Hansen J-test. This Sargan/Hansen J-test shows the extent to which the GMM method is able to give the same results even with slight changes in certain parameters. The interpretation is that the model is robust if the Sargan/Hansen test value is greater than 0.05.

The impact of working capital on the size of companies in the Czech Republic will be expressed using the following equation, which is consistent with Hall (2005):

$$S_{it} = \alpha_1 + \beta_1 * \Delta S_{it-1} + \beta_2 * X_{1it} + \beta_3 * X_{2it} + \cdots + \beta_n * X_{nit} + \varepsilon_{it}, \tag{24.1}$$

where S_{it} represents the dependent variable (size of the enterprise), which is represented by the indicator of total assets and the indicator of sales, which capture the size of the *i-th* enterprise within the Czech Republic at time *t*, $\Delta S_{it\text{-}1}$ is an explanatory variable representing the delayed value *S* z the previous year, and X_{nit} includes explanatory variables that are considered to be elements of working capital that may have an impact on the size of enterprises. These are mainly the cash conversion cycle (including inventory turnover time, receivables turnover time, and liability turnover time), current assets ratio (CAR), current liabilities ratio (CLR), and working capital ratio. The characters α_1, β_0, and ε_t are a constant model and the residual component in the model.

The impact of working capital on the profitability of companies in the Czech Republic will be expressed using the following equation, which is consistent with Hall (2005):

$$P_{it} = \alpha_1 + \beta_1 * \Delta P_{it-1} + \beta_2 * X_{1it} + \beta_3 * X_{2it} + \cdots + \beta_n * X_{nit} + \varepsilon_{it}, \tag{24.2}$$

where P_{it} represents a dependent variable (profitability of the company), which is represented by the indicator of gross operating profit (or other indicators capturing the profitability of companies), which captures the profitability of individual business performance of the *i-th* company in the Czech Republic at time *t*, $\Delta P_{it\text{-}1}$ is an explanatory variable that represents the delayed value of *P* from the previous year, and X_{nit} includes explanatory variables that are considered to be elements of working capital that may have an impact on the profitability of enterprises. These are mainly the cash conversion cycle (including inventory turnover time, receivables turnover time, and liability turnover time), current assets ratio, current liabilities ratio, and working capital ratio. The characters α_1, β_0, and ε_t are a constant model and the residual component in the model.

24.4 Results and Discussion

In this part of the article, the results of the comparison method and the generalized method of moments (GMM method) will be presented. All conclusions will be interpreted and related to the business practice of companies operating in the manufacturing industry and the retail and wholesale sector in the Czech Republic.

24.4.1 Manufacturing Industry: Comparison Method

The comparison method was first used to find out how working capital and its management affect the size of companies and the profitability of companies operating in the manufacturing industry in the Czech Republic.

Figure 24.1 shows the development of operating profit, total assets, and total sales in the manufacturing industry in the Czech Republic from 2009 to 2019.

Operating profit, total assets, and total sales represent endogenous variables (dependent variables) in research. The company's profit is represented by operating profit. The size of the company is represented by total assets and total revenues. Based on Fig. 24.1, it can be stated that operating profit and total assets showed an increasing trend throughout the analyzed period. It should be noted that companies show a positive operating profit (i.e., profit), but the amount of operating profit does not show a significant volume. On the contrary, total sales showed an alternating

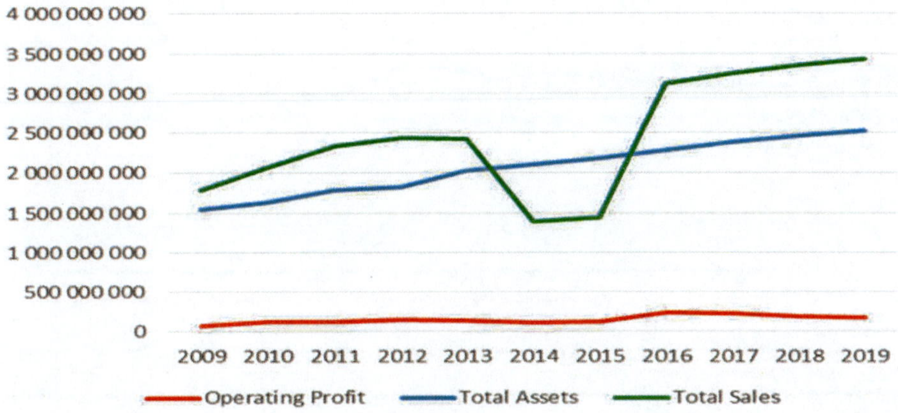

Fig. 24.1 Development of operating profit, total assets, and total sales in manufacturing industry in the Czech Republic from 2009 to 2019 (in CZK)

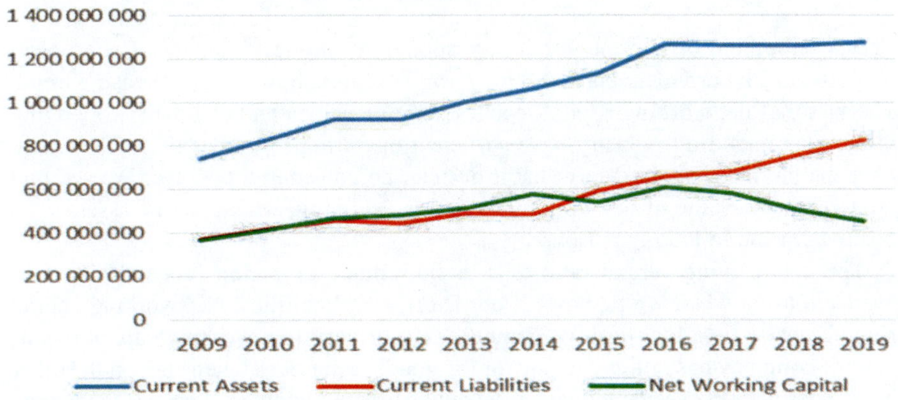

Fig. 24.2 Development of Net Working Capital and its Components in Manufacturing Industry in the Czech Republic from 2009 to 2019 (in CZK)

trend, when in 2014 and 2015 they fell to the lowest level of the entire analyzed period. After 2015, total sales increased and reached a maximum throughout the analyzed period. Interestingly, despite higher sales, companies report low operating profit. Companies should focus on managing costs that are likely to be high and reduce operating profit.

Figure 24.2 shows the development of net working capital and its components such as current assets and short-term liabilities in the manufacturing industry in the Czech Republic from 2009 to 2019.

From Fig. 24.2 it can be stated that current assets are higher than current liabilities, and companies thus have enough current assets to cover current liabilities.

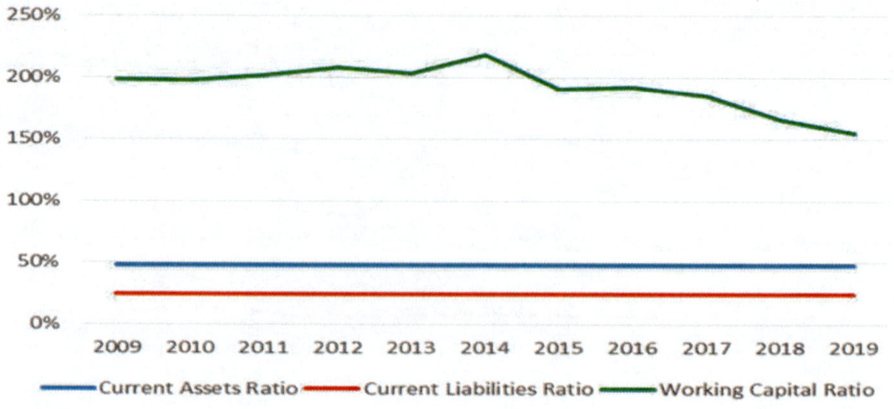

Fig. 24.3 Development of current assets ratio, current liabilities ratio, and working capital ratio in manufacturing industry in the Czech Republic from 2009 to 2019 (in %)

The development of current assets corresponds to the development of short-term liabilities, with current assets and short-term liabilities showing an increasing trend. The fact that net working capital reaches positive values and companies operating in the manufacturing industry have sufficient operating resources that will remain after the payment of short-term liabilities can be considered positive. We see that after 2016, the value of net working capital is declining, which can be assessed as positive for the following reasons.

The net working capital ratio tells us how much operating funds will remain available to us when we pay off all our short-term liabilities. Net working capital should ideally be a low positive number. Zero or very low working capital means that the company has nothing to pay for the goods or services taken and, on the other hand, does not receive any money on account from its customers, because the money received will result in an increase in the indicator to positive values. In this case, the company does not have sufficient capital for its operation. On the other hand, the higher the positive number, the more the company's operations are financed from long-term external sources or from its own resources.

Figure 24.3 shows the development of the current assets ratio, the current liabilities ratio, and the working capital ratio in the manufacturing industry in the Czech Republic from 2009 to 2019.

From Fig. 24.3, it can be stated that the development of current assets ratio and current liabilities corresponds to the development of current assets and current liabilities (Fig. 24.2). We see that current assets contribute to assets to a greater extent than current liabilities. Thus, companies operating in the manufacturing industry have a higher share of current assets than current liabilities. Both the current assets ratio and the current liabilities ratio show a steady development trend throughout the analyzed period. Current assets represent almost 50% of the total assets, while current liabilitites represent almost 25% of the total assets of companies. The working capital ratio showed a declining development trend. In the

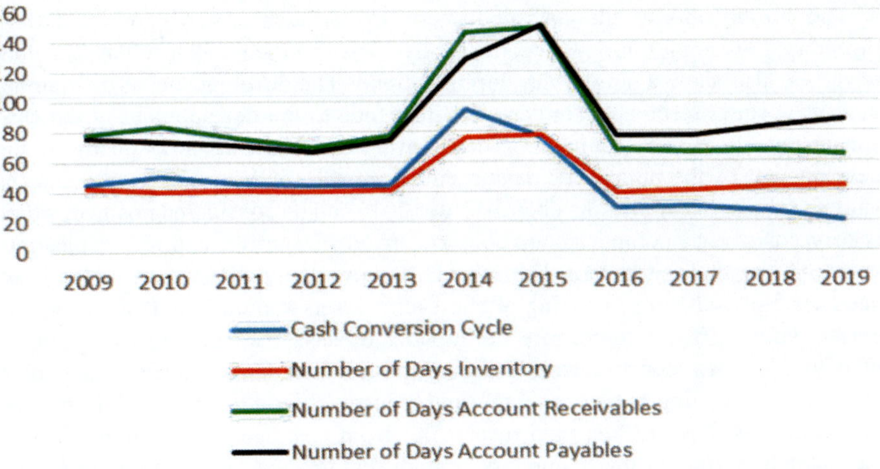

Fig. 24.4 Development of cash conversion cycle and its components in manufacturing industry in the Czech Republic from 2009 to 2019 (in days)

first half of the analyzed period, the working capital ratio reached the recommended values (from 1.8 to 2.5; from 180% to 250%). After 2014, the working capital ratio decreased. Companies should pay attention to declining values, as a decline in the working capital ratio signals solvency risk. On the other hand, the working capital ratio is slightly below the recommended values, and it can be stated that there is no risk associated with the solvency of companies.

Figure 24.4 shows the development of the cash conversion cycle and its components such as number of days inventory, number of days account receivables, and number of days account payables in the manufacturing industry in the Czech Republic from 2009 to 2019.

Cash conversion cycle shows how many days you need to sell inventory and then how many days you need to collect debts and how many days the company needs to pay on average payables. To put it simply, cash conversion cycle means the time needed to convert short-term assets into cash and pay short-term liabilities. In a cash flow management context, the more the longer the cash conversion cycle is, the more resources are needed to finance short-term assets, and as a rule, funding is more expensive and vice versa.

Based on Fig. 24.4, it can be stated that the development of the cash conversion cycle shows an alternating development trend. The cash conversion cycle reached its highest value in 2014, when the cash conversion cycle value was approximately 90 days. It thus took companies about 90 days to convert current assets into cash and settle their short-term liabilities. The value of the cash conversion cycle decreased after 2014, which meant that companies took less time to convert current assets into cash and pay their liabilities, which meant that companies needed fewer resources to finance current assets.

The components of the cash conversion cycle, such as the number of days inventory, the number of days account receivables, and the number of days account payables, also show a similar development trend. The development of the number of days account receivables indicator corresponds to the development of the cash conversion cycle. The number of days inventory indicator corresponds to the development of the number of days account payables indicator. The fact that the values of the above indicators decrease after 2016 can be considered positive, which is very positive, as companies are able to convert inventories and receivables into cash and pay their short-term liabilities in a shorter time interval and there is no need for more cash for financing of short-term assets. Companies have set up the correct collection policy because the number of days inventory and the number of days account receivables are less than the number of days account payables. Companies operating in the manufacturing industry should not be at risk of generic insolvency, as they are first paid receivables from customers and then companies pay their liabilities to their suppliers, employees, financial institutions, and other business entities.

24.4.2 *Manufacturing Industry: GMM Method*

The GMM method was also used to find out how working capital and its management affect the size of companies and the profitability of companies operating in the manufacturing industry in the Czech Republic.

Table 24.2 presents the resulting impact of working capital on the profitability and size of companies operating in the manufacturing industry in the Czech Republic. The Sargan/Hansen test shows that the robustness of the model has been demonstrated in the three models mentioned above. All results were tested and confirmed at a statistical significance of 1% (probability is 0.0000).

The first model examined the influence of variables such as cash conversion cycle (CCC), current assets ratio (CAR), current liabilities ratio (CLR), and working capital ratio (WCR) on the profitability of companies operating in the manufacturing industry in the Czech Republic. Using the GMM method, variables

Table 24.2 The influence of working capital and its components on the profitability and size of companies in the manufacturing industry

Variables	Delayed variable	CCC	CAR	CLR	WCR	J-statistic
OP	0.3649	−0.0589	−0.0392	−0.0521	2.2845	28.5749
Probability	(0.0000)	(0.0000)	(0.0000)	(0.0000)	(0.0000)	
TS	0.2562	0.2648	−0.3976	2.1098	1.5352	38.5574
Probability	(0.0000)	(0.0000)	(0.0000)	(0.0000)	(0.0000)	
TA	0.8785	0.4902	1.8307	0.2094	2.9449	18.3594
Probability	(0.0000)	(0.0000)	(0.0000)	(0.0000)	(0.0000)	

Source: Authors' calculations

such as cash conversion cycle (CCC; regression coefficient −0.0589), current assets ratio (CAR; regression coefficient −0.0392), and current liabilities ratio (CLR; regression coefficient −0.0521) were found to negatively affect the profitability of the above enterprises. If these independent variables increase in companies, their profitability is also likely to decline. In other words, if you increase the cash conversion cycle (CCC) by one unit, for example, the company's operating profit is likely to decrease by 0.0589 units. Furthermore, variables such as working capital ratio (WCR; regression coefficient +2.2845) and operating profit previous period (delayed variable; regression coefficient +0.3649) were found to have a positive effect on operating profit. If a company's working capital ratio (WCR) and operating profit of the previous period increase, the operating profit of the current period is likely to increase.

The second model examined the influence of variables such as cash conversion cycle (CCC), current assets ratio (CAR), current liabilities ratio (CLR), and working capital ratio (WCR) on the size of companies operating in the manufacturing industry in the Czech Republic. In this model, the size of companies was represented by the indicator of total sales. The results of the GMM method showed that the current assets ratio (CAR; regression coefficient −0.3976) has a negative effect on total sales. This means that if the value of the current assets ratio increases, there will be a decrease in the total revenues of companies operating in the manufacturing industry in the Czech Republic. The model also pointed to the positive effect of variables such as cash convergence cycle (CCC, regression coefficient 0.2648), current liabilities ratio (CLR; regression coefficient 2.1098), working capital ratio (WCR; regression coefficient 1.5352), and total sales previous period (regression coefficient 0.2562) on total sales. Thus, it can be stated that if, for example, the current liabilities ratio increases by one unit, total sales will increase by 2.1098 units.

The third model examined the influence of variables such as cash conversion cycle (CCC), current assets ratio (CAR), current liabilities ratio (CLR), and working capital ratio (WCR) on the size of companies operating in the manufacturing industry in the Czech Republic. In this model, the size of companies was represented by the indicator of total assets. Based on the GMM method, the total assets previous period (regression coefficient 0.8785), cash conversion cycle (CCC; regression coefficient 0.4902), current assets ratio (CAR; regression coefficient 1.8307), current liabilities ratio (CLR; regression coefficient 0.2094), and working capital ratio (WCR; regression coefficient 2.9449) positively affect the value of total assets of companies operating in the manufacturing industry. For example, if the value of the current assets ratio increases by one unit, total assets will increase by 1.8307 units.

24.4.3 *Wholesale and Retail Trade Sector: Comparison Method*

The comparison method was first used to find out how working capital and its management affect the size of companies and the profitability of companies operating in the wholesale and retail trade sector in the Czech Republic.

Figure 24.5 shows the development of operating profit, total assets, and total sales in the wholesale and retail trade sector in the Czech Republic from 2009 to 2019.

Based on Fig. 24.5, it can be stated that operating profit and total assets showed an increasing trend throughout the analyzed period. It should be noted that the values of operating profit, total assets, and total sales show a similar development trend in this sector as the values of operating profit, total assets, and total sales in the manufacturing industry. It is clear that companies show a positive operating profit (i.e., profit), but the amount of operating profit does not show a significant volume. On the contrary, total sales showed an alternating trend, when in 2014 and 2015 they fell to the lowest level of the entire analyzed period. After 2015, total sales increased and reached a maximum throughout the analyzed period. Interestingly, despite higher sales, companies report low operating profit. Also in this sector, companies should focus on managing costs that are likely to be high and reduce operating profit.

Figure 24.6 shows the development of net working capital and its components such as current assets and short-term liabilities in the wholesale and retail trade sector in the Czech Republic from 2009 to 2019.

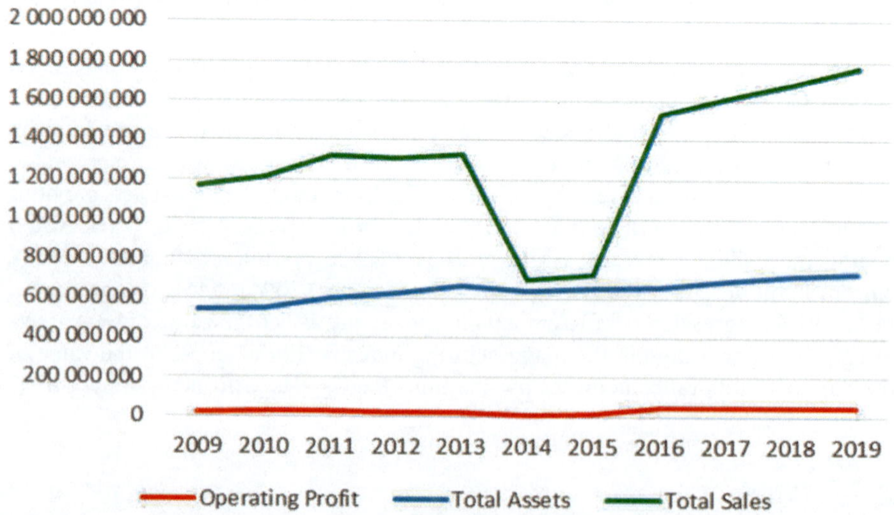

Fig. 24.5 Development of operating profit, total assets, and total sales in wholesale and retail trade sector in the Czech Republic from 2009 to 2019 (in CZK)

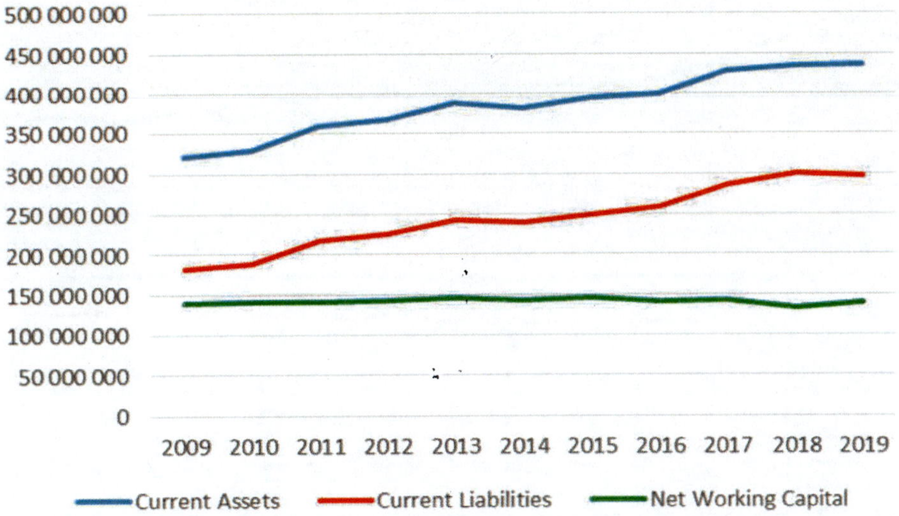

Fig. 24.6 Development of net working capital and its components in the wholesale and retail trade sector in the Czech Republic from 2009 to 2019 (in CZK)

Figure 24.6 shows that current assets are higher than current liabilities and companies have sufficient current assets to cover current liabilities. These conclusions also correspond to the conclusions of companies operating in the manufacturing industry. The development of current assets corresponds to the development of short-term liabilities, with current assets and short-term liabilities showing an increasing trend. The fact that net working capital reaches positive values and companies have sufficient operating funds to pay their liabilities and ensure the operation of the company can be considered positive. The value of net working capital began to decline after 2013, which can be considered positive, as companies need less long-term external resources or own resources to finance their operations.

Figure 24.7 shows the development of the current assets ratio, the current liabilities ratio, and the working capital ratio in the wholesale and retail trade sector in the Czech Republic from 2009 to 2019.

From Fig. 24.7, it can be stated that the development of current assets ratio and current liabilities corresponds to the development of current assets and current liabilities (Fig. 24.6). We see that current assets contribute to assets to a greater extent than current liabilities. Thus, companies operating in the wholesale and retail trade sector have a higher share of current assets than current liabilities. Both the current assets ratio and the current liabilities ratio show a steady development trend throughout the analyzed period. Current assets represent almost 60% of total assets, while current liabilitites represent almost 40% of companies' total assets. The working capital ratio showed a declining development trend throughout the period analyzed. The working capital ratio did not reach the recommended values throughout the analyzed period (from 1.8 to 2.5; from 180% to 250%). Companies

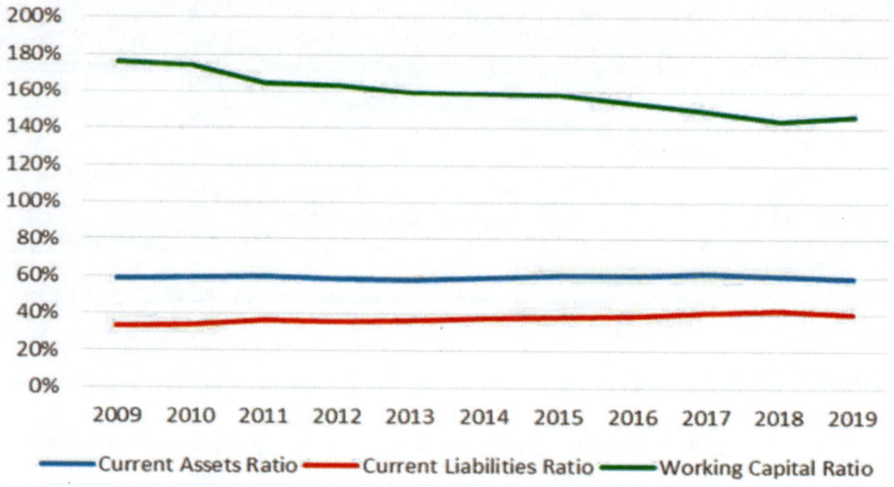

Fig. 24.7 Development of current assets ratio, current liabilities ratio, and working capital ratio in wholesale and retail trade sector in the Czech Republic from 2009 to 2019 (in%)

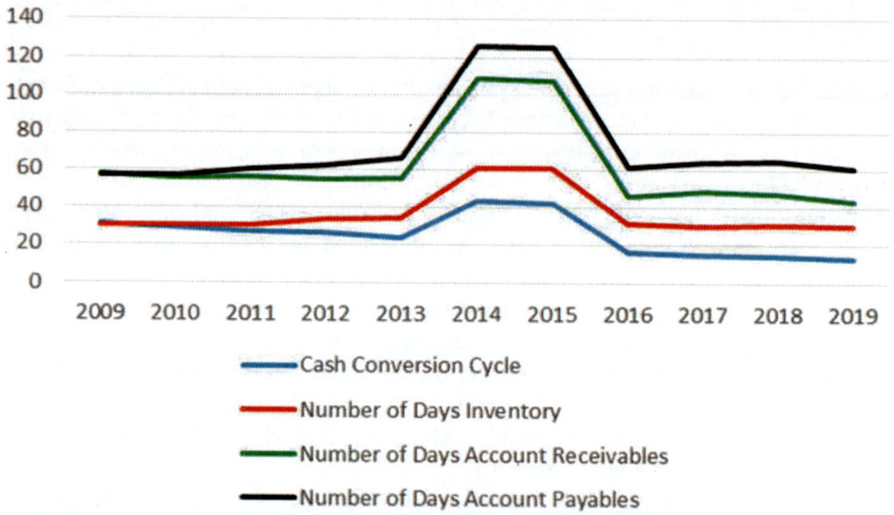

Fig. 24.8 Development of cash conversion cycle and its components in wholesale and retail trade sector in the Czech Republic from 2009 to 2019 (in days)

should pay attention to declining values, as a decline in the working capital ratio signals solvency risk. On the other hand, the working capital ratio is slightly below the recommended values, and it can be stated that there is no risk associated with the solvency of companies.

Figure 24.8 shows the development of the cash conversion cycle and its components such as number of days inventory, number of days account receivables, and number of days account payables in the wholesale and retail trade sector in the Czech Republic from 2009 to 2019.

Figure 24.8 shows that the development of the cash conversion cycle shows an alternating development trend. The cash conversion cycle reached its highest value in 2014, when the cash conversion cycle value was approximately 40 days. It thus took companies about 40 days to convert current assets into cash and pay off their short-term liabilities. The value of the cash conversion cycle decreased after 2014, which meant that companies took less time to convert current assets into cash and pay their liabilities, which meant that companies needed fewer resources to finance current assets.

The components of the cash conversion cycle, such as the number of days inventory, the number of days account receivables, and the number of days account payables, also show a similar development trend. The development of the number of days account receivables indicator corresponds to the development of the cash conversion cycle, the number of days inventory indicator, and the number of days account payables indicator. The fact that the values of the above indicators decrease after 2015 can be considered positive, which is very positive, as companies are able to convert inventories and receivables into cash and pay their short-term liabilities in a shorter period of time and there is no need for more cash for financing of short-term assets. Companies have set up the correct collection policy because the number of days inventory and the number of days account receivables are less than the number of days account payables. Companies operating in the wholesale and retail trade sectors should not be exposed to generic insolvency in the same way as companies operating in the manufacturing industry.

24.4.4 Wholesale and Retail Trade Sector: GMM Method

The GMM method was also used to find out how working capital and its management affect the size of companies and the profitability of companies operating in the wholesale and retail trade sector in the Czech Republic.

Table 24.3 presents the resulting impact of working capital on the profitability and size of companies operating in the wholesale and retail trade sector in the Czech Republic. The Sargan/Hansen test shows that the robustness of the model has been demonstrated in the three models mentioned above. All results were tested and confirmed at a statistical significance of 1% (probability is 0.0000).

The first model examined the influence of variables such as cash conversion cycle (CCC), current assets ratio (CAR), current liabilities ratio (CLR), and working capital ratio (WCR) on the profitability of companies operating in the wholesale and retail trade sector in the Czech Republic. Using the GMM method, variables such as cash conversion cycle (CCC; regression coefficient −0.1767), current assets ratio (CAR; regression coefficient −0.1658), and current liabilities ratio (CLR; regression coefficient −0.0651) were found to negatively affect the profitability of the above enterprises. If these independent variables increase in companies,

Table 24.3 The influence of working capital and its components on the profitability and size of companies in the wholesale and retail trade sector

Variables	Delayed variable	CCC	CAR	CLR	WCR	J-statistic
OP	0.2432	−0.1767	−0.1658	−0.0651	1.5475	32.6497
Probability	(0.0000)	(0.0000)	(0.0000)	(0.0000)	(0.0000)	
TS	0.3843	1.5970	−1.1044	3.5317	−1.2968	25.1403
Probability	(0.0000)	(0.0000)	(0.0000)	(0.0000)	(0.0000)	
TA	1.7572	0.8284	2.2106	0.1638	0.2907	16.8375
Probability	(0.0000)	(0.0000)	(0.0000)	(0.0000)	(0.0000)	

Source: Authors' calculations

their profitability is also likely to decline. In other words, if you increase the cash conversion cycle (CCC) by one unit, for example, the company's operating profit is likely to decrease by 0.1767 units. Furthermore, variables such as working capital ratio (WCR; regression coefficient +1.5475) and operating profit previous period (delayed variable; regression coefficient +0.2432) were found to have a positive effect on operating profit. If a company's working capital ratio (WCR) and operating profit of the previous period increase, the operating profit of the current period is likely to increase.

The second model examined the influence of variables such as cash conversion cycle (CCC), current assets ratio (CAR), current liabilities ratio (CLR), and working capital ratio (WCR) on the size of companies operating in the wholesale and retail trade sector in the Czech Republic. In this model, the size of companies was represented by the indicator of total sales. The results of the GMM method showed that the current assets ratio (CAR; regression coefficient −1.1044) and the working capital ratio (WCR; regression coefficient −1.2968) have a negative effect on total sales. This means that if the value of the current assets ratio indicator and the working capital ratio indicator increases, there will be a decrease in the total sales of companies operating in the wholesale and retail trade sector in the Czech Republic. The model also pointed to the positive effect of variables such as cash convergence cycle (CCC, regression coefficient 1.5970), current liabilities ratio (CLR; regression coefficient 3.5317), and total sales previous period (regression coefficient 0.3843) on total sales. It can therefore be stated that if, for example, the current liabilities ratio is increased by 1, total sales will increase by 3.5317 units.

The third model examined the influence of variables such as cash conversion cycle (CCC), current assets ratio (CAR), current liabilities ratio (CLR), and working capital ratio (WCR) on the size of companies operating in the wholesale and retail trade sector in the Czech Republic. In this model, the size of companies was represented by the indicator of total assets: regression coefficient 2.2106), current liabilities ratio (CLR; regression coefficient 0.1638), and working capital ratio (WCR; regression coefficient 0.2907) positively affect the value of total assets of companies operating in the wholesale and retail trade sector in the Czech Republic. For example, if the value of the working capital ratio increases by 1 unit, total assets will increase by 0.2907 units.

24.5 Conclusion

The aim of this chapter was to find out how working capital and its management affect the size of companies and the profitability of companies operating in the manufacturing industry and wholesale and retail trade sector in the Czech Republic. The method of comparison and the generalized method of moments (GMM method) were used to fulfill the aim of this chapter. The data used in the research covered the period from 2009 to 2019. The sample of data included companies operating in the manufacturing industry and the wholesale and retail sector in the Czech Republic. The analysis included 3645 companies operating in the manufacturing industry and 5257 companies operating in the wholesale and retail sectors.

Within the manufacturing industry and the wholesale and retail trade sector, it was found using a comparative method that operating profit and total assets showed an increasing trend throughout the analyzed period. It should be noted that companies report operating profit, but the amount of operating profit does not show a significant volume. On the contrary, total sales showed an alternating trend throughout the analyzed period. Interestingly, despite higher sales, companies report low operating profit. Companies should focus on managing costs that are likely to be high and reduce operating profit. Furthermore, it was found that current assets are higher than current liabilities, and companies thus have enough current assets to cover current liabilities. The fact that the net working capital reaches positive values and the companies have sufficient operating funds that will remain after the payment of short-term liabilities can be considered positive. Furthermore, it was found that the development of current assets ratio and current liabilities corresponds to the development of current assets and current liabilities. Current assets participate in assets to a greater extent than current liabilities. Thus, companies operating in the manufacturing industry and the wholesale and retail trade sector have a higher share of current assets than current liabilities. Both the current assets ratio and the current liabilities ratio show a steady development trend throughout the analyzed period. The working capital ratio showed a declining development trend throughout the period analyzed. A similar development trend was also shown by the components of the cash conversion cycle, such as the number of days inventory, the number of days account receivables, and the number of days account payables. The fact that the values of the above indicators decrease can be considered positive, which is very positive, as companies are able to convert inventories and receivables into cash and pay their short-term liabilities in a shorter period of time and there is no need for more funds to finance short-term assets.

Using the GMM method, it was found that variables such as cash conversion cycle, current assets ratio, and current liabilities ratio negatively affect the profitability of companies operating in the manufacturing industry in the Czech Republic. It was also found that operating profit was positively affected by variables such as the working capital ratio and operating profit of the previous period. The results of the GMM method showed that the current assets ratio has a negative effect on total sales. The model also pointed to the positive effect of variables such as cash convergence cycle, current liabilities ratio, working capital ratio, and total sales of the previous period on total sales. Furthermore, it was found that the total assets of the previous period, cash conversion cycle, current assets ratio, current liabilities ratio, and working capital ratio positively affect the value of total assets of companies operating in the manufacturing industry.

Within the wholesale and retail trade sector, it was found using the GMM method that variables such as cash conversion cycle, current assets ratio, and current liabilities ratio negatively affect the profitability of the abovementioned companies. If these independent variables increase in companies, their profitability is also likely to decline. It was also found that operating profit was positively affected by variables such as the working capital ratio and operating profit of the previous period. The results of the GMM method showed that the current assets ratio and the working capital ratio have a negative effect on total sales. The model also pointed to the positive effect of variables such as cash convergence cycle, current liabilities ratio, and total sales previous period on total sales. Furthermore, it was found that the total assets of the previous period, cash conversion cycle, current assets ratio, current liabilities ratio, and working capital ratio positively affect the value of total assets of companies operating in the wholesale and retail trade sector in the Czech Republic.

In conclusion, it is necessary to keep the level of net working capital at a level that ensures the smooth functioning of the company and at the same time does not mean unnecessarily high costs of financing from long-term or own resources and thus contributes to generating profit.

Acknowledgment This chapter ensued thanks to the support of the grant **IGS/11/2021** "Aspects of financial accounting and managerial accounting outputs in connection with the decision-making processes of accounting units."

References

Baveld, M. B. (2012). *Impact of working capital management on the profitability of public listed firms in the Netherlands during the financial crisis*. BMS: Behavioural, Management and Social Sciences. Available from https://essay.utwente.nl/61524/

Enqvist, J., Graham, M., & Nikkinen, J. (2014). *The impact of working capital management on firm profitability in different business cycles: Evidence from Finland* (Vol. 32, pp. 36–49). *Research in International Business and Finance*. ISSN 0275-5319.

Hall, A. R. (2005). *Generalized method of moments (Advanced texts in econometrics)*. University Press. ISBN 0-19-877521-0.

Huynh, N. T. (2012). *The influence of working capital management on profitability of listed companies in the Netherlands*. University of Twente: School of Management and Governance. Available from https://essay.utwente.nl/62755/1/Master_thesis_-_Ngoc_Trinh_Huynh_-_final_version.pdf

Lazaridis, M., & Tryfonidis, D. (2006). Relationship between working capital management and profitability of listed companies in the Athens stock exchange. *Journal of Financial Management and Analysis, 19*(1), 26, ISSN 0970-4205.

Prucha, I. R. (2014). Instrumental variables/method of moments estimation. In M. M. Fisher & P. Nijkamp (Eds.), *Handbook of regional science*. Springer. ISBN 978-3-642-23430-9.

Rehn, E. (2012). *Effects of working capital management on company profitability*. Hanken School of Economics. Available from https://helda.helsinki.fi/bitstream/handle/10138/32507/rehn.pdf

Uyar, A. (2009). The relationship of cash conversion cycle with firm size and profitability: An empirical investigation in Turkey. *International Research Journal of Finance and Economics, 24*. ISSN 1450-2887.

Chapter 25
Bankruptcy and Business Consolidation in Greece: An Exploratory Approach

I. Araviadi and A. Kataraxia

Abstract This paper concerns the consolidation process after the amendments to Law 4446/2016. Specifically, the new consolidation process is presented, aiming at rescuing companies in economic crisis. In times of severe economic crisis, as many businesses are overwhelmed by enormous financial difficulties, it was necessary to change and modernize the legislative framework that has been made to facilitate the rescue of viable businesses.

An attempt is made by the Legislator to restore the debtor to the market and its business. The consolidation process could succeed with a collective and honest effort by all parties involved. With these modifications, an attempt was made to address the disadvantages of the process and in general to strengthen the consolidation and prevention of operational bankruptcy, so that it becomes a modern and effective tool for dealing with commercial insolvency for sustainable businesses.

In the same direction and after studying and analyzing the case of the consolidation and rescue of Marinopoulos company, some proposals are made for the existing legislative framework. Our main goal should be to attract investments, so that investors and investment funds could give the opportunity to acquire an existing business that needs liquidity. The interests and claims of the creditors are better secured, since as a rule the creditors will be satisfied more by a functioning company than they would be by the forced sale of its assets. Creating an effective bankruptcy system that will faction as a tool for business recovery would open up a new market.

Keywords Reorganization · Consolidation · Bankruptcy · Economic dimensions · Bankruptcy code · Amendments after Law 4446/2016 · Rescue of enterprises

---

I. Araviadi (✉) · A. Kataraxia
Department of Accounting & Finance, School of Economic Sciences, University of Western Macedonia, Kozani, Greece
e-mail: akatarachia@uowm.gr

N. Tsounis, A. Vlachvei (eds.), *Advances in Quantitative Economic Research*, Springer Proceedings in Business and Economics,
https://doi.org/10.1007/978-3-030-98179-2_25

25.1 Introduction

In today's rapidly changing economic environment, under the influence of a global financial crisis and the prolonged recession in Greece, the restructuring of companies on the verge of bankruptcy seems to be crucial both financially and academically. It is clear from the recent literature review that the consolidation of companies with financial problems, which are either on the verge of bankruptcy or are already bankrupted, is now of great importance, not only in terms of satisfying the creditors of debtor companies but, above all, in terms of their ability to reorganize and possibly reactivate (Broude R, Reorganizations, 2005).

In Greece, the economic crisis has highlighted the structural weaknesses of both companies and the state. The implementation of the measures imposed by the three memorandums led small, medium, and large enterprises to a financial impasse (Pitoska & Katarachia, 2018), forcing them to gradually start applying the Bankruptcy Law that aims at maintaining, utilizing, and restructuring the business. This has many consequences, both for the national economy and for stakeholders. In addition, with the unstable effects that the COVID-19 pandemic has had on global and national economies, it is estimated that many companies in the near future will be in a critical situation on the verge of bankruptcy.

It is an interesting challenge to study and research, from an economic-social point of view, the possibilities that the current legislative/institutional framework provides, as well as to propose possible future amendments, in the direction of restructuring companies instead of them going bankrupt with the safeguarding of all parties.

The provisions for the consolidation process are found in the Greek Bankruptcy Code, as they currently apply after the subsequent amendments, the last of which were made recently, with Law 4446/2016.

With these modifications, an attempt was made to address the disadvantages and in general to strengthen the consolidation and prevention of operational bankruptcy, so that it becomes a modern and effective tool for dealing with commercial insolvency for sustainable businesses.

Bankruptcy and the consolidation process have similarities in terms of the conditions for inclusion, but this does not mean that these two concepts have the same purpose (Archaniotakis, 1997). The purpose of bankruptcy is the collective satisfaction of the creditors through the liquidation of the debtor's property, or in some other way that provides the reorganization and especially the rescue of the debtor's business. The main purpose of the consolidation is to avoid in any way the bankruptcy of viable companies and to rescue the debtor's company (Rokas, 2014).

Therefore, it could be said that the difference is that the collective satisfaction for the bankruptcy is the purpose (Bankruptcy Code, Article 1), while in the consolidation process, the purpose is the limit of the agreement (Perakis, 2017).

If a business does not go bankrupt, it is possible for it to become more attractive and attract new investments, as the investors would prefer to start investing in an existing business that needs liquidity to survive and grow, rather than start again from scratch (Angelakis, 2010).

The study and analysis of the case of the consolidation of the Marinopoulos Company, which was achieved and validated at one stage, is of great interest. Marinopoulos Company was a strong company until 2012, one of the largest supermarket chains in Greece, but finally filed for bankruptcy, as it owed large amounts of money, and both the creditors and their banks pushed for debt repayment. Of particular importance, apart from the study of the course that led to the ratification of the consolidation of this very important Greek company, are the various effects, financial, social, and fiscal, which came out of it in Greece.

25.2 Pre-bankruptcy Consolidation Process

The consolidation process is a collective pre-bankruptcy process, which aims at maintaining, utilizing, and restructuring the business with the agreement provided in the sixth chapter of the Bankruptcy Code, without compromising the collective satisfaction of creditors (Perakis, 2012).

These purposes are pursued with the conclusion and ratification of the resolution agreement, in accordance with the provisions of the above chapter of the Bankruptcy Code. At the same time, after the last amendments of this article, we could characterize the consolidation process as more flexible. In particular, the purpose of the consolidation process is to reach an agreement between the debtor and the creditors, who represent at least 60% of the total receivables – which include 40% of any real or mortgage-secured creditors. After the Law 4446/2016, the stage of opening the consolidation procedure is no longer provided, which included the submission of an application and the issuance of a court decision to open the procedure, by granting a deadline for reaching an agreement and its submission for judicial ratification.

From now on, the consolidation process is completed at one stage that begins with the submission of an application for ratification of the already concluded consolidation agreement, either between creditors and debtor or only between creditors (art. 100 par. 1 and art. 104 par. 1 of the Bankruptcy Code), and ends with the issuance of a court decision on it.

- Who has the right to be included: Any company (or an individual with bankruptcy capacity) can be included in the reorganization process, if there is a present or threatened inability to fulfill its overdue obligations. There is also the possibility of inclusion in the stage where the insolvency of a company is probable, since this risk could be avoided through consolidation.
- Concluding an agreement without the debtor's partnership: The possibility of concluding a resolution agreement by the qualified majority of creditors (i.e., those representing at least 60% of the total claims), which is submitted for ratification without the debtor's partnership, is expressly provided. The

ratification of the above agreement is possible only if the debtor is, at the time of concluding the agreement, in a cessation of payments. In this case, the application for ratification is submitted by any of the contracting creditors.

- Content of a resolution agreement: The resolution agreement usually provides for (a) a change in the terms of the debtor's obligations, such as the write-off of part of his debt, (b) a new loan-financing, (c) an operating restructuring plan, (d) a sale of assets, and (e) transfer of the company or more of the above measures in combination. It is pointed out that the agreement is necessary to regulate all the obligations of the debtor, including debts to the State, insurance funds, and employees.
- Automatic Suspension of Prosecution: From the filing of the resolution agreement for ratification until the issuance of a decision by the Bankruptcy Court (for the ratification or not of the agreement), any enforcement measures against the debtor are automatically suspended for claims made before its application.
- Conditions for ratification of the resolution agreement: The Bankruptcy Court ratifies the resolution agreement if it has been signed by the debtor and the required majority of creditors (or only by the majority of creditors when the agreement has been drawn up without the debtor's partnership). However, the following criteria must be met cumulatively: (a) the viability of the business must be assumed, (b) the collective satisfaction of creditors must not be impaired, (c) the resolution agreement must not be the result of deceit or other wrongdoing or bad faith, and (d) the agreement treats creditors, who are in the same position, equally. If the application is submitted by the creditors without the consent of the debtor, the consent of the debtor is also required. Consent is deemed to have been given if no action has been taken against its acceptance until the application has been heard in court.
- Permissible discrepancies between creditors: Creditors in the same position may not be treated equally only with the consent of the affected creditor or if there are important business or social reasons that justify the above discrepancy set out in the relevant court decision. Indicatively, favorable treatment may be received from customers whose non-satisfaction substantially damages the reputation or the continuation of the proper operation of the business, as well as claims, the repayment of which is necessary for the living of the creditor and his family. Finally, labor requirements are usually met on a preferential basis.
- Effects of ratification: Upon ratification, the resolution agreement is binding on all creditors whose claims are settled, even if they have not voted at all or have voted against it. Creditors whose claims were made after the decision is issued are not bound. It is also possible to provide information on debts to the State and Social Security Institutions, provided that these debts are regulated by the resolution agreement.

25.3 Case Study: The "Marinopoulos" Company

The company Carrefour Marinopoulos was founded in 1999. 50% of it belonged at Marinopoulos and the other 50% at Carrefour. The company owned a total of 823 stores in Greece, Cyprus, and southeast Europe. It also had 13.000 employees.

The company had trouble paying its suppliers. As a result, on July 2015, problems started with the inadequacy of products in its stores, and in August, the deficiencies were so significant that payment cuts ensued.

Until 2012, Marinopoulos Company was a really strong business, when Carrefour Company decided to withdraw because of the Greek financial crisis. That immediately led to a decrease in the market share of the chain.

The end of an era had come for Marinopoulos, one of the largest supermarket chains in Greece. After intense pressure by the suppliers and because of its enormous debt to the banks and the creditors, the company finally applied for bankruptcy.

The company filed for bankruptcy based on Article 106 b and until the court date, on July 1, 2016, was entitled to suspension of any ongoing enforcement proceedings (Tables 25.1 and 25.2).

By filing the application, the main goal of the company's administration was to "freeze" the daily seizures and stop suppliers from withdrawing their products. However, the possible collapse of the company obviously involved the risk for hundreds of other companies to go bankrupt. Panic spread.

In this way, the company gained some months of protection, in order to seek some cooperation and a solution to the impasse. This is how the negotiations between

Table 25.1 Capture of financial problem of Marinopoulos Company

Liability account	
Long-term responsibilities	207.461.330,33
Suppliers	425.568.849,13
Payable bonds	1.315.250,75
Bank accounts for short-term liabilities	49.404.890.14
Staff remuneration payable and due minus advances	4.289.639,58
Current liabilities to affiliated companies	69.923.887,31
Checks payable (postdated)	553.454.357,80
Other current liabilities	2.181.649,61
Liabilities from taxes-fees	49.073.451,44
Insurance agencies	51.765.861,44
Clients-credit institutions	273.961.21
Charges – various – benefits to suppliers	-268.723.430,87
Various charges–others	111.164,23
Financial leases	159.018.990,38
Total	**1.324.683.288,1**

Source: Company balance December 2015

Table 25.2 Capture of financial liabilities of Marinopoulos Company

STATE-public	Liabilities to tax offices	49.073.451,52
Total Liabilities to the State	Liabilities to insurance organizations	57.765.861,44
Total liabilities to the State		**106.839.312,96**
Employees	Employee payroll	4.289.639,58
Total liabilities to employees		**4.289.639,58**
Creditors with collateral	Loans with collateral	126.679.257,55
	Suppliers with collateral	0,00
Total liabilities to creditors with collateral		**126.679.257,55**
Unsecured creditors	Loans without collateral	211.072.332.29
	Leasing	159.018.990,38
	Suppliers and other creditors (no collateral)	722.783.755,41
Total liabilities to unsecured creditors		**1.092.875.077,09**
Total		**1.324.683.288,17**

Source: Company balance December 2015

"Marinopoulos" and "Sklavenitis," the other large supermarket chain, started. On February 2016, an agreement was reached.

Sklavenitis Company, after many months of negotiations with the Marinopoulos Company's creditors and the banks, announced the acquisition of it. The acquisition was approved following a court decision on January 16, and the Hellenic Competition Commission approved it on January 26. The agreement was finally closed on March 2017, and the activities of the companies Marinopoulos, Supermarket Xinos SA, Express Market AE, and Piraiki SA were transferred to the company Hellenic Supermarkets Sklavenitis SA.

In summary, after the ratification of the takeover agreement, the following measures were taken:

- The total debts of the company Marinopoulos amounting to 1,490,755,496 euros were transferred at a rate of 79.4% (€ 1,183,726,841) to the Sklavenitis company. The remaining 20.6% remained at Marinopoulos. The Marinopoulos Company had designed a comprehensive Development Plan, in order to ensure its exit from the existing financial impasse and to ensure its long-term viability and development.
- All the privately owned properties of the company were transferred to the new company as financial leases.
- All claims were transferred to the new company, such as rents, credit cards, and so on, and the Marinopoulos Company maintained some amounts to receive from the Karipidis companies (1.1 million euros) and some others.
- Marinopoulos Company had total liabilities to Alpha Bank of up to 146.9 million euros, of which 26.7 million euros continued to remain in it and were written

off completely, while the remaining 120 million euros were taken over by Sklavenitis. They are expected to be paid within 5 years.

- In addition, half of the credit balances were transferred to the new company to the suppliers by the four companies that are to be reorganized, and an effort was made to transfer all of the suppliers' credit balances that are less than 100,000 euros per supplier.
- The new company was burdened with staff compensation and debts to staff. It is of particular importance that the consolidation of the Marinopoulos Company in this way resulted in the employees continuing to work in it and even in better conditions (since Sklavenitis increased the salaries of the lowest paid employees).
- The debts to the State and the insurance funds were decided to be paid in 250 interest-free equal monthly installments. All interest, fines, surcharges, and other charges are written off.
- Marinopoulos' liabilities to local authorities and public services and utilities (DEKO) were written off by 50%, and the remaining amount will be paid to the new company in 36 interest-free equal monthly installments.
- The company's liabilities to unsecured creditors amounting to 647,155 million euros were written off by 50% (43% is the total of Marinopoulos' debts), and the remaining amount will be paid within 60 working days from the completion of the transaction by the new company.
- Interim financing: In order to be viable the companies that will be transferred and those that are under consolidation, until the completion of the agreement, it was foreseen to make interim financing of 80 million euros by 30/6/2016 through Express. The above amount will be covered by 15 million euros by the company Sklavenitis to buy goods in cash, 10 million euros by the shareholders of the company Marinopoulos to pay salaries and operating expenses, and 55 million euros for loans from banks, of which the 15 million euros were made with the guarantee of the company Sklavenitis, which will help repay some of the overdue rents from the company's stores.

As we can easily understand from the above, Marinopoulos company with its inclusion in the new article 99 of the Bankruptcy Code managed to continue its commercial transactions, to overcome its overdue debts, to repay its self-financed creditors, and to employ full- or part-time staff, contributing to the reduction of unemployment, to continue to pay indirect and direct taxes to the Greek government, and to settle its debts and not to cause any substantial damage to its creditors.

25.4 Conclusions and Some Proposals for Future Improvements of the Law

After the bibliographic review and the study of the case "Marinopoulos," which was important for the national economy and the market, the following can be concluded: The consolidation preserves the value of the company as an "ongoing concern," i.e., as an economic unit that continues to operate, in contrast to the (destructive) scenario of liquidation of the assets of the company that leads to the bankrupt (thesis of Potamitis St. & Roka Al., 2017).

An important issue of the new bankruptcy law is to shift the attention of the protective legislation from the interests of the creditors to these of the bankrupted companies to provide them a second opportunity (Augitidis, 2017; Kavadella, 2018).

There is also a need for a legislative "break" in the near future, which will allow familiarization with the new provisions, as Professor Perakis E. aptly observed in 2017 (Perakis, 2012).

The concept of consolidation of companies that are in a state of impending bankruptcy offers a socially important second opportunity to save jobs, both in the company itself and in the other cooperating companies that do business with it (Pitoska et al. 2017).

A successful business rescue helps attract investment, as it gives investors and investment funds the opportunity to acquire an existing business that needs liquidity but does not lose its intangible value and does not stop its productive activity.

The interests and claims of the creditors are better secured, since as a rule the creditors will be satisfied more by a functioning company, than they would be by the forced sale of its assets.

The progressive implementation of the business consolidation will gradually bring a change in the perception of business failure in Greece, where bankruptcy and liquidation of a business are a heavy stigma and will cultivate a culture of rescue, with an emphasis on reorganization.

A culture of conciliation of all parties involved must be "cultivated," and a more compassionate attitude toward the debtor and his business must be adopted in order to put the agreements in a different context. It is important to have a forecast so that the business does not terminate its activities, preserve its name and not to be placed in social, economic, and moral exclusion due to its debts.

The institution of business reorganization, as regulated by bankruptcy law, will need time and smooth operating conditions of the national economy and market to be assessed and evaluated in terms of its efficiency and completeness.

There is room for improvement/reform of the bankruptcy law, despite its modernization, which in short concerns its flexibility and attractiveness for all parties involved, in order to further improve the process but also to safeguard the interests of all parties (creditors, debtors), judicial authorities, etc.

The process must be adapted to the current socioeconomic reality, to the international trends and jurisprudence so that second opportunity returns dynamically to the field of bankruptcy law. Furthermore, to everyone's satisfaction, stricter conditions must be introduced.

It is very important that the companies that have the possibility to be consolidated present a feasible reorganization plan, with the effort of all stakeholders and with legislative support to succeed. The continuation of the operation of a company ensures that there will be no financial loss.

Finally, collective effort and flexibility are required from all those involved in the process of consolidation of a business in order to keep businesses "alive," with ultimate purpose to satisfy everyone who depends on the viability of the business.

The points that need to be addressed in the future and improved in the next improvement/change of the relevant article of the bankruptcy law are:

A. The utilization of real estate with preservation of their objective value: the proposal here is related to the utilization of the debtor's property in the best possible way, so that it is not liquidated in a hurry, so that the creditors are immediately satisfied by zeroing the debtor morally, psychologically, financially, and ethically. The assets of companies and individuals must be better utilized at a fair price both in the context of consolidation and liquidation. Perhaps the value of the debtor's real estate should be preserved at the level of their fair value, in order to avoid their violent and hasty liquidation, leaving the companies helpless and without any protection under the pressure of the creditors.
B. The training of the involved parties. It is proposed to create an environment that will guarantee and enhance the education and training of the involved parties. Bankruptcy and liquidation law judges should be continuously trained, to have the appropriate knowledge and qualifications, as well as research activity on these subjects. An important component for the development of "rescue culture" is the training of all parties involved (business managers, lawyers, judges) for the operation and unlimited possibilities of the institution of consolidation.
C. Establish rules of supervision in professional organizations which help their members dealing with bankruptcy, in order to ensure high standards of adequacy and integrity.
D. The handling of the consolidation procedures should be done by special Courts and these cases to be undertaken by judges, with experience and combined knowledge in tax, accounting, and labor law.

Creating an effective bankruptcy system that will faction as a tool for business recovery would open up a new market.

References

Angelakis, M., The changes that occurred in the Bankruptcy Code with law 3588/2007 2010 p. 856.

Archaniotakis, G. (1997). *Transfer of property of the company, inclusion of 143 479 AK in the system of protection of creditors from the insolvency of the debtor* (p. 125). Sakkoulas Publications.

Augitidis, D. (2017). *Business Fertilization Through Bankruptcy Agreements* (1st ed.). Sakkoulas Publications.

Broude, R. F. (2005). *Reorganizations Under Chapter 11 of the Bankruptcy Code* (Bankruptcy Series, Lslf Edition)

Kavadella, E. (2018). *Forms, conditions and procedure of article 99 et seq. Of the Bankruptcy Code after law 4446/2016 – Pre-bankruptcy process of business consolidation as well as proposals de lege ferenda*. Diploma Thesis, University of Piraeus.

Perakis, E. (2012). *Bankruptcy Law* (2nd ed.)

Perakis, E. (2017, 20–22 October). *Proceedings & conclusions of the 27th Commercial Law Conference Recent Developments in Bankruptcy Law*, Karpenisi.

Pitoska, E., & Katarachia, A. (2018). Small and medium sized enterprises in the age of Memoranda. In *6th International conference on contemporary marketing issues*, Athens.

Pitoska, E., Katarachia, A., & Tsiavi, M. (2017). *Small and medium sized enterprises, Financing prospects and programs during the Financial International Conference, 2nd International Conference*, Kalamata Greece

Potamitis, S., & Rokas, A. (2017). Debt capitalization as a measure for business consolidation and methods of bypassing the will of shareholders. In *EpiskED 3/2017* (p. 377). 388, Sakkoulas-Online.gr.

Rokas Al. (2014). *Bankruptcy Process of business consolidation 2014* (p. 281). Sakkoulas Publications.

Chapter 26
The European Case: Are There Externalities from the National Toward the Regional R&D Systems That Enhance Their Efficiency?

Cristián Gutiérrez Rojas and Thomas Baumert

Abstract The present chapter studies the externality flows from the national to the regional R&D systems in Europe, analyzing to which degree—if at all—they improve the latter's efficiency. For this purpose, we combine factorial, regression, and cluster analysis with a two-stage data envelopment analysis on a sample of 129 regions from 2000 to 2010. The results obtained confirm the existence of asymmetric spillovers between both system levels and that they indeed have a statistically significant impact on regional efficiency.

Keywords Innovation · Spillovers · Externalities efficiency · Europe · National and regional R&D systems

26.1 Introduction

The present chapter—which complements a previous one by Gutiérrez et al. (2018) which studied the presence of externalities between National and Regional Innovations Systems in Europe—, analyses whether these externalities have a statistically significant effect on the efficiency of the R&D performance of regions.[1] By doing so, it aims to add to an underexploited question in the field of Innovation studies

[1] As might be observed, we now prefer the expression "R&D system"—which we consider more acurate to the Schumpetarian conception of a "spontaneous" innovation—to that of "Innovation

C. G. Rojas
School of Economics and Management, Catholic University Silva Henríquez, Santiago, Chile
e-mail: cgutierrez@ucsh.cl

T. Baumert (✉)
Universidad Nebrija, Madrid, Spain
e-mail: tbaumert@nebrija.es

N. Tsounis, A. Vlachvei (eds.), *Advances in Quantitative Economic Research*, Springer Proceedings in Business and Economics,
https://doi.org/10.1007/978-3-030-98179-2_26

and R&D systems, namely, whether national R&D—or innovation—systems are mainly the aggregate of the regional systems that constitute them (or, from a top-down perspective, whether the regional systems are just the disaggregation of the national supersystem). And, assuming that both are not identical, to which extend there is a reciprocal flow of externalities that improves—or weakens—their respective performances in innovation related issues (in our specific case considering both technological and scientific output). For this purpose, we combine different econometric techniques—Factorial, Regression and Cluster Analysis with a two-stage Data Envelopment Analysis—on a sample of 129 regions and for a time period that spans from 2000 to 2010.

26.2 Theoretical Framework

The efficiency of regional R&D systems in the context of geographic proximity and the presence of externalities has been approached in different ways in the field of the economy of the innovation. Gallaud and Torre (2004) have analyzed the real importance of the geographical proximity in the technological diffusion and the innovative process of the firms and sectors. They conclude that it is important only when there is effective interaction between the agents (transmission channels), that there may be temporal proximity (early stage of R&D), and that it is more relevant for small and medium firms. Beugelsdijk (2007), for his part, studies the role of the regions in the innovative performance of firms incorporating variables that indicate the strategy and structure of each of them.

Other studies have addressed this issue employing spatial econometrics. Moreno et al. (2004) used different techniques (SAR: LM-LAG and Lm-ERR test) to analyze the spatial distribution of innovation in Europe and the role of technological spillovers, testing whether there is a process of dependence on the distribution of the innovative activity between periods and sectors. Modeling the regional innovative behavior under consideration of the spillovers, they concluded that when considering both technological and geographical proximity, the impact on innovation is stronger than if only one is used, thus stressing the importance of national innovation systems in Europe. Marrocu et al. (2011), using spatial autoregressive models (SAR), studied the effect of different measures of proximity in observing the effects of knowledge overflow between regions. All the proximities have a significant and complementary role in generating important flows of knowledge between regions, with the technological ones playing the most relevant role. In addition, the authors demonstrated that in terms of improving the innovative capacity of the regions, human resources are more important than R&D expenditure. Finally, Capello and Lenzi (2013), using SEM and SAR estimates, observed the influence

system" which we believe may induce to consider Innovation, wrongly, as a sistematic process (see for details Gutiérrez & Baumert, 2019).

of regional innovation patterns on the impact of innovation and knowledge on regional economic growth, seeking to demonstrate that knowledge has a positive impact on the latter. They concluded that the benefits to growth from innovation and knowledge are not necessarily consistent with the strengths of the local formal knowledge base.

Other studies have analyzed this subject from very different angles. Duvidier (2013) used the stochastic frontier production function approach to test the impact of urban proximity on the technical efficiency of Chinese agricultural sectors, finding great differences among Chinese macro-regions. Bellmann et al. (2013) studied the exogenous determinants of innovation at the firm level using three-step random-effect logit models for German firms in the period 2006–2010, detecting important effects of the regional unemployment rate and the rate of graduates in scientific and technical careers. Also of relevance is the paper by Capello and Lenzi (2013), who mapped spatial patterns of innovation using cluster analysis of k-means and ANOVA techniques for regional systems in Europe.

On the other hand, there are some studies that have employed Data Envelopment Analysis techniques to reflect the effects of exogenous or environmental variables on efficiency, either in terms of two-stage DEA (Simar & Wilson, 2007), of conditional DEA (Daraio & Simar, 2005), or of m-order DEA (Cazals et al., 2002). Among the most relevant empirical studies in this category, we may highlight the one by Broekel (2008), who uses the m-order efficiency approach to evaluate the externalities of urbanization, location (Marshall), and diversification (Jacobs) on the innovative performance of German industries at the regional level. The author demonstrated that the existence of positive impacts and rescued the utility of using non-parametric approaches. In the same year, Broekel and Meder (2008) evaluated the impact of intra- or interregional cooperation on regional innovative performance, finding both positive and negative effects. Using the conditional boundary approach and non-parametric regressions, they concluded that both types of cooperation are complementary and have important effects on regional innovative performance.

Finally, Simar and Wilson in their already mentioned article of 2007 published a two-stage estimation methodology that has been since then widely used in the treatment of external or environmental variables on efficiency scores within the framework of the DEA, given the weakness of traditional estimation and inference methods which did not adequately address the serial correlation between the efficiency scores obtained by DEA. This methodology uses the assumption of separability between the environmental variables and the efficiency frontier, i.e., they have only a limited impact on the distribution (mean and variance) of the efficiency scores but not on the boundary form. Hence, it is this method that we have chosen in the present chapter to identify the externalities of national innovation systems on the efficiency of regional innovation systems.

26.3 Model Specification

26.3.1 Calculating the Technological Capacity Index

To measure the knowledge flows of the national R&D systems on their respective regions, we run regression models for three sub-samples (clusters), grouping the regions according to their degree of technological capacity, as measured by means of an "index of technological capacity" calculated on the average sample period (see for this Delgado-Márquez & García-Velasco, 2018).

The technological capacity index seeks to quantitatively reflect the elements that can improve the results of innovation systems, in addition to allowing comparisons between them. From an initial regional database (including the technological products of the innovative process), the factorial analysis was repeated in order to identify the factors that make up regional innovation systems. We then proceeded to calculate the weight(s) of the factors and variables and normalize them to finally calculate the index. To calculate the weights, and to maintain statistical objectivity, the results of the factorial analysis were used when weighing the contribution of each variable to the innovation system. We considered that each factor is a subscript within the global index, its weight being determined by the total variability explained by the factor regarding the overall variance explained by the factorial model as a whole. This implies that variables—and, therefore, factors with greater variability—will have a greater influence or weight than those variables that reflect a more homogeneous distribution between regions (see Buesa et al., 2006).

Regarding the variables, their weight within each factor or sub-index is calculated from the coefficient matrix employed to obtain the factor scores in the components. Considering that each variable is assigned to only one factor based on its degree of correlation with it, the relative weight is calculated as a percentage from the correlations between the factor and each variable, and the correlation of the factor with all the variables, as detailed in Annex 1.[2]

26.3.2 Calculation of the Regional Clusters According to Their Technological Capabilities

From the average of the index for the period of years that constitute our database, a cluster analysis was run that resulted in the obtention of three clusters composed by the same number of regions, employing the agglomerative "farther neighbor" hierarchical method, which is based on joining objects according to the so-called

[2] The values of each element of the index are standarized between 0 and 100 as to allow for their comparison.

maximum distance.[3] The three resulting clusters are Cluster 1, which includes 43 regions mainly in southern Europe with low GDP per capita; Cluster 2, which incorporates 43 regions of medium economic development; and Cluster 3, which groups 43 rich regions of western and central Europe which also present well-developed R&D systems, so that we may well consider them as "core" regions (see Map 26.1).

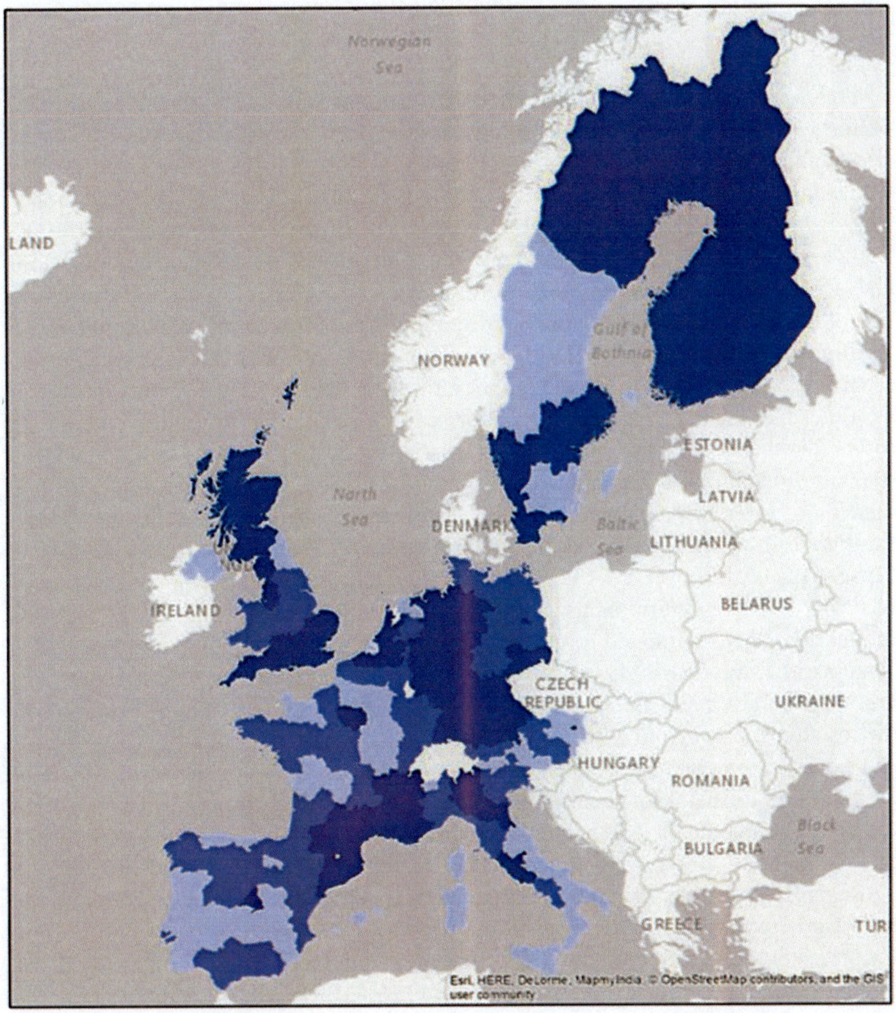

Map 26.1 Clusters by the technological capacity index. Light color: Technologically backward regions; medium color: Technologically moderated regions; dark color: Technologically advanced regions. (Source: Own elaboration)

[3] The Kruskal-Wallis test was performed to corroborate the conformation of the three clusters, rejecting the null hypothesis of equality of means between the three groups at 99%.

26.3.3 *Measuring Regional R&D System's Efficiency: Data*

In order to study the efficiency of regional R&D systems in Europe, we applied a factor analysis that allowed the reduction of information from a broad set of variables (29) to a few hypothetical or unobservable variables (cf. Buesa et al., 2010). Each of the factors reflects the essential aspects (being the different components or subsystems) of the regional R&D system, and these hypothetical variables—called factors—collect almost all the information of the original set of variables, around 83% of the original variance (for details, see Gutiérrez et al., 2018).

Following the criterion by Baumert (2006) regarding the competence in R&D policies of the different European regions, we have chosen to use the following geographical units in our analysis: the Belgian Régions (NUTS 1), the German Bundesländer (NUTS 1), the Spanish Autonomous Communities (NUTS 2), the French Regions (NUTS 2), the Italian Regions (NUTS 2), the Dutch Provinces (NUTS 2), the Austrian Bundesländer, the Portuguese Regional Coordination Commissions (NUTS 2), the Finnish Suuralueet/Storområden (NUTS 2), the Swedish Riksområden (NUTS 2), and the Government Office Regions of the United Kingdom (NUTS 1). In this way, there are 129 DMUs (decision-making units) that will be analyzed from the point of view of the efficiency of their R&D systems. From the factor analysis, five clearly interpretable factors can be distinguished, which correspond to *the Regional Economic Environment*, to the (innovating) *Firms*—which includes the specific activity of creation of technological knowledge—institutions of higher education (*Universities*), that reflect the specific generation of scientific knowledge, the *Public Administration*, and the *Sophistication of Demand* (in the technological sense). As may be observed, the results obtained through the factor analysis coincide basically with the determinants pointed out by the theory. In summary, the factorial model we have estimated provides adequate representation of regional R&D systems in Europe (EU11), as all the statistical and conceptual requirements that are required are met. Therefore, the resulting factors in this model—expressive of the resources, organization, and interrelationships that describe the R&D systems—can be used to address the analysis of the efficiency with which the activities of creation and diffusion of technological knowledge are developed in the European regions. The output variables refer to quantitative indicators that express the results of such systems, including both technological and scientific products (Global EI).[4]

Regarding the determination of efficiency, an important aspect has to do with the time lag between effort in R&D and the time of patent application or publication. Empirical studies seem to show that this relationship is almost contemporary in the case of patents (Schmoch, 1999; Hall et al., 1986; OECD, 2004: 139) but not in the case of articles for scientific publications. On the other hand, among the variables chosen is the stock of technological capital, which, according to its calculation

[4] Cf. Baumert and Gutiérrez (2020).

methodology, incorporates R&D expenditures with delays and stock depreciations, that is, implicitly a delay structure is used. Finally, factor analysis smoothens the time series of data so that the possible divergences in the values from one year to another of a variable are reduced, making the distinction of delays less relevant. In this way, the model presented in this study did not assume explicit delays between the independent variables and the different outputs.[5]

26.3.4 Relationship Between the Technological Capacity Index and the Efficiency Index for European Regional R&D Systems

As can be seen in Fig. 26.1, the index presents a high correlation with the level of efficiency of each of the regions. Yet, as shown in Fig. 26.2, the regions with greater technological capacity evidence a level of efficiency much higher to that of the other two clusters, although all biased to the scientific production more than technological ("European paradox," see Dosi et al., 2006). However, the difference between scientific and technological efficiency on average is increasing to greater technological capacity: 0.13 in cluster 1, 0.15 in cluster 2, and 0.20 in cluster 3.

Finally, and from the perspective of the configurations of the regional R&D systems, it becomes clear that the regions with the greatest technological capacity

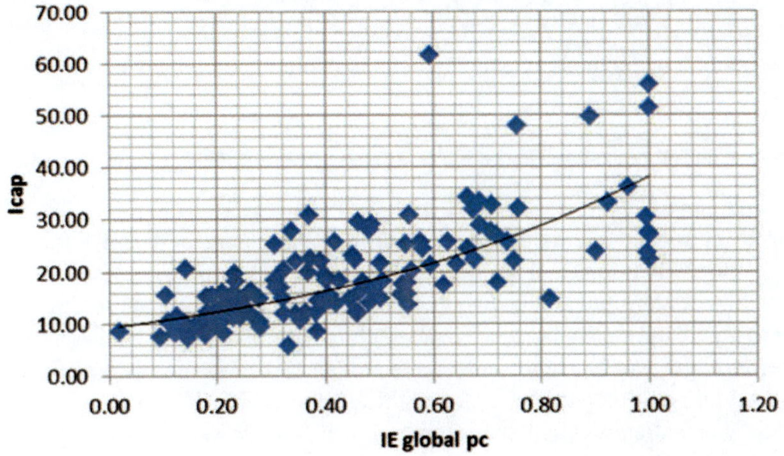

Fig. 26.1 Index of technological capacity (average) and index of global efficiency pc (2010). (Source: own elaboration)

[5] Calculations were also made with 1 year and 2 years' delay. However, they did not change any of the conclusions of the study.

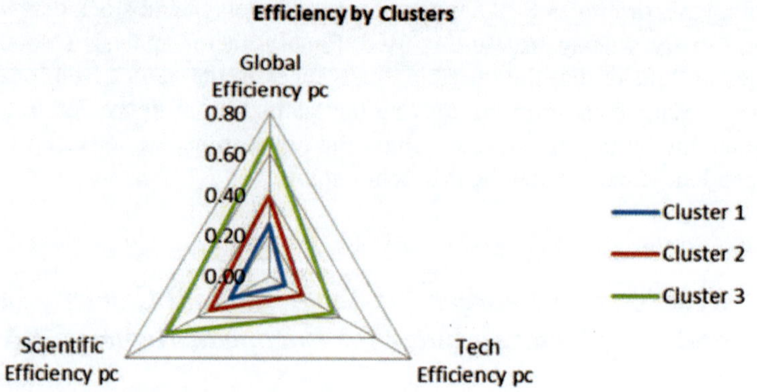

Fig. 26.2 Efficiency year 2010 by *cluster* and output. (Source: own elaboration)

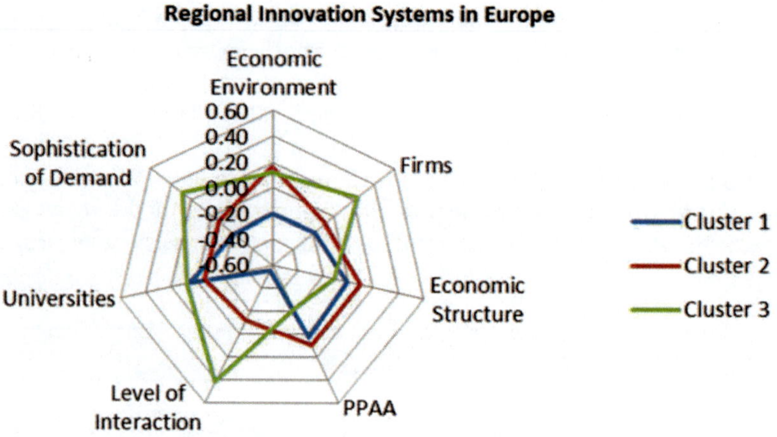

Fig. 26.3 Regional R&D Systems in Europe. (Source: Own elaboration)

belong to national systems that have a strong component of Firms, Universities, Demand Sophistication, and Degree of Interrelation among the system's Agents. Intermediate regions tend to have a strong component of the Economic Environment (large regions) and strong presence of the Public Administration, while regions with less technological capacity to those systems that rest their innovative effort in the Public Administration and in the Universities (see Fig. 26.3).[6]

As has been already stated, the central topic of this chapter—measuring influence of national R&D systems on the efficiency of their regional subsystems—is done following the model originally developed by Simar and Wilson (2007), which consists of a two-step model.

[6] Cf. the results presented by Baumert (2021) when studying the regional R&D performance by their phase of entrance to the EU.

The method starts by constructing and simulating a "sensitive" data generating process. This involves generating independent and identically distributed artificial bootstrap samples from an artificial data generating process. Then standard errors and confidence intervals are constructed through bootstrap simulation to finalize with truncated regressions and estimation by maximum likelihood.

Simar and Wilson propose two algorithms, of which we use the first, since it uses the DEA efficiency scores obtained in the first stage, and thus it is possible to compare it with other estimation methods (MCO and Tobit).

This can be summarized as follows[7]:

1. Estimate θ_i with i = 1, ..., N using DEA.
2. Fitting $\hat{\theta_i} = \beta' z_i + \epsilon_i$ using truncated regression truncadas (obtain estimates $\hat{\beta}$ and $\hat{\sigma_\varepsilon}$).

   Efficient DMUs J $\left(\hat{\theta_J} = 1, J = 1, \ldots, M\right)$ excluded.

   $\epsilon_i = \varepsilon_i + \tau_i \; with \; \tau_i \equiv \hat{\theta_i} - \theta_{i}.$

   $\hat{\theta}_i^I \in (0,\ 1]$ (Input orient.): right-truncation at 1.

3. Loop over the next three steps b times (b = 1, ..., B).

   Draw ε_i^b from N(0, $\hat{\sigma_\varepsilon}$) with right-truncation (input orient.) at (1- $\hat{\beta}' z_i$) for i = M + 1, ..., N.

   Compute $\theta_i{}^b = \hat{\beta}' z_i + \varepsilon_i{}^b$ for i = M + 1, ..., N.

   Estimate $\hat{\beta^b}\; and\; \hat{\sigma_\varepsilon}{}^b$ by truncated regression using the artificial efficiency scores $\theta_i{}^b$ as lhs-variables.

4. Construct standard errors for $\hat{\beta}\; and\; \hat{\sigma_\varepsilon}$ (conf. Interv. For $\beta\; and\; \sigma_\varepsilon$) from simulated distribution of $\hat{\beta^b}\; and\; \hat{\sigma_\varepsilon}{}^b$.

26.3.5 Econometric Results and Analysis: Second-Stage DEA

In order to study the spillovers and possible externalities of the national innovation systems in the efficiency of the regional innovation systems, regressions were run on the grouped data (panel) for the total and for each cluster. In the case of the panel, fixed effects by country and time were used employing dummies, performing two regressions for each model, one using the fixed effects and another using the factors of the national R&D systems obtained previously.[8] We only present the results for the regressions using factors (Table 26.1) according to the following expression:

[7] Using the terminology of Tauchmann based in the first algorithm of Simar and Wilson (2007).

[8] The Wald test was used to confirm the overall significance of the models.

$$K_{it} = \beta_0 + \beta_1 ENV_{it} + \beta_2 IFIR_{it} + \beta_3 STRUC_{it} + \beta_4 ADM_{it} + \beta_5 COOP_{it} + \beta_6 UNIV_{it} + \beta_7 DEM_{it} + +\varepsilon_{it} + v_t$$

where:

K_{it} = *DEA efficiency regional scores obtained in the first stage*
ENVit = Economic environment
IFIRit = Innovatory firms
STRUCit = Economic structure
ADMit = Public Administration
COOPit = Degree of interaction
UNIVit = Universities
DEMit = Sophistication of demand
εit = Overall error term
νt = Specific year

To make the different DEA scores comparable, a new single frontier was calculated for the whole period (2000–2010). Then, to relax the assumption of no-technological change, regressions were repeated for three subperiods, namely, 2000–2003, 2004–2007, and 2008–2010 (Table 26.2).

According to our results, in the global model, there are important differences between countries: while in Germany, Finland, Sweden, and the United Kingdom the national R&D Systems contribute positively to the efficiency of their regional R&D systems, the opposite occurs in Spain, Portugal, France, and Italy. This would ratify the results of the efficiency ranking carried out in the first stage (see also Gutiérrez et al., 2018). Regarding factors of the national R&D system that most influence efficiency are the Degree of Interrelation and Sophistication of Demand with positive impacts on the regional R&D system's efficiency scores and the National Economic Structure with a negative impact. Hence, economies that tend toward more service-oriented structures affect efficiency negatively (Table 26.2). Differences between clusters show that while in cluster 1, the most technologically backward regions receive positive spillovers from the Degree of Interrelation, Demand Sophistication, and Universities, in cluster 3, the most advanced regions receive spillovers from the Public Administration and the Sophistication of Demand, while in cluster 2, it is only received from the latter factor. Finally, in terms of time, it is possible to see how, as the period elapses, the efficiency scores improve progressively, since the coefficients of the dummy variables correspond to the years that are in the middle of the series, 2005, 2006, and 2007, and the of the end, 2009 and 2010.

Table 26.1 Econometric results. Factors NR&DS on RR&DS efficiency. Global Model (technological and scientific output)

	Total			Cluster 1			Cluster 2			Cluster 3		
Factors NIS	OLS	TOBIT	S/W+	OLS	TOBIT	S/W+	OLS	TOBIT	S/W+	OLS	TOBIT	S/W+
Economic environment	*−0.016*	*−0.016*	*−0.016*	*−0.012*	*−0.011*	*−0.018*	*−0.001*	*−0.000*	*0.001*	*−0.020*	*−0.019*	*−0.021*
Innovatory firms	*−0.009*	*−0.009*	*−0.011*	*−0.018*	*−0.019*	*−0.015*	*−0.018*	*−0.019*	*−0.016*	*−0.006*	*−0.006*	*−0.011*
Economic structure	−0.026**	−0.026**	−0.024*	*−0.003*	*−0.001*	*−0018*	*−0.031*	*−0.034*	*−0.017*	*0.007*	*0.006*	*0.012*
Public administration	*0.017*	*0.017*	*0.017*	*−0.012*	*−0.011*	*−0.020*	*0.021*	*0.023*	*0.008*	0.043**	0.043**	0.048**
Degree of interaction	0.037***	0.037***	0.039***	0.042**	0.042**	0.049**	*0.022*	*0.023*	*0.018*	*0.015*	*0.015*	*0.021*
Universities	*−0.001*	*−0.001*	*−0.000*	*0.037*	*0.036*	0.043*	*−0.006*	*−0.007*	*−0.001*	*−0.021*	*−0.022*	*−0.021*
Sophistic. Of demand	0.020***	0.020***	0.020***	0.021**	0.020*	0.026**	0.023**	0.024**	0.023*	0.025***	0.025***	0.029***
Years												
2001	*−0.026*	*−0.025*	*−0.038*	*−0.048*	*−0.050*	*−0.047*	*−0.072*	*−0.077*	*−0.050*	*0.029*	*0.032*	*0.001*
2002	*−0.009*	*−0.009*	*−0.011*	*−0.024*	*−0.027*	*−0.017*	*−0.057*	*−0.062*	*−0.036*	*0.016*	*0.016*	*0.013*
2003	*−0.012*	*−0.012*	*−0.013*	*−0.009*	*−0.012*	*−0.003*	*−0.048*	*−0.053*	*−0.027*	*−0.007*	*−0.007*	*−0.013*
2004	*0.062*	*0.063*	*0.060*	*0.069*	*0.064*	*0.101*	*0.046*	*0.048*	*0.030*	*−0.020*	*−0.020*	*−0.031*
2005	0.099**	0.099**	0.096**	*0.092*	*0.084*	*0.142*	*0.085*	*0.087*	*0.072*	*0.009*	*0.010*	*−0.001*
2006	0.091**	0.091**	0.085**	0.127*	0.124*	0.150*	*0.058*	*0.057*	*0.060*	*0.044*	*0.046*	*0.031*
2007	0.096**	0.096***	0.089**	0.131*	0.127*	0.152**	*0.099*	*0.097*	*0.100*	*0.050*	*0.052*	*0.035*
2008	*−0.001*	*−0.000*	*−0.009*	*0.015*	*0.010*	*0.039*	*0.065*	*0.064*	*0.064*	*−0.003*	*−0.001*	*−0.026*
2009	0.105***	0.106***	0.089***	0.108*	0.113*	*0.087*	0.167***	0.171***	0.155***	0.141***	0.147***	0.117**
2010	0.168***	0.170***	0.147***	*0.031*	*0.034*	*0.011*	0.226***	0.237***	0.164**	0.213**	0.220**	0.180**

(continued)

Table 26.1 (continued)

Factors NIS	Total			Cluster 1			Cluster 2			Cluster 3		
	OLS	TOBIT	S/W+	OLS	TOBIT	S/W+	OLS	TOBIT	S/W+	OLS	TOBIT	S/W+
Constant	0.297***	0.297***	0.300***	0.442***	0.445***	0.429***	0.433***	0.434***	0.433***	0.503***	0.503***	0.516***
N	1419	1419	1419	473	473	473	473	473	473	473	473	473
Adj R^2 (%)	3.78%			5.88%			8.79%			2.21%		
F test (p value)	0.00			0.00			0.00			0.05		
N truncaded		10	10		8	8		6	6		10	10
Chi^2 test (p value)		0.00			0.00			0.00			0.04	
Wald test (p value)			0.00			0.00			0.00			0.04
Log likelihood		176.21	245.86		40.14	80.02		110.01	137.85		61.45	110.63

Source: Own elaboration using software Stata12.0
***; **; *; mean significance of 1%, 5%, and 10%. + Simar & Wilson 2007, first algorithm

Table 26.2 Econometric results. Factors NR&DS on RR&DS efficiency, by sub periods. Global Model

Factors NIS	Total			2000–2003			2004–2007			2008–2010		
	OLS	TOBIT	S/W+	OLS	TOBIT	S/W+	OLS	TOBIT	S/W+	OLS	TOBIT	S/W+
Economic environ-ment	*−0.016*	*−0.016*	*−0.016*	−0.051**	−0.054**	−0.040*	*−0.126*	*−0.126*	*−0.147*	*0.053*	*0.052*	*0.063*
Innovatory firms	*−0.009*	*−0.009*	*−0.011*	*−0.003*	*−0.001*	*−0.014*	*0.060*	*0.059*	*0.072*	*−0.027*	*−0.027*	*−0.031*
Economic structure	−0.026**	−0.026**	−0.024*	*−0.054*	*−0.060*	*−0.025*	*0.038*	*0.037*	*0.052*	*0.007*	*0.003*	*0.029*
Public administra-tion	*0.017*	*0.017*	*0.017*	*0.019*	*0.020*	*0.014*	*0.021*	*0.023*	*0.007*	0.074**	0.075*	0.076**
Degree of interaction	0.037***	0.037***	0.039***	0.071**	0.072**	0.068**	*−0.011*	*−0.008*	*−0.036*	*−0.062*	*−0.061*	*−0.077*
Universities	*−0.001*	*−0.001*	*−0.000*	*−0.009*	*−0.007*	*−0.022*	*−0.058*	*−0.061*	*−0.047*	*−0.015*	*−0.015*	*−0.017*
Sophistic. Of demand	0.020***	0.020***	0.020***	0.031***	0.034***	0.027**	*−0.025*	*−0.028*	*−0.009*	*−0.023*	*−0.021*	*−0.036*
Years												
2001	*−0.026*	*−0.025*	*−0.038*	*0.025*	*0.025*	*0.020*						
2002	*−0.009*	*−0.009*	*−0.011*	*0.056*	*0.057*	*0.054*						
2003	*−0.012*	*−0.012*	*−0.013*	*0.039*	*0.039*	*0.036*						
2004	*0.062*	*0.063*	*0.060*									
2005	0.099**	0.099**	0.096**				*0.031*	*0.030*	*0.037*			
2006	0.091**	0.091**	0.085**				0.107*	0.107*	0.109**			
2007	0.096**	0.096***	0.089**				0.110*	0.110*	0.119**			
2008	*−0.001*	*−0.000*	*−0.009*									
2009	0.105***	0.106***	0.089***							*0.057*	*0.058*	*0.047*
2010	0.168***	0.170***	0.147***							*−0.007*	*−0.001*	*−0.056*

(continued)

Table 26.2 (continued)

	Total			2000–2003			2004–2007			2008–2010		
Factors NIS	OLS	TOBIT	S/W+	OLS	TOBIT	S/W+	OLS	TOBIT	S/W+	OLS	TOBIT	S/W+
Constant	0.297***	0.297***	0.300***	0.321***	0.316***	0.321***	0.287***	0.289***	0.264***	0.512***	0.513***	0.517***
N	1419	1419	1419	516	516	516	516	516	516	387	387	387
Adj R^2 (%)	3.78%			3.89%			2.25%			0.56%		
F test (p value)	0.00			0.00			0.01			0.26		
N truncaded		10	10		14	14		10	10		13	13
Chi^2 test (p value)		0.00			0.00			0.01			0.29	
Wald test (p value)			0.00			0.01			0.04			0.07
Log likelihood		176.21	245.86		−49.55	15.34		8.15	64.74		−5.75	70.72

Source: Own elaboration using software Stata12.0
***; **; *; mean significance of 1%, 5% and 10%. + Simar & Wilson 2007, first algorithm

26.4 Conclusions: Relevance of Externalities from an Evolutionary Perspective

According to econometric results, national factors do have effects on the efficiency of regional R&D systems—albeit of different signs—and they do, thus, affect the distribution of efficiency scores between regions. In other words, the presence of national factors in efficiency estimation models expresses the relevance of national R&D systems in the generation of knowledge at the regional level (although they are clearly asymmetric, as shown in Gutiérrez et al., 2018).

Yet, it has become evident that the evolutionary processes of the regions in terms of their economic development and innovative level, that is, their technological capacity, imply a change in the role of spillovers generated within their national contexts, as the estimates of the moderately developed regions include less national factors than regions with greater technological capability and therefore with greater capacity of absorption. The coefficients do also differ significantly, with much greater impacts in developed regions; less developed regions benefit greatly from their environment, and the technological convergence found is related to this phenomenon. More specifically, in Germany, Finland, Sweden, and the United Kingdom, the national R&D system contributes positively to the efficiency of their respective regional subsystem, while the opposite occurs in Spain, Portugal, France, and Italy.

Appendix

Structure of technological capacity index

	Factors and components						
	Economic environment	Universities	Technological outputs	Innovative firms	Public administration	Sophistication of demand	Regional economic growth
Annual average population (thousand)	9.1%						
Patents per capita (millions of people)			18.6%				
Patents per capita (millions of actives)			17.6%				
High-tech patents per capita (millions of people)			32.0%				
High-tech patents per capita (millions of actives)			31.8%				
Human resources in S&T—core (thousands of people)	8.5%						
Human resources in C&T—education (thousands of people)	8.6%						

Human resources in C&T—employment (thousands of people)	8.4%						
GDP (millions € 2010)	8.9%						
Gross fixed capital formation (millions € 2010)	8.4%						
Wages (millions € 2010)	8.8%						
GAV (millions € 2010)	8.9%						
Number of people employed (thousand)	8.8%						
Firms R&D expenditures (‰ GDP)				20.1%			
Public administration R&D expenditures (‰ GDP)					25.4%		
Universities R&D expenditures (‰ GDP)		20.3%					

(continued)

	Factors and components						
	Economic environment	Universities	Technological outputs	Innovative firms	Public administration	Sophistication of demand	Regional economic growth
Firms R&D staff (HC) ‰ employment				20.0%			
Firms R&D staff (FTE) ‰ employment				19.5%			
Public administration R&D staff (HC) ‰ employment					24.9%		
Public administration R&D staff (FTE) ‰ employment					25.7%		
Universities R&D staff (HC) ‰ employment		21.5%					
Universities R&D staff (FTE) ‰ employment		20.6%					
GDP per worker (€ 2010)						51.2%	
GDP per capita (€ 2010)						48.8%	
Regional 3rd cycle students (% population)		20.8%					

Stock of technological capital firms per capita (€ 2010)				14.0%			
Stock of technological capital universities per capita (€ 2010)		16.7%					
GDPpc rate of growth							50.2%
Regional employment hi-medium tech manufactures (% of employment)				26.4%			
Total expenditure R&D (millions € 2010)	5.5%						
Firms R&D expenditures (millions € 2010)	4.7%						
Firms R&D staff N°	6.4%						
Total R&D staff N°	5.2%						

(continued)

	Factors and components						
	Economic environment	Universities	Technological outputs	Innovative firms	Public administration	Sophistication of demand	Regional economic growth
GDP rate of growth							49.8%
Stock of technological capital public administration per capita (€ 2010)					24.0%		
PONDERATION OF EACH FACTOR IN THE INDEX	**37.30%**	**13.40%**	**12.20%**	**12%**	**11.70%**	**7.02%**	**6.18%**

Source: Own elaboration

References

Baumert, T. (2006) *Los determinantes de la innovación. Un estudio aplicado sobre las regiones de la Unión Europea*. Tesis Doctoral, Universidad Complutense de Madrid

Baumert, T. (2021). Patterns of knowledge creation in European regions: An analysis by the phases of the EU-enlargements. In N. Tsounis & A. Vlachvei (Eds.), *Advances in longitudinal data methods in applied economic research*. Springer.

Baumert, T., & Gutiérrez, C. (2020). Are we spending our scarce R&D resources adequately? Analysing the efficiency of EU's regional innovation systems. In N. Tsounis & A. Vlachvei (Eds.), *Advances in cross-section data methods in applied economic research*. Springer.

Bellmann, L., Crimmann, A., Evers, K., & Hujer, R. (2013). *Regional determinants of establishments innovations activities: A multi-level approach*. Institute for the Study of Labor.

Beujelsdijk, S. (2007). The regional environment and a firm's innovative performance: A plea for a multilevel interactionist approach. *Economic Geography, 83*(2), 181–199.

Broekel, T., & Meder, A. (2008). *The bright and dark side of cooperation for regional innovation performance*. Jena Economic Research Papers 053.

Buesa, M., Heijs, J., & Baumert, T. (2010). The determinants of regional innovation in Europe: A combined factorial and regression knowledge production function approach. *Research Policy, 39*(2010), 722–795.

Buesa, M., Heijs, J., Martínez Pellitero, M., & Baumert, T. (2006). Regional systems of innovation and the knowledge production function: The Spanish case. *Technovation, 26*(4), 436–472.

Capello, R., & Lenzi, C. (2013). Territorial patterns of innovation and economic growth in European regions. *Growth and Change, 44*(2), 195–227.

Cazals, C., Florens, J., & Simar, L. (2002). Nonparametric frontier estimation: A robust approach. *Journal of Econometrics, 106*, 1–25.

Daraio, C., & Simar, L. (2005). Introducing environmental variables in nonparametric frontier models: A probabilistic approach. *Journal of Productivity Analysis, 24*, 93–121.

Delgado-Márquez, B. And García-Velasco, M. (2018). Geographical distribution of the European knowledge base through the lens of a synthetic index. *Social Indicators Research, 136*, 477–496.

Dosi, G., Llerena, P., & Sylos Labini, M. (2006). The relationship between science, technologies, and their industrial exploitation: An illustration through the myths and realities of the so-called 'European paradox'. *Research Policy, 35*, 1450–1464.

Duvivier, C. (2013). Does urban proximity enhance technical efficiency? Evidence from Chinese agriculture. *Journal of Regional Science, 53*(5), 923–943.

Gallaud, D., & Torre, A. (2004). Geographical proximity and the diffusion of knowledge. In G. Fuchs, P. Shapira, & A. Koch (Eds.), *Rethinking regional innovation*. Springer.

Gutiérrez, C., & Baumert, T. (2019). Smith, Schumpeter y el estudio de los sistemas de innovación. In *Tecnología y Sociedad: una mirada multidisciplinaria*. Universidad de Santiago de Chile.

Gutiérrez, C., Heijs, J., & And Baumert, T. (2018). Asymmetric spillovers from National Innovation Systems to knowledge creation processes in their regions. *Revista de Economía Aplicada, 77*(XXVI), 77–100.

Hall, B., Griliches, Z., & Hausman, J. (1986). Patents and R and D: Is there a lag? *International Economic Review, 27*(2), 265–283.

Marrocu, E., Paci, R., & Usai, S. (2011). *Proximity, networks and knowledge production in Europe*. University of Cagliari and CRENOS. 09.

Moreno, R., Paci, R. & Usai, S. (2004). Spatial spillovers and innovation activity in European regions. *44th Congress of the European Regional Science Association*. Porto, Portugal, 25th–29th August, 2004.

OECD. (2004). *Compendium of patent statistics*. Paris.

Schmoch, U. (1999). Eignen sich Patente als Innovationsindikatoren? En R. Boch (Ed.), *Patentschutz und Innovation in Geschichte und Gegenwart*. Frankfurt am Main et al.

Simar, L., & Wilson, P. (2007). Estimation and inference in two-stage, semi-parametric models of production processes. *Journal of Econometrics, 136*, 31–64.

Chapter 27
Tracking Price Trends Using User–Product Interaction Data From a Price Comparison Service

Mattias Rydenfelt

Abstract Using online prices has made it possible to estimate inflation rates at a larger scale and higher time resolution than were previously possible. In this chapter, we introduce a daily updated chain index to track prices in over 2400 different product categories and brands over time using data from online price comparison service Prisjakt. Our price index, among others, allows (1) users to optimize purchase decisions in time using historic trends, (2) stores to revise pricing strategies, (3) data analysts to derive business insights at high temporal and categorical resolution, and the index could (4) aid national statistic offices in inflationary studies. By using user–product interaction data as a proxy for quantities sold, products in the index can be weighted by user popularity. Chaining a price index at high frequency, however, presents challenges with potentially large biases, as has been observed in recent studies on scanner data. Here we show that much of these biases can be handled by carefully constructing product weights, without resorting to more involved multilateral indices. Finally, we compare our price index to matching product categories in the official Statistics Sweden consumer price index.

Keywords Online inflation · Consumer price index (CPI) · Price comparison · E-commerce

27.1 Introduction

E-commerce has by convenience and competitive pricing seized an ever-increasing share of retail spending, 14.3% overall in the United States (US Census Bureau, 2020; OECD, 2020) and over 50% in selected categories in 2020 Q3. E-commerce has now reached a level where it can no longer be ignored in Consumer Price Index

M. Rydenfelt (✉)
Prisjakt Sverige AB, Ängelholm, Sweden

N. Tsounis, A. Vlachvei (eds.), *Advances in Quantitative Economic Research*, Springer Proceedings in Business and Economics,
https://doi.org/10.1007/978-3-030-98179-2_27

(CPI) calculations (Nygaard, 2015; Breton et al., 2015). Through the Billion Prices Project (Cavallo and Rigobon, 2016) and similar efforts, vast numbers of online prices are continually being collected and processed to measure online inflation in near real time. These data have even been used to debunk manipulated official inflation statistics (Cavallo, 2013). Apart from offering higher time resolution and covering a larger cross-section of prices, measuring online inflation from automatically scraped prices is also considerably less labor-intensive compared to traditional inflation studies. Moreover, online indices, unlike traditional CPIs, track products over their entire lifecycle, which also results in "automatic" quality adjustment of the index (see Sect. 27.3.2). Still, estimating inflation from online prices presents challenges. First, a CPI constitutes both goods and services; however, many services are not available for online purchase. Conversely, some items may only be available for online purchase. Second, scraped online prices (unlike scanner data) lack information about quantities sold, as such information is typically proprietary and not publicly available. Therefore, online prices must be complemented with weights from other ("offline") sources, such as consumer expenditure surveys, to be representative of actual consumption patterns. This dependency undoes some of the benefits of an online inflation index. Third, both an online inflation index and a traditional CPI are subject to a number of potential biases, for example, due to changes in product quality or product composition (Hausman, 2003), which might (Goolsbee and Klenow, 2018) or might not (Cavallo, 2017) cause the two indices to diverge.

In this chapter, we attempt to address the second challenge by augmenting online prices with user–product interaction data from online price comparison service Prisjakt. Prisjakt is one of the largest price comparison services in Scandinavia and is currently present (under different names) on seven different markets.[1] The service is used by approximately ten million unique visitors per month and includes about one million products in one thousand categories. Using user–product interaction data as a proxy for a number of initiated purchases allows us to dynamically weight products in the price index by popularity, which makes the index better aligned with actual consumption patterns.

A price comparison service is especially well-positioned to establish an online price index, not only because of the large number of listed and annotated products, and access to user–product interaction data, but also in-house expertise in matching identical products from different stores. This presents a significant challenge when working with unstructured and continuously changing data from disparate sources.

Apart from aiding inflation studies, our online price index provides a powerful tool for deriving business insights, e.g., to identify categories and brands that became more expensive during the Corona pandemic, to measure and compare discounts at different shopping holidays, to alert for price increases before sales

[1] Sweden, Norway, New Zealand, France, Great Britain, Finland, Denmark (ordered by falling market size).

periods, or to observe seasonal trends in different product categories. We will explore these applications in Sect. 27.3.

27.2 Method

27.2.1 Price Index Design Goals

Price index theory remains one of the more well-researched areas of economics. Still, recent studies show that traditional index theory breaks down when indices are chained at high frequency with irregular input data (Ivancic et al., 2011). Proposed solutions, including multilateral indices such as rolling-window GEKS, are powerful but can be hard to communicate to a non-expert audience and be somewhat challenging to implement at scale. In this chapter, we aim to construct a price index that is both well-behaved when chained at high frequency with irregular input data and yet simple to implement. In exchange for simplicity, we sacrifice index properties such as transitivity (ILO et al., 2004), which makes a price index manifestly free from certain types of biases.

There are limitless possibilities to construct an index that tracks the price or value of a quantity of interest over time. In a stock index, companies can be weighted by company size, geographic location, dividend size, volatility etc. (Standard Poor's, 2020). In a consumer price index, products can be weighted to reflect the consumption patterns of urban dwellers or retirees, or to (de)emphasize certain expenditure types such as mortgage interest payments (Office for National Statistics, 2019). An index will only track whatever it is designed to track, and it is up to the index inventor to make sure that the index is informative for the intended purposes.

To constrain the infinite space of possible index definitions, we postulate a number of design goals to guide the construction of an informative price index:

- D1 The index can be updated at high frequency (minimum daily).
- D2 Newly released products will gracefully appear in the index, and old products no longer for sale will gracefully disappear from the index.
- D3 Popular products are given higher weight than less popular products.
- D4 The index has limited chain drift (ILO et al., 2004). This implies that over short time periods, the index agrees to a good approximation with a corresponding fixed base index, where the first time point is used as reference for all consecutive time points. If the price of a product changes and then returns to its original value, the net effect on the price index is approximately zero. We will say that a price index has an inflationary/deflationary bias if the index increases significantly faster/slower relative to a corresponding fixed base index.
- D5 Noisy data is filtered out. A price comparison service of Prisjakt's magnitude receives millions of new product offers and price updates daily, making a certain degree of irregularity in the data (e.g., inaccurate data from stores, or wrongly mapped products) inevitable. To increase the stability and reliability of the

index, raw data is filtered for extreme outliers before being incorporated into the price index.

D6 The index represents a variety of products.

With these design goals in mind, we define the basic functional form of the price index in Sect. 27.2.3 and leave for Sect. 27.2.4 the important question of how to weight products in the index.

27.2.2 Data Collection and Filtering

At Prisjakt, the two primary proxies for product popularity are (1) the number of times users click on a product hyperlink to visit the store selling a product (*clicks*, the "demand") and (2) the number of stores selling a product (*stores*, the "supply"). A product click does not necessarily lead to a purchase; however, as long as the constant of proportionality between the number of clicks and initiated purchases is preserved across different products, weighting by clicks is equivalent to weighting by the number of initiated purchases. This hypothesis could in principle be validated against scanner data but regretfully, to the best of our knowledge, no such public access and up-to-date dataset exists (Kilts Center for Marketing, 2013). As anecdotal evidence, we verified that the most clicked products in selected categories such as TVs, mobile phones, and running shoes were indeed listed as popular products on large Swedish e-commerce websites.

User traffic to a price comparison service is, however, not representative of typical household consumption. For example, few people use a price comparison service before making a food-related purchase, even though food makes a sizable contribution to a typical household budget. This bias can partly be corrected by complementing the price index with data from household expenditure surveys, for product categories available in both datasets. This correction does, however, not make the price index a "faithful" CPI, as many services and product categories are not available for online comparison.

In this chapter, we aggregate prices to the level of unique products, by defining the price of a product as the cheapest price available on Prisjakt, recorded daily, and the number of product clicks as the total number of clicks across all stores selling the product. Since the majority of Prisjakt users interacts only with product offers at or around the cheapest price, the aggregated data fairly well approximate the unaggregated data. Aggregating the data makes it straightforward to weight products, and it offers technical advantages, such as reducing the storage capacity required for raw data. The price index definition of Sect. 27.2.3, however, is agnostic about whether data were aggregated or not.

To reduce the impact of extreme outliers, we cap the daily price change of a product to at most a factor of three (Design Goal D5). Moreover, we consider the price index of a product category to be undefined if the effective number of products (see Sect. 27.2.4.1) is less than ten (Design Goal D6).

27.2.3 *Price Index Mathematical Formulation*

Consider prices $P_i^{t_n}$ for a set of products at time point t_n. We define the index change between two time points t_{n-1} and t_n for this set of products as the number α_n that, according to some yet to be defined cost function $C(\alpha_n)$, minimizes the regression error

$$P_i^{t_n} = \alpha_n P_i^{t_{n-1}}. \tag{27.1}$$

One straightforward choice is the mean-squared error (MSE) cost function

$$C^{\mathrm{BAD}}(\alpha_n) = \mathrm{MSE}(\alpha_n) \propto \sum_i \left(P_i^{t_n} - \alpha_n P_i^{t_{n-1}}\right)^2; \tag{27.2}$$

however, this puts a lot of emphasis on expensive products that will dominate the sum. As we have no motivation to favor expensive products, we instead choose the weighted mean-squared logarithmic error (MSLE) cost function

$$C(\alpha_n) = \mathrm{MSLE}(\alpha_n) = \sum_i w_i^{t_n} \left[\ln\left(P_i^{t_n}\right) - \ln\left(\alpha_n P_i^{t_{n-1}}\right)\right]^2 \tag{27.3}$$

$$= \sum_i w_i^{t_n} \ln\left(\frac{P_i^{t_n}}{\alpha_n P_i^{t_{n-1}}}\right)^2, \tag{27.4}$$

where we also introduced (non-negative time-dependent) product weights $w_i^{t_n}$. These product weights will be discussed in detail in Sect. 27.2.4. The logarithmized cost function of Eq. (27.3) is more robust to outliers than MSE and associates a penalty that is independent of the absolute price scale. To find the index change α_n that minimizes this cost function, we differentiate Eq. (27.3) with respect to α_n and set the derivative to zero

$$\ln(\alpha_n) = \sum_i w_i^{t_n} \ln\left(\frac{P_i^{t_n}}{P_i^{t_{n-1}}}\right) \stackrel{\mathrm{def}}{=} \left\langle \ln\left(\frac{P_i^{t_n}}{P_i^{t_{n-1}}}\right)\right\rangle, \tag{27.5}$$

where we assume that the product weights are normalized $\sum_i w_i^{t_n} = 1$. After exponentiation, Eq. (27.5) is equivalent to a weighted geometric average, as is used by many traditional price indices such as Geometric Lowe, Geometric Young, and Törnqvist.

To find the total accumulated index change α_{tot} over multiple time steps, we multiply the corresponding $\alpha_1, \alpha_2, \ldots, \alpha_n$ factors for each pair of consecutive time points together

$$\alpha_{tot} \stackrel{\mathrm{def}}{=} \alpha_1 \alpha_2 \cdots \alpha_n. \tag{27.6}$$

By using a chain index, the set of products need not be the same over the entire time window (Design Goal D2). This follows by the same logic that a stock index such as Dow Jones can be traced back to 1896, even though the underlying composition of companies has changed dramatically since.

When the product weights $w_i^{t_n}$ are time-independent, it is easy to show that the accumulated price index is identical to a fixed base index, computed directly from the initial and final product prices, in agreement with Design Goal D4

$$\begin{aligned}\ln(\alpha_{tot}) &= \ln(\alpha_1) + \ln(\alpha_2) + \ldots + \ln(\alpha_n)\\ &= \left\langle \ln\left(\frac{P_i^{t_n}}{P_i^{t_{n-1}}}\right)\right\rangle + \left\langle \ln\left(\frac{P_i^{t_{n-1}}}{P_i^{t_{n-2}}}\right)\right\rangle + \ldots + \left\langle \ln\left(\frac{P_i^{t_1}}{P_i^{t_0}}\right)\right\rangle\\ &= \left\langle \ln\left(\frac{P_i^{t_n}}{P_i^{t_{n-1}}}\frac{P_i^{t_{n-1}}}{P_i^{t_{n-2}}}\cdots\frac{P_i^{t_1}}{P_i^{t_0}}\right)\right\rangle\\ &= \left\langle \ln\left(\frac{P_i^{t_n}}{P_i^{t_0}}\right)\right\rangle. \end{aligned} \tag{27.7}$$

We are allowed to combine brackets in Eq. (27.7) because product weights are constant in time. Later in Sect. 27.2.4, we will show that when product weights are time-dependent, the chain index will gradually drift from the corresponding fixed base index.

27.2.4 Weighting Products by Demand and Supply

The interest garnered by different products follows a highly skewed distribution. At Prisjakt, the effective number of products is less than 1% of the total number of products when weighting products by the number of user clicks (Eq. (27.8)). If prices for this small fraction of highly popular products were to follow a different trajectory than the majority of other, less desired, products, it could potentially have a large impact on how price changes are perceived by the average consumer. To take this into account, we incorporate product popularity into the price index (Design Goal D3). An advantage with using data from a large price comparison service is that both product prices and user–product interaction data can be readily obtained. At Prisjakt, such data is available at high time resolution for roughly one million products, permitting us to update the price index and the corresponding product weights frequently.

In Sect. 27.2.4.1, we will investigate how product weights can be constructed from user–product interaction data in accordance with our Design Goals. In Sect. 27.2.4.2, we will separately address the question of how to time-average user–product interaction data in order to reduce index bias due to negative correlation between product price and demand.

27.2.4.1 Exploring Functional Forms for Product Weights

The way product weights are constructed will affect index properties such as bias and volatility. In a traditional price index, the weight of a product scales linearly with quantities sold, but such linear scaling might not be the optimal in all circumstances. To explore different functional forms of product weights, we start from a set of five candidates (neglecting a normalization constant)

$$\begin{aligned} w_0 &= 1 \qquad w_1 = \text{clicks} \qquad w_2 = \text{clicks} \cdot \text{stores} \\ w_3 &= \sqrt{\text{clicks}} \; w_4 = \sqrt{\text{clicks} \cdot \text{stores}} \, . \end{aligned}$$

We deliberately do not weight products by price, to avoid expensive products dominating the index. For a homogeneous group of similarly priced products, analogous to elementary indices (ILO et al., 2004) of a traditional CPI, this decision will have little impact on the index. To calculate an aggregated price index across multiple categories, weights from expenditure survey data could be used to reduce bias due to unrepresentative product sampling at a price comparison service.

Propagating the different candidate functional forms for 1 year (Fig. 27.1a) results in an index spread of more than 10% between the most inflationary ($w_0 = 1$) and the most deflationary (w_2 = clicks · stores) functional form, emphasizing that the construction of product weights has a profound impact on the index. To study this more closely, we calculate the price index change for all categories and markets in Fig. 27.1c. We observe that the number of stores selling a product, i.e., the *competition*, has a clear deflationary effect on the price index, as could be expected.

The different functional forms have a strong influence on the volatility of the price index. In Fig. 27.1b, we see an abrupt 10% price index drop in the headphones category when scaling product weights linearly with the number of clicks. After closer inspection, this whole drop can be attributed to a transient discount on one single product—Apple AirPods—the most popular product in the category. Such sensitivity on individual products is not acceptable for our price index (Design Goal D6), leading us to discard the two functional forms scaling linearly with the number of product clicks ($w_{3,4}$). In Fig. 27.1d,e, we confirm that the functional forms scaling linearly with the number of clicks have an increased day-to-day index volatility (RMS), and a reduced effective number of products contributing to the index (Kish, 1965)

$$n_{eff} = \frac{\left(\sum_i w_i\right)^2}{\sum_i w_i^2}. \tag{27.8}$$

For the remainder of this chapter, we will, unless stated otherwise, use $w = w_4 = \sqrt{\text{clicks} \cdot \text{stores}}$ as functional form, by virtue of having both a comparably large effective number of products in the index (Fig. 27.1e) and low bias relative to the official Statistics Sweden CPI (Statistics Sweden, 2021) (see Sect. 27.3.4). We acknowledge that this exploration of functional forms is by no means exhaustive, and that much remains to be understood regarding the construction of product weights.

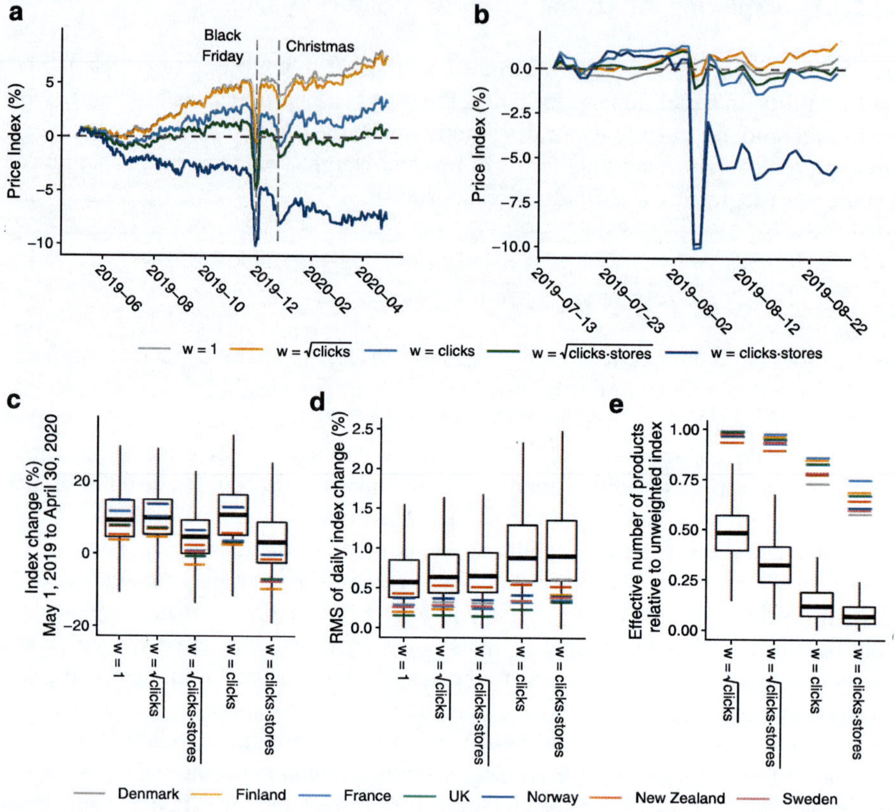

Fig. 27.1 Weighting products by "demand" (the number of clicks) and "supply" (the number of stores selling a product). (**a**) Price index aggregated across all product categories (Sweden). (**b**) Price index for headphones (Sweden). The price index drop on August 5 is due to a transient discount on one single product—Apple AirPods—the most popular product in the category. ((**c**))–(**d**) Boxplots: distribution of start-to-end price index change (**c**) and root mean square (RMS) of daily price index change (**d**) between May 1, 2019 and April 30, 2020 for $M \times K$ different indices, corresponding to all categories ($K \approx 1000$) on all markets ($M = 7$). Colored lines: corresponding values when aggregating the price index across all product categories for each market. (**e**) Boxplot: the average effective number of products in the index (Eq. (27.8)) relative to the unweighted price index, calculated for all categories on all markets. Colored lines: the average number of categories for each market with an effective number of products greater than ten relative to the unweighted price index. User–product interaction data is time-averaged as described in Sect. 27.2.4.2. The price index is aggregated (when applicable) without using any external data sources (e.g., expenditure surveys)

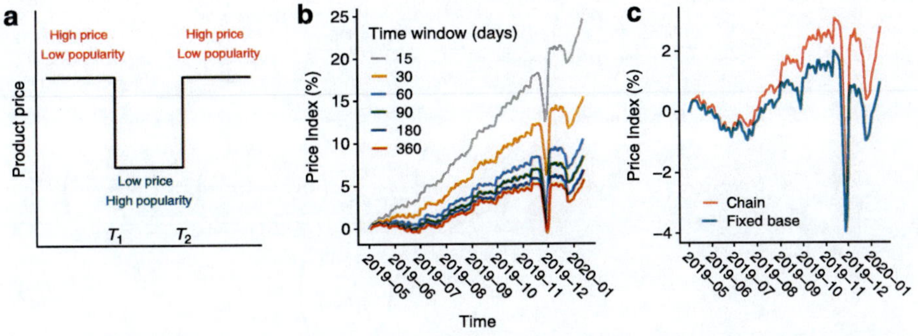

Fig. 27.2 Time-averaging of user–product interaction data. (**a**) Cartoon: The demand of a product increases when the price drops. When the price is restored to its original value at time T_2, the product has greater index weight than when the price drops at time T_1. As a consequence, the product will over its lifetime have a net inflationary effect on the price index. (**b**) Price index for the Swedish market with user–product interaction data averaged over different time windows (days): 15 (top curve), 30, 60, 90, 180, and 360 (bottom curve) ($w = \sqrt{\text{clicks}}$). (**c**) The accumulated chain index (red) slowly diverges from the corresponding fixed base index (turquoise), computed using the first time point as reference for all consecutive time points (w = clicks)

27.2.4.2 Time-Averaging User–Product Interaction Data Reduces Inflationary Bias

The demand for a product is strongly negatively correlated with the product price. Since products are weighted by demand in the price index, it follows that the weight of a product increases when the price drops. Furthermore, price increases will contribute more to the price index than price drops, as is illustrated in Fig. 27.2a. We will denote this type of chain drift *price fluctuation bias*. Before time T_1, a product is expensive and attracts little customer interest; hence, the price drop at time T_1 has little impact on the price index. The price drop, however, sparks an interest in the product, and consequently, its weight in the price index increases. As the price is restored to its original value at time T_2, the product has a greater impact on the price index. The product will over its lifetime have a net inflationary effect on the price index, even though the initial and final prices are identical, hence creating an inflationary bias in the index. Mathematically, one can show that the accumulated price index of Eq. (27.6) is no longer a telescopic product that reduces to a fixed base index, instead

$$
\begin{aligned}
\ln(\alpha_{tot}) &= \ln(\alpha_1) + \ln(\alpha_2) + \ldots + \ln(\alpha_n) \\
&= \sum_i w_i^{t_n} \ln\left(\frac{P_i^{t_n}}{P_i^{t_{n-1}}}\right) + \ldots + \sum_i w_i^{t_1} \ln\left(\frac{P_i^{t_1}}{P_i^{t_0}}\right)
\end{aligned}
$$

$$
\begin{aligned}
&= \underbrace{\sum_i w_i^{t_n} \ln\left(\frac{P_i^{t_n}}{P_i^{t_0}}\right)}_{\text{Fixed base index}} - \sum_i (w_i^{t_n} - w_i^{t_1}) \ln\left(\frac{P_i^{t_{n-1}}}{P_i^{t_0}}\right) \\
&+ \sum_i \left(w_i^{t_2} - w_i^{t_1}\right) \ln\left(\frac{P_i^{t_{n-1}}}{P_i^{t_1}}\right) + \sum_i \left(w_i^{t_3} - w_i^{t_2}\right) \ln\left(\frac{P_i^{t_{n-1}}}{P_i^{t_2}}\right) \\
&+ \ldots + \sum_i \left(w_i^{t_{n-1}} - w_i^{t_{n-2}}\right) \ln\left(\frac{P_i^{t_{n-1}}}{P_i^{t_{n-2}}}\right). \qquad (27.9)
\end{aligned}
$$

When product weights are time-dependent, a correction term, whose size depends on the weight shift, will cause the chain index to drift from the fixed base index, as shown in Fig. 27.2c. The price fluctuation bias will be most prominent when user–product interaction data is averaged over a time window that is narrower than $\Delta T = T_2 - T_1$ of Fig. 27.2a. Extending the time window beyond ΔT will reduce the effect of the price fluctuation bias, since the weight of the product remains relatively constant within the time window $[T_1, T_2]$, and the price index will agree better with a corresponding fixed base index. We study the impact of the price fluctuation bias for different time windows in Fig. 27.2b. For short time windows, the price fluctuation bias inflates the price index by almost 25% in 9 months. For longer time windows, the price fluctuation bias quickly tapers off until the window reaches approximately 360 days, after which extending the time window even further has little impact on the index. For the remainder of this chapter, we will use a time window of 360 days.

Choosing a large time window, however, means that it takes longer for new products to enter the index and that the weights of products remain artificially inflated for some time even after they have reached their peak popularity. To partly offset these effects, we instead use the average number of clicks per day from the beginning of the time window, or from the release date of a product (minimum 30 days), whichever comes later. This allows newly released products to enter the index more quickly. Moreover, by weighting products by the "supply" (the number of stores selling them), obsolete products will get downweighted in the index as they are sold by fewer stores (see Fig. 27.1).

27.3 Results

27.3.1 Price Trends During Shopping Holidays

With Black Friday and Christmas sales in close succession, the fourth quarter stands out in terms of shopping activity on all markets where Prisjakt is present. The surge in sales around this period shows that consumers are willing to adapt their shopping behavior around changes in pricing. In Fig. 27.3a, we see that significant discounts

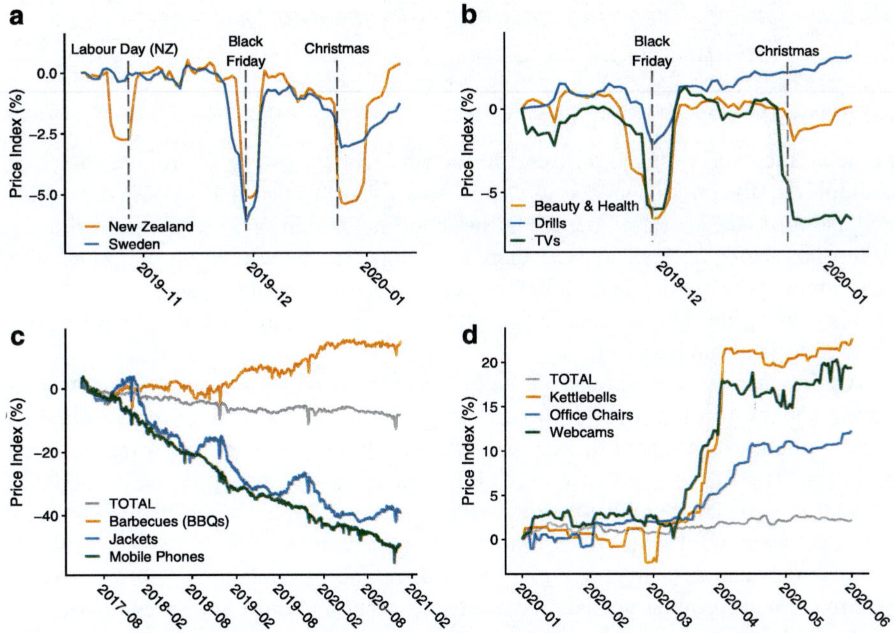

Fig. 27.3 Price index for selected categories and markets. (**a**) The aggregated price index over all product categories drops significantly during shopping holidays. (**b**) Some categories are heavily discounted on both Black Friday and Christmas sales (e.g., TVs), other categories only on Black Friday (e.g., beauty and health), and other categories are barely discounted at all (e.g., drills). (**c**) Price index for selected categories during 2017–2020. Fashion categories such as jackets exhibit strong annual cycles and a deflationary trend, which is a possible sign of quality improvement in the category. The aggregated index across all product categories is slightly deflating, in part due to an overrepresentation of consumer electronics products in the index. (**d**) Price index increases in selected home office and home training categories at the onset of the Corona pandemic. Unless stated otherwise, data shown refer to the Swedish market. The price index is aggregated (when applicable) without using any external data sources (e.g., expenditure surveys)

are offered both during Black Friday and Christmas sales and on Labor Day in New Zealand. The offered discounts vary between categories, with some categories being heavily discounted on both Black Friday and Christmas sales, whereas others are not much discounted at either of these shopping holidays (Fig. 27.3b). The price index could help customers to decide whether it is best to buy a product on Black Friday or if it is worth holding out until Christmas sales for potentially bigger savings.

A common consumer concern regarding shopping holidays is that stores might surreptitiously raise prices before the start of sales. Although this can be seen for individual products, the effect is small enough not to affect the price index as a whole for the year of 2019, neither in Sweden nor in New Zealand.

27.3.2 Categories with Seasonal Patterns and Long-Term Trends

Some product categories exhibit annual cycles, which can be seen as cyclic modulations over a long-term trend in the price index. In Fig. 27.3c, we show for example that the price of jackets goes up distinctly each year (2017–2019) from mid-August until Black Friday, before falling continuously in price until the beginning of the next cycle. In this category, there is a long-term deflationary trend, as a result of old models being discounted before getting replaced by new ones. In Fig. 27.3c, we also show, for comparison, mobile phones, with a deflationary trend but without noticeable seasonal patterns.

A falling price index should not be interpreted as falling average prices. Despite strong deflation in the mobile phones category (2017–2020), the average price of mobile phones on Prisjakt in fact went *up* during the same period. A deflationary price index can be a sign of quality improvements in a category, when updated product models create additional perceived customer value. When two versions of a product coexist for some time, one can intuitively think of the price gap between the two versions as a measure of quality difference (Armknecht, 1989). *Quality* is here defined from the perspective of the customer and must not necessarily agree with objective measures, such as screen resolution or memory capacity. A traditional CPI will likely overestimate inflation unless adjusted for quality changes, e.g., using hedonic regression (ILO et al., 2004). A complete discussion of quality adjustment in price indices falls beyond the scope of this study, and we refer readers to resources such as (Aizcorbe et al., 2003; Silver and Heravi, 2005).

Finally, as an example of an inflationary category with annual cycles, we consider barbecues in Fig. 27.3c. Naively, one might expect barbecues to be discounted at the end of summer, but in fact sales start already in the end of May and last until mid-August (Sweden, 2017–2019). This is in agreement with Prisjakt user–product interaction data, which show that the interest in buying barbecues peaks already in the spring and then falls during the summer. After the end of sales in mid-August, the prices on barbecues continuously go up until the beginning of the next cycle.

27.3.3 Price Trends During the Corona Pandemic

The onset of the Corona pandemic in 2020 caused an abrupt shift in consumption patterns that could not be immediately accommodated by a corresponding shift in the production chain. This led to higher prices or shortages for certain goods (Hamilton, 2021). In Fig. 27.3d, we show that prices on home office equipment, such as webcams and office chairs, and home training equipment rose by 10–20% in 1 month between March and April of 2020. At the time of writing, 1 year later, the prices remain high in these categories, suggesting that the market has not yet returned to its previous equilibrium point.

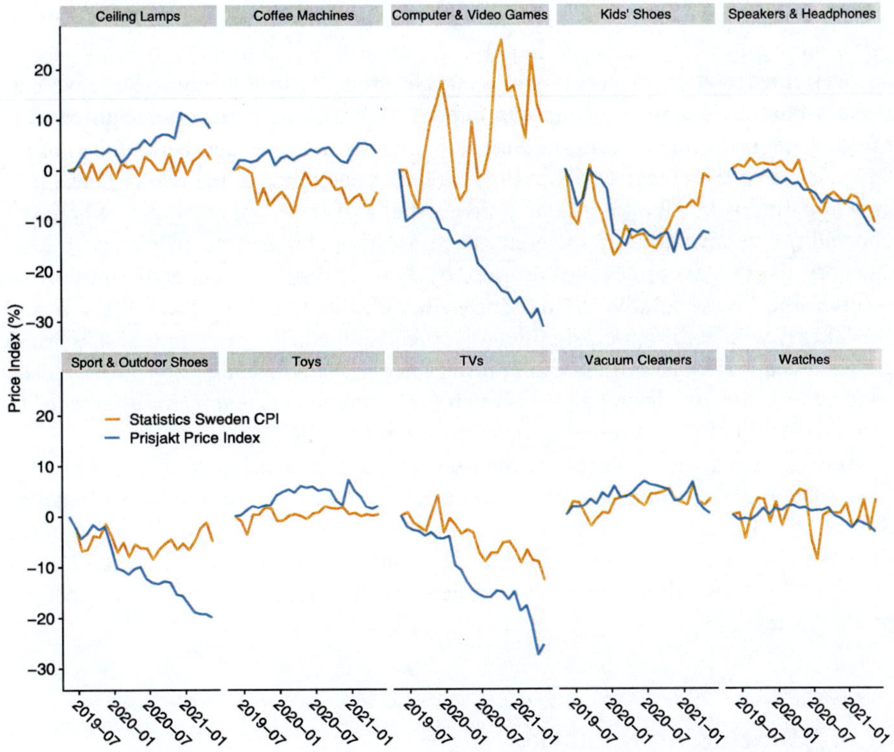

Fig. 27.4 Prisjakt price index vs. Statistics Sweden CPI for the top ten matching categories with most user traffic on Prisjakt

The Corona pandemic did not only trigger a shift in *what* consumers bought, but also *how* they bought it. As some consumers, not the least the age group 65+ (Postnord, 2020), started to view online shopping as a potentially safer alternative to visiting physical stores, e-commerce grew by 49% year over year in Sweden (Postnord, 2020) and slightly less in the United States (OECD, 2020) in 2020 Q2. The growth in e-commerce due to the Corona pandemic has been clearly visible also in Prisjakt user traffic data.

27.3.4 Comparison to Statistics Sweden CPI

User traffic to different product categories of a price comparison service does not follow the same distribution as measured through consumer expenditure surveys. For this reason, our price index will be biased relative to an official CPI when aggregated across multiple categories. This is apparent from Fig. 27.3c, where the aggregated price index drops by 9.5% between May 2017 and December 2020, whereas the official Statistics Sweden CPI (Statistics Sweden, 2021) increased by 5.5% during the same time period. We attribute this deflationary bias in part to an overrepresentation of consumer electronic products in the index. Still, we can make a fairer comparison of the two indices by matching product categories. Out of 357 categories included in the Statistics Sweden CPI, 51 can be matched to an equivalent Prisjakt category. From Fig. 27.4, we conclude that the two indices often agree qualitatively, albeit not quantitatively, but that there are categories where the two indices behave notably different, such as computer and video games. In this category, the Prisjakt price index dropped by 31% during the considered time period, whereas the (more volatile) Statistics Sweden CPI increased by 9%. Although the Prisjakt price index dropped significantly, the average price of computer and video games listed on Prisjakt did not fall during the considered time period, which leads us to believe that the discrepancy between the two indices amounts to differences in how product quality and product substitutions are handled.

Across all matched categories, the unweighted average index change between May 2019 and May 2021 was almost identical for the two indices, 0.02% (Statistics Sweden CPI) and 0.05% (Prisjakt), from which we conclude that our price index does not appear to be significantly biased relative to the Statistics Sweden CPI at the category level, although the two indices can deviate considerably for specific product categories.

27.4 Concluding Remarks

A drawback with measuring inflation using online price scrapers is a lack of information about quantities sold. In this chapter, we attempt to address this shortcoming by using user–product interaction data from price comparison service Prisjakt as a proxy for product popularity, in order to construct a daily updated chain index. Incorporating product popularity into a price index makes it better aligned with the price changes seen by the average consumer. We show that our price index does not have any apparent biases when compared to the Statistics Sweden CPI at the level of product categories, although there is a strong deflationary bias when aggregated across all product categories. We attribute this bias in part to a strong overrepresentation of consumer electronic products in the index. To reduce this bias, the price index could be complemented with data from consumer expenditure surveys, for product categories available in both datasets.

Weighting products in a price index by user–product interaction data presents a number of challenges. Negative correlation between product price and demand leads to a strong inflationary bias unless interaction data is time-averaged over a sufficiently large time window. Such bias has previously been reported from studies on scanner data. Here we show that this bias can be handled by carefully constructing product weights, without resorting to more involved multilateral indices such as rolling-window GEKS. Another challenge is that the functional form of product weights has a significant impact on index properties such as bias and volatility. We acknowledge that our exploration on functional forms has been far from exhaustive and that much remains to be understood.

Aside from being a potential aid for inflationary studies, we have shown that our price index, among others, provides a powerful tool for users to optimize purchase decisions in time using historic trends, and that it allows data analysts to derive business insights at a higher time resolution and finer level of categorization than available through a traditional CPI.

Acknowledgments The author wishes to thank Peter Stark for originally proposing the idea to construct a daily updated price index at Prisjakt. The author wishes to thank Henrik Leijon for valuable suggestions on product weighting. The author wishes to thank Marcin Zawalski for valuable help scaling up the index to cover a greater number of product categories and brands. The author wishes to thank Henrik Leijon, Kevin Fox, Peter Stark, Laura Patel-Smith, Magdalena Henrysson, and Kyle van de Langemheen for valuable comments on the manuscript.

Conflict of Interest
Mattias Rydenfelt is an employee of Prisjakt Sverige AB.

Financial Disclosure
None reported.

References

Aizcorbe, A. M., Corrado, C. A., & Doms, M. E. (2003). When Do Matched-Model and Hedonic Techniques Yield Similar Measures? In *FRB of San Francisco Working Paper*

Armknecht, P. (1989). Adjustments for quality change in the U.S. consumer price index. *Journal of Official Statistics, 5*, 107–123.

Breton, R., Clews, G., Metcalfe, L., Milliken, N., Payne, C., Winton, J., & Woods, A. (2015). Research indices using web scraped data. In *Office for National Statistics*.

Cavallo, A. (2013). Online and official price indexes: Measuring Argentina's inflation. *Journal of Monetary Economics, 60*(2), 152–165.

Cavallo, A. (2017). Are online and offline prices similar? evidence from large multi-channel retailers. *American Economic Review, 107*(1), 283–303.

Cavallo, A., Rigobon, R. (2016). The Billion prices project: Using online prices for measurement and research. *Journal of Economic Perspectives, 30*(2), 151–178.

Goolsbee, A. D., Klenow, P. J. (2018). Internet rising, prices falling: Measuring inflation in a world of E-Commerce. *AEA Papers and Proceedings, 108*, 488–492.

Hamilton, R. (2021). Scarcity and coronavirus. *Journal of Public Policy & Marketing, 40*(1), 99–100.

Hausman, J. (2003). Sources of bias and solutions to bias in the consumer price index. *Journal of Economic Perspectives, 17*(1), 23–44.

ILO, IMF, OECD, Eurostat, UNECE, Bank, W. (2004). *Consumer price index manual: Theory and practice*. Geneva: International Labour Organization.

Ivancic, L., Erwin Diewert, W., & Fox, K. J. (2011). Scanner data, time aggregation and the construction of price indexes. *Journal of Econometrics, 161*(1), 24–35.

Kilts Center for Marketing (2013). *Dominick's Data Manual*. Chicago.

Kish, L. (1965). *Survey Sampling*. New York: Wiley.

Nygaard, R. (2015). The use of online prices in the Norwegian Consumer Price Index. In *Paper prepared for the meeting of the Ottawa Group, Tokyo, Japan, May 20–22, 2015*. http://www.stat.go.jp/english/info/meetings/og2015/pdf/t1s2p5_pap.pdf.

OECD (2020). E-commerce in the time of COVID-19. https://www.oecd-ilibrary.org/content/paper/3a2b78e8-en.

Office for National Statistics (2019). *Consumer prices indices technical manual*. https://www.ons.gov.uk/economy/inflationandpriceindices/methodologies/consumerpricesindicestechnicalmanual2019.

Postnord (2020). e-barometern. https://www.postnord.se/siteassets/pdf/rapporter/e-barometern-q2-2020.pdf.

Silver, M., Heravi, S. (2005). A failure in the measurement of inflation: Results from a hedonic and matched experiment using scanner data. *Journal of Business and Economic Statistics, 23*(3), 269–281.

Standard Poor's (2020) *Index Mathematics: Methodology*. https://www.spglobal.com/spdji/en/documents/methodologies/methodology-index-math.pdf.

Statistics Sweden (2021). http://www.scb.se.

US Census Bureau (2020). *E-Commerce retail sales as a percent of total sales*. St. Louis: Federal Reserve Bank

Chapter 28
Differences in Generational Cohort Satisfaction from a Public Hospital Medical Personnel: Insights from Generation Cohorts X, Y, and Z

Irene Kamenidou, Spyridon Mamalis, Aikaterini Stavrianea, and Ifigeneia Mylona

Abstract This research paper aims to investigate citizens' satisfaction from a public hospital in Greece, based on eight satisfaction statements referring to the healthcare personnel (nurses, doctors, and medical personnel with a degree as a healthcare provider, such as assistant nurses). The sample consisted of 352 citizens of three generational cohorts (X, Y, Z). A questionnaire provided with the eight statements rated satisfaction on a 5-point satisfaction scale. Results reveal that in all cases, MS > 4.00. Thus, the three cohorts seem to be satisfied with the personnel, while in few cases, they tend to be very satisfied (MS > 4.51). Additionally, generational cohort differences do exist, with the younger cohort being the most dissatisfied. Guidelines for accomplishing future patient satisfaction from medical personnel and from public hospitals are provided.

Keywords Patient satisfaction · Healthcare sector · Generational cohorts · Hospital · Medical personnel · Marketing communication

JEL Codes M10, M30, M31, M37, M39, I12, I18

I. Kamenidou (✉) · S. Mamalis · I. Mylona
Department of Management Science and Technology, School of Business and Economics, International Hellenic University, Kavala, Greece
e-mail: rkam@mst.ihu.gr; mamalis@econ.auth.gr; imylona@mst.ihu.gr

A. Stavrianea
Department of Communication and Media Studies, National and Kapodistrian University of Athens, Athens, Greece
e-mail: aikstavria@media.uoa.gr

N. Tsounis, A. Vlachvei (eds.), *Advances in Quantitative Economic Research*, Springer Proceedings in Business and Economics,
https://doi.org/10.1007/978-3-030-98179-2_28

28.1 Introduction

Grönroos (1988) has pointed out the complexity of service encounter satisfaction, asserting that because "quality is what customers perceive" (Grönroos, 1988, p. 11), it is entirely of a subjective manner. It is widely accepted that the healthcare sector is an extremely sensitive sector. Vogus and McClelland (2016) state, "Healthcare presents two additional and unique challenges to achieving high customer satisfaction and service quality. First, the potential consequences for the patient (i.e., customer) and, recently, the organization (i.e., hospitals and other healthcare delivery settings) are qualitatively different in healthcare. Care delivery carries with it a high risk for harm from services performed relative to other industries." Patient satisfaction evaluation is affected by actual experiences but also by individual factors (Bjertnaes et al., 2012). Researchers also indicated that these particular factors affecting patient satisfaction could be demographic, such as age (Crow et al., 2002), or physical and psychological (Mitropoulos et al., 2018). Age is considered as one of the most significant demographic factors affecting patient satisfaction. While there are many studies that acknowledge that patient's age is associated with her/his satisfaction toward hospital-related services, they are not conclusive, and findings are contradictory. For example, Cohen (1996) found that elderly patients are more satisfied than younger ones from medical care, while Lee and Kasper (1999) in their study found "a significant negative association between age and highly positive ratings of care in the elderly; the old-old are less likely than the young-old to give very favorable opinions." Ghuloum et al. (2010), in their research, found that the highest satisfaction level came from the youngest age group (18–34 years old), while Satibi et al. (2015) did not find any association between patient age and their satisfaction level. Overall, the inconsistencies of findings referring to patient satisfaction develop the need to further investigate the effect of age on patient satisfaction.

Even more, contemporary researchers consider that generational cohorts are better demographic indicators as compared to age, since cohorts have consistent behavior and one cohort has different behavior from another (Kamenidou et al., 2020; Meredith et al., 2002).

Additionally, it is widely recognized that patient satisfaction affects clinical outcomes, patient retention, and medical malpractice claims (Prakash, 2010). The abovementioned set aside, patient feedback should be taken into consideration for service improvement (Marley et al., 2004) because patient satisfaction is an indicator of healthcare quality (Lyu et al., 2013; Noor et al., 2009; Abd Manaf & Nooi, 2007; Cleary & McNeil, 1988).

The Committee on Quality of Health Care in America; Institute of Medicine (2001 in the US Office of Disease Prevention and Health Promotion, 2020) states that "Health care quality is a broad term that encompasses many aspects of patient care. Quality health care is care that is safe, effective, patient-centered, timely, efficient, and equitable." This quality healthcare is given to patients among others (e.g., up-to-date medical machinery) through healthcare providers (doctors, nurses, and medical personnel with a degree as a healthcare provider, such as assistant nurses). Thus, patient satisfaction feedback from these providers is essential, especially for Greece, since budget decreases have been applied for the national healthcare system (Kentikelenis & Papanicolas, 2011). Consequently, a decline in public healthcare has been acknowledged (Mpouzika et al., 2018).

Under this context and taking to account that personal factors, such as age, affect patient satisfaction, this research has as its aim to explore patient satisfaction from a public hospital in Greece, and more specifically, it explores two issues:

1. The satisfaction level of patients from hospital healthcare providers (doctors, nurses, and medical personnel with a degree as a healthcare provider, such as assistant nurses).
2. The existing statistically significant differences between three Greek generational cohorts (generation X, generation Y, and generation Z) and their satisfaction from medical personnel.

Generational cohorts have been applied in this research since academics consider cohorts as better demographic indicators than age. Members of a cohort have a more homogeneous behavior due to the same life-changing situations that have affected them, while simultaneously, one cohorts' behavior differs from another (Dries et al., 2008; Kupperschmidt, 2000).

Taking all the beforementioned into account, this research centers on the General Hospital of Kavala, Greece, a hospital that serves the surrounded area of the prefecture of Kavala (95 towns and villages).

28.2 Literature Review

The academic research on hospital patient satisfaction is abundant (Batbaatar et al., 2017; Jackson et al., 2016; Prakash, 2010; Quintana et al., 2006; Sacks et al., 2015; Sitzia & Wood, 1997; Tsai et al., 2015; Young et al., 2000; Zineldin, 2006). Some published articles focus exclusively on patient-doctor satisfaction (Baker et al., 2003; Drossman et al., 2021; Jalil et al., 2017; Lehmann et al., 1988; Shah et al., 2021; Williams et al., 1998). Additionally, some refer to patient-nurse interaction and patient satisfaction (Johansson et al., 2002; Kim-Soon et al., 2021; Yusuf et al., 2020), while others tackle both patient-doctor/nurse interaction and their satisfaction (DeBehnke & Decker, 2002; Hitawala et al., 2020; Mayer et al., 1998). Though addressing patient characteristics, and primarily generational cohorts in patient satisfaction studies, these are relatively few. Precisely, a search with keywords "health care," "generational cohort," "patient satisfaction," and "hospital" provided 143 articles on https://scholar.google.com/, on the first of July 2021, the vast majority of which concern job satisfaction and generational cohorts in the workforce. Likewise, only 79 articles deal with "generational differences," "health care," "generational cohort," "patient satisfaction," and "hospital" on the same search channel and date. Again, almost all deal with generational differences in the workplace or from the healthcare providers' perspective and not from the patient perspective (Berkowitz & Schewe, 2011; Hisel, 2017; Keith, 2021; Kramer, 2010; Wakim, 2014). Only one study was found that have investigated generational cohort differences in patient satisfaction from medical personnel (Farooq et al., 2020). Specifically, Farooq et al. (2020) identified the total knee arthroplasty (TKA) patient satisfaction predictors (N = 897 after 1-year follow-up) using 15 variables; among them were doctor (doctor A and doctor B) satisfaction from the procedure. They found that overall, 85.3% of patients were satisfied. They also found that the older generational cohorts were more satisfied than the younger ones. Specifically, the Traditionalist/Baby Boomer group was 2.9 times more likely to be satisfied than the Generation X/Millennial group. Lastly, they found that surgeon A patients were 1.9 times more likely to be satisfied than surgeon B patients.

The current study draws after prior research and suggests that differences between patients' generational cohort and their satisfaction from the medical personnel exist. Thus, the research hypothesis is the following:

H1: Statistically significant differences exist between generational cohorts and their satisfaction from the medical personnel.

Since eight statements were used for measuring satisfaction from medical personnel, the above hypothesis is extended to the eight statements, thus producing from the general hypothesis eight sub-hypotheses.

28.3 Materials and Methods

The research strategy implemented in this study is a case study-based quantitative research. As regards to the research design, it has as follows. The study targeted three generational cohorts in the Kavala area (generation X, Y, and Z). Data was collected via a questionnaire. The questionnaire pertained to eight statements measuring patient satisfaction that was adopted by previous research. Specifically, seven of the eight items were adopted from Elleuch (2007), and one item (item no.2) was adopted from Clucas and St Claire (2010). These statements were slightly modified to fit the aim and objectives of the study. Specifically, the items that were tested were:

1. The medical personnel is willing to help me.
2. The medical personnel respects me (from Clucas & St Claire, 2010).
3. The medical personnel behaviors transmit trust and confidence to me.
4. I feel safe in receiving medical care from the medical personnel.
5. The medical personnel is courteous when dealing with me (good communication manner, consideration).
6. The medical personnel has the knowledge to answer my questions (knowledge and skill regarding medical and health information).

7. The medical personnel gives me individual attention (learning a patient's specific medical history, flexibility, and accommodating the individual patient's requirements).
8. The medical personnel listens to me and keeps me informed.

The Likert-type satisfaction scale was used to assess patient satisfaction. Answer ratings were in the range 1–5, whereas answer 1 = completely dissatisfied up to 5 = completely satisfied, and with the neutral response 3 = neither satisfied nor dissatisfied. Criteria were set in order for a person to be part of the research sample. The main criteria that a participant had to fulfill were:

1. To be an adult 18–52 years of age, thus belonging in one of the generational cohorts: X, Y, or Z.
2. To have been an inpatient at the hospital in the last year.
3. To have knowledge on computers and the Internet and have an e-mail or Facebook account.
4. To give consent to use their answers for data analysis.

If one of the above criteria were not satisfied, the questionnaire would be discarded. Acquaintances of the researchers were sent an e-mail or Facebook invitation with the distributed link. Additionally, they were requested to invite their friends or acquaintances that met the above criteria to take part in the research, thus utilizing a mixed-method data sampling method (convenience, criteria, and snowball). These two methods (online data collection and sampling technique) are considered the most appropriate because it provides with the following advantages:

1. It is cost-efficient, since it is free of charge.
2. It gathers quickly data due to easy access to the questionnaire and due to the mixed sample method utilized.
3. The participant can answer the questionnaire at his/her convenience since it is asynchronous.
4. It collects data from individuals that live in remote areas, where access would be very difficult due to time and economic constraints.
5. The targeted audience of this research are individuals that are technologically knowledgeable, and as for the youngest cohort, it is technological savvy, and technology consists of its main way of their communication (social media—Facebook).

The research concerned the General Hospital of Kavala (public hospital) and was realized in January 2019. During a 1-month period, a valid sample of 352 inpatients was gathered that met the above criteria. Data encompassed descriptive statistics, reliability analysis, one-way ANOVA, and multiple comparisons of means. All tests were preset at $a = 0.05$.

Ethical approval. There are no ethical issues involved in the processing of the questionnaire data used in the study. The necessary consents have been obtained by the persons involved, and the anonymity of the participants has been secured. All procedures performed in studies involving human participants were in accordance with the ethical standards of the International Hellenic University research committee and with the 1964 Helsinki declaration and its later amendments or comparable ethical standards.

28.4 Results

28.4.1 Sample Profile

As to gender, 47.1% were males and 52.9% females, while age ranged from 18 to 52 years old, with the mean age being 33.55 (StD = 10.791). As to generational cohorts, generation Z is 29.5% (N = 104), generation Y is 37.8% (N = 133), and generation X is 32.7% (N = 115). As to marital status, 42.3% were married, 50.9% single, and 6.8% were widowed or divorced. As to their health insurance, 10.6% had OGA (federal insurance for farmers), 51.0% had EOPPY (federal insurance in the public and private sector), 9.2% had no insurance at all, 5.4% had a private insurance company, and 23.8% had other types of government insurance (such as for businessmen, sailors, taxicab drivers, student insurance, etc.). As to education, 44.4% had basic obligatory education (lyceum), 1.1% had post-secondary, and 46.7% had at least graduate education. Additionally, 47.5% were people with a monthly salary (civil servants or private sector employees or on a pension), 13.2% were businessmen and farmers, and 39.3% were dependent on others (housekeepers, university students, unemployed). Lastly, as to family net monthly income, 26.9% fell in the low-income category (up to 600€), 21.4% from 600.01 to 1000.0€, 37.4% in the 1000.01–2000.00€ category, and 17.3% with a net family monthly income of more than 2000.00 €.

28.4.2 Patient Satisfaction Ratings

Regarding the eight presented statements, patient satisfaction may be considered relatively high, since in all cases mean score (MS) per item was MS > 4.00, as Table 28.1 presents. Moreover, from Table 28.1, it is evident that the highest satisfaction comes from the statement "the medical personnel are courteous when dealing with me (good communication manner, consideration)" (MS = 4.61), followed by the statement "the medical personnel is willing to help me" (MS = 4.55). The statement that has the lowest satisfaction rating is "I feel safe in receiving medical care from the medical personnel" (MS = 4.28), followed by the statement "the medical personnel gives me individual attention (learning my specific medical history, flexibility, and accommodating my requirements)" with MS = 4.37. Table 28.1 presents the satisfaction toward the medical personnel in descending order and percentages (columns under the numbers 1–5) and MS. In the first row, the numbers 1–5 represent the answers from the Likert-type scale.

Table 28.1 Patient satisfaction from the medical personnel (%)

Statements	1	2	3	4	5	MS
1. Medical personnel are courteous when dealing with me (good communication manner, consideration).	4.8	10.8	29.3	38.6	16.5	4.61
2. Medical personnel are willing to help me.	6.3	12.2	28.4	38.9	14.2	4.55
3. Medical personnel behaviors transmit trust and confidence to me.	8.0	11.4	29.3	34.1	17.3	4.51
4. Medical personnel respects me.	6.3	15.6	23.9	37.2	17.0	4.50
5. Medical personnel have the knowledge to answer my questions (knowledge and skill regarding medical and health information).	6.3	12.8	23.6	40.1	17.3	4.47
6. Medical personnel listens to me and keeps me informed.	5.8	11.8	30.8	35.2	16.4	4.47
7. Medical personnel gives me individual attention (learning my specific medical history, flexibility, and accommodating my requirements).	8.0	13.6	24.7	36.9	16.8	4.37
8. I feel safe in receiving medical care from the medical personnel.	4.8	9.7	29.0	41.8	14.8	4.28

Source: the authors

28.4.3 Generational Differences

The central hypothesis that was examined was:

H1 = There are differences between generational cohorts and their satisfaction from the medical personnel of the General Hospital of Kavala, Greece. This hypothesis is presented statistically as:

$H_1 0$ = There are no statistically significant differences between the generational cohorts and their satisfaction from the medical personnel of the General Hospital of Kavala, Greece (a = 0.05).

$H_1 1$ = There are statistically significant differences between the generational cohorts and their satisfaction from the medical personnel of the General Hospital of Kavala, Greece (a = 0.05).

Since eight statements were examined for patient satisfaction, these statements one by one were the sub-hypothesis of the abovementioned central hypothesis.

28.4.3.1 ANOVA Tests

At first, factor analysis was conducted in order to explore dimensions of patient satisfaction toward the medical personnel. Factor analysis with Principal Component Analysis (Varimax rotation) provided one factor explaining 63.4% of the total variance (KMO = 0.932; BTS =1627.467; df = 28; Sig. =0.000). Therefore,

Table 28.2 ANOVA tests between generational cohorts satisfaction from the medical personnel statements

Statements	F	Sig.
Medical personnel are willing to help me	5.598	0.004
Medical personnel respects me	3.182	0.043
Medical personnel behaviors transmit trust and confidence to me	3.629	0.028
I feel safe in receiving medical care from the medical personnel	4.596	0.011
Medical personnel are courteous when dealing with me (good communication manner, consideration)	5.173	0.006
Medical personnel have the knowledge to answer my questions (knowledge and skill regarding medical and health information)	4.614	0.011
Medical personnel gives me individual attention (learning my specific medical history, flexibility, and accommodating my requirements)	2.423	0.090
Medical personnel listens to me and keeps me informed	5.700	0.004

ANOVA tests were performed for each item separately to have an in-depth insight into generational differences and patient satisfaction per item.

Table 28.2 presents the results of the hypotheses testing by the one-way ANOVA model. In all cases, the eight statements examined for patient satisfaction were the dependent variable, and the generational cohorts ($n = 3$) were the independent variable.

The one-way ANOVA test revealed significant differences between generational cohorts for seven out of eight hypotheses tested ($a = 0.05$). Specifically, the null hypothesis is rejected for the following statements regarding patient satisfaction from the medical care personnel and generational cohort differences:

1. The medical personnel are willing to help me [F (2.349) = 5.598, p = 0.004].
2. The medical personnel respects me [F (2.349) = 3.182, p = 0.043].
3. The medical personnel behaviors transmit trust and confidence to me [F (2.349) = 3.629, p = 0.028].
4. I feel safe in receiving medical care from the medical personnel [F (2.349) = 4.596, p = 0.011].
5. The medical personnel are courteous when dealing with me (good communication manner, consideration) [F (2.349) = 5.173, p = 0.006].
6. The medical personnel has the knowledge to answer my questions (knowledge and skill regarding medical and health information) [F (2.349) = 4.614, p = 0.011].
7. The medical personnel listens to me and keeps me informed [F (2.349) = 5.700, p = 0.004].

In all the abovementioned seven cases, the null hypothesis is rejected. Only for one hypothesis, one-way ANOVA did not reveal significant differences between generational cohorts: The medical personnel gives me individual attention (learning my specific medical history, flexibility, and accommodating my requirements) [F (2.349) = 2.423, p = 0.090]. As a result, the null hypothesis cannot be rejected.

28.4.4 *Multiple Comparison of Means*

For all the cases where one-way ANOVA presented statistically significant differences between cohorts (null hypothesis rejected), multiple comparisons of means were conducted to examine the specific differences. Table 28.3 displays the multiple comparisons of means for the seven statements, using the post hoc Tuckey B comparisons test. In Table 28.3, each row with the same letter does not present significant differences, while different letters beside the mean scores reveal that statistically significant differences exist. In all cases, the starting point is with "a" for the highest mean score.

Referring to the statements "The medical personnel is willing to help me" and "The medical personnel is courteous when dealing with me (good communication manner, consideration)," the first thing that is noticed is that the older generational cohorts are more satisfied than the younger ones. Specifically, the generation Y and generation X cohort tend to be satisfied, while the generation Z cohort is neither satisfied nor dissatisfied. The second issue noticed is that the Tuckey's B test indicated that the mean scores for the older cohorts are statistically significantly higher than the youngest cohort (Generation Z). It also reveals that the generation Y and generation X cohort compared do not show statistically significant differences in their satisfaction in both cases. In contrast, both cohorts have statistically significant differences compared to the generation Z cohort.

Likewise, in all the other cases, the generation Z cohort was the least satisfied, while generation Y was the most satisfied one. In two cases, i.e., "I feel safe in receiving medical care from the medical personnel" and "The medical personnel listens to me and keeps me informed," the Tuckey's B test indicated that the MS for the older cohorts is statistically significantly higher as compared to the youngest cohort (Generation Z). It also reveals that in both cases, the generation Y and generation X cohort compared do not have statistically significant differences in their satisfaction. In contrast, both cohorts have with the generation Z cohort.

Table 28.3 Tuckey B HSD test between generational cohorts and satisfaction from the medical personnel

Statements	Gen Z	Gen Y	Gen X
Medical personnel are willing to help me	3.13b	3.54a	3.56a
Medical personnel are courteous when dealing with me (good communication manner, consideration)	3.24b	3.60a	3.65a
I feel safe in receiving medical care from the medical personnel	3.27b	3.63a	3.62a
Medical personnel listens to me and keeps me informed	3.16b	3.61a	3.52a
Medical personnel respects me	3.20b	3.56a	3.50ab
Medical personnel behaviors transmit trust and confidence to me	3.17b	3.56a	3.46ab
Medical personnel have the knowledge to answer my questions (knowledge and skill regarding medical and health information)	3.28b	3.71a	3.44ab

Source: the authors

In the last three cases, i.e., "The medical personnel respects me," "The medical personnel behaviors transmit trust and confidence to me," and "The medical personnel have the knowledge to answer my questions (knowledge and skill regarding medical and health information)," the statistically significant differences unveiled were between the generation Z cohort and the generation Y cohort. Specifically, the Tuckey's B test indicated that the MS for the generation Y cohort was statistically significantly higher as compared to the youngest cohort (generation Z), while the generation X and the generation Z did not provide with statistically significant differences.

28.5 Discussion and Implications

The findings of this study, even though they cannot be directly compared with previous studies, can be indirectly compared to. Specifically, as previously stated, only one research paper was found dealing simultaneously with patient satisfaction from medical personnel and the generational cohort theory. Specifically, Farooq et al. (2020), in their study, found that overall, 85.3% of patients were satisfied, which is partially in line with our findings, as satisfaction MS present. Our results reveal that the highest-rated items, and thus the statements that patients are most satisfied toward are "the medical personnel are courteous when dealing with me (good communication manner, consideration)" and "the medical personnel is willing to help me," whereas about half of the sample was satisfied by these statements (55.1% and 53.1%, respectively). While satisfaction does seem to exist, this is relatively lower than the study of Farooq et al. (2020), while the comparison is made indirectly since this study researched different issues.

Prior research has shown the significance of medical personnel and patient interaction for high satisfaction levels. Focusing on the issues that this research deals with, studies reveal that good communication and manners from the medical personnel toward the patient raise patient satisfaction (Lotfi et al., 2019; Onyechi & Babalola, 2020; van Osch et al., 2017; Williams et al., 1998). The same outcome derives from the caring connection between doctor and the patient which also increases patient satisfaction (Teutsch, 2003). Likewise, medical personnel that respects their patients increases satisfaction levels (Clucas & St Claire, 2010; Wright et al., 2004). In the same vein, the medical personnel that is willing to help patients (Zulkarnain & Winardi, 2020) and the information feedback that patients require and have from the medical personnel also raise satisfaction level (Chen et al., 2020; Garg et al., 2016; Merkouris et al., 2004). Individual attention (learning the specific medical history, flexibility, and accommodating my requirements) also increases patient satisfaction (Clucas & St Claire, 2010).

Additionally, the medical personnel's knowledge as evaluated by patients in the context of answering their medical-related questions also accelerates patient satisfaction (Chen et al., 2020; Clucas & St Claire, 2010). Lastly, it is very important for patient satisfaction to occur, that the medical personnel transmit trust and confidence (Birkhäuer et al., 2017; Pellegrini, 2017), and the feeling that the patient gets that he/she is safe when receiving medical care from the medical personnel (Zulkarnain & Winardi, 2020). All these issues mentioned reveal their significance for patient satisfaction and can, as pointed out, only indirectly be compared since they did not deal with generational cohorts. The statement with the lowest satisfaction rating was "I feel safe in receiving medical care from the medical personnel." Even though it has the lowest rating, patients, in general, are satisfied (MS = 4.28; 56.6% were at least satisfied). This outcome can be justified if an in-depth investigation occurs. First of all, there has been an extensive brain drain of medical personnel due to the economic crisis, which significantly impacted healthcare provision. Second, the age of doctors and their position, if they are permanent doctors or are interns, are an issue that reflects on their knowledge, patient trust, and perception of their safety. This research did not investigate medical personnel's age in order to reveal if this is the case, nor did it explore the specific working status of the medical personnel.

As to generational cohort differences, as previously stated, only one research paper was found, i.e., Farooq et al. (2020), in their study, found that the older generational cohorts were more satisfied than the younger ones, which is partially in line with our findings since they measured patient satisfaction from surgery. Also, Farooq et al. (2020) used older cohorts than this study.

Based on the results and taken to account that the youngest generational cohort (generation Z) is the most dissatisfied one, but simultaneously is the future of each country, marketing communication and new technology should be adopted. This generation is technological savvy (Williams & Page, 2011) and uses their trusted community and the Internet for seeking information, which is pointed out by Chung et al. (2010), who consider that younger people are expected to see online communities as beneficial.

Furthermore, Sun and Zhang (2006) state that young people perceive that new technology is valuable and functional. As such, it could affect their adoption of telemedicine and mobile health (m-health). For so, telemedicine and m-health can be adopted by the specific hospital, which would easily be approved by the young generational cohort as well as people living in remote areas. If this is adopted, the hospital can communicate these innovations through social media and specifically through Facebook and Instagram, which have the highest percentage of use in Greece.

28.6 Conclusions and Limitations

This study presented research exploring three-generation patient satisfaction from medical personnel using a case study, the General Hospital of Kavala, Greece. It also explores generational differences based on their satisfaction. The aim and objectives of the study were completed through an online quantitative research, including three generational cohorts (X, Y, and Z). Based on the results and the differences derived, the hospital managers should employ high-tech healthcare techniques such as telemedicine or m-medicine to gain high patient satisfaction from the technological-savvy generation. Also, it is imperative to implement communication techniques for people to gain awareness of these methods used, as well as to communicate its mission and the work that is provided by its medical personnel.

This study has several restrictions that could lead to future research and possibly validate the findings of the current one. This study incorporated only one hospital, the General Hospital of Kavala, which does not generalize results. Additionally, it focused on a public hospital, which operates differently from a private one. Moreover, it addressed eight statements referring exclusively to the medical personnel, and for so, there could be additional items that should have been included.

Despite the fact that this study has the beforementioned limitations, it continues to be very important since it offers hospital managers as well as government officials with inpatient evidence about medical staff satisfaction of different generational cohorts and, therefore, may aid in any future improvements and reforms on the part of the hospital administration.

References

Abd Manaf, N. H., & Nooi, P. S. (2007). Patient satisfaction as an indicator of service quality in Malaysian public hospitals. *Asian Journal on Quality, 8*(3), 113–122.

Baker, R., Mainous Iii, A. G., Gray, D. P., & Love, M. M. (2003). Exploration of the relationship between continuity, trust in regular doctors and patient satisfaction with consultations with family doctors. *Scandinavian Journal of Primary Health Care, 21*(1), 27–32.

Batbaatar, E., Dorjdagva, J., Luvsannyam, A., Savino, M. M., & Amenta, P. (2017). Determinants of patient satisfaction: A systematic review. *Perspectives in Public Health, 137*(2), 89–101. https://doi.org/10.1177/1757913916634136

Berkowitz, E. N., & Schewe, C. D. (2011). Generational cohorts hold the key to understanding patients and health care providers: Coming-of-age experiences influence health care behaviors for a lifetime. *Health Marketing Quarterly, 28*(2), 190–204.

Birkhäuer, J., Gaab, J., Kossowsky, J., Hasler, S., Krummenacher, P., Werner, C., & Gerger, H. (2017). Trust in the health care professional and health outcome: A meta-analysis. *PLoS One, 12*(2), e0170988.

Bjertnaes, O. A., Sjetne, I. S., & Iversen, H. H. (2012). Overall patient satisfaction with hospitals: Effects of patient-reported experiences and fulfilment of expectations. *BMJ Quality and Safety, 21*(1), 39–46.

Chen, S., Guo, X., Wu, T., & Ju, X. (2020). Exploring the online doctor-patient interaction on patient satisfaction based on text mining and empirical analysis. *Information Processing & Management, 57*(5), 102253.

Chung, J. E., Park, N., Wang, H., Fulk, J., & McLaughlin, M. (2010). Age differences in perceptions of online community participation among non-users: An extension of the technology acceptance model. *Computers in Human Behavior, 26*(6), 1674–1684.

Cleary, P. D., & McNeil, B. J. (1988). Patient satisfaction as an indicator of quality care. *Inquiry*, 25–36. https://www.jstor.org/stable/29771928

Clucas, C., & St Claire, L. (2010). The effect of feeling respected and the patient role on patient outcomes. *Applied Psychology. Health and Well-Being, 2*(3), 298–322. https://doi.org/10.1111/j.1758-0854.2010.01036.x

Cohen, G. (1996). Age and health status in a patient satisfaction survey. *Social Science & Medicine, 42*(7), 1085–1093.

Committee on Quality of Health Care in America; Institute of Medicine. (2001). *Crossing the quality chasm: A new health system for the 21st century*. National Academy Press. Chapter 1. Available from http://www.nap.edu/catalog/10027/crossing-the-quality-chasm-a-new-health-system-for-the

Crow, H., Gage, H., Hampson, S., Hart, J., Kimber, A., Storey, L., & Thomas, H. (2002). Measurement of satisfaction with health care: Implications for practice from a systematic review of the literature. *Health Technology Assessment, 6*(32) https://uhra.herts.ac.uk/bitstream/handle/2299/1073/102382.pdf

DeBehnke, D., & Decker, M. C. (2002). The effects of a physician-nurse patient care team on patient satisfaction in an academic ED. *The American Journal of Emergency Medicine, 20*(4), 267–270.

Dries, N., Pepermans, R., & De Kerpel, E. (2008). Exploring four generations' beliefs about career: Is "satisfied" the new "successful"? *Journal of Managerial Psychology, 3*(8), 907–928.

Drossman, D. A., Palsson, O., Stein, E., Ruddy, J., & Lennon, A. M. O. B. (2021). What elements in the physician-patient relationship (PPR) contribute to patient satisfaction: Development of a short form PPRS-Patient Version (PPRS-Patient SF) Questionnaire. *Neurogastroenterology and Motility*, e14191. (early view).

Farooq, H., Deckard, E. R., Ziemba-Davis, M., Madsen, A., & Meneghini, R. M. (2020). Predictors of patient satisfaction following primary total knee arthroplasty: Re-sults from a traditional statistical model and a machine learning algorithm. *The Journal of Arthroplasty, 35*(11), 3123–3130.

Garg, R., Shen, C., Sambamoorthi, N., Kelly, K., & Sambamoorthi, U. (2016). Type of multimorbidity and patient-doctor communication and trust among elderly Medicare beneficiaries. *International Journal of Family Medicine*. Article ID 8747891, 13 pages. https://downloads.hindawi.com/archive/2016/8747891.pdf

Ghuloum, S., Bener, A., & Burgut, F. (2010). Ethnic differences in satisfaction with mental health services among psychiatry patients. *The Open Psychiatry Journal, 4*(1), 19–24.

Gronroos, C. (1988). Service quality: The six criteria of good perceived service. *Review of Business, 9*(3), 10–13.

Hisel, M. E. (2017). Exploring generational differences of level of work engagement among veteran, baby boomer, generation X, and millennial nursing cohorts (Doctoral dissertation, Grand Canyon University). https://www.proquest.com/openview/227709e911152c5059fa5f975043e9e1/1?pq-origsite=gscholar&cbl=18750&diss=y

Hitawala, A., Flores, M., Alomari, M., Kumar, S., Padbidri, V., Muthukuru, S., ... Michael, M. (2020). Improving physician-patient and physician-nurse communication and overall satisfaction rates: A quality improvement project. *Cureus, 12*(4), e7776.

Jackson, K., Drew, K., & Shaw, J. (2016). Y doesn't Gen Y like 2 w8? *The Australian Journal of Advanced Nursing, 33*(3), 29.

Jalil, A., Zakar, R., Zakar, M. Z., & Fischer, F. (2017). Patient satisfaction with doctor-patient interactions: A mixed methods study among diabetes mellitus patients in Pakistan. *BMC Health Services Research, 17*(1), 1–13.

Johansson, P., Oleni, M., & Fridlund, B. (2002). Patient satisfaction with nursing care in the context of health care: A literature study. *Scandinavian Journal of Caring Sciences, 16*(4), 337–344.

Kamenidou, I. E., Stavrianea, A., & Bara, E. Z. (2020). Generational differences toward organic food behavior: Insights from five generational cohorts. *Sustainability, 12*(6), 2299.

Keith, A. (2021). The influences of generational membership and practice environment on nurse manager job satisfaction. Electronic Theses and Dissertations, 2020-.516. https://stars.library.ucf.edu/etd2020/516/

Kentikelenis, A., & Papanicolas, I. (2011). Economic crisis, austerity and the Greek public health system. *The European Journal of Public Health, 22*(1), 4–5. https://doi.org/10.1093/eurpub/ckr190

Kim-Soon, N., Abdulmaged, A. I., Mostafa, S. A., Mohammed, M. A., Musbah, F. A., Ali, R. R., & Geman, O. (2021). A framework for analyzing the relationships between cancer patient satisfaction, nurse care, patient attitude, and nurse attitude in healthcare systems. *Journal of Ambient Intelligence and Humanized Computing*, 1–18.

Kramer, L. W. (2010). Generational diversity. *Dimensions of Critical Care Nursing, 29*(3), 125–128.

Kupperschmidt, B. R. (2000). Multigeneration employees: Strategies for effective management. *The Health Care Manager, 19*(1), 65–76.

Lee, Y., & Kasper, J. D. (1999). Age differences in ratings of medical care among older adults living in the community. *Aging Clinical and Experimental Research, 11*(1), 12–20.

Lehmann, F., Fontaine, D., Bourque, A., & Côté, L. (1988). Measurement of patient satisfaction: The Smith-Falvo patient-doctor interaction scale. *Canadian Family Physician, 34*, 2641–2645.

Lotfi, M., Zamanzadeh, V., Valizadeh, L., & Khajehgoodari, M. (2019). Assessment of nurse–patient communication and patient satisfaction from nursing care. *Nursing Open, 6*(3), 1189–1196.

Lyu, H., Wick, E. C., Housman, M., Freischlag, J. A., & Makary, M. A. (2013). Patient satisfaction as a possible indicator of quality surgical care. *JAMA Surgery, 148*(4), 362–367.

Marley, K. A., Collier, D. A., & Meyer Goldstein, S. (2004). The role of clinical and process quality in achieving patient satisfaction in hospitals. *Decision Sciences, 35*(3), 349–369.

Mayer, T. A., Cates, R. J., Mastorovich, M. J., & Royalty, D. L. (1998). Emergency department patient satisfaction: Customer service training improves patient satisfaction and ratings of physician and nurse skill/practitioner response. *Journal of Healthcare Management, 43*(5), 427.

Meredith, G. E., Schewe, C. D., & Karlovich, J. (2002). *Defining markets, defining moments: America's 7 generational cohorts, their shared experiences, and why businesses should care*. Wiley.

Merkouris, A., Papathanassoglou, E. D., & Lemonidou, C. (2004). Evaluation of patient satisfaction with nursing care: Quantitative or qualitative approach? *International Journal of Nursing Studies, 41*(4), 355–367.

Mitropoulos, P., Vasileiou, K., & Mitropoulos, I. (2018). Understanding quality and satisfaction in public hospital services: A nationwide inpatient survey in Greece. *Journal of Retailing and Consumer Services, 40*, 270–275.

Mpouzika, M. D., Mpouzika, E., & Papathanassoglou, E. (2018). The effect of the Greek financial crisis on the operation of public intensive care units. *Connect: The World of Critical Care Nursing, 12*(2), 48–51. https://doi.org/10.1891/1748-6254.12.2.48

Noor Hazilah, A. M., & Phang, S. N. (2009). Patient satisfaction as an indicator of service quality in Malaysian public hospitals. *The Asian Journal of Quality, 10*(1), 77–87.

Onyechi, N., & Babalola, Y. (2020). Doctor-patient communication: Perception of doctors' communication skills among patients in selected hospitals in Ibadan Nigeria. *Journal of Management and Social Sciences, 9*(2), 858–872.

Pellegrini, C. A. (2017). Trust: The keystone of the patient-physician relationship. *Journal of the American College of Surgeons, 224*(2), 95–102.

Prakash, B. (2010). Patient satisfaction. *Journal of Cutaneous and Aesthetic Surgery, 3*(3), 151.

Quintana, J. M., González, N., Bilbao, A., Aizpuru, F., Escobar, A., Esteban, C., ... Thompson, A. (2006). Predictors of patient satisfaction with hospital health care. *BMC Health Services Research, 6*(1), 1–9.

Sacks, G. D., Lawson, E. H., Dawes, A. J., Russell, M. M., Maggard-Gibbons, M., Zingmond, D. S., & Ko, C. Y. (2015). Relationship between hospital performance on a patient satisfaction survey and surgical quality. *JAMA Surgery, 150*(9), 858–864. https://doi.org/10.1001/jamasurg.2015.1108

Satibi, Diah, A. P., Sendy, S., & Putu, D. C. (2015). Factors affecting patient satisfaction in JKN system: Study on patient characteristics, JKN services, and pharmacy services. *Indonesian Journal of Pharmacy/Majalah Farmasi Indonesia, 26*(4), 233–240.

Shah, A. M., Yan, X., Tariq, S., & Ali, M. (2021). What patients like or dislike in physicians: Analyzing drivers of patient satisfaction and dissatisfaction using a digital topic modeling approach. *Information Processing & Management, 58*(3), 102516.

Sitzia, J., & Wood, N. (1997). Patient satisfaction: A review of issues and concepts. *Social Science & Medicine, 45*(12), 1829–1843. https://doi.org/10.1016/S0277-9536(97)00128-7

Sun, H., & Zhang, P. (2006). The role of moderating factors in user technology acceptance. *International Journal of Human-Computer Studies, 64*(2), 53–78.

Teutsch, C. (2003). Patient–doctor communication. *Medical Clinics of North America, 87*(5), 1115–1145. https://doi.org/10.1016/s0025-7125(03)00066-x

Tsai, T. C., Orav, E. J., & Jha, A. K. (2015). Patient satisfaction and quality of surgical care in US hospitals. *Annals of Surgery, 261*(1), 2–8. https://doi.org/10.1097/SLA.0000000000000765

US Office of Disease Prevention and Health Promotion. (2020). About Health Care Quality. https://health.gov/our-work/health-care-quality/about-health-care-quality

van Osch, M., van Dulmen, S., van Vliet, L., & Bensing, J. (2017). Specifying the effects of physician's communication on patients' outcomes: A randomised controlled trial. *Patient Education and Counseling, 100*(8), 1482–1489. https://doi.org/10.1016/j.pec.2017.03.009

Vogus, T. J., & McClelland, L. E. (2016). When the customer is the patient: Lessons from healthcare research on patient satisfaction and service quality ratings. *Human Resource Management Review, 26*(1), 37–49.

Wakim, N. (2014). Occupational stressors, stress perception levels, and coping styles of medical surgical RNs: A generational perspective. *The Journal of Nursing Administration| JONA, 44*(12), 632–639.

Williams, K. C., & Page, R. A. (2011). Marketing to the generations. *Journal of Behavioral Studies in Business, 3*, 37–53.

Williams, S., Weinman, J., & Dale, J. (1998). Doctor–patient communication and patient satisfaction: A review. *Family Practice, 15*(5), 480–492. https://doi.org/10.1093/fampra/15.5.480

Wright, E. B., Holcombe, C., & Salmon, P. (2004). Doctors' communication of trust, care and respect in breast cancer: Qualitative study. *British Medical Journal, 328*, 864–869.

Young, G. J., Meterko, M., & Desai, K. R. (2000). Patient satisfaction with hospital care: Effects of demographic and institutional characteristics. *Medical Care, 38*(3), 325–334. https://www.jstor.org/stable/3767196

Yusuf, A., Kusumaningrum, T., & Suhron, M. (2020). Nurses communication model to increase patient satisfaction: Evidence from Indonesia hospital. *Indian Journal of Public Health Research & Development, 11*(4), 841–845.

Zineldin, M. (2006). The quality of health care and patient satisfaction. *International Journal of Health Care Quality Assurance, 19*(1), 60–92.

Zulkarnain, M. R., & Winardi, B. (2020). Analysis of maternity patients' satisfactory to maternity room installment in Dr. Soetomo Hospital Surabaya. *Majalah Obstetri & Ginekologi, 28*(1), 3–15.

Chapter 29
An Engineering Financial Analysis of a Research Sea Platform

Fotis Mavromatakis, Ioannis Katsigiannis, Hara Haritaki, Kyriakos Siderakis, and Giorgos Stavrakakis

Abstract This chapter presents a financial and operational analysis of a sea platform that is used for research purposes and is planned to be located north of Heraklion city, Crete Island. The operation of the platform will be based mainly on renewable energy technologies, such as photovoltaics and wind turbines. In order to utilize properly the renewable energy potential, the sea platform will also include batteries and diesel generator, whereas the option of grid interconnection with Crete Island is also examined, in order to purchase and sell its electricity when needed. The alternative options that are examined include different battery autonomy, various funding options, and sensitivity analysis of the results regarding different lending parameters. The financial indices used in this analysis are: net present value, internal rate of return, discounted payback period, and weighted average cost of capital. The results show that the operation of the sea platform can be economically viable if annual incomes of a few hundred thousand euros exist, provided by platforms research activities.

Keywords Renewable energy sources · Photovoltaic technology · Wind power · Energy storage · Net present value · Internal rate of return · Payback period

---

F. Mavromatakis · I. Katsigiannis · K. Siderakis
School of Engineering, Department of Electrical and Computer Engineering, Hellenic Mediterranean University, Estavromenos, Crete, Greece
e-mail: fotis@hmu.gr; katsigiannis@hmu.gr; ksiderakis@hmu.gr

H. Haritaki (✉)
School of Management and Economics Sciences, Department of Accounting and Finance, Hellenic Mediterranean University, Estavromenos, Crete, Greece
e-mail: haritaki@hmu.gr

G. Stavrakakis
School of Electrical and Computer Engineering, Technical University of Crete, Chania, Crete, Greece
e-mail: gstavrakakis@isc.tuc.gr

N. Tsounis, A. Vlachvei (eds.), *Advances in Quantitative Economic Research*, Springer Proceedings in Business and Economics,
https://doi.org/10.1007/978-3-030-98179-2_29

29.1 Introduction

The Hellenic Mediterranean University participates in the project "Centre for the study and sustainable exploitation of Marine Biological Resources (CMBR)," which is financed by the General Secretariat for Research and Innovation under the Action "Reinforcement of the Research and Innovation Infrastructure." The specific action is funded by the Operational Programme "Competitiveness, Entrepreneurship and Innovation" (NSRF 2014–2020) and co-financed by Greece and the European Union (European Regional Development Fund). This project aims to design a sea-based platform that will offer unique opportunities to scientists to perform high value research. Specifically, researchers from academia may design and execute large-scale interdisciplinary projects, create networks with the national and international research community, and exploit the capabilities of platform's infrastructure (aquaculture, mesocosm experimental facilities, bioactivity control, etc.). Furthermore, users from the industry may explore processes related to natural products of high commercial value, develop new cultivates like micro algae, and also explore new technologies for energy production and offshore aquaculture.

This sea platform is scheduled to operating near the island of Dia, which is north of Heraklion city, Crete, Greece. In this location, significant amounts of solar and wind energy can be reached. This characteristic makes an ideal option the installation of renewable energy technologies, such as photovoltaics (PVs) and wind turbines (WTs) (Mavromatakis et al., 2016; Manwell, 2004). However, these technologies are dependent on a resource that is unpredictable and depend on weather and climatic changes, so they face increased problems related to their operation and control. The basic ways to solve these problems are: (1) the parallel operation of renewable energy technologies with battery storage combined with the installation of a diesel generator and (2) the interconnection of the system with the power grid, which may increase significantly the cost of the system (Katsigiannis et al., 2016).

A large number of case studies can be found in bibliography, which optimize the operation of a renewable-based autonomous power system that can be located either in a small remote island (He et al., 2021) or in the mainland (Katsigiannis et al., 2012). The operation of sea platforms shares many characteristics with the above-mentioned systems. The majority of existing sea platforms is used for oil and gas extraction (Tiong et al., 2015; Edalat et al., 2019), so the concept of a sea platform operation for scientific purposes is novel and it has never implemented before in Greece.

This chapter is organized as follows: Sect. 29.2 presents the basic characteristics of sea platform system regarding renewable energy potential, load demand, and system components properties. Additionally, this section describes and analyzes the financial metrics that are used for the evaluation of the system. Section 29.3 presents the results for a variety of scenarios including autonomous and interconnected operation of the sea platform, different options regarding autonomy from batteries (half a day, 1 or 2 days), various funding options, as well as sensitivity analysis of the results regarding different lending parameters. Section 29.4 concludes the paper.

29.2 The Power System of the Sea-Based Laboratory

The sea platform is expected to offer research capabilities in the fields of aqua culture, biology, energy production as well as a test bed for relevant activities. The scenario we examine here refers to an average consumption of 679 kWh per day all year round and a peak power demand of 229 kW. In order to match these requirements, we adopt a power system consisting of a photovoltaic system, wind generator, energy storage, and a generator for safety reasons. The annual average solar potential is 5.1 kWh/m^2 per day at the horizontal level and an average wind speed of 5.5 m/sec. A range of peak power for every component is assumed, while storage is managed to provide 12 hours, 24 hours, and 48 hours of autonomy. It is noted here that the larger the storage, the larger the the corresponding costs and the weight. The weight is in important parameter due to the installation on a sea platform. At this stage, we adopt proven lithium-ion technology batteries despite their higher costs since these offer substantially improved properties over, e.g., sulfur acid-based batteries. Furthermore, the field of energy storage is evolving rapidly, and it is expected that both the weight and the cost per nominal stored kWh will drop significantly. We run all possible combinations based on the data listed in Table 29.1, but subsequently, we select those matching criteria related to the photovoltaic and inverter power ratio and the contribution of renewable energy sources to the energy production. We also assume that in the case of no sun and no wind conditions, appropriate load shedding will take place to avoid oversizing the generator. In the first series of scenarios, we consider the platform as an off grid system where the energy is produced by its power systems, part of it is stored, and a significant part of the energy is serving the loads. However, there is also the case where energy is produced but the load requirements are low, and thus, this energy cannot be exploited. This is a known and common characteristic of off grid systems. The excess energy could be used to produce hydrogen, but at this stage, we do not consider this case due to the limitations imposed by the platform design. The second series of scenarios involves the possibility of a grid connection to the main land of Crete allowing energy exchange. For safety reasons, the generator remains

Table 29.1 Basic data of the power system

Photovoltaic power (kW)	60	70	80	100
Inverter power (kW)	60	70	80	100
Wind power (kW)	50	100	150	
Generator power[a] (kW)	80	100	120	
Battery storage (kWh)	430	860	1720	

[a] Assume $cos(\phi) = 1$

part of the platform's energy system. In this case, energy can be drawn from the main grid at a certain price, and energy can be sold back to the grid at another lower price. In both series of scenarios, we explore the case where interested parties (e.g., organizations, users from academia, industry) may make use of the infrastructure under an agreement including economic terms.

29.2.1 Financial Evaluation Model

The financial evaluation of all candidate feasible solutions is implemented according to the following criteria: (1) weighted average cost of capital (*WACC*), (2) net present value (*NPV*), (3) internal rate of return (*IRR*), and (4) discounted payback period (Sullivan et al., 2020). All of these criteria are based on the principle of time value of money, which explains how time affects the monetary worth of things (Brigham and Ehrhardt, 2002). In this section, the calculation of *NPV* will be analytically presented for all components of the sea platform that are needed for electricity generation and storage, because it includes information that is based on their operational characteristics.

The first parameter of *NPV* is the component Net Present Cost (*NPC*), which is expressed in Euros (€) and is calculated as follows (Farret and Simoes, 2006):

$$NPC = \frac{C_{ann,tot}}{CRF(i, R_{proj})}, \tag{29.1}$$

where $C_{ann,tt}$ is the total annualized cost (€/yr), *CRF* is the capital recovery factor, *i* is the discount rate, and R_{proj} is the project lifetime (yr). $CRF(i,R_{proj})$ is the ratio used to calculate the present value of an annuity and is calculated from

$$CRF(i, R_{proj}) = \frac{i \cdot (1+i)^{R_{proj}}}{(1+i)^{R_{proj}} - 1}. \tag{29.2}$$

The total annualized cost $C_{ann,tot}$ is the sum of the annualized costs of system's components. For each one of them, the annualized cost is equal to the sum of its annualized capital cost $C_{a,cap}$, its annualized replacement cost $C_{a,rep}$, its annual operation and maintenance (O&M) cost, and its annual fuel cost (for the case of diesel generator). $C_{a,cap}$ is calculated from

$$C_{a,cap} = C_{cap} \cdot CRF(i, R_{proj}), \tag{29.3}$$

where C_{cap} is the initial capital cost of the component. $C_{a,rep}$ is calculated from

$$C_{a,rep} = C_{rep} \cdot f_{rep} \cdot SFF(i, R_{comp}) - S \cdot SFF(i, R_{proj}). \tag{29.4}$$

In the above equation, C_{rep} is the replacement cost of the component, f_{rep} is a factor arising because the component lifetime can be different from the project lifetime, *SFF* is the sinking fund factor, and R_{comp} is the component's lifetime (yr). The factor f_{rep} is given by

$$f_{rep} = \begin{pmatrix} CRF(i, R_{proj})/CRF(i, R_{rep}) & R_{rep} > 0 \\ 0 & R_{rep} = 0 \\ . & \end{pmatrix} \tag{29.5}$$

R_{rep} represents the replacement cost duration and is given by

$$R_{rep} = R_{comp} \cdot INT\left(\frac{R_{proj}}{R_{comp}}\right), \tag{29.6}$$

where *INT* is the integer function, returning the integer portion of a real value. Variable *SFF* in $C_{a,rep}$ equation represents the sinking fund factor, which is a ratio used to calculate the future value of a series of equal annual cash flows. *SFF* is calculated from

$$SFF(i, R) = \frac{i}{(1+i)^R - 1}, \tag{29.7}$$

where i is the discount rate and R is the lifetime of component/project. Variable S in $C_{a,rep}$ equation represents the salvage value of the component at the end of the project lifetime. It is assumed that component's salvage value is proportional to its remaining life. Therefore, S is given by

$$S = C_{rep} \cdot \frac{R_{rem}}{R_{comp}}, \tag{29.8}$$

where R_{rem} represents the remaining life of the component at the end of the project lifetime and is given by

$$R_{rem} = R_{comp} - (R_{proj} - R_{rep}). \tag{29.9}$$

After having calculated the *NPC* of sea platform's electrical components, the corresponding *NPV* can be estimated according to the following formula:

$$NPV = C_{an,rev} \cdot PVIFA(i, R_{proj}) - NPC - C_{an,loan} \cdot PVIFA(i_{loan}, R_{loan}), \tag{29.10}$$

where $C_{an,rev}$ are the after-tax annual revenues of the sea platform operation, $C_{an,loan}$ is the annual loan repayment, i_{loan} is the lending rate, R_{loan} is loan duration, and *PVIFA* is the present value interest factor of an annuity, which estimates the present value of a series of future annuities. For a specific lifetime R and discount rate i, *PVIFA* is calculated as follows:

Table 29.2 Component characteristics

Component	Capital cost	O&M costs	Lifetime
Wind generator	3,000 €/kW	90 €/(kW yr)	20 yr
Photovoltaic system	600 €/kW	40 €/(kW· yr)	25 yr
Battery	650 €/kWh	0 €	
Converter	600 €/kW	20 €/(kW· yr)	15 yr
Diesel generator	400 €/kW	0.010€/(kW· hr)	15,000 hr

$$PVIFA(i, R) = \frac{1 - (1 + i)^{-R}}{i}. \tag{29.11}$$

29.2.2 *Financial Assumptions*

The project lifetime R_{proj} is assumed to be 20 years, and the annual discount rate i is set equal to project's *WACC*, which is a widely accepted criterion in after-tax engineering economy studies Sullivan et al. (2020). Lending rates are taken as 4, 5, 6, 7%, while the fractional equity capital for the specific costs is initially assumed to be 70%. The costs and lifetime characteristics of the sea platform system components are summarized in Table 29.2. For each one of them, the replacement cost is considered to be equal to the capital cost. The fuel cost of diesel generator is taken as 1.4 €/L.

Several activities are foreseen to be carried out at the sea platform. Users from academia, other organizations, industry interested in the relevant scientific fields may conduct research or test new products or technologies. In this respect, formal agreements will regulate the details of the actions to take place, the use of the infrastructure, and the corresponding costs. In this chapter, we assume an annual fixed amount of money as the income from such activities. Since the sea platform is currently at the design phase, we consider the financial data of the energy system alone. We examine the following, economic related, cases (a) include initial costs (purchase and installation) of the energy system as would be the case for a private company, (b) reduce initial costs from the calculations in the case where the sea platform will be partially financed by other sources, such as national and EU funds. In both cases, we include replacement as well as operation and maintenance costs.

29.3 Results

As already mentioned (Sect. 29.2), we select scenarios which satisfy specific criteria as the following: the inverter power lies within 15% of the photovoltaic peak power, the renewable energy fraction is higher than 85% and make use of the least, possible quantity of conventional fuel. A sufficient number of scenarios is

Table 29.3 Typical power system combinations

Scenarios	1	2	3	4	5	6	7
Photovoltaic power (kW)	100	80	100	100	80	100	100
Inverter power (kW)	100	80	100	100	80	100	100
Wind power (kW)	150	150	150	100	150	150	100
Generator power (kW)	80	80	80	100	80	80	80
Fuel mass (tn/yr)	5.5	6.7	8.2	9.3	9.5	9.8	13.8
Renewable fraction (%)	97	96	95	93	94	94	89
Battery autonomy (hours)	48	48	24	48	24	12	12
Energy production (MWh/yr)	600	570	610	460	580	610	480

fulfilling these constraints. Here we summarize just a few possible scenarios with their major characteristics (Table 29.3). A common property of these scenarios is that the energy produced is substantially higher than the consumption. This is explained by the following facts: (a) available space is limited and thus, the installed photovoltaic power is limited although the solar potential in Crete is very high, (b) the wind potential is low and consequently, a wind generator will be operating at its lower areas of the power curve producing less power than its nominal value, (c) load peaks must be matched by the instantaneous power, and (d) the excess energy cannot be stored because this would require very large battery banks leading to increased overall weight and cost. Excess energy could be used to produce hydrogen, which could be stored and then, it could be used for energy production when needed. However, due to space limitations and safety reasons, we do not consider this possibility. If we try to reduce the peak power of the installed power systems, we find, on average, that the total electrical production is reduced by 12%, the renewable energy production is reduced by 14%, the fuel requirements of the generator increase by 25%, while the life time of the generator reduces by 20%. These differences may seem small but if we consider specific scenarios, the difference are actually much larger.

The second series of scenarios examines the case where the power system is connected to the main grid and is capable of injecting energy to the grid as well as retrieving energy from the grid. The generator is still considered part of the platform's power system for safety reasons. It will contribute to the energy requirements of the platform whenever the main grid is not available (power failures or scheduled maintenance). In those exceptional cases, the loads of the platform will be arranged in way, so that the generator will provide sufficient power to match them. In the first economic scenario, it is assumed that all initial costs (100%) are handled by the organization. The second scenario assumes that 75% of all initial costs are supplied by an external source and thus, the organization should handle the remaining 25% (e.g. funding through national or EU projects). Here we present preliminary results from scenarios 2 and 6 as listed in Table 29.3 where the platform is considered an autonomous energy source. It is evident that the only case for a positive cash flow is by hosting activities of users from other

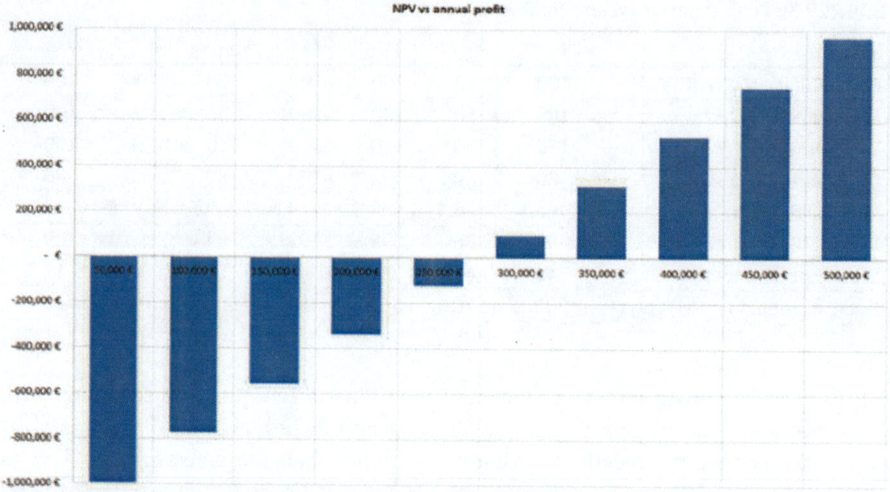

Fig. 29.1 The net present value in Scenario No 2 remains negative up to almost an annual income of 300 K€ per year. The income that may arise from activities that involve third parties is the only source of cash flow that could make such a facility profitable under economic terms

Table 29.4 Grid connected power system

Scenarios	1	2	3	4
Photovoltaic power (kW)	100	80	70	80
Inverter power (kW)	100	70	70	70
Wind power (kW)	150	150	150	150
Generator power (kW)	80	80	80	80
Energy to the grid (MWh)	361	338	327	319
Energy from the grid (MWh)	38	43	45	26
Renewable fraction (%)	94	93	92	96
Battery autonomy (hours)	12	12	12	48
Energy production (MWh/yr)	576	547	533	547

organizations. Figure 29.1 shows how the *NPV* develops, for a 20 year period, as a function of this income in Scenario No 2. It is clear that the *NPV* becomes positive, approximately, above 300 K€. For simplicity reasons we have assumed a fixed amount of income from such activities. Table 29.4 summarizes four possible scenarios for grid-connected power systems. We also explore the variation of the *NPV* as a function of lending rate and loan ratio, which is the ratio of loan over the sum of the loan and the equity of the project (Table 29.5). Scenario No 6 in Table 29.3 refers to a system of higher power but of lower energy storage. The current costs of batteries are quite high and take up a large share of the initial cost, although, their cost is expected to drop in the near future. More specifically, mid cost projections for utility scale lithium bsttery costs show reduction of initial cost up to 50% at the end of this decade (Cole and Frazier, 2019). Figure 29.2 shows that in this case the *NPV* becomes positive for an annual income of around 200 K€, while Table 29.6 summarizes basic economic parameters of this scenario.The discounted

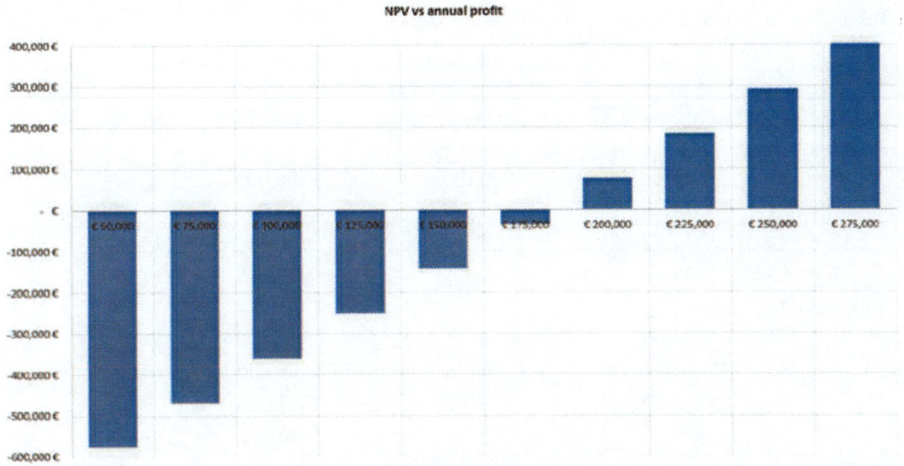

Fig. 29.2 The net present value in Scenario No 6 remains negative up to almost an annual income of 200 K€ per year. The significant reduction in the income required to present a positive *NPV* is due to lower storage capacity and corresponding costs

Table 29.5 Scenario 2: Financial data without funding

	WACC (%)	Discounted Payback Period (yr)	*NPV* (€)	*IRR* (%)
Lending rate (%)				
4	11.08	15.3	98,000	12.15
5	11.29	16.0	78,000	12.14
6	11.52	16.9	56,000	12.14
7	11.75	17.9	34,000	12.13
Loan ratio (%)				
30	11.08	15.3	98,000	12.15
55	8.24	15.7	141,000	9.57
65	7.10	15.9	162,000	8.53
75	5.96	16.1	186,000	7.50

'Data based on a fixed annual income of 300 K€

payback period is 13–16 years for the parameters range assumed in this work which is more than 50% of the project's duration. At the same time, *IRR* is higher than *WACC* by 1 to 2% in absolute units. Figure 29.3 shows the change in *NPV* of Scenario No 6 for different values of the annual income as a function of the reduction in the cost of the storage media. The 0% case corresponds to the currently assumed cost of storage reported in Table 29.1. The above data show that it will be difficult to set up the energy system of the platform without additional financial support. It is clear that the whole platform constitutes a unique pilot project and its cost is expected to be much higher than the cost of the energy generation facilities.

Table 29.6 Scenario 6: Financial data without funding

	WACC (%)	Discounted Payback Period (yr)	*NPV* (€)	*IRR* (%)
Lending rate (%)				
4	11.08	13.0	75,000	12.67
5	11.29	13.5	65,000	12.67
6	11.52	14.7	53,000	12.66
7	11.75	16.1	42,000	12.66
Loan ratio (%)				
30	11.08	13.0	75,000	12.67
55	8.24	13.8	99,000	10.06
65	7.10	14.5	111,000	9.02
75	5.96	15.4	125,000	7.97

Data based on a fixed annual income of 200 K€

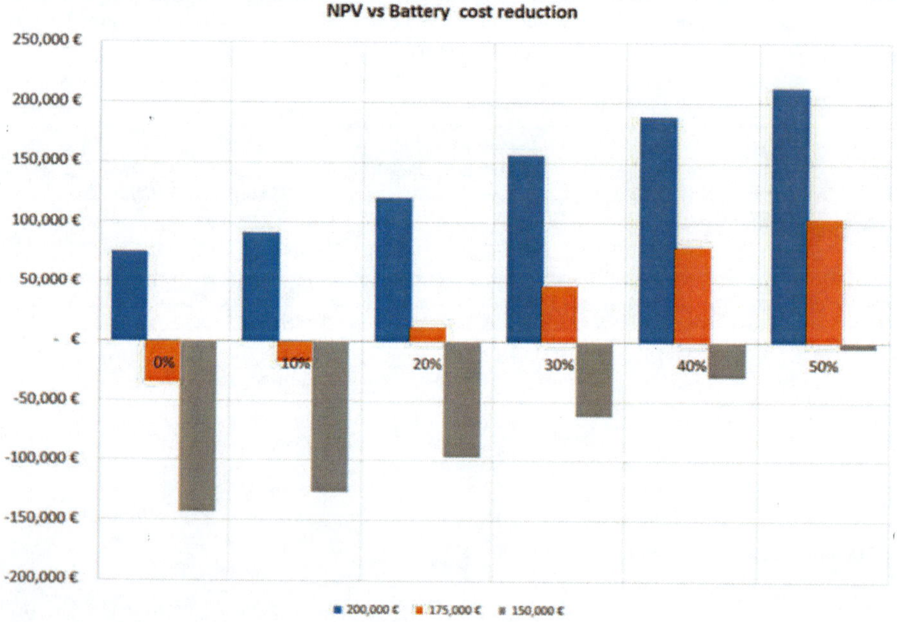

Fig. 29.3 The *NPV* in Scenario No 6 changes as a function of the drop in the prices of storage. Adopted values change from 0% (current pricing) up to a drop of 50%. Two more different levels of income are adopted apart from the current one of 200 K€

However, given technological advances and the need to explore fields like aqua culture or energy generation at the sea we expect the cost to drop significantly as more and more facilities are installed. Here, we also explore the case where the initial energy costs are funded by 75% from other funds (e.g. national or EU

Table 29.7 Scenario 2: Financial data with a 75% funding

	WACC (%)	Discounted Payback Period (yr)	*NPV* (€)	*IRR* (%)
Lending rate (%)				
4	11.08	9.8	70,000	14.22
5	11.29	9.9	65,000	14.22
6	11.52	10.2	59,000	14.21
7	11.75	10.6	53,000	14.21
Loan ratio (%)				
30	11.08	9.8	70,000	14.22
55	8.24	10.6	85,000	11.58
65	7.10	11.1	92,000	10.51
75	5.96	11.5	100,000	9.43

Data based on a fixed annual income of 125 K€

Table 29.8 Scenario 6: Financial data with a 75% funding

	WACC (%)	Discounted Payback Period (yr)	*NPV* (€)	*IRR* (%)
Lending rate (%)				
4	11.08	7.6	58,000	16.51
5	11.29	7.7	55,000	16.51
6	11.52	7.8	51,000	16.51
7	11.75	7.9	49,000	16.51
Loan ratio (%)				
30	11.08	7.6	58,000	16.51
55	8.24	7.9	64,000	13.67
65	7.10	8.1	66,000	12.49
75	5.96	8.4	69,000	11.29

Data based on a fixed annual income of 110 K€

funds) and the organization running the platform should deal with just the rest of the 25%. Table 29.7 summarizes the results following a 75% funding from any other source without additional costs. It must be made clear that the *NPV* becomes positive, approximately, at an annual income of 125,000€ compared to 300,000€ of the same scenario (Table 29.5) without any funding. The difference between *IRR* and *WACC* increases and ranges from 2.5% to 3.5%. Table 29.8 lists the financial data of scenario 6 when available funding amounts to 75% of the initial costs. The discounted payback period now drops to 7–8 years, while the difference between the internal rate of return and the weighted average cost of capital increases to around 5%. As we have already mentioned, the improved results in this scenario are directly related to the lower storage capacity which greatly reduces the initial installation costs. Finally, we present results in the case where the platform is connected to the

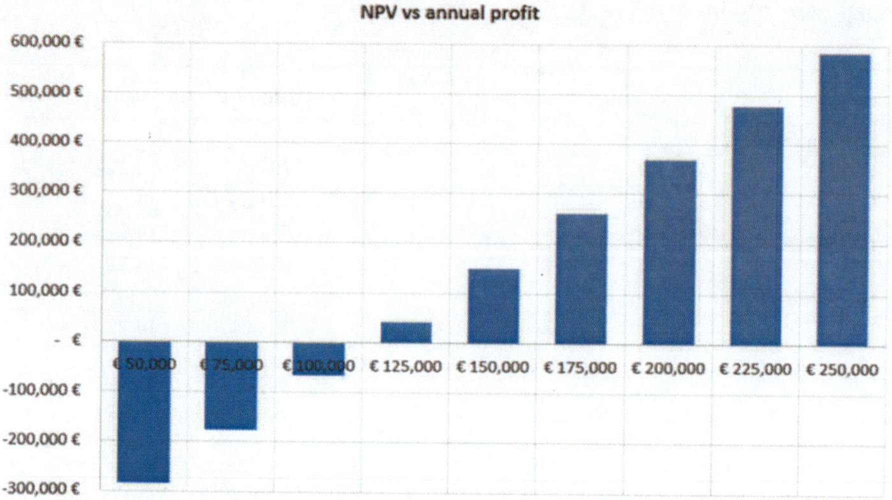

Fig. 29.4 The variation of the *NPV*, of the system described as Scenario 1 in the grid connected case, is shown as a function of the income from activities of third party users. The typical income resulting from the selling of the excess energy to the grid is around 22 K€

main grid and is able to retrieve energy from the grid at a given price as well as sell back excess energy to the grid at a lower price. Consequently, an additional source of positive cash flow is introduced. The actual income depends on the installed power for the given loads but a typical value is approximately 22,000€ per year. The backup generator is still considered as part of the energy system for safety reasons, although its use is quite limited in the presence of grid power. Table 29.4 lists a small number of possible scenarios but several more are available. Despite the high initial costs, the income from selling energy and making available the platform's capabilities to third parties allow for discounted payback times in the range of 10–12 years, *NPV* in the range of 114 K to 152 K€, while the difference between *IRR* and *WACC* varies from 2.5% to 3.7%. Keeping all other parameters fixed, we performed a sensitivity analysis on the dependence of the *NPV* upon the value of the unit energy sold to the grid (€/kWh). In general, sensitivity analysis helps to identify those investment plans for which small variations in parameters lead to large fluctuations in the degree of return on investment (Jain et al., 2011). A 14% reduction in the unit energy results in a 8% increase in the discounted payback time and a 17% decrease in the actual net present value. Figure 29.4 shows the variation of the net present value of Scenario 1 (Table 29.4) as a function of the income from activities of third party users and the injection of the excess energy to the grid. The reduction in the minimum annual cash flow seen in this figure is mainly due to the reduction of the energy storage costs specific to this scenario and the additional income related to the excess energy sold to the grid.

29.4 Conclusions

In this work we have explored basic parameters that affect the economics of the installation and operation of a sea platform for a period of 20 years. It is assumed that the platform is operated by an organization ruled as a Société Anonyme under the Greek law. Storage costs are the highest among the various components of the energy system. Their effect upon the economics of the project is very strong. A drop in the prices will affect profoundly the net present cost. In the case of an electrically autonomous platform the minimum annual income to have a small but positive *NPV* is of the order of a few hundred thousand euros. It is mainly a technical and safety matter to decide whether an energy autonomy of half a day, a day or 2 days is required. A 2 day autonomy requires 300% additional storage costs with respect to the minimum storage allowing for half a day of operations. The discounted payback period is well above 10 years in the off grid case, while the internal rate of return is 12%. If the platform is grid connected then the costs are also reduced mainly due to reduction in energy storage and to a lesser extend, due to income from the energy sold to the grid. The main source of incoming cash flow is the use of the platform by third parties.

Acknowledgments This work received financial support from the project "Centre for the study and sustainable exploitation of Marine Biological Resources (CMBR)" financed by the General Secretariat for Research and Innovation under the Action "Reinforcement of the Research and Innovation Infrastructure", funded by the Operational Programme "Competitiveness, Entrepreneurship and Innovation" (NSRF 2014–2020) and co-financed by Greece and the European Union (European Regional Development Fund).

References

Brigham E. F., & Ehrhardt M. C. (2002). *Financial management: Theory and practice* (10th ed.). San Diego: Harcourt, Inc.

Cole, W., & Frazier, A. W. (2019). *Cost projections for utility-scale battery storage*. New York: National Renewable Energy Laboratory. Technical Report NREL/TP-6A20-73222 7.

Edalat, P., Salehi, G. R., & Shahriari, S. (2019). Techno-economic assessment power supply in offshore platform by renewable and conventional source. *Petroleum Business Review, 3*(3), 1–14.

Farret, F. A., & Simoes, M. G. (2006). *Integration of alternative sources of energy*. London: Wiley.

He, W., Tao, L., Han, L., Sun, Y., Campana, P. E., & Yan, J. (2021). Optimal analysis of a hybrid renewable power system for a remote Island. *Renewable Energy, 179*, 96–104. https://doi.org/10.1016/j.renene.2021.07.034.

Jain, R., Grabner, M., & Onukwugha, E. (2011). Sensitivity analysis in cost-effectiveness studies. *Pharmacoeconomics, 29*(4), 297–314.

Katsigiannis, Y. A., Georgilakis, P. S., & Karapidakis, E. S. (2012). Hybrid simulated annealing tabu search method for optimal sizing of autonomous power systems with renewables. *IEEE Transactions on Sustainable Energy, 3*(3), 330–338.

Katsigiannis, Y. A., Kanellos, F. D., & Papaefthimiou, S. (2016). A software tool for capacity optimization of hybrid power systems including renewable energy technologies based on a hybrid genetic algorithm? tabu search optimization methodology. *Energy Systems, 7*(1), 33–48.

Manwell J. F. (2004). Hybrid Energy Systems. *Encyclopedia of Energy, 3*(2004), 215–229. https://doi.org/10.1016/B0-12-176480-X/00360-0.

Mavromatakis F., Vignola F., & Fraghiadakis Y. (2016). Photovoltaic power model, Engineering. *Technology & Applied Science Research, 6*(5), 1115.

Sullivan, W. G., Wicks, E. M., & Koelling, C. P. (2020). *Engineering economy* (17th ed.). Pearson, UK: Global Edition.

Tiong, Y. K., Zahari, M. A., Wong, S. F., & Dol, S. S. (2015). The feasibility of wind and solar energy application for oil and gas offshore platform. In IOP Conference Series: Materials Science and Engineering (Vol. 78, No. 1, p. 012042). New York: IOP Publishing.

Chapter 30
Identification of Environmental and Economic Indicators: A Case Study of EU Countries with the Use of the DEA Method

Dimitrios Niklis, Pavlos Stamatiou, and Chaido Dritsaki

Abstract Economic development is crucial for all the authorities, in both local and national level. On the other hand, environmental protection is an issue of increased interest, especially in the last decades. There is a debate how likely is to achieve sustained growth without deterioration of the environment. The aim of this study is to identify the relationship between environmental and economic indicators with a use of a non-parametric method, namely, DEA (Data Envelopment Analysis), among EU-27 countries. For this purpose, two environmental indicators (greenhouse gas emissions per capita and greenhouse gas emissions in ESD sectors) will be used as inputs and two economic indicators (GDP per capita and real expenditure per capita) as outputs by following input-oriented approach. Moreover, to identify the balance between efficient and non-efficient countries and the potential improvements of environmental inputs without changing the economic outputs. Dataset consists of EU countries, for the period 2015–2019. The results would lead to strategies and policies that can be proposed and help governments or policymakers to obtain more sound decisions, guided by economic as well as environmental development.

Keywords Economic growth · Environmental indicators · DEA method · EU countries

JEL Classification C14, C54, C67, D57, Q51

D. Niklis (✉) · C. Dritsaki
Department of Accounting and Finance, University of Western Macedonia, Kozani, Greece
e-mail: dniklis@uowm.gr; cdritsaki@uowm.gr

P. Stamatiou
Department of Applied Informatics, University of Macedonia, Thessaloniki, Greece
e-mail: stamatiou@uom.edu.gr

N. Tsounis, A. Vlachvei (eds.), *Advances in Quantitative Economic Research*,
Springer Proceedings in Business and Economics,
https://doi.org/10.1007/978-3-030-98179-2_30

30.1 Introduction

Economic development is of upmost importance for all authorities, in both local and national level. On the other hand, environmental protection is an issue of increased interest, especially in the last decades. There is a broad discussion how likely it is to achieve sustained growth without deterioration of the environment. For example, are variables as income, capital, consumption, and GDP growth affected in case we take measures for environment protection? According to the environmental Kuznets curve, there is a negative relationship between economic growth and environmental development. Other studies focus on economic growth and energy consumption, and finally the third category examines the dynamic interdependence between economic growth, energy consumption, and environmental pollutants. The aim of this study is the identification of countries that can be used as good examples to other EU countries, when there is a decrease in environmental inputs, together with the changes that non-efficient countries should follow in order to become efficient. The dataset consists of selected EU countries. The result would act as guideline to policymakers in order to achieve an optimum between economic growth and environmental protection. The rest of the chapter is organized as follows: Section 30.2 describes literature review, while Sect. 30.3 focuses on methodological background. In Sect. 30.4, the data are presented together with the empirical results, and in Sect. 30.5, conclusions are given.

30.2 Literature Review

There are generally three categories of studies on examining the relationship between environmental and economic development. The first category focuses on the relationship between environmental pollutants and economic growth and explores the validity of the Kuznets (1955) environmental curve. The second category explores the relationship between economic growth and energy consumption, and finally the third category examines the dynamic interdependence between economic growth, energy consumption, and environmental pollutants.

Regarding the first category, some indicative studies are the following. Stern et al. (1996) critically examine the concept of the environmental Kuznets curve (EKC). They state that there is an inverted U shape relation between environmental degradation and income per capita, so that, eventually, growth reduces the environmental impact of economic activity. Akbostancı et al. (2009) examine the relationship between income and environmental quality for Turkey. The authors investigate the relationship between the CO_2 emissions and per capita income by using a time series model and in another stage the relationship between income and air pollution. Their results are opposite of the environmental Kuznets curve hypothesis. López-Menéndez et al. (2014) investigate the relationship between CO_2 emissions and GPD on a EU-27 panel. Their results provide evidence about the significant impacts of renewable energies on CO_2 emissions, suggesting the existence of an extended EKC. Congregado et al. (2016) analyze the existence of the environmental Kuznets curve using quarterly data from 1973 to 2015. Their results depict the existence of the environmental Kuznets curve (EKC) in the USA only when they allow for structural breaks. Churchill et al. (2018) test the environmental Kuznets curve (EKC) hypothesis for OECD nations. Authors find support for the EKC hypothesis for the panel as a whole. Moreover, country-specific results provide mixed support for the EKC hypothesis. Kaika and Zervas (2013) present basic critiques on the EKC concept. They come up to result that the original Kuznets theory, which laid the groundwork for the EKC concept, does not seem to solve income inequality problems.

The second category explores the relationship between economic growth and energy consumption. Xepapadeas (2005) states that environmental pollution is introduced both as a joint product and as a source of disutility in growth models. Many questions are posed regarding the relationship between growth and pollution (e.g., how are the levels, the paths, or the growth rates of crucial variables such as capital, income, consumption, or environmental pollution affected if we take into account the environment?). Moreover, how can total factor productivity be decomposed into its sources once we account for the fact that an economy produces not only the desired output but also undesirable output (environmental pollution)? Saidi and Hamami (2015) attempt to investigate the impact of economic growth and CO_2 emissions on energy consumption for a global panel of 58 countries using dynamic panel data model estimated by means of the generalized method of moments (GMM) for the period 1990–2012. The empirical evidence indicates significant positive impact of CO_2 emissions on energy consumption. There is also a positive impact between economic growth and energy consumption. Arbex and Perobelli (2010) propose a methodology that integrates a growth model with an input-output model to analyze the impacts of economic growth on the consumption of energy. The authors apply this methodology to study the energy consumption of eleven economic sectors in Brazil. They conduct experiments involving changes in technological progress growth rate, extraction, and regeneration rates of both renewable and nonrenewable resources and population growth to analyze the impact of changes in the parameters of the model on the sectoral output growth rate and, consequently, on the consumption of energy in each economic sector. Waheed et al. (2019) examine the survey of earlier literature that deals with economic growth, energy consumption, and carbon emission, both single-country studies as well as multi-county studies that cover the period until 2019. The results of their study are controversial for developed and developing countries. For developed countries, there is dependence among economic growth, energy consumption, and carbon emission, whereas for developing countries, the above dependence is not clear and significant.

The third category refers to the dynamic interdependence between economic growth, energy consumption, and environmental pollutants. Menyah and Wolde-Rufael (2010) examine the long-running causal relationship between economic growth, pollutant emissions, and energy consumption for South Africa for the period 1965–2006. They found a short-running as well as a long-running relationship among the variables with a positive and a statistically significant relationship between pollutant emissions and economic growth. The econometric evidence suggests that South Africa has to sacrifice economic growth or reduce its energy consumption per unit of output or both in order to reduce pollutant emissions. Ang (2008) examines the long-running relationship between output, pollutant emissions, and energy consumption in Malaysia during the period 1971–1999. The results indicate that pollution and energy use are positively related to output in the long run. Ozturk and Acaravci (2010) examine the long-running causal relationship issues between economic growth, carbon emissions, energy consumption, and employment ratio in Turkey by using autoregressive distributed lag bounds testing approach of co-integration. Their results indicate that energy conservation policies, such as rationing energy consumption and controlling carbon dioxide emissions, are likely to have no adverse effect on the real output growth of Turkey. Omri, 2013, examines the nexus between CO_2 emissions, energy consumption, and economic growth using simultaneous-equations models with panel data of 14 MENA countries over the period 1990–2011. Their empirical results show that there exists a bidirectional causal relationship between energy consumption and economic growth. The study suggests that environmental and energy policies should recognize the differences in the nexus between energy consumption and economic growth in order to maintain sustainable economic growth in the MENA region. Soytas and Sari (2009) investigate the long-running Granger causality relationship between economic growth, carbon dioxide emissions, and energy consumption in Turkey, controlling for gross fixed capital formation and labor. The most interesting result is that carbon emissions seem to Granger cause energy consumption, but the reverse is not true.

30.3 Methodology

30.3.1 Data Envelopment Analysis

The non-parametric DEA method was first introduced by Charmes, Cooper, and Rhodes (1978), known as the "CCR model." Few years later, Banker et al. (1984) introduced the "BCC model." Lozano-Vivas and Pastor (2002) evaluate the technical efficiency of the banking industry of different countries through the DEA model. They consider "n" basic inputs and "m" basic outputs for each bank and apply the BCC input-oriented model. The mathematical formulation of this model is:

$$\min_{\theta,\tau} \ \theta \text{ subject to } Y_\tau \geq Y_0$$

$$\tau \geq 0_n \ \ X_\tau \leq \theta X_0 \tag{(30.1)}$$

$$e^T \tau = 1$$

$$\tau \geq 0_n$$

where:

Y is the matrix of output vectors
X is the matrix of input vectors
(X0, Y0) is the unit being rated
eT denotes a row-vector of 1's
τ is the vector of intensity variables and
θ is the so-called efficiency score—a quantity between 0 and 1

If $\theta < 1$, a proportional decrease of all inputs is required in order to achieve the efficient frontier. This decrease is given by (1-θ) X_0, which means that the projected unit given by (θ X_0, Y_0) is efficient in Debreu-Farrell terminology or weakly efficient in DEA terminology. No further radial decrease of all inputs is possible given the current amount of outputs. It is possible that, in order for DEA to be efficient, further individual reduction in some inputs and/or increase in some outputs is required. To evaluate these mixed inefficiencies, we need to resort to a more complex BCC model, in which a non-Archimedean element in the target function is multiplied by the sum of the dummy variables. However, if the dummy variables are not important, we do not need to enhance this model further. The model considered in this first example is called the "basic" model.

Nowadays, this method has become widely known in measuring efficiency of different sectors or countries. Based on Fethi and Pasiouras (2010), "DEA is a mathematical programming technique for the development of production frontiers and the measurement of efficiency relative to these frontiers." The obvious advantages of DEA approach are that:

- It implies successfully with small samples.
- It does not require undertaking any assumptions concerning the distribution of inefficiency.
- It does not require a specific type of data in order to determine the most efficient countries.

However, in the same research, it is mentioned that there are two well-known limitations of this method. "The first is that DEA assumes data to be free of measurement error and the second one, that it is sensitive to outliers."

In this approach, the units (countries in our case) which convert the inputs to outputs are referred to as decision-making units (DMUs). In addition, the DEA efficiency value for a decision-making unit (DMU) is not determined by a specific level, but it is determined in comparison to the other DMUs of the examined sample. That characteristic differentiates the DEA approach from the parametric approaches, which require particular functional form (Casu and Molyneux, 2003). According to Pasiouras (2008), DEA can estimate the technical efficiency of each DMU under the hypothesis of constant returns to scale (CRS) or variable returns to scale (VRS).

Every unit in the effective frontier is considered to be efficient, which means that the examined unit uses the suitable sources and it is not possible to increase the production of certain goods, while its efficiency is equal to 1. On the other hand, the units below the efficient frontier line present efficiency less than 1. Consequently, each unit can receive an efficiency score ranging from 0 to 1. (Wozniewska, 2015). So, "each country with higher score indicates a more efficient country, relatively to other countries in the sample."

DEA model can be either input-oriented model or output-oriented model. The input-oriented technical efficiency measures address the question "By how much can input quantities be proportionally reduced without changing the output quantities produced?", and the output-oriented measures of technical efficiency address the question "By how much can output quantities be proportionally expanded without altering the input quantities used?" (Coelli et al., 2005) In our case, input-oriented model was chosen under the hypothesis of constant returns to scale (CRS). The reason is that it could be easier to minimize inputs (environmental factors here) than maximize the outputs (economic factors), which are more difficult to control.

30.4 Data and Empirical Results

30.4.1 Data

In this study, we measure the efficiency of European countries over the period 2015–2019, though the method of Data Envelopment Analysis (DEA). The data obtained from Eurostat database. For the efficiency analysis, the software "Frontier Analyst Professional" was used.

Table 30.1 depicts the inputs and outputs used for this analysis. As it is earlier mentioned, inputs refer to environmental indicators, whereas outputs refer to economic indicators. Table 30.2 shows the countries that consist the data sample.

Input 1 is greenhouse gas emissions per capita. The indicator measures total national emissions of the so-called Kyoto basket of greenhouse gases, including carbon dioxide (CO_2), methane (CH_4), nitrous oxide (N_2O), and the so-called F-gases (hydrofluorocarbons, perfluorocarbons, nitrogen trifluoride (NF_3), and sulfur hexafluoride (SF_6)). Using each gas' individual global warming potential (GWP), they are being integrated into a single indicator expressed in units of CO_2 equivalents. Emissions data are submitted annually by the EU Member States as part of the reporting under the United Nations Framework Convention on Climate

Table 30.1 Inputs/outputs

Inputs	Outputs
1. Greenhouse gas emissions per capita	1. GDP per capita
2. Greenhouse gas emissions in ESD sectors	2. Real expenditure per capita

Table 30.2 Sample data: average values (2015–2019)

Countries	Greenhouse per capita	Greenhouse gas emissions in ESD	GDP per capita	Real expenditure per capita
Austria	9.372	88.88	128.4	360608.6
Belgium	10.732	91.2	119	433374.6
Bulgaria	8.36	118.38	50.2	114154.4
Croatia	5.944	93.4	62.6	82951.2
Cyprus	11.348	99.92	88	24366.8
Czechia	12.228	102.14	90.6	308167.6
Denmark	8.8	81.8	129	237888.2
Estonia	14.452	115.04	80.2	33772
Finland	10.52	88.72	111.2	196008.6
France	7.004	87.44	105.4	2264991
Germany	10.848	93.7	123.4	3259853
Greece	8.86	71.9	67.4	232642.2
Hungary	6.612	88.86	70.4	221271.8
Ireland	13.4	93.74	185.2	285669.8
Italy	7.304	81.62	97.2	1878321
Latvia	5.912	106.64	67.2	41869.8
Lithuania	7.316	105.56	78.8	71993.4
Luxembourg	20.216	87.06	265.4	50665.8
Malta	5.224	122.32	99.2	15030.8
Netherlands	11.668	78.98	129.6	710523.6
Poland	10.708	113	70.4	866296.6
Portugal	6.872	84.16	78.2	258020
Romania	5.948	99.7	63	396011.4
Slovakia	7.644	90.48	72.6	126157.6
Slovenia	8.464	92.42	85.8	56835.8
Spain	7.408	84.7	91.6	1369567
Sweden	5.46	74.04	122.8	394605.2

Change (UNFCCC). The average population of the reference year (calculated as the arithmetic mean of the population on the first of January of 2 consecutive years) is used as denominator (per capita).

Input 2 is greenhouse gas emissions in ESD sectors. The indicator calculation is based on the emissions covered under the Effort Sharing Decision (406/2009/EC). The Effort Sharing Decision sets national annual binding targets for emissions not covered under the EU emission trading scheme (ETS). The ESD emissions are calculated by deducting ETS-verified emissions, CO_2 emissions from domestic aviation, and NF3 emissions from national total emissions.

Output 1 is GDP per capita. Gross domestic product (GDP) is a measure for the economic activity. It is defined as the value of all goods and services produced less the value of any goods or services used in their creation. The volume index of GDP per capita in Purchasing Power Standards (PPS) is expressed in relation to the European Union average set to equal 100. If the index of a country is higher than 100, this country's level of GDP per head is higher than the EU average and vice versa. Basic figures are expressed in PPS, i.e., a common currency that eliminates the differences in price levels between countries allowing meaningful volume comparisons of GDP between countries.

Output 2 is real expenditure per capita. Purchasing power parities (PPPs) are indicators of price level differences across countries. PPPs tell us how many currency units a given quantity of goods and services costs in different countries. PPPs can thus be used as currency conversion rates to convert expenditures expressed in national currencies into an artificial common currency (the purchasing power standard, PPS), eliminating the effect of price-level differences across countries.

The main use of PPPs is to convert national accounts aggregates, like the gross domestic product (GDP) of different countries, into comparable volume aggregates. Applying nominal exchange rates in this process would overestimate the GDP of countries with high price levels relative to countries with low price levels. The use of PPPs ensures that the GDP of all countries is valued at a uniform price level and thus reflects only differences in the actual volume of the economy.

PPPs are also applied in analyses of relative price levels across countries. For this purpose, the PPPs are divided by the current nominal exchange rate to obtain a price level index (PLI) which expresses the price level of a given country relative to another, or relative to a group of countries like the EU Member States.

30.4.2 Results

In this subsection, the results of the analysis are presented. Table 30.3 depicts the efficiency levels of the countries. If a country has a value of 100, this means that it is efficient and does not have to change the parameters (in this case, no change should be done in input parameters). If the value is less than 100, this means that there should be a reduction in input parameters in order to be able to achieve efficient levels (value of 100). From Table 30.3, we can observe variations in efficiency scores from 25% to 100%. This indicates that there are differences among the countries, regarding the examined parameters. Another interesting element is the small efficiency change per country through the examined period.

Table 30.4 shows the number of countries that are efficient through the examined period. Additionally, the number of countries that are non-efficient (efficiency levels less than 50%). We can observe that there is a stable number in the first category (four countries per year, namely, France, Germany, Luxemburg, and Sweden). On the other hand, countries with efficiency level less than 50% come from eastern and northern Europe. This could be an indicator of how environment-friendly and concerned are some countries in contrast with other ones. Another reason could be the integration of more environment laws in the efficient countries. Moreover, it could be the level of economy, whereas efficient countries are the ones with more advances economies.

Table 30.3 Efficiency scores 2015–2019 (in %)

	Year					
Country	2015	2016	2017	2018	2019	Average
Austria	77.9	76.08	73.85	76.77	73.92	75.70
Belgium	66.64	65.72	67.75	65.64	65.6	66.27
Bulgaria	25.05	27.14	25.91	27.65	28.59	26.87
Croatia	45.71	48.35	46.56	48.81	47.34	47.35
Cyprus	42.91	43.81	43.87	46.19	44.04	44.16
Czechia	43.85	43.04	44.9	46.52	44.04	44.47
Denmark	78.9	77.06	81.86	81.19	84.6	80.72
Estonia	32.28	30.84	31.37	33.53	37.9	33.18
Finland	61.02	58.21	62.54	61.62	63.4	61.36
France	100	100	100	100	100	100.00
Germany	100	100	100	100	100	100.00
Greece	47	46.56	45.55	45.81	47.1	46.40
Hungary	49.14	49.56	46.83	47.69	47.61	48.17
Ireland	85.41	81.22	87.6	89.78	94.02	87.61
Italy	90.78	93.02	94.81	89	88.08	91.14
Latvia	51.29	53.23	52.08	50.9	49.43	51.39
Lithuania	46.68	48.52	48.13	49.93	49.01	48.45
Luxembourg	100	100	100	100	100	100.00
Malta	74.66	90.1	85.06	86.54	82.45	83.76
Netherlands	76.86	74.38	76.92	79.95	79.98	77.62
Poland	43.24	41.36	40.2	39.55	41.72	41.21
Portugal	54.49	54.67	54.18	54.44	53.88	54.33
Romania	46.42	51.27	52.34	51.71	54.95	51.34
Slovakia	50.41	47.84	44.44	44.34	42.78	45.96
Slovenia	50.53	49.25	51.72	51.96	53.62	51.42
Spain	77,22	78.79	79.16	75.32	76.09	77.32
Sweden	100	100	100	100	100	100.00

Table 30.4 Efficient countries per year

	2015	2016	2017	2018	2019
Number of countries	27	27	27	27	27
Efficient (100%)	4	4	4	4	4
Non-efficient (<50%)	10	11	10	10	11

Figure 30.1 presents the average efficiency results per year for the examined countries. As it is earlier mentioned in Table 30.5, there is a significant number of countries with low efficiency scores. From the below figure, we can observe a light improvement, which is positive, but cannot lead to safe remarks. Moreover, on average, the efficiency results are far from 100%, which means that inefficient countries should make significant changes in input parameters in order to become efficient.

Fig. 30.1 Average efficiency scores per year

Table 30.5 Potential improvements per year (%)

Potential improvements (%)	2015	2016	2017	2018	2019
Greenhouse gas emissions per capita	−16.52	−16.83	−16.74	−16.55	−15.75
Greenhouse gas emissions in ESD sectors	−15.66	−15.49	−15.58	−15.33	−14.63
GDP per capita	0	0	0	0	0
Real expenditure per capita	67.83	67.68	67.68	68.12	69.62

Table 30.5 depicts the potential improvements that should be done in order for all countries to become efficient. In this analysis, as far as it is input oriented, focus is given in input reduction. For example, in the year 2015, if greenhouse gas emissions per capita decrease by 16.52% and greenhouse gas emissions in ESD sectors decrease by 15.66%, this could cause an improvement by 67.83% in real expenditure per capita and no change in GDP per capita. With a more thorough look in all examined period, the first input (greenhouse gas emissions per capita) should be decreased from 15.75% to 16.83% in order for all countries to become efficient. For second input (greenhouse gas emissions in ESD sectors), changes vary from 14.63% to 15.66%. Another interesting fact is that 2019 is the year with the smaller potential changes. This has to do with the fact that in 2019, higher efficiency levels are met. This is the general frame, as there are variations from one country to another. Regarding outputs, there would be no change in first output (GDP per capita), whereas second output (real expenditure per capita) would be affected significantly around 68%. This is also interesting and maybe further elaborated, as the target in this analysis is the minimization of inputs. If this decrease causes a significant increase in an output, maybe it is a sign that environment protection is positively correlated with economic growth.

30.5 Conclusions

This study provides an approach to modeling country efficiency. It employs the Data Envelopment Analysis (DEA) method on annual data to construct the efficiency frontiers. It examines the performance of EU-27 countries. The examined period is the years 2015–2019. The study uses as inputs (a) the greenhouse gas emissions per capita and (b) greenhouse gas emissions in ESD sectors and as outputs (a) GDP per capita and (b) real expenditure per capita. The data obtained from the Eurostat database, in order to have accurate and easily comparable information. For the efficiency analysis, the software "Frontier Analyst Professional" was used. The aim of this study is to examine if the change in input parameters has an impact on country performance by using the DEA technique. The efficient scores of the DEA analysis, for every examined country in each year, derive from the specific data and are used as inputs and outputs. Therefore, in the case of changing the sample of countries or another parameter, the efficiency level could be changed.

The results show that the DEA efficiency scores and the number of efficient countries are quite stable. Specifically, the same four countries are efficient throughout the examined period, while a significant number of countries (ten or eleven) have efficient levels less than 50%. That is an interesting finding that should be further elaborated. For example, maybe a split in the sample (Western and Eastern countries) could lead to more meaningful results, as these countries have more similarities in both environmental and economic indicators. Moreover, the change or enrichment of the examined parameters (inputs and outputs) could lead to different results.

The rapid evolutions of the last years in the global economy (and the need for economic growth) together with a greater concern for environment lead to the conclusion that analysis of this issue (environment and economy balance) is absolutely essential and difficult for regulators and policymakers. On one hand, we have environment protection (a topic that is critical for all citizens for the existence of humanity) and on the other hand, the economic growth, also important for society to be able to have an accepted level of life. It is important for all countries to take measures and regulations for environment protection, especially in Eastern European countries where efficiency levels are quite low. In those countries, there should be a general campaign to citizens in order to become environment-friendly. Moreover, incentives should be given to businesses in order to keep all standards for environment protection. In that way, more countries could become efficient, and this will contribute to overall economic growth and stability.

References

Akbostancı, E., Türüt-Aşık, S., & Tunç, G. İ. (2009). The relationship between income and environment in Turkey: is there an environmental Kuznets curve? *Energy Policy, 37*(3), 861–867.

Ang, J. B. (2008). Economic development, pollutant emissions and energy consumption in Malaysia. *Journal of Policy Modeling, 30*(2), 271–278.

Arbex, M., & Perobelli, F. S. (2010). Solow meets Leontief: Economic growth and energy consumption. *Energy Economics, 32*(1), 43–53.

Banker, R. D., Charnes, A., & Cooper, W. W. (1984). Some models for estimating technical and scale inefficiencies in data envelopment analysis. *Management Science, 30*(9), 1078–1092.

Casu, B., & Molyneux, P. (2003). A comparative study of efficiency in European banking. *Applied Economics, 35*(17), 1865–1876.

Charmes, A., Cooper, W. W., & Rhodes, E. (1978). Measuring the efficiency of decision making units. *European Journal of Operational Research, 63*, 429–444.

Churchill, S. A., Inekwe, J., Ivanovski, K., & Smyth, R. (2018). The environmental Kuznets curve in the OECD: 1870–2014. *Energy Economics, 75*, 389–399.

Coelli, T. J., Rao, D. S. P., O'Donnell, C. J., & Battese, G. E. (2005). An introduction to efficiency and productivity analysis. Springer Science & Business Media.

Congregado, E., Feria-Gallardo, J., Golpe, A. A., & Iglesias, J. (2016). The environmental Kuznets curve and CO_2 emissions in the USA. *Environmental Science and Pollution Research, 23*(18), 18407–18420.

Fethi, M. D., & Pasiouras, F. (2010). Assessing bank efficiency and performance with operational research and artificial intelligence techniques: A survey. *European Journal of Operational Research, 204*(2), 189–198.

Kaika, D., & Zervas, E. (2013). The environmental Kuznets curve (EKC) theory. Part B: Critical issues. *Energy Policy, 62*, 1403–1411.

López-Menéndez, A. J., Pérez, R., & Moreno, B. (2014). Environmental costs and renewable energy: Re-visiting the Environmental Kuznets Curve. *Journal of Environmental Management, 145*, 368–373.

Lozano-Vivas, A., Pastor, J. T., & Pastor, J. M. (2002). An efficiency comparison of European banking systems operating under different environmental conditions. *Journal of Productivity Analysis, 18*(1), 59–77.

Menyah, K., & Wolde-Rufael, Y. (2010). Energy consumption, pollutant emissions and economic growth in South Africa. *Energy Economics, 32*(6), 1374–1382.

Omri, A. (2013). CO2 emissions, energy consumption and economic growth nexus in MENA countries: Evidence from simultaneous equations models. *Energy Economics, 40*, 657–664.

Ozturk, I., & Acaravci, A. (2010). CO_2 emissions, energy consumption and economic growth in Turkey. *Renewable and Sustainable Energy Reviews, 14*(9), 3220–3225.

Pasiouras, F. (2008). Estimating the technical and scale efficiency of Greek commercial banks: the impact of credit risk, off-balance sheet activities, and international operations. *Research in International Business and Finance, 22*(3), 301–318.

Saidi, K., & Hammami, S. (2015). The impact of CO_2 emissions and economic growth on energy consumption in 58 countries. *Energy Reports, 1*, 62–70.

Soytas, U., & Sari, R. (2009). Energy consumption, economic growth, and carbon emissions: challenges faced by an EU candidate member. *Ecological Economics, 68*(6), 1667–1675.

Stern, D. I., Common, M. S., & Barbier, E. B. (1996). Economic growth and environmental degradation: the environmental Kuznets curve and sustainable development. *World Development, 24*(7), 1151–1160.

Waheed, R., Sarwar, S., & Wei, C. (2019). The survey of economic growth, energy consumption and carbon emission. *Energy Reports, 5*, 1103–1115.

Wozniewska, G. (2015). Methods of measuring the efficiency of commercial banks: an example of Polish banks. *Ekonomika, 85*, 81–91.

Xepapadeas, A. (2005). Economic growth and the environment. *Handbook of Environmental Economics, 3*, 1219–1271.

Chapter 31
Application of Methods of Comprehensive Evaluation of a Company in the Conditions of the Visegrad Group's Countries

Tomáš Pražák

Abstract For groups of users of business information, from owners through potential investors, management, or employees, it is important to find out the financial situation of the company and its future development. The financial health of a company can be determined in many ways, most commonly through financial analysis indicators. The aim of this chapter is to evaluate the applicability of methods for comprehensive assessment of the financial situation of Visegrad Group companies. The basis for the evaluation of the applicability of the methods of enterprise assessment will be the analysis of the applicability of bankruptcy models. The results of the bankruptcy models will be compared with the real numbers of bankruptcies of enterprises. The sensitivity analysis showed that the IN05 index was the most suitable for practical use on businesses in the Visegrad countries.

Keywords Financial distress · Bankruptcy models · Sensitivity analysis · Visegrad Group countries

31.1 Introduction

The financial situation of a company can be determined in many ways, most often through indicators of financial analysis. A company's financial distress arises in situations where the company has serious payment difficulties that cannot be resolved other than by a radical change in its activities or structure. The criterion for financial distress is usually defined not only by a capital restructuring of the firm or large-scale redundancies but also by the failure to pay dividends on preference shares, default on bond obligations, accumulated losses of the firm, or repeated

T. Pražák (✉)
School of Business Administration in Karviná, Department of Business Economics and Management, Silesian University in Opava, Karviná, Czechia
e-mail: prazak@opf.slu.cz

N. Tsounis, A. Vlachvei (eds.), *Advances in Quantitative Economic Research*, Springer Proceedings in Business and Economics,
https://doi.org/10.1007/978-3-030-98179-2_31

negative cash flow. According to Baker and Powell (2005), financial distress occurs in a firm when it has difficulty meeting contractual obligations associated with debt financing. In this case, there is a general weakening of the firm's financial condition caused by enormous debt, with bankruptcy being the extreme case of financial distress.

However, the process of financial analysis, as a basic tool for assessing the financial health of a company, requires relatively lengthy and demanding procedures, and ultimately, its results may not provide sufficient information.

Bankruptcy models are an appropriate way of interpreting the results obtained in a comprehensive and comprehensible way to assess the health of a company. They are able to predict with a certain degree of probability the future financial performance assessment of an undertaking. In particular, they can determine whether or not an enterprise is heading toward a zone of potential financial distress.

Bankruptcy models (the Altman bankruptcy model, the Taffler bankruptcy model, or the IN credibility indices) are used as early warning systems of potential financial distress, capturing events typical of a firm's future bankruptcy. Through bankruptcy or creditworthiness prediction models, it is possible to model whether a firm will meet its obligations in a timely and sufficient manner. The formulas and financial ratios developed are used to predict whether a company is heading toward bankruptcy or is thriving. The bankruptcy prediction can be determined several years before the actual bankruptcy.

The aim of this paper is to evaluate the applicability of methods for comprehensive assessment of the financial situation of Visegrad Group companies. The basis for the evaluation of the applicability of the methods of enterprise assessment will be the analysis of the applicability of bankruptcy models. The results of the bankruptcy models will be compared with the real numbers of bankruptcies of enterprises. The expected finding will be whether the models fulfill the basic function of predicting potential financial distress of enterprises. The period under study is the period between 2008 and 2016 based on data availability. The mutual relationship will be analyzed at the national level for the Visegrad Group countries (Czechia, Hungary, Poland, Slovakia).

The remainder of this chapter is organized as follows. The relevant literature is reviewed in Sect. 31.2. The data and the methodology used in this chapter are introduced in Sect. 31.3. The results of the empirical estimation are reported in Sect. 31.4. The conclusions and summary of the main findings are contained in the Conclusion part.

31.2 Literature Review

Altman (2006) or Senbet and Wang (2012) have addressed the root causes of corporate financial distress. According to them, the most common reasons for financial distress are insufficient legislation, macroeconomic factors, deregulation in key industries (financial services, aviation, healthcare, energy industry), or growing international competition and globalization. The basic models for predicting financial distress and corporate bankruptcy based on financial ratios are those of Beaver (1966) and Altman (1968). The prediction models are based on the hypothesis that a firm's financial distress can be identified by the values of its financial ratios before it actually manifests itself. The Taffler bankruptcy model (Taffler, 1983) was also developed on this basis. The first step in constructing this model was to calculate more than 80 selected ratios of all industrial firms between 1968 and 1976 and 46 randomly selected solvent industrial firms. The predictive ability of the Taffler model over the years has been confirmed by Agarwal and Taffler (2007).

Given that the paper is focused on the V4 countries, studies will be presented that dealt with the application of bankruptcy models to these countries. Opinions on the applicability of bankruptcy models vary widely. However, a common feature of the monitored studies dealing with the practical application of bankruptcy models is the opinion on the need for their combination.

According to Neumaierová and Neumaier (2005), the specifics of Czech financial statements and the economic situation in the Czech Republic are reflected in the IN credibility index. Similarly to previous bankruptcy models, this index contains an analysis of activity, profitability, debt, and liquidity ratios. Based on these analyses, four variants of the index were sequentially constructed. The IN95 index is a bankruptcy model created from a creditor's perspective, and unlike the Altman model, its indicators do not include the market value of the company. This modification is suitable for conditions of a poorly liquid capital market. In contrast, the IN99 index is a creditworthiness model constructed from the perspective of the owner. This index was constructed by applying a discriminant analysis to revise the weights of the IN95 indicators. These two models were then followed by the so-called comprehensive analysis IN01, which combined the previous two models. Subsequently, in 2005, a modified comprehensive index IN05 was created to assess the financial situation of an enterprise using a single number. According to Neumaierová and Neumaier (2005), the IN05 index is similarly successful in identifying the threat of bankruptcy as the Altman bankruptcy analysis in predicting potential bankruptcy.

The financial situation of firms, especially the prediction of financial distress and bankruptcy, was the subject of a study by Lizal (2012) using the Czech Republic as a case study. In the Czech Republic, the main factors affecting the probability of bankruptcy in the period 1993–1999 were analyzed. The basic bankruptcy models are compared on the basis of neoclassical theory, financial ratios, and corporate governance indicators. It is the evaluation of financial ratios that has proved to be the most appropriate for monitoring corporate activities. Thanks to them, enterprises that were at risk of financial distress during the period under review were identified. The importance of the practical use of bankruptcy models in the Czech Republic is also highlighted by Škerlíková and Rudolfová (2015), where the instability and risk of the overall economic environment in recent years have emphasized the need for accurate tools for predicting bankruptcy and assessing the overall performance of enterprises. In their article, they also draw attention to the threat of late filing for insolvency proceedings.

Karas and Režňáková (2014) and Basovníková et al. (2018) analyzed the practical application of Altman's bankruptcy model in the condition of Czechia. They point out that while the Altman model is suitable for use in predicting potential financial distress, they also recommend monitoring other financial ratios, in particular return on equity. Machek (2014) or Čamská (2016) dealt with the comparison of individual models and their ability to identify a company in financial distress in the Czech Republic. In his article, Machek (2014) analyzed Kralick's Quick test, Taffler's bankruptcy model, IN99 and IN05 indices, and Altman's Z′score in the case of Czech companies from 2007 to 2010. Based on the results of individual models, which predicted the company's financial distress, he found that the most suitable models for the practical use of the prediction of financial distress are Altman's Z′score and the indices IN99 and IN05. On the contrary, Kralick's Quick test is the least suitable. Although Taffler's model was able to draw attention to companies in financial distress, its predictive power was low compared to other bankruptcy models. In her article, Čamská (2016) compared the predictive power of both bankruptcy and creditworthiness models in the manufacturing industry during the global financial crisis. The bankruptcy models that achieved the highest telling values were IN01, IN05, or Altman's Z′score, thus confirming Machek's (2014) conclusions.

Based on previous research in the Slovakian context, Gavurová et al. (2017a) and Gavurová et al. (2017b) established a portfolio of four models (Altman model, Ohlson model, and indices IN01 and IN05), which were validated on a sample of 700 Slovakian firms. They assessed the accuracy of financial distress prediction at three levels. Based on the results, they showed that the most suitable model applicable to the Slovak business environment is the IN05 index. The prediction of financial distress of enterprises in Poland was the goal of Gruszczynski (2014). Based on the results of each model, they concluded that the sudden increase in the ratio of short-term liabilities to total assets should be continuously monitored and thoroughly investigated. The study also confirmed the high predictive ability of bankruptcy models in the short term.

The available research shows that the suitability of applying the bankruptcy models differs in terms of the country where the analyzed firms operate. While in the case of Altman's models and IN indices the opinions on their applicability prevail, the opposite is the case for Taffler's model. In terms of the observed applicability, it will then be possible to recommend an appropriate model. For the preparation of the analysis, the necessity to combine available bankruptcy prediction models when assessing the financial situation of firms, to compare the resulting values of the bankruptcy models with each other, and to focus in particular on the comparison with the actual values of the number of bankrupt firms is taken into consideration.

31.3 Data and Methodology

The first phase of the research involved the creation of a database of corporate data and selected macroeconomic factors of the V4 countries. The corporate data used are taken from the annual reports of companies recorded in the corporate data databases of Bureau van Dijk (BvD) Orbis or Amadeus. For reasons of data availability and to obtain a sufficient time series, both databases were used. Based on the BvD company identification number and by using advanced functions in MS Excel, it was possible to link the two available databases. In the second phase of the research, bankruptcy models were processed using MS Excel, which yielded the results of the assessment of the financial situation of V4 enterprises in the years under study. In the Czech Republic, a total of 3736 enterprises were monitored as part of the analysis. In Hungary, a total of 1502 enterprises are monitored, in Poland a total of 4006 enterprises are monitored, and in Slovakia a total of 985 enterprises are monitored.

The main focus of this study is on models that are able to predict possible financial distress early. As Sedláček (2001) argues, bankruptcy models can be classified as ex ante analyses that point to possible threats to the financial health of firms and can predict the future course of the firm over the next 3–5 years. The basic method for predicting financial distress is the Altman bankruptcy model. Edward I. Altman in 1968 first constructed a model for equity companies traded on capital markets based on multiple discriminant analysis (called the Z′score). For the purpose of predicting financial distress, he selected five indicators with the highest predictive ability from the original 22 financial analysis indicators and assigned weights according to their significance using a computer algorithm. The original Altman's Z′score is expressed according to Altman (2006) as follows:

$$Z'\text{Score} = 0.717X_1 + 0.847X_2 + 3.107X_3 + 0.42X_4 + 0.998X_5 \quad (31.1)$$

where:

X_1 = (current assets – current liabilities)/total assets.
X_2 = retained earnings/total assets.
X_3 = earnings before interest and taxes/total assets.
X_4 = book value of equity/total equity.
X_5 = sales/total assets.

The resulting qualification of the company will be done according to the following:

Z′score > 2.9 enterprise is in a good situation.
1.2 < Z′score < 2.9 gray zone of unresolved results.
Z′score < 1.2 for bankruptcy is very likely.

The other variant of Altman's model is designed to evaluate firms operating in emerging markets (Z//EM Score). For the purpose of constructing the model, X_5

(sales/assets) is abstracted, and the coefficient weights are also adjusted. Due to the reduced number of indicators, the weights are increased compared to previous models, with the weight of net working capital/assets being increased the most. In order to be able to compare the resulting value of the bankruptcy model for companies operating in emerging markets with the US bond rating, a constant of 3.25 was added to the model for non-manufacturing companies. The resulting values of the Z//EM model for assessing the financial health of non-US firms and for emerging markets allow the monitored firms to be assigned an adequate rating that indicates the ability of the entity to meet its obligations in a timely manner. According to Altman (Altman, 2006), the different models are quantifiable as follows:

$$Z''EM = 3.25 + 6.56X_1 + 3.26X_2 + 6.72X_3 + 1.05X_4, \quad (31.2)$$

where:

X_1 = net working capital/assets.
X_2 = retained earnings/assets.
X_3 = EBIT/assets.
X_4 = market value of equity/debt.

Based on the changes in the construction of the model, it was also necessary to change the individual boundaries of the intervals. The boundary points of the intervals in this case are 4.35 and 5.85.

Z//EM > 5.85 enterprise is in a good situation.
4.35 < Z//EM <5.85 gray zone of unresolved results.
Z′score < 4.35 for bankruptcy is very likely.

A reaction to Altman's original bankruptcy model was the creation of the Taffler Index (Taffler, 1983). British economists Taffler and Tisshaw analyzed the financial situation of British companies on more than 80 ratios, from which they selected four key ratios and assigned them specific weights. The Taffler Index is known in two versions: the original and a modified version. The modified version of the model (Tfm) differs from the original by adjusting the last ratio X_4. In the modified version, the X_4 ratio captures the ratio of sales to total assets. The individual weights of the ratios remain unchanged. The modified version no longer considers the existence of a gray zone category, which includes firms that could not be classified as having a low or high probability of failure. The cutoff points in this variant are 0.2 and 0.3. The Taffler model (Tfm) is expressed by the following equation according to Taffler (1983):

$$\text{Tfm} = 0.53X_1 + 0.13X_2 + 0.18X_3 + 0.16X_4 \quad (31.3)$$

where:

X_1 = EBIT/current liabilities.

X_2 = fixed asset additions/depreciation.
X_3 = EBIT/markets.
X_4 = Sales/total assets.

Tfm > 0.3 – Low probability of financial distress.
0.2 < Tfm < 0.3 – gray zone of companies with potential threat of financial distress
Tfm < 0.2 high probability of the upcoming financial distress of the company.

The last methods is modified complex variant IN05. The IN05 index was developed in 2005 as an updated version of IN01. The modified version of IN05 focuses on the prediction of financial distress, but also on the ability to create value for owners:

$$\text{IN05} = 0.13X_1 + 0.04X_2 + 3.97X_3 + 0.21X_4 + 0.09X_5 \quad (31.4)$$

X_1 = total assets/foreign capital.
X_2 = EBIT/interest expenses.
X_3 = EBIT/total assets.
X_4 = sales/total assets.
X_5 = current assets/current liabilities.

The resulting qualification of the company will be done according to the following:

IN05 > 1.6 The company creates added value.
0.9 < IN01 < 1.6 Gray zone of unresolved results
IN05 < 0.9 Enterprise does not create added value.

31.3.1 Correlation Analysis

Correlation analysis is used to analyze the sensitivity of the evolution of lagged values of bankruptcy models and their comparison with the evolution of real bankrupt firms. Liou and Smith (2007) concluded that the number of bankruptcies increases during recessions, while the number of bankruptcies decreases. Correlation is a mutual relationship between changes in two variables that takes values in the interval <−1;1>.

$$r_{xy} = \frac{\sum (x_i - \overline{x})(y_i - \overline{y})}{(n-1)\, s_x s_y}. \quad (31.5)$$

31.4 Results

31.4.1 Czechia

Figure 31.1 shows that the largest number of Czech firms at risk of financial distress by model was in 2009. Conversely, the number of bankruptcies suggests that 2009 was an accelerating year for the number of bankruptcies, with a peak in the maximum number of businesses that went out of business only seen in 2012. Another year where an increased number of businesses in financial distress can be observed was 2013. The number of bankruptcies for the Czechia between 2008 and 2016 ranged between 7.51% and 9.58%.

When comparing the number of bankruptcies with the results of bankruptcy prediction models, it is clear that only the Taffler model classified fewer firms as financially distressed than actually exited over the entire period. From this perspective, it can be argued that its use is not appropriate in the Czech Republic. A similar number of firms in financial distress as actually went bankrupt can be observed in the results of the original Altman Z′score. The other two models, Altman's Z//EM Score and IN05, classified more firms as potentially financially distressed than actually went bankrupt. From this perspective, it can be concluded that it is the Z//EM and IN05 that fulfill their function as an early indication of financial distress.

At the same time, it can be observed in Table 31.1 that, according to the sensitivity analysis, there is a correlation between the lagged values of Z//EM and IN05 and the actual number of bankruptcies. A similarity can also be observed between the actual Z′score values and the real numbers of bankruptcies.

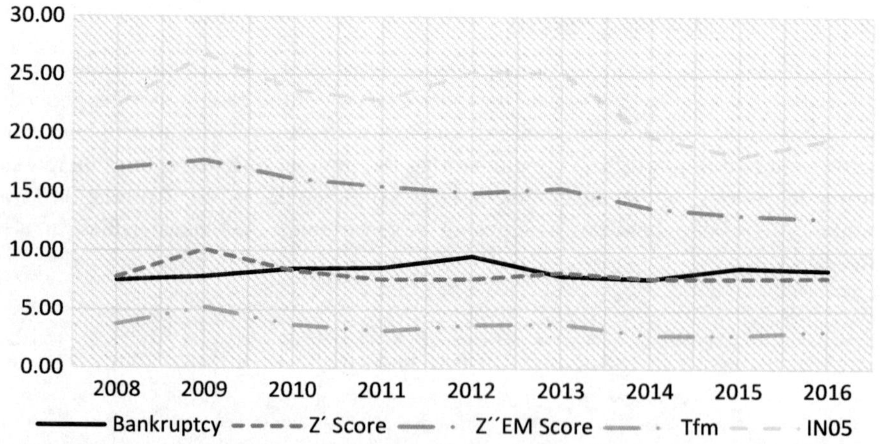

Fig. 31.1 Resulting values of the number of bankruptcies and firms in financial distress in Czechia in %. (Source: Creditreform 2018, Author's calculations)

Table 31.1 Sensitivity analysis between values of real bankruptcies and selected models in Czechia

Czechia	Z′score	Z//EM	Taffler	IN05
Bankruptcy	0.318	0.519	−0.108	0.598

Source: Author's calculations

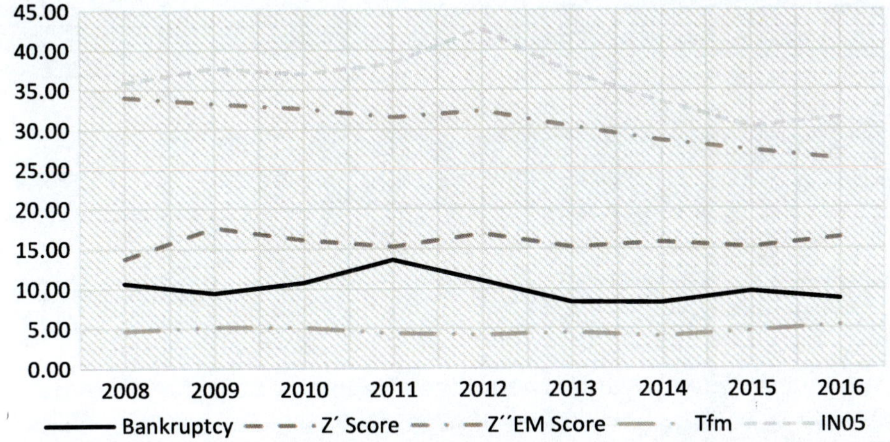

Fig. 31.2 Resulting values of the number of bankruptcies and firms in financial distress in Hungary in %. (Source: Creditreform 2018, Author's calculations)

31.4.2 Hungary

Compared to the evolution of the number of business bankruptcies in the Czech Republic, the highest number of bankruptcies in Hungary was already in 2011, when the indicator reached 13.6%. The number of bankruptcies for Hungary between 2008 and 2016 ranged between 8.29% and 13.60%.

Looking at Fig. 31.2, it can be seen that only the Taffler model included a smaller number of enterprises with potential financial distress than actually went bankrupt. The other three models assigned more firms to the potential financial distress category than the number of bankruptcies, fulfilling their primary function of providing an early warning of firms in financial distress. It can also be observed that according to the sensitivity analysis, there is a correlation between lagged Z′score and IN05 values and the actual number of bankruptcies. A similarity can also be observed between the actual Z//EM values and the real numbers of bankruptcies of firms in Hungary (Table 31.2).

Table 31.2 Sensitivity analysis between values of real bankruptcies and selected models in Hungary

Hungary	Z′score	Z//EM	Taffler	IN05
Bankruptcy	0.489	0.285	0.114	0.535

Source: Author's calculations

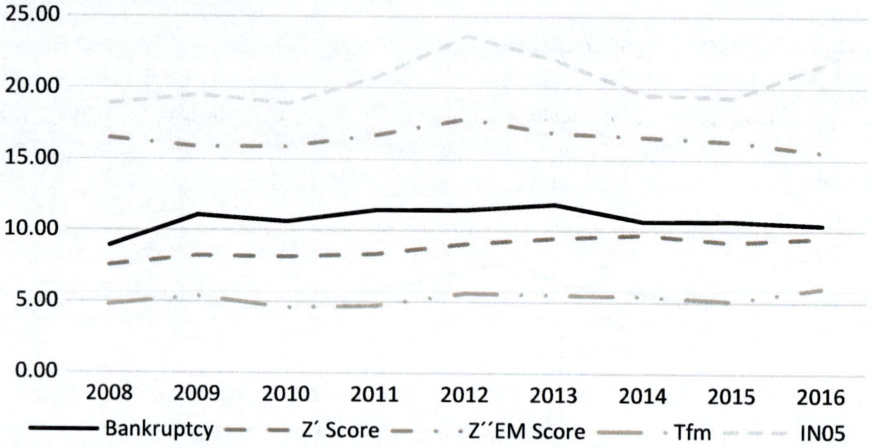

Fig. 31.3 Resulting values of the number of bankruptcies and firms in financial distress in Poland in %. (Source: Creditreform 2018, Author's calculations)

31.4.3 Poland

The number of corporate bankruptcies in Poland has been mostly in the range of 10–12% during the period under review (Fig. 31.3). The highest increase compared to the previous year was achieved in 2009. After a slight decline in 2010, the number of bankruptcies gradually increased until a peak in 2013. Despite the subsequent decline, the percentage of bankrupted firms has not recovered to the pre-crisis level.

When compared with other models that predicted financial distress for firms that did not close down during the period under review, Tfm and Z′Score models classified less than 10% of firms at risk of financial distress. The other two models, Z′em Score and IN05, classify more than 15% of enterprises as being at risk. The Z//EM and IN05 models fulfil their function as early warnings of financial distress. At the same time, it can be observed in Table 31.3 that, according to the sensitivity analysis, there is a correlation between lagged Z//EM values and the actual number of bankruptcies.

Table 31.3 Sensitivity analysis between values of real bankruptcies and selected models in Poland

Poland	Z′score	Z//EM	Taffler	IN05
Bankruptcy	0.512	0.601	0.277	0.466

Source: Author's calculations

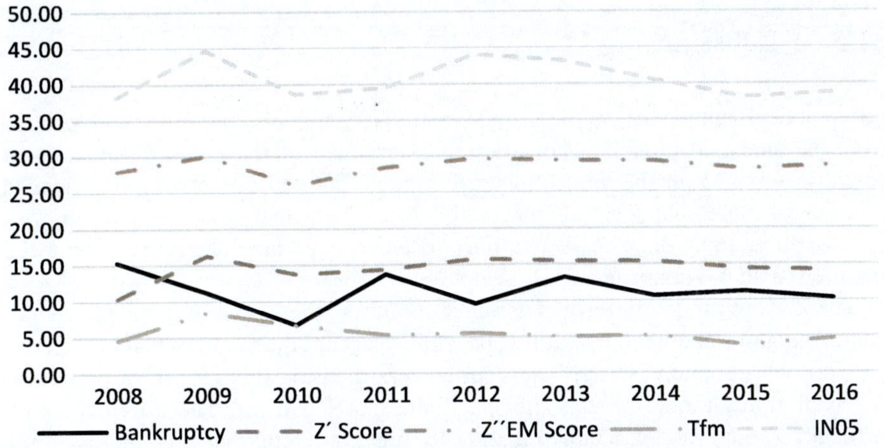

Fig. 31.4 Resulting values of the number of bankruptcies and firms in financial distress in Slovakia in %. (Source: Creditreform 2018, Author's calculations)

31.4.4 Slovakia

Slovakia is the only V4 country where the highest number of corporate bankruptcies was already recorded in 2008. A high fluctuation of the measured values in the number of bankrupt enterprises can be observed between 2008 and 2014. Figure 31.4 further shows a large difference between the measured values of the financial performance of enterprises. The number of bankruptcies for the Slovakia between 2008 and 2016 ranged between 6.70% and 15.35%.

The lowest number of enterprises in potential financial distress is recorded by the Tfm model. The bankruptcy model Z′score classified on average about 15% of enterprises in the distressed category in the period under review. The second observed Altman Z//EM score model classified 26–30% of enterprises as vulnerable in the period under review. The last model analyzed, IN05, classified between 38% and 45% of the enterprises as vulnerable. From this point of view, it can be concluded that Z′EM and IN05 are fulfilling their function as an early warning of financial distress. At the same time, it can be observed from Table 31.4 that, according to the sensitivity analysis, there is a correlation between the lagged values of Z//EM and IN05 and the actual number of bankruptcies.

Table 31.4 Sensitivity analysis between values of real bankruptcies and selected models in Slovakia

Slovakia	Z′score	Z//EM	Taffler	IN05
Bankruptcy	0.166	0.499	0.043	0.664

Source: Author's calculations

31.5 Discussion

For practical applicability, the Z//EM and IN05 models can be recommended from the analyzed models. The resulting assessment of the financial situation of enterprises based on the values of these models pointed to a worsened financial situation of more enterprises than actually closed their operations. As a result, they fulfilled their function of early warning of enterprises in a deteriorated financial situation in all V4 countries.

The Z′score model performed its function only in the case of enterprises operating in Hungary. In other cases, it was possible to accept the views of Gavurová et al. (2017a), who pointed out the inappropriateness of using this model. In particular, this bankruptcy model reflects the specificities of US firms. The difference with Altman's Z//EM model, adapted mainly to emerging economies, is mainly in the tracking of firms' liquidity through working capital. While the working capital to total assets ratio is assigned the fourth highest weight in the Z′Score model, it is assigned the second highest weight in the Z′EM model after EBIT/total assets.

Differences causing the different results in the two Altman models can also be found in the retained earnings/total assets ratio. Despite the higher coefficient in the Z//EM model, it is assigned only the third highest weight compared to the others. In the Z′score model, it is assigned the second highest weight and favors companies that have been on the market longer and have built up sufficient reserves. Thanks to these observations, we can also agree with the studies by Karas and Režňáková (2014); Basovníková et al. (2018); Csikosová et al. (2019); and other authors pointing out the appropriateness of using Altman's Z′EM.

The worst results in all V4 countries were achieved by the Taffler model. As pointed out by Machek (2014), this model does not fulfil the function of an early warning for firms at risk of financial distress. Due to its construction including only basic information about the firm as well as inappropriate thresholds for assessing the financial situation, it is not possible to recommend this model for practical use in the V4 countries.

The opposite results were found for the applicability of the IN05 model. The dissertation reaches the same conclusions as Machek (2014); Csikosová et al. (2019); or Dorgai et al. (2016), who recommend the model for practical use in the V4. The undeniable advantage of the model is its construction to the conditions of the business environment in the Czechia, where the focus is mainly on the ability to cover the company's own assets with its own profits or revenues. However, the results of the study recommend its application to other V4 countries.

31.6 Conclusion

There are countless methods and procedures for assessing the creditworthiness of companies and predicting possible bankruptcies. Financial institutions usually keep their procedures secret because they are about their know-how. However, financial indicators play a significant role in all models. Simpler approaches include various indicator systems allocating points. To the more complex ones, sophisticated statistical procedures work with historical data series and calculate different probabilities of company failure based on certain values of financial indicators. Comprehensive evaluation of financial indicators and construction of bankruptcy models proved their importance. The overall economic environment in recent years has highlighted the need for precise tools to anticipate financial distress and assess the overall financial situation of companies.

Bankruptcy models are used to evaluate the financial situation of companies. The construction of the models is based on the assumption that companies in financial difficulties experience certain anomalies several years before their bankruptcy. Their use is appropriate not only for current and future managerial decision-making but also for the assessment of companies by the banking sector. The aim of the chapter was to evaluate the applicability of bankruptcy models in the V4 countries.

Based on a literature review, four bankruptcy models suitable for analyzing the financial performance of companies were selected. In the practical part of the work is used the application of Taffler model, Altman model Z′score, Altman model Z//EM Score, and Credibility Index IN05.

The main tool for evaluating the suitability of the selected bankruptcy models is the statistical significance of the models obtained after performing a mutual sensitivity analysis. The individual results confirm the theory of the combination of the models for practical use. In addition to the differences within each of the observed categories, the results show that at least one model was always significant for a given country. While for Hungary and Poland the combination of Altman's bankruptcy models Z′score and Z′EM seems to be appropriate, the analyzed relationship in Czechia and Slovakia is best captured by the IN05 model. Unlike Altman's models, IN05 also focuses on the liquidity of enterprises and the ability to create value for the owners of the enterprise. When investigating the practical use of bankruptcy models, it was possible to notice the limited use of the IN05 model on Polish companies and the Z//EM model on Slovak companies.

Acknowledgments Publication of this paper was supported by the Internal Grant System of Silesian University in Opava within the project "Methods of comprehensive evaluation of the company and their use in the conditions of selected countries of the Visegrad Group." The support is greatly acknowledged.

References

Agarwal, V., & Taffler, R. (2007). Twenty-five years of the Taffler Z-score model: Does it really have predictive ability? *Accounting and Business Research*, 285–300.

Altman, E. (1968). Financial ratios, discriminant analysis and the prediction of corporate bankruptcy. *Journal of Finance, 23*(4), 589–609.

Altman, E. (2006). *Corporate financial distress and bankruptcy* (3rd ed.). Wiley.

Baker, H. K., & Powell, G. E. (2005). *Understanding financial management*. Blackwell Publishing.

Basovníková, M., Konečný, M., Dubový, R., & Masařová, A. (2018). The use of the Altman model in evaluation of economic performance of a corporation in the crisis period in the building sector in the Czech Republic. *Acta Universitatis Agriculturae et Silviculturae Mendelianae Brunensis, 66*, 409–421.

Beaver, W. (1966). Financial ratios as predictors of failure. *Journal of Accounting Research, 4*(1), 71–111.

Csikosova, A., Janoskova, M., & Culkova, K. (2019). Limitation of financial health prediction in companies from post-communist countries. *Journal of Risk and Financial Management, 12*(15).

Dorgai, K., Fenyves, V., & Sutó, D. (2016). Analysis of commercial enterprises solvency by means of different bankruptcy models. *Gradus, 3*(1), 341–349.

Gavurová, B., Janke, F., & Packová, M. (2017a). Analysis of impact of using the trend variables on bankruptcy prediction models performance. *Journal of Economics, 65*(4), 370–383.

Gavurová, B., Packová, M., Misanková, M., & Smrčka, L. (2017b). Predictive potential and risks of selected bankruptcy prediction models in the Slovak business environment. *Journal of Business Economics and Management, 18*, 1156–1173.

Gruszczynski, M. (2014). Financial distress of companies in Poland. *International Advances in Economic Research, 10*(4), 249–256.

Karas, M., & Režňáková, M. (2014). To what degree is the accuracy of a bankruptcy prediction model affected by the environment? The case of the Baltic States and the Czech Republic. Procedia – Social and behavioral sciences, 19th international scientific conference. *Economics and Management, 2014*, 564–568.

Liou, D., & Smith, M. (2007). Macroeconomic variables and financial distress. *Journal of Accounting –Business and Management, 14*, 17–31.

Lízal, L. (2012). *Determination of financial distress: What drives bankruptcy in a transition economy?* (William Davidson Working Paper). The Czech Republic Case.

Machek, O. (2014). Long-term predictive ability of bankruptcy models in the Czech Republic: Evidence from 2007–2012. *Central European Business Review, 3*, 14–17.

Neumaierová, I., & Neumaier, I. (2005). Index 05. In *Evropské finanční systémy: Sborník příspěvků z mezinárodní vědecké conference* (pp. 143–146). Masarykova univerzita v Brně.

Sedláček, J. (2001). *Účetní data v rukou manažera – finanční analýza v řízení firmy*. Computers Press.

Senbet, L. W., & Wang, T. Y. (2012). *Corporate financial distress and bankruptcy: A survey foundations and trends in finance* (pp. 2243–2335).

Škerlíková, T., & Rudolfová, L. (2015). Possible causes of delay in default in the Czech Republic. *International Journal of Economic Policy in Emerging Economies*, 305–317.

Taffler, R. (1983). The assessment of company solvency and performance using a statistical model. *Accounting and Business Research, 15*(52), 295–308.

Chapter 32
Determinants of Customer Loyalty Toward Internet Service Providers in Albania

Alma Braimllari (Spaho) and Sauda Nerjaku

Abstract The Internet has brought significant changes to individuals' lifestyles and many aspects of society and also has an impact on economic development. Diffusion and usage of the Internet vary greatly according to the social and economic conditions of the country. During the last years, the number of subscribers of fixed broadband Internet access services has been increased for all main operators in Albania. The purpose of this study was to identify the determinants of customer loyalty to Internet service providers in Albania. The target population of this study consisted of individuals who have a fixed broadband Internet connection at their home. Data of 235 respondents were analyzed using logistic regression analysis. The results of binary logistic regression analysis indicated that network quality, price perception, and perceived value were statistically significant and positively related to customer loyalty, whereas the employment status of the respondent was statistically significant and negatively related to customer loyalty toward the Internet service provider. The findings of this study provide useful information for managers of Internet service providers to design the promotions strategies and to offer loyalty programs for building enduring loyalty with consumers.

Keywords Fixed broadband Internet access · Network quality · Price perception · Perceived value · Logistic regression analysis

32.1 Introduction

The development of Information technology has reduced the costs of information processing, and the Internet has facilitated and revolutionized communications. The Internet has a significant economic effect and will impact the quality of life in developing countries in a long term (Kenny 2003). The Internet has experienced

A. Braimllari (Spaho) · S. Nerjaku (✉)
Faculty of Economy, University of Tirana, Tirana, Albania
e-mail: sauda.nerjaku@unitir.edu.al

N. Tsounis, A. Vlachvei (eds.), *Advances in Quantitative Economic Research*, Springer Proceedings in Business and Economics,
https://doi.org/10.1007/978-3-030-98179-2_32

exponential growth; however, diffusion rates across countries differ enormously. At the end of January 2021, there were 4.66 billion active Internet users worldwide, about 59.5% of the world population (Statista 2021). At the end of December 2020, the number of Internet users in Albania was 2.16 million (Internet World Stats 2021), and Internet diffusion has achieved the maturity level (Braimllari and Sala 2017).

Even though the world history of the Internet started in the early 1960s, in Albania, the Internet service was provided for the first time in 1996, and the need for operators that offer this service emerged. An Internet service provider (ISP) offers access to the Internet and other Internet services to individuals and businesses. The first private ISP started to offer paid Internet service in 1998, and directly after that, three other ISPs entered the Albanian market. Somewhat greater access to the Internet began only after 2000 when the state operator ALBtelecom started to provide the Internet service, in addition to other private ISPs. The Internet access of Albanian families was at a low rate until 2007, and the number of subscribers with a fixed broadband Internet connection was about 1800 in 2007. In succeeding years, with the large investments made to increase Internet access through a fixed broadband connection, the number of subscribers with fixed broadband access has been increasing.

Electronic and Postal Communications Authority in Albania reported that about 174 operators have provided fixed broadband Internet services in 2020. At the end of 2020, Albania exceeded for the first time the figure of 500,000 subscribers with fixed broadband access, with an increase of 15% higher than in 2019. In the first quarter of 2021, the number of subscribers with fixed broadband networks amounted to 505.9 thousand, which is an increase of 13.8% compared to the first quarter of 2020. The number of subscribers of fixed broadband Internet access services has been growing, and all major operators (ALBtelecom, ASC, Vodafone, Abissnet, Nisatel) have increased their number of subscribers in recent years (Electronic and Postal Communications Authority, 2021).

Customer loyalty is customers' willingness to buy a brand frequently over all other brands. In the service business sector, customer loyalty plays an important role to increase the business; it also focuses on establishing good relationships with their customers. Loyal customers are the main source of generating profits and bringing more new customers into the business. Customer loyalty increases business profits, improves sales, and provides opportunities for sustainable growth.

This study aimed to find the factors that significantly influence customer loyalty toward Internet service providers in Albania. Network quality, price perception, perceived value, monthly payment of the Internet service, experience in years with ISP, and individual characteristics of the respondent were considered in this study.

32.2 Literature Review

Customer loyalty is a condition in which the consumer has a positive attitude toward a brand, is committed to the brand, and intends to continue purchasing in the future (Mowen and Minor 2002). There are several studies about factors influencing customer satisfaction and customer loyalty to ISPs in the literature.

In the telecommunications industry, *network quality* includes the quality and strength of the network signal (Wang et al. 2004), the number of errors, downloading and uploading speed, and system response time (Vlachos and Vrechopoulos 2008). Related to network quality provided by ISPs, the stability and transmission speed of the Internet are important to users, and they will consider shifting to other service providers due to stability and speed (Junoh and Yaacob 2011). Moreover, the uptime of service was found to have a significant impact on customer satisfaction and customer loyalty (Wang et al. 2004). The study of (Nerjaku and Braimllari 2021) showed that network quality was positively related to customer satisfaction. Results of (Khoi and Van Tuan 2018) indicated that network quality was significantly and positively related to customer loyalty through customer satisfaction. The study of (Joudeh and Dandis 2018) found that service quality influences customer satisfaction and customer satisfaction influences customer loyalty. The findings of (Thaichon et al. 2014) revealed that service quality is influenced by network quality, customer service, information support, privacy, and security, and also service quality impacts customer loyalty attributes, including satisfaction, value, trust, and commitment.

Price perception has a great influence on consumers' buying decision process. Consumer's price perception depends on many factors, some of which are subjective, and it is not the real monetary value of the product or service. The consumer is more willing to buy the product or service when the perceived price approximates the real price. When the perceived price is lower than the real price, the customer is reluctant to make a purchase. When the perceived price is higher than the real price, the customer has doubts about the quality of the product or service. In the perception of price, an important role is played by the marketing of the product or service.

Even though Internet broadband users are disposed to pay more for better service, they will consider shifting to another Internet service provider because of the price (Junoh and Yaacob 2011; Khoi and Van Tuan 2018). Hence, customers of Internet services are sensitive to price. According to (Suharyono and Elfahmi 2021), price perception has a positive and significant indirect effect on customer loyalty through customer satisfaction.

Customer trust is a key success factor for building and maintaining all businesses. Trust refers to customers' perceptions of their service provider, including the ability, integrity, and benevolence of the provider, and includes perceptions of customers relating to the capacity of a brand to fulfill its promises (Thaichon et al. 2014). When Internet users have trust in Internet service providers, they are likely to continue using other services offered by their Internet service provider without the need for advertising. The study of (Gul 2014) found a significant and positive relationship between trust and customer loyalty, so increment of trust enhances customer loyalty. According to (Kishada and Wahab 2013), trust has a significant positive influence on customer loyalty. The results of (Leninkumar 2017) found a significant positive association between customer trust and customer loyalty.

Customer perceived value is one of the most important elements for gaining a competitive edge and is considered to be a significant predictor of customer satisfaction and loyalty (Gallarza and Saura 2006). According to (Faber et al. 2004), the perceived value can be defined as "the value seen as the perceived benefits and total costs (or sacrifice) of (obtaining) a product or service." The costs of a product can be defined by the money paid for the service. So, as less money is paid for a high-quality product, the more positive the service is perceived. Customer perceived value is positively associated with customer loyalty as supported by (Yang and Peterson 2004). The study of (Chiou 2004) showed that perceived value is very important in generating overall customer satisfaction and loyalty toward an ISP and that the perceived trust of an ISP increases perceived value, overall satisfaction, and loyalty. The study of (Khoi and Van Tuan 2018) found that the customer perceived value was significantly and positively related to customer loyalty through customer satisfaction.

Consumer satisfaction has a vital role for businesses to gain and maintain a competitive advantage. Fulfilling customer expectations for the product or service determines the level of customer satisfaction (Oliver 2010). The customer is satisfied if the perceived performance is above its expectations. It is increasingly important that researchers consider the customer satisfaction measurement to achieve loyalty. The results of (Khoi and Van Tuan 2018; Leninkumar 2017; Mandira et al. 2018) indicated that customer satisfaction had a positive and significant effect on customer loyalty. Also, the results of (Cheng et al. 2008) indicated that customer satisfaction had the greatest influence on customer loyalty, compared to price perception.

32.3 Research Methodology

The target population of the study was composed of individuals aged more than 18 years old with a fixed broadband Internet connection at their home and that use the Internet at least once a month. Data were collected through a self-administered questionnaire in the period January 10 to February 20, 2021, and only 235 questionnaires were valid to use for data analysis. Non-probability (purposive) sampling was used to collect the data.

The questionnaire included questions about experience in years, monthly payment, name and location of ISP; network quality, price perception, perceived value, trust, customer satisfaction, and customer loyalty; and the respondent profile such as age, gender, employment, education level, and family monthly income level.

The items for network quality, price perception, perceived value, trust, customer satisfaction, and customer loyalty, adopted from the literature (Khoi and Van Tuan 2018; Thaichon et al. 2014; Cheng et al. 2008), were measured on a 5-point Likert scale, ranging from 1 = "strongly disagree" to 5 = "strongly agree." To ensure that the items comprising constructs produced a reliable scale, Cronbach's alpha coefficient was calculated (Annex, Table 32.2). Reliability over 0.7 is generally considered to be acceptable (Hair et al. 2009). A composite score was used to represent each construct by taking the average score of all items for that construct.

To identify the determinants of customer loyalty, three logistic regression models with a binary response were modeled, and each model estimates probabilities of the response occurring (Hosmer and Lemeshow 2004). The binary logistic regression equation has the following form:

$$\ln\left(\frac{p}{1-p}\right) = \beta_0 + \beta_1 x_1 + \cdots + \beta_k x_k \tag{32.1}$$

where p is the estimated probability that the customer is loyal and $x_1, x_2, \ldots, x_k$ are the independent variables considered in this study. A customer is considered to be loyal toward an ISP if its composite score for the customer loyalty construct is higher than the overall average of the sample for that construct.

The maximum likelihood method was used to estimate the odds ratios ($p/(1-p)$). Values of odds ratios lower than 1 indicate a negative association, odds ratios equal to 1 indicate no association, and odds ratios higher than 1 indicate a positive association between independent variables and the binary dependent variable of the model, customer loyalty.

STATA12 was used to perform the data analysis.

32.4 Results and Discussion

32.4.1 Descriptive Analysis

About 41% of the respondents live in Tirana, 71% were female, and 58% were between 18 and 24 years old. About 46% of the respondents hold a university diploma, and 38.3% have a master's diploma. The majority of the respondents (56.2%) were employed; 32.8% of the respondents have declared family monthly income between ALL 60,001 and 90,000 and 27.7% between ALL 30,001 and 60,000. Also, around 34% of the respondents have been using at-home Internet service for 2 to 3 years and 25% for 5 years or more. About 31.6% of the respondents use the Internet service of ALBtelecom, 19% ABcom, 12% Tring, 6.5% Abissnet, and 6% Digicom. For the Internet service, 42.5% of the respondents pay between

ALL 1001 and 1500, and 35% pay between ALL 1501 and 2000; only 8.5% pay more than ALL 2000.

32.4.2 *Logistic Regression Analysis*

The results of binary logistic regression models, shown in Table 32.1, indicated that each model was statistically significant (p-value <0.05). The values of Pseudo-R^2 were between 46.21% and 51.89%, whereas the percentages of cases correctly classified were between 82.13 and 84.68.

Two independent variables, trust and customer satisfaction, showed high correlation values with other variables ($r > 0.7$, p-value <0.05) and were not included in the logistic regression models.

The odds ratios values in Table 32.1 indicated that the network quality was statistically significant and positively related to customer loyalty for each model, indicating that customers with very good network quality were more likely to be loyal to their ISP. This finding was consistent with the results of (Khoi and Van Tuan 2018).

The results of Table 32.1 indicated that the price perception was statistically significant and positively related to customer loyalty for each model, that is, customers that had a good perception of price were more likely to be loyal to their ISP. This finding was consistent with the results of (Mandira et al. 2018; Cheng et al. 2008).

The results indicated that the customer perceived value was statistically significant and positively related to customer loyalty for each model, that is, customers with a good perceived value about the service were more likely to be loyal to their ISP. This finding was consistent with the results of (Chiou 2004) and in contrast to the finding of (Thaichon et al. 2014), in which customer value had no significant impact on customer loyalty.

For models 2 and 3, experience in years of the customer was not statistically significant at the 5% level. However, more experienced customers were less likely to be loyal to their ISP. Also, the region was not statistically significant, but it indicates that customers from Tirana were less likely to be loyal to their ISP (perhaps because they have more options). The other variable, monthly payment for Internet service, was not statistically significant at the 5% level, but positively related to customer loyalty, that is, customers who paid more for the Internet service were more likely to be loyal toward their ISP.

In model 3, among customers' characteristics, only employment status was statistically significant at 5% level, indicating that employed respondents were less likely to be loyal to their ISP. This finding was in contrast to the finding of (Khoi and Van Tuan 2018) that job had no significant impact on customer loyalty. Other variables such as age, gender, education level, and family monthly income were

Table 32.1 Results of binary logistic regression models (odds ratios)

Variable	Model 1	Model 2	Model 3
Network quality	3.015*	3.074*	4.375*
Price perception	2.918*	3.361*	4.304*
Perceived value	3.543*	3.359*	3.076*
Region			
Tirana		0.603	0.693
Other (RC)		1.000	1.000
Experience			
Less than 1 year (RC)		1.000	1.000
1–2 years		0.798	0.872
2–3 years		0.735	0.521
More than 3 years		0.633	0.550
Monthly payment for internet service (ALL)			
Less than 1500 (RC)		1.000	1.000
More than 1501		1.298	1.318
Age			
Less than 25 years (RC)			1.000
25 years or more			1.629
Gender			
Female (RC)			1.000
Male			0.432
Education level			
High school (RC)			1.000
University			2.748
Master +			2.216
Employment status			
Yes			0.287*
No (RC)			1.000
Family monthly income (ALL)			
<60,000 (RC)			1.000
60,001–90,000			2.705
>90,000			0.886
Constant	0.00002*	0.0000*	0.0000*
LR χ^2 (df)	150.09 (3)	152.63 (8)	168.54 (15)
Prob > χ^2	0.0000	0.0000	0.0000
% correctly classified	84.26	82.13	84.68
Pseudo-R^2	46.21%	46.99%	51.89%

Note: RC indicates the reference category. * indicates the 5% level of significance not statistically significant; however, adult customers (25 years old or more) and more educated customers (with university or master diploma) were more likely to be loyal, whereas male customers were less likely to be loyal to their ISP. The findings of age and gender were consistent with the findings of (Khoi and Van Tuan 2018). The finding of monthly income was not supported by the finding of (Khoi and Van Tuan 2018) that income had a positive impact on customer loyalty.

32.5 Conclusions

This study aimed to analyze the ISPs in Albania regarding factors influencing the loyalty of their customers.

The results of logistic regression analysis indicated that network quality, price perception, and perceived value were statistically significant and positively related to customer loyalty, whereas employment status was negatively related to customer loyalty to their ISP. These results revealed that the customers with good network quality, good perception of price, and high value for the service were more likely to be loyal to their ISP, whereas employed customers were less likely to be loyal to their ISP. Customer loyalty toward the ISP could be achieved by enhancing network quality and perceived value and improving the price perception of the ISP customers.

The findings of this study are useful for managers of Internet service providers. This valuable information about network quality, consumers' price, and value perceptions can be used by ISPs to improve their network quality, to design their promotions strategies, and to offer customer loyalty programs to encourage their customers on continuous shopping. Enduring loyalty is about relationships and builds on a deep understanding of the customers, their needs, and behaviors. With the maturation of the ISP market, Internet service providers that pay attention to building good relationships with their customers will gain a competitive advantage.

This study has some limitations. Firstly, other factors can be studied, and composite scores for constructs are used to model the data. Secondly, the sample was relatively small and not representative of the country. Lastly, nonprobability (purposive) sampling was used to collect the data in a short time and at a low cost.

In future research, other factors such as service quality, switching cost, brand image, etc. that can influence customer loyalty can be studied using other statistical methods.

A.1 Annex

Table A.1 Descriptive statistics for items

Item/construct	Mean	Std. dev.
Network quality (NQ) (alpha = 0.88)		
NQ1: The upload and download speed of the network is always strong	3.01	1.13
NQ2: The uptime of the network is always available without interruption	2.89	1.19
NQ3: The connection quality is always reliable	3.11	1.07
NQ4: You can access the network at any time without delay	3.23	1.12
Price perception (PP) (alpha = 0.77)		
PP1: The price charged by your ISP is reasonable	3.35	1.16
PP2: The service's price of your ISP is cheaper than others	3.02	1.04
PP3: Service supplied by your ISP is equivalent to its price	3.11	1.06
PP4: Service offered by your ISP is better value for money than what you would pay for the same service as others	3.17	1.05
PP5: You are willing to pay more for better service quality	3.10	1.15
Perceived value (PV) (alpha = 0.90)		
PV1: The customer service staff of your ISP gives me adequate support	3.49	1.13
PV2: Whenever you have a problem with services, your ISP takes corrective action without delay	3.30	1.23
PV3: Your ISP keeps you informed of things that you need to get the best use of the service	2.99	1.18
PV4: You feel comfortable with the willingness of assistance and support from your ISP	3.27	1.14
PV5: Overall, the chosen offerings are worth your money, effort, and time	3.26	1.08
Trust (T) (alpha = 0.89)		
T1: You believe that your ISP will be ready and willing to offer me assistance and support	3.34	1.12
T2: You believe that your ISP always fulfills the promises that it makes to its customers	3.00	1.04
T3: You believe that your ISP has the necessary ability and knowledge to fulfill its tasks	3.48	1.00
T4: You believe that your ISP always puts the interests of its customers first of all	3.13	1.05
Customer satisfaction (CS) (alpha = 0.95)		
CS1: You are satisfied with your decision to use this company as ISP	3.31	1.07
CS2: Your choice to choose this company as an ISP was a wise one	3.33	1.09

(continued)

Table A.1 (continued)

Item/construct	Mean	Std. dev.
CS3: You did the right thing when you choose this ISP	3.31	1.15
CS4: Your experience with this ISP has been enjoyable	3.28	1.13
CS5: Overall, you are satisfied with the ISP offering the services	3.37	1.13
Customer loyalty (CL) (alpha = 0.92)		
CL1: You say positive things about your ISP to other people	3.31	1.03
CL2: You would recommend your ISP to those who seek your advice about such matters	3.29	1.11
CL3: You would encourage friends and relatives to use your ISP	3.22	1.11
CL4: You would post positive messages about your ISP on some internet message board	2.89	1.11
CL5: You intend to continue to do business with your current internet service provider	3.50	1.09
CL6: You intend to do more business with your current internet service provider	3.11	1.08

References

Braimllari, A., & Sala, E. (2017). Modeling of Internet diffusion in Balkan countries. In *Proceedings in conference of informatics and management sciences (ICTIC-2017), March 26–30, Slovakia* (pp. 53–57). https://doi.org/10.18638/ictic.2017.6.1.319

Cheng, T. E., Lai, L. C., & Yeung, A. C. (2008). The driving forces of customer loyalty: A study of Internet service providers in Hong Kong. *International Journal of E-Business Research, 4*(4), 26–42.

Chiou, J. S. (2004). The antecedents of consumers' loyalty toward Internet service providers. *Information & Management, 41*(6), 685–695.

Electronic and Postal Communications Authority (2021). https://akep.al/wp-content/uploads/2021/08/Raport-T1_2021_-docx.pdf. Accessed 5 July 2021.

Faber, E., Haaker, T., & Bouwman, H. (2004) *Balancing requirements for customer value of mobile services*. In 7th bled e-commerce conference eGlobal Bled, Slovenia, June 21–23, 2004.

Gallarza, M. G., & Saura, I. G. (2006). Value dimensions, perceived value, satisfaction, and loyalty: An investigation of university students' travel behavior. *Tourism Management, 27*(3), 437–452.

Gul, R. (2014). The relationship between reputation. *Customer Satisfaction, Trust, and Loyalty, Journal of Public Administration and Governance, 4*(3), 368–387.

Hair, J. F., Black, W., Babin, B. J., & Anderson, R. E. (2009). *Multivariate data analysis* (7th ed.). Pearson.

Hosmer, D. W., & Lemeshow, S. (2004). *Applied logistic regression* (2nd ed.). Wiley.

Internet World Stats. (2021). Internet in Europe Statistics. https://www.internetworldstats.com/europa2.htm. Accessed 5 July 2021.

Joudeh, J. M., & Dandis, A. (2018). Service quality, customer satisfaction and loyalty in an Internet service providers. *International Journal of Business and Management, 13*(8), 108–120.

Junoh, A. S., & Yaacob, M. R. (2011). Determinants of customer satisfaction towards broadband services in Malaysia. *International Journal of Business, Humanities, and Technology, 1*(2), 123–134.

Kenny, C. (2003). The Internet and economic growth in less-developed countries: A case of managing expectations? *Oxford Development Studies, 31*(1), 99–113.

Khoi, B. H., & Van Tuan, N. (2018). Using smart PLS 3.0 to analyze Internet service quality in Vietnam. In L. H. Anh, L. S. Dong, V. Kreinovich, & N. N. Thach (Eds.), *Econometrics for financial applications, studies in computational intelligence* (Vol. 760, pp. 430–439). Springer.

Kishada, Z. M. E., & Wahab, N. A. (2013). Factors affecting customer loyalty in Islamic banking: Evidence from Malaysian banks. *International Journal of Business and Social Science, 4*(7), 264–273.

Leninkumar, V. (2017). The relationship between customer satisfaction and customer trust on customer loyalty. *International Journal of Academic Research in Business and Social Sciences, 7*(4), 450–465.

Mandira, D. A., Suliyanto, S., & Nawarini, A. T. (2018). The influence customer trust, service quality, and perceived price on customer satisfaction and customer loyalty. *Journal of Research in Management, 1*(1), 16–21.

Mowen, J. C., & Minor, M. (2002). *Customer loyalty*. Erlangga.

Nerjaku, S., & Braimllari, A. (2021). Network quality, Price perception, and customer satisfaction: Case of internet service providers in Albania. In *Proceeding of the 4th international conference on recent trends and applications in computer science and information technology, Albania, May 21–22, 2021* (pp. 84–93) http://ceur-ws.org/Vol-2872/paper12.pdf

Oliver, R. L. (2010). *Satisfaction: A behavioral perspective on the consumer*. M.E. Sharpe.

Statista (2021). *Worldwide digital population as of January 2021*. https://www.statista.com/statistics/617136/digital-population-worldwide/. Accessed 5 July 2021.

Suharyono, S., & Elfahmi, M. (2021). The effect of product quality, price perception, and promotion on customer satisfaction and its impact on customer loyalty of PT Makmur Jaya agro pesticides. *Open Access Indonesia Journal of Social Sciences, 4*(1), 157–172.

Thaichon, P., Lobo, A., & Mitsis, A. (2014). An empirical model of home Internet services quality in Thailand. *Asia Pacific Journal of Marketing and Logistics, 26*(2), 190–221.

Vlachos, P. A., & Vrechopoulos, A. P. (2008). Determinants of behavioral intentions in the mobile Internet services market. *Journal of Services Marketing, 22*(4), 280–291.

Wang, Y., Lo, H. P., & Yang, Y. (2004). An integrated framework for service quality, customer value, satisfaction: Evidence from China's telecommunication industry. *Information Systems Frontiers, 6*(4), 325–340.

Yang, Z., & Peterson, R. (2004). Customer perceived value, satisfaction, and loyalty: The role of switching costs. *Psychology and Marketing, 21*(10), 799–822. https://doi.org/10.1002/mar.20030

Chapter 33
Strategic Agility and Economic Environment's Friendliness-Hostility in Explaining Performance of Polish SMEs in the Phase of COVID-19 Pandemic

Tomasz Sikora and Ewa Baranowska-Prokop

Abstract The main purpose of this article is to present the relationship between two factors: perceived environmental hostility (or friendliness) and strategic agility with market performance of Polish SMEs from medium-tech and high-tech industries during COVID-19 pandemic. This research directly refers to analogical study analyzing the role of the two variables in the period just before COVID-19 (Sikora & Baranowska-Prokop, Advances in longitudinal data methods in applied economic research, Springer Proceedings in Business and Economics, 2021).

Research results revealed that respondents interviewed during the period of entire second lockdown in December 2020–January 2021 evaluated external environment as more friendly (none of the respondents evaluated environment as "unfriendly") compared to their pre-COVID counterparts interviewed during May–July 2019. Moreover, in contrast to the previous research, neither strategic agility nor environmental hostility–friendliness showed significant relationships with firms' results. These unexpected findings may be explained in regards to several factors:

- In general, industry was hit less severely by lockdowns than services (most of respondents declared only "moderately" negative impact of COVID-19-related restrictions on the environment their firm operated and the relationship between the declared number of COVID-19 related consequences and market performance was weak).
- Efficacy of government's programs within the framework of "Anti-crisis Shield" (introduced in Poland end-March 2020) providing subsidies for enterprises (to maintain financial liquidity and employment).
- Favorable macro-environment in which the local currency (considered as undervalued) helped both exporters making them more price-competitive and manu-

T. Sikora (✉) · E. Baranowska-Prokop
SGH Warsaw School of Economics, Warsaw, Poland
e-mail: tsikora@sgh.waw.pl

N. Tsounis, A. Vlachvei (eds.), *Advances in Quantitative Economic Research*, Springer Proceedings in Business and Economics,
https://doi.org/10.1007/978-3-030-98179-2_33

facturing firms operating on the local market by "insulating" them from cheaper imports.

In our opinion, friendly macro-environment, availability of public assistance programs, and firms' capability to get money from them (which need further research) were decisive factors influencing Polish firms' performance, whereas strategic agility, as operationalized in this study and in the previous one, did not matter as significant predictor of firms' success.

Keywords Strategic agility · Environmental hostility · Competitive strategies · SMEs · COVID-19 pandemic · **JEL code**: L11 · M10 · M16 · M31

33.1 Introduction

The coronavirus (COVID-19) pandemic has negatively affected the global economy at virtually all levels. The OECD (2020) observes that the results of this crisis will be noticeable for years to come, and the Asian Development Bank (2020) warns that the global cost of COVID-19 could hit $8.8 trillion. However, the impact of COVID-19 has not been equally spread across countries, sectors, and firms of different sizes.

The SMEs were particularly vulnerable for several reasons. Primarily, they tend to be more prevalent in regions and sectors seriously affected by the crisis. Also, SMEs are more sensitive to some of the pandemic's channels of impact than larger firms within the same country and sector. Moreover, in the World Bank report, Adian et al. (2020) indicated that due to pandemic (COVID-19) "... *small and medium enterprise sales shrink by more and their cash drains faster than large firms in the same sector and country. Among them, fast growing firms experience the demand shock somewhat less severely, but they are more exposed to international trade disruption, supply, and finance shocks*". The report points that SMEs are more likely to suffer from decreased liquidity or cash flow availability due to COVID-19 than larger firms by an average of 10 percentage points. The longer the crisis persists, the more likely problems with liquidity will result in insolvency and SME's bankruptcy.

Findings of the Adian et al. (2020) research clearly show that SMEs are more than 8 percent more likely to temporarily shut down due to COVID-19 than larger firms, across all countries and sectors in the sample. SMEs can also have fewer tools to respond to a number of pandemic threats so the responsive and agile strategy might be seen as crucial for their survival.

The concept of strategic agility has been coined in the mid-1980s. Aaker and Mascarenhas (1984) concluded that growing uncertainty and turbulent changes in environment were resulting in significant problems in application of conventional methods of firm management. As an outcome, the concept of strategic agility understood as an ability to adapt to rapid, intense, and difficult-to-forecast changes in firm's environment has been introduced. However, strategic agility, like majority of social science concepts, can be shaped in many definitions. Morton et al. (2018)

indicated that strategic agility is the "practice of continuously adjusting and adapting strategic direction in core business in a flow of strategy praxis over time, as a function of strategic ambitions and changing circumstances".

One of the most frequently cited definitions has been coined by Weber and Tarba (2014) and goes as follows: *Strategic agility is an ability of management to constantly and rapidly sense and respond to a changing environment by intentionally making strategic moves and consequently adapt the necessary organizational configuration for its successful implementation.* Challenges faced by firms operating in global, turbulent, and unpredictable environment inspired a significant number of researchers to underline in proposed definitions the ability of firms to survive in adverse economic environment.

At the beginning of globalization era, Kumar and Motwani (1995) define strategic agility as capacity to take accelerated action in critical situations, starting with identification of market needs and finishing with delivering the final product to customers. Gunaskaran (1998) describes entrepreneurial agility as the ability of firms to survive and cope with challenges in turbulent environment.

Meredith and Francis (2000) characterize it as an organizational capacity to gain competitive advantage due to intelligent, fast, and proactive grabbing of opportunities and appropriate response to environmental threats. Narasimhan et al. (2006) define strategic agility as a capacity to introduce a performant change at a firm's operational level as an answer to uncertainty and changing market requirements.

Bernardes and Hanna (2009) stress that strategic agility is a managerial concept focused on achieving competitive advantage in turbulent environment and ability to manage uncertainty through feasible options within current resources configuration and predetermined limits. Weber and Tarba (2014) pointed that challenges encountered by firms in highly competitive global environment necessitate a better understanding of strategic agility and its implications for firm performance.

Morton et al. (2018) and Doz and Kosonen (2016) indicated that in order to be strategically agile, enterprise should develop three elements: strategic sensitivity, resource fluidity, and leadership unity. Strategic sensitivity is defined as sharpness of perception, awareness, and attention; resource fluidity is described as the capability to reconfigure systems and redeploy resources rapidly; and leadership unity is the ability of top management to make decisions quickly and apolitically.

Application of strategic agility could also be an effective tool for competitive strategy of SMEs in Poland. According to PARP (2020) report, the number of Polish SMEs before the pandemic crisis was constantly growing. It reached the number of 2.1 million and accounted for 99.8 percent of all enterprises in Poland. Polish SMEs are operating mainly in commerce and service sector (75.7 percent), followed by construction sector and manufacturing. Throughout the period of several years before COVID-19 crisis, the number of newly formed firms was outgrowing the number of eradicated. In 2018, all groups of Polish enterprises have increased their income: small firms by 4 percent, big by 7.7 percent, and medium-sized by 8 percent. In this period, the Polish economy has increased by 5.1 percent and shows one of the highest scores in the EU. The pandemic (COVID-19) came as a shock. At the beginning of COVID-19 crisis, nearly 90 percent of SMEs in Poland expected a decrease in turnover, and 75 percent planned to stop pay increases anticipating problems with liquidity (Statista, 2021). The main challenges for SME sector in Poland were lack of capital, necessity to meet changed market requirements, and shortage of sufficient specialists (Report Salesforce 2019).

As in our previous research (Sikora & Baranowska-Prokop, 2021), we asked interviewed managers if companies tend to offer similar conditions to all clients or if they differentiate conditions according to groups of clients. We consider that "multi-strategy" represents a higher level of strategic agility than mono-strategy, because it implies a higher level of adaptation to the existing situation and potential changes in markets and environment. Two marketing tools or strategies have been used in the presented research as a basis for strategic agility operationalization, i.e., price and product quality. Our operationalization of strategic agility can be seen as a behavioral one, based on the description of what firms actually do, unlike some other operationalizations based on multi-item scales (see Roberts & Grover, 2012).

Applied operationalization of environmental friendliness–hostility concept is based on Khandwalla (1977) (a 3-item bipolar scale measuring the degree of environment friendliness–hostility). It has been later used by Covin and Slevin (1989). For the purposes of the presented research, the fourth item has been added to this scale.

33.2 Research Method and Hypotheses

Interviews with companys' owners and managers have been conducted by Indicator (a certified research company) in December 2020–January 2021 through questionnaires sent to a representative sample of Polish SMEs (random selection within two strata of small- and medium-sized companies and two strata of exporters and non-exporters) established after 1995 (firms with exports amounting to at least 15 percent of their sales or not exporting at all). This sample is not directly comparable to the previous sample of Polish SMEs (Sikora & Baranowska-Prokop, 2021), because only managers of companies from medium-tech and high-tech industries, serving either B2B clients only or B2B and B2C, have been interviewed. There were no such restrictions applied to the pre-COVID-19 sample.

Data collection was conducted through the Internet questionnaire (CAWI) and telephone interviews (CATI). The total sample size was 219 firms selected from the database of 1395 Polish SMEs firms that met the sampling criteria. The share of exporters is 49.8 percent, and the share of non-exporters in the sample is 50.2 percent. The share of medium-sized and small-sized enterprises constitutes 37.9 percent and 62.1 percent, respectively.

Hypotheses are also in line with the previous study (Sikora & Baranowska-Prokop, 2021) for comparability reasons. According to Roberts and Grover (2012) (p.579): "in today's hypercompetitive environment, firms that are agile tend to be more successful." They also found positive relationships between agility measures and enterprises' performance. Analogous to these findings, our first hypothesis assumes positive relationship between strategic agility and measures of enterprises' performance:

H1: Agile (multi-strategic) firms achieve better results compared to non-agile (mono-strategic) firms.

According to Miller and Friesen (1983) and previously quoted research, hostility of external environment reduces resources, decreases profit margins, and handicaps maneuverability. Taking into account the restraining role of hostile environment and favorable role of friendly environment, the hypothesis concerning relationship between environment and market performance may be formulated as follows:

H2: There is a positive relationship between the degree of external environment friendliness and market performance (alternatively, the more hostile external environment the worse economic results).

The third hypothesis is based on expected interaction and addresses the "core" of strategic agility usefulness: it should be particularly useful in hostile, risky, and turbulent environment and less useful in a stable or friendly environment.

H3: Superiority of multi-strategic or more agile firms over mono-strategic or less agile firms is positively related to the degree of external environment's hostility (or negatively related to the degree of external environment's friendliness).

Next we present distribution and characteristics of independent variables, dependent variables, and analyses aimed at tests of hypotheses.

33.3 Research Results

33.3.1 Independent Variables: Strategic Agility and Environment Friendliness–Hostility

Operationalization of all variables is identical to the one in our previous study (Sikora & Baranowska-Prokop, 2021). Thus, strategic agility is operationalized through distinction between mono-strategy and multi-strategy in two aspects: price strategy (setting one price level, or better, having one price-setting orientation for all customers vs applying multiple price levels depending on customer) and product quality strategy (producing all goods at a given quality level vs producing the same goods at different quality levels depending on customers' requirements and/or their ability to detect quality variations).

Table 33.1 presents answers of interviewed managers concerning price strategy.

Single price formation strategies are implemented by the majority of enterprises. Exporters were no more likely to adopt multi-strategy in regards to price than

Table 33.1 Single price level strategy vs multiple price levels strategy

		Frequency	Percent
Valid	Single price level strategy	142	64.8
	Multiple price levels strategy	77	35.2
	Total	219	100.0

Source: Own elaboration

Table 33.2 Single quality level strategy vs multiple quality levels strategy

		Frequency	Percent
Valid	Single quality level strategy	138	63.0
	Multiple quality levels strategy	81	37.0
	Total	219	100.0

Source: Own elaboration

non-exporters (36.7 percent against 33.6 percent, the difference is not significant). The difference between small- and medium-sized firms (25.7 percent against 50.6 percent) is significant: $\chi^2 = 13.981, p < 0.0001$.

Since the phenomenon of multi-strategy is considered to be an aspect of strategic agility, exporters do not appear to be more strategically agile than non-exporters. The different observation is in the case of medium-sized firms, compared to the small ones.

Table 33.2 presents data about the second measure of strategic agility: mono- and multi-strategies related to product quality.

For product quality level strategy, majority of respondents (63 percent) declared pursuing a single quality standard strategy (the proportion is comparable to the price strategy).

This time exporters have been more willing to apply multi-strategy (48.6 percent) compared to non-exporters (25.5 percent), and the difference is significant: $\chi^2 = 12.610$, $p < 0{,}0001$. The disparity between medium-sized and small-sized firms in this respect (36.0 percent against 38.6 percent) is not significant.

The two measures of strategic agility are not correlated.

Operationalization of hostility–friendliness of external environment is based on a three-item scale proposed by Khandwalla (1977) and presented by Covin and Slevin (1989), to which the fourth item has been added. The items are preceded by a question: "How would you characterize the external environment within which your firm operates." They are formulated as follows:

- Very safe, little threat to the survival and well-being of my firm vs very risky, a false step can mean my firm's undoing.
- Rich in investment and marketing opportunities vs very stressful, exacting, hostile, very hard to keep afloat.
- An environment that my firm can control and manipulate to its own advantage, such as a dominant firm has an industry with a little competition and few hindrances vs a dominating environment in which my firm's initiatives count for very little against the tremendous competitive, political, or technological forces.

Table 33.3 Descriptive statistics for the environment friendliness–hostility scale, Dec. 2020–Jan. 2021

	N	Mean	Std. deviation	Skewness		Kurtosis	
	Statistic	Statistic	Statistic	Statistic	Std. error	Statistic	Std. error
Very safe [1] –very risky [7]	219	2.66	0.936	0.215	0.164	−0.230	.327
Friendly, opportunity-rich [1] – Stressful, hostile [7]	219	2.55	0.835	0.094	0.164	−0.586	.327
Controllable [1] – non-controllable, dominating [7]	219	2.82	0.997	−0.215	0.164	−0.909	.327
Stable, foreseeable [1] – Unstable, changing [7]	219	2.59	0.751	0.446	0.164	−0.195	.327
Valid N (listwise)	219						

Source: Own elaboration, 7-point scale

One item has been added by the authors: stable, foreseeable vs unstable, changing.

In the tables below, the items (measured on a seven-point scale) are referred to as:

- Very safe vs very risky.
- Friendly, opportunity-rich vs stressful, hostile.
- Controllable vs non-controllable, dominating,
- Stable, foreseeable vs unstable, changing.

Table 33.3 presents descriptive statistics for the scale of external environment-friendliness—hostility as perceived by respondents in December 2020 and January 2021.

Means much below the midpoint of the scale (4) indicate that majority of respondents perceived external environment as very friendly or friendly.

Table 33.4 presents similar data from our previous study (Sikora & Baranowska-Prokop, 2021) when questions have been asked during the pre-COVID period of May–July 2019.

Means of answers in Table 33.4 are only slightly below the midpoint (4), so, when they are compared with those in Table 33.3, it appears paradoxically that during COVID-19 pandemic, respondents perceived external environment in Poland as safer, more friendly, controllable, and stable than prior to COVID-19 (most of the differences between means from Tables 33.3 and 33.4 are superior to 1 point of the scale).

Reliability of this scale is worse compared to the earlier study, because the Cronbach alpha coefficient is 0.681, which is a "borderline" value; the Guttman's L coefficients (2–6) are between 0.64 and 0.72 (as compared to the level above 0.8 in

Table 33.4 Descriptive statistics for the environment friendliness–hostility scale, May–July 2019

	N	Mean	Std. deviation	Skewness		Kurtosis	
	Statistic	Statistic	Statistic	Statistic	Std. error	Statistic	Std. error
Very safe [1] – Very risky [7]	240	3.74	1.344	−0.301	0.157	0.255	0.313
Friendly, opportunity-rich [1] – Stressful, hostile [7]	240	3.58	1.314	−0.302	0.157	−0.100	0.313
Controllable [1] – non-controllable, dominating [7]	240	3.86	1.377	−0.189	0.157	0.286	0.313
Stable, foreseeable [1] – Unstable, changing [7]	240	3.85	1.325	−0.218	0.157	0.366	0.313
Valid N (listwise)	240						

Source: Own elaboration, 7-point scale

Table 33.5 Environment hostility–friendliness scale: Two categories of environment

		Frequency	Percent
Valid	Very friendly environment	111	50.7
	Friendly-to-neutral environment	108	49.3
	Total	219	100.0

Source: Own elaboration

the previous study). Values of the items have been added, and the final single scale has values between 4 (very friendly or benign environment) and, theoretically, 28 (very difficult, hostile environment) with the midpoint at 16. However, the highest value given by one respondent is 18, which can still be considered as neutral environment.

Unlike the previous study, where categories of "friendly," "neutral," and "hostile" environment could be distinguished, in the presented research, it is only possible to distinguish two categories of the external environment: "very friendly" and "friendly-to-neutral."

Table 33.5 presents a classification of answers within two categories of environment friendliness.

As concerns differences in perception of environmental hostility–friendliness between exporters and non-exporters and between small- and medium-sized enterprises, univariate analysis of variance shows that one main effect is significant (exporters vs non-exporters with non-exporters perceiving environment as less friendly). The interaction is significant, which means, in this case, that medium-sized exporters perceived environment in most friendly terms, medium-sized non-exporters in the least friendly, but still friendly terms and with virtually no difference between small exporters and small non-exporters.

33.3.2 Dependent Variables: Indicators of Firms' Performance

The concept of firm performance is one that has not been a unanimously accepted definition over the years. Some researchers measure it using quantitative indices such as profitability, return on investment (ROI), market share, etc. From another perspective, it is perceived as a degree in which the objectives of the organization are achieved (Wales et al., 2012). In this approach, performance is measured using qualitative descriptions such as employee performance, customer satisfaction, competitive advantage, etc. Ledwith and O'Dwyer (2009) suggest to assess SME's performance by the accomplishment of tasks by the employees of a firm as well as the quality of these completed tasks at the close of a specific business period as measured against predetermined targets or aims.

Due to the impossibility in our research of obtaining precise figures about profits and sales, descriptive questions about market performance in 2019 and 2020 had to be applied.

Respondents from companies evaluated, in general terms, the level of profits/losses and sales dynamics on 5-point scales. The degrees of the profit/loss scale include substantial loss (1), small loss (2), result close to zero (3), small profit (4), and substantial profit (5). The degrees of scale measuring sales dynamics include substantial decrease by 2-digit percent (1), decrease by 1-digit percent (2), no change (3), increase by 1-digit percent (4), and substantial increase by 2-digit percent (5).

The period of data collection, i.e., December 2020 and January 2021, is characterized by uncertainty about 2020 results; therefore, they have been referred to as "estimated" in the questionnaire.

Table 33.6 presents descriptive statistics related to measures of firms' performance.

Analysis of frequencies reveals that the situation was not that "dramatic" as one might have expected due to COVID-19 pandemic lockdowns, supply chain disruptions, and other restrictions and problems. The share of firms declaring heavy or light losses was 14.6 percent, those with result "close to zero" – 31.1 percent and profitable firms accounted for 54.4 percent of the total. The picture was less positive

Table 33.6 Descriptive statistics related to market performance

	N	Mean	Std. deviation	Skewness		Kurtosis	
	Statistic	Statistic	Statistic	Statistic	Std. error	Statistic	Std. error
Financial results in 2020 (estimated)	219	3.36	0.945	−1.042	0.164	0.685	0.327
Sales dynamics in 2020 (estimated) compared to 2019	219	2.99	0.995	0.525	0.164	−0.602	0.327
Valid N (listwise)	219						

Source: Own elaboration; financial results and sales dynamics have been measured on 5-point scales for sales dynamics estimates with 37.4 percent of firms declaring a decrease (in which 1.4 percent of respondents declared "substantial" decrease), 34.2 percent – no change and 28.3 percent small or substantial sales increase.

According to the univariate analysis of variance, every measure of financial results has been better evaluated by exporters compared to non-exporters. Differences between small- and medium-sized firms are not significant. Interactions are significant in the way that small exporters have evaluated market performance measures at the highest levels and small non-exporters at the lowest ones.

33.3.3 Influence of COVID-19 Pandemic-Related Restrictions on Firms' Market Performance

Two measures have been applied to assess the influence of COVID-19 pandemic-related restrictions on a firm's financial results and turnover evolution.

The first, indirect measure aimed at assessing the impact of restrictions on macro- and microenvironment was a question: "Did the Covid-19 pandemic deteriorate or improve situation in the environment your firm operates?" measured on a 7-point scale. There is the following distribution of answers: "strongly deteriorated," 1.4%; "deteriorated," 30.1%; "rather deteriorated," 50.2%; "no change," 18.3%; and "rather improved," 1,4% (N = 219).

This measure is, unexpectedly, not significantly correlated neither with the environment hostility–friendliness scale ($r = -0.019$, $p = 0.779$) nor with the measure of estimated financial results for 2020 ($r = 0.085$, $p = 0.208$) or estimated sales dynamics for 2020 compared to 2019 ($r = 0.084$, $p = 0.215$).

Another measure of consequences of COVID-19 restrictions was based on questions related to positive and negative phenomena which were due to the pandemics.

Among four types of negative consequences, respondents indicated supply chain disruptions (53.4%), increase of losses or decrease of profits (35.6%), customers' bankruptcy/insolvability (14.2%), and the lack of suppliers (6.8%).

However, some respondents declared that their firms had experienced also positive consequences of the pandemic, specifying up to three elements such as some competitors went bankrupt (8.2%), increase in demand for firm's products (1.4%), and increase of profits or decrease of losses (1.4%).

An index of the strength and directions (negative to positive) based on the abovementioned answers could have been created in the way that each of the negative consequences was marked as "−1" and each of positive consequences as "1." Since most of the companies indicated several consequences and some of them both negative and positive ones simultaneously, all consequences have been added, and a "balance of consequences" has been calculated for each company.

The distribution of the COVID-related consequences balance ranged from −3 (either three negative consequences or an excess of negative consequences over the positive ones by the number of three) to 3 (three positive consequences; since no firm declared more than three positive consequences this figure means that no negative consequences have been declared by the companies at the positive end of the scale).

The distribution of this index is skewed toward the predominance of negative consequences with the balance of −3 for 1.4% of companies, −2 for 13.2%, −1 for 76.3%, 0 for 3.2%, 1 for 4.6%, 2 for 0.9%, and 3 for 0.5% (N = 219).

The balance of COVID-19 consequences is not significantly correlated with the environment hostility–friendliness scale ($r = -0.032$, $p = 0.638$), but it is significantly correlated, and in a logical direction, with both the measure of estimated financial results for 2020 ($r = 0.197$, $p = 0.03$) and estimated sales dynamics for 2020 compared to 2019 ($r = 0.185$, $p = 0.06$), although these correlations are very weak. The interpretation of positive correlations with both market performance measures is that the more positive balance of COVID-related consequences (or given the shape of this variable distribution – the less negative balance), the better market performance.

33.3.4 Verification of Hypotheses Related to the Relationship Between Strategic Agility and Performance

Hypothesis 1 implied positive relationship between strategic agility and performance, i.e., the achievement of better results by multi-strategic firms compared to mono-strategic firms.

Tables 33.7a and 33.7b present descriptive statistics related to market performance measures declared by single- and multi-strategic firms with regard to price strategy and results of robust tests of equality of means (available in the SPSS software for ANOVA analysis).

Table 33.7a Descriptive statistics concerning market performance measures related to price strategy

		N	Mean	Std. deviation
Financial results in 2020 (estimated)	Single price level strategy	142	3.31	0.976
	Multiple price levels strategy	77	3.45	0.882
	Total	219	3.36	0.945
Sales dynamics in 2020 (estimated) compared to 2019	Single price level strategy	142	2.96	0.985
	Multiple price levels strategy	77	3.04	1.019
	Total	219	2.99	0.995

Source: Own elaboration

Table 33.7b Robust tests of equality of means related to price strategy

		Statistic[a]	df1	df2	Sig.
Financial results in 2020 (estimated)	Welch	1.245	1	170.094	0.266
	Brown-Forsythe	1.245	1	170.094	0.266
Sales dynamics in 2020 (estimated) compared to 2019	Welch	0.271	1	151.591	0.604
	Brown-Forsythe	0.271	1	151.591	0.604

Source: Own elaboration
[a]Asymptotically F distributed

Table 33.8a Descriptive statistics concerning market performance measures related to product quality strategy

		N	Mean	Std. deviation
Financial results in 2020 (estimated)	Single quality level strategy	138	3.27	1.043
	Multiple quality levels strategy	81	3.52	0.726
	Total	219	3.36	0.945
Sales dynamics in 2020 (estimated) compared to 2019	Single quality level strategy	138	2.93	1.020
	Multiple quality levels strategy	81	3.09	0.951
	Total	219	2.99	0.995

Source: Own elaboration

Table 33.8b Robust tests of equality of means related to product quality strategy

		Statistic[a]	df1	df2	Sig.
Financial results in 2020 (estimated)	Welch	4.354	1	210.647	0.038
	Brown-Forsythe	4.354	1	210.647	0.038
Sales dynamics in 2020 (estimated) compared to 2019	Welch	1.229	1	177.206	0.269
	Brown-Forsythe	1.229	1	177.206	0.269

Source: Own elaboration
[a]Asymptotically F distributed

Although numerically multi-strategic firms achieved better results than mono-strategic firms, the difference is small and nonsignificant, and we cannot conclude that higher level of strategic agility related to price strategy leads to better results.

Tables 33.8a and 33.8b present descriptive statistics related to market performance measures declared by single- and multi-strategic firms with regard to product quality strategy as well as results of robust tests of equality of means.

For both performance measures, multi-strategic firms achieved better results, but the difference is significant for financial results only.

When all outcomes are taken into account in the context of analyzed variables, the support for H1 is very weak, i.e., one out of four results supports it, but the remaining three are not supporting it (although it should be added that there has been no significant result against this hypothesis). However, when we look from a broader perspective to explain firms' performance and when univariate analysis of variance is applied with more variables included and taken into account together with strategic agility (exporters and non-exporters, small- and medium-sized firms and two categories of an external environment), the difference between mono- and multi-strategic firms from Tables 33.8a and 33.8b is no longer significant, so, finally, H1 in a broader context is not confirmed (see Tables 33.13 and 33.14 in the statistical annex).

As far as the second hypothesis is concerned, there is no direct relationship between the characteristics of external environment and firms' performance, because correlation coefficients (Pearson's r and Kendall's tau-b) between the environmental friendliness–hostility scale and the two market performance measures are close to zero (in the range from 0.016 to −0.041) and thus not significant, and results of nonlinear regression show that there is neither quadratic nor cubic form of relationship. Therefore H2 is not confirmed.

Hypothesis 3 assumed that environment might play the role of moderating variable between strategic agility and market performance. The more hostile environment, the more useful role of high strategic agility in achieving better results compared to less strategically agile competitors. However, in contrast to the pre-COVID study, the evaluation of external environment has been so favorable that the cases of hostile environment have not been indicated and cannot be analyzed leaving room for two categories: "very friendly environment" and "friendly-to-neutral environment."

In conclusion, we can imply from Hypothesis 3 that the advantage of multi-strategic (and thus more strategically agile) firms over mono-strategic (and less agile) firms would be smaller in very friendly environment compared to friendly-to-neutral environment.

Tables 33.9a and 33.9b present the results of data analysis concerning relationship between strategic agility and market performance in the case of price strategy for firms operating in a very friendly environment.

In a very friendly environment, higher strategic agility in terms of price strategy did not lead to significant competitive advantage over less strategically agile firms.

Table 33.9a Descriptive statistics concerning market performance measures related to price strategy in a very friendly environment

		N	Mean	Std. deviation
Financial results in 2020 (estimated)	Single price level strategy	74	3.30	0.947
	Multiple price levels strategy	37	3.51	0.804
	Total	111	3.37	0.904
Sales dynamics in 2020 (estimated) compared to 2019	Single price level strategy	74	3.03	1.020
	Multiple price levels strategy	37	3.05	1.026
	Total	111	3.04	1.017

Source: Own elaboration
[a]Environment hostility–friendliness scale (2 categ.) = very friendly environment

Table 33.9b Robust tests of equality of means related to price strategy in a very friendly environment[a]

		Statistic[b]	df1	df2	Sig.
Financial results in 2020 (estimated)	Welch	1.581	1	83.501	0.212
	Brown-Forsythe	1.581	1	83.501	0.212
Sales dynamics in 2020 (estimated) compared to 2019	Welch	0.017	1	71.735	0.896
	Brown-Forsythe	0.017	1	71.735	0.896

Source: Own elaboration
[a]Environment hostility–friendliness scale (2 categ.) = very friendly environment
[b]Asymptotically F distributed

Table 33.10a Descriptive statistics concerning market performance measures related to product quality strategy in a very friendly environment

		N	Mean	Std. deviation
Financial results in 2020 (estimated)	Single quality level strategy	70	3.24	1.042
	Multiple quality levels strategy	41	3.59	0.547
	Total	111	3.37	0.904
Sales dynamics in 2020 (estimated) compared to 2019	Single quality level strategy	70	2,96	1.013
	Multiple quality levels strategy	41	3.17	1.022
	Total	111	3.04	1.017

Source: Own elaboration
[a]Environment hostility–friendliness scale (2 categ.) = very friendly environment

Table 33.10b Robust tests of equality of means related to product quality strategy in a very friendly environment[a]

		Statistic[b]	df1	df2	Sig.
Financial results in 2020 (estimated)	Welch	5.148	1	107.965	0.025
	Brown-Forsythe	5.148	1	107.965	0.025
Sales dynamics in 2020 (estimated) compared to 2019	Welch	1.136	1	83.303	0.290
	Brown-Forsythe	1.136	1	83.303	0.290

Source: Own elaboration
[a]Environment hostility–friendliness scale (2 categ.) = very friendly environment
[b]Asymptotically F distributed

Tables 33.10a and 33.10b present the results of data analysis concerning relationship between strategic agility and market performance in the case of product quality strategy for firms having declared operating in a very friendly environment.

More strategically agile firms declared better financial results compared to the less agile companies in the context of analyzed variables, and it is a support for H1, but again, when other variables are taken into account (exporters vs non-exporters, small- vs medium-sized firms) in univariate analysis of variance, this difference is

Table 33.11a Descriptive statistics concerning market performance measures related to price strategy in a friendly-to-neutral environment[a]

		N	Mean	Std. deviation
Financial results in 2020 (estimated)	Single price level strategy	68	3.32	1.014
	Multiple price levels strategy	40	3.40	0.955
	Total	108	3.35	0.989
Sales dynamics in 2020 (estimated) compared to 2019	Single price level strategy	68	2.90	0.949
	Multiple price levels strategy	40	3.03	1.025
	Total	108	2.94	0.975

Source: Own elaboration
[a]Environment hostility–friendliness scale (2 categ.) = friendly-to-neutral environment

Table 33.11b Robust tests of equality of means related to price strategy in a friendly-to-neutral environment[a]

		Statistic[b]	df1	df2	Sig.
Financial results in 2020 (estimated)	Welch	0.154	1	85.858	0.696
	Brown-Forsythe	0.154	1	85.858	0.696
Sales dynamics in 2020 (estimated) compared to 2019	Welch	0.414	1	76.837	0.522
	Brown-Forsythe	0.414	1	76.837	0.522

Source: Own elaboration
[a]Environment hostility–friendliness scale (2 categ.) = friendly-to-neutral environment
[b]Asymptotically F distributed

no longer significant, and H1 is not supported (see Tables 33.13 and 33.14 in the statistical annex). To observe if the H3 is confirmed or not, data from a less friendly environment should be taken into account.

Tables 33.11a and 33.11b present the results of data analysis concerning the relationship between strategic agility and market performance in the case of price strategy for firms operating in a friendly-to-neutral environment.

Despite the numerical superiority of results achieved by strategically agile firms, the differences are not significant.

Tables 33.12a and 33.12b present the results of data analysis concerning the relationship between strategic agility and market performance in the case of product quality strategy for firms having declared operating in a friendly-to-neutral environment.

Again, in spite of numerically higher results declared by respondents from more strategically agile firms, differences are small and not significant.

Finally, unlike in the previous research (Sikora & Baranowska-Prokop, 2021), none of the three hypotheses has been confirmed due to nonsignificant statistical differences between mono- and multi-strategic firms in terms of market performance

Table 33.12a Descriptive statistics concerning market performance measures related to product quality strategy in a friendly-to-neutral environment[a]

		N	Mean	Std. deviation
Financial results in 2020 (estimated)	Single quality level strategy	68	3.29	1.052
	Multiple quality levels strategy	40	3.45	0.876
	Total	108	3.35	0.989
Sales dynamics in 2020 (estimated) compared to 2019	Single quality level strategy	68	2.91	1.033
	Multiple quality levels strategy	40	3.00	0.877
	Total	108	2.94	0.975

Source: Own elaboration
[a]Environment hostility–friendliness scale (2 categ.) = friendly-to-neutral environment

Table 33.12b Robust tests of equality of means related to product quality strategy in a friendly-to-neutral environment[a]

		Statistic[b]	df1	df2	Sig.
Financial results in 2020 (estimated)	Welch	0.686	1	93.917	0.410
	Brown-Forsythe	0.686	1	93.917	0.410
Sales dynamics in 2020 (estimated) compared to 2019	Welch	0.223	1	92.680	0.638
	Brown-Forsythe	0.223	1	92.680	0.638

Source: Own elaboration
[a] Environment hostility–friendliness scale (2 categ.) = friendly-to-neutral environment
[b] Asymptotically F distributed

and due to lack of significant relationship between evaluations of external environment hostility–friendliness and market performance of analyzed firms.

33.4 Conclusions

We suggest that the result of our research, i.e., nonsignificant relationships in most cases between strategic agility and firms' performance measures, may be explained by the series of actions counteracting the COVID-19 consequences taken by the Polish government. A surprisingly favorable evaluation of external environment, a more favorable one compared to what was declared by respondents during the pre-COVID period, may support our assumption.

On March 31, 2020, the Parliament has enacted "Anti-crisis Shield," the act which aims to eliminate the negative economic effects of COVID-19. The package of around 66.3 billion Euros, which is the largest economic support in Poland's modern history, has been introduced. It provides entrepreneurs with the possibility to suspend or defer social security payments for 3 months, subsidies up to 40 percent of the average 2019 salary for employees in crisis-stricken companies, it offers income support for the self-employed and strengthens the financial system.

The large scale of governmental support was, in our opinion, a decisive factor for firms' financial results. Moreover, the Polish currency was considered to be undervalued. This factor gave support to exporters and to at least some manufacturers delivering for the local market, which improved results related to the second measure of market performance – changes in sales of produced goods.

Strategic agility was probably revealed in a form of efficient application for available government compensation programs rather than in aspects we analyzed in our study.

33.5 Limitations and Further Research

Firstly, other operationalizations of strategic agility and environmental friendliness–hostility may be envisaged. For COVID-19 period, strategic agility may consist in establishing teams capable to get as much aid from public assistance programs as possible.

Secondly, more in-depth knowledge can be gained if less and more agile firms from homogeneous branches of industry or services are compared. However, the sample is very fragmented as far as the number of industrial branches is concerned, and such an analysis is difficult in our case.

Thirdly, when analyzing relationships with univariate analysis of variance including all discussed variables simultaneously to explain firms' performance measures, i.e., two aspects of strategic agility, size of companies, the fact of exporting or not exporting and two categories of environment, the results indicate that main effects of strategic agility on market performance measures are not significant and the effect of interaction between them is not significant either. However, both the first and second strategic agility form (i.e., based on price strategy and product quality strategy) appear involved in various significant less or more complex interactions with other variables. Therefore, looking into these interactions may lead to the elaboration of a more complex theory about the effects of strategic agility on firms' performance.

A.1 Statistical Annex

Table A.13 Results of univariate analysis of variance for financial results in 2020 (estimated) as a dependent variable (excerpt without most of the interactions)

Tests of between-subjects effects					
Dependent variable: Financial results in 2020 (estimated)					
Source	Type III sum of squares	df	Mean square	F	Sig.
Corrected model	62.463[a]	31	2.015	2.854	0.000
Intercept	684.855	1	684.855	969.922	0.000
Balance COVID conseq	**3.597**	**1**	**3.597**	**5.094**	**0.025**
Small- vs medium-sized	**3.430**	**1**	**3.430**	**4.857**	**0.029**
Exporters vs non-exporters	**8.119**	**1**	**8.119**	**11.499**	**0.001**
Environment	**0.142**	**1**	**0.142**	**0.202**	**0.654**
Agility price	**0.107**	**1**	**0.107**	**0.152**	**0.697**
Agility quality	**0.009**	**1**	**0.009**	**0.012**	**0.911**
Smallmdmszd * expnonexp	0.484	1	0.484	0.686	0.409
Smallmdmszd * envir	0.169	1	0.169	0.239	0.625
Smallmdmszd * agilprice	1.234	1	1.234	1.748	0.188
Smallmdmszd * agilquality	0.528	1	0.528	0.748	0.388
Expnonexp * envir	3.446	1	3.446	4.880	0.028
Expnonexp * agilprice	1.031	1	1.031	1.460	0.228
Expnonexp * agilquality	1.171	1	1.171	1.658	0.199
Envir * agilprice	0.470	1	0.470	0.666	0.416
Envir * agilquality	0.607	1	0.607	0.859	0.355
Agilprice * agilquality	0.001	1	0.001	0.002	0.964
(……)	(……)	(……)	.	.	.
Error	132.039	187	0.706		
Total	2668.000	219			
Corrected total	194.502	218			

Source: Own elaboration

[a]R Squared =,321 (Adjusted R Squared = 0.209)

Table A.14 Results of univariate analysis of variance for sales dynamics in 2020 (estimated) compared to 2019 as a dependent variable (excerpt without most of the interactions)

Tests of between-subjects effects					
Dependent variable: Sales dynamics in 2020 (estimated) compared to 2019					
Source	Type III sum of squares	df	Mean square	F	Sig.
Corrected model	54.985[a]	31	1.774	2.060	0.002
Intercept	552.721	1	552.721	641.995	0.000
Balance COVID conseq	**5.657**	**1**	**5.657**	**6.570**	**0.011**
Small- vs medium-sized	**3.186**	**1**	**3.186**	**3.700**	**0.056**
Exporters vs non-exporters	**11.684**	**1**	**11.684**	**13.571**	**0.000**
Environment	**0.502**	**1**	**0.502**	**0.583**	**0.446**
Agility price	**0.218**	**1**	**0.218**	**0.253**	**0.616**
Agility quality	**0.271**	**1**	**0.271**	**0.315**	**0.575**
Smallmdmszd * expnonexp	0.034	1	0.034	0.040	0.842
Smallmdmszd * envir	1.007	1	1.007	1.170	0.281
Smallmdmszd * agilprice	0.909	1	0.909	1.055	0.306
Smallmdmszd * agilquality	1.619	1	1.619	1.881	0.172
Expnonexp * envir	7.202	1	7.202	8.365	0.004
Expnonexp * agilprice	0.065	1	0.065	0.076	0.783
Expnonexp * agilquality	3.895	1	3.895	4.524	0.035
Envir * agilprice	2.788	1	2.788	3.239	0.074
Envir * agilquality	2.283	1	2.283	2.651	0.105
Agilprice * agilquality	0.166	1	0.166	0.193	0.661
(......)	(......)	(......)	.	.	.
Error	160.996	187	0.861		
Total	2175.000	219			
Corrected total	215.982	218			

Source: Own elaboration

[a]R Squared =, 255 (adjusted R squared = 0.131)

References

Aaker, D., & Mascarenhas, B. (1984). The need for strategic flexibility. *Journal of Business 417 Strategy, 5*(2), 74–82.

Adian, I., Doumbia, D., Gregory, N., Ragoussis, A., Reddy, A., & Timmis, J. (2020). Small and medium enterprises in the pandemic: Impact, responses and the role of development finance. Policy Research Working Paper No. 9414. World Bank

Asian Development Bank (2020). COVID-19 Economic Impact Could Reach $8.8 Trillion Globally — New ADB Report. Available at: https://www.adb.org/news/covid-19-economic-impact-could-reach-8-8-trillion-globally-new-adb-report. Retrieved June 26, 2020

Bernardes, E. S., & Hanna, M. D. (2009). A theoretical review of flexibility, agility and responsiveness in the operations management literature: Towards a conceptual definition of customer responsiveness. *International Journal of Operations & Production Management, 29*(1), 30–53.

Covin, J. G., & Slevin, D. P. (1989). Strategic management of small firms in hostile and benign environments. *Strategic Management Journal, 10*(1), 75–87.

CSM. (2020). Anti-crisis shield. The impact of new regulations on conducting business in Poland. https://cms.law/en/media/local/cms-cmno/files/publications/publications/anti-crisis-shield-english-version?v=2 (http://www.psik.org.pl)

Doz, Y., & Kosonen, M. (2016). The dynamics of strategic agility: Nokia's rollercoaster. *California Management Review, 50*(3), 95–118.

Georgieva, K. (2020). IMF forecast for 2020 is negative. Press release no 20/98. Available at: https://www.imf.org

Gunaskaran, A. (1998). Agile manufacturing: Enablers and implementation framework. *International Journal of Production Research, 36*(5), 1223–1247.

Khandwalla, P. N. (1977). The Design of Organizations. Harcourt Bruce Jovanovich, New York, NY, cited after Covin, J. G., Slevin, D. P, Strategic management of small firms in hostile and benign environments, Strategic Management Journal; Jan/Feb 1989, 10(1), 75–87

Kumar, A., & Motwani, J. (1995). A methodology for assessing time-based competitive advantage of manufacturing firms. *International Journal of Operations & Production Management, 15*(2), 36–53.

Ledwith, A., & O'Dwyer, M. (2009). Market orientation, NPD performance, and organizational performance in small firms. *Journal of Product Innovation Management, 26*(6), 652–661.

Meredith, S., & Francis, D. (2000). Journey towards agility: The agile wheel explored. *The TQM Magazine., 12*, 137–143.

Miller, D., & Friesen, P. H. (1983). Strategy-making and environment: The third link. *Strategic Management Journal, 4*(3), 221–235.

Morton, J., Stacey, P., & Mohn, M. (2018). Building and maintaining strategic agility: An agenda and framework for executive IT leaders. *California Management Review, 61*(1), 94–113.

Narasimhan, R., Swink, M., & Kim, S. (2006). Disentangling leanness and agility: An empirical investigation. *Journal of Operations Management, 24*(5), 440–457.

OECD: Business at OECD (BIAC). (2020). Economic Policy Survey "Views from the frontline" https://biac.org/wp-content/uploads/2020/05/Business-at-OECD-2020-Economic-Policy-Survey.pdf

PARP. (2020). Raport o stanie sektora małych i średnich przedsiębiorstw w Polsce 2020. https://www.parp.gov.pl/component/publications/publication/raport-o-stanie-sektora-malych-i-srednich-przedsiebiorstw-w-polsce-2020. Retrieved June 26, 2020.

Roberts, N., & Grover, V. (2012). Investigating firm's customer agility and firm performance: The importance of aligning sense and respond capabilities. *Journal of Business Research, 65*(5), 579–585.

Salesforce (2020). 4th Edition Small & Medium Business Trends Report. https://www.salesforce.com/form/pdf/2020-small-business-trends-report/. Retrieved June 26, 2020.

Sikora, T., & Baranowska-Prokop, E. (2021). The role of strategic agility and economic Environment's friendliness-hostility in explaining success of polish SMEs. In N. Tsounis & A. Vlachvei (Eds.), *Advances in longitudinal data methods in applied economic research* (pp. 267–284). Springer Proceedings in Business and Economics. https://doi.org/10.1007/978-3-030-63970-9_19

Statista. (2021). Coronavirus (COVID-19) in Poland. Statista Dossier. https://www.statista.com/study/71486/coronavirus-covid-19-in-poland/#professional. Retrieved June 26, 2020.

Wales, W., Parida, V., & Patel, P. (2012). Too much of a good thing? Absorptive capacity, firm performance, and the moderating role of entrepreneurial orientation. *Strategic Management Journal, 34*(5), 622–633.

Weber, Y., & Tarba, S. Y. (2014). Strategic agility: A state of the art. *California Management Review, 53*(2), 271–286.

Chapter 34
Brand Evangelism as an Emerging Marketing Approach Among Fashion Businesses

Eleni Mavragani, Fragiskos Archontakis, Maria Koiou, and Stavroula Laspita

Abstract This study examines the relationships between brand evangelism, brand preference and purchase intentions decisions on clothing. Using data from online questionnaires and through probit regression analysis, we investigate the contemporary purchase behaviour and social media interaction between customers and enterprises in Greece. In doing so, we attempt to add more insights to the understanding of the interaction between brand page commitment and brand evangelism.

Keywords Brand evangelism · Marketing · Probit regression · Clothing industry

34.1 Introduction

The advent and rapid adoption of internet-based applications have recently changed the traditional way of communication and marketing strategy. The social media revolution has transformed the traditional one-way communication into a multidimensional communication allowing people to share an increasing volume of information (Hutter et al., 2013). In terms of marketing, that implies consumers often resort to social media either to obtain or to exchange information about brands (e.g. social media fashion influencers: Quelhas-Brito et al., 2020).

E. Mavragani
Department of Accounting and Finance, University of Macedonia, Thessaloniki, Greece
e-mail: mavragani@uom.edu.gr

F. Archontakis · M. Koiou
University Center of International Programmes of Studies, International Hellenic University, Thessaloniki, Greece

S. Laspita (✉)
Department of Economics, University of Western Macedonia, Kastoria, Greece
e-mail: slaspita@uowm.gr

N. Tsounis, A. Vlachvei (eds.), *Advances in Quantitative Economic Research*, Springer Proceedings in Business and Economics,
https://doi.org/10.1007/978-3-030-98179-2_34

Thus, the effect of social media on the branding process may seem fairly ambiguous. On the one hand, social media offer customers the opportunity to have more of say in the products (Gaber & Wright, 2014), share information, brand experiences or perspectives about particular brands and, in general, virtually interact throughout brand community-oriented websites. On the other hand, social media offer contemporary companies the ability to have online presence in several social media outlets (e.g. Facebook, Instagram, Twitter, etc.), increase their attractiveness and, through social media brand communities, establish and foster a long-term relationship with their customers (Hsu, 2019; Parganas et al., 2015). These social networking relationships and interactions have transformed brands into a social process where value is co-created both by brand's marketing activities and by consumer's brand advocacy (Hutter et al., 2013).

The new challenge faced by brand managers is how to manage the new, online customer-brand relationships for this interaction to result in a sustainable competitive advantage for their companies. One of the most prominent methods they often use is customer's commitment to their online brand communities. Brand community commitment is said to be an effective way of recruiting even the most novice customers and making them attached and loyal to the brand (Park & Kim, 2014). The manager's main difficulty, though, lies in cultivating their customers' brand advocacy. Brand advocacy or word-of-mouth (WOM) marketing refers to the customer's messaging of positive recommendations for a particular brand to another customer. When this behaviour becomes aggressive, it is often called *brand evangelism*, and the customers contributing to this behaviour are called brand evangelists (Forbes, 2015). Although it is said to be "the most effective form of promotion" (Forbes, 2015), brand evangelism or evangelism marketing, especially within the context of social media, still remains a challenging and complex process for brand managers.

The present paper aims to shed light on this topic and help managers understand whether this "new media brand engagement" (Hennig-Thurau et al., 2010, p. 314) affects consumer's brand evangelistic behaviours which can contribute both to their sales and the ultimate value of their company (Becerra & Badrinarayanan, 2013).

Many researchers have individually investigated the topics of customer's brand evangelism and brand page commitment without, though, providing a more holistic feedback on the interplay between them. With regards to the consumer-brand relationships, today's practitioners lead the way into phenomena such as brand love, brand zealotry, as well as brand evangelism (Hutter et al., 2013). Brand evangelism has recently gained the interest of many researchers and managers. Research on this heightened form of consumer brand advocacy has revealed methods of how companies can gain competitive advantage just by leveraging relationships with key consumers who can contribute to the co-creation of brand value (Becerra & Badrinarayanan, 2013; Doss & Carstens, 2014). However, these surveys do not incorporate the factor of social media and whether it contributes or not to consumers-brand evangelistic behaviours. At the same time, participation in offline brand communities is found to positively affect customer's commitment, dependability and evangelistic behaviours (Algesheimer et al., 2005). Other researchers have examined the positive effect of social media marketing activities individually on customer's brand awareness, brand trust, brand identification, brand loyalty and positive WOM (Hutter et al., 2013; Park & Kim, 2014). These studies, though, again fail to capture a more holistic view of the impact that online brand page commitment has on brand evangelism. In the traditional way of branding, it is well known that, in order to achieve higher levels of involvement, managers should turn the simple visitors of their brand communities first into members, then into contributors and, finally, into brand evangelists (Algesheimer et al., 2005). Little is known, though, about whether social media, and especially consumer's brand page commitment, does influence consumer's brand awareness, brand trust and consequently three, main, brand evangelistic behaviours: positive brand referrals, oppositional brand referrals and brand purchase intention (Becerra & Badrinarayanan, 2013). Therefore, this study seeks to add more insights to the understanding of the interaction between brand page commitment and brand evangelism.

Greece has recently witnessed an economic crisis which altered the budget of the majority of Greek people, consequently affecting their consumption patterns (e.g. Gerstberger & Yaneva, 2013). A prominent example of this phenomenon is the underlying change of their perceptions towards clothing brands, as many people who were used to purchase only famous clothing brands, now are also buying the cheaper generic.

The main purpose of this work is to examine whether Greek customers' commitment to their favoured clothing brand page can transform them into brand evangelists as well as to influence their perception towards clothing brands. Although several scholars have already investigated the brand evangelism concept (Becerra & Badrinarayanan, 2013; Doss & Carstens, 2014), there is limited systematic research in this subject considering the Greek public. In addition, academics and practitioners have seldom paid their attention to the effect of social media marketing activities, and especially that of brand page commitment, on specific brand evangelistic behaviours (Zailskaitė-Jakštė & Kuvykaitė, 2016). Another important objective of this study is to enable a greater understanding of how this kind of social media marketing affects Greek customers' perception of famous versus generic clothing brands. Even though word-of-mouth (WOM) behaviour is one of the oldest forms of marketing, brand evangelism marketing remains a relatively new domain. Consequently, it would be of great importance for contemporary managers working in the clothing industry to better understand the relation between online brand community commitment and customers' brand evangelistic behaviours.

To achieve the purpose before mentioned, this study poses two main questions:

1. Does Greek customers' commitment to online clothing brand pages affect their brand evangelistic behaviours?
2. Does Greek customers' commitment to online clothing brand pages affect their perception of famous over generic clothing brands?

The structure of the rest of the paper is as follows: Sect. 34.2 provides the literature review, while methods and data are in Sect. 34.3. Section 34.4 presents the results; finally, Sect. 34.5 discusses and concludes.

34.2 Literature Review

34.2.1 The Concept of Brand Evangelism and Relevant Theories

The term "brand evangelism" refers to a strong consumer-brand relationship that goes far beyond a positive consumer-to-consumer WOM communication. It combines the universal word brand, meaning the name, the term, the symbol, the sign or the design of a product or even a combination of them (Kotler and Keller, 2012, p. 265) and the Greek word *evangelismos* that people know today as evangelism, meaning the propagation of good news. Brand evangelism was first used by Kawasaki (1991) in an attempt to describe the behaviour of customers who are inherently motivated to fervently spread WOM (Shaari & Ahmad, 2016). Since then, and especially during the internet boom of the late 1990s, "evangelism" became a business buzzword being used, not only in religious but also in the marketing context (Cheng et al., 2015). It extended the simple WOM, namely, the vocal support of a brand, to an advanced, more active level including the behavioural support, too (Rashid & Ahmad, 2014). The people who support and communicate the character and the features of a specific brand aiming to impact on others' consumption behaviour are accordingly called brand evangelists (Smilansky, 2017; Riivits-Arkonsuo et al., 2015). In the literature review, they can also be found as brand zealots, brand advocates, customer apostles, brand ambassadors, brand militants, brand devotees or brand missionaries, all meaning the same (Maltzer et al., 2007; Doss & Carstens, 2014). So, what evangelism profiles is the missionary component of that customer group (Kautish, 2010).

Although, individually, the words included in the term of brand evangelism are simple and easily understood, as a behavioural concept, it is quite complicated and evolves from an amalgam of components. As Becerra and Badrinarayanan (2013, p. 379) say "brand evangelism cannot be bought and has to be carefully cultivated". One could claim that this cultivation has its early stage on AIDA, one of the most famous hierarchy of effects models, which determines the customer's decision-making process (Hutter et al., 2013). It actually explains the four mental stages of a customer relationship with a specific brand: awareness, interest, desire and action (AIDA). Brand awareness or brand salience refers to the ability of a customer to effortlessly recognize and recall a brand and together with brand image are the most important elements of brand knowledge (Schivinski & Dabrowski, 2015; Zailskaitė-Jakštė & Kuvykaitė, 2016). Interest and desire are what Albert (2008) name as attraction and passion in his survey on the 11 dimensions of brand love

(Riivits-Arkonsuo et al., 2015). Customer's love for a specific brand is also linked to positive emotions, spreading of love for the brand extrovertly (WOM), resistance to negative information, brand loyalty, as well as consumer repurchase intentions, namely, the last stage of AIDA model (Carrol & Ahuvia, 2006; Batra, 2012). Except, though, for the mental and the emotional stage, consumer's passionate love for a brand can subsequently be translated into brand adoption and brand advocacy, behaviours whose combination consists of what researchers call "brand evangelism" (Becerra & Badrinarayanan, 2013). As it still remains a relatively new concept in the marketplace, brand evangelism has limited systematic research upon it. Among the first who recognized that WOM underplays the meaning of brand evangelism was Maltzer (2007) who defined it as an active and committed way of disseminating positive thinking of a specific brand in an attempt to convince others of becoming engaged with the same brand (Swimberghe et al., 2014). For Maltzer (2007) "consumers who evangelize are passionate about their brand and feel the need to share emotions with others" (Riivits-Arkonsuo et al., 2015, p. 7). His approach, though, was restricted only to vocal communication, without taking into account the customer's behavioural component. The journey from the first experience with a brand to the customer becoming brand evangelist was also analysed in the analytical model of a five-stage pyramid adopted by Tarssanen and Kylänen (2007) and Tynan and McKechnie (2009). Consumers in each of these five stages modify their tone of speaking so as to evangelize their meaningful brand experiences and persuade others to engage with their favoured brand (Riivits-Arkonsuo et al., 2015). Scarpi (2010), on the other hand, separated brand evangelism into two main categories: brand-related, caused by affect towards a brand, and community-related, caused by loyalty towards a community. However, similar to Maltzer (2007), Tynan and McKechnie (2009), he focused again only on the emotional and psychological factors overlooking the behavioural factors supporting this strong WOM behaviour.

During the last years, some researchers tried to give a more precise feedback on brand evangelism literature. Among them are Becerra and Badrinarayanan (2013) who supported that, in order for brand firms to cultivate their customers' strong evangelistic behaviours, they should create brands that customers both trust and identify with. Brand trust, namely, the consumer's willingness to rely on a brand's expertise, together with brand identification, namely, the brand's ability to satisfy the consumer's self-definitional needs, are the two "essential building-blocks" which generate three supportive brand-related actions: brand purchase intentions, positive brand referrals and oppositional brand referrals (Becerra & Badrinarayanan, 2013). These actions are not only a proof of vocal but mainly a proof of behavioural brand support. Brand purchase intentions describe consumer's actual willingness to act towards a brand. Referral intention, when positive, means that customers try to persuade others to purchase the same brand, and when negative, means that they try to deter others from buying competitor's brands (Rashid & Ahmad, 2014). Doss (2015) also showed that, apart from brand trust and brand identification, other elements leading to brand evangelism include brand satisfaction, brand salience, as well as opinion leadership. In addition, based on the Big Five Personality Traits

(Goldberg, 1993), he proved that, among them, only extraversion and openness are positively related to brand evangelistic behaviours. Especially extrovert customers are important advocates of a brand and can automatically become passionate opponents if they are disappointed by this particular brand (Matzler et al., 2005; Becerra & Badrinarayanan, 2013). So, extraversion is what actually motivates "brand champions" (Doss, 2014) to freely evangelize their ideas, feelings and information regarding a specific brand aiming to proselytize others to that brand. The investigation of how strong customer-brand relationships lead to specific brand evangelistic behaviours is an important topic not only for researchers but also for managers. In today's "referral powered" (Shaari & Ahmad, 2016, p. 80) community, brand evangelists could play a crucial role acting as volunteer salespeople and actively embracing a particular brand (Doss, 2014). Customers have now become the drivers of brand value and can significantly contribute to the brand value creation process. Recent research, though, suggests that, in order for brand managers to generate and maintain their customers' loyalty, WOM and resistance to negative information, they first have to focus on transitioning their liked into loved brands (Becerra & Badrinarayanan, 2013). Similar to that, they need to empower their customers to actively participate and involve in marketer-sponsored communities turning them from simple visitors, into members, contributors and, finally, into brand evangelists (Algesheimer et al., 2005). Only under these conditions, they will have the opportunity to integrate them in the creation of their brand equity. Managers do recognize the significance of community brand evangelism (Scarpi, 2010), that's why they usually try to create brands that consumers both trust and identify with (Becerra & Badrinarayanan, 2013). Offline cultivation and encouragement of brand evangelistic behaviours for the benefit of their brand is something that managers have already got acquainted with. However, during the past few years, the centre of their attention is whether online brand communities do equally have the ability to generate customer's brand evangelism. The following section sheds light on this particular topic.

34.2.2 Social Media Marketing and Brand Evangelism

Social media defines all the Internet-based applications which form both the ideological and the technological base of Web 2.0. and contribute to the creation and exchange of information, experiences and perspectives throughout various community-oriented websites (Gaber & Wright, 2014; Parganas et al., 2015). This information-exchange, taking place in online social networks, is usually characterized in the literature review as electronic word of mouth (eWOM), microblogging word of mouth (MWOM) or social networking (Barreda et al., 2015). Online social networks involve common sites such as *Facebook*, *Instagram*, *Twitter*, *YouTube*, *Pinterest*, forums, etc., whose greatest benefit is the creation of a virtual, online environment where users can communicate and interact with each other by posting comments, reviews, videos and pictures (Erkan & Evans, 2016; Saravanakumar &

SuganthaLakshmi, 2012). When social networks are used by businesses for the promotion of their brands, as well as for the approach of online customers, they are often called brand social networks or online brand communities (Gong, 2018; Park & Kim, 2014). Accordingly, social media marketing explains exactly that kind of business activity conducted through social media websites and social networks. Also known as digital marketing or e-marketing, social media marketing facilitates the approaching of new customers and the engaging of existing customers. What managers are planning to do or hoping to achieve for their business by utilizing social media defines what researchers call social media marketing strategy.

The creation of an online brand community is one of the most important social media marketing strategies. Customer's commitment to an online brand community (e.g. fan page, follower) describes the psychological state or attitude towards the maintenance of a relationship with a particular brand. It can either be affective, caused by emotional connection to the brand, or calculative caused by anticipated costs of leaving the relationship with a brand. In this paper, customer's brand page commitment refers to the degree of his emotional attachment (affective) to a particular brand. Studies examining brand page commitment have also identified that it can positively affect brand performance, such as brand loyalty. Other studies support a positive relationship between online brand communities and customer's identification, showing stronger attachment to brand relationship quality (Hur et al., 2011). Despite its significance as an individual component, little is known about the significance of customer's brand page commitment on brand evangelism.

The undeniable social media revolution during the last decade has transformed them into a new, hybrid tool for integrated marketing communication (Mangold & Faulds, 2009); not only do they support firm's brand image, but they also create lasting brand equity. On the one hand, the virtual interactivity and the reduced anonymity in online environments provide customers with system and information quality (Barreda et al., 2015), as well as the ability to create their own episodic memories. These memories become brand experiences which they later on share with their online friends contributing to e-WOM and value co-creation for companies (Gaber & Wright, 2014; Park & Kim, 2014). As a result, they are automatically transformed from passive to active creators and influencers adding a 5th "P", i.e. Participation, in the 4 Ps (Price, Product, Promotion and Place) of marketing mix (Gaber & Wright, 2014). On the other hand, marketers, apart from paid and owned media (firm-generated content controlled by company itself), seek to utilize the earned media (user-generated content or e-WOM) for their brand advertising (Stephen & Galak, 2012). Particularly for clothing/fashion industry (Juggessur & Cohen, 2009; O'Cass & Choy, 2008), the majority of the brands often use social media to provide information about their new products and seasoned trends or Facebook fan pages to promote coupons or discounts among online consumers (Schivinski & Dabrowski, 2015). Companies carefully monitor or even participate in online conversations with their customers, not only because their customers perceive it positively but mostly because the companies themselves can gain direct and cost-free insights into their customer's perception of their brand (Parganas et al., 2015). To maintain a strong relationship with their consumers, managers also try, using their social media outlets, to demonstrate a high level of both relationship quality and behavioural loyalty which are by definition positively related (Park & Kim, 2014). The ultimate aim of their attempt is to assure their customers' brand engagement, which in social media glossary is translated into customer brand page commitment. According to Cestare and Ray (2019), brand sentiment has impact on brand evangelism and consumer's loyalty.

Contrary to e-marketing customer engagement, which refers to the company's intention to increase the time or the attention their customers give to its brand on the web or across multiple channels (Sashi, 2012), brand page commitment requires together the physical, cognitive and emotional attachment of the customer to the brand community (Huttere et al., 2013; Gong, 2018). It is not only awareness, purchase, satisfaction, retention and loyalty but the feeling of intimacy that turns loyal customers into ardent advocates of a brand, namely, into brand evangelists (Gong, 2018; Sashi, 2012). Social media marketing bolsters customer's in-role behaviour (Gong, 2018, p. 11), namely, his intimacy and trust on a brand, aiming to strengthen even more his extra-role behaviour, namely, customer's brand engagement and brand evangelistic behaviour (Gong, 2018; Pentina et al., 2018). The degree of his engagement in a brand page is inter alia positively related to his openness to new brand experiences, one of the Big Five Personality Traits (*OCEAN* model) which is also positively related to brand evangelism (Zailskaitė-Jakštė & Kuvykaitė, 2016). On their last survey on brand evangelism, Becerra and Badrinarayanan (2013) mentioned that both the velocity of e-WOM communication and the large size of communication network give online environments the potential to become platforms of brand evangelism manifestation without, though, examining the consequences on each of the three evangelistic behaviours. Shaari and Ahmad (2016) showed that brand page commitment would only lead to positive brand referrals, but not oppositional. To be exact, participation in such online communities results in providing positive feedback and does not go beyond comparing competing brands (Shaari & Ahmad, 2016). What Shaari (2016) proved is that marketing through online brand communities only contributes to positive brand referrals, brand purchase intentions and constructive complaint (Hennig-Thurau et al., 2010). Oppositional brand referrals are not necessarily driven by customer's brand community commitment.

From a managerial point of view, understanding the power that social media brand commitment has on the generation of brand evangelism is of great importance. Many managers, although recognizing that social networking has become a global movement and undeniably influences customer care, they often feel uncertain as to how they can utilize it for marketing goals (Nadeem, 2012). The reason is, they do not know how to monetize the benefit of social media. On the other hand, they feel intense pressure to actively engage in online community relationships with their customers being afraid that, if they do not do so, they might be perceived as out-of-tech firms. The following study's primary goal is to help managers to gain a better insight on whether customer's brand page commitment does contribute to brand evangelism, so as to cost-free foster their company's profile, sales and financial growth.

34.3 Methods and Data

34.3.1 Research Questions

Over the past decade, online brand communities have developed the nature of both web and fan pages, which facilitates fast and easy communication between customers and brands and among customers themselves (Gong, 2018). Nowadays, marketers usually use their Facebook and Instagram pages to post their new products and seasoned trends, not only to inform their online customers but also to empower them to actively engage in interaction with their brand content (e.g. follow, like, comment) (Zailskaitė-Jakštė & Kuvykaitė, 2016). By clicking to the option "Like", the users of social network systems agree on receiving the advertisements from a brand page and, thus, work voluntarily for that brand (Erkan & Evans, 2016).

We regard brand page commitment as an independent variable, and at the same time, consumer's engagement in such fan pages has been found to be strongly correlated to customer's brand awareness (Schivinski & Dabrowski, 2015), namely, the strength of a brand's presence in consumer's mind. As stated earlier, our two research questions are:

1. Does Greek customers' commitment to online clothing brand pages affect their brand evangelistic behaviours?
2. Does Greek customers' commitment to online clothing brand pages affect their perception of famous over generic clothing brands?

The statistical analysis carried out aimed to answer the two research questions initially stated. First, it was investigated how brands' social media marketing activities and, especially, Greeks' social media use and commitment to brands' online pages involves either the cultivation or the intensification of brand evangelism. Secondly, it was tested whether that kind of individuals' social media commitment influences their perception of famous and generic clothing brands.

34.3.2 Data Collection and Preliminary Data Analysis

In an attempt to answer the two research questions and test the aforementioned hypotheses, apart from the literature review, this study provides also a deductive, exploratory survey. The main instrument used for this survey, aiming to collect primary data, was a standardized, online questionnaire based on the model proposed by Google Forms. Respondents were invited to answer this by clicking on the link of the questionnaire broadcasted through Facebook messages and e-mails. All the respondents promised anonymity, and their participation in the survey was voluntary. In order, though, to test the survey's efficacy, a pilot survey was first conducted. During this probationary period, a pretest, online questionnaire was sent to 50 Greek respondents randomly selected among Facebook and e-mail contacts.

This was done primarily to check whether the answers given could somehow explain the dependent variables of the two research models. Subsequently, using systematic, convenience and random sampling to our online Greek contacts, a total of 250 usable responses were collected and considered for the analysis.[1]

The data collection was based on well-established measures from existing studies with some, slight variations. To simplify the survey and enhance the feasibility of data analysis, a one-item, two-point scale was chosen. To start with the demographic section, gender was obviously measured with a one-item, two-point (male or female) scale with males being coded as 0 and females as 1. Age was measured using a one-item, five-point scale (e.g. 15–24 years old). The scale used for the measurement of education was the one-item, four-point scale (e.g. highschool graduate). As for the monthly income, the measurement used was the one-item, five-point scale (e.g. below 500€). Moving forward with the third section, all items tested were measured on a two-point scale. The customers' preference on famous or generic clothing brands was measured by using a one-item, two-point (famous or generic) scale with famous being coded as 1 and generic as 0. The customer's brand page commitment was measured on a two-item, two-point (yes or no) scale (e.g. "I frequently visit my favorite brand page") (Hutter et al., 2013) with "yes" being coded as 1 and "no" as 0. Their trust, or in other words, loyalty to their favoured clothing brand was measured using a one-item, two-point (yes or no) scale (Becerra & Badrinarayanan, 2013) with 1 indicating "yes" and 0 "no". Brand awareness was similarly measured using a one-item, two-point (yes or no) scale (Hutter et al., 2013) with "yes" coded as 1 and "no" as 0. Respondents' brand evangelistic behaviour was revealed in the following questions. Customers' positive brand referral intention (e.g. "I Like/Follow/Tweet a brand in social media") and their oppositional brand referral intention (e.g. "I Dislike/ Un-follow a brand in Social media") (Becerra and Badrinarayanan, 2013) were measured on a two-item, two-point (yes or no) scale with "yes" coded as 1 and "no" as 0. Finally, a two-item, two-point (yes or no) scale was also used for the measurement of respondents' brand purchase intention (e.g. "I buy the brand more often") (Hutter et al., 2013, Becerra & Badrinarayanan, 2013) with 1 indicating the "yes" and 0 indicating the "no" answers.

From the answers provided, the measurements used for the data analysis are the following:

From Table 34.1, we observe that 45 percent were male and 55 percent were female respondents, while 54 percent were aged between 15 and 24 and 28 percent were aged between 25 and 34. Only 17 percent of the respondents were over 34, while the average age was 27.18. The majority of the respondents (77 percent) were either undergraduate or postgraduate university students, whereas only 23 percent of them were teenagers studying at high school. Regarding their income, 48 percent of the respondents answered earning less than 500€ per month, 32 percent of them answered earning between 500€ and 1000€ per month and only 20 percent of the respondents has a monthly income higher than 1000€.

[1] The data collection took place in October 2018.

Table 34.1 Measurements of demographic variables

Variable (questionnaire code)	Obs.	Mean	Std. Dev.	Min	Max
Gender (Q2.1)	250	0.552	0.498	0	1
Age (Q2.2)	250	0.708	0.960	0	4
Education (Q2.3)	250	1.092	0.747	0	2
Monthly income (Q2.4)	250	0.776	0.939	0	4

Note: *Gender* variable was coded as "male" = 0 and "female" = 1; *age* (in years) was coded as "15–24" = 0, "25–34" = 1, "35–44" = 2, "45–54" = 3 and "over 55" = 4; *education* was coded as "secondary school graduate" = 0, "high school graduate" = 1, "undergraduate" = 2 and "post-graduate/PhD" = 3; finally, *monthly income* was coded as "below €500" = 0, "€501–€1000" = 1, "€1001–€2500" = 2, "€2501–€4000" = 3 and "over €4000" = 4

Table 34.2 Cross tabulation of gender (Q2.1) vs brand preference (Q3.1) variables

	Q2.1		
Q3.1	0	1	Total
0	29	79	108
1	83	59	142
Total	112	138	250

Table 34.3 Descriptive statistics of dependent and independent variables

Variable (questionnaire code)	Obs.	Mean	Std. dev.	Min	Max
Brand preference (Q3.1)	250	0.568	0.496	0	1
Influence from social media (Q3.10)	250	0.312	0.464	0	1
Intention of purchase (Q3.11)	250	0.800	0.401	0	1
New designs follower (Q3.2)	250	0.352	0.479	0	1
Company social media follower (Q3.3)	250	0.564	0.497	0	1
Brand recognition (Q3.5)	250	0.624	0.485	0	1
Social media reaction – e.g. "like" (Q3.6)	250	0.328	0.470	0	1
Web-page recommendation (Q3.7)	250	0.100	0.301	0	1

Note: All variables were binary, coded as "no" = 0 and "yes" = 1. Dependent variables are Q3.1, Q3.10 and Q3.11

In addition, from Table 34.2, we observe that the males' preference on popular clothing exceeds that of the female Greek citizens.

In Table 34.3, we provide the variables regarding branding preferences.

From Table 34.3, we note the high mean and corresponding low standard deviation for variable intention of purchase (Q3.11).

34.4 Econometric Model Results

The correlation matrix of all the variables is provided in Table 34.4. It does not suggest high correlations, and thus, there is not an evident problem of multicollinearity. Thus, we deduce that we can go ahead with the regression analysis models.

Table 34.4 Correlation matrix

	Q31	Q310	Q311	Q21	Q22	Q23	Q24	Q32	Q33	Q35	Q36	Q37
Q31	1.00											
Q310	0.06	1.00										
Q311	0.25	0.32	1.00									
Q21	−0.31	0.14	0.03	1.00								
Q22	0.02	0.01	−0.07	−0.13	1.00							
Q23	−0.00	−0.01	−0.05	−0.09	0.61	1.00						
Q24	0.22	−0.09	0.07	−0.24	0.62	0.50	1.00					
Q32	0.14	0.35	0.20	0.34	−0.14	−0.08	−0.04	1.00				
Q33	−0.00	0.38	0.29	0.38	−0.13	−0.10	−0.10	0.53	1.00			
Q35	−0.03	0.29	0.25	0.10	−0.10	−0.10	−0.09	0.16	0.28	1.00		
Q36	0.13	0.27	0.18	0.17	−0.00	−0.14	−0.09	0.43	0.36	0.23	1.00	
Q37	−0.06	0.18	0.17	0.14	−0.02	−0.01	−0.03	0.17	0.21	0.15	0.25	1.00

Given the binary nature of the dependent variables, we opt for the probit model (see, e.g. Greene, 1990). Dependent variables are Q3.1, Q3.10 and Q3.11; thus, three models are run; see Table 34.5. Table 34.5 includes also the corresponding marginal effects of the independent variables (i.e. all the partial derivatives, with respect to the independent variables x, of the linking probit function F as specified in the Stata respective command[2]). The Stata software was used for the analysis.[3]

From Table 34.5, we observe that for the model with brand preference (Q3.1) as a dependent variable, the variables gender (Q2.1), monthly income (Q2.4), new designs follower (Q3.2) and social media reaction (Q3.6) are statistically significant. Thus, the brand preference is correlated with gender (negatively), monthly income (positively), new designs follower (positively) and social media (positively); the corresponding marginal effects are also indicative for the same variables: for instance, the change to a higher income category (in Q2.4) suggests a 0.174 higher probability for brand preference.

In Table 34.6, we provide a robustness check of how dependent variables (from Table 34.5) may be somehow related.

We observe an overall fairly good spread of preferences (with the possible exception of joint "1"s between Q3.1 and Q3.11).

34.5 Discussion and Conclusion

Our findings demonstrate that brand page commitment has positive effects on customers' brand trust, brand awareness, positive brand referral intention as well as

[2] Source: https://www.stata.com/support/faqs/statistics/marginal-effects-methods/

[3] Stata: statistical software for data science, see www.stata.com/

Table 34.5 Probit regression

	Dependent variable: Q31	Marginal effects	Dependent variable: Q310	Marginal effects	Dependent variable: Q311	Marginal effects
Variables	Coefficient	dF/dx	Coefficient	dF/dx	Coefficient	dF/dx
Q21	−1.07***	−0.393***	−0.21	−0.068	−0.25	−0.067
Q22	−0.22	−0.084	0.31**	0.100**	−0.26*	−0.071*
Q23	−0.12	−0.048	0.04	0.012	−0.02	−0.004
Q24	0.45***	0.174***	−0.32**	−0.104**	0.37**	0.099**
Q32	0.64***	0.241***	0.67***	0.226***	0.20	0.052
Q33	0.54	0.021	0.81***	0.248***	0.62**	0.169
Q35	−0.14	−0.055	0.71***	0.212***	0.53**	0.148
Q36	0.46**	0.173**	0.06	0.020	0.16	0.043
Q37	−0.36	−0.144	0.31	0.106	N/A	N/A
Constant	0.46**		−1.75***		0.18	
	LR chi2(9) = 60.77***		LR chi2(9) = 69.93***		LR chi2(8) = 33.11***	
	Pseudo R^2 = 0.18		Pseudo R^2 = 0.23		Pseudo R^2 = 0.14	
	Number obs = 250		Number obs = 250		Number obs = 225	

Note: Stata dropped variable Q3.7 from the third model since Q3.7 = 0 predicts "success" perfectly; as a result, the Q3.7 was dropped, and 25 obs were not used. A cross-check in the actual data set confirmed this issue

Table 34.6 Cross tabulation of brand preference (Q3.1) variables vs Q310 and Q311

	Q310				Q311		
Q31	0	1	Total	Q31	0	1	Total
0	78	30	108	0	34	74	108
1	94	48	142	1	16	126	142
Total	172	78	250	Total	50	200	

their brand purchase intention. Results further indicate that customers' involvement to brand social networks does not affect their oppositional brand referral intention, namely, their attempt to dissuade others from purchasing competing clothing brands. Moreover, findings relative to the second issue imply that Greek customers' brand page commitment could also impact their perception of famous or generic clothing brands, without, though, being always so. Below are explained the theoretical and practical implications of this survey.

As we observe that the males's preference on popular clothing exceeds that of the female Greek citizens, the communication mix of the clothing brands should be aligned with the willing and wants of that segment and focus on satisfying the men segment that appears to be really active in terms of branding. It comes out of the analysis that for the brand preference, the gender, the monthly income, the new designs follower and the social media reaction are statistically significant. For example, the change to a higher income category suggests a 0.174 higher probability for brand preference. The brand preferences relate to the level of income. Also, the new designer's followers and social media players interact with the brand preference.

The present paper aims to shed light on this topic and help managers understand whether this new media brand engagement affects consumer's brand evangelistic behaviours which can contribute both to their sales and the ultimate value of their company. Future studies can expand the research especially in the new e-commerce environment and under extraordinary conditions like pandemic or other crises.

References

Algesheimer, R., Dholakia, U. M., & Herrmann, A. (2005). The social influence of brand community: Evidence from European car clubs. *Journal of Marketing, 69*(3), 19–34.

Barreda, A. A., Bilgihan, A., Nusair, K., & Okumus, F. (2015). Generating brand awareness in online social networks. *Computers in Human Behaviour, 50*, 600–609.

Batra, R., Ahuvia, A., & Bagozzi, R. P. (2012). Brand love. *Journal of Marketing, 76*(2), 1–16.

Becerra, E. P., & Badrinarayanan, V. (2013). The influence of Brand Trust and brand identification on brand evangelism. *Journal of Product & Brand Management, 22*(5/6), 371–383.

Carroll, B. A., & Ahuvia, A. C. (2006). Some antecedents and outcomes of brand love. *Marketing Letters, 17*(2), 79–89.

Cestare, T. A., & Ray, I. (2019). The tribes we lead: Understanding the antecedents and consequences of brand evangelism within the context of social communities. *Journal of Marketing Development and Competitiveness, 13*(4).

Cheng, V., Rhodes, J., & Lok, P. (2015). The relationship between online reviews, brand trust, and willingness to buy. In *Strategic E-commerce systems and tools for competing in the digital marketplace* (pp. 139–161). IGI Global.

Doss, S. K. (2015). "Spreading the good word": Toward an understanding of brand evangelism. In M. Dato-on (Ed.), *The sustainable global marketplace. Developments in marketing science: Proceedings of the Academy of Marketing Science*. Springer.

Doss, S. K., & Carstens, D. S. (2014). Big five personality traits and brand evangelism. *International Journal of Marketing Studies, 6*(3), 13–22.

Erkan, I., & Evans, C. (2016). The influence of eWOM in social media on consumers' purchase intentions: An extended approach to information adoption. *Computers in Human Behaviour, 61*, 47–55.

Forbes, D. (2015). The identity motive. In *The science of why* (pp. 75–92). Palgrave Macmillan.

Gaber, H. R., & Wright, L. T. (2014). Fast-food advertising in social media. A case study on Facebook in Egypt. *Journal of Business and Retail Management Research, 9*(1), 52–63.

Gerstberger, C., & Yaneva, D. (2013). Analysis of EU-27 household final consumption expenditure—Baltic countries and Greece still suffering most from the economic and financial crisis. Eurostat Statistics in focus 2/2013

Goldberg, L. R. (1993). The structure of phenotypic personality traits. *American Psychologist, 48*(1), 26.

Gong, T. (2018). Customer brand engagement behaviour in online brand communities. *Journal of Services Marketing, 32*(3), 286–299.

Greene, W. (1990). *Econometric analysis*. Macmillan.

Hennig-Thurau, T., Malthouse, E. C., Friege, C., Gensler, S., Lobschat, L., Rangaswamy, A., & Skiera, B. (2010). The impact of new media on customer relationships. *Journal of Service Research, 13*(3), 311–330.

Hsu, L. C. (2019). Investigating the brand evangelism effect of community fans on social networking sites. *Online Information Review, 43*(5), 842–866.

Hur, W. M., Ahn, K. H., & Kim, M. (2011). Building brand loyalty through managing brand community commitment. *Management Decision, 49*(7), 1194–1213.

Hutter, K., Hautz, J., Dennhardt, S., & Füller, J. (2013). The impact of user interactions in social media on brand awareness and purchase intention: The case of MINI on Facebook. *The Journal of Product and Brand Management, 22*(5/6), 342–351.

Juggessur, J., & Cohen, G. (2009). Is fashion promoting counterfeit brands? *Journal of Brand Management, 16*(5–6), 383–394.

Kautish, P. (2010). Empirical study on influence of extraversion on consumer passion and brand evangelism with word-of-mouth communication. *Review of Economic and Business Studies, 6*, 187–198.

Kotler, P., & Keller, K. L. (2012). *Marketing Management* (14th ed.). Pearson.

Mangold, W. G., & Faulds, D. J. (2009). Social media: The new hybrid element of the promotion mix. *Business Horizons, 52*(4), 357–365.

Matzler, K., Faullant, R., Renzl, B., & Leiter, V. (2005). The relationship between personality traits (extraversion and neuroticism), emotions and customer self-satisfaction. *Innovative Marketing, 1*(2), 32–39.

Matzler, K., Pichler, E. A., & Hemetsberger, A. (2007). Who is spreading the word? The positive influence of extraversion on consumer passion and brand evangelism. *Marketing Theory and Applications, 18*(1), 25–32.

Nadeem, M. (2012). Social customer relationship management (SCRM): How connecting social analytics to business analytics enhances customer care and loyalty?

O'Cass, A., & Choy, E. (2008). Studying Chinese generation Y consumers' involvement in fashion clothing and perceived brand status. *The Journal of Product and Brand Management, 17*(5), 341–352.

Parganas, P., Anagnostopoulos, C., & Chadwick, S. (2015). 'You'll never tweet alone': Managing sports brands through social media. *Journal of Brand Management, 22*(7), 551–568.

Park, H., & Kim, Y. K. (2014). The role of social network websites in the consumer–brand relationship. *Journal of Retailing and Consumer Services, 21*(4), 460–467.

Pentina, I., Guilloux, V., & Micu, A. C. (2018). Exploring social media engagement Behaviours in the context of luxury brands. *Journal of Advertising, 47*(1), 55–69.

Quelhas-Brito, P., Brandão, A., Gadekar, M., & Castelo-Branco, S. (2020). Diffusing fashion information by social media fashion influencers: Understanding antecedents and consequences. *Journal of Fashion Marketing and Management, 24*(2), 137–152.

Rashid, M. H. A., & Ahmad, F. S. (2014). The role of recovery satisfaction on the relationship between service recovery and brand evangelism: A conceptual framework. *International Journal of Innovation, Management and Technology, 5*(5), 401–405.

Riivits-Arkonsuo, I., Kaljund, K., & Leppiman, A. (2015). Consumer journey from first experience to brand evangelism. *Research in Economics and Business: Central and Eastern Europe, 6*(1), 5–28.

Saravanakumar, M., & SuganthaLakshmi, T. (2012). Social media marketing. *Life Science Journal, 9*(4), 4444–4451.

Sashi, C. M. (2012). Customer engagement, buyer-seller relationships, and social media. *Management Decision, 50*(2), 253–272.

Scarpi, D. (2010). Does size matter? An examination of small and large web-based brand communities. *Journal of Interactive Marketing, 24*(1), 14–21.

Schivinski, B., & Dabrowski, D. (2015). The impact of brand communication on brand equity through Facebook. *Journal of Research in Interactive Marketing, 9*(1), 31–53.

Shaari, H., & Ahmad, I. S. (2016). Brand evangelism among online brand community members. *International Review of Management and Business Research, 5*(1), 80–88.

Smilansky, S. (2017). *Experiential marketing: A practical guide to interactive brand experiences*. Kogan Page Publishers.

Stephen, A. T., & Galak, J. (2012). The effects of traditional and social earned media on sales: A study of a microlending marketplace. *Journal of Marketing Research, 49*(5), 624–639.

Swimberghe, K. R., Astakhova, M., & Wooldridge, B. R. (2014). A new dualistic approach to brand passion: Harmonious and obsessive. *Journal of Business Research, 67*(12), 2657–2665.

Tarssanen, S., & Kylänen, M. (2007). A theoretical model for producing experiences – A touristic perspective. In M. Kylänen (Ed.), *Articles on experiences 2, Lapland centre of expertise for the experience industry* (pp. 134–154). Lapland University Press.

Tynan, C., & McKechnie, S. (2009). Experience marketing: A review and reassessment. *Journal of Marketing Management, 25*(5–6), 501–517.

Zailskaitė-Jakštė, L., & Kuvykaitė, R. (2016). Conceptualizing the social media communication impact on consumer based brand equity. *Trends Economics and Management, 10*(25), 68–74.

Chapter 35
Income Inequality and Shadow Economy in the EU. A Panel Cointegration and Causality Analysis

Simona-Gabriela Masca, Madalina Drutu, and Andrada-Maria Pojoca

Abstract Current political and economic discourse in Europe is often animated by public concerns about the income gap between the rich and the poor on one hand, and the informal economy on the other hand. As researchers argue, the two phenomena do not produce independently; there is some connection between them. This study explores the interrelation between shadow economy and income inequality in the 28 European Union countries over the 2007–2017 period, by means of panel cointegration and causality tests. The hypothesis under test is that the two variables experience a long-term relationship and one of them is a predictor factor for the other. The results lead to the conclusion that there is a long-run relationship between income inequality and shadow economy in our panel. The VECM is estimated, concluding that income inequality does cause shadow economy in EU-28 countries, but shadow economy does not cause income inequality. Our findings are valid under robustness tests, guiding to important policy implications.

Keywords Income inequality · Shadow economy · Panel cointegration · Causality · **JEL classification:** H26 · O15

35.1 Introduction

Income inequality and shadow economy are two acute problems that EU countries are facing, producing large concerns for national and European authorities as it imped economic development. The hypothesis that income inequality and shadow economy are two interrelated phenomena creates supplementary concerns about the way this puzzle should be managed. The importance, from public policy perspective, of a possible interplay of the two major questions in the European

S.-G. Masca (✉) · M. Drutu · A.-M. Pojoca
Faculty of Economics and Business Administration, Finance Department, Babeş-Bolyai University, Cluj-Napoca, Romania
e-mail: simona.masca@econ.ubbcluj.ro

N. Tsounis, A. Vlachvei (eds.), *Advances in Quantitative Economic Research*, Springer Proceedings in Business and Economics,
https://doi.org/10.1007/978-3-030-98179-2_35

countries, and the scarcity of the contributions in the research field motivate us to explore the subject. The main policy challenge is to put behind distribution, and informal economy concerns the convergent politics which are meant to balance the relationship between the two goals.

This study researches the evolution and the interconnection between shadow economy and income inequality in the 28 European Union countries over the 2007–2017 period. The methodology employed is based on panel cointegration and causality tests. By approaching the link between income distribution and informal sector, our study joins the particular strand of literature that includes the contributions of Bloomquist, Berdiev or Elveren.

Nevertheless, the subject is rarely tackled in a causality framework, as panel regressions are generally preferred, with few exceptions (Berdiev & Saunoris, 2019). Testing the cointegration and causality in our paper allows checking for the bidirectional connection between the variables, instead considering only one-way relation. EViews software was exploited together with a variety of tests like Pedroni, Kao or Johansen-Fisher's tests that rend our results well-grounded and robust.

The sample of the European Union countries is seldom considered in this particular part of the literature. Christie and Holzner (2006)'s paper and Gasteratos et al. (2016)'s study investigate the relationship between tax evasion (or shadow economy) and income inequality based on some European countries data. Our contribution consists in delimitating the analysis strictly to EU-28 sample and considering the period until 2017. In this way, a homogenous sample from policy perspective is considered, and the newest data is exploited.

In our sample, the inequality average value based on GINI coefficient is almost 30, and the mean value of the shadow economy is around 16% of GDP. In 2017, Bulgaria experienced the largest income inequality in the EU (Gini coefficient of 40.2), while Slovakia had the smallest value of Gini coefficient (23.2). As regards the shadow economy, the highest value (25.2% of GDP) was recorded by Cyprus and the lowest value (7.1% of GDP) by Austria.

Our data reveal that the EU-28 averages didn't change significantly for both variables on income inequality and shadow economy, over the 2007–2017 period. We notice yet a large heterogeneity among European countries. In some particular cases, we remark improvements, while in others there were deteriorations over time (see Figs. 35.1 and 35.2). No common trend occurs in our sample, in which both variables are concerned. Though, out of our sample, the same 11 countries (Bulgaria, Croatia, Cyprus, Greece, Italy, Latvia, Lithuania, Poland, Portugal, Romania and Spain) recorded both income inequality and shadow economy values above the EU average, over the 2007–2017 period. This observation leads us to consider the hypothesis under which income inequality and shadow economy might experience a long-run and causal interaction.

The study is structured in four parts. After the introductory reflections, the second chapter presents the main contributions in the research field, by inventorying samples, methods and results. The third chapter consists in presenting the data, empirical strategy and our own results. The last part is dedicated to conclusions and policy implications.

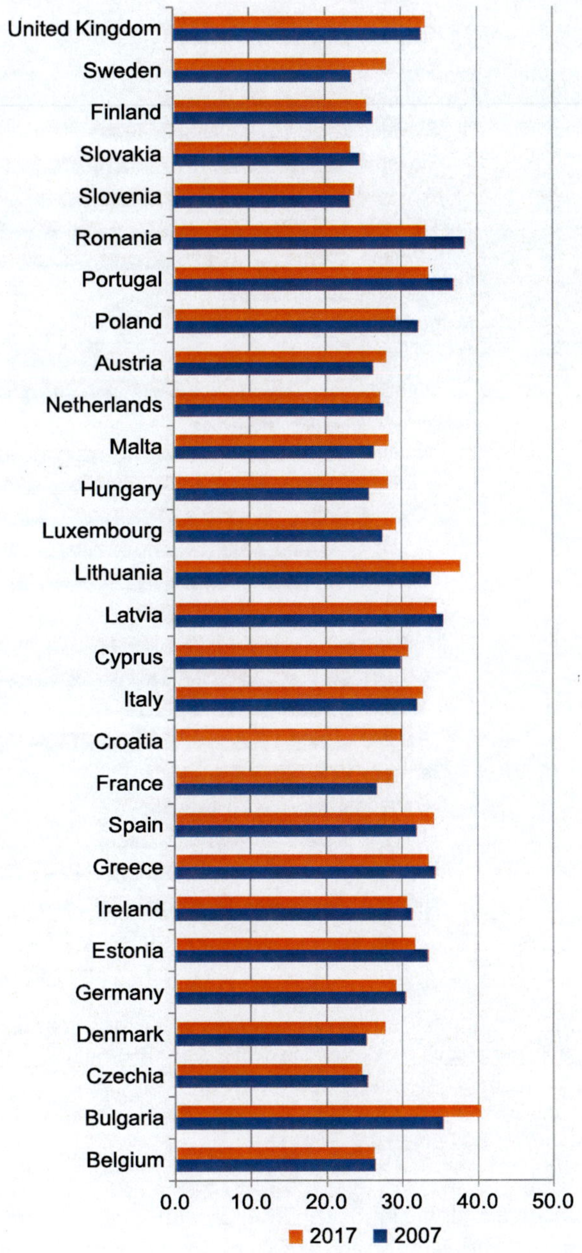

Fig. 35.1 Gini coefficient for the EU-28 countries, 2007 and 2017 periods. (Source: Authors' processing based on Eurostat data)

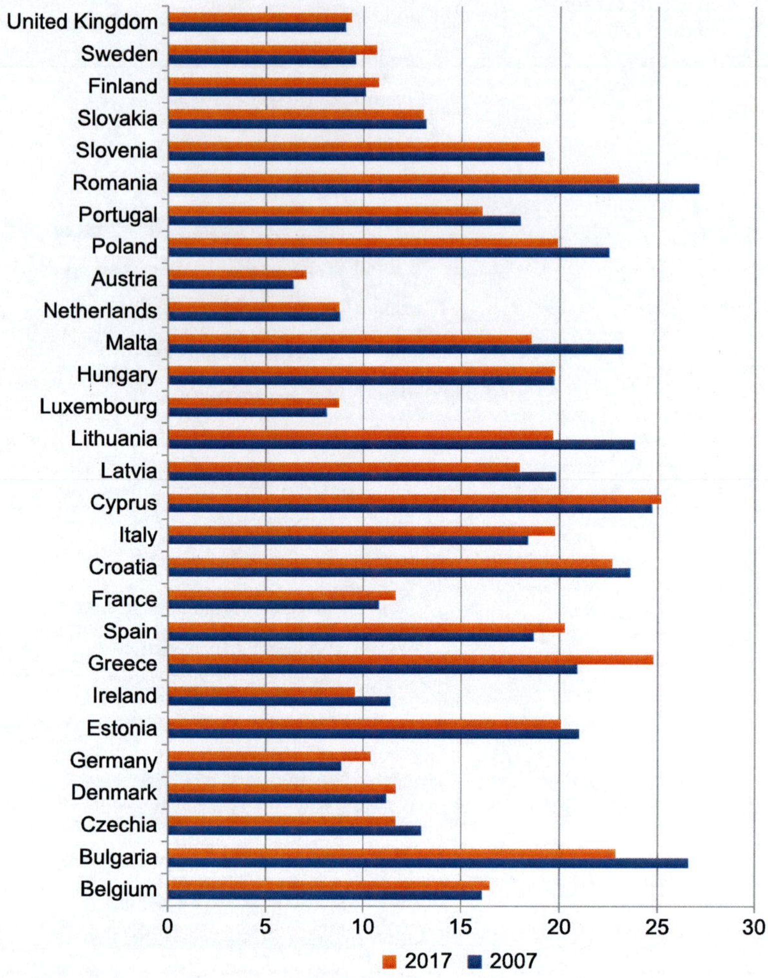

Fig. 35.2 Shadow economy in the EU-28 countries, 2007 and 2017 periods. (Source: Authors' processing based on Medina and Schneider (2019) data)

35.2 Literature Review

Income and wealth distribution as well as the informal economy, taken separately, have been largely addressed by researchers, for many years. Yet, the linkage between income inequality and the size of shadow economy recently became a topic of interest in the research field. The aim of this chapter is to highlight the significant findings from earlier contributions and underlying our own contribution to this particular literature strand.

The reasoning that stays behind a possible interrelation between distribution and unofficial economy is based on several hypotheses.

More of the economic activity is unofficially conducted, less tax revenues will be collected and social security programmes will be damaged, causing more inequality. As the budget deficit gets larger, higher tax rates are expected, and tax payers are likely to go towards the informal sector. Tax moral problems, unfair tax liabilities distribution, unfair firms' competition, inefficient allocation of resources and goods and services produced at lower standards are mentioned as consequences of the informal economy, leading to more unequal income distribution. Larger is the portion of the activities conducted in the informal sector, greater would be the difference between the rents of individuals involved in the formal and unofficial sectors. Shadow economy may increase income inequality, but it also may lead to a more equal society if individuals acquire new skills in the underground that are further exploited in the official economy.

Causal mechanism may operate also in the reverse direction, as increasing inequality leads to weaker social solidarity and government trust, and therefore parts of the economic activity shift towards informal sector. Less wealthy individuals and firms are likely to prefer the informal sector for their activities, where the returns are higher. Underground activities may be the choice of the low-skilled and poor educated individuals due to the lack of opportunities in the official economy and to the augmented flexibility and autonomy in the unofficial sector. Government response itself to high inequality, by introducing the progressive tax system meant to finance the redistributive programmes, creates the incentives for rich individuals to retreat to the unofficial economy.

We will rely on different studies that approach the nexus of income inequality and shadow economy in a cointegration and causality framework. In addition, the interplay between the two is reviewed from a broader perspective, by documenting research papers that make use of a variety of methodologies.

Among the few papers addressing the income inequality and shadow economy nexus, we mention Berdiev and Saunoris (2019), Rosser et al. (2000) and Elveren and Ozgur (2015) studies. There is some agreement in their results about the mentioned interplay, but neither concerns the EU countries' sample over recent years.

Analysing the link between income inequality and the output produced in the informal economy for a sample of 16 transition economies over the 1987–1994 period, Rosser J.B. et al. (2000) find out a positive and significant relationship, both for levels and changes in variables. Apparently, this study is the first one that addresses the interrelation between the two variables, though Rosser (2000)'s paper presents some limitations in what data used and method are concerned. Simple bivariate OLS regressions are exploited, and less conventional measure for informal sector is used.

Addressing the same question, Elveren and Ozgur (2015) employ a time-series analysis with the Johansen cointegration test, a vector error correction model and the Granger causality tests within a country-level case study. The authors investigate the long-term relationship between income inequality and informal economy in

Turkey during the period of 1963–2008. Trade liberalisation is viewed as the driving force of both income inequality and the informality of labour market. Foreign trade competitiveness would reduce the wages of unskilled workers, and consequently, the demand for low-quality products would increase. The manufacturing pay inequality index (Theil) and Elgin's index for the informal economy are used in the empirical analysis. The results suggest that an increase in income inequality leads to an expansion of the informal sector.

Berdiev and Saunoris (2019)'s paper has the merit to investigate the dynamic of the interrelationship between income inequality and shadow economy. The main hypothesis is that association between the two phenomena is a process that develops over time. As the authors assess, in the short run, the shadow economy has a counter-cyclical effect by disturbing both the official sector and income inequality, while in the long run, the unofficial economy alters institutions which, at their turn, impact the nexus of income distribution with the informal sector. Using panel data for 144 countries over the period 1960–2009, a panel VAR methodology is applied which is appropriate to estimate the dynamic endogenous connection between inequality and shadow economy. The authors' findings reveal a bidirectional positive relationship between the two. They show that the interaction varies over time, in a way that at the very first stages income inequality does not significantly impact the unofficial economy, but the spread of shadow economy contributes to lower equality. On the contrary, in the long run, the inequality effect becomes positive and significant, while the informal economy effect turns insignificant.

Another contribution discloses one possible non-linear relationship between income inequality and shadow economy, the hypothesis that is confirmed for a panel of both developed and developing countries, observed over the 2000–2007 period (Yap et al., 2018). The link between the two variables is found depending on the size of shadow economy.

Bloomquist (2003) found a positive correlation between the underreporting rate for wage and salary income and the top decile wage share, for the US sample observed over the period 1947–2000.

Bloomquist's hypothesis that lower equality leads to higher tax evasion is verified by Christie and Holzner (2006) in a sample of European countries over the 2000–2003 period, by applying the methodology of panel data random effects. The hypothesis is confirmed in the case of particular types of taxes such as personal income tax, excise tax and social security contributions. On the other hand, the link between VAT compliance and income inequality seems to be insignificant.

This being said, we can conclude that even if the revised studies are based on different research methodologies, the results are similar, generally indicating a positive correlation between the income inequality and shadow economy.

35.3 Data, Methodology and Results

In this study, we analyse the cointegration and causality relationship between shadow economy and income inequality. Data derived from Medina and Schneider (2019) is used as proxy for the shadow economy variable, expressed as a percentage of GDP. Income inequality is proxied by GINI coefficient of equivalised disposable income, originated from EU-SILC survey, Eurostat database. The panel under study consists of the 28 European Union countries observed over the period 2007–2017. The EViews programme was the key to getting results throughout the paper. Descriptive statistics are available in the Annex – Figs. 35.3 and 35.4.

The methodology we rely on for testing the statistical relationship between shadow economy and income inequality in the EU-28 countries is specific to the cointegration and causality framework. We test if there is a long-term relationship between the developments of the two variables or, in other words, if one variable is a predictor factor for the other. Checking for the long-term relationship is achievable by applying the cointegration analysis and the VECM.

Our sample has the structure of a non-stationary data panel. The stationary series is obtained by differentiation. The first differences of the variables are stationary. Variables are integrated of order one. In Figs. 35.5 and 35.6 from the Annex, it can be observed that the series has become stationary. But these observations have to be confirmed by stationary tests. We apply the Augmented Dickey-Fuller (ADF) test to examine the stationary of the variables (see Fig. 35.7). According to the ADF unit root test results, all our variables have unit roots, but the first differences of the variables are stationary.

The aim of the most empirical studies is to determine whether a change in one variable causes a change or helps to predict another variable. The Granger causality modelling approach is one of the most popular in the experimental fields. In this paper, Granger causality and cointegration tests were used in empirical modelling for stationary variables (first difference).

If two variables are cointegrated, Granger causality must exist in at least one direction (Pfaff & Gentleman, 2008). However, it is appropriate to test the causality of the Granger of panel type (PGC), to assess whether shadow economy (RTAX) can be used to predict income inequality (RGINI) and vice versa. The results obtained by applying the Granger causality test are presented in Fig. 35.8.

For a significance threshold of 10%, we can reject the second hypothesis (8.35%) which reveals that the income inequality Granger causes shadow economy. On the other hand, shadow economy does not Granger-cause income inequality in our panel.

We further apply a vector error correction model (VECM) to examine the short-term and the long-term interdependencies for the relationship of the two variables. The ECM vector is appropriate when the economic variables are interlinked and share long-term and short-term relationships (Asteriou & Hall, 2011; Wooldridge, 2008; Hill et al., 2011). In order to estimate a VECM, certain conditions have to be met, which include that the series must be integrated in the same order and cointegrated.

Descriptive Statistics for GINI
Categorized by values of COUNTRY
Date: 03/24/21 Time: 14:04
Sample: 2007 2017
Included observations: 305

COUNTRY	Mean	Median	Max	Min.	Std. Dev.	Skew.	Kurt.	Obs.
Austria	27.41818	27.50000	28.30000	26.20000	0.540034	-0.711981	3.756309	11
Belgium	26.36364	26.30000	27.50000	25.90000	0.436515	1.589299	5.359469	11
Bulgaria	35.64545	35.40000	40.20000	33.20000	2.067058	0.840873	3.195746	11
Croatia	30.61250	30.65000	31.60000	29.80000	0.640173	0.137033	1.757764	8
Cyprus	31.11818	30.80000	34.80000	29.00000	1.897271	0.676794	2.291758	11
Czechia	24.94545	25.00000	25.30000	24.50000	0.254416	-0.460457	2.073491	11
Denmark	26.76364	26.90000	27.70000	25.10000	0.905840	-0.841032	2.587041	11
Estonia	32.63636	32.50000	35.60000	30.90000	1.486118	0.817921	2.603983	11
Finland	25.67273	25.60000	26.30000	25.20000	0.371728	0.408940	1.864091	11
France	29.45455	29.80000	30.80000	26.60000	1.117465	-1.470094	5.029929	11
Germany	29.58182	29.50000	30.70000	28.30000	0.715288	-0.065015	2.167524	11
Greece	33.84545	34.20000	34.50000	32.90000	0.587135	-0.362788	1.502137	11
Hungary	26.82727	27.20000	28.60000	24.10000	1.642005	-0.474215	1.655552	11
Ireland	30.22727	30.40000	31.30000	28.80000	0.732244	-0.387321	2.382785	11
Italy	32.27273	32.40000	33.10000	31.20000	0.549711	-0.466932	2.493274	11
Latvia	35.65455	35.40000	37.50000	34.50000	1.010310	0.936267	2.840166	11
Lithuania	35.30000	35.00000	37.90000	32.00000	1.945251	-0.179189	1.865351	11
Luxembourg	28.52727	28.50000	30.40000	27.20000	0.999090	0.387656	2.147658	11
Malta	27.75455	28.00000	28.60000	26.30000	0.700519	-0.664740	2.678350	11
Netherlands	26.46364	26.70000	27.60000	25.10000	0.905840	-0.177275	1.573494	11
Poland	30.89091	30.90000	32.20000	29.20000	0.864239	-0.391132	2.784275	11
Portugal	34.59091	34.20000	36.80000	33.50000	1.006434	1.071545	3.090318	11
Romania	34.95455	34.60000	38.30000	33.10000	1.644606	0.927905	2.759177	11
Slovakia	24.67273	24.50000	26.10000	23.20000	0.972719	0.101577	1.751147	11
Slovenia	23.87273	23.80000	25.00000	22.70000	0.658925	-0.022559	2.376178	11
Spain	33.68182	34.00000	34.70000	31.90000	0.925006	-0.745422	2.328982	11
Sweden	26.13636	26.00000	28.00000	23.40000	1.247616	-0.628138	3.381386	11
United Kingdom	32.26364	32.40000	33.90000	30.20000	1.033705	-0.451384	2.665029	11
All	29.92721	29.80000	40.20000	22.70000	3.813801	0.183997	2.039693	305

Fig. 35.3 Descriptive statistics Gini coefficient. (Source: Authors' processing in EViews software)

Descriptive Statistics for TAX_EVASION
Categorized by values of COUNTRY
Date: 03/24/21 Time: 14:04
Sample: 2007 2017
Included observations: 308

COUNTRY	Mean	Median	Max	Min.	Std. Dev.	Skew.	Kurt.	Obs.
Austria	7.045455	7.000000	7.800000	6.400000	0.461224	0.034083	2.007061	11
Belgium	16.51818	16.60000	17.40000	15.50000	0.586205	-0.199672	2.038059	11
Bulgaria	24.94545	24.80000	26.60000	22.90000	1.135221	-0.022897	2.204411	11
Croatia	23.75455	23.80000	24.70000	21.60000	0.927754	-1.161606	3.679979	11
Cyprus	25.83636	26.00000	27.10000	23.10000	1.170703	-1.143110	3.700945	11
Czechia	12.57273	12.40000	13.80000	11.70000	0.634178	0.728778	2.548382	11
Denmark	11.96364	12.00000	13.30000	10.90000	0.748696	0.318391	2.296762	11
Estonia	20.90000	20.90000	24.10000	19.30000	1.409965	1.143621	3.513693	11
Finland	10.84545	11.10000	11.50000	9.700000	0.559220	-0.811107	2.666803	11
France	11.51818	11.70000	12.20000	10.10000	0.643146	-0.958685	3.148524	11
Germany	9.909091	9.900000	11.00000	8.700000	0.759545	-0.228424	1.836134	11
Greece	23.32727	23.60000	25.40000	19.70000	1.760733	-0.796411	2.828524	11
Hungary	20.12727	19.90000	21.20000	18.90000	0.654356	-0.107640	2.413329	11
Ireland	11.23636	11.70000	12.60000	9.500000	1.132495	-0.602482	1.832321	11
Italy	19.85455	20.00000	21.20000	18.10000	1.026025	-0.437772	2.021272	11
Latvia	19.23636	19.10000	21.30000	17.90000	1.077286	0.646565	2.479030	11
Lithuania	21.96364	21.50000	25.20000	19.70000	1.772158	0.497548	2.105711	11
Luxembourg	8.545455	8.700000	9.200000	7.900000	0.432120	-0.279022	1.964626	11
Malta	22.31818	23.10000	24.00000	18.60000	1.680963	-1.135089	3.198750	11
Netherlands	8.954545	9.000000	9.400000	8.400000	0.304512	-0.146794	2.445698	11
Poland	20.66364	20.30000	22.50000	19.40000	1.021051	0.769085	2.279815	11
Portugal	17.54545	17.50000	19.10000	16.10000	0.831100	0.232040	2.778290	11
Romania	24.85455	24.40000	27.40000	23.00000	1.576936	0.462728	1.762263	11
Slovakia	13.24545	13.10000	14.30000	12.60000	0.498726	0.929025	2.939554	11
Slovenia	20.33636	20.70000	21.90000	18.30000	1.163849	-0.331192	1.959205	11
Spain	20.66364	21.10000	21.90000	18.60000	1.079141	-1.117575	2.924279	11
Sweden	10.29091	10.20000	11.50000	9.500000	0.628418	0.339242	2.357762	11
United Kingdom	9.600000	9.500000	10.70000	8.700000	0.558570	0.462195	2.779832	11
All	16.73474	18.05000	27.40000	6.400000	5.950917	-0.037742	1.598059	308

Fig. 35.4 Descriptive statistics for the shadow economy. (Source: Authors' processing in EViews software)

As all variables are first-order integrated, cointegration rank tests can be used to investigate a long-term relationship between these variables. Once a cointegrated vector is found, a vector error correction mechanism can be defined. In our study, we rely on cointegration tests for panel data.

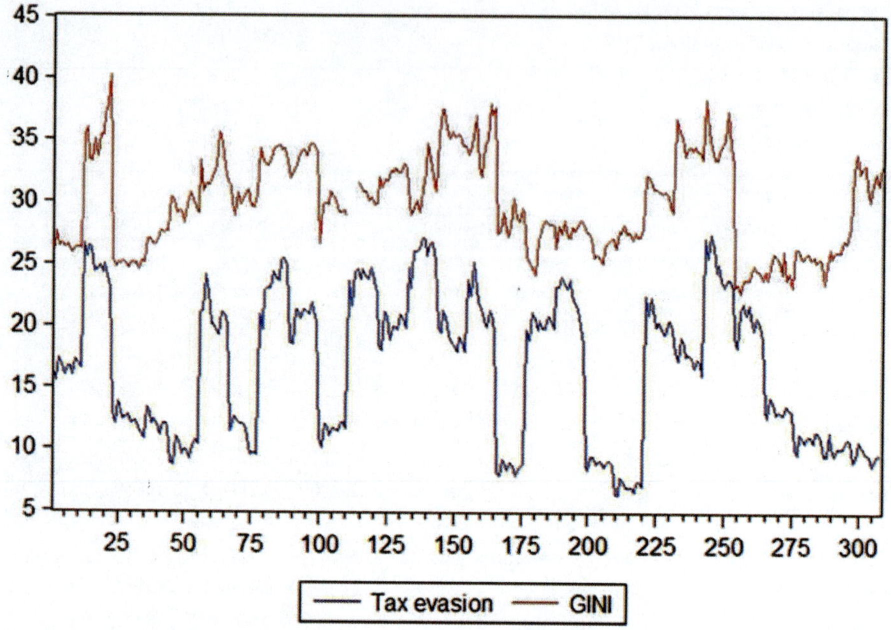

Fig. 35.5 Graphical representation of non-stationary variables. (Source: Authors' processing in EViews software)

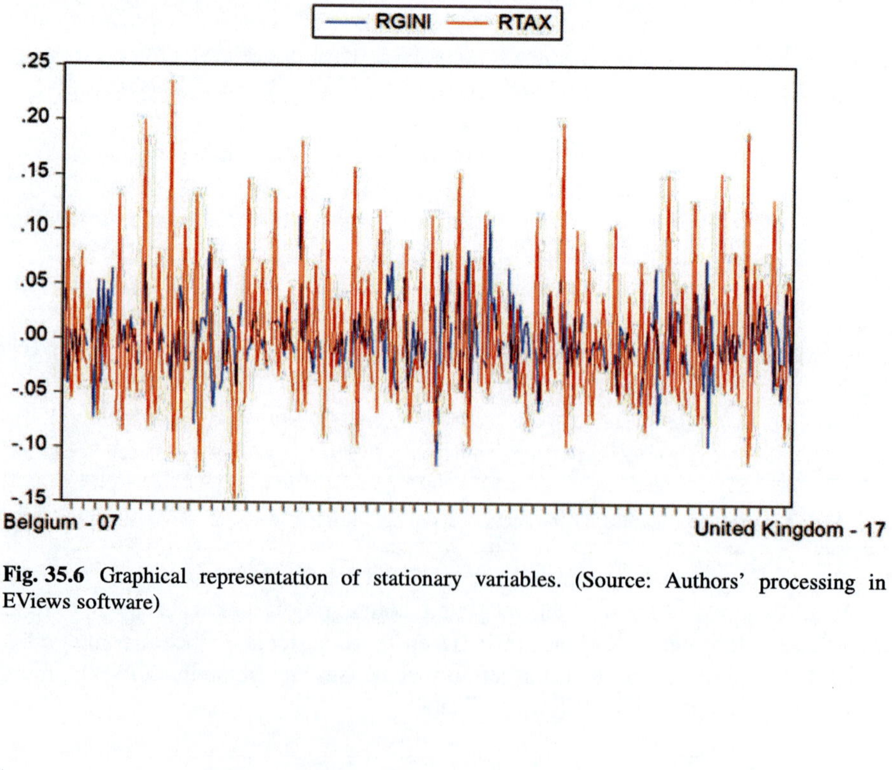

Fig. 35.6 Graphical representation of stationary variables. (Source: Authors' processing in EViews software)

Panel unit root test: Summary
Series: D(RTAX)
Date: 05/04/21 Time: 23:32
Sample: 2007 2017
Exogenous variables: None
User-specified lags: 1
Newey-West automatic bandwidth selection and Bartlett kernel
Balanced observations for each test

Method	Statistic	Prob.**	Cross-sections	Obs
Null: Unit root (assumes common unit root process)				
Levin, Lin & Chu t*	-39.2680	0.0000	28	196
Null: Unit root (assumes individual unit root process)				
ADF - Fisher Chi-square	465.084	0.0000	28	196
PP - Fisher Chi-square	513.600	0.0000	28	224

Panel unit root test: Summary
Series: D(RGINI)
Date: 05/04/21 Time: 23:37
Sample: 2007 2017
Exogenous variables: None
User-specified lags: 1
Newey-West automatic bandwidth selection and Bartlett kernel

Method	Statistic	Prob.**	Cross-sections	Obs
Null: Unit root (assumes common unit root process)				
Levin, Lin & Chu t*	-20.7119	0.0000	28	193
Null: Unit root (assumes individual unit root process)				
ADF - Fisher Chi-square	293.060	0.0000	28	193
PP - Fisher Chi-square	490.148	0.0000	28	221

Fig. 35.7 Augmented Dickey–Fuller test (ADF). (Source: Authors' processing in EViews software)

The best-known panel cointegration tests are those proposed by Pedroni (1999, 2004) and Kao (1999). Johansen (1988) proposes two different approaches. One of them is the likelihood ratio statistics tracking and the other is the maximum eigenvalue statistics, to determine the presence of cointegration vectors in non-stationary time series. The following sections briefly describe the test procedures.

Approaching the *Johansen test* (1988) for cointegration, Maddala and Wu (1999) propose an alternative to the previous two tests to examine the cointegration in a full panel by combining the tests for individual cross-sections.

Pairwise Granger Causality Tests
Date: 05/06/21 Time : 00:35
Sample : 2007 2017
Lags : 2

Null Hypothesis :	Obs	F-Statistic	Prob.
RTAX does not Granger Cause RGINI	221	0.09437	0.9100
RGINI does not Granger Cause RTAX		2.51121	0.0835

Fig. 35.8 Granger causality test. (Source: Authors' processing in EViews software)

Unrestricted Cointegration Rank Test (Trace and Maximum Eigenvalue)

Hypothesized No. of CE(s)	Fisher Stat.* (from trace test)	Prob.	Fisher Stat.* (from max-eigen test)	Prob.
None	281.9	0.0000	252.2	0.0000
At most 1	131.1	0.0000	131.1	0.0000

Fig. 35.9 Johansen/Fisher cointegration test. (Source: Authors' processing in EViews software)

Our own results by applying the Johansen cointegration test are presented in Fig. 35.9.

As it can be observed, the probability is significant for both scenarios, being equal to 0, suggesting that there is a cointegration relationship between the two variables – income inequality and shadow economy. As Trace and Maximum Eigenvalue indicate the existence of a cointegration relationship, we can assert the existence of a long-term relationship between the two variables, and therefore, we will perform the VECM.

First, we choose income inequality as the dependent variable, following all the steps to determine whether or not there is a long-term cointegration relationship. The results of this test (available by request) confirm that there is no causal relationship between GINI coefficient and shadow economy.

The next step is to analyse the shadow economy as a dependent variable. The cointegration equations, vector error correction estimates as well as the coefficients are presented in Figs. 35.10 and 35.11. C(1) represents the error correction term or the balance adjustment speed. As our results reveal, the coefficient C(1) is negative and significant, which suggests the existence of a long-term causality (long run) from the income inequality towards te shadow economy. The lag values of GINI coefficient are correlated with lead values of shadow economy in our panel.

The short-run causality can be verified by applying the Wald test (see Fig. 35.12), whose null hypothesis consists in $C(4) = C(5) = 0$. The probability recorded is below the significance threshold of 5%, which leads to the rejection of the null

Vector Error Correction Estimates
Date: 05/07/21 Time: 23:17
Sample (adjusted): 2010 2017
Included observations: 221 after adjustments
Standard errors in ( ) & t-statistics in [ ]

Cointegrating Eq:	CointEq1
TAX_EVASION(-1)	1.000000
GINI(-1)	0.213637 (0.54250) [0.39380]
C	-23.23391

Error Correction:	D(TAX_EVAS...	D(GINI)
CointEq1	-0.020693 (0.00649) [-3.18658]	0.003933 (0.01010) [0.38942]
D(TAX_EVASION(-1))	-0.145162 (0.04269) [-3.40052]	-0.030587 (0.06640) [-0.46066]
D(TAX_EVASION(-2))	-0.314821 (0.04138) [-7.60863]	-0.062000 (0.06436) [-0.96337]
D(GINI(-1))	0.110457 (0.04307) [2.56460]	-0.106801 (0.06699) [-1.59426]
D(GINI(-2))	0.088838 (0.04084) [2.17542]	-0.074968 (0.06352) [-1.18027]
C	-0.224516 (0.04177) [-5.37451]	0.057093 (0.06498) [0.87868]

Fig. 35.10 The cointegration equation. Error correction. (Source: Authors' processing in EViews software)

D(TAX_EVASION) = C(1)*(TAX_EVASION(−1) + 0.213637127855*GINI(−1) - 23.2339060614) + C(2)*D(TAX_EVASION(−1)) + C(3)*D(TAX_EVASION(−2)) + C(4) *D(GINI(−1)) + C(5)*D(GINI(−2)) + C(6)}
D(GINI) = C(7)*(TAX_EVASION(−1) + 0.213637 127855*GINI(−1) - 23.2339060614) + C(8)*D(TAX_EVASION(−1)) + C(9)*D (TAX_EVASION(−2)) + C(10)*D(GINI(−1)) + C(11)*D(GINI(−2)) + C(12)

	Coefficient	Std. Error	t-Statistic	Prob.
C(1)	-0.020693	0.006494	-3.186585	0.0015
C(2)	-0.145162	0.042688	-3.400525	0.0007
C(3)	-0.314821	0.041377	-7.608633	0.0000
C(4)	0.110457	0.043070	2.564597	0.0107
C(5)	0.088838	0.040837	2.175419	0.0301
C(6)	-0.224516	0.041774	-5.374510	0.0000
C(7)	0.003933	0.010101	0.389417	0.6972
C(8)	-0.030587	0.066397	-0.460663	0.6453
C(9)	-0.062000	0.064357	-0.963368	0.3359
C(10)	-0.106801	0.066991	-1.594257	0.1116
C(11)	-0.074968	0.063518	-1.180268	0.2385
C(12)	0.057093	0.064976	0.878678	0.3801
Determinant residual covariance		0.326357		

Fig. 35.11 Estimation of coefficients. (Source: Authors' processing in EViews software)

hypothesis or, in other words, we can assert the presence of short-term causality from income inequality towards shadow economy ($c(4) \neq 0$ and $c(5) \neq 0$). So, the Wald test suggests that there is also a short-run relationship between the two variables.

Wald Test:
System: {%system}

Test Statistic	Value	df	Probability
Chi-square	10.06431	2	0.0065

Null Hypothesis: C(4)=C(5)=0
Null Hypothesis Summary:

Normalized Restriction (= 0)	Value	Std. Err.
C(4)	0.110457	0.043070
C(5)	0.088838	0.040837

Restrictions are linear in coefficients.

Fig. 35.12 Wald test results. (Source: Authors' processing in EViews software)

Null Hypothesis: No cointegration
Trend assumption: No deterministic trend
Automatic lag length selection based on SIC with lags from 0 to 1
Newey-West automatic bandwidth selection and Bartlett kernel

Alternative hypothesis: common AR coefs. (within-dimension)

	Statistic	Prob.	Weighted Statistic	Prob.
Panel v-Statistic	0.352703	0.3622	-1.480769	0.9307
Panel rho-Statistic	-4.444977	0.0000	-3.748562	0.0001
Panel PP-Statistic	-12.10301	0.0000	-12.08960	0.0000
Panel ADF-Statistic	-11.29730	0.0000	-11.04751	0.0000

Alternative hypothesis: individual AR coefs. (between-dimension)

	Statistic	Prob.
Group rho-Statistic	-1.377941	0.0841
Group PP-Statistic	-17.68064	0.0000
Group ADF-Statistic	-14.06154	0.0000

Fig. 35.13 Pedroni test results. (Source: Authors' processing in EViews software)

In what follows, some robustness tests are performed to test the soundness of the results.

Pedroni (1999, 2004) introduced several statistical tests for the null hypothesis of lack of cointegration in non-stationary panels. The test allows for panel heterogeneity (Neal, 2014). The Pedroni cointegration test contains two scenarios, the Panel type and the Group type. The 2 scenarios include 7 tests, respectively, 11 probabilities that will be considered for testing the cointegration relationship in our study. As shown in Fig. 35.13, for a significance threshold of 10%, we can reject

Kao Residual Cointegration Test
Series: RGINI RTAX
Date: 05/07/21 Time: 22:36
Sample: 2007 2017
Included observations: 308
Null Hypothesis: No cointegration
Trend assumption: No deterministic trend
Automatic lag length selection based on SIC with a max lag of 1
Newey-West automatic bandwidth selection and Bartlett kerne

	t-Statistic	Prob.
ADF	-6.552191	0.0000
Residual variance	0.002254	
HAC variance	0.000641	

Fig. 35.14 Kao test results. (Source: Authors' processing in EViews software)

6/7 tests, respectively, 9/11 probabilities, which means that there is a cointegration relationship between the Gini coefficient and shadow economy in most cases.

The *Kao test* (1999) is based on the Dickey-Fuller test (DF) and the Augmented Dickey-Fuller test (ADF) (Dickey & Fuller, 1981) and exams the null hypothesis of the lack of cointegration relationship (Kao, 1999). By the means of this test, the initial result, according to which there is a long-term cointegration relationship between the two variables, is once again confirmed. Thus, in Fig. 35.14, we can see how the null hypothesis is rejected for a significance threshold of 5%.

35.4 Conclusions and Policy Implications

Current political and economic discourse in Europe is often animated by public concerns about the income gap between the rich and the poor on one hand, and the informal economy on the other hand. As more and more researchers argue, the two phenomena do not produce independently; there is some connection between them. Identifying the way shadow economy and income inequality interrelate is of great importance from public policy perspective.

Analysing the recent strand of literature in this particular area, we found arguments for a positive correlation between the informal economy and income inequality, even a bidirectional causal relationship. The two variables evolve in the same way, as there are common factors that impact them (e.g. trade liberalisation as found in Elveren and Ozgur, 2015). In addition, the way shadow economy and income distribution interrelate changes over time, as Berdiev and Saunoris (2019) suggest, or follow a non-linear shape as proved by Yap et al. (2018).

The present study investigates the relationship between the income inequality measured by Gini coefficient and shadow economy, in a panel of the EU-28 countries, over the 2007–2017 period. By approaching the subject in a cointegration and causality framework, by limiting the analysed sample to a country group that experiences convergent politics and by coming near the recent years, our paper significantly contributes to the literature segment mentioned above.

Our own empirical strategy includes unit root test, Johansen cointegration test and PVECM of Engle and Granger. The results indicate that variables are integrated of order one. A long-run relationship between income inequality and shadow economy is identified, as expected. The PVECM is estimated, concluding that income inequality does cause shadow economy in EU countries, but shadow economy does not cause income inequality. So, there is a unidirectional long-term relationship from income inequality to shadow economy. In addition, the Wald test suggests a short-run causality. Robustness tests are conducted to test the validity of the results. Pedroni and Kao cointegration tests confirm the previous results.

The outcomes are in line with those deriving from previous studies. Yet, we identify a unidirectional relationship instead of a bidirectional one.

Some policy implications could be drawn based on our empirical results.

Simultaneously managing the income distribution and informal economy in a society could be challenging, as the two variables jointly develop and income inequality is the cause for shadow economy. Fiscal and non-fiscal public interventions meant to reduce the income inequality should be carefully analysed from the perspective of their impact on the informal economy too. For instance, one fiscal policy aiming to support the poorest segment of the population or the firms encountering financial problems, by transfer payments from the public budget, eventually could encourage tax evasion and informal economy. The number of potential beneficiaries of those aids could insincerely increase by under-declaring revenues practices.

The context of the COVID-19 pandemic crises amplifies the problems generated by income inequality and shadow economy all over the world. The most vulnerable people are the poorest as they cannot adapt to the challenge of the new setting (Filauro & Fischer, 2021). The less favoured individuals redirect their activities towards the non-formal sector where they remain trapped for a long time. International Labour Office (2020) highlights the huge development of the informal economy during COVID crises and their trait for income distribution and long-term development. Fiscal policy responses are expected to counteract income losses induced by crises, especially for the poorest.

New research directions occur in this area, for example, by testing the cointegration and causality relationship between the income share of the poorest and the dimension of the shadow economy during the COVID-19 pandemic crises. Another target would be to test for the effectiveness of COVID-related fiscal policy measures in amending the income distribution and the relative amount of formal and non-formal activities.

References

Asteriou, D., & Hall, S. G. (2011). *Applied econometrics* (2nd ed.). Palgrave Macmillan.

Berdiev, A. N., & Saunoris, J. W. (2019). On the relationship between income inequality and the shadow economy. *Eastern Economic Journal, 45*, 224–249.

Bloomquist, K. M. (2003, January). Tax evasion, income inequality and opportunity costs of compliance. In *Proceedings. Annual Conference on Taxation and Minutes of the Annual Meeting of the National Tax Association* (Vol. 96, pp. 91–104). National Tax Association.

Christie, E., & Holzner, M. (2006). *What explains tax evasion? An empirical assessment based on European data.* (No. 40). WIIW Working Paper.

Dickey, D. A., & Fuller, W. A. (1981). Likelihood ratio statistics for autoregressive time series with a unit root. *Econometrica: Journal of the Econometric Society*, 1057–1072.

Eleveren, Y. A., & Özgür, G. (2015). The effect of informal economy on income inequality: Evidence from Turkey. *Panoeconomicus, 2016, 63*(3), 293–312.

Filauro, S., & Fischer, G. (2021). *Income inequality in the EU: General trends and policy implications*, VOX^{EU} CEPR, available online at: https://voxeu.org/article/income-inequality-eu-trends-and-policy-implications?fbclid=IwAR2FN4WaI VxK17FlTlqWhRGDge_iB8UoQnYTaCw1YdGCOzXtv QTUDL2pUkc

Hill, R. C., Griffiths, W. E., & Lim, G. C. (2011). *Principles of econometrics* (4th ed.). Wiley.

Gasteratos, I., Karamalis, M., & Koutoupis, A. (2016). Shadow economy worsens income distribution. *International Journal of Economics & Business Administration (IJEBA), 4*(3), 80–92.

International Labour Organization Brief (2020). COVID-19 crisis and the informal economy. *Immediate responses and policy challenges*, available online at https://www.ilo.org/wcmsp5/groups/public/%2D%2D-ed_protect/%2D%2D-protrav/%2D%2D-travail/documents/briefingnote/wcms_743623.pdf

Johansen, S. (1988). Statistical analysis of Cointegration vectors. *Journal of Economic and Control, 12*, 231–254.

Kao, C. (1999). Spurious regression and residual-based tests for Cointegration in panel data. *Journal of Econometrics, 90*, 1–44.

Maddala, G. S., & Wu, S. (1999). A comparative study of unit root tests with panel data and A new simple test. *Oxford Bulletin of Economics and Statistics, 61*, 631–652.

Medina, L., & Schneider, F. (2019). Shedding light on the shadow economy: A global database and the interaction with the official one, CESifo Working Papers, December 2019.

Neal, T. (2014). Panel cointegration analysis with xtpedroni. *The Stata Journal, 14*(3), 684–692.

Pedroni, P. (1999). Critical values for Cointegration tests in heterogeneous panels with multiple Regressors. *Oxford Bulletin of Economics and Statistics, 61*(S1), 653–670.

Pedroni, P. (2004). Panel cointegration: Asymptotic and finite sample properties of pooled time series tests with an application to the PPP hypothesis. *Econometric Theory, 20*(3), 597–625.

Pfaff, B., & Gentleman, R. (2008). *Analysis of integrated and cointegrated time series with R* (2nd ed.). Springer.

Rosser, J. B., Jr., Rosser, M. V., & Ehsan, A. (2000). Income inequality and the informal economy in transition economies. *Journal of Comparative Economics, 28*, 156–171.

Wooldridge, J. M. (2008). *Introductory econometrics: A modern approach* (4th ed.). South Istern Cengage Learning.

Yap, Weng, W., Sarmidi, T., Shaari, A. H., & Said, F. F. (2018). Income inequality and shadow economy: a nonparametric and semiparametric analysis. *Journal of Economic Studies.*

Chapter 36
Social Media Usage and Business Competitiveness in Agri-Food SMEs

Ourania Notta, Venetia Raikou, and Aspasia Vlachvei

Abstract The purpose of this work is first the presentation and implementation of social media in Greek agri-food small and medium firms and second, the evaluation of the impact of the use of social media on the competitiveness of agri-food SMEs. We use the BCCP MODEL (brand building, community building, customer satisfaction and performance) which is a conceptual framework for understanding, implementing, and measuring Social Media effectiveness for the firm involved. Brand building, community building and engagement, and customer satisfaction and loyalty have no direct financial results while Economic performance has financial results. In the case of the impact of social media on financial performance, it has emerged that even with the minimum daily involvement of social media, firms save more money and achieve the increase in their profits.

Keywords Social media · Competitiveness · Performance · Agri-food SMEs

36.1 Introduction

As social media users are around 3.01 billion in 2021 (Statista, 2017), social media are becoming an important part of an organization's media mix (Hoffman and Fodor, 2010; Hoffman and Novak, 2011). Social media allows companies to reach and communicate with consumers and interact with them, and new strategic and tactical

O. Notta (✉)
Department of Agriculture, Program of Agricultural Economics & Entrepreneurship, International Hellenic University, Thessaloniki, Greece
e-mail: ournotta@ihu.gr

V. Raikou
MSc in Agricultural Entrepreneurship – Innovative Systems of Sustainable Agricultural Production, International Hellenic University, Thessaloniki, Greece

A. Vlachvei
Department of Economics, University of Western Macedonia, Kastoria, Greece

N. Tsounis, A. Vlachvei (eds.), *Advances in Quantitative Economic Research*, Springer Proceedings in Business and Economics,
https://doi.org/10.1007/978-3-030-98179-2_36

marketing approaches have been developed to deal with the singularities of this type of media (Hennig-Thurau et al., 2010; Wang et al., 2017). The adoption of social media in business as a key tool of competitiveness has led to new forms of activities, especially in the context of the promotion, development, and assimilation of social media.

According to the results obtained from Vlachvei and Notta (2014) survey, it appeared that Greek food companies are sufficiently informed about new developments on the Internet. It is obvious that the sampling companies have successfully adopted new trends and users are able to appreciate the new features that technology can offer in thousands of ways. The integration of social media into the operating processes of a business has been shown to have a positive influence on sales and revenue growth, brand name building, and brand awareness and can affect consumers' view of a product or service (Weinberg et al., 2011). It is also a very important instrument that helps to acquire new customers and maintain existing ones (Beier, 2016). Customer service and customer satisfaction are two other areas in which business communication with their customers through social media is expanded, which is a key function of this medium (Weber, 2009). Businesses seek to create communities on social media because through them the engagement of users is increased and by extension "loyal customers" are created (Smith, et al., 2015).

According to Vlachvei and Notta (2015), there are three ways to get financial results from using social media. The first is through social media to drive perspectives on an e-commerce page. This means that we can measure the success of social media campaign by increased sales, revenue per customer, recurring purchase rate, and average customer life. The second way is to identify the profits the company has through savings. This means that a business can substantially reduce the cost of customer service by managing a customer complaint through social media. By comparing the cost of traditional customer service with the cost of social media customer service, companies can make a calculation about whether they have improved efficiency using social service (Turner and Shah, 2014). But a business can also have a significant reduction in the cost of traditional advertising through effective social participation of SMEs. Measures that can be used are: reduced advertising costs, reduced customer retention costs, and reduced customer complaint management costs. The third way is to make money through social media (when the company's campaign is designed to do so), which can be measured by increased sales or produce new products. If the goal is to increase sales, measuring the success of the social media program should take into account: web traffic, time spent on the site, dropout rate, recurring visits, content acceptance rate, followers, social references, and voice share.

Based on the work of Vlachvei and Notta (2015), it was attempted to provide a framework where it is clear that the effectiveness of social media involvement has to do with the company's determination and whether the appropriate goals are linked to the social media application. Before a business can enter social media, it must first identify and understand the value of some initially nonmeasurable sizes for the customer and the business at the same time. According to the BCCP model, four goals presented: (B) brand building, (C) community building, (C) customer satisfaction and loyalty, (P) and financial performance.

For each of these objectives, the effectiveness of participation in social media can be measured by the proposed measurements. The introduction of these objectives in essence also signals the company's ability to create a purely cognitive background that can measure the expected benefits accurately and effectively. However, it is not enough for businesses to simply introduce social media, for example, in the form of creating a Facebook page or Twitter account. To make effective use of social media, businesses need to have a strategy for using them and consider why they use it, as well as, in particular, how they can support business goals (Stockdale et al., 2012). Although it can be argued that only financial gains can be measured in monetary value, nonfinancial gains from social media can be just as beneficial resulting in a range of rewards, such as better communication with customers, brand awareness, etc. However, although these may be advantages for each business, measuring these unspecified benefits is problematic. While metrics such as "increasing friends on Facebook" or "increasing Twitter followers" don't have to be related to increased sales, it's clear that a company's presence on social media platforms can ultimately lead to financial gain. Taylor (2011) argues that social media itself has no value as measurable sizes and you can only measure the business results achieved by applying them to the company's operational structure and overall performance by comparing the previous period of non-application with the subsequent in which their use has been integrated into the core functions of the business.

The purpose of this work is first, the presentation and implementation of social media in Greek agri-food small and medium firms and second, the evaluation of the impact of the use of social media on the competitiveness of agri-food SMEs. We use the BCCP MODEL, which is a conceptual framework for understanding, implementing, and measuring social media effectiveness for the firm involved. Brand building, community building and engagement, and customer satisfaction and loyalty have no direct financial results, while economic performance has financial results.

36.2 Empirical Research

Greek food and beverage industry is one of the most important industries in the secondary sector of the economy which together with the processing and distribution significantly affect the whole of Greek production in agricultural products. The sector operates approximately 15.7 thousand enterprises with a turnover of 15.1 billion euros and a number of employees at 111 thousand. This sector of the economy shows a medium-weighted revenue growth of 1.86% for the years 2009 to 2016 and a gross value added of 3.1 billion euros.

The sample of the research is 203 agri-food companies in Greece with at least an account on a social media site. The method is quantitative research; we distribute questionnaire scans through a personal interview and electronically in the form of a

Table 36.1 Incentives for businesses to invest in social media

	Valid values	Average price
Increase company awareness in the market	203	4.23
Communication improvement/customer interaction	203	4.22
Attract new customers	203	4.15
Increase traffic of the corporate site	203	4.14
Approach specific market share	203	3.81
Profitability	203	3.68

Table 36.2 Contribution of the use of social media to businesses

	Valid values	Average price	St. dev.
Brand building and awareness	203	4.19	0.794
Community building and engagement	203	3.83	0.891
Customer satisfaction and loyalty	203	3.62	0.928
Economic performance	203	3.56	0.934

Google Drive form. The duration of the research was from February 2019 to April 2019.

The distribution per branch in the sample is representative from all the sectors of agri-food industry, and the majority of the companies are Greek-owned. Regarding the size of the firms, a large percentage of the companies (62%) in the sample employ less than ten employees.

Based on the number and type of social media in which these companies operate, we found that Facebook (98%) is the dominant media following by Instagram (55,2%), and this is in line with the general rule that these media are the most popular in large parts of the population. The degree of activity of each company with social media and the daily time spent operating the company on a daily basis are two main factors assessing the importance and weight that companies give to the efficiency and utilization of the means for business benefit. The 37.3% use social media daily followed by 24.63% every 2–3 days, but 61.1% spent less than an (1) hour per day on social media.

First, we examine the incentives for businesses to invest in social media (Table 36.1). According to our results, firms invest in social media: first, to increase company awareness in the market (mean = 4.23); second, to improve the communication and interaction with customers (4.22); third, to attract new customers (4.15); fourth, to increase the corporate site traffic (4.14); fifth, to approach a specific market share (3.81); and last, to increase the profitability (3.68).

In order to examine the contribution of the use of social media to businesses, we used the BCCP model (Table 36.2). We found out that companies believe that the use of social media first contributes to build and enhance the brand and awareness (mean = 4.19) and then to build community engagement (3.83), customer satisfaction and loyalty (3.62), and ultimately financial performance (3.56).

Table 36.3 Contribution of the use of social media to businesses in the case of SMEs for each goal separately (BCCP)

Brand building and awareness	Average price	St. dev.
Increase page/account traffic	4.19	0.819
Improve ranking in search engines	3.96	0.892
Monitoring positive/negative comments	3.93	0.898
Time spent on the page	3.54	0.945
Increase in job applications	2.92	1.059
Community building and engagement		
The number of friends/followers	3.9	0.804
Retweets/shares	3.81	0.911
Recommendations	3.75	0.9
Response to reviews	3.76	0.888
Call to action	3.69	0.909
Increase newsletter enrolment	3.57	0.975
References and observations	3.64	0.898
Customer satisfaction and loyalty		
Customer response	3.96	0.884
Feedback	3.92	0.861
The number of customer complaints	3.67	1.021
The adjustment	3.66	0.902
On line product service	3.42	1.033
Economic performance		
Electronic transactions	3.72	0.971
Profits	3.53	0.951
Cost reduction ratio savings	3.36	0.972

Regarding brand building and awareness, the majority of responders strongly believe that the use of social media leads to increasing page/account traffic (4.19), the improving of ranking in search engines (3.96), and the monitoring positive/negative comments (3.93) (Table 36.3).

Regarding community building and engagement, the use of social media is strongly evaluated in the majority of responders with the number of friends/followers in the media (3.90), the retweets and shares (3.81), the recommendations (3.75), the response to reviews (3.76), and the call to action (3.69). The majority of responders strongly believe that customer satisfaction and loyalty is assessed based on customer response (3.96) and feedback (3.92). The majority of respondents strongly believe that the economic performance resulting from the use of social media is measured primary by the electronic transactions (3.72) and secondly by the profits (3.53) and the cost of reduction ratio savings (3.36).

We find that respondents strongly believe that the creation of innovation (4.07) and sales growth (3.89), as factors in evaluating profits and therefore a direct result of the competitiveness of the company from the use of social media (Table 36.4).

Table 36.4 Contribution of the use of social media to business performance

Profits	Average price	St. dev.
Sales growth	3.89	0.894
Innovation (product development due to customer feedback at various stages)	4.07	4.139
Saving money		
Reducing advertising costs	3.76	1.059
Reducing customer service costs	3.59	1.003
Reducing customer retention costs	3.54	0.929
Reducing complaint management costs	3.45	0.986
Electronic transactions		
Market repetition	3.85	0.953
Sales growth	3.72	0.961
The average customer retention	3.67	0.914
Revenue per costumer	3.47	0.935

The majority of the respondents believe that first the reduction in advertising costs (3.76), and then the reduction of customer service costs (3.59) are the main factors of saving money. The respondents strongly believe that the market repetition (3.85), the sales growth (3.72) are the main estimates of electronic transactions.

Then, we utilized a principal component factor analysis. Factor analysis is a statistical method used to describe variability among observed, correlated variables in terms of a potentially lower number of unobserved variables called factors. Principal component analysis seeks a linear combination of variables such that the maximum variance is extracted from the variables.

Through the analysis of the principal component method, five factors have been identified explaining together 65.2% of the variance in the items. The analysis of these coefficients explains the presence of five leading profiles in the sample survey:

- The first factor explains 40.72% of the explained variance and is characterized as community building and customer satisfaction oriented, since there is significant correlation in parameters concerning community engagement and customer loyalty.
- The second factor explains 10.27% of the explained variance and is characterized as profit oriented since there is significant correlation in variables associated with profits and savings.
- The third factor explains 5.21% of the explained variance and is characterized as electronic transactions oriented since there is significant correlation in parameters exclusively related to electronic transactions.
- The fourth factor explains 4.67% of the explained variance and is characterized as brand-building oriented since there is significant correlation in questions related to building/enhancing the brand.

- The fifth and final factor explains 4.29% of the explained variance and is related to the creation of innovation, and the increase in its price indicates a greater impact on this issue.

In order to test the impact of the use of social media on the competitiveness of agri-food enterprises in Greece, we examine the correlations between the five factors with the scale of the use of social media. There is a statistically significant difference between the daily time and the dimensions of community building and engagement and customer satisfaction and loyalty (p-value $0.005 < 0.05$) and between the daily time and the dimensions of profits and saving money (p-value $0.011 < 0.05$). The maximum effect on community building and customer satisfaction is achieved when the daily engagement with social media is from 4 to 5 hours. There is statistically significant dependency between daily time and dimensions of profits and savings. In the case of the impact of social media on financial performance, it has emerged that even with the minimum daily involvement of social media, they save more money and achieve an increase in their profits.

36.3 Conclusions

The use of social media creates business advantage. Companies believe that the use of social media first contributes to building and enhancing the brand and then building the community, customer satisfaction, and ultimately financial performance. Social media, despite their ability to create habits and consumer behavior through information, cannot be clarified whether they help to strengthen/build the brand, something that is done at the later stage of the product's recurrent purchase by the consumer. The use of media creates and highlights a new type of social behavior with exchange of views, common interests, reflections that lead to the creation, and building of the community which is constantly evolving rapidly through the addition of new members and trends. This view is verified and seen as a key conclusion that reinforces the growth trend and the evolution of media in networking communities.

The information provided in the first place by social media and the subsequent infinite possibilities created from online orders, feedback, etc. create an enhanced satisfaction and confidence of the customer that translates into a purchasing response on his part. The use of social media has a positive impact on financial performance through increased sales and savings as well as performance through profits. In the case of agri-food firms, the use of social media builds long-term relationships of trust and mutual respect between entrepreneur and consumer that is being built in a new social environment and is rapidly evolving into a new economic and social entity with similar consumer behavior.

References

Beier, M., & Wagner, K. (2016). *Social media adoption: Barriers to the strategic use of social media in SMEs*. Twenty-fourth European Conference on Information Systems (ECIS).

Hennig-Thurau, T., Malthouse, E. C., Friege, C., Gensler, S., Lobschat, L., Rangaswamy, A., & Skiera, B. (2010). The impact of new media on customer relationships. *Journal of Service Research, 13*(3), 311–330.

Hoffman, L., & Fodor, M. (2010). Can you measure the ROI of your social media marketing. *MIT Sloan Management Review, 52*(1), 41–49.

Hoffman, D. L., & Novak, T. P. (2011). Social media strategy. In V. Shankar & G. S. Carpenter (Eds.), *Handbook on marketing strategy*. Edward Elgar Publishing, Ltd..

Smith, T., Blazovich, K., Janell, L., & Smith, M. L. (2015). Social media adoption by corporations: An examination by platform, industry, size, and financial performance. Academy of marketing. *Studies Journal, 19*(2), p127–p143. 17p.

Statista. (2017). Number of social media users worldwide 2010–2020, available at: www.statista.com/statistics/278414/number-of-worldwide-social-network-users/

Stockdale, R., Ahmed, A., & Scheepers, H. (2012). Identifying business value from the use of social medial an SME perspective. Proceedings of IS Innovation in Pacific Asia, PACIS, 2012, Vietnam, 11–15 July 2012.

Taylor, P., (2011). Making use of social media for business. *Financial Times*, Sept 17, 2011.

Turner, J., & Shah, R. (2014). *How to make money with social media: An insider's guide to using new and emerging media to grow your business*. Pearson Education LTD..

Vlachvei, A., & Notta, O. (2014). Social media adoption and managers' perceptions. *International Journal on Strategic Innovative Marketing, 01*(2014), 61–73. https://doi.org/10.15556/IJSIM.01.02.001

Vlachvei, A. & Notta, O. (2015). "Understanding Social Media ROI in SMEs" Book of Proceedings published by International Organization for Research and Development – IORD. ISSN: 2410-5465 Book of Proceedings ISBN: 978-969-7544-00-4.

Wang, Y., Rod, M., Ji, S., & Deng, Q. (2017). Social media capability in B2B marketing: Toward a definition and a research model. *The Journal of Business and Industrial Marketing*.

Weber, L. (2009). *Marketing to the social web* (2nd ed.). Wiley.

Weinberg, B. D., & Pehlivan, E. (2011). Social spending: Managing the social media mix. *Business Horizons, 54*(3), 275–282.

Chapter 37
Cultural Production as a Means of Acculturation of Global Consumer Culture for Luxury Brands: A Content Analysis

Koronaki Eirini, Aspasia Vlachvei, and Anastasios Panopoulos

Abstract This chapter aims to present how luxury brands engage in cultural production and strategically use it for the acculturation of a global consumer culture. A content analysis is adopted from interviews of luxury brands' creative designers were analyzed through content analysis. Our findings underpin the relevance of cultural production for luxury brands and indicate how the combination of the above can be strategically used. Managerial and academic implications are discussed.

Keywords Arts · Cultural production · Global consumer culture · Acculturation to global consumer culture · Luxury brand

37.1 Introduction

The luxury market is an economic sector of heterogeneous companies and products that has grown dramatically over the past 20 years; from 1996 to 2019, its worth shifted from 76 billion euros to 281 billion euros (Statista, 2019). Today, luxury involves a much wider concept than exclusive, affluent, prestigious, or craftsmanship work. Nowadays, it is about acquiring meaningful experiences (Thomsen et al., 2020), which renders luxury consumption highly contextual (Stiehler, 2016; Wang & Chen, 2020). Each individual's background influences the perception of what luxury should be (Miller & Mills, 2012). In an attempt to respond to these challenges, luxury brands have been increasingly adding artistic elements to their strategies (Chailan, 2018). Whether this refers to collaboration with established or

K. Eirini (✉) · A. Vlachvei
University of Western Macedonia, Kastoria, Greece
e-mail: ekoronaki@uowm.gr

A. Panopoulos
University of Macedonia, Thessaloniki, Greece

N. Tsounis, A. Vlachvei (eds.), *Advances in Quantitative Economic Research*, Springer Proceedings in Business and Economics,
https://doi.org/10.1007/978-3-030-98179-2_37

emerging artists, finding inspiration from famous artistic creations, creating branded spaces at art fairs, investing in brand-hosted art exhibitions, and even establishing museums, all these tactics aim to create a meaningful connection to their consumers, building on the fact that "one of the many powers of an artist is to turn any object into an artwork" (Dion & Arnould, 2011, p. 508).

Venkatesh and Meamber (2006) describe such practices as cultural production, through which cultural products such as possessions, works of art, experiential objects, services, and various other forms of art are created, altered, and added to consumer culture (Lash et al., 1993). Meaning transfer is based on the notion that products are infused with symbolism through marketing strategies and that they subsequently communicate the desired meanings to individuals (McCrakcen, 1986). Especially when using meaning based on the arts and aesthetics, one can leverage on the identified role that they can have in the construction of consumer culture (Firat & Venkatesh, 1995). Thus, it becomes evident that signs and symbols endowed with arts and aesthetics will influence consumer culture (Baudrillard, 1993). Such practices of luxury which are based on arts and aesthetics are frequently linked to "escapism" (Banister et al., 2020), which is based on the ideas of fantasies and cultural capital. Since consumers undergo self-transformation and satisfy their different selves when experiencing nonmaterialistic moments of luxury (Hemetsberger et al., 2012; von Wallpach et al., 2020) and these moments are linked to aesthetic concerns (Tynan et al., 2010), the question arises of whether such luxury moments endowed with artistic elements can still leverage on the positive outcomes of the arts and create the desired cultural meaning (Venkatesh & Meamber, 2006).

One of the ideas that luxury has been linked to is global consumer culture. Alden, Steenkamp, and Batra (1999) define global consumer culture (GCC) as a system of cultural phenomena recognized as exceeding national cultural systems. Appadurai (1990, p. 299) proposes a framework of diffusion for global consumer culture through five paths of global cultural flow, including mediascapes, which offer multifaceted ranges of "images, narratives and 'ethnoscapes'." From these sources, imaginary lives of individuals from various consumer groups can be presented (Appadurai, 1990). The construction of consumers' identities and self-concept is assisted by meanings promoted by foreign cultural meanings through acculturation (Askegaard et al., 2005). Cleveland and Laroche (2007) operationalized acculturation to GCC (AGCC) as a multifaceted construct to encapsulate how people "acquire the knowledge, skills, and behaviors that are characteristic of a nascent and deterritorialized global consumer culture" (p. 252). This process is assisted through the seven dimensions of acculturation to the global consumer culture, namely, cosmopolitanism (COS); exposure to marketing activities of multinational companies (EXM); exposure to/use of the English language (ELU); social interactions, including travel, migration, and contacts with foreigners (SIN); global/foreign mass media exposure (GMM); openness to and desire to emulate global consumer culture (OPE); and self-identification with global consumer culture (IDT) (Cleveland & Laroche, 2007). It is argued, using the semiotics perspective as an underlying theory, that certain consumers will seek out for consumption experiences perceived as a sign of such a script, in order to show that they are a part of this world (Alden et al., 1999). As they mention, through the diffusion of such imagery and consumers' desire for real or imagined participation in the depicted consumer culture, certain product categories become signs of global cosmopolitanism and modernity.

This paper sets out to examine whether cultural production from luxury brands, identified as the inclusion of arts and aesthetics elements in their marketing practices, affects consumers acculturation of global consumer culture and the subsequent outcomes. The first part of the paper discusses the literature regarding art and luxury branding, while the second part presents the literature connecting luxury and acculturation to global consumer culture. Finally, a conceptual framework is presented, which is then examined through content analysis.

37.2 Literature Review

37.2.1 Art and Luxury Brands

The use of the arts by luxury brands is a multifaceted activity with multiple purposes. Marketers and scholars have argued that the adoption of artistic elements is a favorable way to induce consumers into buying the product (Baumgarth, 2018). Hagtvedt and Patrick (2008) studied the phenomenon of "art infusion" "the general influence of the presence of art on consumer perceptions and evaluations of products with which it is associated" (p. 379)—by carrying out an empirical research to measure and analyze the perception and evaluation of consumers toward the presence of visual arts in products. The results showed that products that contain visual arts in their packages seem to be more sophisticated, luxurious, prestigious, and expensive. Logkizidou et al. (2019) also identify the positive effects of art infusion on the product's perceived luxuriousness. Peluso et al., (2017) stress how the use of a painter's recognizable style in advertising can increase the perceived luxuriousness. Lee et al. (2015) also discuss that the inclusion of visual art can increase consumers' perceived prestige value, and specifically perceived conspicuous value, perceived unique value, perceived quality value, and perceived hedonic value.

Leveraging on the arts has also been examined in relation to the retail store. Vukadin et al. (2016) acknowledged that the inclusion of artistic cues offers a differentiation, through hedonic and symbolic elements. Furthermore, the store is not perceived solely as having a commercial purpose. Termed as "M-Art worlds" by Joy et al. (2014), such retail stores can simultaneously provide a feeling of visiting a gallery and visiting a store. Arts marketing within a store has been identified to lead to increased bonds, through value co-creation (Choi et al., 2016).

In fact, the future of the relationship between luxury and arts has been linked to successful marketing strategies. Jelinek (2018) stressed that if the arts are used strategically in luxury brand management, they can significantly enhance brand authenticity and thus increase brand equity. In the same way, Chailan (2018) examined the role of art in the creation of luxury uniqueness and identified four approaches that link luxury brands with the world of art: artistic mentoring, patronage, foundations, and artistic collaboration. In such a context, Grassi (2020) discusses that a foundation such as Fondazione Prada can increase consumer engagement, considering that it increased the interaction and dialogue with its audience and promote its key values and also increase the promotion of contemporary art.

In some cases, brands participate in more than one type/approach of collaboration. Koronaki, Kyrousi, and Panigyrakis (2018) discuss how the art-based initiatives create emotional value for consumers. According to them, the benefits of art-based initiatives are twofold: to promote societal well-being (public benefits) and to benefit the consumer as an individual (private benefits). The experience of the consumers is positive when they gain hedonic value from their purchase, following an emotional connection to the brand which later transforms into loyalty and affective commitment. While an increasing amount of researchers have examined the relationship between the arts and luxury brand management, it has yet to be established how art can be strategically connected to luxury brand management.

In many cases, luxury brands enhance their artistic nature through the promotion of their creative director or designer (Dion & Arnould, 2011). This leverages on their personal style, aesthetic preferences, and on the increased levels of taste that they can offer in the prevailing brand discourse. That is also the reason for which they are also frequently promoted as a fundamental element of the brand's identity.

The following research question thus emerges:

RQ1: Is there a relationship between luxury brands that engage in cultural production and the acculturation of a global consumer culture?

37.2.2 *Acculturation of Global Consumer Culture and Luxury*

Studies have connected luxury consumption to global consumer culture, due to its symbolic nature and its connection to cultural change (Dubois & Duquesne, 1993). Luxury consumption has been identified as indicative of belonging to a global group of people that are like-minded (Seo & Buchanan-Oliver, 2019). This builds on the fact that the use of a certain brand can strengthen consumers' identification, since it allows them to use cultural cues that satisfy their perceptions of selves on a regular basis (Sobol et al., 2018). Consequently, consumers that value global communities and use global brands experience high levels of satisfaction (Bartsch et al., 2016). Thus, acculturation to global consumer culture has been identified as an antecedent of luxury consumption (Cleveland et al., 2016; Sobol et al., 2018). In fact, Nwankwo et al. (2014) underline that global consumer culture can function as a moderator to luxury consumption, while Tsai et al. (2013) find a positive connection between Chinese international students' acculturation into American culture and the respective cultural prevailing beliefs and their luxury consumption choices.

A significant element of acculturation of global consumer culture is cosmopolitanism, which has also been frequently linked to luxury consumption. An individual is described as a cosmopolitan if they travel on a regular basis, interact with individuals from numerous countries, and function as a gate to other cultures (Hannerz, 1992). Moreover, they can significantly influence which aspects of other cultures will be adopted and maintained in their home country (Hannerz, 1992). Cleveland et al. (2009) identify cosmopolitanism as an antecedent of global consumer culture for luxury goods. Fastoso and González-Jiménez (2018) underline that cosmopolitanism is positively related to emotional brand attachment for brands with high levels of ideal self-congruity, and Khare (2014) finds that cosmopolitanism linked to lifestyle affects Indian consumers' involvement.

Luxury brands have been identified as a part of materialism (Arli et al., 2016), since they are based on the concept of indulgence and are not linked to basic needs (Bian & Forsythe, 2012). Materialism has been defined as "the importance ascribed to the ownership and acquisition of material goods in achieving major life goals or desired states" (Richins, 2004, p. 210). Materialistic values have been identified as going in line with global consumer culture (Cleveand et al., 2013; Cleveland et al., 2015), since consumers desire products and then acquire them because they help them to show that they belong to a global consumer culture (Belk et al., 2003). Materialism has also been positively connected to emotional brand attachment toward brands high in ideal self-congruity (Fastoso & González-Jiménez, 2018). They further find that consumers are attached to global brands, regardless of their aspirational value. Especially in BRIC countries, individuals who feel closely connected to global consumer culture have shown high levels of materialism (Strizhakova & Coulter, 2013). In a world were globalization rules in every market, being part of a specific global consumer culture can assist a brand in staying relevant. Since acculturation to global consumer culture teaches consumers how to behave and things they need to know about their consumption, we argue that the use of the arts can facilitate acculturation to global consumer culture.

Thus, the second research question emerges:

RQ2: Does the acculturation to global consumer culture affect responses toward luxury brands?

37.3 Methodology

This study examines the discursive elements of luxury brands, building on the fact that brand meaning is constructed socially (O'Reilly, 2005) and following other studies that have adopted this approach in luxury consumption (e.g., Roper et al., 2013). According to this approach, brand stories can be used by consumers as cultural elements in their identity-building and self-project (Brown et al., 2003). We thus aim to examine how luxury brands are constructed to incorporate a cultural production element, leveraging on the power of the arts and how this leads to

Table 37.1 Interviewees, brands, and positions

Interviewee	Brand(s)	Position
Tory Burch	Tory Burch LLC	Fashion designer, chief creative officer
Robert Storey	Hermès and Prada	Spatial designer
Elin Kling	Totem	Co-founder
Lindsey Adelman	Lindsey Adelman studio	Lighting designer and artist
Paul Andrew	Salvatore Ferragamo	Creative director
Wes Gordon	Carolina Herrera	Creative director
Daniel Humm	Davies and brook restaurant at Claridge's	Chef and restaurateur
Kim jones	Dior	Men's artistic director
Alvaro Maggini	Panerai	Creative director
Jessica McCormack	Jessica McCormack	Jeweller
Fanny Moizant	Vestiaire collective	Co-founder
John Harrison	Gieves & Hawkes	Creative director
Peter Pilotto	Peter Pilotto	Designer
Gaia Repossi	Gaia Repossi	Designer
Claire Choisne	Boucheron	Creative director
Elza Wandler	Wandler	Founder
Adrien Sauvage	House of a Sauvage	Menswear designer
Bella Freud	Bella Freud	Designer

acculturation of global consumer culture. The role of the creative director and fashion designer is fundamental when investing in the ratification of the luxury brand (Kapferer, 2014), which means that they have a crucial role to play in constructing and enhancing the artistic elements of the luxury brand. Thus, the interviews analyzed in this study belong to creative directors of established luxury brands, since in content analysis, it is accepted to use data derived from online forums, interviews, and websites (Roper et al., 2013).

The source from which the 18 interviews of luxury brand designers or creative directors were taken was the Financial Times online magazine "How To Spend It" and specifically its section "The Aesthete." The persons interviewed were the following ones (see Table 37.1).

The interviews included a series of questions, which were linked to a construct related to our hypotheses (see Table 37.2). The questions that were not relevant to our study were not included for analysis (If I weren't doing what I do, I would be, My favourite room in my house, In my fridge you'll always find, During lockdown, I've been..., With time on my hands...). Each interview was first studied separately, to reassure that any information related to our research question would be included. Then, the answers of each responded were classified per question, based on the classification in Table 37.2, and a text of 28 pages (4344 words) emerged for analysis.

Table 37.2 Questions and related constructs

Questions in interview and associated construct
Personal style
• My personal style signifier. • My style icons. • The grooming staple I'm never without is/the beauty staple I'm never without is.
Cultural product, arts
• The best book I've read in the past year/I've also been reading. • The last music I downloaded/and the music I'm enjoying is. • The one artist whose work I would collect if I could.
Cultural product, arts, and digital marketing
• The podcast I'm listening to/my favorite apps are. • My favorite website. • The tech I couldn't do without/the gadgets I couldn't do without are.
Cultural product and exploration
• I've recently discovered. • A recent "find".
Gift-giving and materialism and cultural product, arts
• The best gift I've given recently. • And the best gift I've received recently.
Materialism
• I have a collection of. • The last item of clothing I added to my wardrobe. • The last thing I bought and loved. • An object I would never part with/the item of clothing I'll keep to pass on. • The next thing on my wishlist. • An indulgence I would never forgo is.
Materialism and social interaction-travel
The best souvenir I've ever brought home
Social interaction-travel
• A place I'd love to return to. • If I had to limit my shopping to one neighborhood in one city, I'd choose. • If I didn't live in New York, I would live in.

37.4 Findings

The first set of questions was related to the personal style and related options of the interviewee. In this case in the question regarding the personal style, some interviewees referred to specific clothing options or clothing styles. Others referred to specific accessories. It was also interesting to see that some of them linked their personal style, with moments to remember, such as wedding rings or gift from a friend or the memory of the city in which it was bought.

Regarding style icons, there were some inferences to aspects of personality of the individuals mentioned as icons. In many cases, the profession of the icon was also included in the description. Another interesting element was that some references were to everyday people of the interviewees' partners.

Finally, a question linked to personal style was related to grooming options or beauty products. In this case, a series of specific products and brands were mentioned, whether referring to perfume, face products, or even toothpaste.

The second set of questions related to the cultural product and artistic elements. In this case, the interviewee was asked about their recent findings on various cultural aspects, such as books, music, etc. Regarding the book, it was interesting to see that many books were biographies of inspirational individuals or entrepreneurs. Also, a series of novels was suggested, in line with health and sustainability-related books. In every case, a description of the author was also given, justifying the chosen book. As far as the music is concerned, again a variety of artists from around the world such as London and Turkey were referred to. Furthermore, a soundtrack of a movie was mentioned, as well as a specific type of music. In many cases, the memories that the music is linked to were also discussed. The next question in this context related to the artist they would collect if they had a chance and included a variety of artists from classical ones such as Matisse and Rothko to contemporary ones from painters to sculptors and photographers. Again, in many cases, a story linked to when paintings from the artist were seen either for the first time or recently is discussed.

Next, a series of questions related to digital marketing and cultural production. When asked which podcast they were currently listening to, a variety of entrepreneurial, sustainability-oriented, designer-linked, or even novels were mentioned. Regarding the apps, there was a reference to meditation apps, fitness apps, design inspiration apps, and some shopping apps, while regarding the websites, auction websites were included, in line with museums, and film-databases or journalism and design sites. Finally, regarding the gadget, numerous options were mentioned, varying from headphones to phones and related products, watches, camera, and even an iron.

The next section of the interview is linked to cultural aspects and the notion of new and discovery. In this case, the first question was related to a recent "find" in which case a variety of options were mentioned, ranging from rare books from foreign countries, shops, bookstores, or restaurants in other countries or in one's city of residence, activities such as auctions, specific products or brands, or artists and their work.

An important element that was discussed and is a key area in luxury branding is gift giving. In this case, questions were asked both regarding gift giving and gift receiving. In case the respondent was the gift provider, cases such as a trip, pieces of art, an event, a rare object, a museum membership, and even everyday food such as eggs were mentioned. In the case in which the interviewee was the receiver, again unique products were mentioned in many cases for which the brand's story was also frequently included. Some referred to artistic objects or books, while a percentage referred to objects of sentimental value such as the preparation of a dinner or a mug.

The next set of questions is associated with the notion of materialism. The first question referred to the collections possessed, and answers such as ceramics or pottery, books, vases, and photographs were given, in line with fashion clothing and accessories choices. An interesting choice was linked to natural objects taken from travels. In the question related to specific clothing items recently bought, specific unique brands, from specific stores and brands, were mentioned, whereas for the thing last bought, again specific brands were mentioned. In some cases, connections were also made to the store from which they were purchased. Similarly, the next questions referred to objects one could not leave behind, and the answers included unique brands, in many cases with sentimental value due to connections with significant individuals in one's life. Many choices included products designed by the interviewee themselves, while an interesting answer by a small number of respondents was that they did not want to be attached to objects. Next, the question included unique rare products that they would pass on to the next generation and included vintage, expensive, and difficult to find products, which in some cases were linked to family members, whereas unique brands, furniture, travels, a bike, or a piece of art were chosen as the next thing they wish to buy. Finally, they mentioned indulgences they could not let go of, and in many cases, it related to food objects, in some cases from a specific store from another city, while there were some answers linked to services such as a massage, or to products and another answer linked to family time.

The next set of questions related to the global consumer culture elements and specifically that if human interaction and travel as well as with materialism. The question included souvenirs from other countries, and the answers ranged from fashion accessories, design objects, and country-of-origin unique products. In some cases, the receiver of the souvenir (e.g., a family member) was also mentioned. It was also interesting to see that a small reference to each city from which the souvenir was brought was also made. Finally, the two next questions included recent travels that the individuals had gone to, and numerous countries from around the world were mentioned from India, Egypt, Bali, Sri Lanka, and Peru, to name a few. The interviewees' knowledge from various shopping areas of the world was also made clear with a question asking from which area of the world they would shop and included cities from London, New York, and Paris. Finally, they were also asked in which other city of the world they would like to live, and numerous options from different continents emerged.

37.5 Conclusion

This study sets out to examine how cultural production through the arts from luxury brands leads to increased acculturation of global consumer culture. Furthermore, we linked the aspect of acculturation of global consumer culture to positive outcomes from luxury brands. Content analysis was conducted in interviews from creative directors or fashion designers of acknowledged luxury brands. Our findings find the charismatic persona of the designer, or the director can be used to promote aspects of cultural products and to inspire toward acculturation of global consumer culture, thus enhancing the prestige of the luxury brand.

Our findings are in line with studies examining luxury products as artistic products (Freire, 2014) and iconic products (Kapferer, 2014). This is associated with the fact that they have aesthetic value due to the craftsmanship needed to produce them and the expensive materials (Dion & Arnould, 2011). Our findings are in line with studies indicating that the prestige value increases with the inclusion of artistic elements (Peluso et al., 2017). Furthermore, this study agrees with the importance ascribed to materialism and luxury consumption (e.g., Kamal et al., 2013; Lim et al., 2020; Sun et al., 2014), as well as on the connection drawn between cosmopolitanism and luxury consumption (Cleveland et al., 2009; Fastoso & González-Jiménez, 2018). Another important aspect with which we agree is on the importance of cultural capital in the setting of our study (e.g., Banister et al., 2020; Bourdieu, 1984; Chailan, 2018; Holt, 1998). Finally, the connection between global consumer culture and luxury consumption was identified, through the importance associated with social interaction and travel and openness to other cultures (e.g., Bartikowski et al., 2019; Bartikowski & Cleveland, 2017; de Mooij, 2019).

We can conclude that the application of cultural production and the use of the arts in its majority satisfy numerous aspects of acculturation to global consumer culture. Our study contributes to existing research by proposing that art can be strategically used as a tool to lead to acculturation to a global consumer culture. We thus respond to current calls in research of how experiential and ephemeral unconventional luxury can be satisfied through products, services, servicescapes (Thomsen et al., 2020). We also respond to the need to identify how networks of art lovers can be satisfied through the creation of respective meaning (Baumgarth, 2018).

Luxury brands are experts in establishing long-term relationships with the consumers, which can lead to various positive outcomes such likelihood of repeat purchase behavior. Even though they have managed to maintain their place in their customers minds through the satisfaction of their psychological needs, the strategic use of artistic elements can further enhance this connection. We found that various researchers have examined luxury brands from different viewpoints in the art adoption process, zooming into different elements of artistic practices. Our paper emphasizes how beneficial the use of the arts would be for the acculturation of a global consumer culture. The collaboration between the arts and luxury brands, although is a popular and current trend in the international luxury industry, is not a recent phenomenon. Marketers and scholars have argued that the adoption of artistic elements is a favorable way to induce consumers into buying the product. The purpose of this work was to analyze how these artistic elements can cultivate the acculturation of global consumer culture and to give recommendations for future studies and approaches.

Establishing themselves as contemporary Medicis of Renaissance Florence, luxury brands leverage on the fundamental power that art can have in social settings. Through such a connection, they aim to move away from the perception of luxury as something ephemeral and conspicuous, to something deeply meaningful, indicative of cultural taste and permanent. This use of art to establish and enhance the luxury brand mantra has been continuously increasing within the last years (Kapferer,

2014). What started as something tactical and linked to communication purposes has gained significant attention from brand managers and seems to be becoming a fundamental aspect of building and maintaining a luxury brand (Chailan, 2018). The question arises of whether the use of the arts in luxury brand management can assist in building the desired contemporary image of luxury.

References

Alden, D. L., Steenkamp, J. B. E., & Batra, R. (1999). Brand positioning through advertising in Asia, North America, and Europe: The role of global consumer culture. *Journal of Marketing, 63*(1), 75–87.

Appadurai. (1990). A. Disjuncture and difference in the global economy. *Theory Cultural Sociology, 7*(2/3), 295–310.

Arli, D., Cherrier, H., & Tjiptono, F. (2016). God blesses those who wear Prada. *Marketing Intelligence & Planning*.

Askegaard, S., Arnould, E. J., & Kjeldgaard, D. (2005). Postassimilationist ethnic consumer research: Qualifications and extensions. *Journal of Consumer Research, 32*(1), 160–170.

Banister, E., Roper, S., & Potavanich, T. (2020). Consumers' practices of everyday luxury. *Journal of Business Research, 116*, 458–466.

Bartikowski, B., & Cleveland, M. (2017). "Seeing is being": Consumer culture and the positioning of premium cars in China. *Journal of Business Research, 77*, 195–202.

Bartikowski, B., Fastoso, F., & Gierl, H. (2019). Luxury cars made-in-China: Consequences for brand positioning. *Journal of Business Research, 102*, 288–297.

Bartsch, F., Diamantopoulos, A., Paparoidamis, N. G., & Chumpitaz, R. (2016). Global brand ownership: The mediating roles of consumer attitudes and brand identification. *Journal of Business Research, 69*(9), 3629–3635.

Baudrillard, J. (1993). *The transparency of evil: Essays on extreme phenomena*. Verso.

Baumgarth, C. (2018). Brand management and the world of the arts: Collaboration, co-operation, co-creation, and inspiration. *The Journal of Product and Brand Management*.

Belk, R. W., Ger, G., & Askegaard, S. (2003). The fire of desire: A multisited inquiry into consumer passion. *Journal of Consumer Research, 30*(3), 326–351.

Bian, Q., & Forsythe, S. (2012). Purchase intention for luxury brands: A cross cultural comparison. *Journal of Business Research, 65*(10), 1443–1451.

Brown, S., Kozinets, R. V., & Sherry, J. F., Jr. (2003). Teaching old brands new tricks: Retro branding and the revival of brand meaning. *Journal of Marketing, 67*(3), 19–33.

Bourdieu, P. (1984). *Distinction: A social critique of the judgement of taste*. Harvard university press.

Chailan, C. (2018). Art as a means to recreate luxury brands' rarity and value. *Journal of Business Research, 85*, 414–423.

Choi, E., Ko, E., & Kim, A. J. (2016). Explaining and predicting purchase intentions following luxury-fashion brand value co-creation encounters. *Journal of Business Research, 69*(12), 5827–5832.

Cleveland, & Laroche. (2007). Acculturation to the global consumer culture: Scale development and research paradigm. *Journal of Business Research, 60*(3), 249–259.

Cleveland, M., Laroche, M., & Papadopoulos, N. (2009). Cosmopolitanism, consumer ethnocentrism, and materialism: An eight-country study of antecedents and outcomes. *Journal of International Marketing, 17*(1), 116–146.

Cleveland, M., Laroche, M., & Hallab, R. (2013). Globalization, culture, religion, and values: Comparing consumption patterns of Lebanese Muslims and Christians. *Journal of Business Research, 66*(8), 958–967.

Cleveland, M., Laroche, M., & Takahashi, I. (2015). The intersection of global consumer culture and national identity and the effect on Japanese consumer behavior. *Journal of International Consumer Marketing, 27*(5), 364–387.

Cleveland, M., Rojas-Méndez, J. I., Laroche, M., & Papadopoulos, N. (2016). Identity, culture, dispositions and behavior: A cross-national examination of globalization and culture change. *Journal of Business Research, 69*(3), 1090–1102.

de Mooij, M. (2019). Fairy tales of global consumer culture in a polarizing world. *International Marketing Review*.

Dion, D., & Arnould, E. (2011). Retail luxury strategy: Assembling charisma through art and magic. *Journal of Retailing, 87*(4), 502–520.

Dubois, B., & Duquesne, P. (1993). The market for luxury goods: Income versus culture. *European Journal of Marketing*.

Fastoso, F., & González-Jiménez, H. (2018). Materialism, cosmopolitanism, and emotional brand attachment: The roles of ideal self-congruity and perceived brand globalness. *Journal of Business Research*.

Firat, A. F., & Venkatesh, A. (1995). Liberatory postmodernism and the Reenchantment of consumption. *Journal of Consumer Research, 22*(3), 239–267.

Freire, N. A. (2014). When luxury advertising adds the identitary values of luxury: A semiotic analysis. *Journal of Business Research, 67*(12), 2666–2675.

Grassi, A. (2020). Art to enhance consumer engagement in the luxury fashion domain. *Journal of Fashion Marketing and Management: An International Journal, 24*, 327–341.

Hagtvedt, H., & Patrick, V. M. (2008). Art infusion: The influence of visual art on the perception and evaluation of consumer products. *Journal of Marketing Research, 45*(3), 379–389.

Hannerz, U. (1992). *Cultural complexity: Studies in the social Organization of Meaning*. Columbia University Press.

Hemetsberger, A., von Wallpach, S., & Bauer, M. (2012). Because I'm worth it-luxury and the construction of consumers' selves. *ACR North American Advances*.

Holt, D. B. (1998). Does cultural capital structure American consumption? *Journal of Consumer Research, 25*(1), 1–25.

Jelinek, J. S. (2018). Art as strategic branding tool for luxury fashion brands. *The Journal of Product and Brand Management*.

Joy, A., Wang, J. J., Chan, T. S., Sherry, J. F., Jr., & Cui, G. (2014). M (art) worlds: Consumer perceptions of how luxury brand stores become art institutions. *Journal of Retailing, 90*(3), 347–364.

Kamal, S., Chu, S. C., & Pedram, M. (2013). Materialism, attitudes, and social media usage and their impact on purchase intention of luxury fashion goods among American and Arab young generations. *Journal of Interactive Advertising, 13*(1), 27–40.

Kapferer, J. N. (2014). The artification of luxury: From artisans to artists. *Business Horizons, 57*(3), 371–380. https://doi.org/10.1016/j.bushor.2013.12.007

Khare, A. (2014). Antecedents to fashion clothing involvement: Role of global self-identity, cosmopolitanism, and normative influence. *Journal of Global Fashion Marketing, 5*(1), 39–59.

Koronaki, E., Kyrousi, A. G., & Panigyrakis, G. G. (2018). The emotional value of arts-based initiatives: Strengthening the luxury brand—Consumer relationship. *Journal of Business Research, 85*, 406–413.

Lash, S. M., Urry, S. L. J., & Urry, J. (1993). *Economies of signs and space* (Vol. 26). Sage.

Lee, H. C., Chen, W. W., & Wang, C. W. (2015). The role of visual art in enhancing perceived prestige of luxury brands. *Marketing Letters, 26*(4), 593–606.

Lim, W. M., Phang, C. S. C., & Lim, A. L. (2020). The effects of possession-and social inclusion-defined materialism on consumer behavior toward economical versus luxury product categories, goods versus services product types, and individual versus group marketplace scenarios. *Journal of Retailing and Consumer Services*, 102158.

Logkizidou, M., Bottomley, P., Angell, R., & Evanschitzky, H. (2019). Why museological merchandise displays enhance luxury product evaluations: An extended art infusion effect. *Journal of Retailing, 95*(1), 67–82.

McCracken, G. (1986). Culture and consumption: A theoretical account of the structure and movement of the cultural meaning of goods. *Journal of Consumer Research, 13*(1), 71–84.

Miller, K. W., & Mills, M. K. (2012). Probing brand luxury: A multiple lens approach. *Journal of Brand Management, 20*(1), 41–51.

Nwankwo, S., Hamelin, N., & Khaled, M. (2014). Consumer values, motivation and purchase intention for luxury goods. *Journal of Retailing and Consumer Services, 21*(5), 735–744.

O'Reilly, D. (2005). Cultural brands/branding cultures. *Journal of Marketing Management, 21*(5–6), 573–588.

Peluso, A. M., Pino, G., Amatulli, C., & Guido, G. (2017). Luxury advertising and recognizable artworks: New insights on the "art infusion" effect. *European Journal of Marketing.*

Richins, M. L. (2004). The material values scale: Measurement properties and development of a short form. *Journal of Consumer Research, 31*(1), 209–219.

Roper, S., Caruana, R., Medway, D., & Murphy, P. (2013). Constructing luxury brands: Exploring the role of consumer discourse. *European Journal of Marketing.*

Seo, Y., & Buchanan-Oliver, M. (2019). Constructing a typology of luxury brand consumption practices. *Journal of Business Research, 99*, 414–421.

Sobol, K., Cleveland, M., & Laroche, M. (2018). Globalization, national identity, biculturalism and consumer behavior: A longitudinal study of Dutch consumers. *Journal of Business Research, 82*, 340–353.

Statista. (2019). Value of the personal goods market worldwide from 1996 to 2019. Retrieved from: luxurv-goods-market-worldwide/https://www.statista.com/statistics/266503/value-of-the-personal-luxury-goods-market-worldwide/

Stiehler, B. E. (2016). *Co-creating luxury brands in an emerging market: Exploring consumer meaning making and value creation.* An International Journal.

Strizhakova, Y., & Coulter, R. A. (2013). The "green" side of materialism in emerging BRIC and developed markets: The moderating role of global cultural identity. *International Journal of Research in Marketing, 30*(1), 69–82.

Sun, G., D'Alessandro, S., & Johnson, L. (2014). Traditional culture, political ideologies, materialism and luxury consumption in China. International Journal of Consumer Studies, 38(6), 578–585.

Thomsen, T. U., Holmqvist, J., von Wallpach, S., Hemetsberger, A., & Belk, R. W. (2020). Conceptualizing unconventional luxury. *Journal of Business Research.*

Tsai, W. S., Yang, Q., & Liu, Y. (2013). Young Chinese consumers' snob and bandwagon luxury consumption preferences. *Journal of International Consumer Marketing, 25*(5), 290–304.

Tynan, C., McKechnie, S., & Chhuon, C. (2010). Co-creating value for luxury brands. *Journal of Business Research, 63*(11), 1156–1163.

Venkatesh, A., & Meamber, L. A. (2006). Arts and aesthetics: Marketing and cultural production. *Marketing Theory, 6*(1), 11–39.

von Wallpach, S., Hemetsberger, A., Thomsen, T. U., & Belk, R. W. (2020). Moments of luxury – A qualitative account of the experiential essence of luxury. *Journal of Business Research, 116*, 491–502.

Vukadin, A., Lemoine, J. F., & Badot, O. (2016). Opportunities and risks of combining shopping experience and artistic elements in the same store: A contribution to the magical functions of the point of sale. *Journal of Marketing Management, 32*(9–10), 944–964.

Wang, Y., & Chen, H. (2020). Self-presentation and interactivity: Luxury branding on social media. *Journal of Product & Brand Management.*

Chapter 38
Clustering the Social Media Users Based on Users' Motivations and Social Media Content

E. Iliopoulou and A. Vlachvei

Abstract The power of social media has grown in recent years and is a new approach that can be used by businesses to shape consumer buying behavior. Businesses are aware of the changing nature of customers' engagement with branding and that is why they are trying to build engagement through social media. The ways of communication between companies and customers have changed, and companies need to integrate new communication practices into their communication marketing. Thus, this study focuses on what are the main reasons that users react to the brands' posts and identifies the different types of consumers related to social media brand content and users' motivations of visiting brand page. An online survey was conducted with 503 questionnaires, where the data were collected. The results show two main factors in customers' engagement to brand posts which are interactivity and customization of information. The paper identifies two groups on users' reaction to offensive brand content, which are passive and active users. In addition, the research grouped social media users in five categories according to their motives of following a brand page and grouped social media content into three users groups.

Keywords Social media motives · Social media users groups · Users content groups

38.1 Introduction

The study provides multiple contributions to the brands because it has managed to combine four different research pieces and come to valuable conclusions for brand managers. Firstly, they have been found the motivations of consumers' reactions to the social media brand posts. Secondly, two groups of consumers have been

E. Iliopoulou (✉) · A. Vlachvei
University of Western Macedonia, Kastoria, Greece
e-mail: p200056@uowm.gr

N. Tsounis, A. Vlachvei (eds.), *Advances in Quantitative Economic Research*, Springer Proceedings in Business and Economics,
https://doi.org/10.1007/978-3-030-98179-2_38

revealed regarding their reactions to offensive brand content. Thirdly, they have been categorized the users into groups when they follow a social media brand page. Lastly, they have been categorized the users of social media that involved in the content of the brand pages. This study helps brand managers to develop strategies for effectively targeting the most desirable consumer groups.

Know and Wen (2010) defined social networks "as sites that allow people to build online relationships, gathering useful information and sharing it with other people." The number of active accounts from social networks in the world in April 2021 showed that Facebook is the market leader with 2.797 billion active users. It is followed by YouTube with 2.291 billion active users per month (Tankovska, 2021). Social media can also create groups with common interests and interact with each other. Social media are virtual sites that try to meet the needs of specific populations. People with the same interests are trying to communicate, build relationships, discuss ideas, and exchange views with each other (Raacke & Bonds-Raacke, 2008). Muntinga et al. (2011) are able to link motivations to specific brand-related activities, such as consumption, contribution, and creation, and identify three groups of users by activity. Focusing on five broad categories of motivation (social influence, information seeking, entertainment, trust, and reward) related to social media use, Azar et al. (2016) investigated four types of consumers who interact with the brand. When consumers engage with social media, they exhibit different behaviors. Dolan et al. (2016) categorize the content of social media into four groups (informative, entertaining, paid, and relational) so they identified seven different types of consumer behavior that are involved in social media.

Related to the above, the purpose of this paper is to find different user groups according to different types of motivations. Specifically, the study analyzes users' motives to interact with a brand's posts on social media and classifies the users into different groups according to their motivations. The survey was conducted on users in Greece where there are no previous relevant surveys.

The results of the study show that there are two different types of motivations that lead users to react to a brand's posts (doing "like," "share," or "comment"), such as interactivity and customization of information. Other useful results are that the study has classified users into different groups according to the ongoing motives. For example, there are two groups of users who react to offensives posts on brands pages. These are passive and active users. Also, the study identifies five main clusters of social media users who follow the brand page according to specific motives. The main cluster includes users who participate in a brand page for remuneration. Last, three main user's clusters were found which push users to participate in social media brand content, and the main cluster includes users who interact in challenging and entertaining content of the brand page. All these results are very important for the brand's managers because they give them useful information about the social media market which is really important for their products. Understanding the user's motivations in following a social media brand page and grouped them into different categories, managers can pay attention to market needs and become more flexible in user requirements. In their quest to attract new users, brands build enjoyable pages. They will also be ready to give users exactly what they need, before their competitors.

38.2 Literature Review

38.2.1 Social Media User Motivations

According to Malthouse et al. (2013), the company to attract users and create loyalty with them offers rich and satisfying content on its pages. It's important for brand marketing to understand why consumers reject or accept social media. Ng (2016) suggests that users use social media to communicate and connect with other users, search for information, and belong to a community. Lim and Kumar's study (2018) found four main motives that push consumers to engage with social media. These are information, financial benefits, entertainment, and connectivity. In addition, the research of Ladhari et al. (2019) led to similar motives for social media users: the financial and content benefits (offers and information). In the research of Kim et al. (2007), the motivations of social media were categorized into two main groups: cognitive and emotional. The work of Lin et al. (2011) found that the main factor of social media users is enjoyment, and the second main factor is usefulness.

The findings of the study by Arli (2017) proved that the usefulness that users gain from social media is a key feature toward the acceptance of social media. However, the main motivation that determines the social media attitude of users is entertainment, as the pages by creating games, contests, and rewarding users attract consumers and encourage them to share posts with other users. In addition, information has a positive effect on consumers if it allows them to react to relevant posts, asking questions, commenting, congratulating, or even directly complaining about the company. Information is the point of contact with consumers, and the brand must provide sufficient information in relation to the product or service that offers, for example, regular announcements about special prices. However, it is very important that companies do not flood social media pages with information. On the contrary, irritability, which can include provocative or annoying posts and unpredictable consequences on the website, seems to negatively affect the attitude of consumers.

Social media can be annoying to the consumer due to the intense use of media, because people spend more time dealing with social media. So brand posts should be large enough to engage consumers and not tire them out and be considered annoying. In addition, the marketing techniques used by companies affect loyalty, brand recognition, and ultimately the purchase intention. In particular, the recognition of the brand has a stronger impact on the purchase intention. In terms of age, it plays an important role in how consumers accept social media. Older consumers do not readily accept new and innovative media features, compared to younger ones (Arli, 2017).

Chen (2011) showed that users have used social media for information exchange and social interaction to communicate with each other and feel members of a community. Subsequent study has provided similar consumers' motives for involving in social media such as social interaction, entertainment, financial benefits, information, and enhancing consumer value (Berger, 2014). Park and Kim (2014) researched four benefits of a brand social media page: informational benefits (information acquisition), hedonistic benefits (enjoyment of browsing a page), financial benefits (discount coupons), and social benefits (connection with the brand community).

38.2.2 Consumer Groups

Communities created on corporate social media can contribute to the dissemination of brand-related content by increasing brand visibility, recognition, and engagement (Jahn et al., 2012). Azar et al. (2016) study categorizes users as follows: the first category of consumers (Brand Detached) consists of people who interact little with the pages, spend a little time with social media, and do not like to comment or share content. The second group, are consumers (Brand Profittes) whose interaction is medium with social media, spend more time on them and do not easily participate in brand publications unless they are going to benefit from good offers. Consumers in the third category (brand companions) spend a significant part of their time in the media, but the interaction is moderate. They usually participate to get in touch with other users (friends), for fun, and are mainly motivated by their emotions, while the latest category of consumers (brand reliant) includes people who are enthusiastic and dedicated to the pages of companies, spend a lot of time navigating the pages, and have a high level of response to the invitations of brands.

The research of Muttinga et al. (2011) highlighted two groups of users: the consumption group, where users seek out brand information and they aren't getting involved with the brand engagement. Contribution group, where consumers want to respond to brand activities, talk to other consumers about brand issues and critique branded posts and videos. Creation group, where consumers write, publish, and share the content of brand publications, in their profiles.

Dolan et al. (2016) analyze different types of users groups. Co-creators are at the highest level of positive behavior. On social media, they participate in the co-creation of a brand content and disseminate their knowledge to other consumers (Brodie et al., 2013). Positive contribution is a group which consumers are in the middle of positive behavior on social media. They are usually involved with positive actions in the already existing content of the page in the brand, doing "like" and "share" (Chu, 2011). Another group is consumption which reflects the lowest level of positive consumer behavior. The behavior is passive, does not create content, and does not affect other users. Passive participation could be the search for information, while active is the publication of comments (Shang et al., 2006). Dormancy is a behavior of zero action and contribution, a state of inactive passive engagement of consumers on social media of the brand (Brodie et al., 2013). Detachment refers to a negatively low level of consumer behavior that represents a state of constant disengagement from the brand page (Brodie et al., 2013). Negative contribution is a group which customers represent a mediocre level of negative behavior where they can act negatively on the content of a brand post. Their goal is to influence the perceptions of other consumers (Jaakkola & Alexander, 2014). Last group is co-destruction which social media users display a high level of negative behavior and create negative content on the pages in order to reduce the value of the brand (Plé & Cáceres, 2010).

38.2.3 Social Media Content

According to Peters et al. (2012), the content may consist of four main aspects, which may overlap to some extent. These aspects are the quality of the content, the domain, the strength of the content, and the volume of the content. The quality of the content of social media pages has a positive effect on consumer behavior (Zhang et al., 2015). One of the main motives that users have to use social media is the need they have to receive information from the brand itself (Lin & Lu, 2011). Consumers interact with a brand by looking for information about its brand features and some of the benefits they can have. This tour can have a serious impact (favorable or unfavorable) on the consumer experience of the brand (Ho & Wang, 2015). In addition, the consumer with this individual experience, seeking to find useful information, will enhance his knowledge of the brand (Hamilton et al., 2016). Entertainment content pleases users while creating the need for them to engage with the brand and the desire to return to the site (Raacke et al., 2008). Also, relational content is related to the desire of users to share ideas, information, and opinions and become members of the community (Leung, 2009).

Hollebeek et al. (2014) argue that there are types of consumer activity that are more important to companies; users can create brand content or they can join other users' content. They can comment on brand content and rate products and interact with brand-related content created by others. These activities usually require high or moderate levels of consumer involvement and refer to the favorable behavior of users in terms of participation and communication of brand content. The research of Carlson et al. (2018) showed four characteristics of social networking pages that push the user to have positive behavior. The features that stand out are good contact with the customer (fast and direct communication, correct information about products), sociability (communication of users with common interests and ideas), quality content (direct and up-to-date information), and page interactivity (appropriate page design to attract users to interact with others).

De Vries et al. (2017) identified activities related to the brand and related to two important types of activities: the "creation of activities" where consumers create social media content, reproduce it, and pass it on to other consumers (e.g., the consumer writes in a branding blog) and "activity contributions" in which users collaborate with other users on social media content (e.g., engages in branding online discussions). Creating activities means more dedication because it takes more effort and time while contributing activities means moderate dedication because it requires less effort and time. Consumers can participate in the above two types of activities because they want to be informed about the company and its products. When consumers comment on a post, ask for information about a product brand, rate a product, or engage in discussions, it increases their knowledge of the brand.

De Veirman et al. (2016) provide a comprehensive picture of consumer behavior and motivation when engaging in specific brand-related activities. It initially identified two different types of consumer behavior in relation to activity level and publicity: "lurking" and "posting." The "lurking" is related to the passive attitude of users on the page of a brand, without actively participating and contributing substantially to the brand community, but enjoying the benefits offered by other users. On the contrary, the "posting" concerns the active behavior of users and their public participation in the brand community. These two types of behavior are driven by activities out of a need for social interaction. So, social interaction is considered the primary motivation for participating in brand-related activities. The motivation is the need for entertainment but only in the behavior of the "lurking." This means that consumers may like a page of a brand for entertainment purposes, as they find the content of the page fun, with no further commitment. Motivation for reward, self-promotion, and empowerment has no effect on ambush behavior. On the contrary, the main motivation after the social interaction for "posting" is empowerment.

Calder et al. (2016) defined consumer involvement in the brand as "a psychological state that occurs due to interactive, co-creative experiences of customers with a focal factor under a specific set of conditions and exists as a dynamic repetitive process." Due to the interactive and co-creative nature of social media, consumer brand engagement can be measured by consumer agreement expressions, ratings, comments, and notifications of consumer publications (Barger & Labrecque, 2013).

Kujur, F. and Singh, S. (2020) have shown that there are specific motivations that lead to customer loyalty on a brand's pages. The most important motives for engagement are those that include informative and entertaining content. They also showed that users were not actively involved in the brand pages of Facebook but only passively looked at videos, images, and posts of the brand. In addition, the activities of creation and contribution do not seem to show particular results since their operation requires the active participation of users. Finally, it turned out that the users who are actively involved with the brand page are those who are loyal to the brand.

Research by Barger et al. (2016) referred to the factors that influence consumer commitment to brands. He came up with the following factors. Brands where consumers share a video posted by the company not necessarily because they like the video itself but because they like the company. Product factor includes hedonistic products versus common products, where hedonistic products have increased consumer involvement. Consumer factor includes consumers who engage with a company's social media to socialize and get information about the products they are interested in. Content factor should evoke emotion, and its message should be commercial, its form should be interactive, and the way of obtaining the content is considered important, while the social media factor leads to the intention of consumers to engage with social media and the features of the various platforms. It has also been found that when branded posts include video, they are more preferred and more attractive to users (Ladhari et al., 2019). On the other hand, it has been observed that videos, because of the longer duration watching them, create less interaction (Luarn et al., 2015).

Barger et al. (2016) said that in the same way that brands hope that consumers will engage with their content, so do consumers hope that businesses will engage with content created by the users themselves. So brands can react to consumer comments by doing "likes" and "hearts," letting them know that their opinion has been heard by the brand. In addition, brands can respond by responding to the content of consumer publications, thereby providing customer support or customer interaction resulting in brand trust. Brands can also share with their followers, interesting user content so as to create additional content on their page and reward users who actively participate and engage in it. The brand itself is involved in publications, and this commitment that develops between the brand and the consumer requires the active participation of the company as well as a continuous response.

38.3 Methodology

This paper was created to study the motivations of social media and to highlight the research results, through primary data as the information has not been evaluated. The quantitative research methodology has been chosen, as the study investigates phenomena with statistical methods and numerical data. In addition, secondary data were collected through the literature review. A well-structured questionnaire was designed to collect the primary data and passed to the "Google Forms" tool for distribution to the public. The questionnaires were channeled to social media, as it has been emphasized in the literature, their rapid use by consumers. An internet search was conducted. A random sample, representative of the population, was selected, and the respondents were selected as active consumers and social media users. 503 questionnaires were answered within a period of 3 weeks from March to April 2020, in Greece.

The questions of the questionnaire according to the thematic unit are divided into three categories. The demographic data of the sample are contained in the first section and which concern questions about gender, age, occupation, and educational level. The motivations that push users to interact with the brand are contained in the second section and include a list of 27 items related to motivations (De Vries et al., 2017; Ladhari et al., 2019; Mutinga et al., 2011). The content of the posts of a brand (Dolan et al., 2016, Carlson et al., 2018) as well as consumer behavior toward brand postings (Dolan et al., 2016; Carlson et al., 2016) are included in the third section. The Likert scale (1 = strongly disagree to 5 = strongly agree) was used to conduct the results.

38.4 Results

During the research, the primary data were collected from the 503 fully completed questionnaires. Table 38.1 shows the respondents' profile.

According to Table 38.1, the largest percentage of respondents are women with a percentage of 60.8%, while the age group of the sample is 18–34 years old with a percentage of 53.7%, followed by the age group 35–54 years with 39.2% and the age group 55+ with 7.2%. The largest part comes from private employees with 33.2%, followed by the self-employed with 18.9%, the civil servants with 18.7%, the students with 13.5%, the unemployed with 7.8%, the housewives with 4.8%, and retirees with 3.2%. Also, the educational level of the sample is graduates of higher education institutions with 40.6%, basic obligatory education—Lyceum 38.6%, and holders of postgraduate-doctoral studies with 20.9%.

38.4.1 Factor Analysis-Users' Engagement to Brand Posts

To study users' engagement in branding posts, the survey provided nine items to respondents, which were studied and considered appropriate for factor analysis. All the measures indicated that the correlation matrix was suitable. So, the Kaiser-Meyer-Olkin measure was extremely adequate (KMO = 0.898), using Varimax factor rotation with Kaiser normalization and Bartlett's sphericity test was 0.000, Table 38.2.

Table 38.1 Demographic data of 503 responders

Sample features		Percentage %	Frequency N
Gender	Male	39.2	197
	Female	60.8	306
Age	18–34	53.7	270
	35–54	39.2	197
	55+	7.2	36
Working status	Civil servant	18.7	94
	Private employee	33.2	167
	Freelance	18.9	95
	Retired	3.2	16
	Households	4.8	24
	Student	13.5	68
	Unemployed	7.8	39
Educational level	Elementary – high school – vocational training institution	38.6	194
	Bachelor degree	40.6	204
	Master degree – PhD	20.9	105

Table 38.2 KMO and Bartlett's test of users' engagement with brand posts

KMO and Bartlett's test		
Kaiser-Meyer-Olkin measure of sampling adequacy		0.898
Bartlett's test of sphericity	Approx. Chi-square	2467.044
	Df	36
	Sig.	0.000

Table 38.3 Factors of users' engagement to brand posts

Rotated component matrix items motives Following a business on social media, what is your behavior?	Factor 1	Factor 2
I "like" posts	**0.611**	
I share company posts on social media	**0.877**	
I share company posts outside of social media	**0.862**	
I comment on the posts	**0.715**	
I review the content	**0.653**	
I participate with my own content (photos, videos)	**0.654**	
I ask the company for a product or service that interests me		**0.781**
I complain to the company when something bothers me		**0.784**
I participate in competitions		**0.713**

Table 38.4 Cronbach's alpha for the factors of users' engagement to brand posts

Factors	Cronbach's alpha	N of items
1 + 2	0.899	9
1	0.894	6
2	0.890	3

Component analysis of the nine items identified two factors and jointly account for 66.772% of the "Total Explained Variance," according to Table 38.3.

Cronbach's alpha is very high for variables, and the scales that are created are considered reliable, Table 38.4.

In Table 38.3, two main factors identify as follows:

- **Interactivity (factor 1).** People by participating in the content of the brand, they confirm that they are part of a separate group that creates a sense of shared social identity. They have a common passion, and that is the brand. This makes people feel a strong relationship with each other, a strong bond. The process of creating content allows them to become known, publicize their knowledge, socialize, and be entertained.
- **Customization of information (factor 2).** People participate in the content in order to gain some personal benefits. This can be a prize in a competition, additional information about a product they are interested in or benefit from a complaint they will make to the company.

38.4.2 Factor Analysis-Users' Reactions to Offensive Brand Content

To study users' reactions to offensive brand content, the survey provided six items to respondents, which were studied and considered appropriate for factor analysis. All the measures indicated that the correlation matrix was suitable. So, the Kaiser-Meyer-Olkin measure was extremely adequate (KMO = 0.726), using Varimax factor rotation with Kaiser normalization, and Bartlett's sphericity test was 0.000, Table 38.5.

Component analysis of the six items identified two factors and jointly account for 72.902% of the "Total Explained Variance," according to Table 38.6.

Cronbach's alpha is very high for variables, and the scales that are created are considered reliable, Table 38.7.

In Table 38.6, two main factors for users' reactions to offensive brand content identify as follows:

- **Passive users (factor 1)**. They are people who do not react to the company's posts even if the posts contain offensive content. Passively read the posts and do not get involved in the content. They usually ignore brand's posts.

Table 38.5 KMO and Bartlett's test of users' reactions to offensive brand content

KMO and Bartlett's test		
Kaiser-Meyer-Olkin measure of sampling adequacy		0.726
Bartlett's test of sphericity	Approx. Chi-square	1278.055
	Df	15
	Sig.	0.000

Table 38.6 Factors of users' reactions to offensive brand content

Rotated component matrix items motives Suppose you are a loyal follower on social media of a reputable company. If the content of her posts becomes offensive, how do you react?	Factor 1	Factor 2
Stop following the business	**0.901**	
Block its contents	**0.836**	
Ignore her posts	**0.720**	
Boycott it		**0.690**
You respond negatively to her posts		**0.919**
Share your reaction		**0.841**

Table 38.7 Cronbach's alpha for the factors of users' reactions to offensive brand content

Factors	Cronbach's alpha	N of Items
1 + 2	0.816	6
1	0.794	3
2	0.806	3

Table 38.8 The final clusters centers of users' social media motivations

Factors	Cluster 1	Cluster 2	Cluster 3	Cluster 4	Cluster 5
Factor 1 (social interaction)	−0.183	−0.273	0.705	−1.202	−0.300
Factor 2 (contribution)	−0.008	1.875	−0.298	−0.876	0.664
Factor 3 (entertainment)	−0.137	−1.434	−0.241	0.849	0.841
Factor 4 (remuneration)	0.410	−0.884	−0.117	0.464	−0.859
Factor 5 (information)	−0.773	0.363	0.506	0.806	0.351

- **Active users (factor 2).** These are people who react to most of the brand's posts. If the publication is offensive, they do not hesitate to freely express their opinion and dissatisfaction with the company. Usually act against the company and respond to it in a similar way.

38.4.3 Cluster Analysis-Users' Social Media Motivations

According to Chatfield and Collins (1980), what cluster analysis does is to be able to group observations in such a way that in each group the observations are similar and lead to specific factors. This is done through the k-Means cluster analysis where in this case, it tries to group the users of social media according to their motives.

Our previous study had identified five key factors that users follow a social media brand page. These factors are information, contribution, social interaction, remuneration, and entertainment. According to these factors, we grouped the users. The research found the best solution of the structure that was five clusters, which include users' motivations to follow a brand page. The values of the distances between the groups are quite good, and the ANOVA analysis shows that there are significant differences among the segments (Asymptotic Significance is $0.000 < 0.05$ for all clusters). Table 38.8 shows the final clusters centers.

Cluster 1, which includes 198 people and represents 39.36% of the sample, is the largest cluster, which shows that the remuneration motivates users to visit and follow a social media brand page. Users become members of a page for personal gain. In this group of users, the main goal is the profit whether it concerns their participation in a competition, by winning discount coupons or other prizes.

Cluster 2, which includes 22 individuals, shows that the aim of users is to contribute content to the brand. They are willing to socialize and therefore react to the brand's posts on social media, participate in the brand's publications with their own content, and are active users. Also, they like to be informed about the brand and its products. So contribution and information characterize this group.

Cluster 3 includes 166 individuals and represents 33% of the sample, showing that social interaction is the main reason that users follow a brand page. People chat with each other online and exchange opinions and information about the brand. Also, the brand information that they take is useful for them.

Cluster 4 includes 44 individuals. In this group, entertainment is the main motivator of users, and they are involved in the brand's postings because they like to be entertained through the brand. In addition, in this group, some users are interested in getting information and win remuneration.

Cluster 5 includes 73 individuals. People seem to enjoy talking about their common interests and sharing tips and tricks related to the brand. Entertainment, contribution, and information characterize this group, where users engage with the brand without expecting any personal benefit, just enjoying the brand page.

38.4.4 Cluster Analysis-Social Media Content

This analysis will categorize the users of social media involved in the content of the brand pages. Our previous study had identified three key factors that involve the users with the brand page to social media. These factors are call to action, informational content, and challenging content.

According to these factors, we grouped the users. The research found the best solution of the structure that was three clusters, which include social media users' motivations to involve with brand social media content. The values of the distances between the groups are quite good, and the ANOVA analysis shows that there are significant differences among the segments (Asymptotic Significance is 0.000 < 0.05 for all clusters). Table 38.9 shows the final clusters centers.

Cluster 1, which includes 278 individuals and represents 55.26% of the sample, is the largest group in the analysis. In this group users engaged with the brand content because they like to react and participate in the brand posts. They usually engaged with challenging content and entertainment content.

Cluster 2, which includes 128 individuals and represents 25.44% of the sample, shows that one of the consumer's main pleasures is searching, receiving information about a brand and call for action. Users want to interact directly with the brand and participate actively in the brand content. Call to action is the main factor for consumers to engage with the brand content.

Cluster 3, which includes 96 individuals, reported that social media users are attracted to informative content that provides information on a topic of interest and also entertainment content. They like to learn the brand news but also to spend their time happily.

Table 38.9 The final clusters center according to social media content

Factors	Cluster 1	Cluster 2	Cluster 3
Factor 1 (informational content)	−0.547	0.477	0.949
Factor 2 (call to action)	0.036	0.827	−1.208
Factor 3 (challenging content)	0.378	−0.726	−0.125

38.5 Conclusion and Discussion

Gangadharbatla et al. (2012) noted that nowadays social media are an integral part of people's daily lives. Levinson et al. (2010) deduced that people using social media are able to communicate with each other, find others with common interests, spread their ideas, and be informed about things that interest them. Social media has helped users interact with branding directly (Dijkmans et al., 2015). Indeed, companies around the world are trying to promote their products through social platforms, which have grown rapidly and are taking the place of physical stores. So there is concern about the marketing policy that will be followed so that the platforms attract more customers and their advertising campaigns are attractive.

The present research provides a factor analysis and a clustered-based categorization regarding social media users. The aim of the research is to study the users' motives that engage them with the brand posts and to categorize the users according to their reactions to offensive brand content. In addition, this work classifies users according to their social media brand motivations and social media content. The first findings of user's engagement in brands posts were categorized into two motives: interactivity and customization of information. According to these motives, users react to brand content by doing comments or sharing or participating, or asking. Users' active engagement with the brand content drives them to join a social media community. They like to interact and learn more about the brand which they prefer.

Another important result of this paper is that users' reactions to offensive brand content are divided into two groups: passive and active users. In this case, some users don't react to their brand page offensive posts; they ignore them and some other users react to offensive posts and answering or sharing the posts. Age is a keyword to this reaction. Ages 55+ are critical and respond negatively to offensive company posts. Categorizing social media brand pages that users follow, the study identifies five groups. Into groups, we see that different motives are dominant. Remuneration, contribution, social interaction, entertainment, and information characterize the five different main groups of users. The biggest group is that with the remuneration motives. The last finding of the study categorizes users according to social media content. The study identifies three users groups. The first group is being characterized by the challenging content, the second group is being characterized by call to action, and the third group is being characterized by informational content.

38.6 Limitation and Future Research

Social media has grown significantly over the last decade. They provide huge growth opportunities in many business sectors. They represent a completely different communication environment between companies and consumers. By understanding the customer profile and the motivations that visit the pages on social media, companies can further develop communication with customers as well as improve their corporate image.

There are several limitations to this research that could be taken into account in a future study. Some of these limitations are that the factors studied in the present research are far fewer than they actually are. Therefore, future research may include more factors in terms of both social media brand content and the users' motivations of visiting brand page. In addition, the sample size could be considered a constraint, as the larger sample could show other results. Finally, the profile of the sample is limited as data were collected from a specific country, Greece. Future studies could increase the number of surveyed countries.

References

Arli, D. (2017). Does social media matter? Investigating the effect of social media features on consumer attitudes. *Journal of Promotion Management, 23*(4), 521–539.

Azar, S. L., Machado, J. C., Vacas de Carvahlo, L., & Mendes, A. (2016). Motivations to interact with brands on Facebook – Towards a typology of consumer-brand interactions. *Journal of Brand Managment, 23*, 153–178.

Barger, V. A., & Labrecque, L. I. (2013). An integrated marketing communications perspective on social media metrics. *International Journal of Integrated Marketing Communications, 5*, 64–76.

Barger, V., Peltier, J. W., & Schultz, D. E. (2016). Social media and consumer engagement: A review and research agenda. *Journal of Research in Interactive Marketing, 10*(4), 268–287.

Berger, J. (2014). Word of mouth and interpersonal communication: A review and directions for future research. *Journal of Consumer Psychology, 24*(4), 586–607.

Brodie, R. J., Ilic, A., Juric, B., & Hollebeek, L. (2013). Consumer engagement in a virtual brand community: An exploratory analysis. *Journal of Business Research, 66*, 105–114.

Calder, B. J., Malthouse, E. C., & Maslowska, E. (2016). Brand marketing, big data and social innovation as future research directions for engagement. *Journal of Marketing Management, 32*(5–6), 579–585.

Carlson, J., Rahman, M., Voola, R., & De Vries, N. (2018). Customer engagement behaviours in social media: Capturing innovation opportunities. *Journal of Services Marketing, 32*(1), 83–94.

Chen, G. M. (2011). Tweet this: A uses and gratifications perspective on how active Twitter use gratifies a need to connect with others. *Computers in Human Behavior, 27*(2), 755–762.

Chu, S. (2011). Viral advertising in social media: Participation in Facebook groups and responses among college-aged users. *Journal of Interactive Advertising, 12*, 30–43.

De Veirman, M., Cauberghe, V., & Hudders, L. (2016). *Why are people interacting with brands on Facebook: Unraveling consumers' motivations for lurking and posting on Facebook brand pages*. EMAC.

De Vries, L., Peluso, A. M., Romani, S., Leeflang, P. S. H., & Marcati, A. (2017). Explaining consumer brand-related activities on social media: An investigation of the different roles of self-expression and socializing motivations. *Elsevier, 75*, 272–282.

Dijkmans, C., Kerkhof, P., & Beukeboom, C. J. (2015). A stage to engage: Social media use and corporate reputation. *Tourism Management, 47*, 58–67.

Dolan, R., Conduit, J., & Fahy, J. (2016). Social media engagement behaviour: A uses and gratifications perspective. *Journal of Strategic Marketing, 24*(3–4), 261–277.

Gangadharbatla, H., Hopp, T., & Sheehan, K. (2012). Changing user motivations for social networking site usage: Implications for internet advertisers. *International Journal of Internet Marketing and Advertising, 7*(2), 120–135.

Hamilton, M., Kaltcheva, V., & Rohm, A. (2016). Social media and value creation: The role of interaction satisfaction and interaction immersion. *Journal of Interactive Marketing, 36*, 121–133.

Ho, C., & Wang, Y. (2015). Repurchase intentions and virtual customer relationships on social media Brand community. *Human-centric Computing and Information Sciences, 5*(18), 1–16.

Hollebeek, L. D., Glynn, M. S., & Brodie, R. J. (2014). Consumer brand engagement in social media: Conceptualization, scale development and validation. *Journal of Interactive Marketing, 28*(2), 149–165.

Jaakkola, E., & Alexander, M. (2014). The role of customer engagement behavior in value co-creation: A service system perspective. *Journal of Service Research, 17*, 247–261.

Jahn, B., & Kunz, W. (2012). How to transform consumers into fans of your brand. *Journal of Service Management, 23*(3), 344–361.

Kim, J., Fiore, A. M., & Lee, H. H. (2007). Influences of online store perception, shopping enjoyment, and shopping involvement on consumer patronage behavior towards an online retailer. *Journal of Retailing and Consumer Services, 14*(2), 95–107.

Kujur, F., & Singh, S. (2020). Visual communication and consumer-brand relationship on social networking sites-uses & gratifications theory perspective. *Journal of Theoretical and Applied Electronic Commerce Research, 15*(1), 30–47.

Kwon, O., & Wen, Y. (2010). An empirical study of the factors affecting social network service use. *Computers in Human Behavior, 26*(2), 254–263.

Ladhari, R., Rioux, M. C., Souiden, N., & Chiadmi, N. E. (2019). *Consumers' motives for visiting a food retailer's Facebook page* (Vol. 50, pp. 379–385). Elsevier.

Leung, L. (2009). User-generated content on the internet: An examination of gratifications, civic engagement and psychological empowerment. *New Media & Society, 11*, 1327–1347.

Levinson, J., & Gibson, S. (2010). *Guerilla social media marketing*. Entrepreneur Press.

Lim, H., & Kumar, A. (2018). Variations in consumers' use of brand online social networking: A uses and gratifications approach. *Journal of Retailing and Consumer Services, 51*, 450–457.

Lin, K. Y., & Lu, H. P. (2011). Why people use social networking sites: An empirical study integrating network externalities and motivation theory. *Computers in Human Behavior, 27*(3), 1152–1161.

Luarn, P., Lin, Y. F., & Chiu, Y. P. (2015). Influence of Facebook brand-page posts on online engagement. *Online Information Review, 39*(4), 505–519.

Malthouse, E. C., Haenlein, M., Skiera, B., Wege, E., & Zhang, M. (2013). Managing customer relationships in the social media era: Introducing the social CRM house. *Journal of Interactive Marketing, 27*, 270–280.

Muntinga, D. G., Moorman, M., & Smit, E. G. (2011). Introducing COBRAs: Exploring motivations for brand-related social media use. *International Journal of Advertising, 30*(1), 13–46.

Ng, M. (2016). Factors influencing the consumer adoption of Facebook: A two-country study of youth markets. *Computers in Human Behavior, 54*, 491–500.

Park, H., & Kim, Y. K. (2014). The role of social network websites in the consumer – brand relationship. *Journal of Retailing and Consumer Services, 21*(4), 460–467.

Peters, K., Chen, Y., Kaplan, A. M., Ogniben, B., & Pauwels, K. (2012). Social media metrics – A framework and guidelines for managing social media. *Journal of Interactive Marketing, 27*, 281–298.

Plé, L., & Cáceres, R. C. (2010). Not always co-creation: Introducing interactional co-destruction of value in service-dominant logic. *Journal of Services Marketing, 24*, 430–437.

Raacke, J., & Bonds-Raacke, J. (2008). MySpace and Facebook: Applying the uses and gratifications theory to exploring friend-networking sites. *Cyberpsychology & Behavior, 11*(2), 169–174.

Shang, R. A., Chen, Y. C., & Liao, H. J. (2006). The value of participation in virtual consumer communities on brand loyalty. *Internet Research*, 398–418.

Tankovska, H. (2021, Jan 29). *Global social networks ranked by number of users 2021.* Ανάκτηση 06 02, 2021, από https://www.statista.com/statistics/272014/global-social-networks-ranked-by-number-of-users/

Zhang, H., Lu, Y., Wang, B., & Wu, S. (2015). The impacts of technological environments and co-creation experiences on customer participation. *Information & Management, 52*(4), 468–482.

Index

A
Acculturation to global consumer culture, 539–549
Agri-food SMEs, 531–537
Altruism, 93, 95, 99–110
Amendments after Law 4446/2016, 362, 363
ARIMA model, 113–128
Arts, 37, 272, 289, 540–545, 547–549
Audience development, 273–282

B
Bankruptcy, 66, 192, 262, 361–370, 452–463, 478, 486
Bankruptcy code, 362, 363, 367, 369
Bankruptcy models, 452–457, 461–463
Behavioral economics, 78
Behavioral finance, 190, 193, 194, 200
Box, 5, 116, 117, 127, 130
Brand evangelism, 497–510
Budget balance, 131, 132, 136
Business recycling practices, 328

C
Cash conversion cycle (CCC), 21, 23–28, 341–344, 346, 349–351, 354–358
Causality, 442, 513–529
Circular economy, 327–336
City redesigning, 287–290, 293, 294, 297
Clothing, 68, 70, 71, 73, 327–336, 499, 503, 505–507, 510, 545, 546
Clothing industry, 327–336, 499
Clothing life cycle, 330, 336
Cognitive errors, 189–200
Competitiveness, 48, 50–52, 54–56, 58, 205, 226, 227, 286, 287, 291, 292, 320, 324, 328, 329, 336, 340, 393, 426, 437, 468, 472, 479, 480, 482, 489, 498, 517, 531–537
Consolidation, 362–369
Consumer price index (CPI), 50, 114, 116, 117, 393–395, 399, 404–407
Coopetition, 218, 219, 222, 223, 226, 227
Corruption, 47–58, 295, 316–319
COVID-19, 39, 63–75, 78, 86, 109, 229–252, 256, 257, 260, 320, 322, 478–493
COVID-19 pandemic, 17, 20, 39, 63–75, 86, 230, 234, 251, 271, 318, 362, 478–493, 528
COVID-19 pandemic period, 16–29
Creativity, 144, 154, 275, 276, 281
Cultural centre, 273–282
Cultural production, 183, 539–549
Culture, 1, 51, 68–70, 72, 74, 144, 150, 155, 156, 161, 244, 274, 275, 281, 286, 289–291, 304, 368, 369, 426, 427, 434, 539–549
Culture and creative industry, 275

D
DEA method, 373, 379–380, 439–449
Decision-making, 3, 10, 11, 79, 80, 83, 109, 190, 191, 196, 289, 304, 316, 318, 376, 443, 463
Declining interest rates, 16, 17, 20, 27, 29
Demographic differences, 206

N. Tsounis, A. Vlachvei (eds.), *Advances in Quantitative Economic Research*, Springer Proceedings in Business and Economics,
https://doi.org/10.1007/978-3-030-98179-2

Determinants of gender equality, 230, 231, 244, 247
Digital communication, 146, 204, 279, 282

E
E-commerce, 393, 396, 405, 510, 532
Economic crisis, 230, 231, 234, 239, 243, 244, 250, 252, 362, 419, 499
Economic destabilization, 129–140
Economic dimensions, 77
Economic games, 86
Economic growth, 32, 33, 136, 137, 166, 244, 252, 327, 339, 373, 386, 388, 390, 440–442, 448, 449
Economics, 19, 78, 79, 87, 107, 109, 143–151, 325, 395, 437, 477
Educational management, 301, 303–304, 306–309
Education organisations, 300–313
Efficient market theory, 190, 199, 200
Electoral fiscal cycles, 130, 131, 136, 137
Emerging markets, 31–45, 456, 497–510
Emotional errors, 189–200
Employment, 165–187, 230, 252, 329, 336, 387–389, 442, 468, 470–472, 477
Energy storage, 427, 432, 436, 437
Enforceability of political accountability, 48–50
Environmental hostility, 477–495
Environmental indicators, 439–449
EU countries, 329, 439–449
Europe, 63–65, 247, 260, 328, 332, 340, 365, 371–390, 446
Event window, 16–20, 22–26, 29
Experiential Values, 204–213
Exponential and hyperbolic discounting, 78, 80, 82
Externalities efficiency, 371–390

F
Financial distress, 451–455, 457–463
Financial health, 63–75, 261, 455, 456
Financial performance, 255–270, 463, 533, 534, 537
Fixed broadband Internet access, 466
Forecasting, 31, 113–127, 165–167, 171–187, 192, 261, 368, 478
Foundation, 86, 143–151, 153–162, 542

G
Gender equality, 229–252
Generalised autoregressive conditional heteroscedasticity (GARCH), 32, 35, 36, 38, 39, 43–45
Generational cohorts, 410–420
Global Competitiveness Index, 48, 50, 51, 54–56
Global consumer culture, 539–549
GMM method, 339, 343, 345, 346, 350, 351, 355–358
Government expenditure, 131, 246
Government transparency, 49, 50, 317–320, 325
Greece, 118, 127, 129–139, 165–187, 213, 240, 285, 287, 292, 296, 300, 313, 328–331, 336, 361–369, 415, 420, 426, 437
Greek economy, 168, 187

H
Headline inflation, 113–127
Healthcare sector, 410
Heritage, 144–151, 153–162, 275, 279, 288–290, 297
Hospital, 325, 409–421

I
Impatience, 99–110
Income inequality, 441, 513–529
Industry cartel, 218, 226, 227
Innovation, 50, 146, 147, 217–227, 274, 275, 311, 316, 329, 336, 340, 371–374, 379, 419, 426, 437, 535–537
Insurance companies, 255–271, 414
Internal rate of return (IRR), 428, 433–437
Inventory, 289, 340–346, 349, 350, 354, 355, 357, 395, 514

J
Jenkins methodology, 116–118, 127

K
Kozani city, 287, 292

L
Labor market, 165–187, 229–252
Liabilities, 68, 259, 262, 343–358, 365–367, 454–457, 516

Logistic regression analysis, 470–472
Luxury brand, 539–549

M
Marketing, 144–151, 154, 158, 159, 161, 274, 276, 279, 280, 286, 290–292, 396, 467, 480, 482, 497–510, 532, 540, 541, 545, 546, 555, 565
Marketing communication, 419, 503
Medical personnel, 410–420
Memory, 33, 144, 153–162, 191, 404, 503, 545, 546
Monetary losses, 10, 77–83, 86, 87, 94–97, 99–110

N
National and regional R&D systems, 371
Net present Value, 342, 432, 433, 436
Network quality, 466–473

O
Occupation, 95, 101, 165–187
Online Booking, 204–213
Online inflation, 394

P
Pandemic, 15–29, 39, 63–75
Panel cointegration, 513–528
Patient satisfaction, 410–416, 418–420
Payback Period, 432–437
Perceived value, 466, 468–473
Performance, 177, 179, 183, 184, 187, 217, 218, 231, 255–270, 282, 300, 301, 304, 309, 310, 317, 346, 372, 373, 378, 449, 452, 453, 461, 463, 468, 477–495
Philanthropy, 153–162
Photovoltaic technology, 427, 430, 431
Place marketing, 286, 291
Political budget cycles, 129–139
Preference reversal, 77–83, 95
Press freedom index, 51–53, 56, 58
Price comparison, 393–407
Price competition, 218, 220, 222, 227
Price perception, 466–473
Probit regression, 231, 509
Procurement, 318–320, 324
Product innovation, 217–227
Profitability of companies, 339–358
Prosocial behaviour, 85, 86, 92
Public sector accounting, 316

Q
Quality education, 300–313

R
Random coefficient modeling, 166, 176, 187
R&D investments, 218–220, 222, 224, 226, 227
Receivables, 68, 340–346, 349, 350, 354, 355, 357, 363
Recycling, 328–334, 336
Reinsurance, 255–271
Renewable energy sources, 156, 426, 427
Reorganization, 362, 363, 368
Repositioning, 286, 287, 291, 292, 297
Rescue of enterprises, 362, 368
Reuse, 328–333, 336

S
Sensitivity analysis, 427, 436, 458–463
Shadow economy, 54, 513–528
Size of companies, 340, 341, 343–346, 350–352, 355–357, 493
Small-and medium-sized enterprises (SMEs), 63–75, 477–495
Social cooperation, 3, 10, 11, 156
Social discounting, 86–88, 91, 95, 99–104
Social exchange, 1–11
Social media, 144–147, 150, 154, 156, 161, 162, 208, 273–282, 333, 413, 419, 497–499, 502–508, 510, 531–537, 553–566
Social media motives, 554, 555, 557, 563, 565
Social media users groups, 556
Spillovers, 217–219, 221, 226, 227, 372, 379, 380, 385
Strategic agility, 477–495
Stylised facts, 32–34, 36–38, 41, 45
Sustainable fashion, 328

T
The rule of law index, 48, 49, 51–53, 55
The transparency of the political system, 48–50, 58
Tourism, 66, 68, 69, 71, 72, 74, 144–151, 156, 160, 204, 205, 212, 213, 256, 274, 279, 286, 287, 292, 295, 328
Trading volume, 16, 19, 21–29, 34, 37, 38, 41, 43, 45, 66

U
Users content groups, 557

V
Visegrad Group countries, 451–463
Volatility indices, 31–45

W
Warsaw Stock Exchange (WSE), 16, 17, 20–29
Wind power, 427, 431, 432
Working capital, 339–358, 456, 462